PERSPECTIVES in Whole Language

Julia E. De Carlo

LONG ISLAND UNIVERSITY
C.W. POST CAMPUS

Allyn and Bacon
Boston • London • Toronto • Sydney • Tokyo • Singapore

Editor in Chief, Education:	Nancy Forsyth
Series Editor:	Virginia Lanigan
Editorial Assistant:	Nicole DePalma
Production Administrator:	Susan McIntyre
Editorial-Production Service:	Ruttle, Shaw & Wetherill, Inc.
Cover Administrator:	Suzanne Harbison
Cover Designer:	Dan De Carlo
Manufacturing Buyer:	Louise Richardson

Copyright © 1995 by Allyn & Bacon
A Simon & Schuster Company
Needham Heights, MA 02194

All rights reserved. No part of the material protected by this copyright notice may be reproduced or utilized in any form or by any means, electronic or mechanical, including photocopying, recording, or by any information storage and retrieval system, without the written permission of the copyright owner.

Library of Congress Cataloging-in-Publication Data

De Carlo, Julia E.
    Perspectives in whole language / Julia E. De Carlo.
      p. cm.
    Includes bibliographical references and index.
    ISBN 0-205-15328-3
    1. Language experience approach in education. 2. Reading (Elementary)—Language experience approach. 3. Literacy.
I. Title.
LB1576.D313 1995
372.6—dc20   94-5842
                                                        CIP

This textbook printed on recycled, acid-free paper.

Printed in the United States of America

10 9 8 7 6 5 4 3 2 1   99 98 97 96 95 94

*This book is dedicated to Jim
for all his encouragement, patience, assistance and understanding.
Without his ardent support, this book would not have been completed.*

CONTENTS

PREFACE xi

1 Understanding Whole Language 1

WHAT IS WHOLE LANGUAGE? 1
DIVERSE DISCUSSIONS 2
REFERENCES 3
FOR FURTHER STUDY 4

Defining and Describing Whole Language 5
Dorothy J. Watson

Whole Language and the Practitioner 17
D. Ray Reutzel and Paul M. Hollingsworth

Myths of Whole Language 24
Judith M. Newman and Susan M. Church

CHAPTER DISCUSSIONS AND ACTIVITIES 31

2 Whole Language versus Traditional Reading Instruction 33

THE BASAL READER 39
WHOLE LANGUAGE AND SKILL-BASED INSTRUCTION 34
CHANGES IN READING INSTRUCTION 36
REFERENCES 37
FOR FURTHER STUDY 38

Beyond the Basal 39
Gayle Glidden Flickinger and Emily S. Long

Transitions in Reading Instruction: Handling Contradictions in Beliefs and Practice 43
Maureen Siera and Martha Combs

Whole Language and Its Predecessors 51
Jeannette Veatch

Reading Instruction: Plus Ça Change . . .   *58*
Walter H. MacGinitie

CHAPTER DISCUSSIONS AND ACTIVITIES   63

3   Instructional Considerations   65

INSTRUCTION DEFINED   65
BASAL-READER CLASSROOM   66
THE WHOLE-LANGUAGE CLASSROOM   68
READING INSTRUCTION IN NEW ZEALAND   69
LITERATURE-BASED READING INSTRUCTION   70
REFERENCES   71
FOR FURTHER STUDY   71

Organizing and Managing a Whole Language Classroom   *72*
James F. Baumann

A Practical Guide to Whole Language in the Intermediate Classroom   *83*
Patricia Gannon Smith

Saying the "p" Word: Nine Guidelines for Exemplary Phonics Instruction   *92*
Steven A. Stahl

Learning to Read in New Zealand: The Balance of Skills and Meaning   *100*
Claude Goldenberg

Let's Free Teachers to Be Inspired   *108*
Gerard G. Duffy

CHAPTER DISCUSSIONS AND ACTIVITIES   116

4   Using Literature with Whole Language   119

UNDERSTANDING CHILDREN'S LITERATURE   120
LITERACY ELEMENTS   121
GENRES IN CHILDREN'S LITERATURE   122
READING INSTRUCTION WITH CHILDREN'S LITERATURE   125
REFERENCES   126
CHILDREN'S LITERATURE REFERENCES   127
FOR FURTHER STUDY   127

Whole Language and Children's Literature   *129*
Bernice E. Cullinan

Being Literary in a Literature-Based Classroom   *134*
Daniel D. Hade

Literature-Based Theme Units 146
Maribeth Henney

Literature—S.O.S.! 152
Louise M. Rosenblatt

Give Us Books!.. But Also ... Give Us Wings! 157
Nancy Larrick

CHAPTER DISCUSSIONS AND ACTIVITIES 161

5 The Writing Connection 163

THE WRITING PROCESS 163

THE USE OF COMPUTERS IN THE WHOLE-LANGUAGE CLASSROOM 166

REFERENCES 167

FOR FURTHER STUDY 168

Authorship: A Key Facet of Whole Language 170
Linda Leonard Lamme

The Reading/Writing Connection in Whole Language 177
Martha Grindler and Beverly Stratton

The What, Why, When and How of Reading Response Journals 180
Julia Shinneman Fulps and Terrell A. Young

Is There a Place for Computers in Whole Language Classrooms? 184
Linda DeGroff

CHAPTER DISCUSSIONS AND ACTIVITIES 189

6 Whole Language in the Multicultural Classroom 191

CULTURALLY AND LINGUISTICALLY DIVERSE STUDENTS 192

LEARNING DISABLED AND REMEDIAL READING STUDENTS 194

MAINSTREAMED STUDENTS 195

GIFTED STUDENTS 196

REFERENCES 198

FOR FURTHER STUDY 200

Literacy Development in a Multilingual Kindergarten Classroom 201
Shareen Abramson, Ileana Seda, and Candy Johnson

Whole Language Content Classes for Second-Language Learners 207
Hwa-Ja Lee Lim and Dorothy J. Watson

Working with New ESL Students in a Junior High School Reading Class 218
Beth M. Arthur

Adopting a Whole Language Program for Learning Disabled Students: A Case Study 223
Pamela J. Farris and Carol Andersen

Whole Language Reading Instruction for Students with
Learning Disabilities: Caught in the Cross Fire   227
Nancy Mather

An Affective Approach to Reading: Effectively Teaching
Reading to Mainstreamed Handicapped Children   241
*Michael O. Tunnell, James E. Calder, Joseph E. Justen III,
and Phillip B. Waldrop*

Reading and Writing for the Gifted: A Whole
Language Perspective   245
Selina J. Ganopole

CHAPTER DISCUSSIONS AND ACTIVITIES   254

7   Content Areas and Whole Language   255

NARRATIVE AND EXPOSITORY READING   255

CONTENT-AREA TEXTS COMPARED TO BASAL READERS   256

CONTENT AREAS AND WHOLE LANGUAGE   257

REFERENCES   258

FOR FURTHER STUDY   259

Children's Nonfiction Trade Books: A Complement to Content
Area Texts   260
Barbara Moss

Using Adolescent Literature in Social Studies and Science   267
Dixie Lee Spiegel

Whole Concept Mathematics: A Whole Language Application   272
Cheryl L. Brown

Whole Language: Three Themes for the Future   278
Elfrieda H. Hiebert and Charles W. Fisher

CHAPTER DISCUSSIONS AND ACTIVITIES   281

8   Assessment   283

ASSESSMENT IN THE TRADITIONAL CLASSROOM   283

ASSESSMENT DEFINED   284

ASSESSMENT IN THE WHOLE-LANGUAGE CLASSROOM   285

REFERENCES   287

FOR FURTHER STUDY   288

Learning about Language Learners: The Case for Informal Assessment
in the Whole Language Classroom   289
Bruce Gutknecht

A Portfolio Approach to Classroom Reading Assessment:
The Whys, Whats, and Hows   298
Sheila Valencia

Literacy Portfolios: Helping Students Know Themselves   *302*
Jane Hansen

A MAP for Reading Assessment   *306*
Teri Bembridge

Grading and Evaluation Techniques for Whole Language Teachers   *309*
Wayne M. Linek

CHAPTER DISCUSSIONS AND ACTIVITIES   *318*

9 Teachers and Parents with Whole Language   319

THE SCHOOL STAFF AND WHOLE LANGUAGE   *319*

PARENTS AND WHOLE LANGUAGE   *321*

REFERENCES   *323*

FOR FURTHER STUDY   *324*

From Recipe Reader to Reading Professional: Extending the Roles of the Teacher through Whole Language   *325*
Jill Burk and Joyce Melton-Pagés

Charting a New Course with Whole Language   *332*
Robert J. Monson and Michele M. Pahl

Realities of "Whole Language"   *336*
Sean A. Walmsley and Ellen L. Adams

Talking and Writing: Explaining the Whole Language Approach to Parents   *347*
Marjorie V. Fields

Parent Communication in a Whole Language Kindergarten: What We Learned from a Busy First Year   *351*
Beverly Bruneau, Timothy Rasinski, and Martha Shehan

Putting Children before Grown-ups   *358*
Philip Vassallo

CHAPTER DISCUSSIONS AND ACTIVITIES   *361*

10 Research Signposts   363

EDUCATIONAL RESEARCH   *363*

RESEARCH IN WHOLE LANGUAGE   *364*

REFERENCES   *367*

FOR FURTHER STUDY   *368*

Whole-Language Research: Foundations and Development   *369*
Kenneth S. Goodman

Using "Real" Books: Research Findings on Literature-Based Reading Instruction   *382*
Michael O. Tunnell and James S. Jacobs

The Role of Literature in Reading Achievement 391
Pamela J. Farris and Marjorie R. Hancock

Analysis of Writing Samples of Students Taught by Teachers Using Whole Language and Traditional Approaches 396
Mary Ellen Varble

Teachers' Awareness of Reading Terms 407
Vincent E. Hamman

CHAPTER DISCUSSIONS AND ACTIVITIES 410

Author Index   411

Subject Index   416

PREFACE

Perspectives in Whole Language is a response to change. The child of today is far different from the child of the 1970s or 1980s. There have been changes in society as well as in the family structure. The media and new technology are having a profound impact on elementary school children. Instruction in the teaching of reading is evolving and educators are taking a closer look at new ways of teaching youngsters to read.

Throughout the United States and Canada, there is an increasing interest in the whole language movement. Whole language is held in high regard by many educators and is questioned by others. The philosophy of whole language is causing educators to question and ponder the entire process of literary development. This text was written to focus attention on this emerging philosophy and the practices that make whole language a viable entity. This text is designed to serve as a "portfolio" for the graduate or undergraduate student who is interested in pursuing ideas, considering issues, and thinking about problems related to whole language.

The word *portfolio* is usually used to describe the collection of works of art by an artist or the accumulation of photographs prepared by a photographer. In recent years the term has been adopted to describe an alternative strategy to assess the scholar's academic effort and achievement. This text takes a *portfolio* approach, in that I have carefully selected appropriate articles from the professional journals. They are clear, specific, concrete, and detailed essays with a unique focus that has classroom relevancy for a prospective or practicing teacher.

A great deal has been written about whole language in major education journals published within the last eight to ten years. I have examined over four hundred articles and selected forty-eight that I believe offer the reader "food for thought" in this grass-roots movement. The articles come from twenty-four different journals and provide the reader with a broad view of what professionals are thinking and experiencing with whole language. The beginning of each chapter includes background information to help the reader focus on pertinent ideas that are related to whole language. Key questions precede the articles to call attention to the common understandings and sometimes different viewpoints expressed by various experts. Discussions and activities at the end of each chapter offer students a chance to share and cooperatively learn from one another. Thus, this text offers the reader an opportunity to examine varying ideas and opinions that exist in education concerning whole language. It also provides a means for the reader to expand and develop a personal portfolio in addition to the one provided by the text.

The purpose of this text is to enable the reader to arrive at conclusions regarding the following: what whole language is; how it differs from the basal reader; how a teacher uses whole language; the place that children's literature has in the whole language classroom; the connection between the writing process and whole language; how whole language can be used within a multicultural setting; how whole language affects the learning process in the content areas; how a teacher assesses the development of the whole language student; what the roles of teachers and parents are in whole language; and what research shows about the use of whole language in teaching students to read.

Throughout the text, in terms of style and references, I have attempted to follow—albeit not slavishly—the third edition of the *Publication Manual of the American Psychological Association*, published in 1983 by the American Psychological Association, Washington, D.C. The major departure from this style manual occurs in the references with regard to the designation of issue numbers; colleagues and librarians have agreed that the inclusion of issue numbers within all periodical references facilitates the process of locating specific journal articles. Since the majority of my references were drawn from periodicals, I felt that this departure was warranted.

I wish to thank the many authors and publishers who generously agreed to have their material reprinted. Their contributions are the core of this text and the center of the portfolio. I want to thank the future and practicing teachers in my various college classes who have inspired me with their interest and creativity. Their questioning minds and tireless concern for the education of children provide much hope for the future.

Acknowledgment is made to the following reviewers who provided thoughtful feedback about the manuscript: John Beach, University of Nevada-Reno; Marlys Boschee, University of South Dakota; Susan Daniels, University of Akron; Patricia DeMay, Livingston University; Cheryl Dickinson, Southern Connecticut State University; Jeannette Sites, Brescia College; and Joyce Willis, Youngstown State University. Warm appreciation, also to Virginia Lanigan, Series Editor, and Nicole DePalma, Series Editorial Assistant, at Allyn and Bacon for all their help and support. I also wish to thank Thomas J. Conville, III, Project Manager of Ruttle, Shaw and Wetherill, Inc. for handling the editorial production of the book.

Special thanks to the Long Island University librarians at C.W. Post Campus who helped me locate information: Jo Bianco, Ralph Cambardella, Robert Delaney, Jacqueline Elsas, Janet Jennings, Emily Lehrman, Ellen Perlow, Louis Posha, Diane Podell, Wendy Roberts, Melvin Sylvester, and Maria Zarycky. Their patience and assistance greatly appreciated.

My gratitude to M. Ronald Minge, Professor in the Department of Special Education and Reading at the C.W. Post Campus for his reaction, comments, and suggestions concerning research in education, which assisted me in the preparation of Chapter 10, "Research Signposts."

I am proud to acknowledge the creativity and talent of my nephew, Dan De Carlo who designed and illustrated the cover of this text.

I am especially grateful to James E. McCann who encouraged, supported, and inspired me to keep on going. His editorial help and keen, questioning mind directed me on a clear course. He often reminded me to consider the remarks expressed in "Dr. Seuss at 72—Going Like 60," an article by Don Freeman published in the March, 1977 issue of the *The Saturday Evening Post*. In it, Theodor S. Geisel, warmly known to millions of children and adults as Dr. Seuss, offered:

> If I were a genius, why do I have to sweat so hard at my work? I know my stuff all looks like it was rattled off in twenty-three seconds but every word is a struggle and every sentence is like the pangs of birth. (p. 8)

J.D.C.

CHAPTER 1

Understanding Whole Language

Whole language is a term that has gained increasing interest within education in the past two decades. It has been defined, discussed, accepted, and questioned by teachers, administrators, parents, researchers, and university professors. It offers for many an alternate way of dealing with literacy and perhaps preventing the continuous mounting of the illiteracy rate in the United States. It opens up a different avenue for youngsters to become actively, completely, and directly involved in their learning; an opportunity for teachers to consider the teaching–learning process from a viewpoint quite different from how they themselves were taught; and, most importantly, a chance for all of us to review, and perhaps revise, our perceptions of learning.

In order to fully understand "whole language," it is necessary to look carefully at the various definitions that have evolved and to consider the diverse discussions that have emerged.

WHAT IS WHOLE LANGUAGE?

As part of her master's thesis, Bergeron (1990) reviewed over sixty-four definitions of whole language. Noting this vast array of meanings in the literature, she prepared the following definition:

> Whole language is a concept that embodies both a philosophy of language development as well as the instructional approaches embedded within, and supportive of,

that philosophy. This concept includes the use of real literature and writing in the context of meaningful, functional, and cooperative experiences in order to develop in students motivation and interest in the process of learning. (p. 319)

Goodman (1992) states that "whole language aims to be an inclusive philosophy of education." Involved in whole language are these elements: language (written as well as oral), learning, teaching, curriculum, and the learning community. He further states that

> Whole language is producing a holistic reading and writing curriculum, which uses real, authentic literature and real books. It puts learners in control of what they read and write about. But it also produces new roles for teachers and learners and a new view of how learning and teaching are related. Whole language reemphasizes the need for curriculum integrated around problem solving in science and social studies with pupils generating their questions and answering them collaboratively. Whole language revalues the classroom as a democratic learning community where teachers and pupils learn together and learn to live peacefully together. (p. 196)

In the professional literature, whole language is widely viewed as a theory of knowledge as well as a theory of language, learning, and schooling. Harste and Lowe (1991) point out that in a whole-language classroom, children should be enmeshed completely in their learning. There should be a personal involvement, so that further questions generate from the child. Learning is ongoing and continuous. In a literacy curriculum, the children should have the opportunity to investigate language in all its intricacy, as well as to concentrate on learning (Harste, 1990).

Whole language also has an influence on various trends in education. According to Wood and O'Donnell (1991), reading instruction is moving towards more process orientation, which stems from cognitive psychology, and focuses on more literature-based instruction rather than the product-orientation instruction that is rooted in behavioral psychology related to basal-reader programs.

Looking Ahead

Watson (1989) in her article defines and describes whole language, while Reutzel and Hollingsworth (1988) offer a depiction of whole language by comparing such a classroom to the typical public-school classroom.

DIVERSE DISCUSSIONS

Not everyone is one hundred percent behind whole language nor agrees that it is a total, brand new concept. Aaron (1991) states that whole language rests on various philosophical foundations, which include "humanistic education; emphasis on meaning so that reading is purposeful and interesting; and the integration of reading and writing into a unified learning task" (p. 128). He notes further that although these are sound principles of education, "these ideas are neither innovative nor unique to whole language and, therefore, do not separate whole language from other teaching approaches" (p. 128).

Although Pearson (1989) sees some very positive aspects of whole language, he believes there are some concerns that need to be addressed. He feels that these concerns are a result of miscommunication and raises the following questions: Do teachers take only a back-seat role in reading instruction in the whole-language classroom? Are whole-language programs well suited to children from nonmainstream backgrounds (Hispanics, blacks, and the urban and rural poor)? Is there something inherently good about reading and writing in the real world? Are there certain words, because of their metaphorical significance, that block open communication between conventional scholars and whole-language advocates? Will the all-or-nothing approach to whole language "run the risk of overwhelming us with too much too fast?" (p. 240) Is it naive to assume that whole language will completely eliminate the use of basals and tests?

Although Chaney (1990) believes that whole language has much to offer students as they acquire literacy, she has some cautions. "If whole language does not include systematic teaching of the alphabetic code or leaves the learning of metalinguistic skills to chance, then it is not supporting students in *all* aspects of language as it claims to do" (p. 248).

According to Yetta Goodman (1989), the term *whole language* should not be considered immutable, but should reflect the changes flowing from the debate currently taking place. "Regardless, the educational theories and beliefs that represent what whole language is today will be fundamental to educational practices of the future" (p. 125).

Looking Ahead

In the article by Newman and Church (1990), the authors identify and examine nineteen myths about whole language.

The purpose of the readings in this chapter is to understand the various meanings of *whole language*. The issues that will be addressed include:

- Can we compare and contrast various definitions of whole language that have been offered?
- What are some of the major principles related to whole language?
- Can we contrast whole language to what it is as opposed to what it is not?
- Why have some myths about whole language emerged? Why should we examine some of these myths?

REFERENCES

Aaron, P. G. (1991). Is there a hole in the whole language? *Contemporary Education, 62*(2), 127–133.

Bergeron, B. S. (1990). What does the term whole language mean? Constructing a definition from the literature. *Journal of Reading Behavior, 22*(4), 301–329.

Chaney, C. (1990). Evaluating the whole language approach to language arts: The pros and cons. *Language, Speech and Hearing Services in Schools, 21*(4), 244–249.

Goodman, K. S. (1992). I didn't found whole language. *The Reading Teacher, 46*(3), 188–199.

Goodman, Y. M. (1989). Roots of the whole-language movement. *The Elementary School Journal, 90*(2), 113–127.

Harste, J. (1990). Jerry Harste speaks on reading and writing. *The Reading Teacher, 43*(4), 316–318.

Harste, J. C., & Lowe, K. S. (1991). Whole language: Getting the act together. *Contemporary Education, 62*(2), 76–81.

Newman, J. M., & Church, S. M. (1990). Myths of whole language. *The Reading Teacher, 44*(1), 20–26.

Pearson, P. D. (1989). Reading the whole language movement. *The Elementary School Journal, 90*(2), 231–241.

Reutzel, D. R., & Hollingsworth, P. M. (1988). Whole language and the practitioner. *Academic Therapy, 23*(4), 405–416.

Watson, D. J. (1989). Defining and describing whole language. *The Elementary School Journal, 90*(2), 129–141.

Wood, M., & O'Donnell, M. P. (1991). Directions of change in the teaching of reading. *Reading Improvement, 28*(2), 100–103.

FOR FURTHER STUDY

Altwerger, B., Edelsky, C., & Flores, B. M. (1987). Whole language: What's new? *The Reading Teacher, 41*(2), 144–154.

Cazden, C. B. (1992). *Whole language plus.* New York: Teachers College Press.

Church, S. M. (1994). Is whole language really warm and fuzzy? *The Reading Teacher, 47*(5), 362–370.

Clarke, M. A. (1987), Don't blame the system: Constraints on "whole language" reform. *Language Arts, 64*(4), 384–396.

Fountas, I. C., & Hannigan, I. L. (1989). Making sense of whole language: The pursuit of informed teaching. *Childhood Education, 65*(3), 133–137.

Goodman, K. S. (1986). *What's Whole in Whole Language.* Portsmouth, NH: Heinemann.

Harste, J. C. (1989). The future of whole language. *The Elementary School Journal, 90*(2), 243–249.

Hoffman, A. R., & Daniels, S. J. (1993). Protecting the future of the whole language literacy movement: Past lessons and present concerns. *Reading Horizons, 34*(2), 170–183.

McCaslin, M. M. (1989). Whole language: Theory, instruction, and future implementation. *The Elementary School Journal, 90*(2), 223–229.

Mersereau, Y., Glover, M., & Cherland, M. (1989). Dancing on the edge. *Language Arts, 66*(2), 109–118.

Morgan, N. B. (Producer & Director). (1992). *Whole language: A philosophy that works* [Videotape]. Evanston, IL: Universal Dimensions.

Myers, J. W. (1993). *Making sense of whole language: Fastback 346.* Bloomington, IN: Phi Delta Kappa Educational Foundation.

Routman, R. (1991). *Invitations: Changing as teachers and learners, K–12.* Portsmouth, NH: Heinemann.

TV Ontario Production Company (Producer), & Novak, A. (Director). (1992). *The whole language classroom.* [Videotape]. Princeton, NJ: Films for the Humanities and Sciences.

Shanklin, N. L., & Rhodes, L. K. (1989). Transforming literacy instruction. *Education Leadership, 46*(6), 59–63.

Stanek, L. W. (1991). Whole language for whole kids. *School Library Journal, 37*(9), 187–189.

Defining and Describing Whole Language

Dorothy J. Watson

"Whole language"—two words that have become a label for an exciting grass-roots teacher movement that is changing curricula around the world. Two words that have to do with teachers being heard and students becoming visible. Two words that conjure up diverse definitions and strong reactions. Two words that need clarification by way of definition and description. Two words that are much more than two words.

WHY DEFINE WHOLE LANGUAGE?

Whole language, whatever it is—a spirit, a philosophy, a movement, a new professionalism—is leaving its imprint on students, educators, and parents from Wollongong, Australia; to Winnipeg, Canada, to Nashville, U.S.A.

Whole-language teachers talk enthusiastically about students who have become eager and joyful readers and writers; teachers back up their claims by showing countless examples of pupils' creations. In more and more college courses, *preservice teachers* study the research and theory of whole language and expect to find practical application of the research and theory when they walk into student-teaching classrooms. *Parents* read or hear about literacy programs involving process writing, authors' circles, literature replacing basals, even invented spelling, and they ask for such a curriculum for their children. *Administrators* in increasing numbers are listening to and supporting teachers who advocate and can articulate the principles and practices of whole language. And *researchers and teachers* working together describe the new curriculum and the classrooms in which it is in place; they encourage other teams of educators to become involved in such collaborative inquiry.

Despite growing enthusiasm, some educators, parents, and researchers have serious doubts about the merits of whole language. Those on the periphery of the movement may be impressed with a second grader's interviewing techniques, be pleased with a school's increased circulation of library books, and even show amazement at junior high special-education students' insightful discussion of a book they have read, but they have questions about "the basics" of this innovative literacy program. Many are willing to attribute students' increased interest in and love of reading and writing to the influence of whole-language curriculum, but those same educators and parents become cautious, even fearful, when they cannot get a clear definition of a term that identifies a perspective on literacy that is felt so deeply and is moving so rapidly and with such great force into classrooms around the world. "After all," advocates are asked, "if whole language is not defined precisely, how can we . . . know when it is happening, test the results of it, and report its influence?"

No matter how much intellectual energy and practical experience go into the formation of a whole-language curriculum—no matter how hard it is studied and worked at—if educators cannot talk clearly about whole language in terms of its theory and its practice, some critics will be quick to diminish or discredit it entirely. An administrator once reported that she was pleased with the school's first-grade whole-language curriculum, but was surprised and dismayed that neither first-

---

From "Defining and Describing Whole Language." by D. Watson, 1989, *The Elementary School Journal*, 90, pp. 129–141. Copyright © 1989 by The University of Chicago. All rights reserved. Reprinted by permission of Dorothy Watson and The University of Chicago Press.

grade teacher could clearly define whole language. She readily admitted that she needed and was counting on their expertise and their words to help her talk with parents and with the superintendent about the program. It is not enough to say that whole language is something that all good teachers do and were doing long before the term emerged. Nor is it sufficient to call whole language an essence, a way of thinking, or something that has changed the lives of teachers and students. Such definitions may be accurate, even needed, but they leave the inquirer with the same question, "What is whole language?"

Whole language must be defined not only for those outside the movement but for whole-language educators as well. Doing so helps teachers become mindful of three important dimensions of this powerful point of view: first, of the *research* in literacy and learning that is accepted as credible by whole-language advocates; second, of the pedagogical *theory* that emerges from that research; and finally, of the *practice* that is consistent with the theory. For example, based on research in miscue analysis and on writing as a process, teachers cannot define whole language as an integrative use of the systems of language and then in practice rely heavily on phonics for reading instruction and on parsing of sentences for writing instruction. If a teacher says that whole language involves integrating the language arts across the content areas, that teacher must then turn a critical eye toward the way listening, speaking, reading, and writing are used in order to teach math and science. If a teacher says whole language involves putting students at the center of the curriculum, that teacher must be able to show how children influence what happens academically and socially in the classroom. It is not enough to define whole language; educators must make sure that what occurs in classrooms is supported by and consistent with their definition.

By the same token, when publishing companies and curriculum planners say that their materials and methods are whole language, their definitions must be grounded in whole-language research and theory. I have seen "whole-language reproducibles (ditto sheets)," "whole-language basals," "whole-language reading kits," "whole-language directed reading activities," and "whole-language worksheets to be used with literature," all advertised and promoted by "whole-language publishers and curriculum planners." I have also seen harmful imitations of materials that are regularly found in whole-language classrooms; it can no longer be said that all big books and computer writing programs are suitable for whole-language classrooms. It does not take a genius to detect the inconsistencies between what is stated about these materials and what in truth exists. The practice of such companies is in conflict with the research and theories of whole language and therefore should not be labeled as such.

A final need for a definition and description of whole language can guide us into the future—into an exploration of the potential of language and of learners. For example, when whole language is defined or described as student centered, meaning focused, and involving real literature, teachers are motivated to inquire into the curricular possibilities that can materialize when these three dimensions do indeed exist. Many whole-language teachers have grown to realize that their definition of whole language is in process, that tomorrow it will be sharpened and refined.

WHY WHOLE LANGUAGE IS DIFFICULT TO DEFINE

Whole language is difficult to define for at least three reasons. First, most whole-language advocates reject a dictionary-type definition that can be looked up and memorized. Teachers have arrived at whole language by way of their own unique paths. Because of this, their definitions reflect their personal and professional growth, and their definitions vary. Additionally, to arrive at one's own definition, a teacher must enter what has been called a discomfort zone of whole language, uncomfortable because it requires great honesty in evaluating one's own past, as well as patience and time for reflection. Some educators are hesitant to take on such an introspective inquiry. If they do, the inquiry will reflect their own personal histories; the results will have similarities, but there will be significant and important differences.

Second, whole language is often difficult to define because many of its advocates are intensely passionate about it, while those who demand a definition may disapprove of it just as intensely. For whatever reason, the emotion against or for whole language could be so strong that it keeps opponents from asking reasonable and inoffensive questions, or so intense that it keeps advocates from providing nondefensive answers and an unambiguous definition. One of the most miserable evenings of my life was one in which I was questioned in minute detail about whole language. I perceived the questioning as an offensive and senseless interrogation, when in truth, it is possible that my passion clouded my judgment to the extent of misunderstanding the intentions of the questioners. At any rate, there was no possibility of clarification or meeting of minds—the emotion on both sides was too strong.

Third, the experts in whole language who can provide the richest answers to questions about it—the teachers—have not often been asked. Knowledgeable teachers remained silent. This has changed. Increasingly, whole-language teachers are being consulted; they are receiving recognition for their experience and professional information. Acknowledgment of a teacher's abilities and encouragement to speak up often come first from the teacher's own support group (sometimes called TAWL—Teachers Applying Whole Language). Whole-language teachers are now appearing on national and international conference programs and are writing for recognized professional journals about their experiences with whole-language practice, theory, and research.

All this is not to say that whole language or some major dimension of it cannot be defined. It can be. It has been. The following "definitions" were taken from works in which the authors discussed whole language. I believe it was not their intention to present an all-inclusive definition of it.

"DEFINITIONS"

> Whole language is clearly a lot of things to a lot of people; it's not a dogma to be narrowly practiced. It's a way of bringing together a view of language, a view of learning, and a view of people, in particular two special groups of people: kids and teachers. [Kenneth Goodman, 1986, p. 5]

> ... those who advocate a whole language approach emphasize the importance of approaching reading and writing by building upon the language and experiences of the child. [Constance Weaver, 1988, p. 44]

> *Whole Language:* Written and oral language in connected discourse in a meaningful contextual setting. [Gordon Anderson, 1984, p. 616]

> It is built on practical experience and the research of educators, linguists and psychologists. Whole language utilizes all the child's previous knowledge and his/her growing awareness of the aspects of language. [Members of the Southside Teacher Support Group, Edmonton Public Schools, 1985, p. 1]

> ... "whole language" is a shorthand way of referring to a set of beliefs about curriculum, not just language arts curriculum, but about everything that goes on in classrooms.... "Whole language" is a philosophical stance; it's a description of how some teachers and researchers have been exploring the practical applications of recent theoretical arguments which have arisen from research in linguistics, psycholinguistics, sociology, anthropology, philosophy, child development, curriculum, composition, literary

theory, semiotics and other fields of study. [Judith Newman, 1985, p. 1]

Whole language is a way of thinking, a way of living and learning with children in classrooms. [Lois Bird, 1987, p. 4]

These definitions may lack sameness, but they never go outside the boundaries of an acceptable definition of some dimension of whole language. The definitions are diverse because the personal and professional histories of the authors are different. This variety frees those who have studied and practiced whole language to generate their own definitions, then to revise their definitions again and again.

A few years ago I defined whole language primarily in linguistic terms (Watson, 1982). Language remains an important focus for me, but involvement with whole-language teachers, students, and researchers has made me realize that whole language is more than beliefs about language. Through the years my definition has become more inclusive and more helpful to me as a teacher. In truth, it became so inclusive (of language, learner, teacher, curriculum, politics, etc.) that friends suggested a short definition might be useful. For me that short definition became: Whole language is a label for mutually supportive beliefs and teaching strategies and experiences that have to do with kids learning to read, write, speak, and listen in natural situations. And it is much more. Over the years, that definition has become: *Whole language is a perspective on education that is supported by beliefs about learners and learning, teachers and teaching, language, and curriculum.* This definition calls for the following elaboration.

Because of the term itself, *whole language*, I begin with a linguistic definition that emphasizes the wholeness of language. On first consideration, the words may appear to be redundant: Is language not always whole? Who ever heard of half, or three-quarters language? In natural situations language *is* whole and intact. In many non-whole-language instructional settings, however, language is broken into small segments in the belief that students can master it more easily and that teachers can more closely monitor readers' and writers' acquisition of it. Whole language is a point of view that language is inherently integrative, not disintegrative. It follows that language is learned and should be taught with all its systems intact. That is, all the systems of language —semantics, syntax, and graphophonemics (call it phonics if you must)—are maintained and supported by pragmatics (language in natural use) and must not be torn apart if language is to be learned naturally. Pragmatics includes the situational context in which language is used as well as the learner's prior knowledge activated in that situational context. Because language develops within a culture, the students' culture must be a consideration in the understanding of the language itself and in how language is learned.

Many educators define whole language first in terms of learners and learning. This is understandable, for if it were not for teachers' deep concern for learners, there would be no whole-language movement. Whole language involves whole learners (with all their strengths and needs) who, when given real and continuous opportunities in safe and natural environments, can initiate learning, generate curriculum, direct their own behavior, and evaluate their own efforts.

Frank Smith (1973) said that to help students become proficient language users, teachers need to find out what kids are trying to do and then help them do it. Yetta Goodman (1978) added that the way teachers find out what students are trying to do is to become enlightened observers of them; she calls it "kid watching." For whole-language teachers, students are curricular informants (Harste, Woodward, & Burke, 1984). Based on what they learn about their students and what they know about subject areas, literature, language, and learning, teachers develop curriculum *with* their students. Whole language involves teachers who are classroom researchers, participants, coaches, learners, resource persons, and perhaps most important, listeners. Whole language involves teachers who, even outside their classrooms, are activists and advocates for students, for themselves, and for their curriculum.

It has been said that curriculum is everything that goes on in students' heads; Jerry Harste calls it the learner's "mental trip." Whole-language curriculum also includes what *potentially* can go on in students' heads. In keeping with this notion, whole-language teachers approach curriculum on a "planning to plan" basis. This important curricular step is taken before teachers meet their students on the first day of school and it is taken every day thereafter. This prelude to curriculum replaces a prescribed and permanent program and is based on all that teachers know about students, subject areas, literature, language, learning, and teaching. It involves generating numerous possibilities for study and being knowledgeable about human resources, suitable inquiry, and materials. In whole-language classes, students are at the heart of curriculum planning; nothing is set into classroom motion until it is validated by learners' interests and motivated by their needs.

WHAT WHOLE LANGUAGE IS NOT

Inappropriate definitions of whole language dismay advocates. Such misconceptions do, however, prompt whole-language educators to formulate acceptable definitions in order to clear up the confusion as well as to think about what causes the misleading and inadequate views.

Up to a point, one can define whole language by saying what it is not. For example, whole language does not mean the whole-word (look–say, sight word) approach to reading, nor is it another name for language experience. Whole language has been defined in terms of a particular strategy or materials: "It is just process writing and big books." It also has been said that whole language means "anything students do is okay, including reading words wrong, spelling any way they want, not caring about proper grammar, and talking a lot in class." These are not whole language, nor is it, as one teacher heard his classroom described, ". . . a place where they spend an awful lot of time cooking and singing, and they hate phonics."

As Altwerger, Edelsky, and Flores (1987) point out, the problem with these definitions/accusations is that there is a grain of truth in some of them. For example, any authentic attempt made by students to communicate is valued in a whole-language classroom; language experience is occasionally used in whole-language programs; process writing, big books, cooking, and singing are often seen and heard in whole-language classrooms; and phonics, as a prescribed skill-and-drill program rather than a cue to be used in concert with all the cues of language, is incompatible with a whole-language perspective on reading and therefore is rejected.

Implicit in the above is that whole language is not a program, package, set of materials, method, practice, or technique; rather, it is a perspective on language and learning that *leads to the acceptance* of certain strategies, methods, materials, and techniques, such as using predictable language books, literature discussion groups, acceptance of invented spelling, and so on. Despite the concern for accuracy, I find it easier to talk about "whole-language programs" and "whole-language practices" (Watson & Crowley, 1988) than to work my way around the accurate but awkward "whole-language-based programs," or "whole-language-theory-inspired practices."

FROM DEFINITION TO DESCRIPTION

A single visit in a whole-language classroom is worth more than a hundred definitions, for it is in the classroom that the definitions, the theory, and the stated practices come alive. In visiting whole-language classes, it becomes evident that no two are exactly alike, but even so there is never any question about the model of literacy instruction that underlies the curricula. Although whole-language classrooms vary and have their own personalities, it is inevitable that within the ebb and flow of the day, certain strategies are included no matter what the age, grade, or label given the students. These strategies (Gilles et al., 1988; Y. Goodman & Burke, 1980; Watson, 1988) can be observed daily in self-contained, English as a second language (ESL), special education, speech, Chapter 1, remedial reading, kindergarten, or adult education classes. The strategies are consistent with whole-language teachers' beliefs about language and learning and reflect teachers' respect and regard for story, learner, community of learners, and for the student's life outside the classroom.

Reading and Telling Stories

Teachers read to their students or tell them stories every day. *Story* refers not only to narrative but also to poetry, songs, rhymes, riddles, jokes, informational pieces, plays, and any other authentic and appropriate text. By daily reading and telling stories to students, teachers make a declaration—story, along with the students, is at the heart of the curriculum. Time devoted to listening to stories indicates something very basic in a whole-language classroom. It says that self-understanding is important and that hearing or reading about others can help students know themselves more clearly and completely. It says also that if students are to become authors and readers, story must be bone and marrow to their existence as literate persons.

The content and form of stories heard expand students' experiences with literature and subject areas as well as provide a base for both reading and writing. The sounds of stories provide a story grammar, a frame on which students can create meaning. Literature heard adds to the shared knowledge of the community of learners and sets the stage for listeners to extend a story by linking it with other stories having similar theme, setting, plot, characterization, and content. Listeners may respond to literature through drama, art, and music; by reading more stories by the same author, or even by adding another chapter, verse, or incident to the story heard. When teachers read or tell stories as a natural part of the curriculum, there is no pressure; students are in safe harbors in which they can draw on their own backgrounds in order to create meaning. And, of course, awareness of literature from other cultures promotes understanding of those cultures as well as a deeper regard for one's own.

Students in whole-language classrooms read stories of their own choosing every day. Good literature (that which readers can go back to again and again and never "use up") is at the heart of the curriculum. Other reading materials from authentic and suitable sources inside and outside school, however, are found in a whole-language program. Through reading quality stories and other real texts, students practice their reading, feel the support provided by the author's language, and become more successful and joyful readers.

Writing

Students and story are celebrated through student writings. Writing in whole-language classrooms involves generating ideas, revising, editing when necessary, and celebrating (publishing, presenting, sharing) pieces chosen by the author. After learners have experiences with stories, poems, notes, letters, orders, newspapers, lists, reports, and journals, the invitation to use these forms in their own writing comes through demonstration. For example, students receive the invitation to write a poem by listening to, seeing, and reading a great deal of poetry. In whole-language classrooms children learn to write—with conviction and conventions—by writing.

Personal and Social Connections

The whole-language curriculum encourages individuals to make personal links to meaning through reading and writing. Students constantly have opportunities for private reading and writing—to work alone if they want, but never in a lonely classroom. Because language is learned collaboratively as well as personally, students in whole-language classrooms socialize with each other in ways similar to human socialization outside the classroom: learners talk with each other about what they are writing, the books they are reading, the problems they are solving or not solving, and the experiments they are conducting. Within the community of the classroom there are real reasons to read, write, listen, and speak.

In the context of a classroom that is natural and appropriate for every learner in it, whole-language teachers never do for students what students can do for themselves. When help is needed, it is forthcoming, usually from learners who dig deep to answer their own questions, but often from other students. If a spirit of collaboration has been fostered in the classroom, students can help each other when it may be impossible for a teacher to do so. Whole-language communities maximize the possibility of learners helping each other through partner and small-group work and through students taking on the role of teacher and resource person.

Students talk with each other not only about the content of the stories they are reading and writing but also about the processes of reading and writing. That is, children and their teachers bring to a conscious awareness what is going on in their heads when they read and write. They talk about what happens when things go right or wrong and about when they do not go at all. Whole-language students readily offer each other suggestions for more proficient and efficient reading and writing; the suggestions are given when they are most appropriate and immediately applicable. This attention to the processes of reading and writing takes the place of formalized, direct, and prescribed instruction and happens naturally during group discussions, individual conferences, partner work, and during teacher-initiated strategy lessons.

Planning to Plan

The great authenticity of life outside the school, the experiences and knowledge gained there, and the needs that must be met in order to live in that world provide powerful and immediate motivation for learning. For these reasons, whole-language teachers do not finalize curricula before meeting their students. Rather, whole-language teachers, "plan to plan." Before school starts they explore a variety of units, themes, and lessons. A topic may be *considered* for a variety of reasons: former students have enjoyed the subject; the materials are easily available; the teacher has an abiding interest in the subject; parents encourage the study; the topic is covered on a district-, state-, or province-mandated test; the study is traditional. The topics are *chosen* after the students' larger worlds are brought into the classroom. When students begin to inform teachers about their lives and interests, teachers with the learners can then weave a curriculum that is meaningful, appropriate, and applicable.

PRINCIPLES SUPPORTING WHOLE LANGUAGE

Whole language is more than a definition and a list of mainstay activities. It is a spirit, an enthusiasm for teaching and learning that is supported by beliefs about teaching and learning. As an authentic and natural curriculum develops within the classroom, whole-language teachers refer to these beliefs again and again. There may be no limit to the number of beliefs, but following are some often mentioned by whole language teachers.

Choice is the beginning of ownership in both reading and writing. Within the classroom, choice occurs when students are offered curricular invitations. In orchestrating their invitations, whole-language teachers use all they know about students, the learning process, language, and subject matter. Interestingly, students usually accept whole-language invitations because teachers orchestrate them as carefully as the most gracious host or hostess might. It is also interesting that whole-language teachers accept their own invitations: they too read books, write stories, and participate in the community of learners. Whole-language teachers value the creative and generative powers of students and help them make good choices by offering them good and appropriate invitations.

Student Responsibility for Learning

Students can take ownership and responsibility for their own learning. To empower learners, whole-language teachers do not select all the books to read and the topics to write about, correct students' nonstandard forms at the point of production, spell on demand, or revise and edit for students. In other words, teachers do not do things for students that students can do for themselves. They do, however, facilitate a rich environment within which learners are led not into the impossible but into the delightfully difficult. There, learners grasp patterns, see similarities, make connections, take "mental trips," go beyond "minimal competencies," beyond "stated objectives" —often beyond the teachers themselves.

Acceptance of Errors

There is no such thing as perfectibility of the linguistic form (Cary, 1985). If students and teachers are not bound to someone else's standards of perfection, they can then become linguistic risk takers. When the notion of perfection is dispelled, an uptight, must-be-right model of literacy is dispelled and concepts involving "mastery" are replaced by ideas of language learning through natural use.

Language users can learn as much from getting language wrong (producing a nonstandard form) as they can from getting it right, and maybe more. When readers, writers, listeners, and speakers take risks, inevitably there will be mistakes, miscues, misinterpretations, and misconceptions. The personal logic of children as well as their rough drafts in both reading and writing are valued in whole-language classrooms. In a healthy learning environment students grow from their mistakes, that is, they grow through the process, through the pursuit of language.

Emphasis on Meaning

Stopping students at the point at which they are producing meaning (through either oral or written language) in order to make surface-level corrections may result in stopping students in their linguistic and cognitive tracks. When attention is drawn away from the composing process, the construction of meaning can falter and the language user may never regain the moment, the momentum, or the motivation. Attention to conventions and standard forms is a part of whole-language programs but is not confused with the construction of meaning through reading, writing, listening, and speaking.

Integrating the Language Arts

The language arts are integrative and integrated in a whole-language program just as they are in life outside the classroom. Within the language arts of writing, reading, listening, and speaking, children learn conventions such as standard grammar, spelling, handwriting, and articulation by using them naturally and in concert with each other.

Content Areas

The content areas are grist for the literacy mill. Students listen, speak, write, and read about science, art, music, math, social studies, games and sports, cooking, sewing, nutrition—anything that is important in their lives. Whole-language teachers understand that the interpretation of concepts basic to content areas precedes or parallels the interpretation of words that are peculiar to a specific knowledge domain. Because of this understanding teachers value, respect, and make use of the content areas to promote oral and written language as they use the language arts to support the content areas.

Classroom Environment

The classroom itself is a strategy that promotes learning. Whole-language classrooms facilitate learning communities in which students live comfortably and productively. Not only the atmosphere of the classroom but the physical aspects of it indicate to students that this is their home and that it deserves respect and care. There is a working order within the room that allows its occupants to meet with partners and in small groups, or to have privacy.

Parental Involvement

Children's language and thought have their roots at home and in the community. Teachers make it a point to work with, not without and not for, parents. Whole-language teachers do not assume that all students' problems stem from the home. Rather than assigning blame, whole-language teachers act positively—they invite mothers and fathers to become whole-language parents.

Evaluation

Whole-language teachers believe that the purpose of evaluation is primarily to inform learners themselves. When this is accomplished, then teachers (and therefore the curriculum), parents, and the public (including legislators) will be informed. When this order is reversed and the primary aim becomes to inform the public, students and teachers are lost in the attempt to boil a learner's efforts down to a single number or grade. As scores become important, students become invisible.

Whole-language teachers are cautious about what they accept as evidence of students' abilities and learning. Through student self-evaluation, "kid watching," and other whole-language assessments (K. Goodman, Y. Goodman, & Hood, 1988), teachers break away from narrowly conceived testing that masks students' achievements and that curricularly leads nowhere. Teachers know that it is difficult to get critics to understand and appreciate the wealth of information available through whole-language evaluation; nevertheless, they never stop recommending that the portfolio of written work, pictures, anecdotes, and tapes, along with conferences and written comments, replace letter and numerical grading. Whole-language teachers urge learner-referenced evaluation over norm-referenced and criterion-referenced testing.

These and dozens of other theoretical assumptions powerfully influence whole-language teachers and support their teaching. No one would ever accuse such teachers of being atheoretical, without intention, or without strong groundings in research and experience.

IS IT WORTH THE EFFORT?
A STUDENT ANSWERS

Many whole-language teachers have the respect and encouragement of colleagues and parents. Some, however, have felt strong resistance. When teachers are fortunate enough to belong to a support group such as TAWL (Teachers Applying Whole Language), it is easier to weather the storms. But too often whole-language teachers must stand alone. When this is the case, these teachers turn to their own students for confirmation that their efforts are justified, that they are worthy of learners. Children such as Patty renew the spirit and determination of whole-language teachers.

Patty was a natural and eager user of language. Her parents could not remember exactly when she began to read and write, but they were sure that her "reading readiness" consisted of being read to every day, watching them read and write, reading (remembering encouraged) favorite stories, reading (guessing encouraged) print in her own world, reading (pretending encouraged) to her dolls, getting and leaving notes on the refrigerator door, and writing stories and letters for her friends and relatives.

In kindergarten Patty and her language were valued by a teacher who understood child development and enjoyed child logic. Patty grew as a reader and writer who daily experienced the communicative nature of reading and writing, and who felt the power that comes naturally to a child who is surrounded by oral and written language. Patty considered herself to be a reader and writer, and during the summer after kindergarten she wrote the following story for her most appreciative audience—her grandmother. (Figure 1 shows Patty's original story as she wrote it.)

Patty's Story
[Once upon a time there was a little girl whose name was Jane. And Jane was absolutely a beautiful princess. One day Jane said, "I am so bored that I am going out in the world to find some adventure. I think I'm going in space to catch my adventure." So Jane found a star beam and went high in outer space. If you want to know more about Jane's adventures read the next chapter in my book.]

In almost 6 years of living in a language-filled world—of hearing literature, paying attention to interesting print, creating oral and written discourse herself—Patty had developed a sense of story. She used a conventional opening (Once upon a time), had a motivation for action (Jane is bored), used a traditional character (an absolutely beautiful princess), utilized an often-used setting (outer space), and employed a continued-next-week ending. Patty categorized speech sounds in her head and invented appropriate spellings. She at-

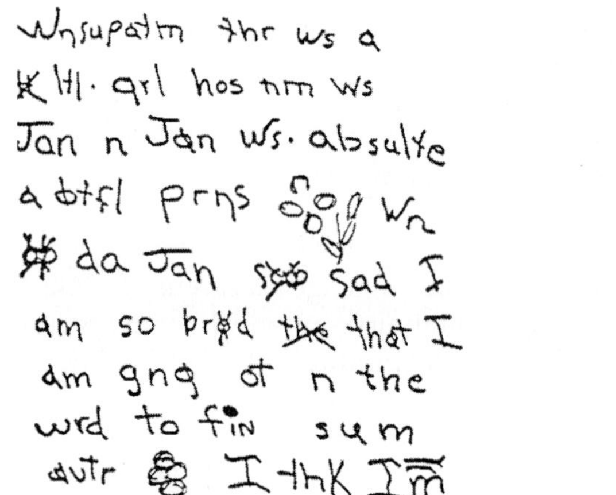

FIGURE 1
PATTY'S STORY

tended to punctuation. The flowers Patty drew after each of the first two sentences served nicely as periods. One sentence ends with four dashes spaced upward (toward outer space?). Two wavy lines over the "m" in *I'm* indicates that Patty was becoming aware of the apostrophe. She used writing conventions and she showed a sense of audience and a sense of humor.

Within one month after entering first grade as a natural reader and writer, Patty stopped writing. She moved from a whole-language attitude about literacy, both at home and in kindergarten, to a first-grade class in which she was directed to master the smallest units of language before moving on to larger ones and to do it in a setting in which risk taking was discouraged.

In the "eleven basic areas of readiness" in which she was diagnostically tested at the beginning of the year, Patty fell below 80 percent competency on sequencing, recognizing causal relations, and recognizing stylistic devices (humor). She was placed in a "basic prerequisite for reading readiness" program. Some of Patty's "reading and writing activities" were

1. Visually discriminating between circles, squares, and triangles, and between capital A, B, and C.
2. Circling the upside-down apple and the bug without a mouth.
3. Recognizing upper- and lower-case letters.
4. Tracing a path from left to right (left-right progression).
5. Copying step by step the teacher's picture from the board to a piece of paper (eye–hand coordination).
6. Listening for the same sounds at the beginning of words.
7. Drawing rings around pictures whose names began with given sounds.
8. Finding the sound that was the same in a group of three letters.
9. Writing lines of letters.
10. Writing words leaving one finger space between words and two fingers for margins.
11. Copying perfectly a poem from the board.

After 2 months without receiving a story from her favorite author, Patty's grandmother begged her to try her hand at another story. After telling her parents that she could not write because she could not spell and that she did not know what to write about, Patty tearfully sat down and wrote "Patty's Nonstory" (Figure 2). An honest critic of her own work, Patty drew an *x* across the story and pushed it aside.

Patty ended the first grade no longer concerned with the communicative nature of language; she now wanted her text to be error free, which meant using words that she was sure she could spell and spending a great deal of time erasing and forming the letters perfectly. Instead of writing stories and poems and reading self-selected books, Patty read short, controlled-vocabulary stories in basals and worked on endless workbook pages.

Patty's second-grade, whole-language teacher recognized the fragile condition of this potentially strong language user and on the first day of school firmly moved Patty back into

FIGURE 2
PATTY'S NONSTORY

real reading and real writing. Within 2 weeks Patty:

1. Heard her teacher tell stories, riddles, and jokes.
2. Told a story and made up a riddle.
3. Heard her teacher read Sid Fleischman's *Mr. Mysterious's Secrets of Magic.*
4. Put on a magic show (complete with posters, handbills, and program) with four other children.
5. Wrote "How to Make a Coin Disappear" for *Our Magic Book.*
6. Wrote a text for Margaret Harteliu's wordless picture book, *The Chicken's Child.*
7. Read *Owl at Home* by Arnold Lobel and *Strega Nona* by Tomie de Paola during silent reading time.
8. Wrote notes to her teacher and friends and a letter to her sixth-grade picture-and-pen pal.
9. Copied the lyrics of a song into her own *Song and Poetry Book.*
10. Wrote in her journal every day.
11. Wrote a letter to the giant telling him how she would spend her gold coin after hearing *Jim and the Beanstalk* by Raymond Briggs.
12. Wrote and illustrated a new story for her very happy grandmother.

"Whole language"—two words that symbolize a kindergarten teacher's awareness and acceptance of the language abilities and needs of all children who enter her classroom. Two words that represent the rich and supportive program into which a second-grade teacher lovingly invited a fragile language user. Two words that offer hope, not hype or helplessness, to discouraged parents. Two words that identify all the research, theory, and practice that restored the confidence of a little girl named Patty.

CONCLUSION

Never in the history of literacy education has there been such genuine excitement on the part of educators. Teachers, many discouraged and burned out, are ignited by a new professionalism. Students, many labeled as lost causes, are regaining their strength and finding their way. Parents, many disheartened and desperate, are realizing that their children need not be diminished by a label and a numbing curriculum. An alternative is available. At the heart of this alternative are learners with their teachers—learners inquiring into life and literature by using language fully, teachers taking on the roles of researcher, learner, and educator. This new professionalism, movement, philosophy, spirit is called whole language.

REFERENCES

Altwerger, B., Edelsky, C., & Flores, B. (1987). Whole language: What's new? *Reading Teacher, 41,* 144–154.

Anderson, G. (1984). *A whole language approach to reading.* New York: University Press of America.

Bird, L. (1987). What is whole language? In "Dialogue," D. Jacobs (Ed.), *Teachers networking: The whole language newsletter, 1*(1). New York: Richard C. Owen.

Carey, R. (1985, October). *Toward a new methodology for research in literacy.* Paper presented at the meeting of the Semiotic Society of America, Bloomington, IN.

Gilles, C., Bixby, M., Crowley, P., Crenshaw, S., Henrichs, M., Reynolds, F., & Pyle, D. (1988). *Whole language strategies for secondary students.* New York: Richard C. Owen.

Goodman, K. S. (1986). *What's whole in whole language?* Portsmouth, NH: Heinemann.

Goodman, K. S., Goodman, Y. M., & Hood, W. J. (1988). *The whole language evaluation book.* Portsmouth, NH: Heinemann.

Goodman, Y. (1978). Kid watching: An alternative to testing. *Journal of National Elementary Principals, 57,* 41–45.

Goodman, Y., & Burke, C. (1980). *Reading strategies: Focus on comprehension.* New York: Holt, Rinehart & Winston.

Harste, J. C., Woodward, V. A., & Burke, C. L. (1984). *Language stories and literacy lessons.* Portsmouth, NH: Heinemann.

Newman, J. (Ed.). (1985). *Whole language theory and use.* Portsmouth, NH: Heinemann.

Smith, F. (1973). *Psycholinguistics and reading.* New York: Holt, Rinehart & Winston.

Southside Teacher Support Group (Eds.). (1985). *What is the whole language approach? A pamphlet for parents.* (Available from Edmonton Public Schools, Edmonton, Alberta, Canada)

Watson, D. J. (1982). What is a whole language reading program? *Missouri Reader, 7,* 8–10.

Watson, D. J. (Ed.). (1988). *Ideas and insights: Language arts in the elementary school.* Urbana, IL: National Council of Teachers of English.

Watson, D. J., & Crowley, P. L. (1988). How can we implement a whole language approach? In C. Weaver (Ed.), *Reading process and practice* (pp. 232–279). Portsmouth, NH: Heinemann.

Weaver, C. (1988). *Reading process and practice: From sociopsychololingistics to whole language.* Portsmouth, NH: Heinemann.

Dorothy J. Watson is a faculty member in the Department of Curriculum and Instruction at the University of Missouri at Columbia.

Whole Language and the Practitioner

D. Ray Reutzel
Paul M. Hollingsworth

During the 1970s, the American public became disenchanted with the quality of public school education. The reported slide of reading and writing skills became the focus of pointed attacks on the public education system (Copperman 1980). In response to these attacks, American school leaders were hearing a cry to offer only the basic curriculum. To assure that children were acquiring the necessary basic language and mathematical skills, many states and school districts developed meticulously designed lists of skills to be taught by teachers and learned by children. These skill lists were accompanied by technologically elegant record-keeping systems and mandated testing programs. Teachers and children became so caught up in record keeping, completing independent worksheets, and testing, little time was left for instruction. Despite these problems, test scores continued to improve. Thus, the practices associated with the basic curriculum remain entrenched in many schools.

Recently, dissatisfaction with schools is growing anew. Parents, teachers, and researchers have begun to notice a neglect of the real "basics" in schools—time spent engaged in actual reading and writing. Worksheets and tests have proliferated at such an alarming rate that both teachers and students scramble to "get through the materials" by the end of the school year. More and more time is devoted to worksheets and tests, and less and less time is given to reading and writing. Anderson, Hiebert, Scott, and Wilkinson (1985) stated that "an estimate of silent reading time in the typical primary school class is seven or eight minutes per day, or less than 10 percent of the total time devoted to reading." They also noted that 70 percent of reading instructional time was spent on independent seatwork employing worksheets. Out of a growing concern over the limited time spent on reading and writing each school day, a small but growing number of educators and parents have joined forces under the banner of *whole language* theory.

Leaders in the field of literacy education appear to be headed for another major debate on how children ought to be taught to read and write. As in decades past, this debate is sure to influence the way reading and writing will be taught well into the next decade. The majority of parents and educators confronted with the whole language philosophy for the first time find themselves confused about how their beliefs on teaching reading and writing differ from whole language (Goodman 1986). Unlike previous debates, the differences between

From "Whole Language and the Practitioner" by D. R. Reutzel and P. M. Hollingsworth, 1988, *Academic Therapy, 23,* 405–416. Copyright (1988) by PRO-ED, Inc. Reprinted by permission.

whole language practices and current practices in schools with respect to reading and writing instruction are both complex and comprehensive. The constructs of whole language theory reach well beyond the narrow boundaries of previous debates to embrace not only methodological issues, but also philosophical issues, research methodologies, principles of learning, the classroom environment, and teacher and child behavior.

Whole language practices stand in stark contrast to the prevailing views of schooling, the schooling process, and the place of children and teachers in this process. Ken Goodman (1986) indicates that whole language theory is "a way of bringing together a view of language, a view of learning, and a view of people, in particular two special groups of people: kids and teachers." Judith Newman (1986) points out that whole language is not just an instructional approach but rather a philosophical stance. Harste, Woodward, and Burke (1984) assert that whole language practices require new ways of thinking about the curriculum and the classroom as well as the use of novel methods of research and inquiry to provide fresh insights into children's language learning. To help teachers and parents understand the differences between current practices and beliefs and those of whole language theorists, it appears that an answer to "What are the implications of whole language theory for classroom practitioners" is needed.

WHAT IS THE WHOLE LANGUAGE PHILOSOPHY ON TEACHING CHILDREN TO READ AND WRITE?

In contrast to the current views of American education, which place the teacher and curriculum at the center of the schooling enterprise, whole language proponents place children and their needs at the heart of schooling. Children should be active participants in the design and direction of the schooling process rather than merely passive recipients of institutional knowledge and skill. Ostensibly, children should be respected and trusted as competent learners who have learned much prior to formal teaching. Whole language theorists denounce the view that children do not know how to learn until taught.

Language is viewed as essentially indivisible. Reading and writing instruction should begin with whole and connected language because whole, undivided language is both familiar and natural for children to learn. Instead of beginning reading instruction with the parts of language, such as letter names and sounds, whole language instruction in reading and writing would begin with stories, poems, signs, and print from the child's environment, e.g., candy wrappers, cereal boxes, road signs, et cetera.

DOES RESEARCH SUPPORT WHOLE LANGUAGE PRACTICES?

Whole language proponents largely reject the findings and traditional research methods of psychology and education. Rather, whole language researchers draw their support from ethnographic or descriptive investigations into how infants and children acquire their native language. These studies indicate that children learn oral language naturally from immersion in a society in which the whole, connected language is used by other members of that society (Smith 1985).

Don Holdaway (1979), a proponent of whole language theory, strongly advocates that reading and writing ought to be taught in a way that parallels and complements early oral language learning. Few children, Holdaway insists, would learn language in infancy if they were taught to speak the same way they are taught to read and write in schools. To demonstrate this pint, Holdaway asks the reader to imagine a mother or father dutifully leaning over an infant's crib and presenting a daily lesson on the name and sounds of the letter "a" or any other alphabet letter in an attempt to teach the infant to speak. When related to the teaching of reading and writing in schools, the logic seems less clear-cut. As a result, many parents and teachers continue to insist that children be taught to read by daily phonics lessons and by reading books containing controlled, sometimes meaningless language.

HOW DO CHILDREN ACQUIRE LANGUAGE?

Advocates of whole language practices assert that children acquire literacy through a series of successive approximations from the whole to the part. Downing and Leong (1982) indicate that children usually approach learning to read and write in a state of cognitive confusion about the purposes and conventions of printed language. However, through immersion in a print-rich environment, children become familiar with meaningful printed materials and naturally progress toward a state of cognitive clarity. Thus, children extract from whole language used in the social context the information needed to facilitate language acquisition and use. At the beginning and throughout life, language is used in a variety of social settings and for personally relevant purposes. Consequently, Newman suggests that children learn to read and write by beginning with familiar language contexts such as their own dictation and writing and move toward the more unfamiliar language contexts of others.

In short, whole language theorists assert that language learning progresses from the whole of language to an understanding of the parts. Language learning and use is largely based on intrinsic motivation or personal relevance rather than on extrinsic rewards and the proddings of others. And finally, whole language advocates are quick to point out that language is naturally learned from exposure and use rather than from instruction.

WHAT IS DIFFERENT ABOUT THE WHOLE LANGUAGE CLASSROOM?

A visit to the typical classroom in most public schools reveals neatly arranged rows of students' desks, bare floors, and artistic bulletin boards carefully constructed by the teacher. A visit to the whole language classroom reveals on the other hand a more home-like environment. Bathtubs are filled with pillows where children curl up with their favorite books. Desks are pushed aside and replaced with large pillows, reading lofts, round tables and chairs, bean-bag chairs, and old couches. Lap boards and large carpeted areas for reading, discussing, or teaching adorn the whole language classroom. Ceilings, walls, floors, and windows are graced with children's compositions, dictations, and art work, all as natural outgrowths of their reading and writing involvement.

Instruction in whole language classrooms frequently occurs in learning centers focusing on a single topic or theme, e.g., kites, karate, or Independence Day. A reading center focused on Independence Day may contain various trade and reference books. A writing center could include various suggestions for compositions related to Independence Day. The social studies center may focus on the historical significance of Independence Day, and the music center may contain various songs, tapes, and records of patriotic music. In whole language classrooms, in-depth study of a topic or theme replaces the learning of reading and writing skills like "getting the main idea" or "writing thesis sentences."

Grouping children for reading instruction according to their measured ability on a standardized test of reading achievement or ability grouping resulting in three reading groups—

high, medium, and low—is foreign to whole language classrooms. If groups are used at all in whole language classrooms, these groups are often formed on the basis of a common need or interest.

In traditional classrooms, reading, writing, spelling, and handwriting instruction are often scheduled and taught as separate subjects during the school day. A whole language classroom integrates the teaching of reading, writing, spelling, and handwriting into a single period often called language arts instruction. As previously stated, the integration of reading, writing, spelling, and handwriting instruction in whole language classrooms is often achieved by focusing instruction on a single topic or thematic unit.

The learning climate or atmosphere in a whole language classroom also differs from traditional classrooms. In traditional classrooms, children are often seated quietly and working independently. Children in whole language classrooms are often working collaboratively on a common interest or goal and appear noisy and busy.

Paper and pencil tests, worksheets, and standardized national achievement tests have come to be the accepted measures of student achievement in traditional classrooms. Testing or evaluation methods used in whole language classrooms would be considered unconventional by many parents and teachers and typically take the form of teacher observations (kidwatching), interviews, discussions, video or audio recordings of children's reading, and selected samples of children's compositions, handwriting, and artistic works.

WHAT DO TEACHERS DO IN A WHOLE LANGUAGE CLASSROOM?

A visit to a whole language classroom reveals noticeable contrasts in teacher behaviors. In the whole language classroom, teachers are often hard to spot. Rather than directing the class from the center of attention, whole language teachers usually participate with their students in organized reading and writing activities. If the children are writing and sharing their compositions, the whole language teacher is also writing and sharing her compositions with the children.

Whole language teachers encourage children's attempt to read and write through frequent praise, although these attempts are often only approximations of mature reading and writing behaviors. Conversely, teachers in traditional classrooms stress correctness over trying. Praise or recognition is only given when children's reading and writing conform to conventional standards of correctness.

Whole language teachers often include children in planning instruction to foster a feeling among students of ownership of the curriculum and their own learning. Rather than predetermining every detail of the curriculum and daily lessons, whole language teachers request children's input into the structure, planning, and content of lessons. Thus, whole language teachers can make on-the-spot modifications of the learning activities to meet the needs and expanding interests of their students.

Reading lessons often begin with the whole language teacher's reading stories and poetry aloud to children to build story background and interest. Children are often encouraged to reread favorite stories on large charts or in big books as a whole group. Whole language teachers take what some might consider to be an informal approach to reading instruction. Reading skills are taught as a by-product of actual reading rather than as a prerequisite for reading. For example, phonics skills are taught from known sight words in books and charts the children have been reading and rereading together as a group rather than in an isolated lesson on the names and sounds of letters to be applied at some later time to lists of unfamiliar or nonsense words.

Although building background for reading is important in both traditional and whole language classrooms, the process is often different. In traditional classrooms, the teacher typically builds background by telling students about the story, providing outlines, or asking questions about what students know about the topic of the story. Contrastingly, whole language teachers use techniques like brainstorming and predicting to build story background. Children become actively involved in sharing their knowledge about the story topic and in making predictions about the setting, plot, and resolution of the story. Thus, reading becomes a process of prediction and confirmation.

Whole language teachers do not use direct instruction techniques to teach children reading and writing. They believe that as teachers, they are living demonstrations of learning and how to learn, never knowing when or how a child will choose to use their example as an aid to learning. An isolated, teacher-led lesson on a specific skill at a given time during the day would not coincide with a whole language teacher's belief on how children learn. In short, whole language teachers seem to be more concerned with how children learn rather than with how teachers should teach.

WHAT DO CHILDREN DO IN A WHOLE LANGUAGE CLASSROOM?

Children are the focus in whole language classrooms. This principle is exemplified by the behaviors of the children in whole language classrooms. In writing activities, children often choose their own topics for composition rather than responding to a teacher-imposed topic. During reading, children read trade books rather than basal readers, use reference books to gather information for an anticipated composition, and even assist one another in reading and writing. And finally, children often spend copious amounts of time engaged in sustained silent reading and writing activities.

Children in whole language classrooms use language as a tool for exploring their world and expressing their growing knowledge of that world. As a direct outgrowth of using language as an exploratory tool for learning, children often make mistakes in reading and writing. However, they realize that to risk and make mistakes is a natural consequence of learning and developing language facility.

Classroom peers are used as mentors, sounding boards, sources of knowledge, and supporters in the enterprise of learning rather than as someone to compete with for grades or other rewards. Children in whole language classrooms learn to recognize both the purpose and joy of learning for learning's sake rather than learning for extrinsic rewards. In short, children in whole language classrooms respond to an intrinsic and purposeful motivation for learning rather than responding to outside enticements.

HOW WHOLE IS WHOLE?

There is always a danger in attempting to contrast anything with something else. The temptation is to paint a picture of opposites or mutually exclusive categories. However, this is seldom the case in reality. This article was meant not to prescribe how to become, as Goodman puts it, *"wholier"* than other teachers. Rather, the intent was to help clarify by contrast what is and what is not consistent with the whole language approach or theory to reading and writing instruction. Table 1 (on page 22) is presented in an attempt to summarize the contrasts presented as well as other possible contrasts between whole language and traditional beliefs and practices.

After examining the information in Table 1, the majority of teachers will likely find themselves somewhere between the two extremes presented. In all probability, however, many teachers after reading this article will have discovered that they also believe in or even practice some if not many of the tenets of the whole language theory of literacy education. As Harste, Woodward, and Burke (1984) have said, learning should be an invitation not an assignment.

TABLE 1
CONTRASTING WHOLE LANGUAGE THEORY

What It Is ...	What It Isn't ...

Philosophical Views about Children and Language

1. Humanism is the philosophical base.	1. Essentialism is the philosophical base.
2. Children already know how to learn.	2. Teachers must teach children how to learn.
3. Process is most important.	3. Product is most important.
4. Language is indivisible.	4. Language is divisible.

Research Support

1. Ethnographic and qualitative research methods predominate.	1. Experimental and quantitative research methods predominate.
2. Instruction is based on language acquisition and development research.	2. Instruction is based on scientific analysis of learning research.

How Children Learn Language

1. Whole to parts learning is emphasized.	1. Parts to whole learning is emphasized.
2. Learning begins with the concrete and moves to the abstract.	2. Learning begins with the abstract and moves to the concrete.
3. Instruction is based on transactional/transformational theories in reading.	3. Instruction is based on transmission/interactive theories in reading.
4. Instruction is associated with theories of gestalt psychology.	4. Instruction is associated with theories of cognitive and behavioristic psychology.
5. Language learning is based on personal relevance and experience.	5. Language learning is based on a hierarchy of skills.
6. Learners use language for personal purposes.	6. Learners use language to satisfy others.
7. Inward forces motivate learning.	7. Outward forces motivate learning.
8. No extrinsic rewards are given for learning or behavior.	8. Extrinsic rewards are given for learning and behavior.
9. Language is learned through immersion.	9. Language is learned through imitation and shaping.

Classroom Environment

1. School learning is like home.	1. School learning is different from home.
2. Environment is "littered" with children's and teacher's printed language.	2. Environment is often teacher made professional bulletin boards or exhibit children's perfect papers.
3. Centers focus on a topic or theme, i.e., kites, karate, etc.	3. Centers focus on skill acquisition.
4. Groups are flexible and often formed by interest.	4. Groups are inflexible and often formed by achievement.
5. Classroom fosters cooperation and collaboration.	5. Classroom fosters competitiveness and isolation.

Teacher Behavior

1. Teachers facilitate learning.	1. Teachers direct learning.
2. Teachers do not label or categorize children.	2. Teachers often label children, e.g., LD, dyslexic, buzzards, weeds, etc.
3. Instruction is informal and discovery based.	3. Instruction is formal, direct and systematic.
4. Teachers give children choices.	4. Teachers often do not give children choices.

(continued)

(Table 1—*continued*)

What It Is . . .	What It Isn't . . .
5. Teachers emphasize trying and taking risks.	5. Teachers emphasize correctness and accuracy.
6. Teachers emphasize the meaning of language.	6. Teachers often emphasize the isolated parts of language.
7. Instruction takes place in sentence level language units or larger.	7. Instruction focuses on small steps in skill acquisition.
8. Phonics principles are taught in known sight words using the analytic approach.	8. Phonics principles are often taught in isolation using the synthetic approach.
9. Teachers instruct with whole stories, books or poems.	9. Teachers instruct with learning letter names/sounds and basal readers.
10. Brainstorming is used to build background experiences for instruction.	10. Advanced organizers are used to build background for instruction.
11. Teachers are always teaching by example.	11. Teachers often teach only by precept.
12. Teachers participate with students in reading and writing.	12. Teachers seldom participate in assigned tasks on an equal basis with children.
Child Behavior	
1. Children often plan their own learning.	1. Children follow the plan set by the teacher.
2. Children often choose their own topics/purposes for writing.	2. Children follow the assigned purposes for writing.
3. Children often assist one another in reading and writing.	3. Children often compete with one another in reading and writing.
4. Children use language to learn about their language.	4. Children learn language conventions to use language.
5. Children participate more often in discussion, etc.	5. Children often work privately and quietly at their desks.
Evaluation	
1. Evaluation is informal—kidwatching, tapes, samples.	1. Evaluation is formal—standardized or criterion referenced.

REFERENCES

Anderson, R. C., Hiebert, E. H., Scott, J. A., and Wilkinson, I. A. G. 1985. *Becoming a nation of readers*. Washington, D.C.: National Institute of Education.

Copperman, P. 1980. *The literacy hoax*. New York, NY: Morrow Quill Paperbacks.

Downing, J. and Leong, C. K. 1982. *Psychology of reading*. New York, NY: Macmillan.

Goodman, K. 1986. *What's whole in whole language?* Portsmouth, NH: Heinemann.

Harste, J., Woodward, V. and Burke, C. 1984. *Language stories and literacy lessons*. Portsmouth, NH: Heinemann.

Holdaway, D. 1979. *Foundations of literacy*. Portsmouth, NH: Heinemann.

Newman, J. 1986. *Whole language: Theory in use*. Portsmouth, NH: Heinemann.

Smith, F. 1985. *Reading without nonsense*. New York, NY: Teachers College Press.

D. Ray Reutzel and Paul M. Hollingsworth are both on the faculty of the Department of Elementary Education, Brigham Young University, Provo, Utah.

Myths of Whole Language

Judith M. Newman
Susan M. Church

It seems everywhere we turn these days, someone has something to say about "whole language." The term has become prominent in journal articles, books, conference presentations, publishers' advertising, and the media. Teachers, school administrators, researchers and theoreticians, parents and politicians have all contributed to the whole language literacy discussion. The problem is, however, that a good deal of what people have had to say reflects a serious misunderstanding of what whole language is really about. A number of myths and misconceptions are causing confusion and anxiety among both educators and the public.

The myths take a variety of forms. There are misconceptions about specific instructional decisions. There are overgeneralizations that keep teachers from seeing what their students are trying to accomplish. There are orthodoxies that undermine students' learning. And there are large overriding myths that conflict dramatically with the theoretical underpinnings of whole language philosophy. We feel very much like Frank Smith must have felt when he wrote his "Myths of Writing" in 1981: "Not all teachers harbor all or even many of these misconceptions. Nevertheless [we] believe they are sufficiently egregious both in school and out to warrant their exposure and examination" (p. 792).

What follows is a close look at some of the myths about whole language. These myths are widespread. We've met them head-on all over the continent—here at home in Nova Scotia, in Alberta and Ontario, in Texas, Maine, and California. We present the myths not to criticize teachers but to help us all examine our pedagogical assumptions and to learn from the contradictions we find there. (We have written as "we" to make it clear that although we as authors have other responsibilities, we are first and foremost whole language teachers ourselves.)

MYTHS ABOUT SKILLS

Myth: *You don't teach phonics in whole language.*

Reality: No one can read without taking into account the graphophonemic cues of written language. As readers all of us use information about the way words are written to help us make sense of what we're reading. But these cues aren't the only clues readers use. We use a variety of other language cues: cues about meaning (semantic cues) and cues about the structure of a particular text passage (syntactic cues). We use pictorial cues when they're available, we bring our general knowledge about the subject into play, and we bring all our previous experience with reading and writing to bear when we read. Whole language teachers do teach phonics but not as something separate from actual reading and writing. We might offer students some phonics hints at an appropriate moment when they are writing and aren't sure how to spell something; we might draw their attention to graphophonic cues after they've successfully figured out an unfamiliar word. Readers use graphophonic cues; whole language teachers help students orchestrate their use for reading and writing.

Myth: *You don't teach spelling or grammar in a whole language classroom.*

Reality: Within a whole language framework, these aspects of language are a means to an end rather than an end in themselves. Spelling, punctuation, and handwriting are important because they help the writer to make meaning clearer for readers. Knowledge of grammar is helpful to both readers and writers as they construct meaning. Learning to read and write begins with engaging reading and writing experiences that have strong personal and shared meaning rather than with instruction in isolated skills. As children use language, they learn about language, discovering much on their own and through interaction with peers. When it seems appropriate, the teacher might provide information or assistance through short, focused lessons with individuals, groups, or the whole class. When children have real audiences for their writing, they have reasons to pay attention to the conventions of written language. They have reasons to learn how to revise and edit. As they become more proficient, they become increasingly independent at using conventional spelling and punctuation in final drafts.

MYTHS ABOUT INSTRUCTION

Myth: *Whole language means a literature-based curriculum.*

Reality: Although many whole language teachers often use literature as a vehicle for shaping classroom learning, we don't limit ourselves to activities that fit into a particular theme or even to texts of a particular genre. Many whole language teachers plan their literacy curriculum around investigations in math, science, and social studies. We try to capitalize on opportunities prompted by our students' interests in the world outside the classroom. We encourage students to be on the lookout for important current community or world events around which to develop learning enterprises. Because we believe it's important to offer our students multiple texts and different genres in conjunction with a broad range of hands-on experiences, we don't worry about forcing everything that goes on in the classroom into a single theme. A number of investigations may be going on simultaneously. The students may be involved in the exploration of some aspect of measurement or classification while at the same time investigating family issues from a number of different perspectives. Or they may be engaged in a project on fables as well as conducting a local community census using a broad range of tools to help them organize and interpret their data.

Myth: *Whole language is a way of teaching language arts; it doesn't apply to other subject areas.*

Reality: Whole language philosophy underlies the entire curriculum. Inquiries in science, social studies, and mathematics provide many opportunities for learners to be actively involved in solving meaningful problems. Students can explore with concrete materials, carry out investigations, relate what they learn outside and inside the classroom, and, in the process, use oral and written language as well as other communication systems to reflect upon and extend their learning. A look at an African legend, for example, might lead to the investigation of legends in the students' own culture. The exploration of legends could raise an interest in the function of musical instruments in African societies. This interest in musical instruments could move to the exploration of the physics of sound and the making of instruments. To consolidate their investigation, students might write their own legends, compose some accompanying music, and then publish and/or perform their efforts. In such a curricular enterprise, the students' knowing is strengthened by exploration between and among these many diverse perspectives.

Myth: *In a whole language classroom you don't have to teach.*

Reality: Teachers working from a whole language perspective are active participants in the learning context. We continually work at structuring an environment in which learners can engage in purposeful activities. We collect curriculum resources such as trade books, magazines, science, math, and social studies support materials, and we consider and reconsider their location in the classroom. We initiate learning activities. We pose questions, offer procedural suggestions, and suggest explorations. We are ever on the alert for opportunities to present learners with challenges that gently push them beyond their current strategies and understanding. We are constantly observing our students, asking questions, and inviting contributions from all members of the class in order to judge when learners can best use articular information. We make time to reflect on how learning is proceeding and change direction when it becomes apparent that things aren't going as well as expected or when students propose better alternatives. All of these activities are integral aspects of teaching.

✓ **Myth:** *A whole language classroom is unstructured.*
Reality: A whole language classroom is highly structured. Both teachers and students contribute to the organization. The teacher has thought about the placement of furniture, what specific resources to offer and their location within the classroom, the grouping of the students, the nature and flow of activity, the approximate amount of time to allocate, and some possible ways for students to present what they have learned. While long-range objectives have been carefully considered, the moment-to-moment decision-making is fluid. Students are encouraged to suggest alternative strategies or to propose new directions for themselves. Whole language teachers make every effort to merge students' interests with overall instructional goals thereby creating a flexible, yet comprehensive curriculum.

MYTHS ABOUT EVALUATION

Myth: *There's no evaluation in whole language.*
Reality: Teachers working from a whole language perspective are always evaluating. We observe and interact with students to discover not only what but how they're learning. We are constantly gathering information that we use to make decisions about future instruction. We notice when a student tries a new strategy or demonstrates awareness of a writing convention. We keep tabs on how groups are progressing. We examine students' work often, looking for evidence of their latest discoveries. We share what we learn with students so they, in turn, can learn to judge how they're doing for themselves. When this kind of ongoing evaluation occurs, both teachers and students have a clear understanding of accomplishments and needs. Moreover, we can communicate this understanding to parents and others.

Myth: *In whole language classrooms there are no standards; anything goes.*
Reality: In open, generative learning environments the standards are set by the situation and the participants. When the focus of learning and teaching is the construction and communication of meaning, standards are intrinsic. When learners are engaged in purposeful experiences, success lies in fulfilling the intended purpose and progress is judged on the basis of students' ability to handle increasingly complex language and thinking tasks. Teachers who are guided by a whole language framework set expectations based upon our theoretical knowledge, and we encourage learners to impose increasingly demanding expectations for themselves.

Myth: *Whole language teachers deal just with process; the product doesn't matter.*
Reality: Whole language teachers are very concerned about the quality of our students' efforts. However, we also value the process

whereby assignments, stories, reports, and projects are produced. We know the value of distinguishing between work-in-progress and finished products. Work-in-progress is allowed to be rough. The point of taking some assignments, stories, reports, and projects through to completion is to help students learn the strategies for making sure that their intended meaning is clear, that conventions have been followed, and that the format is attractive and appropriate. But not all work needs to be perfected. Many assignments and written efforts are intended to increase fluency—to help students discover and articulate ideas. The important thing is assisting students to discern when conventions matter and when they don't.

MYTHS ABOUT LEARNERS

Myth: *Whole language philosophy applies only to teaching children in the early grades.*
Reality: Although the majority of teachers who are attempting to implement whole language philosophy in their classrooms are elementary teachers, the theoretical arguments apply equally to the teaching of 15-year-old and 35-year-old students. The principles guiding whole language instruction are appropriate regardless of the learner's age. Whether in primary classrooms or in graduate classes, students need to be actively engaged in making sense for themselves.

Myth: *Whole language won't work for kids with special needs.*
Reality: Children having difficulty in school for whatever reason are the very ones who benefit most from a learning context that encourages them to take risks and to experiment. For so many of these children their problems have been exacerbated by the fragmented, right answer skills-based literacy instruction they've been receiving. The instruction, rather than helping them sort out what reading and writing are all about, has interfered with their strategies for making sense, rendering them dependent, cautious learners. Many of these children have stopped believing they can learn. A whole language-based learning environment invites these children to see themselves as learners once again.

OTHER MYTHS

Myth: *There is little research to support whole language.*
Reality: The research base for whole language philosophy is broad and multidisciplinary. It includes research in linguistics, psycholinguistics, sociology, anthropology, philosophy, child development, curriculum, composition, literary theory, semiotics, and other fields of study. Increasingly, we are gaining insights into language learning and language instruction through collaborative classroom inquiry, wherein teachers and researchers pursue issues of common concern. Through this kind of research, teachers and researchers alike have made, and are continually making, important discoveries about what happens in highly complex, multifaceted classroom and real-world environments.

Myth: *All you need for whole language is a "whole language" commercial program.*
Reality: Published programs attempt to provide short-cuts for teachers. Many publishers are now prepackaging reading materials and lessons that incorporate aspects of methodology associated with whole language philosophy. There is nothing intrinsically wrong with these materials—many programs use high quality literature and a range of interesting activities. But they do not, in themselves, create a whole language learning environment. Furthermore, to use any materials in a way that is supportive of individual learners, we must first understand some of the theoretical basis of whole language. We must question our beliefs about instruction, and we must be

willing to watch and learn from our students. The danger with adopting a commercially-prepared reading program is that teachers will apply sets of procedures rather than structure experiences appropriate for their particular students and their individual needs. To create a whole language-based classroom, we must learn to observe our students closely and be reflective about our teaching.

Myth: *Whole language is a methodology.*

Reality: Whole language is a philosophy of learning and teaching based on a number of fundamental assumptions. Some of these include the following:

> Learning
>   is social;
>   requires risk-taking and experimentation;
>   involves constructing meaning and relating new information to prior knowledge;
>   occurs when learners are actively involved,
>   when they have real purposes,
>   when they make choices and share in decision-making;
>   uses language, mathematics, art, music, drama, and other communication systems as vehicles for exploration.

Teachers working from these assumptions try to create open learning environments. Our methodology is dynamic and continually evolving—guided by our observations of students and our ever-changing understanding of theory. We use a variety of teaching strategies and materials depending upon the needs of individual students. We base our instructional decisions upon what we know about learning and about the individual learners in our classroom. Whole language is practical theory. It argues for theoretically-based instructional practice.

MYTHS ABOUT BECOMING A WHOLE LANGUAGE TEACHER

Myth: *Giving teachers a few whole language tips makes them into whole language teachers.*

Reality: The difficult part of becoming a whole language teacher is learning to recognize the beliefs that underlie instructional decisions. The trouble with presenting teachers with 50 nifty tips is that it leaves people believing whole language merely consists of using particular materials or doing certain specific activities. Tips perpetuate unreflective teaching; they misrepresent the complexity of what is involved in creating a learner-centered classroom. In fact, every teaching action, every decision, every response in the classroom is based on some set of assumptions about teaching. Helping people become whole language teachers means helping everyone engage in a serious and ongoing examination of pedagogical beliefs and instructional practices.

Myth: *You need only a few inservice sessions to change teaching practice.*

Reality: Since whole language is a philosophy rather than a methodology, teachers need ongoing opportunities to explore both the theory and implications for classroom practice. Traditional, one-shot inservices may give teachers a few new ideas, but they leave people without the analytic tools to be able to figure out where to go next or why. This kind of inservice does not lead to the examination of assumptions so necessary for change in beliefs and practice. Anyone taking a leadership role—principals, curriculum supervisors, as well as classroom teachers—must recognize the complexity of the process and consider realistic time expectations. Curriculum leaders need to create many different kinds of learning situations so that everyone is supported in a long-term exploration of learning and teaching.

Myth: *Whole language simply involves a change in classroom practice; it's business as usual for administrators.*

Reality: Because whole language is not a program to be defined and mandated but a belief system that is in a constant process of evolution and implementation, everyone involved in implementing whole language philosophy has to become a learner. Administrators need to recognize that changing one's philosophical stance involves the same learning processes that teachers are trying to establish for students in the classroom. Like students, teachers also need to be helped to identify their strengths and to build upon them. Teachers need to feel it's safe to take risks and to experiment. That means providing a supportive environment. It's not enough to tell people what *they* should be doing. It means everyone should be working together to identify a specific curricular problem we would like to address and then explore possible instructional alternatives. We all need to reflect on what happens in a collaborative, learning-focused environment. And that can't happen unless administrators are working from the same philosophical position they are attempting to help teachers implement. Therefore, principals and district-level administrators must also examine their beliefs about learning and teaching and about teacher development.

THE GRAND MYTHS

Myth: *There is one right way to do whole language.*

Reality: This grand myth subsumes a long list of misconceptions about whole language: "You only work in small groups." "Every piece of writing has to go through the '3' or the '5' steps in the writing process." "You never spell a word for a child." "You never tell them what a word is." "You never do any grading." Statements like these are easily identified as misconceptions—each represents an orthodoxy. They embody the belief that there is some magic, correct solution to the many complexities of instruction. But the reality is that there is no one right answer to any question about teaching. Every question can and must be answered by "It depends." It depends on what has gone on before, on what the students seem to know, on the strategies they have at their disposal at the moment, on how ready they seem to be to forge ahead, on the resources at hand, on how much time is available, on how far we teachers think we can push the conventional expectations and values of the school and the community. Every instructional decision requires a judgment—a judgment made at the moment, by the teacher who is right there in the classroom. And as with all judgments, sometimes they'll be wrong. However, as we teachers become more adept at examining assumptions and learning from students, we will become better able to take new theoretical ideas and explore them in our classrooms.

Myth: *Whole language is only for superteacher.*

Reality: Although lots of people think you've got to be a special, intelligent, well-read, ambitious, sensitive, brilliant person to teach from a whole language perspective, the truth is that anyone willing to take some risks can begin the exploration. Any teacher can handle the decision-making. Every teacher can create the subtle structures that help shape the learning context. Every teacher can discover that there is no elusive right way for implementing whole language. With some support, every teacher can find his or her own way.

DISPELLING THE MYTHS

So how do we begin to dispel the myths? We begin by assuming responsibility for our personal ongoing professional development. It's as difficult and as simple as that.

Taking charge of our own professional development is not easy. From our own schooling experiences to preservice education and through much of our graduate education and inservice, we teachers have been faced with a transmission view of learning and teaching. At every turn we are told how and what we should teach. Rarely are we encouraged and helped to think a situation through for ourselves. Instead, district-wide adoption of published programs in all areas of the curriculum conveys the not-so-subtle message that we can't be trusted to make sensitive, intelligent instructional decisions; someone else is the expert.

However, it is possible to learn to value our own experience and trust our own instructional judgments. The strategies are varied yet simple. Some people have become researchers in their own classrooms (see Bissex & Bullock, 1987). Not big R researchers, but careful observers. We have made a commitment to finding out for ourselves. We have begun with a question, "I wonder how predictable books support these beginning readers?" "Can journal writing help develop students' writing fluency?" "How does freewriting help my students learn science?" We do our best to keep track of what is happening: jotting notes to ourselves during the day about what we've seen going on, keeping track of students' conversation and written work and examining it regularly for indications of progress or difficulty, interviewing students periodically to ascertain how they see themselves progressing. Through our research efforts, we have uncovered some of the contradictions inherent in our assumptions about teaching and between espoused beliefs and instructional practices. As a result of careful observation, we have been able to eradicate some personally-held misconceptions about whole language-based instruction.

Another useful reflective strategy is the recording and sharing of critical incidents (Newman, 1987; 1990). A critical incident is an occurrence that lets us see with new eyes some aspect of what we're doing. When we're unsettled about something that's happened and reflect on it, we can learn both about our students and about the impact our teaching might be having on them. A comment overheard, a direct question, a reaction in a journal or personal log, something we read that conflicts with our experience or opens possibilities we haven't considered previously can allow us to examine our pedagogical assumptions and refine what we do with students. "I didn't think I was allowed to do that," says a student and the teacher questions what she has done to have conveyed a particular orthodoxy. "The teacher said I should," remarks another student, and we're forced to reconsider the assistance we have just offered. "The difficulty with teaching is to find a balance between imposing judgment and allowing for students' spontaneity, between controlling students' actions and offering free rein" writes a researcher, and we think about an assignment we've just given. Moments like these, if examined, may help us clarify our assumptions and contemplate contradictions within our practice. Potential critical incidents can be found everywhere, not just in the classroom, and they present important opportunities for us to become reflective practitioners. But first we have to become aware of these moments and the possibilities they offer.

Whole language teachers have made a commitment to professional development in a variety of ways. We take courses to help sort out the issues and debates about literacy instruction. We make time to read new books and professional journals in order to stay current with research on theories of literacy development and instructional implementation. We have formed study groups that meet regularly both to share ideas for practice and to discuss classroom, school, and school district problems. A few of us have written about our experiences as a way of sorting out what we have learned and to offer insights to fellow teachers. All of these activities lead to reflective practice and help dispel the myths.

In turn, as we become more strongly reflective, we find ourselves in a position to help others become reflective: our students, their parents, administrators, as well as the public at large. It's important for students to become reflective about what they know and how they learn. By openly sharing our ways of finding out with them, we allow them to become independent and responsible learners. Parents, too, need to understand the theoretical basis of a whole language perspective. By inviting them to participate in class projects by allowing them to share in the celebration of the learning, we can help them understand how a whole language-based instructional context really supports their children's learning and let them see the many different ways their children are developing. Administrators need to become reflective as well. They are responsible for the tone and morale of a school or school district. By inviting them to participate in the students' learning, either directly or vicariously through our writing, we can help them consider contradictions between their pedagogical assumptions and their administrative practices. And the public needs to be informed about what is really happening in whole language classrooms. We can share our students' achievements and involve the public in celebrating their accomplishments.

Whole language is founded on the belief that learning is a collaborative venture and that we are implicated in each other's learning. Whole language isn't an add-on. It's not a frill. We can't just do a little bit of whole language and leave everything else untouched. It's a radically different way of perceiving the relationships between knowledge and the knower, between compliance and responsibility, between learner and teacher, between teacher and administrator, between home and school. Taking a whole language stance makes for a very different classroom—a classroom in which both teachers and students have a voice.

It's seductive to think we're making some headway when we incorporate new activities or set aside published basal reading series. But these changes are merely surface ones (Shannon, 1989). Real change is far more complex. Real change involves a critical appraisal of our instructional practices, trying to identify contradictions within our theoretical assumptions and their impact on our students. There is no safe middle ground, no convenient compromise. We won't make much progress toward developing a whole language stance, or toward discrediting the myths, unless we are willing to make ourselves vulnerable and become learners too.

REFERENCES

Bissex, G. L., & Bullock, R. H. (1987). *Seeing for ourselves*. Portsmouth, NH: Heinemann Educational Books.

Newman, J. M. (1987). Learning to teach by uncovering our assumptions. *Language Arts, 64*, 727–737.

Newman, J. M. (1990). Finding our own way. In J. M. Newman (Ed.), *Finding our own way: Teachers exploring their assumptions* (pp. 7–24.) Exeter, NH: Heinemann Educational Books.

Shannon, P. (1989). The struggle for control of literacy lessons. *Language Arts, 66*, 625–634.

Smith, F. (1981). Myths of writing. *Language Arts, 58*, 792–798.

Judith M. Newman is a professor at Mount Saint-Vincent University, Halifax, Nova Scotia. Susan M. Church is a curriculum supervisor at Halifax County—Bedford District School Board.

CHAPTER DISCUSSIONS AND ACTIVITIES

1. What definition of whole language would you accept and why? Pair off with a classmate and share your decisions. How alike or different are your definitions?
2. Watson, in discussing whole language, focuses on what whole language is not. Which of these misconceptions do you believe cause confusion for some educators and parents in understanding whole language? Why?

3. If you are able, visit an elementary school classroom. Use your observations to categorize this class as traditional or whole language. Base your decision on the descriptions of a whole-language class noted in the article by Reutzel and Hollingsworth.
4. With a small group of classmates, discuss any misconceptions about whole language that you had before you read the article by Newman and Church. By reading this article, did your awareness of whole language change? How alike or different are your opinions from your classmates in this group?
5. Now that you have read the articles in chapter 1 and thought about some of the educational implications of whole language, what is your reaction to some of the miscommunications about whole language noted by Pearson at the beginning of this chapter?
6. View the videotape entitled "What Is Whole Language?" (1992) produced in 1992 by TV Ontario, directed by Alan Novak and distributed by Films for the Humanities and Sciences, Princeton, New Jersey. How does this description of whole language agree or disagree with the views expressed in the articles by Watson and by Newman and Church?

CHAPTER 2

Whole Language versus Traditional Reading Instruction

Historically, youngsters have learned to read through many different approaches. Over the last hundred years or so, teachers have introduced sounds in isolation, sounds blended in the pronunciation of each word, or pronouncing the whole word. Children have been exposed to the McGuffy readers, basal readers, Initial Teaching Alphabet (i.t.a.), programmed reading, language experience, Words in Color, synthetic phonics, individualized reading, Carden method, Palo Alto approach, linguistic approaches, computer-assisted instruction, SRA, and Alpha I to name just a few. Aukerman, in 1971 and in the revised edition in 1984, put together a book entitled *Approaches to Beginning Reading*, in which he described and discussed the many different ways of teaching reading. In 1981, he prepared a text entitled *The Basal Reader Approach to Reading*, in which he reviewed and analyzed the most significant basal readers in use throughout the nation.

In this chapter, we will examine some of the philosophies underlying the teaching of reading and compare and contrast whole language with some of the more traditional reading approaches.

THE BASAL READER

The one method that has had the most profound influence is the basal reader. One has only to ask a group of adults, "How did you learn to read as a child?" The first response is, "Oh, I don't know, I don't remember." Then you add, "Do you remember Dick and Jane?" They usually respond with the remaining cast of characters, "Sally, Puff, and Spot." You might additionally ask, "How about Jack and Janet?" Someone will usually add, "Don't forget Tip!" What they identified were the main characters in the Scott-Foresman basal reader and the Houghton-Mifflin basal readers twenty-some years ago. However, Dick, Jane and Sally, as well as Jack and Janet, have long since been removed from the picture; the most recent readers contain revised stories and passages or actual excerpts from children's literature books.

Today, most eclectic, analytical and literature-based basal readers have retained the same organizational structure. First, there is an extensive teacher's manual, which usually follows the format of a directed reading activity (DRA). This manual describes in detail how to teach the reading lessons from start to finish. Second, there is a series of children's readers with matching workbooks. Each reader and workbook is structured around a controlled vocabulary with an identified scope and sequence of the skills that will be introduced. The student can move from first grade to eighth grade, basically following the same layout; but, the stories increase in difficulty as do the activities within the workbook. It is important to mention, that in kindergarten there is usually a prereading workbook to be used with teacher direction; children who complete the workbook may advance to the first grade readers.

Although some teachers appreciate the wealth of materials and suggestions that are included in the teacher's manuals, the detailed, highly structured organization and recipe-type teaching strategies have long been criticized. In her observation of sixteen teachers of the first, third, and fifth grades, Durkin (1984) recognizes the many problems inherent in the use of basal reader manuals. She concludes that:

> Giving more time to new vocabulary, background information, prereading questions, instruction on essential topics, and better but fewer assignments, and on the other hand spending less time on oral reading and comprehension questions, is one possible change that is not likely to promote any more problems than were seen in the classrooms. What the different allotment of time may promote, however, is better readers. (p. 744)

WHOLE LANGUAGE AND SKILL-BASED INSTRUCTION

The interest in whole language is causing teachers to take a closer look at how they are instructing their students in their classrooms and to come to terms with the possibility of making changes and moving away from the use of basal readers. The professional literature is full of information about whole language and the various ideas that emanate from discussions about how reading should be taught. These ideas represent a variety of opinions regarding the form and structure that reading instruction should take. McCallum (1988) points out that although basals do have limitations and they alone cannot solve all the problems connected with lack of literacy in our society, they should not be totally discarded. Heymsfeld (1989) cautions, "If basals do not teach skills as we think they should be taught, then we should alter the way they present those skills; and if occasional basal selections are inadequate, we should remember that the same is true of a collection of trade books, which are not all high-quality literature either" (p. 68) She strongly advocates that whole language and basals should join forces. However, advocates of whole language believe that "whole language is much more than an alternative to basals" (Goodman, 1989, p. 69).

One writer, McCarty (1991), equates the ideological differences between whole language and skill-based instruction to the disparities between constructivist and behavioral views of education. Some of her thoughts and ideas have been clarified and reorganized into the following side-by-side comparison of some of these differences:

Constructivism	Behaviorism
Knowledge	
1. Knowledge develops out of the individual's effort to construct meaning from experience.	1. Knowledge exists outside of the self.
2. Facts and skills become knowledge only when they take on personal meaning for the individual.	2. Discrete units (facts, skills, subskills, and rules) must somehow be absorbed into the set of human behavior so that knowledge can be said to exist.
3. Truth is an individual perception, constructed out of personal experience.	3. The existence of truth depends on the application of strict, quantitative proofs applied to postulations about the nature of the world we live in and about the "subject" under examination. If it can be proven quantitatively, then it is true.
Learning	
4. Learning emerges in the flow and continuity of an experience. It is ongoing.	4. Learning occurs only within the context of appropriate reinforced responses to events or stimuli.
5. In the learning environment, all individuals are learners and all are teachers. Children are therefore empowered to become teachers of themselves and of each other. Teachers must be cognizant of their second role: that of a learner.	5. The roles of teacher and learner are assigned and well defined. Each role possesses distinct social and cultural behavioral patterns.
Motivation	
6. Motivation arises out of the task itself; children naturally are goal-setting persons who enjoy striving toward self-determined goals.	6. The value of the task is equal to the perceived value of its extrinsic reward.
7. The teacher gives children the opportunity to initiate their own learning tasks and makes an effort to appeal to their natural curiosity.	7. The teacher is given the task of setting the standard for classifying and reinforcing behavior.

Constructivism	Behaviorism
Materials and Methodology	
8. The teacher uses literature, speech and theater arts as tools for learning to read and to apply accepted literacy principles. The teacher considers herself or himself and the children to be the best teaching resource.	8. Teaching materials largely comprise textbooks, basal readers and workbooks; teacher's manuals assist the teacher in carefully planning each lesson around a specific skill.
9. The teacher makes every effort to provide language experiences. The children themselves become the primary teaching tools.	9. The focus is placed on the parts and subparts of language and the learner is expected to put it all into a coherent whole.
10. Children learn through interaction in a cooperative learning environment. Grouped heterogeneously, the children benefit from the mixture of various developmental levels.	10. Mostly, the teacher uses homogeneous groupings to teach oral-reading skills.
11. The teacher ensures that language learning is incorporated into other areas of the curriculum.	11. Reading and language arts are separated from other areas of the curriculum.
12. Children maintain portfolios of their work in various stages of development so that progress can be continuously monitored by the teacher, the parents and the students.	12. Progress is measured by addressing the knowledge that children do not possess rather than looking at what they actually know. It usually takes the form of short-answer questions, which are considered objective because learning can be quantified without relying on value judgments of the teacher.

Looking Ahead

The article by Flickinger and Long (1990) discusses the differences between basal readers and whole language, while the article by Siera and Combs (1990) looks at the varying ways in which teachers using basal readers can move toward adopting whole language. Veatch (1992) discusses the manner in which whole language is interrelated to other reading move- ments, namely, Key Vocabulary, Individualized Reading and Language Experience.

CHANGES IN READING INSTRUCTION

Smith (1992) focuses his attention on the various controversies related to reading that have evolved over the years. He addresses what he calls the two views of learning, *the official* and *the informal*. While he discusses the three theories of teaching reading, (phonics, whole-word, and whole language) and how they relate to the views of learning, he points out that the "great debate may never end." However, it "could serve to keep teachers—and the public at large—conscious of the profound importance and delicacy of the noble art of teaching" (p. 441).

> ## Looking Ahead
>
> In the last article in this chapter, MacGinitie (1991) addresses the question of whether there should be a complete reform in reading instruction.

As we can see, the way in which youngsters have been taught to read has long been a concern and a cause for debate among educators. We are entering a new era, where the interest in whole language offers educators another way of considering how students should be exposed to learning.

The articles in this chapter will further discuss how whole language can be compared to traditional reading instruction. Some of the issues addressed include:

- What are the specific differences between basal readers and whole language?
- Can basal readers and whole language co-exist?
- How do teachers using a basal reader infuse whole language into the classroom? Or can they?
- What are the specific changes in instruction that occur when whole language is embraced?
- Are there some reading approaches of the past that are related to whole language? If so, how, or if not, why not?
- How can we implement and nourish whole language without discarding the effective features of past approaches?
- Why should extremes in reading instruction be avoided?

REFERENCES

Aukerman, R. C. (1971). *Approaches to beginning reading.* New York: John Wiley.
Aukerman, R. C. (1984). *Approaches to beginning reading* (2nd ed.). New York: John Wiley.
Aukerman, R. C. (1981). *The basal reader approach to reading.* New York: John Wiley.
Durkin, D. (1984). Is there a match between what elementary teachers do and what basal reader manuals recommend? *The Reading Teacher,* 37(8), 734–744.
Flickinger, G. G. & Long, E. S. (1990). Beyond the basal. *Reading Improvement,* 27(2), 149–154.
Goodman, K. S. (1989). Whole language *is* whole: A response to Heymsfeld. *Educational Leadership,* 46(6), 69–70.

Heymsfeld, C. R. (1989). Filling the hole in whole language. *Educational Leadership, 46*(6), 65–68.

MacGinitie, W. H. (1991). Reading instruction: Plus ça change . . . *Educational Leadership, 48*(6), 55–58.

McCallum, R. D. (1988). Don't throw the basals out with the bath water. *The Reading Teacher, 42*(3), 204–208.

McCarty, B. J. (1991). Whole language: From philosophy to practice. *The Clearing House, 65*(2), 73–76.

Siera, M., & Combs, M. (1990). Transitions in reading instruction: Handling contradictions in beliefs and practice. *Reading Horizons, 31*(2), 113–126.

Smith, F. (1992). Learning to read: The never-ending debate. *Phi Delta Kappan, 73*(6), 432–441.

Veatch, J. (1992). Whole language and its predecessors. *Journal of Reading Education, 18*(1), 63–77.

FOR FURTHER STUDY

Aaron, P. G. (1991). Is there a hole in the whole language? *Contemporary Education, 62*(2), 127–133.

Combs, M. (1994). Implementing a holistic reading series in first grade: Experiences with a conversation group. *Reading Horizons, 34*(3), 196–207.

Edelsky, C. (1990). Whose agenda is this anyway? A response to McKenna, Robinson, & Miller. *Educational Researcher, 19*(8), 7–11.

Farr, R. (1988). A place for basal readers under the whole language umbrella. *Educational Leadership, 46*(3), 86.

Goodman, K. S., Shannan, P., Freeman, Y. S., & Murphy, S. (1988). *Report card on basal readers.* Katonah, NY: Richard C. Owen.

Herbert, H. (1990). The heritage of our profession. *Reading Psychology, 11*(3), iii–xxi.

McKenna, M. C., Robinson, R. D., & Miller, J. W. (1990). Whole language: A research agenda for the nineties. *Educational Researcher, 19*(8), 3–6.

McKenna, M. C., Robinson, R. D., & Miller, J. W. (1990). Whole language and the need for open inquiry: A rejoinder to Edelsky. *Educational Reseacher, 19*(8), 12–13.

Mosenthal, P. B. (1989). The whole language approach: Teachers between a rock and a hard place. *The Reading Teacher, 42*(8), 628–629.

Reutzel, D., & Hollingsworth, P. M. (1988). Whole language and the practitioner. *Academic Therapy, 23*(4), 405–416.

Sippola, A. E. (1994). Holistic analysis of basal readers: An assessment tool. *Reading Horizons, 34*(3), 234–246.

Smith, K. J., Reyna, V. F., & Brainerd, C. J. (1993). The debate continues. *Phi Delta Kappan, 74*(5), 407–410.

Smith, F. (1993). The never-ending confrontation. *Phi Delta Kappan, 74*(5), 411–412.

Wood, M., & O'Donnell, M. (1991). Directions of change in the teaching of reading. *Reading Improvement, 28*(2), 100–103.

Beyond the Basal

Gayle Glidden Flickinger
Emily S. Long

The whole language integrated approach to reading and writing offers the classroom teacher and students the opportunity to select and choose materials together. Encouraging teachers to choose materials that meet the developmental needs of their students in the reading/writing activities is an essential component of whole language. When the teacher views learning as an active constructive process in which the child's prior knowledge, interests and self-motivated purposes all have a major impact on learning, he/she will understand the need to modify the basal and to break away from the lock-step sequence of basal teaching.

Now teachers can go beyond the teacher's manuals and meet their students' needs through the integration of all the language arts modes; reading, writing, listening and speaking. Many classroom teachers are attracted to the philosophy of the whole language approach, but may be bound for any number of reasons to using a basal reader series chosen for their grade level. The basal should not be a limiting factor in the teacher's desire to integrate whole language into the language arts: listening, speaking, writing and reading program.

Traditionally the authors of basal reader series defined the curriculum and the teaching approach to be taken. Teachers were given a district framework or curriculum, provided with stage directions from the teacher's manual and told to fit their students into the structure as prescribed without looking at the reading and writing process as a natural outgrowth of oral language development. Adoption decisions were made building or district-wide and the classroom teacher was expected to follow the established guidelines and to cover all the materials offered. Customarily, the students had a reading book, a spelling book, a writing book and a language arts book to master. Each book was taught separately and within a discrete and isolated time period.

Recent research suggests that the language arts (reading, writing, speaking and listening) are all interrelated and develop, from the beginnings as integrated skills (Busching and Schwartz, 1983). Similarities and differences exist between and among all four of these language processes. Their acquisition is similar in that learners seem to begin by trying out the processes first. Children then use those processes to learn the appropriate forms of language. Yet, in traditional language arts instruction the typical presentation sequence proceeds through the development of listening, speaking, reading and writing skills thought to correlate with the stages through which language development progresses. However, some children experiment with writing earlier than they do with reading (Chomsky, 1971). It was established by Durkin (1966) that some children who read prior to starting school are often involved in prewriting and writing activities before they can actually read conventionally. Baghban (1984), Bissex (1980) and Lass (1982) have recently documented children's early interest in both reading and writing, while Harste, Woodward and Burke (1984) have asserted that young children know much more about print than what teachers and beginning reading and writing programs assume. On the basis of these and other reports from parents, teachers and researchers, teachers should not assume that there is a definite sequence in learning to use the four language modes.

From "Beyond the Basal" by G. G. Flickinger and E. S. Long, 1990, *Reading Improvement, 27*, pp. 149–154. Copyright © 1990 by Project Innovation of Mobile. Reprinted by permission.

Schwartz (1983) asserted that children come to school prepared to make sense of what they find there. This search for meaning can be employed in acquiring language competencies by creating the conditions and providing the experiences that stimulate rather than impede the operation of learning. To do this, teachers must provide experiences with language that are integrated, whole, natural, functional and meaningful.

Encouraging teachers to go beyond the basal means giving the teachers the opportunity to take charge of the teaching materials and to make daily decisions about teaching strategies. These decisions are a reflection of the professional education teachers have received to be able to make a match between children and appropriate materials. A different approach from one that fits all the children into the materials and routine of the teacher's edition of the basal reader.

The basal reader, required by the district, can become the launching pad from which to begin. Now teachers are able to take the teacher's manual and say, "What else?" The enrichment activities teachers never had time to use with the whole group previously are now the starting place for extending beyond the basal. No longer should there be the compulsion to read every story or to do every single workbook page regardless of student need. The teacher will instead begin to think of language use as always occurring in a situation and that situations are critical to meaning making. Therefore, communication becomes the main aim of reading and writing activities, rather than merely circling words or letters to complete a work sheet or reading workbook or reading text with a controlled vocabulary.

Integrated whole language can be used to immerse the entire class in writing and reading activities. The decisions about the materials to use will include the student's point of view, the teacher's point of view as well as the point of view of the authors of the basal reader series. Discussions will evolve between students and teacher in an effort to better understand and to empathize with what readers and writers do before, during and after they read (Butler, 1984). The teacher's role will shift from being the director of activities to becoming a model for the commitment to immersion in the reading and writing process, by not only demonstrating, but by taking an active role. The teacher will come to acknowledge the important role social interaction plays in the learning process and will therefore view language as central to learning. When the students observe an adult reading and writing, and furthermore actually enjoying writing about what has been read, they will be provided with a model to emulate. The students, in turn, will be stimulated to look for interaction in their own reading writing process. This functional view of language learning will enable the students to understand that language is learned through actual use to accomplish relevant purposes. Teachers will then view writing as a meaning-making process in which writers make their own connections and construct their own meanings.

Most basal series contain adaptations of quality children's literature and these abbreviated selections can be the starting point for an exploration into an author's perspective on writing and reading. The original story from which the adaptation was taken can be found and read aloud by the classroom teacher or by a student. A comparison of the "real" story, or the original, can be made to the basal adaptation. Such comparisons if carried out in the discussion format can lead to some interesting insights from the students as they begin to read and to listen critically. The use of the basal adaptation may spark an interest in becoming familiar with other stories written by the same author. Additional works written by one author can easily expand into the study of various genre of literature as well. Many authors have written kinds of materials (genre) from descriptive to poetry to expository.

When fables and folk tales selections are found in basal readers, they can become the starting point for the teacher to locate other versions of the same story to share with the students. Encouraging students to listen critically to a form of traditional literature will provide the students and teacher an opportunity for decision making as each one decides which version they prefer. Using various versions can encourage students to retell the folk tales in their own words or in a modern setting. Young students like to hear the familiar story read and reread. It is a little like meeting an old friend and enjoying the comfort of the familiar—no surprises.

Surprise and novelty can become very important if the students are encouraged to take the basal reading selection and to extend the text into a new ending, another chapter or the viewpoint of another character. Several basals use excerpts from *Charlotte's Web* by E. B. White and this beautiful story of friendship can be extended by writing about the adventures of Charlotte's children as told by one of them.

Another way teachers can have their students innovate on the basal text adaptation is by having students make their own wordless books from some of the illustrations and to then write their own version of the story. Teachers may choose to make this a whole class project in an effort to help develop an understanding of the process involved. Students can even write variations on the text of a favorite story, such as "Susie's (or their own name) Very Good, Super Glorious, Very Great Day," as a variation on Judith Viorst's *Alexander and the Terrible, Horrible, No Good, Very Bad Day.*

Enlarged versions of familiar books or Big Books can also be used by the teacher in the classroom. Using an opaque projector or overhead transparencies to make the enlarged copy of a favorite book, students can work together to make a copy of a favorite story to share with younger students. Many old favorites are no longer available in print and this is one way to share old remembered stories. The Big Book is easy for the audience to see and to enter into and to be a part of the reading through immersion in the print itself. Senior citizens would probably appreciate a book talk on a favorite child's book in the Big Book format as well. The teachers need to carefully supervise the selection of the book to be enlarged. The book should suit both the students' and the audience's needs while meeting the developmental or interest levels. There are many advantages to selecting a book that has rhyme, rhythm and repetitive language. When the read-aloud book has these qualities the audience will want to join in and really take part in the reading. The first time through the book should be shared with the audience for the sheer enjoyment of the language and description The second reading can have the audience joining in and completing some of the repetition.

Centering on the reading selection itself, the teacher can prepare the audience by taking time to talk about the aptness of the title, the history or background of the author and illustrator and then to do some predicting about the content. Laura Ingalls Wilder's Little House series are often adapted to be included in basal readers. Any one of the selections lends itself to this approach as the titles often indicate the locality, and a study of the Ingalls and Wilder families can be drawn from the pages of the stories themselves. During subsequent readings of other of the series books, the teacher can decide to work with prediction of events, contrasts in settings, development of characters and plot structure.

The children need to be immersed in the writing activities along with the reading. The activities need to be integrated rather than taught as isolated subjects. The class can choose to write a sequel to a favorite story, to modify the title and write their own versions of the story, or to add additional dialogue for their favorite character in the story. The skills practiced in workbooks take on new meanings when they are practiced and used in real connected text. The skills that are incorporated in the basal workbook can also be put to excellent use in journal writing. There is no better way to practice a skill such as the use of quotation marks than by having the children observe their use in a printed story and then to extend the use to the students' own original writing. The children's writings are another excellent source for the development of skills. Skills take on new meaning when they are a part of what the children need to make their own writing clearer. The workbook authors choose the material on skill development arbitrarily and there is no research to support that there is one specific set of skills that need to be taught at a particular stage of reading or writing development (Smith, 1978). Unfortunately, classroom teachers have no direct input into the materials on skill development that are included in the workbooks and are expected to cover the skills in the pre-set sequence. Simply marking pages in a traditional workbook does not develop lasting reading writing skills. In fact, an analysis of workbook activities (Osborn, 1984) revealed that many pages require only a perfunctory level of reading. Students don't understand how completing isolated workbook pages and skill sheets relate to "real" writing, because they rarely need to draw conclusions or reason on a high level. Few of the workbook activities foster fluency, or constructive and strategic reading. Even fewer pages require any extended writing. Children need to put the skills taught from the basal readers into "real" writing experiences if these skills are to be so thoroughly mastered that they will transfer into everyday usage. Therefore, instead of spending money and ordering additional workbooks, teachers may chose to use the money to purchase children's literature books for the classroom. The teacher's manual included with the basal reader can be used as a guide to make sure that the important skills for that particular grade level are introduced. *Transactions* by Reggie Routman is an excellent resource book for the teacher interested in becoming more involved in whole language, integrated language arts, and the literature approach to reading and writing.

If teachers are to be encouraged to choose teaching materials to match with their students' interests and needs they must be encouraged to make that decision in selecting materials to use in reading and writing. To make these decisions, teachers must have an extended and continuing knowledge base in reading and writing development which can be enhanced through in-service workshops and support group meetings. Teachers, who are involved in whole language or those who want to be, form networks of support groups to share success stories and stories of experiences in progress. These support groups help the teacher deal with feelings of isolation when they first try to involve their students in true literacy experiences.

Integrating the processes of the language arts can only be successful if the teachers give themselves the opportunity and encouragement to try. It must be remembered that language is an active developmental process of thinking which, to be mastered, must be used regularly. Students need to use language for "real" purposes and for a variety of real audiences if they are to become competent language users. It is the classroom teacher's right and responsibility to see that whole language activities develop in the classroom without the traditional total dependency on the authors of the basal readers and workbooks. The teacher must become the leader in the whole language experience and must assume the responsibility of total immersion in language activities: written, spoken, read and heard.

REFERENCES

Baghban, M. (1984). *Our Daughter Learns to Read and Write: A Case Study from Birth to Three*. Newark, DE: International Reading Association.

Bissex, G. L., (1980). *Gnys at Wrk: A Child Learns to Read and Write*. Cambridge, MA: Harvard University Press.

Busching, B. A. and Schwartz, J. I., Eds. (1983). *Integrating the Language Arts in the Elementary School*. Urbana, IL: National Council of Teachers of English.

Butler, A. and J. Turbill. (1984). *Towards a Reading, Writing Classroom*. Portsmouth, NH: Heinemann Educational Book Inc.

Chomsky, C. (1971). Write First, Read Later. *Childhood Education, 47,* 269–299.

Durkin, D. (1966). *Children Who Read Early.* New York, NY: Teachers College Press.

Harste, J. C., Woodward, V. and Burke, C. (1984). *Language Stories and Literacy Lessons.* Portsmouth, NH: Heinemann Educational Books.

Lass, B. (1982). Portrait of My Son as an Early Reader. *The Reading Teacher, 36,* 20–28. Newark, DE: International Reading Association.

Osborn, J. (1984). The Purposes, Uses and Contents of Workbooks and Some Guidelines for Publishers. In R. C. Anderson, J. Osborn, R. J. Tierney (Eds.), *Learning to Read in American Schools: Basal readers and Content Texts* (pp. 45–111.) Hillsdale, NJ.

Schwartz, J. I. (1983). Language Play, In B. A. Busching and J. I. Schwartz (Eds.), *Integrating the Language Arts in The Elementary School* (pp. 81–90). Urbana, IL: National Council of Teachers in English.

Routman, R. (1988). *Transitions: From Literature to Literacy.* Heinemann Press, Portsmouth, NH.

Smith, F. (1978). *Reading Without Nonsense.* Teachers College Press, New York.

Viorst, J. (1972). *Alexander and the Terrible, Horrible, No Good Very Bad Day.* Atheneum, New York.

White, E. B. (1952). *Charlotte's Web.* Harper and Row, New York.

Wilder, L. (1974). *Little House Books.* Harper and Row, New York.

The Whole Language Umbrella
Is a grass roots organization of whole language groups and individuals. The primary purposes of the WLU are to improve the quality of learning and teaching at all levels of education and to provide support for member groups and individuals. For more information about WLU membership contact: Debbie Manning, 4848 N. Fruit, Fresno, CA 93705.

International Reading Association: Whole Language Special Interest Group.

For more information about the group, contact: Jane Baskwill, R.R. 1, Lawrence Town, Anapolis County, Nova Scotia, Canada, BOS 1 MO.

Gayle Glidden Flickinger is Associate Professor of Elementary Education, Curriculum and Instruction, in the College of Education at Illinois State University. Emily S. Long is Faculty Associate, Metcalf Laboratory School in the Department of Curriculum and Instruction, College of Education at Illinois State University.

Transitions in Reading Instruction: Handling Contradictions in Beliefs and Practice

Maureen Siera
Martha Combs

Reconciling whole language philosophy with traditional classroom reading instruction requires redefining beliefs about reading processes that, for most of us, are deeply embedded in years of basal reading instruction. Such redefining has the potential of creating conflicts between curricular beliefs and instructional practices. Whole language and basal skills instruction, according to Goodman (1989), are contradictory and incompatible practices. In contrast, Heymsfeld (1989) suggests that it is appropriate to combine the best aspects of skills instruction and whole language into one approach. While contradictions may exist initially, perhaps such contradictions will resolve themselves as educators redefine professional beliefs.

In support of others who are in transition, we would like to share experiences of two first

From "Transitions in Reading Instruction: Handling Contradictions in Beliefs and Practice" by M. Siera and M. Combs, 1990, *Reading Horizons, 31,* pp. 113–126. Copyright © 1990 by Western Michigan University. Reprinted by permission.

grade teachers, Nancy and Sandra, who were beginning to make a transition from basal reading to a more holistic approach. Nancy and Sandra each discovered that transition is a slow process and that contradictions in beliefs and practice are a very real part of the transition.

A LITTLE BACKGROUND ON NANCY AND SANDRA

Both Nancy and Sandra came from traditional preservice programs, had student teaching experiences which emphasized a basal reading skills program approach and have taught for six and five years respectively. They are employed in different school systems; however, the adopted basal reading programs are the reading curriculum in both districts. During the year prior to the changes described, both teachers enrolled in graduate courses in reading/language arts at different universities and were introduced to whole language philosophy.

At school Nancy was allowed to make some changes in her instruction, but her principal assumed that she would continue to use basal materials in some manner. He expressed concern for children learning "the skills" and for the money that he expended for materials. Sandra's principal expressed similar concerns. Her school system, however, mandated at least three days of basal instruction per week.

NANCY'S TRANSITION

Following two and one-half months of basal readiness letter books combined with language experience, Nancy decided not to move into the preprimers as she had always done in the past. While she was deciding what to do about reading groups, she instituted a form of individualized reading. Using picture books and easy to read books that were leveled from very easy to hard, the children, with Nancy's guidance, chose books to read. They practiced reading the book by themselves, with a partner from their class, with a sixth grade partner, with the teacher, and with their parents until they felt confident to read the book aloud to the class. As Nancy made other changes in her program, time for individual reading remained. At the time, Nancy did not consider this approach as a viable alternative to her basal groups.

In lieu of basal instruction, Nancy decided to alternate weekly between the use of (1) big books, and (2) content language experience (a combination of reading easy informational books and language experience stories). Even though a basal series had been adopted by her district, Nancy chose not to use those materials. She was, however, required to give the end of level tests that would be placed in cumulative folders.

During big book lessons, children were called to reading by table groups, so that the lesson was repeated three times. Nancy felt that the small groups enhanced interaction and attention. Lessons usually began with predictions using the title and pictures; as Nancy read each page aloud, she encouraged children to discuss story events and make new predictions. Nancy would also call attention to such things as word or letter patterns and new vocabulary words. The group then reread the story with Nancy. The reading was followed by a worksheet based upon the story and reinforcing a skill emphasized during the discussion.

Over the course of the week, the children participated in repeated readings, identified skill elements found in the stories, completed follow-up activities, and tape recorded themselves reading. Nancy commented that the first reading seemed tedious, but she did not change this routine.

Content language experience lessons were organized around four or five topics each week for which Nancy could find a variety of books, such as space, famous people, sports, wild animals, or transportation. On Monday, after selecting a topic, the children would choose a book to start reading. Then they would informally share their books with each other. During the week of study, the groups would alternate meeting days with Nancy. Children discussed what they had learned, shared ideas they had written down, and dictated ideas they thought were important to remember. These dictated stories could be reread during future group times or independently. During the week the children also read a number of different books about their topic. Books were checked out to be read and shared at home. While Nancy met with one group of children, other groups were completing seatwork, listening to "skill" tapes and completing worksheets, or doing Workshop Way activities. Children were free to interact during this time, assisting each other.

The morning routine in Nancy's room began with process writing time. During writing children selected their own topics, wrote and often collaborated on stories. Nancy would conference with children. The writing time ended with a few children sharing their pieces at an "author's chair." After reading and responding to questions and comments about their stories, the authors would award a "listening ear" to the best listener. Authors also joined the "author's club" or added another star on the chart by their names for sharing.

Following writing, children were directed to a daily mystery word, sight words that Nancy believed needed to be learned. On 3×5 cards, children copied the word and a sentence, either the one on the board or their own, drew a picture on the reverse side of the card, and filed the card in a box with other mystery words. These cards were often referred to during spelling or writing.

Next came the assigning of seat work to be completed while Nancy met with reading groups. The seatwork often was a combination of work with spelling words, phonics workbook pages, teacher-made practice pages for a skill discussed in reading group or in a mini-lesson, a follow-up activity to a language experience story, a math workbook page, or Workshop Way activities. Later in the year, the children received writing tablets for copying work from the board.

Skill teaching, such as phonics or structural analysis, was also completed as a whole group in mini-lessons. Along with skill knowledge, children were encouraged to think strategically about the skill knowledge that Nancy was presenting. There were usually follow-up activities on other days to reinforce the lesson. The content for these lessons came from Nancy's observations during reading and writing times.

The afternoon included a spelling program in which children selected their own words and practiced with a partner, independent reading, math, or story times, and special classes, such as music, art or physical education. At the end of the day the children would mark their own behavior sheet by either circling a happy or sad face for that day.

SANDRA'S TRANSITION

Because of her school district's mandate of basal instruction three days per week, Sandra decided to use multiple copies of children's literature on the other two days. Initially she chose Tuesdays and Thursdays for literature. On the other three days she conducted her reading groups as she had always done, at least in the beginning of her transition.

On basal days, Sandra moved from the process writing period into an explanation of seatwork activities, which included a variety of reading and math worksheets, basal workbook pages, and handwriting. A literature activity related to each group's book was also explained along with reminders about other classroom choices. In these sessions children were grouped by learning modalities. In these groups Sandra used a combination of story and vocabulary introductions, silent and oral reading, discussion of stories, skill instruction and explanations of workbook pages.

In preparation for the literature groups, Sandra selected four books that she thought her children would enjoy and for which she could get enough copies. For a period of four weeks children would rotate through these books, but in the order they chose. The week before the literature groups met, Sandra read all of the books aloud. On Friday, the children would tell her their choice for the first rotation. Sandra also developed five different extension activities for each book, one for each day of the week. These usually tended to be open ended activities, encouraging creativity and expression.

On Tuesdays, Sandra would introduce the children to the author of the book with interesting tidbits that she had found. Before reading, she would present a chart of vocabulary words, in story context, that she felt were necessary to discuss ahead of time. Then Sandra would read the story aloud again, with the children following along in their own books. The story would be discussed, emphasizing the parts the children enjoyed most and any questions they had about the story, including vocabulary. After the first reading, the book would be repeated with children reading along with Sandra whenever they could. If the group was enthusiastic and time permitted, the reading might be repeated several times. Finally, the children would act out favorite parts or become one of the characters in a new version.

On Thursdays, the second meeting of the literature group, the children would participate in repeated readings and some individual reading of favorite parts. During this group time, Sandra often called attention to certain aspects of the book that she wanted students to notice, such as special words, interesting patterns or how illustrations related to text. As the year progressed, these discussions were built more upon what students noticed in the book.

Over time, the children expressed reluctance to return to the basal stories so Sandra began to make some modifications in both literature and basal groups. In the literature groups, Sandra began to realize that no matter how carefully she selected the vocabulary words, they never seemed to be appropriate for all children. So she encouraged children to select five words from the story that they found interesting or wanted to learn. These words were placed in the child's word book.

Sandra also discovered that after several rotations through the set of four books, the children were very familiar with the stories and were suggesting new activities to extend the books. She learned that children often thought of better extensions than she did; certainly they were more personal.

During the basal lessons, Sandra began to find that students already were familiar with skills she was directed to introduce. Sandra believed that the combination of writing and wide reading was definitely helping. Realizing that students didn't need all of what the basals suggested, she began to alter lessons drastically, focusing on comprehension of the better stories and using the workbook pages less and less. Along with this change, she began to alter morning seatwork into more open ended activities that would allow children more time for exploration. But she was never allowed to completely give up the basal program—and perhaps she wasn't ready to.

During the afternoon, Sandra's students were read to, completed math lessons, did independent reading (often partner reading in one of the four literature group books), and were involved in units or other special activities. Children read a wide variety of texts in the unit activities. Sandra commented on how much easier it seemed to be to bring books into the afternoons than the mornings.

CONTRADICTIONS COME WITH TRANSITIONS

Fullan (1982) suggests that changes in classroom instruction involve (a) use of new and revised materials, (b) use of new teaching approaches, and (c) alteration of beliefs. We will use this as a framework for reflecting on how Nancy and Sandra began to make changes in their classrooms and to consider the question of contradictory practices and beliefs during times of transition.

Use of New and Revised Materials

Both Nancy and Sandra incorporated new materials (children's literature and some follow-up or extension activities) into their reading instruction but in different ways. As they did this, they still retained some of the old materials. While initiating use of big books, information books, and language experience, Nancy still retained many worksheet-type activities that had previously been a part of her reading program. For the most part, Sandra seemed to separate the literature groups from other parts of the day. She did not bring old materials into these groups, but did retain them in most other parts of the morning.

These teachers come out of a basal tradition where change of curriculum is often equated with a change of materials, but not necessarily a change in beliefs or behaviors. In some school districts, it is done every five years or so as new state adoptions take place. Even when the new materials come, we often hold on to the old because it is familiar and comfortable. As the new materials become more familiar, we are better able to make judgments about the relevance or effectiveness of such materials.

Were the materials used by Sandra and Nancy incompatible or contradictory? Yes, they were. It seems, however, that part of the transition from basal to literature may involve a period of time when the materials we use are incompatible and contradictory as we are learning. However, as Nancy and Sandra illustrate, over time we can re-examine our ideas about contrived skill materials as we learn the power and potential of authentic materials.

Some impacts of the contradictions were easier to see than others. Nancy sensed that the big book lessons were not as effective as the content language experience lessons and she was initially defensive about them. Over time, she began verbalizing concerns about the big book lessons, acknowledging that a change was needed but she still wasn't sure what was wrong. Sandra could not elect to end basal instruction altogether, but she could begin to modify it to make it more consistent with the literature groups. Even though she was modifying her materials, Sandra still retained some old materials, such as workbooks and morning seatwork, for which she did not seem to see a new alternative. The process of change followed by the two teachers is summarized in Figures 1 and 2 on pages 48 and 49.

Use of New Teaching Approaches

For at least a portion of the school day, both Nancy and Sandra incorporated new teaching approaches, while maintaining the former approaches. Nancy's content language experience groups led her in new directions for the use of information books, open discussions, using writing as a way of responding to books, and a new teacher behavior for less directed reading groups. Nancy did not use these same behaviors in her big book groups where she was much more directed and used worksheets to isolate and check skill knowledge. She sensed that there was a difference between the two groups, but could not specifically identify what it was.

Except for her initial attempts to preteach vocabulary in stories, the approach that Sandra took in the literature groups was dramatically different than her typical basal teaching behavior. She behaved as if basal and literature groups served different functions. However, Sandra's basal group behavior was modified over the course of the year as she watched

Chapter Two

Basal Readiness Books with LEA

OCT/NOV
- decision not to use basal preprimers
- independent & partner reading (while deciding alternative approach)
- New approaches (alternating weeks)

NOV/DEC
- big book units (3 groups)

Day 1	Day 2/3
predict	reread
teacher read aloud	attention to skills
discuss	worksheets
attention to skills	taped story
choral read	
worksheets	

- content language experience (4–5 groups)

Day 1	Day 2/3	Day 3/4
select from 4–5 topics	share/discuss	share/discuss
select book	dictate LEA	add to LEA
read independently or with partner	exchange books	reread LEA
take book home	take books home	write ideas
	write responses	

FEB/MAR
- Add whole group mini-lessons for phonics and structural analysis. Emphasize strategies.

Note: The chart reflects only major changes in reading instruction.

FIGURE 1
NANCY'S TRANSITION

---

the children demonstrate knowledge of reading processes before the basal introduced the skill.

For both Nancy and Sandra some new behaviors were carried over to other parts of the day. Nancy moved into a more child-directed spelling approach. Sandra's afternoon incorporated a great deal of literature into units of study and she was being trained for Math Their Way, a process approach. Both teachers devoted time each morning to process writing.

Did Nancy and Sandra display incompatible and contradictory teaching behaviors? Yes, they did, but over the course of the year they both began to alter those behaviors. While at the end of the year all of the contra-

Whole Language versus Traditional Reading Instruction

> **SEPT** • basal groups (3 days) (district mandate)
>
> *Day 1*
> introduce story
> introduce vocabulary
> silent reading
> discussion
> workbook
>
> *Day 2*
> oral reading
> skill work
> workbook
>
> *Day 3*
> skill work
> workbook
>
> • literature groups (2 days)
> (4 books–4 groups, rotate weekly for 1 month)
>
> *Day 1*
> introduce vocabulary
> read aloud
> discuss favorite parts
> choral reading
> acting out parts
> responsive activity
>
> *Day 2*
> choral reading
> reread favorite parts
> focus on particular aspects of book
> discuss author
>
> **OCT** • after several rotations students begin suggesting activities
>
> **NOV** • replace vocabulary introduction with personalized vocabulary activities
>
> **JAN/FEB**
> • notice early skill acquisition
> • reduce isolated skill instruction
> • emphasize personal response
> • replace some workbook pages with open-ended activities
>
> **MARCH**
> • become more selective about stories
> • some multiple copies of literature are by student authors
>
> *Note: The chart reflects only major changes in reading instruction.*

FIGURE 2
SANDRA'S TRANSITION

dictions were not resolved, both Nancy and Sandra had learned to take some of their cues from their children and from their intuition about what felt right.

Sensing that our behaviors may not be appropriate can be a long and drawn out process for some of us. We are not used to trusting ourselves. Both Nancy and Sandra needed time to grow into their new approaches, see how they felt, and then begin to reflect. Like materials, some behaviors were more obvious, others were very subtle and remained unchanged at the end of the year.

Alteration of Beliefs

Redefining some of their beliefs initially led Sandra to begin making changes in classroom instruction which continued throughout the year. Both began with a global direction, but had difficulties with the details involved in the redefining that Goodman (1989) suggested must take place. They both seemed to focus on the most obvious at first—a need for new materials. Even though both Nancy and Sandra embraced holistic principles they continued some incompatible practices, such as isolated skill instruction. They seemed to be unable to recognize the contradictions between their espoused beliefs and some of their classroom practices. Even at the end of a year, there were still contradictions between beliefs, materials, and approaches that each teacher could not reconcile on her own.

The sheer number of changes may have actually slowed down Nancy's transition. There were times when Nancy felt overwhelmed with all that was happening in her classroom. Nancy had replaced most all of the traditional landmarks of the morning in a primary classroom with unfamiliar activities. While Sandra experimented with literature, she was still able to tell herself that she was teaching the "skills." This issue—"skills"—may very well be the most difficult aspect of our histories to alter. Nancy had given up the security of basal groups, but did not give up teaching "skills" during that school year. Both teachers needed time to reconcile this issue for themselves.

CONCLUSION

We believe that the experiences of teachers like Nancy and Sandra suggest that while teachers are in transition from basals to more holistic approaches, we should expect that some incompatible and contradictory elements will exist. Unlike Hemysfeld (1989), we do not suggest that the strengths of basals skills and whole language be combined into one approach. What we do suggest is acceptance of the co-existence of contradictory beliefs and practices as natural for a period of time while teachers re-educate themselves about new approaches, materials, and beliefs. Co-existence may mean periods of confusion and uncertainty, but reassurance comes from teachers like Nancy and Sandra, who demonstrate that when we begin to tune into ourselves and our children, new directions slowly become clearer.

REFERENCES

Fullan, M. (1982). *The meaning of educational change.* New York: Teachers College Press.
Goodman, K. (1989). Whole language is whole: A response to Heymsfeld. *Educational Leadership, 46,* 69–70.
Heymsfeld, C.R. (1989). Filling the hole in whole language. *Educational Leadership, 46,* 64–67.

Maureen Siera is a member of the Department of Curriculum and Instruction in the College of Education at Northeastern Oklahoma State University in Tahlequah, Oklahoma. Martha Combs is a faculty member in the Department of Curriculum and Instruction at the University of Nevada in Reno.

Whole Language and Its Predecessors

Jeannette Veatch

Since the rise of the Whole Language movement, I have been wondering whatever happened to (1) Sylvia Ashton-Warner and her Key Vocabulary, (2) Individualized Reading, and (3) the Experience Chart. These are three activities I have enthusiastically espoused for many years. In scanning the many books now available, the omission of these three activities is noteworthy and puzzling. As they seem to me to be so clearly in the child-centered ballpark, and thus so compatible with Whole Language philosophy, why, then, is their absence so noticeable? This is an anomaly that I would like to examine.

Nor am I the only person wondering why certain educators, or activities, especially those prominent before 1970, are so rarely found in current Whole Language literature. For example, Goffin (1991) asks the same question about Carolyn Pratt, a 1930s and 40s educational crusader in New York City (1990). In more general terms Harold H. Herber (1990) deplored the lack of attention to earlier traditional contributors and their contributions to the profession.

There is no doubt that the Whole Language movement, as labeled in *Teacher Magazine* (1991) is a revolution, a wonderful, radical revolution of major proportion. And it is sweeping the country. The Second Whole Language Umbrella Conference in Phoenix in August 1991 served to increase my hopes that the day was closer for the kind of education I have worked for for decades. There I heard teachers—hundreds of them—applaud those speakers making derogatory remarks about basals, workbooks, and other facets of traditional, commercial, educational material. The enthusiasm, the professionalism, the *youth*, the concern for children, of those attending that conference, was exhilarating. I have waited over thirty years for such a reaction. That excitement was certainly in marked contrast to an earlier educational conference I attended in Las Vegas. Maybe those in Las Vegas *felt* the same way, but it did not show like it did in Phoenix.

While it is not the purpose of this paper to evaluate typical on-going practices in the Whole Language classroom, as tempting as that exercise might be, I do wish to raise some questions as to why the above educational approaches are so infrequently found. One reason might be attributed, perhaps, to the rapid pace of the development of the Whole Language movement itself. Certainly such classrooms have been evolving in markedly unique ways than those that have gone before. It is easier to identify one when observing school. Whole Language classrooms are simply different than others, and many of us are very glad for it.

Yet the Whole Language movement is paying a price for this unprecedented singularity. Like Topsy, it has grown so rapidly that it has not yet gotten its act together. Its incredible popular growth has brought about, in many schools and teachers, a "have-you-been-saved" syndrome that is noticeable. To me, this brings back memories, as I, personally, suffered through the same pattern, twenty years ago, during the "Individualized Reading" era. In this instance, history is repeating itself, and a similar backlash is developing. Hostility and antagonism to the very name of Whole Language itself is rearing its head in the same way that the term and practice of "Individualized

---

From "Whole Language and Its Predecessors" by J. Veatch, 1992, *Journal of Reading Education, 18,* pp. 63–77. Copyright © 1992 by the Organization of Teacher Educators in Reading. Reprinted by permission of Jeannette Veatch and the Journal of Reading Education.

Reading" did twenty years ago. This is true not only in the halls of academe, but among many proponents of Whole Language itself. Such hostility toward *both* of these approaches may come from angry personal responses to certain professional accusations, published and spoken. But there is more to it than that.

WHOLE LANGUAGE CHARACTERISTICS

There is no question that Whole Language strength is notable in at least four major areas: (1) learner-centeredness, (2) scorn of commercial behavioristic material, such as basals and workbooks, (3) demand for the integration of all curriculum, especially the language arts, and (4) salutary insistence on authenticity in teaching methodology. These are attributes that I find admirable. Let me now apply these criteria to these three approaches I referred to above to see just how compatible each is with Whole Language Philosophy. First, let us begin with Sylvia Ashton-Warner's Key Vocabulary.

KEY VOCABULARY

In a videotaped demonstration (Jan V Productions, 1986) a teacher elicits a word spontaneously from a child. The teacher does not know what the word might be, but urges that it be a "good" one, *i.e.,* good to the child. The teacher then prints the word on a piece of tag board, and asks the child to identify each letter, referring, if necessary, to the alphabet posted on the nearby wall. Then the child is asked to trace the letters, following the western traditional left-to-right directionality. Finally, the child is asked to "read" the word from the card, which is taken to his desk for incorporating into writing, and related language arts.

Now to compare this with Whole Language philosophy. In Key Vocabulary we find:

1. Learner-centeredness. All words are the child's. NONE are given by the teacher.
2. No commercial materials. No basal readers, or workbooks needed for the activity.
3. Integration. Reading, writing, speaking, listening are all part of the activity.
4. Authenticity. All products are valid personal expressions of the learner. No assignments from outside sources are made, or needed.

Next let us look at Individualized Reading and apply our four characteristics.

INDIVIDUALIZED READING

In this demonstration, also videotaped, (Jan V Productions 1986), reading instruction takes place *only* with books that are chosen by the learner, using the Rule of Thumb for finding appropriate reading level. Individual, one-to-one conferences with the teacher, on a self-selected book (about one out of ten books read) follow. Areas explored are: (a) personal reasons for book choice, (b) main idea presented by author, and appreciation of its literary quality and meaning, (c) phonics and other mechanical details for reading proficiency, and, (d) love of audience appreciation from oral reading. As the teacher confers with each child over the week, records are kept of needs, interests, etc. that would provide a topic for a group to examine and study more intensively. Those elements needing further work or instruction are taken care of by the teacher on individual, group, or class basis. Mini-lessons are prominent and useful. Nor is it precluded that a group could meet on a chosen book with the teacher acting as chair.

Now to compare this activity with the Whole Language philosophy:

1. Learner-centeredness: No book is chosen by the teacher and assigned to a learner. Literature appreciation as a whole class

activity can be developed on teacher-chosen books, but never when the goal is instruction.
2. No commercial materials. No basal readers, workbooks or printed exercises of any kind are desired or needed. Such destroy the personal choice element needed to promote the love of reading.
3. Integration. The total curriculum can be covered by independent seat work while the teacher is conducting individual or group conferences. Projects in writing, math (original story problems), science, history, etc, become part of the school day.
4. Authenticity. No learning is developed on other than that personally chosen book, and other realistic, non-assignment activities.

Finally, the Experience Chart, part of the Language Experience approach, is described and judged.

THE EXPERIENCE CHART

The Experience Chart (Jan V Productions, 1986) is being considered as a part of the Language Experience approach as a whole. Any time children's own language is used (see above with Key Vocabulary, for example) in teaching reading, it constitutes some element of Language Experience. For my present purpose, I wish to deal only with this type of class "newspaper" when the whole class is together, usually in the early grades, to illustrate my argument. In this activity, the teacher elicits from the whole class accounts of those most recent happenings, "that every one would like to hear about." After all listen to the various events, the teacher, *not* the class, chooses that event that has the most dramatic promise. The teacher should be aware of the difference between the oral and written language modalities and so must transmogrify the words spoken into words written on the chalk board or easel. Usually four or five events can constitute one daily chart. This "news" becomes a written record of the children's lives, in and out of school, and can be used as material that children can refer to during the rest of the day when working on individual writing, math, science, etc. projects. The teacher concludes the chart time period by having the class read the "newspaper" aloud, and making the best possible use of instruction to promote literacy.

Now let us compare this activity to Whole Language Philosophy:

1. Learner-centeredness. ALL events are from the children's lives. Never does the teacher ask them to relate an event that conforms to an assigned topic.
2. No commercial material. No drills, texts, or other commercial material are needed or desired.
3. Curriculum integration. As the "news" comes from the class, it can, and does, cover such curriculum aspects as math, history, economics(!), science, etc.
4. Authenticity. As all discussion originates with pupils, all discussion requires authentic topics. To talk about an occurrence that was not part of *that* class' living experience, would not be authentic and so would destroy the drive to learn and find out about the world.

REASONS BEHIND THE LACK OF EMPHASIS?

The above description and discussion redesigned, of course, to bolster my belief that these activities (vocabulary interaction, Individualized Reading and Language Experience) should not be omitted from current practice. Education, in my opinion, has suffered from their absence in the classroom. The obvious question is why are they missing? Perhaps the heart of the matter lies in their differing in certain ways from those current, unique, Whole Language classroom practices.

I am asking why these, and other tried and true learner-centered activities are being ignored? Why are they so unfamiliar to so many budding, young 1992 teachers? Why is the methodology of Whole Language classrooms being developed as if there had never been any other practice, equally learner-centered, equally non-commercial, equally non-behavioristic in its teaching? Why are earlier activities being discouraged, ignored or, at least, not recognized as valid education? Why is it so difficult for Whole Language Proponents to accept divergence, *even when such divergence is clearly compatible with the dearest precepts of the Whole Language philosophy?*

Perhaps it is because divergence is not considered "pure" Whole Language? I think that may well be the case, as the following incident illustrates. A principal of an elementary school known and admired for its Whole Language classrooms, stated, after watching a videotaped demonstration of Sylvia Ashton-Warner's Key Vocabulary, "It is good, but *I am a purist.*" In other words she felt that learner-centered practice *in any other form* than what she considered Whole Language was, to her, not "pure," and therefore, not Whole Language. Is it because such teaching is so different, that many Whole Language classrooms—and their advocates—are coming to be seen as a cultish "If-you-don't-do-it-our-way, you-ain't-doing-it" group. It seems either you belong to the Whole Language club, or you do not.

But, however robust, the Whole Language movement is still very young, about two decades old. Have its current advocates *never* experienced any of these early activities? Have current advocates not chosen to look at previous developments? Could these approaches I have described, and others, have been considered, and *rejected?* If so, I raise the question of "*WHY?*" Could such a decision to reject stem from a *lack of actual classroom teaching experience on the part of Whole Language proponents?* Could that actual experience be at inappropriate grade levels? Answering such questions is difficult. But if earlier practices have been judged unacceptable to many Whole Language proponents, that can explain why current Whole Language classrooms are so different from others, even if those others are not traditional textbook-driven, behavioristic situations.

It is not sinful to to be different, of course, because being different can be desirable. But being different can lead to the development of some of the antagonism and hostility that is now apparent. The phrase "Whole Language" is now being banned in places, to my great regret, and its continued existence could regrettably be in jeopardy. Part of the problems lies in the insistence that "If-you-don't-do-it-our-way, you-ain't-doing-it!" Peace and serenity in schools are more easily obtained when all the teachers know and understand what is going on. But if youth, inexperience, and the excitement of a burgeoning movement affects scholarship, is that former congruous practice overlooked? Is this why earlier "heroines" and approaches, demonstrably analogous to Whole Language philosophy, have been skipped?

ASSESSING BIBLIOGRAPHICAL DATES, PRE-1970

As an expansion of the movement did not take place until the mid 1970s, the matter of dates becomes important in examining causes for the low priority of earlier activities. To begin with, it must be recognized that these three activities I am referring to, whatever their merits, were popular BEFORE 1970. Ashton-Warner's *Teacher* came out in 1962. Dorris May Lee's first book bore a 1943 date, and its second edition with Roach Van Allen was published in 1963. My first article on Individualized Reading appeared in 1954. Willard Olsen's pamphlet in 1952 was the true beginning of literature-based approaches to reading. Other writings analogous to current Whole Language thinking in emergent literacy were even earlier. Alvina Burrows (1939) began the demise of traditional "composition" a decade before. The educational volcano at Teachers College, Columbia, with its Horace Mann Lincoln Laboratory School, its promotion of the Activity Program, block building (Patty Hill), social studies units (Frederick Bonser), and much else, erupted in the 1920s. Alice Keliher effectively destroyed the ideological base of ability grouping (1931). Carolyn Pratt (1948), mentioned earlier, was a notable in private schooling in post-war New York City. Others could be added.

The Importance of the 1970 Date

Thus the date of 1970 becomes important. The current voluminous literature in the Whole Language genre, especially books from Heinemann, have hardly been on the market since 1970. I will now pose questions about the activities cited above which were popular *before* 1970. My reasoning tells me that the pre-1970 activities were not prevalent, nor popular enough, to draw the attention and examination by Whole Language advocates. This leads me to take a look at Whole Language literature and determine the dates in the bibliographies of selected texts.

To examine this problem, I selected five major texts, recognized as important in the field of Whole Language. Their authors are: R.W. Blake (1990), Victor Froese (1990), J. Hansen, T. Newkirk, and D. Graves, (1985), Judith M. Newman (1985), and Constance Weaver (1988). While there are many other texts dealing with Whole Language, I feel safe in assuming that the scope indicated above would not be changed significantly even if other bibliographies were examined. There are, of course, many others, but these should serve my purpose, as will be seen in the following presentation.

Intellectual Incest in Footnotes?

My first impression in studying these bibliographies was, in the words of Yogi Berra, "*deja vu* all over again.*" Years ago a professor of mine, in referring to a flood of curriculum books then on the market muttered, "I do wish they would stop committing intellectual incest by writing footnotes to each other!" That comment of many years ago came to mind, so frequently were the Goodmans, Smith, Harste, Graves, and Calkins listed, that without them, these selected texts would have had much shorter bibliographies! Maybe not better, but certainly shorter!

Frequency of Citation

A tally of the bibliography of each of the above five texts came to 1,424 different entries. Of these, 1,248 citations, or 92%, bore dates *after* 1970, leaving only 176, or 8% that were published *before 1970*. The ratio of 8 to 1 indicates the heavy preference, by authors or editors of the Whole Language texts, for recent writings—*after 1970*. However, there were educators of earlier years included who must be mentioned: Sylvia Ashton-Warner, Alvina Burrows, Dorris May Lee, Roach Van Allen, Mary Ann Hall, Russell Stauffer, Willard Olsen, Jeannette Veatch, Alice Keliher, Winifred Ward, Lev Vygotsky, and Edmund Huey. These people were not only well known before 1970, but held compatible views, in my opinion, to learner-centered education. Their frequency of mention in these five texts is shown in Table 1 on page 56.

Nila Banton Smith, William S. Gray, John Holt, and Rudolph Flesch were also found, but I question their early relationship to the Whole Language movement.

Flesch and Basals

However, of those bibliographies, one page needs special comment. Constance Weaver in *Reading Process and Practice* (1988, p. 467), reveals, I feel, a surprising ignorance about the disputes that have roiled the field of reading

TABLE 1
FREQUENCY OF MENTION IN SELECTED TEXTS

Name of Author/Activity	No. of Times Mentioned in 5 Texts	No. of Times Mentioned in 12 Texts
Sylvia Ashton-Warner	1	8
Key Vocabulary	5	–
Alvina Burrows	0	–
M. Clay	–	10
Kenneth Goodman	–	11
Yetta Goodman	–	8
Edmund Huey	3	–
Alice Keliher	0	–
Language Experience:		
Dorris May Lee	1	–
Roach Van Allen	2	8
Mary Ann Hall	2	7
Russell Stauffer	4	8
None Related to Area	–	9
Willard Olson	1	–
Frank Smith	–	11
R. Strickland	–	7
Jeannette Veatch	2	6
Individualized Reading	4	–
Winifred Ward	0	–
Lev Vygotsky	4	–

for decades. On that page, out of thirteen references, there is not ONE mention of the issue of Language Experience, nor of Sylvia Ashton-Warner, nor of Individualized Reading (to me, the most rancorous omission of all). She does list one reference that has the word "Phonics" in the title. Is "phonics" the *only* problem in the past history of reading?

In addition, Weaver gives prominence to Rudolph Flesch (1955) saying his phonics system was his greatest contribution. Many reading specialists think so, too, but I do not.

On a 1961 platform I shared with him at Lehigh University, I heard *him* say that his contribution was implementing the first allout, and long overdue, attack on basal readers. With this I agree. In 1961 I was a lonely fighter against such commercialism, so I was delighted to find a cohort in that battle that is still not over. But, I am still of the opinion that his phonics are ridiculous. The "whole word" fuss (*i.e.*, the phonics disputes) is, in my opinion, an example of bait-and-switch tactic on the part of traditional reading people who wish to protect the sacred cow of basals. That is, it is better to inveigh against Rudolph Flesch for his phonics ideas, than to accept his quite valid criticism of basal readers. He DID start the ball rolling against basals, although few agree with me that he deserves such credit.

Comparison with Another Study

While the preceding is a brief accounting of the pre- and post-1970 bibliographical references in five Whole Language textbooks, there is another study that sheds light on the same question. Blanchard, Rottenberg, and Jones (1991) selected twelve reading methodology textbooks rather than texts specifically aimed at a Whole Language audience. Their methodology was similar to mine, in that names, rather than separate citations, were tallied as to the number of books in which each was listed. No matter how many books of a given author were included in the body of the book, only the name itself, rather than the number of references, was tallied. Not surprisingly, there were many names listed, covering decades of publishing in reading instruction. Interestingly, he found *no* one name listed in all twelve texts.

For my purposes, I have selected from the many that were tallied, only those who, in my opinion, could be considered valid predecessors to the Whole Language movement, and therefore related to the main inquiry I am pursuing. Table 1 shows the findings.

The question arises in looking at these listings, as to why Sylvia Ashton-Warner is included in eight of those texts selected by Blanchard, and yet mentioned only once in all of the Whole Language bibliographies? Similarly, Van Allen is listed eight times in the Blanchard study, but only twice in the Whole Language Group. Even I, the pariah and early nemesis of basal systems, am referred to in *six* of the reading methodology texts, yet only twice in the Whole Language listing. Those accorded bare mention in the Whole Language references are found far more frequently in the standard, traditionally oriented, reading texts.

The rare mention of those earlier educators, as well as the lack of emphasis on Sylvia Ashton-Warner, Individualized Reading, and the Experience Chart, is revealing. These are evidently not to be considered important or *pure* in the Whole Language sense. Certainly they are not to be classified as seed beds, or even fore-runners of the movement. If prominent and respected Whole Language educators consider writings prior to 1970 to be unworthy of inclusion in their bibliographies, even if demonstrably compatible to their educational philosophy, it is no wonder that there is confusion, puzzlement, and hostility abroad about what Whole Language really is. Indeed, if Whole Language practice is going off in its own direction without acknowledgement or *knowledge* of what has gone before, the current schism in education, fueled by this philosophy, is bound to expand. And that is what is happening.

CONCLUSION

This paper began with my questioning of why certain activities and approaches, popular before 1970, are rarely found in current Whole Language literature. One study, citing specific bibliographies from selected Whole Language texts, revealed the heavy preponderance of items published after 1970. In another study by Blanchard et al., of authors, in the genre of our concern, mentioned in reading methodology texts, were mentioned far more frequently than in the five Whole Language texts. It can be assumed, I think, that proponents of Whole Language chose to ignore, or were ignorant of, those approaches and activities popular before 1970, that were compatible with their philosophy.

I cannot close my discussion without indicating that I find some flaws in the present practice of Whole Language. The most serious of which, in my opinion, is the lack of respect for instruction that is not behavioristic in character. But that is another story, and another paper.

REFERENCES

Ashton-Warner, S. (1962). *Teacher.* New York: Simon & Schuster

Blake, R. W. (Ed.) (1990) *Whole language: Explorations and applications,* Schnectady, NY: New York State English Council

Blanchard, J., Rottenberg, C., & Jones, J. (1991). "In search of a shared paradigm." *Reading Psychology, 12*(4), 291–318.

Burrows, A., Ferebee, J., Jackson, D. and Saunders, D. (1939). *They all want to write.* Indianapolis: Bobbs Merrill.

Flesch, R. (1955). *Why Johnnie can't read.* New York: Harper Row.

Froese, V. (Ed.) (1990). *Whole language, practice and theory.* Scarborough, ONT: Prentice Hall, Canada.

Goffin, S. G. (1991). "Remembering heroines of early childhood education." *Young Children,* 47(1).

Hall, M. A. (1970). *Teaching reading as language experience.* Columbus, OH: C.E. Merrill.

Hansen, J., Newkirk, T. & Graves, D. (1985). *Breaking ground: Teachers relate reading and writing in the elementary school.* Portsmouth, NH: Heinemann.

Herber, H. H. (1990). "The heritage of our profession." *Reading Psychology, 11,* iii–xxi.

Jan V Productions (1986). Videotap series *Showing teachers how #1.* "Getting literacy started." Mesa, AZ.

Jan V Productions (1986). Videotape series. *Showing teachers how #5.* "The experience chart." Mesa, AZ.

Jan V Productions (1986). Videotape series. *Showing teachers how #7.* "How to teach reading with trade books." Mesa, AZ.

Keliher, A. V. (1931). *A critical study of homogeneous grouping.* New York: Teachers College, Columbia University.

Lamoreaux, L.A. & Lee, D. M. (1943). *Learning to read through experience,* New York: Appleton-Century Crofts.

Lee, D. M. & Allen, R. V. (1963). *Learning to read through experience.* 2nd ed., New York: Appleton-Century Crofts.

Newman, M. J. (1985). *Whole language: Theory in use.* Portsmouth, NH: Heinemann.

Olsen, W. C. (1952). "Seeking, self-selection and pacing in the use of books by children." *The Packet,* 7(1), Boston: D.C. Heath.

Pratt, C. (1990 & 1948). *I learn from children.* New York: Harper Row. First Perennial Library Edition 1990, (originally published: New York: Simon & Schuster, 1948).

Veatch, J. (1986). *Reading in the elementary school.* 2nd ed., New York: R.C. Owen Publishers.

Veatch, J. (1954). "Individualized reading: For success in the classroom," *Education Trend.* New London, CT: A.C. Crofts.

Weaver, C. (1988). *Reading process and practice.* Portsmouth, NH: Heinemann.

Jeannette Veatch is Professor Emerita of Arizona State University, Tempe Arizona. She is widely known for her writings on Individualized Reading and has written several textbooks for teachers.

Reading Instruction: Plus Ça Change . . .

Walter H. MacGinitie

This is a time of great change in the teaching of reading . . . again. The French say the more things change, the more they stay the same; their shrug derives from an Old World perspective that extends farther back than ours. The sameness is apparent not so much from one moment to the next as from one cycle of time and events to another—from one life span to another, from one government to another, from one love, one war, one fashion to another, from one reform in education to another.

And so, as things change in reading instruction, passions of the past break through again like jonquils in the spring. And, like jonquils in the spring, many of the old ideas are welcome. But one must wistfully add that they will flower only to die once more. Almost certainly, the new–old ideas will again be oversold, misunderstood, overdone, then overwhelmed by reactions to the excesses. Naively eager, and oblivious of the past, we recreate not only enlightened curriculums but the very conditions that doom them.

COMING AROUND AGAIN

Principles of reading instruction that are now promoted and welcomed as new have fired

From "Reading Instruction: Plus Ça Change . . ." by W. H. MacGinitie, 1991, *Educational Leadership, 48,* pp. 55–58. Copyright © 1991 by ASCD. All rights reserved. Reprinted with permission of the Association for Supervision and Curriculum Development.

the enthusiasms of a former generation of teachers. At one time, the concept of the *language arts* was hailed by those who were frustrated by the unnatural separation of reading and writing instruction and by the virtual absence of concern for listening and speaking skills. The emphasis on the unifying language base of the language arts was wholesome. The term *language arts* continued in use, but the unified curriculum was lost. Now the current enthusiasm for the integration of reading and writing greets that integration as new. Listening and speaking are still largely ignored; I wonder why.

About the time I entered the field of education, more than 40 years ago, a curricular movement emphasizing the education of the *whole child* was very popular. I think the *whole child* beats *whole language.* Louise Rosenblatt (1990), in her acceptance of the NCRE Research Award for Lifetime Research Achievement in the English Language Arts, chided "whole language" for compartmentalizing language. Perhaps it does. Language is used by the whole child.

And this is not the first time that an enthusiasm for using *literature* in the teaching of reading has influenced the curriculum. And I see in the *teacher-as-researcher* many reincarnated principles of *action research.* Why, if we welcome the wholesome contributions of whole language, the integration of reading and writing instruction, the use of literature in reading instruction, did we abandon the similar contributions of the language arts movement and the goal of educating the whole child? Primarily, I believe, because changes in education ("reforms!") are typically promoted as replacements rather than improvements. We never seem to try to improve education; we are forever revolutionizing it. It is undoubtedly more stimulating to participate in a revolution than to do one's job better. But, as Slavin (1989) has put it, if there is to be real generational improvement in education, "the emphasis in staff development must shift from what's new to implementation of what works" (p. 757).

GOING TO EXTREMES

Revolution—political or educational—may seem necessary when conditions have become insufferably bad. In education, conditions can become insufferably bad when good ideas are carried to extremes. When the present way, whatever it may be, has been carried to ridiculous extremes, it may seem that the only way to return to sanity is to throw out the present way entirely.

A recent and familiar example of the extremes to which most educational fads are carried can be seen in the way we broke down reading into innumerable skills. We all know of classrooms where most of the children are quite capable of doing independent reading but where there is little time for it. The children are fully occupied, instead, with a mandatory and seemingly interminable series of exercises and skills tests.

Just a few years ago, the *open classroom* concept was introduced, widely misinterpreted, and carried to extremes that destroyed both the movement and the values it contained. Many of the schools without walls became schools without substance. Earlier, the curriculum for educating the whole child drifted to extremes that frustrated parents' wishes that their children's education include a core of traditional subjects.

I do not believe that these movements—their wholesome beginnings, their irrational growth, and ultimate self-destruction—have yet been thoroughly documented. Scholarly examination of their rise and fall might teach us a great deal about how to retain the positive contributions from whole language and literature-based instruction.

Why is it that concepts in education become fads or movements and get carried to foolish extremes? One reason is a university system that spurs professors to make a name for themselves by promoting something "new." Tenure, advancement, and status depend on having articles published and on getting grant money. The chance of being published is greatly increased if you write about the latest trend. If you were a professor wanting to get published in *The Reading Teacher,* what would you write about? Transfer of learning? No. Thirty years ago you might have written about transfer. Now you would write about whole language or literature-based instruction. Although teachers could profit more from a good article on transfer than from one more article on whole language, what gets published is that article on whole language. And getting grants depends on salesmanship—you must convince a granting agency that your work will attract attention and make the granting agency look good. Since tenure, advancement, and status depend so much on salesmanship, the professor feels impelled to sell a "new and better" product in order to succeed . . . or at least survive.

Often there is a time lag while the professor indoctrinates a sufficient number of doctoral students to constitute a critical mass of new professors committed to the new method and while the extremes of the current curriculum become sufficiently oppressive to make the field ripe for change. Then the new method, promoted by these new professors, sweeps in and prospers for awhile. But, as each of these professors adds a burden of new details, the new method in its turn becomes the "sabertoothed curriculum," ripe for ridicule and replacement by a *new* new approach.

Publishers often get blamed for developing new methods so they can sell more materials. Actually, publishers are not a major source of new developments. The publisher who introduces something too new and different in reading is likely to take a big loss, both in money and in market share. But once it seems clear that a new fad *is* taking hold, then the publishers are right there to add all the bells and whistles they can sell. Publishers also may try to swell profits by extending some new practice up and down the grades. For example, if schools buy primary-grade materials that teach and test a series of decoding skills, publishers will find more difficult skills —of interest only to a language scientist—and build them into lessons and materials for the higher grades. Thus, publishers carry a developing trend to extremes in order to sell more of it. But the schools ask for it. They buy.

Schools do indeed encourage this carrying of educational trends to foolish extremes. Some schools aggressively embrace new fads; others accept faddish developments to defend themselves against crusading critics. Our schools are not well served by those who see no value in any but one idea. As Bartlett Giamatti (1988) told a recent graduating class at the Massachusetts Institute of Technology:

> The diagnosticians for whom all illnesses are similar because all cures are identical; the purveyors of an ism, the dealers in system . . . the Simplifiers who tell you . . . they have boiled life down to a bumper sticker—these are the enemies . . . of the life of the mind (p. 18).

PROFITTING FROM THE PAST

Why can't we profit from our past experience? One reason is that it is sometimes difficult to recognize in the new trends the related ideas of the past. Promoters of a new fad in education, like politicians on the stump, may be very vague about the details of their schemes. Like candidates for office citing isolated horrors, they can be scathing and specific about shortcomings of current practice while their own ideas remain glowing generalities. It is much easier and safer to be explicit about the weaknesses in someone else's scheme than to describe the specifics of one's own.

We educators abet the faddists in this vagueness. Have you noticed that we usually talk about different approaches to the teaching of reading? "A phonics approach," "a psycholinguistic approach," "a skills approach," "a literature-based approach." We need to do more than just *approach* the teaching of reading. Those who seriously wish to improve education must do more than describe a classroom atmosphere; they must describe how that atmosphere can be achieved and maintained and how people function within it. There is a productive middle ground between being stiflingly prescriptive and merely exhortative. It is called good teaching, and those who seek to improve education should practice it.

A second reason we fail to profit from our past is that we choose to ignore it. After learning that some professors of reading were requiring that students' papers contain no references that were more than 10 years old, Herber and Michel (Herber 1990) studied all the references in several recent reading journals. They found that 85 percent of all the references cited in the *Reading Research Quarterly*, the *Journal of Reading*, and *The Reading Teacher* in a recent 5-year period were articles that were no more than 15 years old at the time they were cited. There is an intriguing irony, of course, in the professors' desire that their students know only recent work: they teach their students a style of "scholarship" that insures the professors' own rapid oblivion.

A third reason that we do not use our past as a guide is that it is genuinely hard to know when an idea really does work well. There are so many other factors—public attitudes, television programming, parental assistance, the interests and backgrounds in a particular community—that can influence the outcome of education, often far more than a particular teaching method.

Since it is, in fact, very hard to know how well we are doing and how educational achievements under our present practices compare to what was achieved, or might be achieved, under different practices, the yearning for security is strong. We need to know that what we are doing for the children is the right thing to do. So, if someone says this is the right way, and everyone else seems to be going along, it is hard to resist following. We don't want to risk being wrong. We are told coercively, "If you're not for us, you're against the kids."

These pressures make it difficult for a thoughtful teacher to hang back and maintain a balanced, independent position.

Finally, we embrace each new-old trend without considering our past experience because, old or new, the core of the new trend simply makes sense to us. Behind every fad in education is a reasonable idea. For example, consider the fad of breaking down reading into objectives and skills. It was perfectly reasonable and, indeed, salutary to think about exactly what we were trying to accomplish. It was perfectly reasonable and, indeed, salutary to think about what children needed to be able to do before asking them to do something more advanced. But it was *not* reasonable to ignore goals that could not be stated in objective terms, to impose a fancied sequence where a real one could not be found, to break down tasks into skills so numerous that neither the student nor the teacher could see the ultimate objective, to require students to practice component skills that were difficult only because they had been deprived of their natural context.

MAKING LANGUAGE MEANINGFUL

The current trend toward a curriculum that emphasizes real reading and writing is surely welcome. But as this trend in its turn gets carried to extremes, potential abuses loom ominously. Will whole language lead us to ignore the alphabetic principle on which our written language is based? If it does, the eventual reaction to this neglect will bring demands for phonics instruction that, as they grow extreme, will create again the overemphasis on skills instruction that we are just now escaping.

Some of the champions of whole language tell us that whole language is not anti-phonics. Others interpret whole language as a total rejection of phonics. I think the former must be right, for without the alphabetic principle, written English is not whole. The alphabetic principle is one of the underlying rational principles that relates written English to spoken English, and a principle of all good teaching is that learning should be meaningful, not arbitrary; learning should make sense. The relationship of written language to spoken language should not be presented as arbitrary. The letters *m-o-m* constitute the word *mom* not just because Teacher says so or because *mom* fits the context, but because these letters represent the sounds of the language that compose the spoken word *mom*.

All of reading should make sense. The child should understand not just that written language conveys meaning but that the whole system of our written language is meaningful. But there is a great danger: because whole language is entering the scene in the guise of a replacement, many will interpret whole language as a total rejection of phonics, and the progression of fads will continue. To avoid returning to the excesses of the skills-based movement, we should continue to help students know and use the meaningful system that relates our written language to our spoken language.

Recently I accompanied a four-year-old girl on a trip downtown. She saw a sign larger than many of the others and asked me, "What does that say?"

"It says RESTAURANT," I told her.

She looked at the sign a little longer and declared, "I know how to spell ESTAURANT!"

What the child said sounds a little silly, but it isn't. She had expressed an emerging understanding of the phonemic nature of speech and of its representation in written English. I was able to tell her quite honestly, "Nora, that's wonderful! You have learned the way words are written. You'll be able to read almost anything before long."

Fortunately, a reborn emphasis on writing will help counter the effects of programs that ignore phonics. Experience in writing can make many important contributions to the development of quick and accurate decoding. At a very basic level, constructing words with letters emphasizes the phonemic structure of language—that is, it clarifies that there is a sound system of the language that is represented in alphabetic writing. Writing also provides support for learning the specific relationships between phonemes and graphemes. At a higher level, of course, the experience of writing helps make clear how language may be structured to express ideas in writing.

INCLUDING *ALL* GOOD WRITING

Like whole language, the "literature" movement comes with a built-in possibility for abuse: a narrow definition of literature. There is little room in some of the literature-based reading programs for writings about science, history, geography, economics, art, or music. This narrowing of the curriculum is occurring at a time when American students' illiteracy in science is generating national concern. It is vital to provide students with the reading experiences that will enable them to read a variety of nonfiction materials effectively. Reading science or mathematics requires a different type of effort, a different vocabulary, and familiarity with a different type of text structure than reading stories requires (MacGinitie 1985).

Many teachers read to their classes briefly after lunch or recess to share with their students the joy of reading and to help them become familiar with the structure and vocabulary of poems and stories. This activity is a sound use of the students' time, and it could and should be extended to reading about history, the sciences, the arts.

Perhaps the enthusiasm for literature will grow generous enough to include all good writing. If the effect is to demand better written materials for children in history, science, and other fields, the emphasis on literature will have a double value. We shall see.

Almost predictably, good ideas in education are carried to such extremes that the ideas become deformed. A good idea grows grotesque and then dies out. Most of the good that the movement brought is lost, and a countertrend with its own abuses develops. The sad result is that, not only do children receive the best of each new trend in education, they also receive the worst—the abuses and the foolish extremes.

We owe our children more than half the best and half the worst. We need to embrace and retain the best of new-old trends in education. But we must also reject the excesses. As Paul the apostle counseled:

> Do not quench the spirit, do not despise prophesying, but prove all things; hold fast that which is good (1 Thessalonians 5:19–21).

REFERENCES

Giamatti, A. B. (July 12, 1988). "Commencement Address of A. Bartlett Giamatti." Cambridge, Mass.: Massachusetts Institute of Technology.

Herber, H. L. (1990). "The Heritage of Our Profession." *Reading Psychology 11:* iii–xxi.

MacGinitie, W. H. (1985). "Materials Do Make a Difference." In *Reading Education: Foundations for a Literate America,* edited by J. Osborne, P. T. Wilson, and R. C. Anderson. Lexington, Mass.: D.C. Heath. (pp. 79–84).

Rosenblatt, L. (May 1990). "Presentation in Acceptance of the NCRE Research Award for Lifetime Research Achievement in the English Language Arts" at the meeting of the National Conference on Research in English, Atlanta, Ga.

Slavin, R. E. (1989). "PET and the Pendulum: Faddism in Education and How to Stop It." *Phi Delta Kappan* 70: 752–758.

Walter H. MacGinitie was Professor of Psychology and Education at Teachers College, Columbia University, for twenty years. He is now an independent writer and consultant. His address is P. O. Box 1789; Friday Harbor, WA 98250.

CHAPTER DISCUSSIONS AND ACTIVITIES

1. Pair off with a classmate and prepare a chart listing a comparison between basal readers and whole language. How does your chart compare with the one on constructivism versus behaviorism? How does it compare with the chart found in the article by Reutzel and Hollingsworth in Chapter 1?
2. You are an elementary school teacher using a basal reader and thinking about moving towards the use of whole language. How would you go about making the change? What are some of the implications that need to be considered?
3. Your principal has asked you to serve on a district-wide committee for elementary school teachers to look into the implementation of whole language. Some of the teachers are very concerned about maintaining specific instruction of skills while others are not. Discuss your beliefs and how you would serve on the committee.
4. Select one of the reading movements that Veatch refers to in her article. Review the literature about that movement and discuss how you think it relates or does not relate to whole language. Share your findings with the class.

5. Describe how you think you would respond to the following statement if you were an elementary school teacher who uses a basal reader. Frank Smith, in "Learning to Read: The Never-Ending Debate," published February, 1992 in the *Phi Delta Kappa*, states: "People who do not trust children to learn—or teachers to teach—will always expect a method to do the job" (p. 441).
6. Based on some of the points discussed by MacGinitie, defend or refute the following statement:

    Whole language is a new fad in education and it, too, will fade away in the next ten years.
7. Are there some reasons why it might be desirable for basal-reader teachers to carefully consider the advantages and disadvantages of whole language before deciding to use it in their school building? Pair off with a classmate and discuss your opinions.
8. If possible, visit a basal-reader classroom and a whole-language classroom. Compare what you observe in both classes to the difference between constructivism and behaviorism. Prepare a report summarizing your findings.
9. In this chapter, which suggestion(s) about reading instruction did you like the best? Why? Which did you like the least? Why?

CHAPTER 3

Instructional Considerations

In looking at whole language in the classroom, it is necessary to review and study its instructional framework. There is much in the professional literature that describes and discusses the "what" and the "why" of whole language, but equally important is the "how." The "how" offers teachers some ideas in implementing whole language in the classroom.

There are a number of questions that need to be addressed when looking at the instructional considerations of whole language, namely: what does the term "instruction" mean; how does instruction in a whole-language classroom differ from instructional procedures in a basal-reader classroom; how is instruction in a literature-based reading classroom similar to or different from that found in a whole-language classroom?

INSTRUCTION DEFINED

Instruction means different things to different people. Throughout life, we are instructed directly or indirectly by those around us or by things around us. Directly, by someone showing us how to drive a car, how to sew, or how to figure skate. Indirectly, by reading a manual for the word processor or the computer or watching someone cast a fish line, or modeling someone on a videotape who demonstrates certain exercises. In the teaching of reading, Durkin (1990) states that "instruction refers to what someone or something does or says that has the

65

potential to teach one or more individuals what they do not know, do not understand, or cannot do" (p. 472).

BASAL-READER CLASSROOM

In most basal readers, instruction centers around a *directed reading activity (DRA)*. This is a teaching technique that Burns, Roe, and Ross (1992) note "can be used with a story from a published reading series or with any other reading selections including content area materials or trade books" (p. 333). Basically, the DRA consists of the following steps:

1. **Preparing for reading.** First, the teacher motivates the students to read the story. This can be done by using pictures, posters, stick figures, toy models, or discussing the title of the story—anything or everything that can allow the children to relate this story to their own experiential background. New vocabulary words are presented in meaningful context; these words should not be introduced in isolation, but in sentences that enhance the meaning of the new words.
2. **Guiding the silent reading.** Before the students begin to read the story silently, the teacher asks some questions in order to direct the students to find specific information. These questions may be written on the blackboard or on a prepared chart. By doing this, the teacher sets the purpose for the silent reading. Not all the questions related to comprehension are given to the children at this time because they will then be only reading to find the answers to the specific questions.
3. **Guiding oral reading.** After the students have read the material silently, the teacher might ask the students to read aloud: a part of the story that answers some of the questions they have been asked, the part of the story that they liked the best, the funniest or the saddest part of the story, or parts of the story that they would like to act out. The need for silent reading prior to reading aloud cannot be overemphasized. Without this preparation, students are counting ahead to "their" paragraph or sentence when they should be attending to and comprehending the reading of their classmates. After all, the children want to read their passages clearly and without error, to avoid the possibility of criticism by teacher or peers. Heilman, Blair, and Rupley (1994) caution that "although some stories are meant to be read aloud, reading every story aloud day after day is both a waste of time and a probable cause of such difficulties as word-by-word silent reading and development of poor self-esteem" (pp. 277–278).
4. **Discussing the story.** In this step, the teacher asks other questions to help the students interpret the whole story. Numerous, unduly specific questions are not needed in order to make sure the students comprehend the full meaning of the story. As noted by O'Donnell and Wood (1992), "Ideally, the discussion will involve summarizing the text, interpreting it, and relating it to prior knowledge" (p. 96).

5. **Providing related follow-up activities.** In teaching a reading lesson, the teacher may use a variety of activities, such as further vocabulary development or direct instruction in phonics, structural analysis, or study skills. By using workbook activities, the children may practice various skills and strategies supervised by the teacher or done independently.
6. **Encouraging enrichment.** This final step allows the students to experience the joy of reading by connecting the story that they just have read to art, music, or creative writing. The teacher might ask children to act out or draw a picture of the part that they liked best, write an alternative ending to the story, or to sing songs appropriate to the story's theme. These activities can encourage students to read additional material about a particular topic or other works by the same author (Burns, Roe & Ross, 1992). Unfortunately, due to the constraints of time and the pressure of teaching basic skills, teachers often omit this step (Heilman, Blair, & Rupley, 1994).

As can be seen from looking at these steps, teachers become the prime movers for instruction. They select specific skills directly related to the particular lesson and follow the suggestions described in the teacher's manual. Most critics of basal-reader series decry the overemphasis on these isolated skills, which they believe to be nonconducive to the child's reading progress (O'Donnell & Wood, 1992). In using the traditional basal readers, the teacher asks the questions and the students read to find the answers. But according to Burns, Roe, and Ross (1992) a shift is now taking place through the development of literature-based and language-integrated series. Instead of the purpose-setting being dictated by the teacher, the students are responsible for defining that emphasis, as well as for the tasks of producing and acknowledging predictions.

When using traditional basal readers, the teacher structures the directed reading lesson to accommodate the varying levels of student ability through the use of reading groups. The students are categorized on the basis of their perceived reading levels and instruction takes place with the teacher using from three to five separate reading groups. However, in *Becoming a Nation of Readers,* the authors point out that "because of the serious problems inherent in ability grouping, the Commission on Reading believes that educators should explore other options for reading instruction" (Anderson, Hiebert, Scott, & Wilkinson, 1985, p. 91). Logan, Rux, and Paradis (1991) suggest a number of strategies to overcome many of the weaknesses of traditional heterogeneous grouping; among these are addressing individual needs and interests, varying the pacing of the groups to suit the different reading levels, rotating discussion groups, and using a daily reading schedule to give an overview of each day's activities. Flood, Lapp, Flood, and Nagel (1992) propose the use of flexible grouping patterns. Instead of using ability grouping, Wiesendanger and Bader (1992) recommend and describe cooperative grouping in reading instruction. The authors believe that "in a completely teacher controlled environment, students are less likely to take initiative or be responsible for their own learning" (p. 403). O'Donnell and Wood (1992) point out the advantage in using more flexible and varied grouping in the teaching of reading—and these grouping patterns are never permanent.

THE WHOLE-LANGUAGE CLASSROOM

In the whole-language classroom, instruction is no longer centered around the teacher doing something "to" or "at" children. Rather, it manifests itself in a cooperative environment, in which the teacher and children collaborate on long- and short-term planning, selection, and distribution of materials, and which stresses child-centered activities. As Goodman (1986) points out, "The whole language teacher is clearly in charge, but it may take a visitor a few minutes to locate the busy adult doing many things in many parts of the room" (p. 32). At this point, it should be noted that, while many whole-language advocates insist that teachers should eschew direct instructional methods, others—such as Spiegel (1992) and Slaughter (1988)—believe that direct and indirect instruction can be blended to achieve a cohesive, coordinated style of instruction.

When discussing principles of language learning as related to whole-language instruction, Yatvin (1992) emphasizes that the child should recognize the reasons for reading, writing, speaking, and listening, and that these activities should be integrated across the curriculum. She also notes that quality instruction depends upon the use of unabridged trade books and relies on the language knowledge that children have accrued since birth. She further reiterates that the person most suitably skilled to be directly involved in all these principles is the teacher.

In describing the structure of whole-language instruction in a school district in New Hampshire, Robbins (1990) provides the following ten elements adapted from the prior work of Butler (1987): reading to children; shared book experience; sustained silent reading; guided reading; individualized reading; language experience; children's writing, using the writing process; modeled writing; opportunities for sharing; and content-area reading and writing.

The place of phonics in whole-language instruction is often discussed. Mills, O'Keefe, and Stephens (1992) point out that whether phonics and whole language are compatible or incompatible depends upon the basic meanings of the terms. If phonics is defined as "decontextualized" direct instruction that focuses on a set of rules that establishes the relationship between sounds of letters and their names, then it would be incompatible with whole language. "However, most of the time the word *phonics* is used to mean 'knowledge about sound–symbol relationships in language.' When phonics is defined this way, phonics and whole language are quite compatible" (p. xi). Altwerger (1991) in examining the place of phonics in the whole-language classroom emphasizes the following:

> The relationship between oral and written language for an alphabetic system such as ours is called the 'graphophonic system.' It is an indisputable fact that the graphophonic system exists, and that it is a vital aspect of our written orthography. *Phonics* refers to the direct teaching of the graphophonic system, most often in ways that are behavioristic in nature, and *linguistically inaccurate*.
>
> Whole language teachers *do not* teach phonics per se but we absolutely *do* concern ourselves with helping children learn how to use the graphophonic system. Every time your children write (and attempt to spell words), every time you read to them while they follow along, every time they listen to a tape as they read along in a book, every time they use charts to sing together, and every time they match what they know or can predict to print, they are learning how to use the graphophonic system. (p. 407)

Some principles related to the use of phonics in the whole-language classroom are offered by Freppon and Dahl (1991). They note that phonic instruction should be: student centered, contextualized learning, preceded by foundation concepts, based on students' intended meanings, not taught in isolation, demonstrated by teachers, designed to involve students, and learned in a variety of settings.

Adams (1990) best summarizes the discussion by stating that phonics skills should not be taught in a vacuum, but "within a single integrated and interdependent system" (p. 423). She concludes that "Phonological awareness, letter recognition facility, familiarity with spelling patterns, spelling–sound relations, and individual words must be developed in concert with real reading and real writing and with deliberate reflection on the forms, functions, and meanings of texts" (p. 422).

Looking Ahead

Two articles, one by Baumann (1992) and the other by Smith (1991), offer ideas on organizing and directing a whole-language classroom—one on the primary level and the other on the intermediate. Stahl (1992) presents several suggestions for including phonics in the literary classroom.

READING INSTRUCTION IN NEW ZEALAND

Considering the principles and elements outlined above, one might easily conclude that whole-language instruction bears a remarkable similarity to the manner in which reading is taught in New Zealand. And while the term "whole language" is not used in her country, Mabbett (1990) describes how children are exposed to reading and shares some of the following key principles:

- Reading, talking, and writing are inseparably interrelated.
- The foundations of literacy are laid in the early years.
- Reading for meaning is paramount.
- Books for children learning to read should use natural idiomatic language that is appropriate to the subject.
- There is no one way in which people learn to read. A combination of approaches is needed. (p. 60)

Looking Ahead

Goldenberg (1991), in his article, expands on the description of how reading is taught in New Zealand. He provides an interesting comparison between reading instruction in that country and whole-language instruction in the United States.

LITERATURE-BASED READING INSTRUCTION

In many schools today, there seems to be a renewed interest in the use of quality children's literature in the teaching of reading. Huck (1992) identifies three different kinds of literature-based programs. First, there are the literature-based basal readers, which contain excerpts from the original trade books. Primarily, their organization centers around teachers' manuals and workbooks, very much patterned after the structure of standard basal readers.

With the second type of literature-based program, real books are used, but the teaching strategies remain the same—there are teacher guides for each of the books, which are modeled like those for the standard basal reader. As Huck points out, many teachers do not really understand how to use children's literature and therefore use it in ways that years of teaching from basal readers have taught them—"they basilize it and destroy it in the process" (p. 534).

The third type is a comprehensive-literature program in which real books are the primary focus and permeate the curriculum, and where teachers spend a great deal of time reading to the students. As opposed to the directed-reading lesson, in which the teacher assumes the dominant role, the children select the books to read, to share and to discuss, and not only learn how to read, but as Huck emphasizes, "... they also become *readers*" (p. 524). Using literature in this fashion conforms admirably to the philosophy of whole language (Burns, Roe, & Ross, 1992).

Looking Ahead

In the last article, Duffy (1992) takes a close look at the place of specific instruction in the schools and provides some thought-provoking points.

As you read the articles in this chapter, various strategies related to instruction in the whole-language classroom will be discussed. Some of the pertinent questions that will be addressed include the following:

- What organizational framework exists in a whole-language classroom?
- How alike or different are instructional considerations in a primary grade classroom compared to that found in an intermediate classroom in which whole language is used?
- In what way is instruction in a whole-language classroom different from instruction in a basal-reader program?
- What options does a whole-language teacher have in regard to direct instruction in the teaching of reading?
- Why do some researchers believe that whole language and the instruction of reading in New Zealand are alike? Why do some believe they are different?
- What does "inspired teaching" mean? How does this relate to reading instruction—or does it?

REFERENCES

Adams, M. J. (1990). *Beginning to read: Thinking and learning about print*. Cambridge, MA: M.I.T. Press.

Altwerger, B. (1991). Five tough questions that whole language teachers ask. In K. S. Goodman, L. B. Bird, and Y. M. Goodman (Eds.), *The whole language catalog* (p. 407). Santa Rosa, CA: American School Publishers.

Anderson, R. C., Hiebert, E. H., Scott, J. A., & Wilkinson, I. A. G. (1985). *Becoming a nation of readers: The report of the Commission on Reading*. Washington, D.C.: The National Institute of Education, U.S. Department of Education.

Baumann, J. F. (1992). Organizing and managing a whole language classroom. *Reading Research and Instruction, 31*(3), 1–14.

Burns, P. C., Roe, B. D., & Ross, E. P. (1992). *Teaching reading in today's elementary schools* (5th ed.). Boston: Houghton Mifflin.

Butler, A. (1987). *The elements of whole language*. Crystal Lake, IL: Rigby.

Duffy, G. G. (1992). Let's free teachers to be inspired. *Phi Delta Kappan, 73*(6), 442–447.

Durkin, D. (1990). Dolores Durkin speaks on instruction. *The Reading Teacher, 43*(7), 472–476.

Flood, J., Lapp, D., Flood, S., & Nagel, G. (1992). Am I allowed to group? Using flexible patterns for effective instruction. *The Reading Teacher, 45*(8), 608–616.

Freppon, P. S., & Dahl, K. L. (1991). Learning about phonics in a whole language classroom. *Language Arts, 68*(3), 190–197.

Goldenberg, C. (1991). Learning to read in New Zealand: The balance of skills and meaning. *Language Arts, 68*(7), 555–562.

Goodman, K. (1986). *What's whole in whole language?* Portsmouth, NH: Heinemann.

Heilman, A. W., Blair, T. R., & Rupley, W. H. (1994). *Principles and practices of teaching reading* (8th ed.). New York: Merrill/Macmillan.

Huck, C. S. (1992). Literacy and literature. *Language Arts, 69*(7), 520–526.

Logan, N. L., Rux, J. D., & Paradis, E. E. (1991). Profile of a heterogeneous grouping plan for reading. *Reading Horizons, 32*(2), 85–95.

Mabbett, B. (1990). The New Zealand story. *Educational Leadership, 47*(6), 59–61.

Mills, H., O'Keefe, T., & Stephens, D. (1992). *Looking closely: Exploring the role of phonics in one whole language classroom*. Urbana IL: National Council of Teachers of English.

O'Donnell, M. P., & Wood, M. (1992). *Becoming a reader*. Boston: Allyn and Bacon.

Robbins, P. A. (1990). Implementing whole language: Bridging children and books. *Educational Leadership, 47*(6), 50–54.

Slaughter, H. B. (1988). Indirect and direct teaching in a whole language program. *The Reading Teacher, 42*(1), 30–34.

Smith, P. G. (1991). A practical guide to whole language in the intermediate classroom. *Contemporary Education, 62*(2), 88–95.

Spiegel, D. L. (1992). Blending whole language and systematic direct instruction. *The Reading Teacher, 46*(1), 38–44.

Stahl, S. A. (1992). Saying the "p" word: Nine guidelines for exemplary phonics instruction. *The Reading Teacher, 45*(8), 618–625.

Wiesendanger, K. D. & Bader, L. (1992). Cooperative grouping in literacy instruction. *Reading Horizons, 32*(5), 403–410.

Yatvin, J. (1992). *Developing a whole language program for a whole school*. Midlothian, VA: Virginia State Reading Association.

FOR FURTHER STUDY

Cox, C., & Zarrillo, J. (1993). *Teaching reading with children's literature*. New York: Merrill/Macmillan.

Gothard, H. M., & Russell, S. M. (1990). A tale of two teachers. *Childhood Education, 66*(4), 214–218.

Hauser, M. E. (1992). A prologue: What happens before alternative groupings. *Reading Horizons, 32*(5), 343–348.

Jerolds, B. W., & Thompson, R. A. (1992). Whole language problems and what to do about them: Balanced reading instruction. *Journal of Reading Education, 18*(1), 28–42.

Kucer, S. B. (1991). Authenticity as the basis for instruction. *Language Arts, 68*(7), 532–540.

McCallum, R. D. (1988). Don't throw the basals out with the bath water. *The Reading Teacher, 42*(3), 204–208.

McWhirter, A. M. (1990). Whole language in the middle school. *The Reading Teacher, 43*(8), 562–565.

Morrice, C., & Simmons, M. (1991). Beyond reading buddies: A whole language cross-age program. *The Reading Teacher, 44*(8), 572–577.

Reutzel, D. R., & Cooter, Jr., R. B. (1992). *Teaching children to read: From basals to books.* New York: Merrill/Macmillan.

Staab, C. F. (1990). Teacher mediation in one whole language classroom. *The Reading Teacher, 43*(8), 548–552.

Vann, A. S. (1992). Phonics or whole language? *Principal, 71*(5), 37–39.

Webb, A., Bowers, R., Hietpas, L., Lang, T., & McKinley, L. (1991). Four teachers pilot a whole language program. *Childhood Education, 67*(3), 155–160.

Wepner, S. B., & Feeley, J. T. (1993). *Moving forward with literature: Basals, books and beyond.* New York: Merrill/Macmillan.

Wiggins, R. A. (1994). Large group lesson/small group follow-up: Flexible grouping in a basal reading program. *The Reading Teacher, 47*(6), 450–460.

Organizing and Managing a Whole Language Classroom

James F. Baumann

INTRODUCTION

What is meant by classroom organization and management? What is whole language? Can or should a whole language program be organized and managed? In short, is the notion of organizing and managing a whole language classroom an oxymoron, or might these actually be ideas *en rapport*? In this article, I will respond to each of these questions. First, I present definitions of whole language and classroom organization/management. Second, I will argue that any successful program of literacy instruction—whole language approaches included—must address classroom organizational and management issues. Third, I will describe several plans for organizing and managing a whole language program. Finally, I will present an example that demonstrates how a primary

From "Organizing and Managing a Whole Language Classroom" by J. F. Baumann, 1992, *Reading Research and Instruction, 31*, pp. 1–14. Copyright © 1992 by The College Reading Association. Reprinted by permission.

grade teacher might organize and manage a whole language classroom according to one of these plans.

WHOLE LANGUAGE

Definitions of *whole language* vary and are oftentimes elusive (cf., Goodman, 1986, and Newman, 1985a; see also Bergeron, 1990). As Watson (1989) stated:

> Whole language is difficult to define for at least three reasons. First, most whole-language advocates reject a dictionary-type definition that can be looked up and memorized.... Second, whole language is often difficult to define because many of its advocates are intensely passionate about it, while those who demand a definition may disapprove of it just as intensely. ... Third, the experts in whole language who can provide the richest answers to questions about it—the teachers—have not often been asked (pp. 131–132).

Although acknowledging that it is difficult to define, Watson offered the following general definition of whole language: *"Whole language is a perspective on education that is supported by beliefs about learners and learning, teachers and teaching, language, and curriculum"* (p. 133). Goodman (1986) has specified what these basic beliefs might entail as follows:

- Whole language learning builds around whole learners learning whole language in whole situations.
- Whole language learning assumes respect for language, for the learner, and for the teacher.
- The focus is on meaning and not on language itself, in authentic speech and literacy events.
- Learners are encouraged to take risks and invited to use language, in all its varieties, for their own purposes.
- In a whole language classroom, all the varied functions of oral and written language are appropriate and encouraged. (Goodman, 1986, p. 40)

Thus, for this paper, *whole language involves meaningful, authentic classroom literacy events among respectful, secure children and teachers.*

CLASSROOM ORGANIZATION AND MANAGEMENT

Turning to *Webster's New Collegiate Dictionary* (1980), one finds the following definitions for *organize* and *manage*:

> *organize:* "to arrange to form a coherent unity or functioning whole ... to arrange elements into a whole of interdependent parts" (p. 802)
> *manage:* "to handle or direct with a degree of skill ... to treat with care" (p. 691)

Drawing from these definitions, *I will define classroom organization and management of a whole language program as a teacher's ability to handle or direct with skill and care a functioning, coherent, language learning environment for children.*

CLASSROOM ORGANIZATION/ MANAGEMENT AND WHOLE LANGUAGE: ARE THEY COMPATIBLE NOTIONS?

Goodman (1986, p. 29) stated that whole language teachers "guide, support, monitor, encourage, and facilitate learning, but do not control it." One might infer, therefore, that the idea of classroom organization/management, which has the connotation of control, is incompatible with a whole language view of literacy learning. Certainly, a whole language philosophy presupposes that students assume considerable responsibility for their learning and that it is the teacher's role to promote, support, and facilitate learning, not to govern or dominate it.

However, as Ken and Yetta Goodman have noted, "Teaching children to read is not putting them into a garden of print and leaving them unmolested" (Goodman & Goodman, 1979, p. 139). Indeed, Goodman (1986) acknowledged that cooperative planning and organization are part of whole language classrooms and that "The whole language teacher is clearly in charge" (p. 32). Steinle (1986) also commented on how important planning and organization are in whole language programs:

> It is essential for teachers to *plan with care* what they should teach. This is particularly important in regard to the more flexible approaches to teaching. Indeed it can be argued that the more flexible and informal the style which a teacher adopts, then the greater the need for the teacher to prepare and plan the activities for the year, the term, the week, the day, and the lesson. Such planning must of course result in some form of classroom organization to ensure that the plans are implemented (p. 4).

Somewhat similarly, Newman and Church (1990), when discussing various myths of whole language, stated:

> **Myth:** *A whole language classroom is unstructured.*
>
> **Reality:** A whole language classroom is highly structured. Both teachers and students contribute to the organization. The teacher has thought about the placement of furniture, what specific resources to offer and their location within the classroom, the grouping of the students, the nature and flow of activity, the approximate amount of time to allocate, and some possible ways for students to present what they have learned (p. 22).

Thus, some of the most dedicated whole language advocates emphasize the need to address organizational and structural concerns—classroom management, if you will—when designing and implementing a literacy education program.

SOME ORGANIZATIONAL AND MANAGEMENT PLANS APPROPRIATE FOR WHOLE LANGUAGE CLASSROOMS

What kinds of organizational and management plans are appropriate for whole language classrooms? Sloan and Whitehead (1986) suggest three different approaches are useful when organizing, planning, and scheduling reading-writing classrooms: a contract approach, a priorities list approach, and a blocked approach. I will briefly mention the first two approaches and then focus and elaborate on the third, which I consider to be most useful for organizing and managing a whole language program.

A *contract approach*, which is perhaps the least structured and most flexible, requires children and the teacher to form agreements about what work and activities will be done and when. Refer to Fleet (1986) for specific suggestions about organizing a classroom according to a contract approach.

When using a *priorities list* approach, teachers rank, in order of importance, the goals and accompanying tasks and activities for a given day, week, or month. The teacher then proceeds through the priorities list, rescheduling and modifying the list from day to day and week to week as needed. Refer to Sloan and Whitehead (1986) for a discussion of the underlying assumptions, and the advantages and disadvantages of a priorities list approach.

A *blocked approach* involves "arranging largish blocks of time in which related activities take place" (Sloan & Whitehead, 1986, p. 14). For example, a teacher might structure the day into language arts, cultural studies (art, music, social studies), science/mathematics, and activity/recreation time blocks. A number of elaborated examples of blocked approaches can be found in Sloan and Whitehead (1986) and in Butler and Turbill (1985, chapter 4). Also refer to Cambourne (1988, pp. 89–102) for additional, pragmatic suggestions for how to organize space and resources in a whole language classroom.

The following example of how to organize and manage a whole language primary classroom involves a modified blocked approach. This format was selected because it is the most common and practical management plan. In addition, it is possible to include elements of contract and priorities list approaches within a blocked instructional format.

Because a blocked approach involves setting aside specific times for different curricular areas, one might view it as an organizational structure that could segment the curriculum—a result antithetical to a whole language philosophy. Notice, however, that the following example involves a thematic approach (Gamberg, Kwak, Hutchings, Altheim, & Edwards, 1988) in which projects related to activities introduced in language instruction are integrated across the curriculum to subjects such as science and social studies.

ORGANIZING AND MANAGING A WHOLE LANGUAGE CLASSROOM: AN EXAMPLE

Ms. Marcella Jackson is a second-grade teacher at Sleepy Hollow Elementary, an urban school in a large, midwestern city. She has a class of 23 students of mixed racial, ethnic, and economic backgrounds. She has organized her classroom according to whole language theoretical and practical principles, adopting a flexible blocked scheduling format (Sloan & Whitehead, 1986). Her weekly schedule, which is presented in Figure 1, contains two daily language arts blocks, one each at the beginning of the morning and afternoon sessions. It is November and Ms. Jackson's whole language classroom is running smoothly. The students have settled into a routine (as routine as a whole language classroom can be) and are comfortable with the activities, centers, materials,

	MONDAY	TUESDAY	WEDNESDAY	THURSDAY	FRIDAY
8:30–8:45	Organization and Sharing				
8:45–10:15	Language Arts I				
10:15–10:45	Recess				
10:45–11:45	Math				
11:30–12:15	Lunch				
12:15–1:45	Language Arts II				
1:45–2:15	Recess	Phy. Educ.	Recess	Phy. Educ.	Recess
2:15–2:45	Science	Social Studies	Science	Social Studies	Art 2:15–3:00
2:45–3:15	Music	"Reading Rainbow"	Music	Library	"Friday Celebration"

FIGURE 1
MS. JACKSON'S WEEKLY SCHEDULE

classroom helpers, and instructional formats Ms. Jackson has incorporated into her whole language program.

Ms. Jackson has adopted a theme approach for organizing her whole language curriculum (Gamberg et al., 1988). For periods of one to three weeks, she and her students explore—across the curriculum when appropriate—all facets of a particular theme. Sometimes she chooses the theme; often the students select the theme.

The theme for this week and the following two is friendship/communities. The theme originated from events surrounding the arrival of a new girl, Jennifer Washington, in Ms. Jackson's class three weeks earlier. Although Ms. Jackson and her students had worked hard to develop a compassionate, loving, charitable environment in the classroom, Jennifer's arrival caused quite a stir. Jennifer was attractive and personable and soon achieved a celebrity status as the new student. This threatened several children in the class, resulting in jealousy, quarreling, and cliquish behavior.

Recognizing the problem at hand, Ms. Jackson held a class meeting to discuss it. To provoke thought about the problem situation, Ms. Jackson began the meeting by reading *The New Girl at School* (Delton & Hoban, 1979), a picture book that tells the story of a similar situation. This helped the students recognize their problem and enabled them and Ms. Jackson to arrive at a resolution to it.

One week later when the class met again to decide what the theme would be for their next unit of study, Jennifer herself suggested that they explore friendship—what it means to be a friend, how friends treat one another, how to make new friends, how to keep old friends, and so forth. The other students supported the idea, and Ms. Jackson asked if they could expand on the theme to include the concept of communities, an important part of friendship and cooperative behavior. The students agreed, thus allowing Ms. Jackson to coordinate social studies (a study of their own urban community), science (study of social animals, e.g., bees, wolves), and other aspects of the curriculum (e.g., physical education: team play) with language arts.

Ms. Jackson planned a three-week unit on the theme of friendship/communities. Table 1 presents Ms. Jackson's lesson plans for the first two days of the unit. The following narrative describes in detail the whole language activities that occurred on those days within the Language Arts I and II, Science, and Social Studies time blocks.

Monday

Language arts I. To kick off the unit during the Language Arts I (LA-I) period, Ms. Jackson reads a big book (Holdaway, 1979) version of Cohen and Hoban's (1971a) *Best Friends*, the story of Paul and Jim who are best friends, have a disagreement at school, and then make up and resume their friendship ever more strongly. She reads the story aloud to the children with expression and enthusiasm, modeling for them various book-handling skills; she also tracks the text with her hand as she reads. (Note: If a big book version of *Best Friends* were not available, Ms. Jackson would use the opaque projector to display the story page-by-page on a screen in a darkened classroom.)

After discussing *Best Friends* and how it is similar to and different from *The New Girl at School*, Ms. Jackson reminds the students that they will be reading and learning about friendship and communities of people and animals over the next three weeks. To pique their interest, Ms. Jackson talks briefly about each of several of the friendship books she has assembled. She has chosen to talk about *Will I Have a Friend?* (Cohen & Hoban, 1971b), the story of Jim and Paul's first meeting at school; *Timothy Goes to School* (Wells, 1981), the story of Timothy's difficulties attending a new school; *Two is Company* (Delton & Maestro, 1975), the story of Duck and Bear who are best friends until Chipmunk moves in and makes three a crowd;

TABLE 1
MS. JACKSON'S LESSON PLANS

MONDAY	TUESDAY
LA-I 1. Unit Introduction: Read big book version of *Best Friends*. 2. Do short book talks on *Will I Have a Friend?*, *Timothy Goes to School*, *Two Is Company*, and *Anna's Secret Friend*. 3. Practice reading. Select a friendship book. Mr. Anderson, Ms. Hopkins, and Ms. Watson provide assistance. 4. Reading conferences with Sarah and Jim. Writing conferences with Max and Molly. 5. Contract center time. Promote listening and social studies centers. **LA-II** 1. Read aloud Silverstein's "Hug O'War." Discuss the highs and lows of friendship. 2. Compose a group poem titled "Friendship is . . ." 3. Do oral, echoic, and choral reading of "Friendship is . . ." poem. Distribute hard copies of it in p.m. Remind the students to add new words to their word banks. 4. Strategy instruction for two groups: CVC, CVCe group; handwriting and writing conventions group. Others work in centers or read friendship books. **Science** 1. Show film on bee communities. 2. Preview Wednesday's speaker, Mr. Bennett.	**LA-I** 1. Review purposes and uses of the Message Board. Encourage friends to write one another. 2. Group reading of *A Boy, a Dog, and a Frog*. Compose an oral text for it. Discuss various interpretations. Have students retell the story. 3. Students compose written text for *A Boy, A Dog, and a Frog* or other wordless books. Classroom volunteers assist. 4. Independent choice time: centers, Message Board, silent reading, listen to Ms. Sanford's stories. **LA-II** 1. Journal writing. Recommend theme-related topics. 2. Introduce kindergarten book buddy activity. 3. Informal book talk session. Discuss friendship books and others 4. Model oral reading using Carle's *Do you Want to Be My Friend?* 5. Friendship book selection. Ms. Zieman's 5th grade tutors will help in selection and initial reading. 6. Conferences with Tami, Josh, and others if time. **Social Studies** 1. Brainstorm community helpers. 2. Introduce oral report activity. 3. Discuss reporter/interviewer tasks. Take turns role playing reporter and the person who is interviewed.

and *Anna's Secret Friend* (Tsutsui & Hayashi, 1987), the story of Anna who leaves her old friends behind but finds a new, secret friend when she moves to the mountains in Japan.

After displaying these books, reading brief excerpts from each, and talking about the many other wonderful books that have been written about friendship, Ms. Jackson asks the students to select a friendship book to read. With the assistance of the school library media specialist, Ms. Jackson has assembled about 60 picture books, predictable-pattern books (e.g., Rhodes, 1981; Rhodes & Dudley-Marling, 1988; Tomkins & Webeler, 1983), and wordless picture books that deal with friendship in some fashion. These books were chosen from Ms. Jackson's personal collection of books, the school and public library collections, her classroom library, and books written and contributed by current and former students.

Ms. Jackson enlists the help of several other persons to assist the children in selecting and reading their books for the first time. Mr. Anderson, a retired person, Susan Hopkins, a high school junior enrolled in an early childhood co-op program, and Ms. Watson, a parent volunteer, are there to help in Ms. Jackson's classroom on Monday and Wednesday mornings for LA-I. They will help the students select books that are interesting and readable. They will also read with and to the children, providing positive models and helping them through the first reading of the friendship books. (Additional retired persons, co-op students, and parent volunteers, as well as teacher aides and student teachers, may provide individualized help at other times. Refer to Rauch and Sanacore, 1985, and Rhodes and Dudley-Marling, 1987, chapter 13, for further information about how to involve volunteers in the classroom.)

During the remaining time of LA-I on Monday, Ms. Jackson meets individually with students for conferences. These conferences may be one of two different types. Some may involve discussing the independent reading that the students are doing (Holdaway, 1980; Hornsby, Sukama, & Parry, 1986), in which the teacher and child talk about recent books that the child has read. Ms. Jackson might also ask the student to read aloud a portion of a book they have read in order to informally evaluate their growth and development of reading strategies. The conferences may also be writing conferences (Calkins, 1986; Graves, 1983; Newman, 1985b; Parry & Hornsby, 1985) in which the child and teacher discuss successes, problems, and concerns about compositions that are in progress.

Students who finish reading their friendship books and do not confer with Ms. Jackson may participate in one or more of the classroom centers until the 10:15 A.M. recess break. Among the various centers in Ms. Jackson's classroom are a writing center, a listening center (that also permits students to make audio recordings), a construction center, a math center, a printing center (includes letter and word stamps with colored ink pads and paper), a computer center, an art center, and various science centers.

Ms. Jackson has attempted to make the centers thematically related whenever possible. For example, the listening center has the books and audio tapes for several friendship books. Titles of books on tape in the center include Steven Kellogg's (1986) *Best Friends,* Bernard Waber's (1972) *Ira Sleeps Over,* Judith Viorst's (1974) *Rosie and Michael,* Nicki Weiss' (1983) *Maude and Sally,* and Jeannette Caines' (1982) *Just Us Women.* Ms. Jackson's books-on-tape collection contains some commercially-produced recordings; other tapes have been prepared by Ms. Jackson herself; still others have been produced by former and current second-grade children who rehearsed books, recorded them, and donated the tapes to the classroom collection. Ms. Jackson has found this latter group of tapes to be the most popular with her students.

Another example of a thematically related center is the social studies center, within which Ms. Jackson has included several activity cards (Kwak & Newman, 1985). Activity cards pose questions or problems for children to solve that often involve experimentation or research. For example, one of Ms. Jackson's social studies activity cards required the students to view a filmstrip that discussed family organization and relations. Then the students were directed to construct a family tree which included names and drawings (or photos) of immediate and extended family members. To involve the students' families, they were encouraged to complete the family tree at home with the assistance of family members.

To promote independence and responsibility, as well as to monitor students' work in centers and other independent activities during the week, Ms. Jackson has initiated a contract system (Fleet, 1986). Each Monday morning during the organizing and sharing time, Ms. Jackson displays on a wall chart the centers and independent activities that the students must do and those they may choose to do during the week. Then, on individual contracts, the students decide when they plan to do the required activities and list additional, optional activities they plan to complete during the week. Ms. Jackson has found this helpful for students to develop responsibility and decision-making ability.

Language arts II. After lunch, Ms. Jackson begins the Language Arts II (LA-II) time block with a group speaking and listening activity. She reads aloud Shel Silverstein's (1974) "Hug O' War," a short, entertaining poem about how friendship, hugging, cuddling, and giggling ("hug of war") are superior to fighting and disagreements ("tug of war"). Then she and the students discuss friendship and the trials and tribulations associated with it. She invites the students to discuss their personal experiences as well as those contained in the books they read that morning.

As an extension activity, Ms. Jackson has the students compose a group free verse poem titled "Friendship is . . .", Building upon the suggestions for free verse poetry writing by Kenneth Koch in *Wishes, Lies, and Dreams* (1970), she asks each student to contribute one or more lines that begin with one of the stems "Friendship is . . .", "A Friend . . .", or "Being a friend means . . .". She writes their statements on a large chart and assembles the collaborative poem. Next Ms. Jackson reads the poem aloud to the students, pointing to words and phrases as she reads orally. For a second reading of the poem, she uses an echoic reading technique in which she reads a line and then has the children repeat it after her. Finally, she asks the students to join her in a choral reading of the entire poem.

Before the group breaks up, Ms. Jackson reminds the students that one job they must do yet that afternoon during LA-II is to add to their individual word journals, bound books containing an alphabetical listing of all words each child has used in prior compositions. Students add to their individual journals all new words that were contained in the line(s) that each child contributed to the poem. Also, while Ms. Jackson and the children are reading the "Friendship is . . ." poem, a parent volunteer enters the poem on the class microcomputer. Afterward, the parent prints and duplicates the poem and then distributes a copy to all children before they leave school that afternoon. A copy will also be laminated and placed within the classroom library for future independent reading.

Next Ms. Jackson meets with several small groups of students for instruction in specific language arts strategies. First she works with a group of eight children who need additional help decoding words that follow the CVC and CVCe patterns. She attempts to include thematically related words in such lessons whenever possible (e.g., *pal, hug, like*) and assigns practice and application materials that also match the theme. For example, Ms. Jackson has selected a chapter from *Frog and Toad are Friends* (Lobel, 1970) that contains many CVC and CVCe words. She uses this story for a decoding application exercise.

Ms. Jackson then meets with a second group of children who need some assistance in manuscript letter formation and writing conventions (capital letters and sentence end marks). Ms. Jackson models for the students on the chalkboard how to form letters and punctuate sentences correctly. As an independent activity, the students compose and write on the chalkboard three sentences, selecting words from their word journals as needed. Children who do not meet with Ms. Jackson during this period work in centers or reread the friendship books they selected during LA-I.

Ms. Jackson has identified children in need of these strategies on the basis of informal evaluation procedures (e.g., Goodman, Goodman, & Hood, 1989; Kemp, 1989). Ms. Jackson also has established a literacy portfolio for all students in her class (Mathews, 1990; Valencia, 1990), within which she and her students can place various documents and artifacts that demonstrate the children's growth and development in literacy abilities.

Science. Ms. Jackson has also attempted to coordinate content area instruction with her whole language theme. In keeping with the friendship/communities theme, Ms. Jackson has decided to select activities that examine the social nature of insects. Today the children view a film that tells how different kinds of bees fill different roles within their community. Ms. Jackson has a speaker scheduled for Wednesday—Mr. Bennett, a friend of hers who is a beekeeper. He will bring to class the various tools and paraphernalia used by beekeepers (honey harvesting equipment, protective suit), a part of a honeycomb, and a case of bees for the children to inspect.

Tuesday

Language arts I. Ms. Jackson begins LA-I today with a group meeting at which she reminds the students about the classroom Message Board (Boyd, 1985). The Message Board is a decorated bulletin board on which students can post notes and letters they write to classmates and adults who work in the classroom. Receivers of those messages can also respond in writing, resulting in dialogue between and among Message Board users. The students have not been using the Message Board as much recently, so Ms. Jackson suggests to them that now might be a good time to write a note or message to a friend since their current theme is friendship. Ms. Jackson concludes this brief announcement by reviewing the rules for using the Message Board, which are posted on it:

After the Message Board reminder, Ms. Jackson introduces a large group activity. She has obtained a big book version of Mercer

- **Who may use it?** Everyone.
- **When may you use it?** Before and after class or recess or during quiet, study times during Language Arts.
- **Why might you use it?** To send a personal message to classmates and adults in the classroom.
- **How can you use it?** Use the materials on the Message Board and include the sender's and receiver's names.

(adapted from Boyd, 1985, p. 98)

Mayer's (1967) wordless picture book, *A Boy, a Dog, and a Frog,* the delightful story of a boy and a dog who befriend a frog in their unsuccessful attempt to catch it. She presents the book to the students with the tongue-in-cheek explanation that the author drew a book full of pictures that tell a story but forgot to write any words. Adopting a problem-solving mind set, Ms. Jackson and the students "read" and reread the story and generate an oral text to go with it. She invites volunteers to tell their individual versions of the story. The students compare their interpretations and discuss how they are alike and different and speculate about what the author intended the story to say.

Following the reading and retelling activity, Ms. Jackson asks the students to write their version of *A Boy, a Dog, and a Frog* or another wordless picture book (she has assembled a small collection of wordless books from the school media center; see bibliographies of wordless book in Johns, 1986, and Morrow, 1989). Students may work individually or with a partner. Classroom volunteers assist Ms. Jackson in monitoring and helping the students as they complete this task independently. Once the students get into this activity, several request that this week's "Friday Celebration" period (a special time for students to share their published works) be reserved for them to read their versions of the wordless picture books as the rest of the class views the illustrations.

Students who complete their stories before the end of LA-I may choose to work on contracted items in classroom centers, write Message Board notes, or engage in independent silent reading. Ms. Jackson has also invited Ms. Sanford, a room grandparent, to read aloud to interested students Marjorie Sharmat's (1970) *Gladys Told Me to Meet Her Here* and Russell and Lillian Hoban's (1969) *Best Friends for Frances,* stories dealing with the rocky side of friend relationships.

Language arts II. Ms. Jackson has set aside a journal writing period at the beginning of Tuesday's LA-II block. Although Ms. Jackson has decided that today's journal writing should be an "open entry" (students are free to write what they wish), she suggests to the students a few theme-related topics: (a) write about your best friend, (b) write about a disagreement you may have had with a friend and how you made up, and (c) write about a new friend you made this year.

When students have completed their journal entries, Ms. Jackson announces that she has arranged for each of her students to be a book buddy for two kindergarten children. Specifically, she has arranged for each of her second graders to read orally a picture book, one-to-one, to one child each in Mr. Mansfield's morning and afternoon kindergarten classes. The first book buddy time is scheduled for next Wednesday. Ms. Jackson suggests that the students might select a picture book on friendship from the classroom collection, although they are free to choose whatever book they believe will be interesting and entertaining to kindergarten children.

To familiarize the students with additional friendship books and other titles in their classroom and school library collections, the class engages in an informal book talk session, in which children describe and evaluate the books they have read recently and make recommendations about their suitability for reading aloud to kindergarten children. Ms. Jackson discusses principles of good oral reading and concludes the group meeting by modeling oral reading with Eric Carle's (1971) *Do You Want to Be My Friend?* The students then select a book for their kindergarten tutoring experience. Eight students from Ms. Zieman's fifth-grade class in Sleepy Hollow are available during the remaining time of the LA-II block to help children select their books and read them for the first time. As students are working independently or with the fifth-grade tutors, Ms. Jackson conducts several additional individual conferences.

Social studies. During social studies, Ms. Jackson capitalizes on the friendship/community theme by initiating a discussion of community helpers. After brainstorming a list of persons that contribute to their own urban community (e.g., fire fighters, police officers, sanitation workers, postal workers, nurses, teachers), Ms. Jackson introduces a project to the students. The project requires each student to make a brief, oral report on one community helper. A major source of information for their reports will come from an interview each student will conduct with a community helper. During the remaining part of the social studies class, Ms. Jackson and the students discuss what an interview is and how the "reporter" gets information by asking questions and recording responses. To make this more concrete, Ms. Jackson role plays a reporter and interviews several of her students. Volunteers also model being reporters. In subsequent social studies classes, the students will decide which persons they will interview, determine where and when they will conduct their interviews, write questions they will ask at their interviews, discuss how they will record responses (a tape recorder or an adult transcriber in most instances), work on their reports after the interviews are done, and make their oral presentations.

CONCLUSION

Because the preceding example is so specific, it is limited in scope and range; hence, it presents only a few ideas about how teachers can organize and manage whole language programs. Furthermore, there are no formulas for planning, developing, organizing, and managing a whole language curriculum (Newman & Church, 1990; Watson, 1989); in other words, there are many other permutations and conceptions of what a whole language program is or might be (cf., Cambourne, 1988; Cambourne & Turbill, 1987; Hancock & Hill, 1987; Jensen, 1989; Johnson & Lois, 1987; Routman, 1988; Stewart-Dore, 1986). Nevertheless, all versions of whole language instruction must possess a basic organizational and management plan in order for them to be successful. In the end, however, the design of whole language programs is limited only by the creativity, ingenuity, imagination, and ambition of teachers and students.

REFERENCES

Bergeron, B. S. (1990). What does the term *whole language* mean? Constructing a definition from the literature. *Journal of Reading Behavior, 22,* 301–329.

Boyd, R. (1985). The message board: Language comes alive. In J. M. Newman (Ed.), *Whole language: Theory in use* (pp. 91–98). Heinemann: Portsmouth, NH.

Butler, A., & Turbill, J. (1985). *Towards a reading–writing classroom.* Portsmouth, NH: Heinemann.

Caines, J. (1982). *Just us women.* New York: Harper and Row.

Calkins. L. M. (1986). *The art of teaching writing.* Portsmouth, NH: Heinemann.

Cambourne, B. (1988). *The whole story: Natural learning and the acquisition of literacy in the classroom.* New York: Scholastic.

Cambourne, B., & Turbill, J. (1987). *Coping with chaos.* Rozelle, NSW, Australia: Primary English Teaching Association.

Carle, E. (1971). *Do you want to be my friend?* New York: Crowell.

Cohen, M., & Hoban, L. (1971a). *Best friends.* New York: Macmillan.

Cohen, M., & Hoban, L. (1971b). *Will I have a friend?.* New York: Macmillan.

Delton, J., & Hoban, L. (1979). *The new girl at school.* New York: E. P. Dutton.

Delton, J., & Maestro, G. (1975). *Two is company.* New York: Crown.

Fleet, A. (1986). Contracting. In W. McVitty (Ed). *Getting it together: Organizing the reading-writing classroom* (pp. 49–64). Primary English Teaching Association: Rozelle, Australia. Distributed in the U. S. by Heinemann: Portsmouth, NH.

Gamberg, R., Kwak, W., Hutchings, Altheim, J., & Edwards, G. (1988). *Learning and loving it: Theme studies in the classroom.* Heinemann: Portsmouth, NH.

Goodman, K. (1986). *What's whole in whole language?* Portsmouth, NH: Heinemann.

Goodman, K. & Goodman, Y. M. (1979). Learning to read is natural. In L. B. Resnick & P. A. Weaver (Eds.), *Theory and practice of early reading,* vol. 1, (pp. 137–154). Hillsdale, NJ: Erlbaum.

Goodman, K. S., Goodman, Y. M., & Hood, W. J. (Eds.). (1989). *The whole language evaluation book.* Portsmouth, NH: Heinemann.

Graves, D. (1983). *Writing: Teachers and children at work.* Portsmouth, NH: Heinemann.

Hancock, J., & Hill. S. (Eds.). (1987). *Literature-based reading programs at work.* Heinemann: Portsmouth, NH.

Hoban, R., & Hoban, L. (1969). *Best friends for Frances.* New York: Harper and Row.

Holdaway, D. (1979). *The foundations of literacy.* Sydney: Aston Scholastic.

Holdaway, D. (1980). *Independence in reading,* 2d ed. Sydney: Aston Scholastic.

Hornsby, D., Sukama, D., & Parry, J. (1986). *Read on: A conference approach to reading.* Heinemann: Portsmouth, NH.

Jensen, J. M. (Ed.). (1989). *Stories to grow on: Demonstrations of language learning in K–8 classrooms.* Portsmouth, NH: Heinemann.

Johns, J. L. (1986). *Handbook for remediation of reading difficulties.* Englewood Cliffs, NJ: Prentice-Hall.

Johnson, T. D., & Lois, D. R. (1987). *Literacy through literature.* Heinemann: Portsmouth, NH.

Kellogg, S. (1986). *Best friends.* New York: Macmillan.

Kemp, M. (1989). *Watching children read & write: Observational records for children with special needs.* Portsmouth, NH: Heinemann.

Koch, K. (1970). *Wishes, lies and dreams: Teaching children to write poetry.* New York: Vintage.

Kwak, W., & Newman, J. M. (1985). Activity cards. In J. M. Newman (Ed.), *Whole language: Theory in use* (pp. 137–144). Heinemann: Portsmouth, NH.

Lobel, A. (1970). *Frog and toad are friends.* New York: Harper and Row.

Mathews, J. K. (1990). From computer management to portfolio assessment. *The Reading Teacher, 43,* 420–421.

Mayer, M. (1967). *A boy, a dog, and a frog.* New York: Dial.

Morrow, L. M. (1989). *Literacy development in the early years: Helping children read and write.* Englewood Cliffs, NJ: Prentice-Hall.

Newman, J. M. (1985a). Introduction. In J. M. Newman (Ed.), *Whole language: Theory in use* (pp. 1–6). Heinemann: Portsmouth, NH.

Newman, J. M. (1985b). Conferencing: Writing as a collaborative activity. In J. M. Newman (Ed.), *Whole language: Theory in use* (pp. 123-129). Heinemann: Portsmouth, NH.

Newman, J. M., & Church, S. M. (1990). Myths of whole language. *The Reading Teacher, 44,* 20–26.

Parry, J., & Hornsby, D. (1985). *Write on: A conference approach to writing.* Heinemann: Portsmouth, NH.

Rauch, S. J., & Sanacore, J. (Eds.). (1985). *Handbook for the volunteer tutor.* Newark, DE: International Reading Association.

Rhodes, L. K. (1981). I can read! Predictable books as resources for reading and writing instruction. *The Reading Teacher, 34,* 511–518.

Rhodes, L. K., & Dudley-Marling, C. (1988). *Readers and writers with a difference: A holistic approach to teaching learning disabled and remedial students.* Heinemann: Portsmouth, NH.

Routman, R. (1988). *Transitions from literature to literacy.* Heinemann: Portsmouth, NH.

Sharmat, M. (1970). *Gladys told me to meet her here.* New York: Harper and Row.

Silverstein, S. (1974). *Where the sidewalk ends.* New York. Harper and Row.

Sloan, P. & Whitehead, D. (1986). Organizing space and materials. In W. McVitty (Ed.), *Getting it together: Organizing the reading-writing classroom* (pp. 21–30). Primary English Teaching Association: Rozelle, Australia. Distributed in the U.S. by Heinemann: Portsmouth, NH.

Steinle, J. (1986). Statement of principles. In W. McVitty (Ed.), *Getting it together: Organizing the reading-writing classroom* (pp. 1–4). Primary English Teaching Association: Rozelle, Australia, Distributed in the U.S. by Heinemann: Portsmouth, NH.

Stewart-Doe, N. (Ed.). (1986). *Writing and reading to learn.* Heinemann: Portsmouth, NH.

Tomkins, G. E., & Webeler, M. (1983). What will happen next? Using predictable books with young children. *The Reading Teacher, 36,* 498–502.

Tsutsui, Y., & Hayashi, A. (1987). *Anna's secret friend.* New York: Viking Penguin.

Valencia, S. (1990). A portfolio approach to classroom reading assessment: The whys, whats, and hows. *The Reading Teacher, 43,* 338–340.

Viorst, J. (1974). *Rosie and Michael.*

Waber, B. (1972). *Ira sleeps over.* Boston: Houghton Mifflin.

Watson. D. J. (1989). Defining and describing whole language. *The Elementary School Journal, 90,* 129–141.

Webster's New Collegiate Dictionary. (1980). Springfield, MA: Merriam.

Weiss, N. (1983). *Maude and Sally.* New York: Greenwillow.

Wells, R. (1981). *Timothy goes to school.* New York: Dial.

James F. Baumann is a faculty member at the University of Georgia.

A Practical Guide to Whole Language in the Intermediate Classroom

Patricia Gannon Smith

Whole language in the intermediate classroom is often given less attention in professional books and journals than the primary classroom receives. The result is that many teachers of grades four, five, and six have been at a loss about how to apply whole language in their classrooms. This article is meant to be helpful to that *curious but puzzled* intermediate teacher.

Whole language in the intermediate classroom follows the same basic assumptions as whole language at any level; there is a difference in degree from the primary classroom, but not in kind. The children are more mature; they are able to read and write longer pieces and to understand more sophisticated ways to approach literature and writing. In their writing, intermediate children are often more willing to edit and rewrite than younger children are, especially if their teacher gives them the tools to make that editing and rewriting easier.

From "A Practical Guide to Whole Language in the Intermediate Classroom" by P. G. Smith, 1991, *Contemporary Education,* 62, pp. 88–95. Copyright © 1991 by Patricia Gannon Smith and *Contemporary Education.* Reprinted by permission.

The following is a discussion of what the intermediate teacher using the basic assumptions of whole language does.

1. *Whole language teachers assume that children will learn to read and write just as naturally as they learned to talk if given the proper environment.* This is the most basic assumption of whole language learning. It says that learning to read and write (and spell) are as assuredly developmental processes as is learning to talk. To learn to talk a child needs a speech-rich environment; to learn to read and write, a child needs a print-rich environment. Development of these skills is slow; it takes many years to master them. A child does not become an accomplished writer overnight any more than he/she learns to talk or read overnight; this is as true in the intermediate as in the primary grades. Teachers and parents alike need to be patient as they teach, support, and encourage.

What whole language teaching consists of is providing the *proper* environment, the environment which allows and encourages the child to develop his/her language skills as rapidly as he/she is developmentally able to do. The following characteristics of whole language teaching describe that proper environment in the intermediate classroom.

2. *Whole Language teachers place their emphasis on the meaning in words; not on the mechanics of reading or writing.* Contrary to what Marshall McLuhan said in the 1960s, the medium is not the message. The content is the message. The point of learning to talk, listen, read and write is to communicate meaning. Therefore, the whole language teacher places his/her heaviest emphasis on the meaning of the words children are reading and writing, not on the way they are being read or written.

In practical terms, this means that when reading, the emphasis is put on the sense of the words, not on correct decoding of words; in writing, the initial emphasis is put on the message that a child is trying to convey to his/her reader, not on the mechanics with which it is done. This emphasis on meaning in exemplified in two synonymous terms for whole language reading: "Meaning-Centered" or "Comprehension-Based" reading.

When the emphasis is put on meaning in reading, the child is taught to process constantly his/her reading for the sense it is making, rather than on the proper naming of words. When the emphasis is put on meaning in writing, the child is freed to explore his/her ideas as fully as possible. Not restricted to using only the words he/she can spell properly so as to avoid a red mark on his paper, the child is freed to use any word in his oral vocabulary because he knows there will be no penalty for misspelling that word. His/her teacher is interested in what he has to say, not in how he is saying it.

Thus, in the intermediate classroom, the emphasis in reading is on understanding and in writing the emphasis is on fluency and content of the writing. This is not to say that reading and writing basic skills are not taught; they most emphatically are taught, but the child needs to understand that these are the tools by which thoughts are conveyed, not the be-all and end-all of reading and writing. The skills are taught whenever possible in context, not as separate, stand-alone entities.

For example, take the reading skill of word analysis or word attack. This skill can be meaningfully taught in the context of spelling; that is, use spelling words as a vehicle for practicing word attack skills rather than miscellaneous words on ditto sheets. Use words from the book you are reading aloud; use words from print in the classroom. Emphasize the pronunciation guide in glossaries and the dictionary so that readers can learn to be independent. Do these lessons frequently and informally so that children understand that word attack is a skill to be used all of the time, not just at a reading circle.

Another illustration of the whole language approach is spelling. Many whole language writers encourage teachers to abandon spelling books in favor of word lists made up as much as possible of words which the child him/herself deems useful. For example, a child might keep a list of words he/she has had trouble spelling in daily writing. The teacher might provide a weekly list of words with some words illustrating a spelling concept chosen from a spelling book, some from content areas currently being studied, and also blank space for each child to add those individual words which he/she could not spell easily in a piece of writing. When test days arrive, the children work in pairs to give each other their *independent* spelling words. Children love the chance to choose their own words, and they are learning to spell words which have direct meaning to them.

3. *Whole language teachers encourage risk-taking. They communicate that it's okay to make mistakes.* If the emphasis on learning language is put on the meaning of the words, not in having them in proper form, then it's not only okay, it's expected that children will make mistakes. It's a cliche, but true nevertheless: we learn from our mistakes. Mistakes can be fixed, easily fixed, they need not be a cause for anxiety, they are an opportunity to learn something. The corollary of this is that, for a teacher, a child's mistake is an opportunity to teach.

Therefore, the whole language reading teacher distinguishes between reading errors and miscues. In oral reading, if a child substitutes a word that shows understanding of the text, she doesn't correct. If an error shows lack of understanding of the text, then she asks, "Does that make sense?" She teaches the child to ask continuously the same question of him/herself, continuously to process the sense of what he/she is reading.

The whole language writing teacher discourages children from stopping their writing to find out how to spell a word correctly. He/she encourages them to take an educated guess or to write the first letter plus a line. There is time later to go back and find out the correct spelling of the word from dictionary, friend or teacher. The emphasis should be on the ideas the child is trying to convey in writing, not on the mechanics. Mechanics come later on in the writing process.

4. *Whole language teachers know that children learn to read by reading and learn to write by writing, so they give children a predictable time and opportunity to do a great deal of both.* Frank Smith was the first to make this statement. It took awhile for people to listen, but after research was done to show how many minutes children were actually reading each day in school as opposed to filling in workbook and worksheet blanks, or waiting while someone else read round-robin style in a reading circle—it was well under ten minutes—teachers and administrators started to listen. Now such practices as sustained silent reading are well established, but writing needs the same concentration of time as reading. In fact, it may need more time, because the development of writing skills lags behind other language skills. Many teachers are now encouraging children to write journals daily or several times a week. These journals should be personal writing, though, with no connecting of skills because the emphasis in on the conveying of ideas between writer and reader.

Learning journals are another excellent tool to increase writing fluency; these are journals whose purpose is to help children clarify their thinking about content areas, including math. This writer has used reading journals, in which children write a reflective letter to me about their independent reading books, with excellent success. These letters provide excellent insight into the depth of a child's comprehension of what he is reading and also demonstrate the current status of his/her writing skills.

Children still need instruction in their writing, and this is where the Writer's Workshop enters. Writer's Workshop is a name commonly given to process writing as practiced in the elementary and junior high school. Writer's Workshop means that children are given the opportunity to write daily, or almost daily, on subjects of their own choosing, with the goal of informally publishing some of their writing so that others may read it. A key idea in Writer's Workshop is that children know there will be time to write daily; when this predictable time is made each day, they begin to, in Donald Graves' words, rehearse what they will write next. They begin to think about what they'll write when they're out of class. They'll begin to collect ideas for writing, to plan ahead, to think about words and phrases they might incorporate in their current piece. In other words, they begin to see themselves as writers.

Here are some brief ideas for organizing a Writer's Workshop in your intermediate classroom.

1. Give each child a permanent writing folder; manila folders work well, construction paper is too flimsy. Keep these folders in a central location where children have easy access to them —perhaps in a box so that they can stand on end. If the folders are kept at their desks, they seem to disintegrate. An easy way to keep track of the folders is to ask the children to put both their names and an alphabetical order-by-last-name number on the tab of their folders. In this way, a child helper can quickly figure out whose folder is missing.

2. On one of the inside covers of the folder, after a brainstorming warm-up, ask the children to write a list of things they might want to write about. This list can be updated as children think of other topics. The teacher can model this ongoing thinking about topics by suggesting topics to children based on things that happen or are talked about in class. For example, a child telling the class about a funny or sad occurrence in his or her life can be reminded that this story might be a great writing topic. Although most whole language experts emphasize the idea of self-selected topics, many teachers suggest topics from time to time.

3. Now, write! According to most whole language experts, the teacher should write along with his/her students. This writer has found this to be impossible after the first few writing workshop sessions because children begin to need your help. However, the modeling idea is an important one. It is valuable for a teacher to model the writing process in a formal way to demonstrate that writing is a messy process. Words are changed, sentences and phrases are moved, deleted and/or added. This can conveniently be done on an overhead projector.

4. During the writing process, children are encouraged to consult each other and the teacher. This writer asks children to write their names on the chalkboard under the heading "Writing Conference" at the beginning or during a writing period if they need to talk to the teacher. In this way there is no line of children waiting, wasting their time and disturbing others. If a writer is stuck, he or she—while waiting to see the teacher—should work an another piece of writing, or read, or follow whatever procedure is established.

5. There are several good reasons for these conferences with the teacher. One of those reasons is NOT for the purpose of spelling a word correctly. Encourage a child to make an educated guess at spelling while still writing rough drafts. Remember, it is the content of their ideas that you are emphasizing at this point. One of the good reasons for teacher-writer conferences is to help a writer who is stuck. This often means he has not thought out the plot if writing fic-

tion; if writing non-fiction, help may often be needed with elaboration. Asking such questions as, "How did you feel when this happened?" or "Tell me more about . . . " helps with elaboration, a skill which is difficult for many children.

A second reason for a writer–teacher conference is editing; if a child has decided he/she wants to publish a piece of writing, the editing process begins in full force. A third reason for a writer-teacher conference is simply that a child wants your feedback, encouragement or praise.

6. Publishing is the final stage of writing process. Whole language insists that children have real audiences for their output, again to emphasize the message that we write to communicate our thoughts. Simply put, publishing means that a child decides that a piece of his/her writing is good enough to share with others. Publishing necessitates bringing a piece of writing up to conventional standards of writing–good paragraphing, complete sentences, good punctuation and spelling, and so forth. The child is taught to edit his own work, peers edit, and finally the teacher edits.

The standards you set for editing depends on the skill level of the child. The teacher usually chooses one or two skills to emphasize with each child according to his/her own needs. The final piece may or may not be perfect, but it should be easily readable by others. The piece might actually be put between attractive covers and added to the classroom library; it might be typed by the teacher and hung on a bulletin board; it might be a letter, in which case, mailing the letter to its intended reader constitutes publishing.

5. *Whole language teachers build their curriculum, as much as possible, around the interests of the child; therefore, as much as possible, they encourage the child to choose his/her own topics for writing and his/her own books for reading.* Self-selection of reading material is a controversial subject; there are many writers, such as Jeanette Veatch, who have advocated self-selected reading for decades. This idea has had a hard time being accepted in the age of basal readers. One thing about self-selection has been proven, however: children read more and enjoy books more when they are allowed to choose their own reading matter. Many whole language writers advocate this method; to this writer's knowledge, all whole language writers advocate letting children choose their own topics for writing. This is a central idea in Writer's Workshop. They reason that if a child chooses his/her own topic for writing, they will feel ownership of that writing. They will be more interested in it, they will be more motivated to write, they will take more risks to improve their writing, especially if they are writing for a larger audience than just their teacher.

Writing for an audience beyond the teacher, and, more basically, writing for real purposes are important ideas in the whole language classroom. If the child is writing for his peers, for other children in his school, for audiences even beyond his school, it gives added purpose to his writing. Writing for real purposes such as an opinion piece for a class newspaper, a fan or pen pal letter, or questions to use for an interview, helps the child to see that writing is a useful skill in the real world.

Related to the need for a wider audience for a child's writing, is the development of a sense of audience, of writing differently for different audiences. This sense of audience becomes better developed in the intermediate grades as a child's world widens and he understands that one writes differently for his peers than he does for the readers of the letters to the editor page in the local newspaper. Children at this level should be given the opportunity to write for many audiences: possibilities range from picture books for younger children in their school to letters to manufacturers concerning their products to opinion pieces on current classroom, community, or national issues.

6. *In the whole language classroom, the child is the center of the learning process; the teacher is the facilitator of that process. The child takes responsibility for his/her own learning. The teacher guides, interacts, challenges and provides support and stimulation for growth.* Ownership is a word one often hears in relation to whole language. It means that a child feels in control of his/her learning; and that one's motivation is coming from within oneself rather than from the teacher. For this reason, children are given choice in what they read in the whole language classroom. For this reason they choose their own topics for Writer's Workshop; therefore, each child is the "expert" when it comes to the content of his/her own writing. Donald Graves encourages children to write non-fiction pieces based on their own experiences which, automatically, makes them the most knowledgeable people about the content of their writing. They decide what to include in their piece, when it is finished, and if they want to publish it. Children are given choices and opportunities to make decisions.

Another aspect of this idea of ownership is the way that editing and proofreading of children's writing is done in the Writer's Workshop. Children are taught to do their own editing and proofreading, and they help each other with these tasks. They gain the skills efficiently. The teacher facilitates what can be a tiresome job by teaching the children how to cut and paste their work and how to use editing marks, like the backward, double stemmed P for indicating a new paragraph and the caret mark for insertions. This writer also teaches children tips like writing on every other line when they are composing in order to facilitate making changes and additions to their work later.

In the whole language classroom, it is not the teacher's role or task to correct every word written by each child in the classroom. Imagine how discouraging it is for a child to write a piece of work, probably only to be read by the teacher, and then to have that solitary audience cut and slash the way through that writing with a red pencil.

Why would a child want to write again? Only a piece of writing that a child wishes to publish goes through an exhaustive editing process in order to make it ready for other people to read. The conventions and mechanics of writing become important because they facilitate someone else's reading of that work. Up until this time, attention has been paid almost exclusively to the content and its refinement, that is, making it something other people want to read and will enjoy.

7. *Whole language teachers encourage collaborative learning among children.* Collaborative learning is a *buzzword* now, but even though the phrase may be a fad, the idea is fundamental: children can and do learn from each other. Writer's Workshop encourages this idea in several ways. As they feel the need for feedback or help, children are encouraged to share their work-in-progress with both teacher and friends. They are also encouraged to share it more formally in the *author's chair* in which they present a work-in-progress or a finished piece to the entire class for their help or reaction.

This writer has found that daily informal sharing and collaborating of child-writers—that is, asking a friend or two to listen to what they have written and give their opinion and/or suggestions—is more valuable. If a teacher is concerned about too much ad hoc sharing during writing time, this process can be structured by having a particular place in the room, an author's or consulting or conferencing table or corner, where this sharing may go on. Otherwise the room is a fairly quiet workshop. Many teachers find that there is no need for this kind of limitation once the structure and goals of the workshop have been internalized.

8. *Whole language teachers teach reading and writing by using whole pieces of language not fragments.* Children do not learn language by first learning the small parts, the "a", the "b", and the "c" and then gradually working up to words, phrases, sentences, paragraphs, pages, stories, and whole books. They need first to grasp the whole context—the conversation, the story or book—and then gradually refine their understanding and use of the pieces which make up those wholes. In the intermediate classroom, this foundation statement translates into the whole language belief that children learn how to write best by doing real writing for real purposes, not by filling in blanks in workbooks.

Skills are taught as the need for them appears in the child's writing; the formal study of grammar is put off or at least de-emphasized in favor of the development of the ability of a child to communicate with an audience in a meaningful and satisfying way. In reading, this means there is a strong preference for using whole pieces of literature—whole stories, whole articles, whole books, not pieces of them. If a reading textbook must be used, try to find one which includes the best pieces of writing from the best authors available. Do not be distracted by a beautiful binder full of blackline masters to "enrich" or "reteach." Go for the best selections for the children to read.

9. *Whole language teachers encourage children to read by using the best literature available.* There has been a considerable amount written about the inadequacies of basal texts for reading instruction in recent years. One of the complaints has been about the quality of the reading selections. Sometimes stories are written to fit a skill-lesson with a resulting inane plot because content is second in importance; sometimes a recognized piece of good literature is cut or simplified to fit the needs of the grade level. Whole language espouses using whole pieces of the best literature available to children; if age- and ability-appropriate works are chosen, the interest children have in the well-written works of literature will help to overcome difficult language. We have all had the experience of seeing children read a book supposedly beyond their ability because they are very interested in the content of what they are reading. In the younger years, the best literature means classic folk and fairy tales, good poetry, and the best of picture books, both fiction and non-fiction. In the intermediate years, too, this means making the best writing there is available for children to enjoy. Teachers can read book reviews, consult their librarians and lists of "best books" if they are unsure of what to offer children. The best and most fun course is to read widely in children's literature and discover what you like yourself.

Not only will this strategy help children enjoy reading so that they are more apt to become lifelong readers, but it will also improve their writing. The more good language they read, the more apt you are to see that good language appear in their writing and speaking. When reading aloud to children of any age, stop to admire a fine turn of phrase, a beautifully chosen word, or a passage of great power or beauty. Ask children what they like about the words. Keep a chart of "beautiful words and phrases," note similes and metaphors with older children, talk about character motivation, plot and setting, do a lot of predicting about what might happen next and why. The why is crucial because this helps the child to understand the author's purposes. As a child's appreciation for words, mood, and sense of story grows, so will their own writing. As teachers we will find a great deal more success in this transfer if it happens naturally in the course of talking about books and writing than if we drill with worksheets.

10. *Whole language teachers teach skills in context, as children need them.* If you allow children to make mistakes, when do they ever learn to do things correctly? They learn correct form and mechanics gradually, the same as they do in a skills-based program. However, a skill is taught to an individual child or a group of children when the teacher can see a need for the teaching of that skill, not because the teacher's manual says, if it's the second Tuesday in October, it must be time to teach quotation marks. The reason we have to teach skills over and over and over again is because a child needs to be ready to learn that skill, needs to see the need for quotation marks because he/she wants to have a conversation in his piece of writing; if a child is not ready, if a child does not see the need for that skill for him or herself, then the child will not retain it.

Along the same lines, there may or may not be a worksheet used to practice a skill, but if there is, the worksheet grows out of a need perceived by the teacher in children's reading or writing. The skill is not taught first, and then put to work in a context of real words. The need for a skill is discovered in a child's use of words in real contexts. After the needed skill is identified, then that skill is taught and practiced, preferably still in context.

Many whole language writers, especially Nancie Atwell, encourage intermediate grade teachers to teach mini-lessons of about five or 10 minutes' duration at the beginning of a writing session. The mini-lesson could be a writing mechanics skill such as paragraphing, or a writing expression need such as how to write an opening for a story which captures the reader's attention. Again, these skills lessons are not chosen arbitrarily. They are selected because the teacher sees the need for them in the writing of the children.

What about achievement tests such as the Iowa Test of Basic Skills and ISTEP? Will children be ready for these tests if we don't teach skills directly? Probably not. These tests are written to test skills taught in the fragmented way, by rote and out of context. If your school/school corporation gives these tests and puts a great deal of emphasis on them, a month before the tests, start practicing skills out of context so that your children can "perform" properly for the test writers. Tell the children what you're doing and why you're doing it. Teach them test-taking skills along with the language skills. Then when the tests are over, go back and use words in meaningful contexts, like they are meant to be used.

11. *Whole language teachers, not a distant text-book writer, decides what concept or skill each child needs to learn next.* Mention was made above of the whole language advocacy of the empowerment of teachers as decision makers. This is a strongly held belief when it comes to skills instruction. Whole language pioneers such as Kenneth Goodman exhort us to have faith in our own knowledge of our field and our children. Goodman tells us that we know what each of our children needs to learn next in terms of skills far better than a textbook writer in some far-off publishing house does. We may consult a commercially published scope and sequence as a guide, but we decide when a child needs a skill—his/her reading and writing show us what he needs.

It is easy to make a list of the writing skills usually taught at any given grade level. Keep such a list as a checklist for each child. Encourage your youngsters also to keep a record of the skills they have mastered, for example on the inside cover of their writing folder; perhaps provide them with a form to facilitate this. Make them an aware partner in the process of skills acquisition. Learning journals here again are an appropriate tool for self-awareness and reflection on the progress of their learning.

12. *Whole language teachers recognize that evaluation is a part of the reading and writing process.* Many of us are faced with the neces-

sity of assigning grades to children's writing, even though we may be philosophically opposed to it. Grades are only one way to evaluate writing—there are many ways which will have a more salutary effect on children's writing efforts. What, after all, does an "A" or a "C" tell a child about her or his writing except the teacher's opinion of it. How does it help her or him improve?

There are several evaluation techniques suggested by whole language experts. A checklist was mentioned earlier as one way to account for skills; a checklist of criteria for good writing can also be used to evaluate overall achievement—criteria such as "You choose words which enhance your meaning," "You write effective leads," and "Your story has a beginning, a middle, and an end." Both teacher and child can use checklists which tend to emphasize the positive accomplishments rather than what is wrong with the child's writing. Portfolios are currently being touted as an excellent tool for evaluation. A portfolio is a file of a child's work—for example, samples of his/her writing, over the course of the grading period or year. The key idea is that the teacher and the child together take part in the choosing of the pieces to go into the portfolio because this again encourages the child-writer's self-awareness. The teacher and the child together develop criteria for choosing the pieces which will go into the portfolio, and thus the child is encouraged to think about what is good and what needs improving in his writing.

13. *Whole language teachers integrate different aspects of the curriculum as much as possible.* Themes of study are encouraged by whole language writers, broad themes into which all curriculum areas can be integrated. This is so because life is integrated; in the real world we use reading, writing, and math to help us solve real life problems. Subject areas are not isolated in the real world. Teachers need to choose themes which are broad enough to encompass all areas of the curriculum from math to music. A social studies or science theme is often chosen, such as "community" or "space." Sometimes an even broader and more abstract theme is chosen such as "transformations" or "conflict and cooperation." Reading and writing become the tools of exploration of such a theme.

Whole language in the intermediate is as exciting, satisfying, and successful as it is in the primary classroom. Nine-, 10-, and 11-year-olds respond to the opportunity to read and discuss good pieces of writing and to write and publish on their own choice of topic with the same interest and enthusiasm as younger children do. Please do not think, however, that whole language is a panacea, an answer to all the learning problems in your fourth, fifth, or sixth grade classroom. This is not the case. Though research is showing that whole language techniques are successful with slow learners and even with learning disabled children, there will still be children who are not motivated to learn. This teacher has found, however, that the precepts of whole language go farther than any other set of strategies she has tried toward reaching all of the children in her classroom.

Try it. You'll like it!

Patricia Gannon Smith is Assistant Professor of Elementary Education at University School, Terre Haute, Indiana.

Saying the "p" Word: Nine Guidelines for Exemplary Phonics Instruction

Steven A. Stahl

Phonics, like beauty, is in the eye of the beholder. For many people, "phonics" implies stacks of worksheets, with bored children mindlessly filling in the blanks. For some people, "phonics" implies children barking at print, often in unison, meaningless strings of letter sounds to be blended into words. For some people, "phonics" implies lists of skills that must be mastered, each with its own criterion-referenced test, which must be passed or the teacher is "in for it." For some people, "phonics" somehow contrasts with "meaning," implying that concentrating on phonics means that one must ignore the meaning of the text. For others, "phonics" is the solution to the reading problem, as Flesch (1955) argued and others have concurred (see Republican Party National Steering Committee, 1990), that if we just teach children the sounds of the letters, all else will fall into place.

Because "phonics" can be so many things, some people treat it as a dirty word, others as the salvation of reading. It is neither. With these strong feelings, though, extreme views have been allowed to predominate, seemingly forcing out any middle position that allows for the importance of systematic attention to decoding in the context of a program stressing comprehension and interpretation of quality literature and expository text. The truth is that some attention to the relationships between spelling patterns and their pronunciations is characteristic of all types of reading programs, including whole language. As Newman and Church (1990) explain:

> No one can read without taking into account the graphophonemic cues of written language. As readers all of us use information about the way words are written to help us make sense of what we're reading.... Whole language teachers do teach phonics but not as something separate from actual reading and writing.... Readers use graphophonic cues; whole language teachers help students orchestrate their use for reading and writing. (p. 20–21)

"Phonics" merely refers to various approaches designed to teach children about the orthographic code of the language and the relationships of spelling patterns to sound patterns. These approaches can range from direct instruction approaches through instruction that is embedded in the reading of literature. There is no requirement that phonics instruction use worksheets, that it involve having children bark at print, that it be taught as a set of discrete skills mastered in isolation, or that it preclude paying attention to the meaning of texts.

In this article, I want to discuss some principles about what effective phonics instruction should contain and describe some successful programs that meet these criteria.

WHY TEACH PHONICS AT ALL?

The reading field has been racked by vociferous debates about the importance of teaching phonics, when it is to be taught, and how it is to be taught. The interested reader can get a flavor of this debate by reviewing such sources as Adams (1990), Chall (1983a, 1989), Carbo (1988), and so on. To rehash these arguments would not be useful.

From "Saying the 'p' Word: Nine Guidelines for Exemplary Phonics Instruction" by S. A. Stahl, 1992, *The Reading Teacher, 45*, pp. 618–625. Copyright © 1992 by the International Reading Association. Reprinted with permission of Steven A. Stahl and the International Reading Association.

The fact is that all students, regardless of the type of instruction they receive, learn about letter–sound correspondences as part of learning to read. There are a number of models of children's initial word learning showing similar stages of development (e.g., Chall, 1983b; Frith, 1985; Lomax & McGee, 1987; McCormick & Mason, 1986). Frith, for example, suggests that children go through three stages as they learn about words. The first stage is *logographic* in which words are learned as whole units, sometimes embedded in a logo, such as a stop sign. This is followed by an *alphabetic* stage, in which use children use individual letters and sounds to identify words. The last stage is *orthographic* in which children begin to see patterns in words, and use these patterns to identify words without sounding them out. One can see children go through these stages and begin to see words orthographically by the end of the first grade. Following the orthographic stage children grow in their ability to recognize words automatically, without having to think consciously about word structure or spelling patterns.

These stages in the development of word recognition take place while children are learning about how print functions (what a written "word" is, directionality, punctuation, etc.), that it can signify meanings, about the nature of stories, and all of the other learnings that go on in emergent literacy (see Teale, 1987). Learning about words goes hand in hand with other learnings about reading and writing.

All children appear to go through these stages on their way to becoming successful readers. Some will learn to decode on their own, without any instruction. Others will need some degree of instruction, ranging from some pointing out of common spelling patterns to intense and systematic instruction to help them through the alphabetic and orthographic stages. I want to outline some components of what exemplary instruction might look like. These components could be found in classrooms based on the shared reading of literature, as in a whole language philosophy, or in classrooms in which the basal reader is used as the core text.

EXEMPLARY PHONICS INSTRUCTION . . .

1. *Builds on a child's rich concepts about how print functions.* The major source of the debates on phonics is whether one should go from part to whole (begin by teaching letters and sounds and blend those into words) or from whole to part (begin with words and analyze those into letters). Actually, there should be no debate. Letter-sound instruction makes no sense to a child who does not have an overall conception of what reading is about, how print functions, what stories are, and so on, so it must build on a child's concept of the whole process of reading.

A good analogy is baseball. For a person learning to play baseball, batting practice is an important part of learning how to play the game. However, imagine a person who has never seen a baseball game. Making that person do nothing but batting practice may lead to the misconception that baseball is about standing at the plate and repeatedly swinging at the ball. That person would miss the purpose of baseball and would think it a boring way to spend an afternoon.

Adams (1990) points out that children from homes that are successful in preparing children for literacy have a rich idea of what "reading" is before they get to school. They are read to, play with letters on the refrigerator door, discuss print with their parents, and so on. Other children may have had only minimal or no exposure to print prior to school. The differences may add up to 1,000 hours or more of exposure to print.

For the child who has had that 1,000 hours or more, phonics instruction is grounded in his or her experiences with words. Such a child may not need extensive phonics instruction. Good phonics instruction should help make sense of patterns noticed within words. Just "mentioning" the patterns might suffice. However, for the child with little or no exposure, phonics instruction would be an abstract and artificial task until the child has additional meaningful encounters with print.

To develop this base of experience with reading, one might begin reading in kindergarten with activities such as sharing books with children, writing down their dictated stories, and engaging them in authentic reading and writing tasks. Predictable books work especially well for beginning word recognition (Bridge, Winograd, & Haley, 1983). Stahl and Miller (1989) found that whole language programs appeared to work effectively in kindergarten. Their effectiveness, however, diminished in first grade, where more structured, code-emphasis approaches seemed to produce better results. In short, children benefited from the experiences with reading that a whole language program gives early on, but, once they had that exposure, they benefit from more systematic study.

2. *Builds on a foundation of phonemic awareness.* Phonemic awareness is not phonics. Phonemic awareness is awareness of sounds in *spoken* words; phonics is the relation between letters and sounds in *written* words. Phonemic awareness is an important precursor to success in reading. One study (Juel, 1988) found that children who were in the bottom fourth of their group in phonemic awareness in first grade remained in the bottom fourth of their class in reading four years later.

An example is Heather, a child I saw in our clinic. As part of an overall reading assessment, I gave Heather a task involving removing a phoneme from a spoken word. For example, I had Heather say *meat* and then repeat it without saying the /m/ sound (*eat*). When Heather said *chicken* after some hesitation, I was taken aback. When I had her say *coat* with the /k/ sound, she said *jacket*. Looking over the tasks we did together, it appeared that she viewed words only in terms of their meaning. For her, a little less than *meat* was *chicken*, a little less than *coat* was *jacket*.

For most communication, focusing on meaning is necessary. But for learning to read, especially learning about sound-symbol relationships, it is desirable to view words in terms of the sounds they contain. Only by understanding that spoken words contain phonemes can one learn the relationships between letters and sounds. The alternative is learning each word as a logograph, as in Chinese. This is possible, up to a certain limit, but does not use the alphabetic nature of our language to its best advantage.

Heather was a bright child, and this was her only difficulty, but she was having specific difficulties learning to decode. Other children like Heather, or children with more complex difficulties, are going to have similar problems. We worked for a short period of time on teaching her to reflect on sounds in spoken words, and, with about 6 weeks of instruction, she took off and became an excellent reader. The moral is that phonemic awareness is easily taught, but absence of it leads to reading difficulties.

3. *Is clear and direct.* Good teachers explain what they mean very clearly. Yet, some phonics instruction seems to be excessively ambiguous.

Some of this ambiguity comes from trying to solve the problem of pronouncing single phonemes. One cannot pronounce the sounds represented by many of the consonants in isolation. For example, the sound made by b cannot be spoken by itself, without adding a vowel (such as /buh/).

To avoid having the teacher add the vowel to the consonant sound, however, some basals have come up with some terribly circuitous routes. For example, a phonics lesson from a current basal program begins with a teacher presenting a picture of a key word, such as *bear*, pronouncing the key word and two or three words with a shared phonic element (such as *boat, ball,* and *bed*). The teacher is to point out that the sound at the beginning of each is spelled with a *B*. The teacher might then say some other words and ask if they, too, have the same sound. Next, written words are introduced and may be read by the whole class or by individuals. After this brief lesson, students might complete two worksheets, which both involve circling pictures of items that start with *b* and one which includes copying upper- and lowercase *b*'s.

In this lesson, (a) nowhere is the teacher supposed to attempt to say what sound the *b* is supposed to represent and (b) nowhere is the teacher directed to tell the children that these relationships have anything to do with reading words in text. For a child with little phonemic awareness, the instructions, which require that the child segment the initial phoneme from a word, would be very confusing. Children such as Heather view the word *bear* not as a combination of sounds or letters, but identical to its meaning. For that child, the question of what *bear* begins with does not make any sense, because it is seen as a whole meaning unit, not as a series of sounds that has a beginning and an end.

Some of this confusion could be alleviated if the teacher dealt with written words. A more direct approach is to show the word *bear,* in the context of a story or in isolation, and pointing out that it begins with the letter *b,* and that the letter *b* makes the /b/ sound. This approach goes right to the basic concept, that a letter in a word represents a particular phoneme, involving fewer extraneous concepts. Going the other direction, showing the letter *b* and then showing words such as *bear* that begin with that letter, would also be clear. Each of these should be followed having children practice reading *words* that contain the letter *b,* rather than pictures. Children learn to read by reading words, in stories or in lists. This can be done in small groups or with pairs of children reading with each other independently. Circling pictures, coloring, cutting, and pasting, and so on wastes a lot of time.

4. *Is integrated into a total reading program.* Phonics instruction, no matter how useful it is, should never dominate reading instruction. I know of no research to guide us in deciding how much time should be spent on decoding instruction, but my rule of thumb is that at least half of the time devoted to reading (and probably more) should be spent reading connected text—stories, poems, plays, trade books, and so on. No more than 25% of the time (and possibly less) should be spent on phonics instruction and practice.

Unfortunately, I have seen too many schools in which one day the members of the reading group do the green pages (the skills instruction), the next day they read the story, and the third day they do the blue pages. The result is that, on most days, children are not reading text. Certainly, in these classes, children are going to view "reading" as filling out workbook pages, since this is what they do most of the time. Instead, they should read some text daily, preferably a complete story, with phonics instruction integrated into the text reading.

In many basals, the patterns taught in the phonics lessons appear infrequently in the text, leading students to believe that phonics is somehow unrelated to the task of reading (Adams, 1990). What is taught should be directly usable in children's reading. Juel and Roper/Schneider (1985) found that children were better able to use their phonics knowledge, for both decoding and comprehension, when the texts they read contained a higher percentage of words that conformed to the patterns they were taught. It is best to teach elements that can be used with stories the children are going to read. Teachers using a basal might rearrange the phonics lessons so that a more appropriate element is taught with each story.

Teachers using trade books might choose elements from the books they plan to use, and either preteach them or integrate the instruction into the lesson. A good procedure for doing this is described by Trachtenburg (1990).

She suggests beginning by reading a quality children's story (such as *Angus and the Cat*, cited in Trachtenburg, 1990), providing instruction in a high utility phonic element appearing in that story (short *a* in this case), and using that element to help read another book (such as *The Cat in the Hat* or *Who Took the Farmer's Hat?*). Trachtenburg (1990) provides a list of trade books that contain high percentages of common phonic elements.

Reading Recovery is another example of how phonics instruction can be integrated into a total reading program. Reading Recovery lessons differ depending on the child's needs, but a typical lesson begins with the rereading of a familiar book, followed by the taking of a "running record" on a book introduced the previous session (see Pinnell, Fried, & Estice, 1990, for details). The phonics instruction occurs in the middle of the lesson and could involve directed work in phonemic awareness, letter–sound correspondences using children's spelling or magnetic letters, or even lists of words. The teacher chooses a pattern with which the child had difficulty. The "phonics" instruction is a relatively small component of the total Reading Recovery program, but it is an important one.

5. *Focuses on reading words, not learning rules*. When competent adults read, they do not refer to a set of rules that they store in their heads. Instead, as Adams (1990) points out, they recognize new words by comparing them or spelling patterns within them to words they already know. When an unknown word such as *Minatory* is encountered, it is not read by figuring out whether the first syllable is open or closed. Instead most people that I have asked usually say the first syllable says /min/ as in *minute* or *miniature*, comparing it to a pattern in a word they already know how to pronounce. Effective decoders see words not in terms of phonics rules, but in terms of patterns of letters that are used to aid in identification.

Effective phonics instruction helps children do this, by first drawing their attention to the order of letters in words, forcing them to examine common patterns in English through sounding out words, and showing similarities between words. As an interim step, rules can be useful in helping children see patterns. Some rules, such as the silent *e* rule, point out common patterns in English. However, rules are not useful enough to be taught as absolutes. Clymer (1963) found that only 45% of the commonly taught phonics rules worked as much as 75% of the time.

A good guideline might be that rules might be pointed out, as a way of highlighting a particular spelling pattern, but children should not be asked to memorize or recite them. And, when rules are pointed out, they should be discussed as tentative, with exceptions given at the same time as conforming patterns. Finally, only rules with reasonable utility should be used. Teaching children that *ough* has six sounds is a waste of everyone's time.

6. *May include onsets and rimes*. An alternative to teaching rules is using onsets and rimes. Treiman (1985) has found that breaking down syllables into onsets (or the part of the syllable before the vowel) and rimes (the part from the vowel onward) is useful to describe how we process syllables in oral language. Teaching onsets and rimes may be useful in written language as well.

Adams (1990) points out that letter–sound correspondences are more stable when one looks at rimes than when letters are looked at in isolation. For example, *ea* taken alone is thought of as irregular. However, it is very regular in all rimes, except *-ead* (bead vs. bread), *-eaf* (sheaf vs. deaf), and *-ear* (hear vs. bear). Then rime *-ean*, for example, nearly always has the long *e* sound. Of the 286 phonograms that appear in primary grade texts, 95% of them were pronounced the same in every word in which they appeared (Adams, 1990).

In addition, nearly 500 words can be derived from the following 37 rimes:

-ack	-ain	-ake	-ale	-all	-ame
-an	-ank	-ap	-ash	-at	-ate
-aw	-ay	-eat	-ell	-est	-ice
-ick	-ide	-ight	-ill	-in	-ine
-ing	-ink	-ip	-ir	-ock	-oke
-op	-or	-ore	-uck	-ug	-ump
-unk					

Rime-based instruction is used in a number of successful reading programs. In one such program, children are taught to compare an unknown word to already known words and to use context to confirm their predictions (Gaskins et al., 1988). For example, when encountering *wheat* in a sentence, such as *The little red hen gathered the wheat*, a student might be taught to compare it to *meat* and say "If m-e-a-t is *meat* then this is *wheat*." The student would then cross-check the pronunciation by seeing if *wheat* made sense in the sentence. This approach is comprehension oriented in that students are focused on the comprehension of sentences and stories, but it does teach decoding effectively (see also Cunningham, 1991).

7. *May include invented spelling practice.* It has been suggested that when children work out their invented spellings, they are learning phonic principles, but learning them "naturally." For this reason, many whole language advocates suggest that practice in writing with invented spelling might be a good substitute for direct phonics instruction. Practice with invented spelling does improve children's awareness of phonemes, which, as discussed earlier, is an important precursor to learning to decode.

However, there is very little research on the effects of invented spelling. That research is positive, but I know of only one study that directly addresses the question. Clarke (1989) found that children who were encouraged to invent spelling and given additional time for writing journals were significantly better at decoding and comprehension than children in a traditional spelling program. However, the classes she studied used a synthetic phonics program as their core reading program. These results may not transfer to a whole language program or even to a more eclectic basal program. An evaluation of the Writing-to-Read program, a computer-based program incorporating writing, found that it had little effect on children's reading abilities (Slavin, 1991).

We need not wait for the research needed to evaluate the use of invented spelling. Writing stories and journal entries using invented spelling does not seem to hurt one's reading or spelling abilities and may help them, and it certainly improves children's writing.

8. *Develops independent word recognition strategies, focusing attention on the internal structure of words.* The object of phonics instruction is to get children to notice orthographic patterns in words and to use those patterns to recognize words. Effective strategies, whether they involve having a child sound a word out letter by letter, find a word that shares the same rime as an unknown word, or spell out the word through invented or practiced spelling, all force the child to look closely at patterns in words. It is through the learning of these patterns that children learn to recognize words efficiently.

Good phonics instruction should help children through the stages described earlier as quickly as possible. Beginning with book-handling experiences, story book reading and "Big Books" and other features of a whole language kindergarten support children at the logographic stage. Frith (1985) suggests that writing and spelling may aid in the development of alphabetic knowledge. This can be built upon with some direct instruction of letters and sounds, and showing students how to use that knowledge to unlock words in text. Sounding words out also forces children to examine the internal structure of words, as does rime-based instruction. These can help children make the transition to the orthographic stage. In the next stage, the child develops automatic word recognition skills, or the ability to recognize words without conscious attention.

9. *Develops automatic word recognition skills so that students can devote their attention to comprehension, not words.* The purpose of phonics instruction is *not* that children learn to sound out words. The purpose is that they learn to recognize words, quickly and automatically, so that they can turn their attention to comprehension of the text. If children are devoting too much energy sounding out words, they will not be able to direct enough of their attention to comprehension (Samuels, 1988).

We know that children develop automatic word recognition skills through practicing reading words. We know that reading words in context does improve children's recognition of words, an improvement which transfers to improved comprehension. There is some question about whether reading words in isolation necessarily results in improved comprehension. Fleisher, Jenkins, and Pany (1979–1980) found that increasing word recognition speed in isolation did not result in improved comprehension; Blanchard (1981) found that it did. Either way, there is ample evidence that practice reading words in text, either repeated readings of the same text (Samuels, 1988) or just reading of connected text in general (Taylor & Nosbush, 1983), improves children's comprehension.

Good phonics instruction is also over relatively quickly. Anderson, Hiebert, Wilkinson, and Scott (1985) recommends that phonics instruction be completed by the end of the second grade. This may even be too long. Stretching phonics instruction out too long, or spending time on teaching the arcane aspects of phonics—the schwa, the silent *k*, assigning accent to polysyllabic words—is at best a waste of time. Once a child begins to use orthographic patterns in recognizing words and recognizes words at an easy, fluent pace, it is time to move away from phonics instruction and to spend even more time reading and writing text.

THE "POLITICS" OF PHONICS

Given that all children do need to learn about the relationships between spelling patterns and pronunciations on route to becoming a successful reader, why all the fuss about phonics?

Part of the reason is that there is confusion about what phonics instruction is. A teacher pointing out the "short *a*" words during the reading of a Big Book in a whole language classroom is doing something different from a teacher telling her class that the short sound of the letter *a* is /a/ and having them blend in unison 12 words that contain that sound, yet both might be effective phonics instruction. The differences are not only in practice but in philosophy.

In discussions on this issue, the philosophical differences seem to predominate. These exaggerated differences often find people arguing that "phonics" proponents oppose the use of literature and writing in the primary grades, which is clearly false, or that "whole language" people oppose any sort of direct teaching, also clearly false. The truth is that there are commonalities that can be found in effective practices of widely differing philosophies, some of which are reflected in the nine guidelines discussed here.

In this article, I have proposed some characteristics of exemplary phonics instruction. Such instruction is very different from what I see in many classrooms. But because phonics is often taught badly is no reason to stop attempting to teach it well. Quality phonics instruction should be a part of a reading program, integrated and relevant to the reading and writing of actual texts, based on and building upon children's experiences with texts. Such phonics instruction can and should be built into all beginning reading programs.

REFERENCES

Adams, M. J. (1990). *Beginning to read: Thinking and learning about print.* Cambridge, MA: M.I.T Press.

Anderson, R. C., Hiebert, E. F., Wilkinson, I. A. G., & Scott, J. (1985). *Becoming a nation of readers.* Champaign, IL: National Academy of Education and Center for the Study of Reading.

Blanchard, J. S. (1981). A comprehension strategy for disabled readers in the middle school. *Journal of Reading, 24,* 331–336.

Bridge, C. A., Winograd, P. N., & Haley, D. (1983). Using predictable materials vs. preprimers to teach beginning sight words. *The Reading Teacher, 36,* 884–891.

Carbo, M. (1988). Debunking the great phonics myth. *Phi Delta Kappan, 70,* 226–240.

Chall, J. S. (1983a). *Learning to read. The great debate* (revised, with a new foreword). New York, NY: McGraw-Hill.

Chall, J. S., (1983b). *Stages of reading development.* New York: McGraw-Hill.

Chall, J. S. (1989). Learning to read: The great debate twenty years later. A response to "Debunking the great phonics myth." *Phi Delta Kappan, 71,* 521–538.

Clarke, L. K. (1989). Encouraging invented spelling in first graders' writing: Effects on learning to spell and read. *Research in the Teaching of English, 22,* 281–309.

Clymer, T. (1963). The utility of phonic generalizations in the primary grades. *The Reading Teacher 16,* 252–258.

Cunningham, P. M. (1991). *Phonics they use.* New York: HarperCollins.

Fleisher, L. S., Jenkins, J. R., & Pany, D. (1979–1980). Effects on poor readers' comprehension of training in rapid decoding. *Reading Research Quarterly, 15,* 30–48.

Flesch, R. (1955). *Why Johnny can't read.* New York: Harper & Row.

Frith, U. (1985). Beneath the surface of developmental dyslexia. In K. E. Patterson, K. C. Marshall, & M. Coltheart (Eds.), *Surface dyslexia: Neuropsychological and cognitive studies of phonological reading* (pp. 301–330). Hillsdale, NJ: Erlbaum.

Gaskins, I. W., Downer, M. A., Anderson, R. C., Cunningham, P. M., Gaskins, R. W., Schommer, M., & The Teachers of Benchmark School. (1988). A metacognitive approach to phonics: Using what you know to decode what you don't know. *Remedial and Special Education, 9,* 36–41.

Juel, C. (1988). Learning to read and write: A longitudinal study of fifty-four children from first through fourth grade. *Journal of Educational Psychology, 80,* 437–447.

Juel, C., & Roper/Schneider, D. (1985). The influence of basal readers on first grade reading. *Reading Research Quarterly, 20,* 134–152.

Lomax, R. G., & McGee, L. M. (1987). Young children's concepts about print and reading: Toward a model of reading acquisition. *Reading Research Quarterly, 22,* 237–256.

McCormick, C. E., & Mason, J. M. (1986). Intervention procedures for increasing preschool children's interest in and knowledge about reading. In W. H. Teale & E. Sulzby (Eds.), *Emergent literacy. Writing and reading,* (pp. 90–115). Norwood, NJ: Ablex.

Newman, J. M., & Church, S. M. (1990). Commentary: Myths of whole language. *The Reading Teacher 44,* 20–27.

Pinnell, G. S., Fried, M. D., & Estice, R. M. (1990). Reading Recovery: Learning how to make a difference. *The Reading Teacher 43,* 282–295.

Republican Party National Steering Committee. (1990). *Position paper on teaching children to read.* Washington, DC: Author.

Samuels, S. J. (1988). Decoding and automaticity: Helping poor readers become automatic at word recognition. *The Reading Teacher, 41,* 756–760.

Slavin, R. E. (1991). Reading effects of IBM's "Writing to Read" program: A review of evaluations. *Educational Evaluation and Policy Analysis, 13,* 1–11.

Stahl, S. A., & Miller, P. D. (1989). Whole language and language experience approaches for beginning reading: A quantitative research synthesis. *Review of Educational Research, 59,* 87–116.

Taylor, B. M., & Nosbush, L. (1983). Oral reading for meaning: A technique for improving word identification skills. *The Reading Teacher 37,* 234–237.

Teale, W. H. (1987). Emergent literacy: Reading and writing development in early childhood. In J. E. Readence & R. S. Baldwin (Ed.), *Research in literacy: Merging perspectives, Thirty-sixth yearbook of the National Reading Conference* (pp. 45–74). Rochester, NY: National Reading Conference.

Trachtenburg, P. (1990). Using children's literature to enhance phonics instruction. *The Reading Teacher, 43,* 648–653.

Treiman, R. (1985). Onsets and rimes as units of spoken syllables: Evidence from children. *Journal of Experimental Child Psychology 39,* 161–181.

Steven A. Stahl is an associate professor at the University of Georgia in Athens, Georgia.

Learning to Read in New Zealand: The Balance of Skills and Meaning

Claude Goldenberg

Walk into New Zealand early primary classrooms—as my wife and I did on a recent trip—and you won't see phonics sheets and drills, flashcards, or workbooks, nor will you hear teacher exhortations to "sound it out." Rather, you'll see print-drenched rooms with more books than you thought could fit into a single classroom. You will see stories, pictures, labels, and charts stuck on the walls and hung from the ceiling. Children will be reading and writing at various levels of proficiency while their teacher helps them, either in groups or individually, become increasingly adept at navigating through the world of print.

Although we cannot claim that the 15 or so classrooms we visited (in six schools in three different cities) are necessarily representative or "typical" of all New Zealand early primary classrooms, the programs and practices we did observe offer U.S. educators plenty to think about. This is especially true as we consider the implications of some of our current enthusiasms. There is much more to early reading instruction in New Zealand than some of the labels applied to it—"whole language," "meaning-centered," "literature-based"—seem to imply. (Although New Zealand's approach to reading instruction has been characterized as "whole language" by American commentators [e.g., Anderson, Hiebert, Scott, & Wilkinson, 1985; Goodman, 1987], this is not, however, a term New Zealand educators themselves use to describe what they do.) What we saw was an approach that stressed developmentally organized and sequenced direct experiences with print and a set of curricular and instructional practices that achieve a subtle, but powerful, balance between skills and meaning.

LITERACY FROM THE OUTSET

From the time children in New Zealand enter school on their fifth birthday, the main item on the academic agenda is becoming literate. The entire morning for 5- to 8-year-olds is devoted to language arts—speaking, listening, writing, and reading. Reading itself is allocated an hour or so, for example, from 10:45 to 12. Afternoons are devoted to mathematics.

Reading and writing are taught from the day the child enters school. Teachers emphasize communicating and deriving meaning from texts. Children read, listen to books, and write (or attempt to write) in order to communicate or to make sense of someone else's communication. Except for practicing the alphabet, we saw no drills or exercises that did not involve meaningful text. Sometimes the text consisted of a single word. But it was invariably taken from, then found its way back into, a larger passage.

This focus on meaning did not mean mechanics (or "skills") were ignored. To the contrary, teachers consistently stressed accurate and efficient word recognition, particularly words in context. During reading and writing activities, teachers frequently called children's attention to punctuation marks and their correct usage. Teachers also devoted time to having children learn letters and their corresponding sounds. As one teacher told us, "Children absolutely must have them."

From "Learning to Read in New Zealand: The Balance of Skills and Meaning" by C. Goldenberg, 1991, *Language Arts, 68,* pp. 555–561. Copyright © 1991 by the National Council of Teachers of English. Reprinted with permission.

ORAL READING AND "GUIDED READING"

Accurate, fluent oral reading also received much attention since it is seen as an important bridge between children's spontaneous oral language and later successful silent reading. Children just beginning to read used simple, patterned caption books with texts that are very easy to remember. As children advance, they read progressively more challenging texts requiring higher levels of reading skill.

Instead of using basals, reading instruction in New Zealand centers around one or more series of actual books of gradually increasing difficulty. When teachers meet with reading groups (which are constituted according to children's current reading levels, but can change throughout the year), these are the texts they use. Sometimes teacher and group read a book, or part of a book, in unison. In the lessons we observed, children followed along and participated actively in the choral readings.

At other times, the lesson appeared similar to what is called "round robin reading" in the United States. In New Zealand, they refer to it as "guided reading," which has a different connotation. One difference stems from the fact that New Zealand teachers not only do not use basal readers—neither do they have teachers' guides containing questions they are to ask during oral reading. Consequently, teachers must become thoroughly familiar with the book children are reading in order to engage them in the sort of interactive, nonscripted give-and-take we observed.

In a guided reading session, the teacher typically introduced a book by talking about the entire selection with the group. She first read the title and looked at the cover with the children, perhaps inviting them to speculate what the story would be about. Next, she would go through the story page by page, again inviting the children to construct or anticipate key elements or events. As she went through the story, the teacher called attention to the pictures, explained unfamiliar concepts or bits of information, and pointed out key words, phrases, or passages in the text. Sometimes the teacher would read extended portions of the text—although not the entire story—to the group.

The idea seemed to be to give the children an overall view of the book, the whole picture, but without reading it entirely. Children were thus quite familiar with the story before actually beginning to read it. But there was also an air of expectancy and excitement, since many of the story's important elements had not yet been revealed. The teacher helped build the anticipation by encouraging children to talk, share pertinent ideas and experiences, and make predictions about the selection.

Once the framework for the story had been created in this way, children took turns reading aloud, with everyone else following along silently. At this point, while children and teacher made comments or observations, and the teacher perhaps asked an occasional question (which often seemed more rhetorical than anything else), the focus shifted to correct, fluent reading of the text.

SUPPORTS FOR ORAL READING

Teachers insisted on accurate and fluent oral reading. Accordingly, a crucial part of the instruction was aimed at providing children with the necessary supports for accomplishing this. If a child did not know a word or read it incorrectly, the teacher assisted. She might call the child's attention to context or to sound–symbol cues, although the former was used much more frequently. Children were encouraged to predict or estimate a word they did not recognize, using either visual, semantic, or syntactic cues.

"What would make sense there?" might be appropriate in some instances. In others, the teacher might ask, "What does it look like? Make your mouth ready to say it." If the teacher had chosen the selection well for the group, however, and had done a good job before the actual reading commenced, the number of instances where children were completely stuck would be minimal.

In correcting oral reading errors, the most frequent type of feedback we heard teachers give was, "Does that make sense?" This, of course, caused the children to focus on meaning or syntax as a basis for checking whether they were reading accurately. If the child made an error, but what was read made sense, the teacher would say, "It could be that; that would make sense. But does it look like _____ ?" In this way, the teacher reinforced use of context, while simultaneously prompting students to attend to letter (that is, visual) cues to verify their reading.

Teachers generally did not interrupt to correct an error. Unless the child were completely stuck, the teacher would wait until the end of the page or passage, then go back. If the child read a passage correctly, but haltingly, the teacher might then focus on building fluency by having the child reread the section. We often heard teachers encouraging children to "read just like you talk," thereby further reinforcing the link between written text and spoken language.

INDEPENDENT WORK

While teachers read with small groups or with individual children, the rest of the class engaged in a variety of literacy-related activities—independent reading, playing with alphabet or word games, working crossword puzzles, completing an activity sheet devised by the teacher, writing, answering questions about a story they had read, etc. These activities and materials were not unlike what children in this country do when working independently, although there were some important differences.

One difference was that children—even the 5-and 6-year-olds—seemed to do more independent reading and looking at books. During reading time, children actually read. Also, we saw no busywork, activities whose primary purpose is to keep children quietly engaged in a task while the teacher conducts a group lesson. While working independently, the children we observed either engaged in meaningful reading and writing activities, or else (in the case of the younger ones) played with games and materials designed to help them learn letters and sounds. Perhaps children would listen to a tape recording of a book while they followed along in their own copy. Once we saw a group of children copying a short paragraph from the board ("Today is Friday. It is raining," etc.). Much more often, however, written work consisted of original writing, answering questions about a story, or filling in or completing sentences.

New Zealand teachers do not enjoy the abundance of commercially-produced materials available in the U.S., so they must provide many materials themselves. Since New Zealand does not use basal reading series, teachers do not have the workbooks, ditto sheets, a host of supplementary materials, and extensive teacher's guides with suggested uses and activities. The teachers we met seemed untroubled by this. In fact, we heard from several of them that New Zealand teachers have a tradition of innovation and creativity. This tradition, clearly in evidence in every classroom we visited, includes making their own materials—even their own books.

RELATIONSHIP BETWEEN SKILLS AND MEANING

The entire process of literacy development seemed to involve an exquisitely complex and subtle interplay between acquiring the skills of literacy while focusing on the meaning for which literacy is a vehicle. It is an interplay the teachers we observed handled with great skill, professionalism, and, apparently, after considerable training. Observing the very sophisticated view of literacy acquisition that guided instruction in New Zealand made us ever more aware of the futile debates over skills vs. meaning, process vs. products that rage in some academic and professional reading circles in the United States.

The reading and writing instruction we observed seemed to be based on the assumption that there is a reciprocal and mutually supportive relationship between word recognition skills and deriving meaning from texts. Skills can be practiced in isolation in order to build fluency and automaticity. But assuming the primacy of one over the other (as participants in the "skills" vs. "meaning" debate appear to do) simply does not make sense. Fortunately, although we are still far from a unified and generally accepted view of how children learn to read (McKenna, Robinson, & Miller, 1990a&b), there seems to be a growing awareness in the U.S. of the complementary role played by skills (e.g., phonic decoding) and meaning (e.g., the structure and function of written texts [Adams, 1990]).

Accurate word recognition—either through recalling sight words, using context or letter cues, or through some combination—clearly helped the young readers we observed derive meaning from a text. But knowing what the text was about also helped: They recognized words more quickly and efficiently, since an "expectancy set" of high probability words appeared to be created in their minds. The two processes, sometimes characterized in the reading literature as "bottom-up" and "top-down," complemented, rather than competed with, each other.

READING RECOVERY

Despite the many positive features of literacy instruction in New Zealand, there are children who do not make adequate progress after a year of instruction. These children are candidates for Reading Recovery, an early intervention tutoring program created by Marie Clay (Clay, 1985) which is receiving considerable attention in the United States (Slavin, Karweit, & Madden, 1989). (Also, see "How Reading Recovery Was Established," 1989; Jongsma, 1989; Pinnell, 1989; Pinnell, Fried, & Estice, 1990, for program descriptions and results.) In New Zealand, the Department of Education funds the program at individual schools throughout the country. Children requiring extra help in learning to read spend, on average, 12–14 weeks in the program. Teachers receive special training, including conducting tutoring sessions under close supervision, in order to become Reading Recovery teachers.

Reading Recovery sessions demonstrated most clearly the perspective New Zealand teachers have on literacy—a meaning-making enterprise that requires the skillful coordination of perceptual, linguistic, and cognitive systems. This skillful coordination sometimes requires the direct teaching of specific skills, together with assisting the young learner to integrate and coordinate these skills. Reading Recovery was designed to play this role for children requiring additional help.

In one session we observed, for example, a child was having difficulty reading a simplified version of "Jack and the Beanstalk." The teacher had previously done some exercises with "little," a high-frequency word and a recurring word in this particular text. When the teacher saw the child was having difficulty reading fluently, she again isolated "little" from the text and guided the child to listen for the individual sounds in the word, then to write it out accurately. (New Zealand teachers call this "writing and reading practice," rather than "sounding and spelling exercises," which is how we in the U.S. would tend to characterize this type of activity.)

Next she spent several minutes going over the entire story with the child, page by page, picture by picture, making sure to use key words and phrases in the text, such as "little bean" and "big stalk." She prompted the child to participate in constructing the story with her by asking him questions and encouraging his comments and observations. "If you know what the story's about, it helps you read it," she told him, and she demonstrated this to him (and to us) by having him reread key passages. Upon final reading of the story, he read with much more fluency.

It was a remarkable—and tangible—demonstration of the interplay between skills and meaning. The teacher had helped him integrate visual, linguistic, and cognitive information and knowledge to produce a more successful reading of a text. I could not help but think that in the United States, such a session would have involved far more use of phonic drills and phonetically controlled reading vocabularies.

One of the aspects of Reading Recovery that impressed us greatly was the very good direct teaching in evidence. The Reading Recovery teachers we saw were highly skilled at using basic, fundamental principles of teaching and learning. They were extremely good at modeling correct responses, building automaticity through repeated trials of increased speed (overlearning), and maintaining a brisk, upbeat, and appropriate pace during the half-hour sessions. Moreover, they skillfully broke down complex tasks into more simple ones, but then efficiently worked with children to put the pieces back together so as not to lose sight of the bigger picture. In other words, they helped structure the learning task appropriately while avoiding the sort of reductionism that obscures the purpose and nature of reading.

In one instance where a child was having difficulty with a word, the teacher stopped the reading and declared, "Let's take a look at this word." She got out some plastic letters, formed the word, and had the child look very carefully at it and read it slowly, paying close attention to each letter. "What does that say?" the teacher asked, and the child read it.

The teacher scrambled the letters and had the child put them in order, then read the word carefully. The teacher repeated the procedure twice, each time telling the child—in a challenging, but encouraging way—"do it faster now, see how fast you can do it." The girl accepted each challenge enthusiastically. Once her response was firm, the teacher turned back to the sentence with the problematic word. The child read accurately, but haltingly. "OK, read it again," the teacher said, "but faster." The teacher repeated this two or three times, until the child read the sentence fluently in a normal, conversational tone.

We have known for years that individual tutoring can substantially help students who are falling behind academically (Bloom, 1984; Gates & Bond, 1935–36). Reading Recovery seems to go several steps beyond individual tutoring, incorporating robust direct teaching practices into a highly sophisticated, professionally demanding perspective on the literacy-acquisition process.

PROBLEMS OF ACHIEVEMENT, CLASS, AND ETHNICITY

How many children need Reading Recovery, that is, require intensive, individual assistance in order to progress adequately in reading? The most frequently cited estimate is that about 20% of 6-year-olds—children who have been receiving reading instruction for a full year—will probably require Reading Recovery (Clay, 1985). How many actually receive it, however, depends upon the availability of resources in relation to need at a particular school ("How Reading Recovery Was Established," 1989).

The proportion of children acknowledged to need intensive individual assistance (1 in 5) might seem high. But keep in mind that New Zealand appears to have higher literacy standards than we do in the U.S, an impression supported by international comparisons that suggest high levels of literacy achievement among New Zealand school children (Purves, 1989). After a year of instruction, which begins at age 5, children in New Zealand are expected to read with fluency and good comprehension texts that we estimated to be around the level of a U.S. first reader. It is difficult to say with certainty (and New Zealand educators do not use cut-off scores or criteria for failure or retention), but most children seemed to be beyond the primer stage by age 6. Many children judged not to be making satisfactory progress in New Zealand would therefore, in our estimation, not be identified as needing additional help in the United States.

But allowing for the higher expectations operating in New Zealand, why do a relatively sizeable number of children require additional assistance in the form of Reading Recovery? We heard different plausible explanations. One is that teachers sometimes attempt to push children prematurely. Either because of parent pressure or teachers' own professional motivation, some children might not be given enough time at the "emergent" (that is, prereading) stage. Another explanation suggests that some children simply learn more slowly than others, and they will need not only more time but also more instruction.

A skills-oriented observer from the United States would probably offer another hypothesis: The reading program does not place sufficient emphasis on skills such as phonic decoding, which might help children who have not themselves "cracked the code" by independently inferring the system of sound–symbol correspondence. There might be some truth in each of these possible explanations, but to our knowledge, this set of questions is not being actively investigated in New Zealand.

The need for Reading Recovery seems also to vary according to schools' social-class make-up. One school in Auckland we visited, which had a lower- to higher-middle class, predominantly European ("Anglo") student population, had 6 children enrolled in the program and another 3 on the waiting list. This amounts to 9 children, or 25% of the total 6-year-old school population of approximately 35 children, needing special individual help in order to make adequate progress. (Only 6 out of the 9—17%—were actually receiving such help).

In South Auckland, in contrast, where there is a higher concentration of low-income Maori and Pacific Island families, the need for Reading Recovery appears to be much greater. (The Maori are the indigenous people of New Zealand, who constitute approximately 12% of the country's 3.5 million inhabitants.) Children from these families tend to fare poorly in school. A teacher with whom we spoke, who had previously taught in South Auckland, estimated that as many as 80% of the first-year children in some of these schools needed extra assistance to help them learn to read satisfactorily. This was her own estimate, and we know of no systematic data that would directly confirm or challenge the figure she offered.

Indirect evidence, however, does tend to support the general view that need for Reading Recovery (or at least some form of extra assistance) is related to the socioeconomic and ethnic makeup of the school. Clay and Watson (1982) report that in the Auckland area, "schools in advantaged districts ... have tended not to opt into the [Reading Recovery] programme" (pp. 26–27). In contrast, 4 of the 5 schools that participated in a follow-up study of Reading Recovery had relatively high proportions of Polynesian students. Perhaps most significant was Clay and Watson's finding that 42% of the children who had been in the program in 1978 were Maori or Pacific Islander, a percentage far in excess of these children's numbers in the overall population.

Despite the imperfect data, our discussions with New Zealand educators suggested strongly that the need for Reading Recovery is related to children's ethnic and social class background. Certainly the teachers and administrators we spoke with believed, as do their counterparts in this country, that students' backgrounds strongly affected their school achievement. For all of its excellent features, classroom literacy instruction in New Zealand has not solved the problem of disproportionate underachievement by low-income, nonwhite minorities.

Nor has it obviated the need either for remedial, preventative (such as Reading Recovery), or alternative programs. Some of the schools we visited were exploring the last course. There is an incipient Maori bilingual education movement in New Zealand, which is invariably tied to the community-based education movement. These efforts have very strong political overtones, reminiscent of those in the United States that began in the 1960s (see Spolsky, 1989).

As in the United States, this state of affairs is symptomatic of a much larger problem: a large minority underclass that is disproportionately young, unemployed, and undereducated. Explanations for this condition—and prescriptions for its resolution—vary widely among New Zealanders, as they do among educators and commentators in the U.S. who have tried over the last decades to come to grips with these problems. As in the United States, the problem in New Zealand goes far beyond questions pertaining to reading instruction, with its attendant issues such as the proper role of skills and meaning. No less than here, New Zealand educators face a huge challenge for which there are no simple solutions.

It remains to be seen whether mainstream solutions, such as smaller classes and additional Reading Recovery resources, will meaningfully attenuate the achievement disparities between majority and minority students. It is possible that significant departures from the mainstream—such as Maori-language and community-based instruction—will be required. New Zealand schools are currently undergoing a transformation in their administration and local governance that will provide unprecedented opportunities for local experimentation. Perhaps out of this transformation will evolve innovative and effective solutions.

LITERACY PROBLEMS AND SOLUTIONS

Nevertheless, what remains impressive about New Zealand's approach to literacy is the unequivocal and progressive stance the educational establishment has taken with respect to achieving early, universal literacy for the entire populace. This position is backed up by the allocation of resources, time, and a professional support staff, together with an approach to literacy education that takes into account a range of developmental, instructional, and curricular factors that affect learning.

Teacher education reflects a coherent, substantive view of literacy instruction. Children's school literacy experiences are rich, varied, and intensive in the best sense. Fully half the school day in the early years is devoted to literacy development. Children who are falling behind are given extra help on an individual basis by teachers specially trained to carry out this important task.

Furthermore, the New Zealand Department of Education publishes a number of very high quality professional books which are taken very seriously by the profession and which actually guide classroom literacy instruction throughout the country. The Department also publishes an excellent series of developmentally sequenced children's books which are used instead of basals. This series has become a model that commercial publishers use when developing materials they hope to sell to schools. Local education departments are actively involved in inservice development, training, and supervision. They also employ "Advisers," experienced teachers who work directly with classroom teachers on a wide range of instructional and curricular matters. We got the very clear impression that policy and practice are much more aligned in New Zealand than they are in this country.

Amid the current enthusiasms for whole language, process writing, and meaning- and literature-based curricula, it is perhaps too easy to run one of these banners up the flagpole and proclaim that all of our literacy problems would be solved if only we were to adopt one or more of these as our new dogma. But it would be a superficial response to a problem that requires more than new slogans and labels. If we are truly to learn anything from New Zealand-style literacy instruction, it is that we must take seriously the issues that New Zealand educators seem to have taken seriously—professional education for the professional staff; a substantive understanding of how we can best teach both the skills and knowledge of literacy; universal access by children to quality materials and instruction; and a commitment to developing and implementing policies and practices that are actually used and can be shown to work. We cannot be satisfied with simply adopting a new dogma, however appealing its slogans and labels might be.

REFERENCES

Adams, M. (1990). *Beginning to read: Thinking and learning about print.* Cambridge, MA: MIT Press.

Anderson, R. B., Hiebert, E. H., Scott, J. A., & Wilkinson, I. A. G. (1985). *Becoming a nation of readers: The report of the Commission on Reading.* Champaign, IL: Center for the Study of Reading.

Bloom, B. (1984). The search for methods of group instruction as effective as one-to-one tutoring. *Educational Leadership, 41*(8), 4–17.

Clay, M. (1985). *The early detection of reading difficulties,* (3rd ed.). Portsmouth, NH: Heinemann.

Clay, M., & Watson, B. (1982). *The success of Maori children in the Reading Recovery programme. Part 1: Group analysis.* Auckland, New Zealand: Department of Education, University of Auckland.

Gates, A., & Bond, G. (1935–36). Reading readiness: A study of factors determining success and failure in beginning reading. *Teachers College Record, 37,* 679–685.

Goodman, K. (1987). Who can be a whole language teacher? *Teachers Networking: The Whole Language Newsletter, 1*(1), 10–11.

How Reading Recovery was established. (1989, November). *National Education* (New Zealand), 138–142.

Jongsma, K. (1989). Reading Recovery. *The Reading Teacher, 43,* 184–185.

McKenna, M., Robinson, R., & Miller, J. (1990a). Whole language: A research agenda for the nineties. *Educational Researcher, 19*(8), 3–6.

McKenna, M., Robinson, R., & Miller, J. (1990b), Whole language and the need for open inquiry: A rejoinder to Edelsky. *Educational Researcher, 19*(8), 12–13.

Pinnell, G. (1989). A systematic approach to reducing the risk of reading failure. In J. Allen & J. M. Mason (Eds.), *Risk makers, risk takers, risk breakers: Reducing the risks for young literacy learners* (pp. 178–200.) Portsmouth, NH: Heinemann.

Pinnell, G., Fried, M., & Estice, R. (1990). Reading Recovery: Learning how to make a difference. *The Reading Teacher, 43,* 282–295.

Purves, A. (Ed.) (1989). *International comparisons and educational reform.* Alexandria, VA: Association for Supervision and Curriculum Development.

Slavin, R., Karweit, N., & Madden, N. (1989). *Effective programs for students at risk.* Needham Heights, MA: Allyn and Bacon.

Spolsky, B. (1989). Maori bilingual education and language revitalisation. *Journal of Multilingual and Multicultural Development, 10,* 89–106.

Additional information on reading instruction in New Zealand, and the theory underlying it, can be found in:

Clay, M. (1979). *Reading: The patterning of complex behavior* (2nd ed.). Portsmouth, NH: Heinemann.

New Zealand Department of Education (1985). *Reading in the junior classes.* Wellington, New Zealand: New Zealand Department of Education. (Published in the U.S. by Richard C. Owen Publishers, Inc., New York.)

Claude Goldenberg is an assistant psychologist at UCLA and sometimes teaches in the Lennox (CA) School District.

Let's Free Teachers to Be Inspired

Gerald G. Duffy

No matter what is being taught, there seem to be two prevalent approaches to instruction. One is direct; the other, holistic. I never really understood how we dichotomize our instructional approaches until I returned to school recently to upgrade my skills as a private pilot. In Michigan, pilots don't get to fly much in the winter unless they can fly on instruments alone. Consequently, I decided to become instrument rated. It was this experience that started me thinking about how our tendency to dichotomize instruction contributes to what Gary Sykes calls a lack of "inspired teaching."[1]

FLYING INSTRUCTION

In flying, for instance, there are two ways to learn to be instrument rated. Flyers call the first "ground school." This is where you are supposed to learn how the system governing instrument flight works. In ground school, you learn all about the system in isolation. That is, without actually flying, you learn to answer questions such as these: What obstacle clearance and navigation signal coverage is a pilot assured with the MSA depicted on the approach chart? Where should the bearing pointer of the HSI be located relative to the wingtip reference to maintain the 16 DME range in a left-handed arc with a right crosswind component? You must then select the correct answer from four foils cleverly written to trip up the unsuspecting test-taker.

So I took ground school. It is conducted in the tradition of what we in education call "direct instruction": carefully sequenced, teacher-directed lessons; lots of repetition and drill using workbooks; and frequent quizzes.[2] What counts is passing the Federal Aviation Authority's written exam, which consists of a hundred multiple-choice questions selected at random from the ones that are used in class for practice all semester. Understanding is not emphasized. When I asked my seatmate, who consistently scored better than I did on the quizzes, how he was managing to understand all this stuff, he replied, "Oh, hell. I don't understand it. I just memorize the right answer for each test item." The material is uninspiring, boring, dull, and essentially meaningless.

I did pass the test. But I still couldn't fly my plane in bad weather. I had learned to answer the multiple-choice questions, but I did not understand how the instrument flying system worked.

This worried me. But, like others pursuing an instrument rating, I went on to the second way to learn how to fly my plane in bad weather. Flyers call this "air work." In air work you practice various components of the instrument flying system while actually flying a plane under simulated instrument conditions. My flight instructor would, on any given day, put me in the airplane and say, "Okay, today we're going to shoot the ILS 24 approach," or "Okay, today we're going to do a teardrop entry to a holding pattern south of the NDB on the 210 radial." Then we would just jump in the airplane and go do it.

This method is *not* very structured. It is reminiscent of what reading educators call the whole-language approach: the experience is embedded in real activity, is free of rigid instructional sequencing, is not dominated by teacher direction, and is not evaluated by quizzes.[3] What counts is being able to control the airplane by reference to the instruments while performing certain maneuvers—or what my instructor called "avoiding premature termination of the flight." Although these tasks are

---

From "Let's Free Teachers to Be Inspired" by G. G. Duffy, 1992, *Phi Delta Kappan, 73,* pp. 442–447. Copyright © 1992 by Phi Delta Kappan. Reprinted by permission of Phi Delta Kappan and Gerald G. Duffy.

fun, exciting, and very meaningful (especially if you avoid premature termination), the instruction I received was not inspired teaching, because in the end I still couldn't fly from one place to another in bad weather.

READING INSTRUCTION

As with flying instruction, there seem to be basically two ways to teach children to read. First, there is the "skill-and-strategy" approach. Most basal texts, as well as a variety of other programs, kits, and instructional packages, fall into this category. Students are supposed to learn that reading and writing are governed by a language system. In the skill-and-strategy approach, students learn all about the language system in isolation. That is, without actually sending or receiving written messages of substance, they learn to answer such questions as: What is the best title for this paragraph? Which is the correct punctuation for the following sentence? Then they select the correct answer from among four foils cleverly written to trip up the unsuspecting test-taker.

Like my instrument ground school, classrooms that use this method of teaching reading usually rely on the tradition of direct instruction: very structured, carefully sequenced, teacher-directed lessons; lots of repetition and drill using workbooks; and frequent quizzes. What counts is passing the end-of-unit test or the statewide assessment test. Understanding how to use text to achieve useful purposes does not count toward the grade. Instruction is uninspiring, boring, dull, and essentially meaningless. Still, many students pass the tests. The only problem is that they don't read. They learn to answer test questions but do not become literate because they do not understand how main idea, punctuation, and all the other elements of the language system are used in real reading.

This worried some folks. So they started teaching children to read another way. It is often called the "whole-language" or "literature-based" approach. In this approach, the emphasis is on actually reading books and writing stories. The learning experience is relatively unstructured and unsequenced, there are no quizzes, and the teacher's instructional role is to promote real reading activity without being unduly directive. Students just jump into reading and start. It is fun, exciting, and very meaningful (as long as you already know how to read or can learn how to read without much assistance). But it is not inspired teaching, because many students, particularly at-risk students, still can't use reading to meet their needs in real life—which is what they are supposed to be learning. Without explicit assistance, many at-risk students never figure out that there is a system of language conventions and strategies that governs written communication, and, lacking this understanding, they assume that they are dumb, or they decide that reading and writing aren't really important anyway, or they otherwise fail to become literate.

WHAT'S WRONG?

So what's wrong here? The problem is that, because one philosophy or theory is relied on to the exclusion of the other, instruction is dichotomized. Students receive one-sided messages about what really counts. With a direct-instruction approach, test passing is what counts; with a holistic approach, the number of books you report reading is what counts. Neither emphasizes what we really want literate people to be able to do: use written language to complete authentic and useful tasks successfully.

Teachers, for their part, think that a philosophy or theory is to be *followed* and that any deviation compromises instructional quality. Teachers are encouraged in this belief by professors who argue that to deviate from a theory or philosophy or program is to risk being "atheoretical." As evidence of the heat and passion of such arguments, one need only examine Carole Edelsky's recent defense of whole language and compare it to Walter MacGinitie's appeal for balance, in which he points out, "In education, conditions can become insufferably bad when good ideas are carried to extremes."[4]

Indeed, such dichotomized views are in stark contrast to the picture we get from recent research about what characterizes effective teachers. Deborah Dillon, for instance, reports that her intensive study of teaching indicates that effective teachers construct "a model of teaching that works for each of them in their specific setting and with various groups of students." Along the same lines, Gaea Leinhardt argues that effective teachers develop "craft knowledge" that is contextualized rather than generalized and that this craft knowledge constitutes the wisdom of practice. My own work similarly suggests that effective teaching is associated with being empowered to combine tenets of various positions in order to arrive at instructional decisions that make sense in a particular instructional situation.[5]

The point is not whether direct or holistic approaches to instruction are right or wrong in any empirical sense. Instead, the point is promoting inspired teaching. Inspired teaching does not originate in a particular philosophy, theory, approach, or program. It originates in the creativity of teachers. But a theory or philosophy often becomes more important than that creativity. When this happens, teachers turn over to the philosophy or theory the responsibility for instructional decisions. In following the tenets of a philosophy or theory in compliantly passive ways, teachers are effectively disempowered. Consequently, inspired teaching is more likely to result when teachers are encouraged to use various philosophical and theoretical tenets in what Dillon calls "informed, dynamic, and artful" combinations,[6] and students are more likely to use reading and writing as sources of their own empowerment when teachers themselves are empowered to select intelligently from among various conceptions.

WHAT ABOUT COMBINED APPROACHES?

Does instruction have to be either of the one-dimensional extremes I have described here? Couldn't we select from both the holistic and the direct approaches in devising instructional plans? I think we could, and, in the process, we would create more exciting and more effective teaching. To illustrate, let's return to instrument flying.

First, we would probably use holistic philosophies to think about how to make instruction authentic rather than artificial. In doing so, we would probably change the concept of air work to mean authentic trips from one airport to another to accomplish some purpose important to the flyer. We would encourage the student to plan a series of trips that he or she needed or wanted to make, and then we would organize instruction in the various elements of instrument flying around those trips. Instruction would be embedded in "real flying"—real trips being made for purposes important to the student pilot—not contrived, artificial exercises assigned by teachers. In this sense, instruction would be very holistic. What the student was learning about instrument flying would seem sensible because it would be used in making a real trip for real purposes.

Second, drawing from direct instruction, we would impose an order on the trips to make sure that the first trips are shorter and require relatively simple elements of the instrument flying system, while subsequent trips are longer and call for more complex elements of the system. We would use the earlier trips as an occasion to focus on the "basics"; later trips would focus on refinements. There would, therefore, be a structure and sequence to the curriculum. After deciding what flights would be made first, second, and so on, and what instrument flying procedures the student pilot would need in order to complete each flight, we would provide direct instruction in those procedures.

But that instruction would not occur in an isolated ground school. It would occur in the context of the trip. Before taking off, we would model for the student how to perform the necessary procedures, offer simulated opportunities for the student to try out what we have modeled, and give corrective feedback. During the flight itself, we would monitor the student pilot's use of the procedures, assisting whenever necessary and elaborating on our earlier explanations in light of the student's misconceptions. In the early flights, when there is much the student has not yet learned, we would have to perform some of the flying tasks ourselves, and if unusual situations arose we would simply assume command. In later flights, we would intervene less and less as the student grew in proficiency.

Finally, we would evaluate. What counted would not be whether the student pilot could answer multiple-choice questions about the instrument flying system or use isolated segments of the system but, rather, whether the trip was successfully completed using the instrument flying system. If during the flight the student exhibited weaknesses in particular elements of the system or did not use certain "basic skills" fluently, we would reteach those items in the interval between one flight and the next. It makes sense, doesn't it?

So what makes this approach sensible? In the first place, there is a practical immediacy to instruction, much as proponents of holistic approaches advocate. What is being learned at any given time is used during an authentic flight made that day. In short, learning is situated in meaningful activity.[7] This system motivates the student, and understanding results.

Second, the curriculum is sensibly ordered (i.e., the basics are learned before the refinements), and we are unabashedly direct in assisting the student, much as proponents of direct instruction advocate. In short, instruction is forthright; there is no coyness about the teacher's role as a transmitter and mediator of the instrument flying system.

Finally, what counts is not whether the student pilot can choose the correct multiple-choice answer on a test or fly an isolated segment of an instrument approach without crashing; instead, what counts is the more sensible criterion of whether the instrument flying system is used to achieve the pilot's goal. Therefore, there is congruence between what we want instrument pilots to be able to do and what is evaluated.

Could we do the same thing in reading? What would we do first? Consistent with holistic philosophies, we would base instruction on authentic activity, in which written materials found in the natural environment are used to complete an activity that is important to the students. In contrast to programs using basal texts (which consist of contrived materials that students are forced to read) and literature-based programs (which, while sometimes consisting of self-selected trade books, are seldom organized to fulfill purposes identified by students), we would organize instruction around what students consider to be authentic activity, with instruction in reading and writing occurring as a natural consequence of completing the activity. All instruction would be embedded in "real reading"—completed because it is needed to engage in the activity, not because distant experts prescribed it in a teacher's guide. In this sense, instruction would be holistic. What the student learned about the language system would make a lot of sense because it would contribute to completing an authentic activity.

Second, we would make sure that early encounters are with shorter texts that use "basic elements" of the language system—reading for meaning, left-to-right orientation to the page, recognition of high-utility words, predicting, deciding whether the text's meaning fits the reader's purposes, and using context clues to remove impediments to meaning. Subsequent encounters in later projects would be longer and would require more complex operations—summarizing, drawing conclusions, synthesizing information from several texts, and using various text structures as cues to meaning. There would be a structure and sequence to the curriculum, much as proponents of direct instruction advocate.

Before each encounter with text, we would provide students with direct instruction on what they needed to know about reading so that they could read on that day the text that would help them engage in the authentic activity they wished to complete. We might introduce certain vocabulary words, explain and model how to predict or how to use context or a particular type of text structure, guide students' emerging understandings by helping them complete simulated examples of what we mean by being a good reader, and provide corrective feedback as they completed these simulations. When the students moved to reading the text itself, we would monitor their progress, assisting whenever necessary. When the text to be read included language elements or references beyond the students' experience, we would have to identify difficult words, provide background for alien ideas, or suggest inferences. And in cases in which the reading was particularly difficult, we might even have to read some of the material orally to the students. In later encounters with text, we would intervene less and less.

Finally, we would evaluate. What counted would not be whether students could complete workbook exercises or pass tests but, rather, whether they got from text what they needed in order to complete the authentic activity. If, while they were reading, we noted that some students seemed weak on certain previously taught elements of the language system or were not using certain "basic skills" fluently, we would reteach or arrange for drill and practice before their next encounter with text.

Combining direct instruction and holistic approaches in this way has three advantages. First, the emphasis is on authentic use, not contrived exercises. Because this is so, skills and strategies learned in the context of the genuine activity take on a practical immediacy. They are used to complete the activity, not to do the next exercise in the workbook. The focus, therefore, becomes teaching and learning for understanding. Second, instruction is direct. Because the curriculum is ordered and the teaching is forthright, basics are learned before refinements, and students are not left to figure things out unassisted. Finally, what counts is *not* whether students can complete exercises associated only with school or pass tests that measure "pretend" literacy; what counts is whether, when engaging in authentic activity, students do what literate people do in real life—use reading to complete genuine and useful tasks successfully. There is congruence between what we want literate people to be able to do and what we evaluate.

It is sensible to combine whole language and direct instruction when teaching literacy. But it is not easy. Flight instructors, for instance, have a much easier time of it than reading teachers because they don't have to worry about teaching 25 or 30 students at a time, about how to group, about being with students all day long, about parents, and about the principal sitting in the plane checking things off on a teacher evaluation form. But, despite the difficulties, a combined approach can be adapted to real classrooms.

EMPOWERING TEACHERS

Can teachers creatively combine tenets of both holistic and direct approaches? My work for the last three years with principals and volunteer teachers from eight rural schools in northern Michigan suggests that they can.[8] The goal of my work is to empower teachers to be adventuresome and idiosyncratic in their teaching. I do not want them to adhere to tenets of one approach or another; instead, when they are creating instructional situations, I want them to adapt their professional knowledge to what students need. To help teachers do this, we join them in their classrooms, where we demonstrate and coach adaptive teaching as they work with students who traditionally have difficulty becoming literate.

This is not to say that teachers do not receive information as part of these staff development efforts. They do. We present whole-language concepts about the importance of providing genuine opportunities for reading and writing; about the message-sending, message-getting function of written language; and about the aesthetic and functional purposes of literacy. At the same time, we present direct-instruction concepts about the importance of routine skills and metacognitive strategies, about the power of explicit teacher talk and modeling, and about various ways to create opportunities for ordered and systematic learning of fundamental skills and strategies. In short, we teach *both* whole language and direct instruction (as well as other theories and philosophies), helping teachers see that the key to instruction lies not in following the prescriptions of a particular philosophy or theory but, rather, in using elements of whole language, direct instruction, or both as called for by an instructional situation. This approach puts the teacher, not the theory or philosophy, in charge. Thus teachers are freed to create inspired instructional encounters.

It is much more difficult to create programs that combine various philosophies and theories than to follow a basal text, teach isolated skills, or get students to read a lot of literature books. But, difficult or not, it is being done. The experiences of three teachers are illustrative.

A First-Grade Teacher

Let's look at one of the ways a first-grade teacher synthesizes whole language and direct instruction. This teacher and her class are deciding how to celebrate winter. To help make this decision, they read. For instance, they read picture books about winter, such as Ezra Jack Keats' *Snowy Day*, and poetry about winter. In addition, they write. They are writing language-experience stories about what they have learned from their reading about how to celebrate winter. They are also doing paintings of winter scenes and collecting what they call "winter recipes" of food items they might be able to prepare themselves. The problem of deciding how to celebrate winter provides a real reason for reading and writing, as whole-language advocates suggest.

Within the framework of preparing to celebrate winter, the teacher directly teaches the system for figuring out meaning in text. When examining the books and materials being read in class, the teacher and students talk about reading as message-getting, about how writing makes sense, about thinking of the reader when we write, and about thinking of the author and what the author is trying to tell us when we read. Each activity is preceded with a lesson on how the language system works. For instance, the teacher teaches such skills as left-to-right progression across the page, basic sight words, and the sounds of initial consonants and consonant clusters. She also emphasizes being strategic when reading. Specifically, she directly teaches her students how to make predictions before reading; how to monitor meaning and, if unknown words are encountered, how to use context and phonics during reading; and how to reflect after reading (in this case, about what they have learned that could be used to celebrate winter).

This first-grade teacher, like all good teachers, evaluates. And, like most teachers, she feels the pressure of the testing movement. Her school must give both schoolwide standardized tests and the annual state assessment. However, while she wants her students to do well on these tests and prepares them to do so in the weeks before a test is scheduled, her current evaluation focuses on whether they successfully use written materials to decide how to celebrate winter.

A Third-Grade Teacher

My next example is a third-grade teacher who relies primarily on a basal textbook. However, drawing from whole-language philosophy, she embeds her basal text instruction in authentic activity. For instance, she recently suggested that her students write books for the kindergartners. After exchanging favorite stories about past visits to the school's kindergarten and the way the younger children respond to "older" students' writing, the third-graders agreed that they each wanted to submit something to the kindergarten library. Because the teacher wanted to integrate reading with a science unit on animals, she encouraged students to submit writing about animals.

It was necessary to read and write to engage in this activity. For instance, the students had to read about animals, not only to learn what they could write about animals but also to find out how "real" authors write. They began by reading every selection about animals that was in the basal text. Then they read a trade book, *Not THIS Bear!*, by Bernice Myers; then they moved to selected magazine articles, encyclopedia entries, and informational books on various kinds of animals. And, of course, they read the animal unit in their science book. For seatwork, students read about the animals they planned to write about. This part of instruction was firmly based on holistic principles because the reading was for authentic purposes.

However, this teacher also employs direct instruction. Before reading the science book or the next basal story or the next section in *Not THIS Bear!* or whatever text they are about to use, she presents elements of the language system. For instance, she teaches students to discriminate visually between similar-looking words, such as *where* and *there*, when both words appear in the selection to be read next.

Most of her effort, however, is devoted to strategy instruction. As a "before-reading" strategy, she emphasizes predicting, much as the first-grade teacher did. However, because writing is a major component of this project, she also emphasizes the text structure that authors use when writing stories, as opposed to the text structures used for informational books, poems, and so on. Her direct instruction includes showing students how they can use their knowledge of text structures when reading as well as when writing—that is, if they think about the text structure of what they are about to read, they can predict what will come first and second in the text. For "during-reading" strategies, she continues to emphasize how to figure out unknown words when they are encountered in text, but she also shows students how to make new predictions if, while monitoring meaning during reading, one realizes that the meaning predicted initially is not the meaning the author is conveying. As an "after-reading" strategy, the teacher shows the students how to make semantic maps (sometimes referred to as "webbing") as a way to reflect on and organize what they have gotten from their reading. They can use these maps when it comes time to write what they will submit to the kindergarten.

This teacher has not yet completed her evaluation because the students' books are not yet finished. However, her final evaluation will not consist of giving the end-of-unit test in the basal text or a workbook page on visual discrimination or a multiple-choice test on what to do when you encounter a word you don't know while reading. Instead, she will evaluate how successfully her students—like literate people in the real world—use available materials to complete authentic activity.

A Fifth-Grade Teacher

A fifth-grade teacher I have observed prefers a literature-based program emphasizing recreational reading. However, because his students were neglecting expository text in favor of narrative text, he and his class developed a school newspaper that they sell to other students in the school. Publishing the weekly newspaper is an authentic activity; reading and writing are natural consequences of pursuing that activity.

For instance, consistent with the whole-language emphasis on purposeful reading, the class immersed itself in expository text to learn how to produce the newspaper. The students read books about newspapers and studied various newspapers before visiting a newspaper office.

Now that the newspaper is up and running, they report on events and personalities within the school building itself, read expository text about world and local issues in such news sources as magazines and newspapers, and write reports for their paper. They also continue to read good narratives, but now they write about them for the newspaper's book review section. They also keep up on controversial issues, both within the school and outside the school, and write editorials and feature articles about them.

The teacher also provides direct instruction, particularly on how to be strategic readers and (because they are all writing articles for the paper) on how to be strategic writers. As a "before-reading" strategy, he emphasizes making predictions based on purpose (since one reads differently to find out the score of last week's soccer game than to find out how many times the lead changed hands) and making predictions based on text structure (because a different structure is used for news articles than for feature articles, for instance). As a "during-reading" strategy, he emphasizes rate of reading (because one may wish to scan some parts of a news article and read other parts carefully). Critical reading is a major "after-reading" strategy, in which students learn how to recognize bias in writing and how to make judgments about the validity of what they have read or about what they are writing for their own paper.

This teacher evaluates by noting how effectively his students use reading and writing to produce the newspaper. He does not test isolated aspects of language, such as punctuation or main idea, He assesses students' ability to punctuate by looking at their punctuation in the articles they write for the newspaper; he assesses their ability to determine the gist of an article by looking at both the reading they do when preparing for writing articles and what they ultimately write for the newspaper.

These three teachers are neither whole-language teachers nor direct-instruction teachers. They are empowered teachers—empowered because they exercise professional judgment to select from various conceptions in creating literacy instruction. The result is inspired teaching—meaningful, rigorous, and responsive to the students.

Inspired teaching does not come from a particular philosophy or theory or set of materials. Inspired teaching comes from teachers who analyze their particular situation and create instruction to meet the needs of that situation. Insisting on rigid compliance with one or another approach tends to convince teachers that the key to improved instruction lies outside themselves. In actuality, however, inspired teaching lies within the teacher, because it is the teacher who assesses the particular demands of the situation and creates an instructional mosaic that is at once conceptually coherent, responsive to students, and reflective of a broad range of professional knowledge.

Such empowerment is not easy to come by. Teachers must be committed, hard working, courageous, tenacious, patient, creative, and adaptable. They must harness various ideas, select from a variety of principles, and create different instructional combinations. Perhaps even more difficult, such empowerment for teachers requires teacher educators and staff developers to abandon the practice of promoting a particular philosophy, theory, or program and, instead, to help teachers adapt a variety of philosophies, theories, and programs to the realities of their classrooms.

1. Gary Sykes, "Inspired Teaching: The Missing Element in 'Effective Schools,'" *Educational Administration Quarterly*, vol. 24, 1988, pp. 461–69.
2. Jere Brophy and Thomas Good, "Teacher Behavior and Student Achievement," in Merlin C. Wittrock, ed., *Handbook of Research on Teaching* (New York: Macmillan, 1986), pp. 328–75; and Barak Rosenshine and Robert Stevens, "Classroom Instruction in Reading," in P. David Pearson, ed., *Handbook of Reading Research* (New York: Longman, 1984), pp. 745–98.
3. Kenneth Goodman, "Whole Language Research: Foundations and Development," *Elementary School Journal*, vol. 90, 1989, pp. 207–22; and Dorothy Watson, "Defining and Describing Whole Language," *Elementary School Journal*, vol. 90, 1989, pp. 129–42.
4. Carole Edelsky, "Whose Agenda Is This Anyway? A Response to McKenna, Robinson, and Miller," *Educational Researcher*, November 1990, pp. 7–11; and Walter H. MacGinitie, "Reading Instruction: Plus Ça Change..." *Educational Leadership*, March 1991, p. 56.
5. Deborah Dillon, "Showing Them What I Want Them to Learn and That I Care Who They Are: A Microethnography of the Social Organization of a Secondary Low-Track English-Reading Classroom," *American Educational Research Journal*, vol. 26, 1989, p. 256; Gaea Leinhardt, "Capturing the Craft Knowledge in Teaching," *Educational Researcher*, March 1990, pp. 18–25; Gerald Duffy, "Reading Strategy Instruction: Reevaluating What Is Really Crucial," paper presented at the annual meeting of the American Educational Research Association, Boston, 1990; and idem, "What Counts in Teacher Educating? Dilemmas in Educating Empowered Teachers," paper presented at the annual meeting of the National Reading Conference, Miami Beach, 1990.
6. Dillon, p. 189.
7. John Seely Brown, Allan Collins, and Paul Duguid, "Situated Cognition and the Culture of Learning," *Educational Researcher*, January-February 1989, pp. 32–42; Gaea Leinhardt, "Situated Knowledge and Expertise in Teaching," in James Calderhead, ed., *Teachers' Professional Learning* (London: Falmer Press, 1988), pp. 147–68; and Lauren B. Resnick, "Learning In School and Out," *Educational Researcher*, December 1987, pp. 13–20.
8. Duffy, "What Counts in Teacher Educating?"

Gerald G. Duffy is a professor of teacher education at Michigan State University in East Lansing.

CHAPTER DISCUSSIONS AND ACTIVITIES

1. After reading the articles by Baumann and Smith, compare and contrast the instructional considerations focusing on the following points:
   a. How did each article define whole language? Which definition do you prefer and why?
   b. What active learning was noted in each article?
   c. How was the empowerment of teachers discussed and/or described?
2. Either visit a whole-language classroom or view a videotape about whole language, for example "The Whole Language Movement: From Teacher to Teacher" produced in 1991 by Patricia M. Hart, directed by Eric L. Johnson and distributed by Films for the Humanities and Sciences, Princeton, New Jersey.
   a. How do the activities differ from those of a traditional classroom?
   b. In what ways do teachers reinforce or repudiate the principles of classroom management espoused by Baumann? Do they agree or disagree with the points made by Smith? In what ways?

c. In what way would the teaching of phonics, as described by Stahl in his article be compatible or incompatible with the teaching that you have observed?
d. In what ways are instructional practices similar or dissimilar to those described in Goldenberg's article about New Zealand?
e. What examples of teacher creativity did you observe and how do these relate to the points discussed in the article by Duffy?

Be prepared to share and defend your responses to these questions.

CHAPTER 4

Using Literature with Whole Language

The use of literature in the classroom is becoming a first priority for educators in schools throughout the United States. Through literature, students are exposed to a wide range of challenges: it offers them an opportunity to widen their past experiences and develop new ones; it affords the unfolding of the pleasures of our language; it furnishes a cognitive understanding of human behavior; it expands life experiences; and it yields a sensitivity to the use of language as an important tool in coming to terms with human experiences (Ruddell, 1992).

According to Cullinan (1992a), "good literature, clearly the foundation of an effective language program, is central to reading and writing in whole language classrooms" (p. xii). She notes that the movement is based on three fundamental beliefs: "children learn to read by actually reading and not by doing exercises, reading is a part of language and is learned in the same way as are other forms of language, and learning in any one area of language helps learning in other areas" (p. xii). Because literature is a creative form of communication, and it is at the heart of whole language, teachers need to have a deep and continuous love and knowledge of children's literature. In this chapter, we will be defining children's literature, reviewing the elements involved in book selection, identifying the genres of children's literature and examining the role of literature in the whole-language classroom.

UNDERSTANDING CHILDREN'S LITERATURE

What is children's literature? Tiedt (1979) defines it for us in the following poem:

> Children's literature is . . .
>   stories—exciting, well-loved, satisfying;
>   pictures—joyful, interpretive, enhancing;
>   films—animating, sensory, perceptive;
>   recordings—voicing, hearing, reacting;
> Children's literature is adventurous, informative, and poetic.
> Literature for children is . . .
>   feeling—hurting, laughing, hoping;
>   experiencing—dramatizing, interacting, socializing;
>   sharing—identifying, reaching, understanding;
>   languaging—explaining, questioning, responding;
> Literature for children is drama, song and dance. (p. 17)

Children should be exposed to literature every day in school so that reading becomes a pleasurable habit that stays with them throughout their lives. One has only to ask adults who like to read the question, "What was your favorite book as a child?" Whether it is *Charlotte's Web* or *The Velveteen Rabbit* or *Amelia Bedelia*, smiles cross the respondents' faces and usually you will be told what the book was about. Stewig (1988), in offering some very important reasons for using literature with children, points out that using literature helps children read:

- For simple enjoyment
- To escape from present situations
- To stimulate the imagination
- To gain understanding of themselves
- To gain understanding of the nature of language
- To learn about other times and places
- In quest of information (pp. 24–29)

There is nothing more rewarding for a teacher than to read a book to children and see their faces light up, their eyes brighten and a smile burst forth. The authors of *Becoming a Nation of Readers: The Report of the Commission on Reading* (Anderson, Hiebert, Scott, & Wilkinson, 1985) note that "There is no substitute for a teacher who reads children good stories. It whets the appetite of children for reading, and provides a model of skillful oral reading. It is a practice that should continue throughout the grades" (p. 51). Children's books offer the listener and the reader thoughts, feelings or dreams that are waiting to be discovered.

Many children from literate families appear to develop naturally a love and interest in hearing children's literature as well as in reading it. In *One Writer's Beginnings*, Welty (1983) shares her experiences as a child: "I learned from the age of two or three that any room in our house, at any time of day, was where to read in, or to be read to. My mother read to me" (p. 5). Why is it that Ryan, an eighteen-month-old boy busily playing with his toys, will drop what he is doing and climb up on his mother's lap while she is reading to his four-year-old brother Sean, and readily become involved in the story of *Alexander and the Terrible, Horrible, No Good Very Bad Day*? Ryan's interest is keen, he is totally engrossed in the story and waits patiently as Mom turns each page. Or what about a three-year old who on a Saturday afternoon asks his mother, "What are you doing, Mom?" "I'm reading, Paul," is the response. He goes to his father and asks, "What are you doing, Dad?" The response is, "I'm reading, Paul." Then he goes over to his six-year-old sister and asks her what she is doing. When she replies that she, too, is reading, it becomes just too frustrating for Paul. He stands in the middle of the room and painfully states, "How come everyone is reading and I'm not! Who is going to read to me?" When sharing stories with a child, the delight and enjoyment of books evolve and, in many cases, so does the avid reader. Huck (1992) in recounting her childhood states that "I don't remember learning to read at all; I only remember loving reading" (p. 520).

LITERARY ELEMENTS

Before teachers can comfortably embark on using trade books as the major aspect of reading instruction, it is necessary for them to develop and widen their knowledge of children's literature. In selecting books for classroom use, the teacher needs to have a comprehensive understanding of the literary elements of children's literature, namely: plot, theme, characterization, setting, and style. These terms are defined by Burns, Roe, and Ross (1992) as follows:

- The *plot* is the overall plan for the story.
- The *theme* is the main idea the writer wishes to convey.
- The *characterization* is the way in which the writer makes the reader aware of the characteristics and motives of each person in the story.
- The *setting* consists of time and place.
- The *style* is the writer's mode of expressing thoughts. (p. 517)

We can take a careful look at each of these elements and consider some pertinent questions:

- Plot
  How does the plot move?
  Is it a good story?
  Is this a story that children will enjoy?
  How believable is this plot?
  Does the plot follow a logical sequence?
  Do happenings in the story build to a climax?
  Is the plot well constructed?
  Is this plot suitable for the age level of the students?
  Is this story make-believe or is it realistic?

- Theme
  - Is the theme easily identified?
  - Is it a worthwhile theme?
  - How believable is the theme to the reader?
  - Is the theme suitable for the age level of the children?
  - Is the theme a carefully integrated part of the story?
- Characterization
  - How believable are the characters?
  - How are the characters introduced?
  - Do the characters grow and develop?
  - How can children identify with the characters?
  - Does the reader see the strengths and weaknesses of the characters?
  - How does the author reveal the character's problems?
- Setting
  - How authentic is the setting?
  - Is authenticity of setting an important part of the story? In what way?
  - In what way does the setting influence the characters, theme, action or move of the story?
  - Is time handled appropriately by the author?
  - Is the setting important for the development of the story? Why? Why not?
- Style
  - Is the story well written?
  - Can the children relate to the style of writing?
  - Is there a balance between narrative and dialogue?
  - How does the author use figurative language?
  - Is symbolism, if used, appropriate for this particular story?
  - What aspects of the writing style are unique to this author?

GENRES IN CHILDREN'S LITERATURE

Within children's literature, teachers need to be cognizant of genres or literary forms. These are categorized in different ways by various authorities in the field. In this discussion, these genres are defined as: picture books; traditional literature books—folktales, fables, myths, and legends; modern fantasy; poetry; contemporary realistic fiction; historical fiction; multicultural literature; and nonfiction books—biographies and information books (Norton, 1991).

Picture books cover a wide variety of trade books, progressing from alphabet books for the very young child to picture books with extensive plots that are more appropriate for the older child (Norton, 1991). For the very young child, Tana Hoban's *Count and See* provides easily identified objects in a simple counting book, while *Jambo Means Hello: Swahili Alphabet Book* by Muriel Feelings with illustrations by Tom Feelings could be used very effectively with older children working on a unit about Africa. Huck, Hepler and Hickman (1993) view the picture story book as one that "conveys its message through two media, the art of illustrating, and the art of writing" (p. 197). In the *Polar Express*, Chris Van

Allsburg spins a story about the adventure of a boy on Christmas Eve and his meeting with Santa Claus; the illustrations enhance the story and delight the viewer.

With traditional literature, the tales have no known author because the stories have been handed down by word of mouth over a long span of time. Many of the stories originated before the printing press and were narrated and perhaps embellished by the storyteller. These tales, through the charm of the storyteller, captured the interest of the listeners, children and adults. Although retold and illustrated by modern day writers and illustrators, the stories continue to mesmerize their listening or reading audiences. In *Red Riding Hood* by James Marshall, the incident of this little girl with the wolf is vividly presented with humorous illustrations and probably captures the readers' hearts in much the same manner as the story did hundreds of years ago.

In the genre of modern fantasy, the listener or reader is spellbound by the creativity of a known author. According to Huck, Hepler, and Hickman (1993) "the great fantasies frequently reveal new insights into the world of reality" (p. 394). In modern fantasy, the "author encourages readers to suspend disbelief" (Norton, 1991, p. 295). Through such books, the imagination of children can be developed and nurtured. In *Charlotte's Web*, E. B. White provides a classic story of true friendship between Wilbur, a pig, and Charlotte, a spider—but readers and listeners seldom question such an unusual relationship.

Poetry has much to offer children. "Poetry is filled with carefully selected words that are arranged to call attention to experiences we have not known or fully recognized. . . . Poetry deals with truth—the essence of life and experience" (Cullinan & Galda, 1994, p. 127). Poetry speaks to children in a manner that appeals to their emotions and senses. Poetry can make a child smile, laugh, or giggle, and just as effectively can make a child become somber, sad, and even cry. Farjeon (1951) defines poetry as:

Poetry
What is Poetry? Who knows?
Not a rose, but the scent of the rose;
Not the sky, but the light in the sky;
Not the fly, but the gleam of the fly;
Not the sea, but the sound of the sea;
Not myself, but what makes me
See, hear, and feel something that prose
Cannot: and what it is, who knows? (p. 58)

Perhaps one of the finest books of poetry for classroom use is *The Random House Book of Poetry for Children* edited by Jack Prelutsky, which is an anthology of over five hundred poems arranged by themes.

Contemporary realistic fiction centers on the "now" in a child's life—it focuses on the problems of living today. Norton (1991) states that "the term *contemporary realistic fiction* implies that everything in a realistic story—including plot, characters, and setting—is consistent with the lives of real people in our contemporary world" (p. 408). Children relate well to the stories contained in this genre because they can usually associate the stories to their own experiences or those of a friend. This is vividly portrayed in *The Bear's House,* in which Marilyn Sachs relates the story of a fourth-grade girl trying to deal with severe home problems.

With historical fiction, the reader is taken back to a different time period and through the development of the story, the child can experience the past. In this genre, the author draws from fact as well as imagination. Extensive research, as well as authenticity about the particular period in history, is a major priority for the author of such literature. Patricia MacLachlan illustrates this in *Sarah Plain and Tall,* a story of the children in a frontier family dealing with the loss of their birth mother and their adjustment to a new, mail-order mother.

Multicultural literature "refers to those trade books, regardless of genre, having as the main character a person who is a member of a racial, religious, or language minority" (Lynch-Brown & Tomlinson, 1993, p. 172). The groups identified by the authors include African American; Asian American; Hispanic American; Jewish American; and Native America. In his book, *The Land I Lost: Adventures of a Boy in Vietnam,* Huynh Quang Nhuong depicts his childhood experiences in pre-war Vietnam. Books of this nature can help improve the self-esteem of various individuals and develop in children a sensitivity to the needs of different people in American society. In chapter 6 of this text, we will be looking at a definition of multicultural education that includes exceptional children. In most current children's literature textbooks, books about children with special needs are usually included and discussed in the genre of contemporary realistic fiction. Hopefully, this will be changing within the next few years and trade books about exceptional children will be placed in the genre of multicultural literature.

Nonfiction books include information books as well as biographies. Such books "encourage children to look at the world in new ways, to discover laws of nature and society, and to identity with people different from themselves" (Norton, 1991, p. 608). From information books, children can learn concepts, facts, and ideas that are expressed in expository and narrative children's books. Through information books, the child's knowledge of concepts in social studies, science, math and art, music and the humanities can be expanded and broadened (Wiseman, 1992). For example, in *Cathedral: The Story of Its Construction,* David Macaulay furnishes detailed drawings and extensive explanations of the building of a cathedral. Biography, on the other hand, "deals with the life of an actual person of the past or present with the intent of commemorating the subject and inspiring the reader by example" (Lynch-Brown & Tomlinson, 1993, p. 161). When looking at a biography, one has to make sure that the facts are authentic and they can be verified; the subject is viewed as a person; and the writing contains all the essentials of quality (Sutherland & Arbuthnot, 1991). Using these criteria, Russell Freeman provides a well prepared, documented life of Abraham Lincoln, in his Newbery award-winning book entitled *Lincoln: A Photobiography.*

READING INSTRUCTION WITH CHILDREN'S LITERATURE

An important vehicle for integrating literature into all areas of the curriculum is the thematic unit. As noted by Roser, Hoffman, Labbo, and Farest (1992) themes can "provide a framework for the children's discoveries of the connections among the literature selections" (p. 45). Crook and Lehman (1991) offer ways in which teachers can unify themes used in a whole-language classroom. This can be done by developing a web that connects fiction and nonfiction books within the theme, and within this web, developing integrated units related to such areas as language arts, math, science, social studies, art, music, and drama, and by using what they call literary text sets. "A text set is simply any group of books: folktale variants, books on a similar theme or common topic, books by the same author or illustrator, books with the same story structure or the same character, or books about the same culture" (p. 36).

There are other important considerations that teachers need to weigh when implementing successful reading instruction through the use of literature. First, there should be a wide variety of books housed in the classroom, readily available for selection by the children. Second, within class time, students should be given the opportunity to read and exchange ideas about what they have read through informal discussions. Third, teachers should provide daily blocks of time for sustained silent reading (SSR) or uninterrupted sustained silent reading (USSR). Finally, and most importantly, teachers should read aloud each day a broad selection of books (Frew, 1990).

The role of the teacher in literature selection is very special because it is the teacher, not the author or illustrator who knows the interests of the children. Coody (1992) points out "it is their responsibility, and privilege, to select those books that best fit the needs of the children they teach" (p. 2).

Looking Ahead

Cullinan (1992b) in her article discusses the relationship between whole language and children's literature; Hade (1991) describes a literary classroom; Henney (1992) provides an in-depth review of literature-based theme units; Rosenblatt (1991) provides a provocative view of literature; and Larrick (1991) offers the reader an important concern about the use of literature in the classroom.

When reading these articles about literature and whole language, your may want to consider the following questions:

- How do whole-language advocates view the use of literature in the classroom?
- How does the use of literature in the classroom influence the writing of children as well as their reading achievement?
- In what different ways can teachers use literature in the classroom?

- What is meant by the statement "materials don't teach, teachers do?"
- What are some of the teaching techniques that a teacher can use in a literature-based program?
- What is the purpose of literature-based theme units and what are the major elements to be included?
- How does a teacher prepare the various types of theme units?
- How important is the aesthetic response to literature? How can teachers encourage its use in the classroom?
- What are some of the mistakes that teachers make when using literature in the classroom?

REFERENCES

Anderson, R. C., Hiebert, E. H., Scott, J. A., & Wilkinson, I. A. G. (1985). *Becoming a nation of readers: The report of the Commission on Reading.* Washington, DC: The National Institute of Education, U.S. Department of Education.

Burns, P. C., Roe, B. D., & Ross, E. P. (1992). *Teaching reading in today's elementary schools* (5th ed.). Boston: Houghton Mifflin.

Coody, B. (1992). *Using literature with young children.* Dubuque, IA: Wm. C. Brown.

Crook, P. R., & Lehman, B. A. (1991). Themes for two voices: Children's fiction and nonfiction as "whole literature". *Language Arts, 68*(1), 34–41.

Cullinan, B. E. (1992a). Prologue: Learning with literature. In B. W. Cullinan (Ed.), *Invitation to read: More children's literature in the reading program* (pp. x–xxii). Newark, DE: International Reading Association.

Cullinan, B. E. (1992b). Whole language and children's literature. *Language Arts, 69*(6), 426–430.

Cullinan, B. E., & Galda, L. (1994). *Literature and the child* (3rd ed.). New York: Harcourt Brace.

Frew, A. W. (1990). Four steps toward literature-based reading. *Journal of Reading, 34*(2), 98–102.

Hade, D. D. (1991). Being literary in a literature-based classroom. *Children's Literature in Education, 22*(1), 1–17.

Henney, M. (1992). Literature-based theme units. *Kansas Journal of Reading, 8,* 36–41.

Huck, C. S. (1992). Literacy and literature. *Language Arts, 69*(7), 520–526.

Huck, C. S., Hepler, S., & Hickman, J. (1993). *Children's literature in the elementary school* (5th ed.). New York: Harcourt Brace.

Larrick, N. (1991). Give us books! . . . . but also . . . give us wings! *The New Advocate, 4*(2), 77–83.

Lynch-Brown, C., & Tomlinson, C. M. (1993). *Essentials of children's literature.* Boston: Allyn and Bacon.

Norton, D. E. (1991). *Through the eyes of a child* (3rd ed.). New York: Merrill/Macmillan.

Rosenblatt, L. M. (1991). Literature—S.O.S.! *Language Arts, 68*(6), 444–448.

Roser, N. L., Hoffman, J. V., Labbo, L. A., & Farest, C. (1992). Language charts: A record of story time talk. *Language Arts, 69*(1), 44–52.

Ruddell, R. B. (1992). A whole language and literature perspective: Creating a meaning-making instructional environment. *Language Arts, 69*(8), 612–620.

Stewig, J. W. (1988). *Children and literature* (2nd ed.). Boston: Houghton Mifflin.

Sutherland, Z., & Arbuthnot, M. H. (1991). *Children and books* (8th ed.). New York: Harper Collins.
Tiedt, I. M. (1979). *Exploring books for children.* Boston: Houghton Mifflin.
Welty, E. (1983). *One writer's beginnings.* Cambridge, MA: Harvard University Press.
Wiseman, D. L. (1992). *Learning to read with literature.* Boston: Allyn and Bacon.

CHILDREN'S LITERATURE REFERENCES

Farjeon, E. (1951). *Eleanor Farjeon's poems for children.* New York: Lippincott.
Feelings, M. (1974). *Jambo means hello: Swahili alphabet book.* New York: Dial.
Freeman, R. (1987). *Lincoln: A photobiography.* New York: Clarion.
Hoban, T. (1972). *Count and see.* New York: Macmillan.
Macauley, D. (1973). *Cathedral: The story of its construction.* Boston: Houghton Mifflin.
MacLachlan, P. (1985). *Sarah plain and tall.* New York: Harper and Row.
Marshall, J. (1987). *Red Riding Hood.* New York: Dial.
Nhuong, H. Q. (1982). *The land I lost: Adventures of a boy in Vietnam.* New York: Harper and Row.
Parish, P. (1963). *Amelia Bedelia.* New York: Harper and Row.
Prelutsky, J. (Ed.). (1983). *The Random House book of poetry for children.* New York: Random House.
Sachs, M. (1971). *The bear's house.* New York: Doubleday.
Van Allsburg, C. (1981). *Polar Express.* Boston: Houghton Mifflin.
Viorst, J. (1972). *Alexander and the terrible, horrible, no good, very bad day.* New York: Atheneum.
White, E. B. (1952). *Charlotte's web.* New York: Harper and Row.
Williams, M. (1922). *The Velveteen Rabbit.* New York: George H. Doran.

FOR FURTHER STUDY

Altwerger, B., & Flores, B. (1994). Theme cycles: Creating communities of learners. *Primary Voices K–6, 2*(1), 2–6.
Beach, J. D. (1992). New trends in an historical perspective: Literature's place in language arts education. *Language Arts, 69*(7), 550–556.
Beuchat, C. E. (1993–1994). The writer: Another agent in the development of literacy. *The Reading Teacher, 47*(4), 312–315.
Castro, E. (1994). Implementing theme cycle: One teacher's way. *Primary Voices K–6, 2*(1), 7–14.
Cooter, Jr., R. B., & Griffith, R. (1989). Thematic units for middle school: An honorable seduction. *Journal of Reading, 32*(8), 676–681.
Cox, C., & Many, J. E. (1992). Toward an understanding of the aesthetic response to literature. *Language Arts, 69*(1), 28–33.
Flynn, R. M., & Carr, G. A. (1994). Exploring classroom literature through drama: A specialist and a teacher collaborate. *Language Arts, 71*(1), 38–43.
Fox, M. (1993). Men who weep, boys who dance: The gender agenda between the lines in children's literature. *Language Arts, 70*(2), 84–88.
Fuhler, C. J. (1990). Let's move toward literature-based reading instruction. *The Reading Teacher, 43*(4), 312–315.

Funk, H., & Funk, G. D. (1992). Children's literature: An integral facet of the elementary school curriculum. *Reading Improvement, 29*(1), 40–44.

Hancock, M. R. (1992). Literature response journals: Insights beyond the printed page. *Language Arts, 69*(1), 36–42.

Hiebert, E. H., & Colt, J. (1989). Patterns of literature-based reading instruction. *The Reading Teacher, 43*(1), 14–20.

Hughes, S. M. (1993). The impact of whole language on four elementary school libraries. *Language Arts, 70*(5), 393–399.

Lukens, R. J. (1990). *A critical handbook of children's literature* (4th ed.). Glenview, IL: Scott, Foresman/Little, Brown Higher Education.

McKenna, M. C., & Kear, D. J. (1990). Measuring attitude toward reading: A new tool for teachers. *The Reading Teacher, 43*(9), 626–639.

Pappas, C. C. (1991). Fostering full access to literacy by including information books. *Language Arts, 68*(6), 449–462.

Reimer, K. M. (1992). Multiethnic literature: Holding fast to dreams. *Language Arts, 69*(1), 14–21.

Reutzel, D. R., & Cooter, Jr., R. B. (1991). Organizing for effective instruction: The reading workshop. *The Reading Teacher, 44*(8), 548–554.

Saccardi, M. (1993–1994). Children speak: Our students' reactions to books can tell us what to teach. *The Reading Teacher, 47*(4), 318–324.

Smolkin, L. B., & Yaden, Jr., D. B. (1992). *O* is for *mouse:* First encounters with the alphabet book. *Language Arts, 69*(6), 432–441.

Staab, C. (1991). Classroom organization: Thematic centers revisited. *Language Arts, 68*(2), 108–113.

Swift, K. (1993). Try Reading Workshop in your classroom. *The Reading Teacher, 46*(5), 366–371.

Trelease, J. (1989). Jim Trelease speaks on reading aloud to children. *The Reading Teacher, 43*(3), 200–206.

Villaume, S. K., Worden, T., Williams, S., Hopkins, L., & Rosenblatt, C. (1994). Five teachers in search of a discussion. *The Reading Teacher, 47*(6), 480–487.

Wollman-Bonilla, J. E. (1989). Reading journals: Invitations to participate in literature. *The Reading Teacher, 43*(2), 112–120.

Wicklund, L. K. (1989). Shared poetry: A whole language experience adapted for remedial readers. *The Reading Teacher 42*(7), 478–481.

Wilson, P. J., & Abrahamson, R. F. (1988). What children's literature classics do children really enjoy? *The Reading Teacher, 41*(4), 406–411.

Young, T. A., & Vardell, D. (1993). Weaving Readers Theatre and nonfiction into the curriculum. *The Reading Teacher, 46*(5), 396–406.

Zarnowski, M. (1988). Learning about fictionalized biographies: A reading and writing approach. *The Reading Teacher, 42*(2), 136–142.

Zhang, M., & Breedlove, W. G. (1989). The changing role of imagination in Chinese children's books. *The Reading Teacher, 42*(6), 406–412.

Whole Language and Children's Literature

Bernice E. Cullinan

"So Wilfrid Gordon went home again to look for memories for Miss Nancy because she had lost her own."

(Fox, 1985, unpaged)

Of all the residents at the retirement center near Wilfrid Gordon McDonald Partridge's home, he likes Miss Nancy best. When he learns that she has lost her memory, he prepares a basket of memories for her. Mem Fox's tender story vividly illustrates the connection between whole language and children's literature. We teachers need to fill our students' baskets of memory with sparkling language and memorable experiences from literature.

Whole language and children's literature is a combination that makes sense. I start with a definition, briefly review the research, and then discuss problems and promises in this area. Since whole language means different things to different people, I prefer to focus on literature-based programs or integrated language arts programs. Whatever we call it, it is a vital grass roots movement that is spreading across the nation and around the world.

The whole language movement is grounded in three basic beliefs: that children learn to read by actually reading full texts, not worksheets; that reading is a part of language learning; and that learning in any one area of language helps learning in other areas. Children learn best when language is whole, meaningful, and functional. The language of literature becomes the heart of reading and writing programs; thus, whole language and literature are inseparable.

WHAT DOES RESEARCH TELL US?

Some convincing research on the strong connection between reading and writing comes from DeFord's (1987) study that examined the kinds of writing children do in relation to the kind of reading program they have. The study found that children in strong synthetic phonics programs write only the sounds of language they are taught to read: e.g., "I had a dad. I had a gag." Children in skills classrooms with linguistically consistent word patterns write only the word patterns they know: e.g., "I am Jill. I am Bill. Jill. Bill."

In whole language or literature-rich classrooms where teachers encourage invented spelling, children draw upon a richer fund of language: e.g., "Iran is fighting U.S. 19 bombers down. 14 fighters. We have destroyed Iran. Signing out. Jason." DeFord shows us that children draw upon the language around them. If they read the interesting language of expository and narrative literature, they use it in their writing. This happens in an environment where children feel it is safe to experiment and take risks. So we need to give children the beautiful language of literature in an environment where they are free to experiment with reading and writing. That's what whole language teachers do.

A new area of research documents why story is basic to whole language and focuses on the power of narrative and our hunger for story. Barbara Hardy, Professor of English Literature at the University of London, reminds us that we remember the past in narrative, we plan the future in narrative, and we dream in narrative (Hardy, 1978). Narrative is the way we organize our minds. In order really to live, we make up stories about ourselves and others, about the past and future. Britton (1970), noted for his work on the relationship between language and learning, describes how

From "Whole Language and Children's Literature" by B. E. Cullinan, 1992, *Language Arts, 69*, pp. 426–430. Copyright © 1992 by the National Council of Teachers of English. Reprinted with permission.

we use language to represent and structure our world; this representation actually constitutes the world in which we function. We literally create stories of our lives around the framework of our individual belief systems. During childhood our narratives are fairy tales that verify our interior life (Bettelheim, 1976). Rosen (1984) holds that as we mature, narrative becomes a predisposition of our minds; we lean naturally toward the framework of narrative. We begin with story to get to truth, and the truth is, we must begin with story. The story form is a cultural universal; stories help us to remember by providing meaningful frameworks. Stories make events memorable. Cognitive psychologists have discovered the power of story; it fits in with schema theory—story provides the schema.

Another area of research contributing to the whole language movement is the work in writing process. Graves and his colleagues at the University of New Hampshire, the Bay Area Writing group, and many others have found out what young people can do when they approach writing as real writers do. Calkins (1990) invited writing teachers to meet in book-discussion groups to discuss both children's and adult books. As teacher participants thought about their own talk about books, teachers transferred practices from their book-discussion groups in their classrooms; they stopped quizzing children about little bits and pieces of text and started *talking* with them about books. In a similar vein, author Katherine Paterson (1989) highlights the difference between stoplight readers and flashlight readers. For a long time, we have been trying to train stoplight readers. We ask children to read a little bit of a story, then stop and talk about it. Yet, what we should be working toward is flashlight readers who, after the lights are out, take a book under the covers with a flashlight because they cannot bear to stop reading what may very well seem to be the best book they have ever read. Paterson says, "If you want illumination, a flashlight will beat a stoplight every time" (p. 138).

Do you know any child who took "The Fat Cat Sat on the Mat" to bed or begged to continue reading a textbook?

Finally, the amount of independent, silent reading children are doing in school is significantly related to gains in reading achievement. But children in primary classes actually read only 7 to 8 minutes a day (Dishaw, 1977). By the middle grades, silent reading time may average 15 minutes a day (Dishaw, 1977). The amount of reading students do outside of school is consistently related to gains in reading achievement. But Fielding, Wilson, and Anderson (1986) found that reading from books occupies 1% or less of the free time for the majority of children. Students who read most, read best. These studies emphasize the need for more reading time both inside and outside of school.

Clearly, the research is convincing, and the whole language movement is gaining momentum. But typically, research is slow to be translated into classrooms. Sometimes we find it hard to let go of old ways of doing things. For example, the "phonics first" and "back-to-basics" ideas have held sway for many years. According to some reports, they still do. The rate of change may be slow, but we see promising signs.

WHAT ARE THE PROBLEMS AND PROMISES?

In the summer of 1988, numerous reading professionals were invited to Boston to respond to a draft of Marilyn Adams' manuscript for *Beginning to Read: Thinking and Learning about Print* (Adams, 1990). At an early meeting of the advisory panel a number of my colleagues and I had hoped that the report might bring together the disparate groups in our profession so we could lay the issue of phonics to rest once and for all. We wanted to be sure that Adams included some of the naturalistic research that focuses on what children can *do* with their knowledge of letter–sound correspondences when they face whole and meaningful text. Instead of limiting the review to experimental studies with rigid pretest, post-test, control group design, we encouraged her to include the work of Yetta Goodman, Jerry Harste, Don Holdaway, and other naturalistic researchers. When the report was published, terms such as *reading readiness, prereading skills,* and *systematic code* instruction still dominated its pages. There was virtually no acknowledgement of terms such as emerging literacy, invented spelling, or predictable books. Dorothy Strickland and I wrote an afterword, pointing out some areas where we disagree with what is said or left unsaid. We concur that children need to learn letter–sound correspondences, but much depends upon how the concepts are taught and whether they are taught in the context of whole language. We believe that the child and adult share the responsibility of determining what shall be learned; a predetermined sequence handed out in discrete bits and pieces goes against this belief.

When I started teaching in the 1940s, we were arguing about phonics. Nearly 50 years later, we are still arguing about phonics. I ask myself, Is this the way a grown woman should be spending her time? Aren't we ready to move on from this ridiculous argument and take our cues for teaching from children and teachers themselves and from naturalistic research?

A disturbing situation arises when the general public thinks professionals can't agree on "the right way to teach reading." Certainly, some confusion arises because of the controversy surrounding whole language. Some people call it "holy language" because you have to be a believer to be saved. A problem always arises when extremists insist that their way is best. Members of our profession add fuel to the fire by their reactions. The National Assessment of Educational Progress continues to publish state-by-state rankings of reading achievement test scores. This gives credibility to test scores as the ultimate measure of success. We have tried such rankings before and consistently found a high correlation between academic achievement and the amount of money people spend on schools. Why demonstrate again what we already know? What new insights will we gain? Do the tests reflect what children can actually do? Even with the old tests, children in whole language classrooms are showing up well. Some New York City School districts are moving toward whole language, as well as implementing Reading Recovery programs. One such district, District #2, for example, has moved from near the bottom of the list to fourth from the top in city-wide rankings published annually in the *New York Times*. While we need new assessment procedures, we can also be sure that children who read more will read better, even when measured by traditional tests.

Another concern is the role of the basal reader in whole language. I hear people say, "Throw away the basals!" In fact, some say, "Throw away all the textbooks! Just use tradebooks in the classroom." Certainly, no one believes in using tradebooks in the classroom more than I do, but I think it's time for a word of caution. First of all, I respect teachers and I want *them* to select the materials they use. If they want to wade into whole language gradually and use textbooks and developmental reading programs as they do so, they are the ones who must decide. More importantly, materials don't teach. Teachers do! And teachers have the right to choose the material! The new basal readers are filled with literature because publishers want to publish what teachers ask for.

Despite the problems, there are some promising signs on the horizon. I began to wonder if we whole language people were talking only to ourselves. Are these ideas being picked up by others? Who out there is listening? I wanted to know how far literature-based programs had spread across the U.S. Whenever reading teachers invited me to speak, they always asked me to talk about literature, and I began to think that the world was finally recognizing the value of good literature. Then I realized that the *only* people who ever asked me to speak are the ones who want to hear about literature. In order to be a little more scholarly in studying the spread of whole language programs, I surveyed the Directors of Reading and Language Arts in the 50 states. The results reported in *School Library Journal*, are striking (Cullinan, 1989). At that time, 9 states had statewide initiatives centered on literature. Sixteen others had statewide initiatives focused on an integrated language arts program. Literature played a central role in the integrated programs, however; in many it was the heart. Further, 22 states that did not have statewide initiatives reported that at least 5 to 10 local districts used literature and whole language programs. These states, with strong local control, have districts that reserve the right to select programs and materials. Even the few states whose directors reported continuing the regular basic skills program have individual teachers who use literature-based, whole language programs. In summary, literature-based programs are spreading like wildfire across the country—not only through state departments of education but also in the classrooms of individual teachers as they gain power to make curriculum decisions.

While publishing in general is facing difficult economic times, there is growth in sales of children's books. George Nicholson of Dell Corporation says this is a guarded growth, appearing primarily in books for very young children. Some publishers have success stories to tell; one comes from Kids Can Press in Toronto, Canada. Kids Can Press was founded on a shoe string as a cooperative with a government grant in 1973. During the first year, sales were $17,000 with zero profits. Last year, the publisher reported sales of $2.5 million. About 15% came from international sales, suggesting that we are developing a global community in children's literature.

New children's bookstores are opening in communities across the country. Betty Takeuchi, recent president of the Association of Booksellers for Children, says that 15 years ago, there were fewer than 20 "children's only" bookstores. Today, there are nearly 500. Bookstore owners join teachers and librarians as professionals to help select material and to prepare integrated teaching units.

Parents are paying attention to what their children are reading. Just as they want them to have the best car seats and the best T-shirts, they want them to have the best books. Young parents today are better educated and have more money to spend; fortunately, they spend a good deal of it on books.

Knowledge of children's literature is recognized not as a frill, but as a basic part of teacher education programs. Still not a required course for certification in all states, the number of such offerings is increasing. In talks with teachers, I find many of them knowledgeable and eager to learn more about new children's books. It is reassuring to know that beginning teachers have studied children's literature so they can join those of us who have always shared good books with children.

Further good news comes from the American Association of Publishers who have funded a full-time professional to coordinate efforts to get tradebooks into classrooms. The AAP Reading Initiative, launched in 1989 by its Children's Publishing Committee, conducts market research, sets up a computer networking database, and conducts workshops in an ongoing effort to encourage children to read widely and well. The AAP Reading Initiative is also a clearinghouse for information on projects involving children's books in the classroom; it coordinates efforts related to tradebooks sponsored by numerous professional organizations. In a survey of over 5,000 elementary principals from 21 states (reported in the Spring, 1991, issue of *AAP Reading Initiative News*) more than 5 out of 10 elementary principals encourage their teachers to use children's books in conjunction with their reading textbooks. The survey shows that schools continue to move away from a skill-based reading philosophy, with 60% of principals describing their reading program as a literature-based, integrated language arts or whole language program. One project the AAP group promotes, Teachers as Readers, helps classroom teachers set up teacher reading groups in their schools. This project has a proven track record. Teachers who read and talk about books with their peers create rich literate environments in their classrooms.

The most promising sign comes from what teachers are doing in their classrooms. For example, Joanne Lionetti, teacher in Lynbrook, New York, works with the slow readers in the third grade. She started sharing Tomie dePaola books last fall, and her students fell in love with the man and his work. They have stripped every library in Nassau County of Tomie dePaola books. At last count they had read 55 of his books and are still going strong. They wrote his biography, called "The Art of the Heart Man," and are now working on a book about how Tomie learned to read. The children had a conference telephone call with him, and one child asked, "Are you going to write any more books?" When Tomie said yes, the boy replied, "Oh, thank God!"

Lisa Johnson, teacher in San Jose, California, has 26 different cultural groups in her reading classes. She began a thematic study of the way we celebrate holidays, starting with her own Swedish traditions. Children talked and wrote about their own traditions: special foods, when they open presents, whether they sit at the children's table, and how old they must be to sit with the grownups. They all dug into Patricia Polacco's books (she won the IRA Children's Book Award last year for *Rechencka's Egg*) to learn about Russian traditions. They read *Uncle Vova's Tree*, *Rechencka's Egg*, *Babushka's Doll*, and *The Keeping Quilt*. Teachers like Joanne Lionetti and Lisa Johnson are turning reluctant readers into avid ones. They are also stressing multicultural literature, which is in great demand at this time.

When we look at the high quality books published for children, we can understand why teachers want to use them and the children enjoy reading them. Each year, the Teachers' Choices teams field test hundreds of books and pick 30 outstanding books that work well in the classroom. Teachers looking for a place to start with children's books might begin with Teachers'Choices.

In a similar national field test, 10,000 children select their favorites as Children's Choices. The Children's Choices list contains over 100 books that children love to read—books that are very high in child appeal. Each year the Newbery and Caldecott Committees of the American Library Association select outstanding books that attract critical acclaim from both child and adult readers of children's books. The wealth of excellent children's books continues to grow. You and I have the joyful responsibility of handing these treasures on to children; it's a gift worth giving.

Even with the problems surrounding the whole language movement, whole language and literature-based programs continue to spread across the nation and around the world. Just as Wilfrid Gordon McDonald Partridge collects treasures to put into Miss Nancy's basket of memories, we can fill children's baskets of memory with beautiful language and life experiences from the books we share with them. The memories will last a lifetime.

REFERENCES

Adams, M. J. (1990). *Beginning to read: Thinking and learning about print.* Cambridge, MA: The MIT Press.

Bettelheim, B. (1976). *The uses of enchantment: The meaning and importance of fairy tales.* New York: Alfred A. Knopf.

Britton, J. (1970). *Language and learning.* New York: Penguin Books.

Calkins, L., with Harwayne, S. (1990). *Living between the lines.* Portsmouth, NH: Heinemann.

Cullinan, B. E. (April, 1989). Latching on to literature: Reading initiatives take hold. *School Library Journal, 35*(8), 27–31.

DeFord, D. E. (1981). Literacy: Reading, writing and other essentials. *Language Arts, 58,* 652–658.

Dishaw, M. (1977). *Descriptions of allocated time to content areas for the A-B period. Beginning teacher evaluation study* (Tech. Note IV-11a.) San Francisco, CA: Far West Regional Laboratory for Educational Research and Development.

Fielding, L. G., Wilson, P. T., & Anderson, R. C. (1986). A new focus on free reading: The role of trade books in reading instruction. In T. E. Raphael (Ed.), *The contexts of school-based literacy* (pp. 149–160). New York: Random House.

Hardy, B. (1978). Narrative as a primary act of mind. In M. Meek, A. Warlow, & G. Barton (Eds.), *The cool web: The pattern of children's reading* (pp. 12–23). New York: Atheneum.

Paterson, K. (1989). *The spying heart: More thoughts on reading and writing books for children.* New York: E.P. Dutton Lodestar.

Rosen, H. (1984). *Stories and meanings.* London: The National Association for the Teaching of English.

CHILDREN'S BOOKS CITED

Fox, Mem. (1985). *Wilfrid Gordon McDonald Partridge.* Illustrated by Julie Vivas. Brooklyn, NY: Kane/Miller.

Polacco, Patricia, (1988). *The keeping quilt.* New York: Simon & Schuster.

Polacco, Patricia. (1988). *Rechencka's eggs.* New York: Philomel.

Polacco, Patricia. (1989). *Uncle Vova's tree.* New York: Philomel.

Polacco, Patricia, (1990). *Babushka's doll.* New York: Simon & Schuster.

Bernice E. Cullinan is a professor at New York University and a past president of the International Reading Association.

Being Literary in a Literature-Based Classroom

Daniel D. Hade

One reason for using children's literature in classrooms, upon which nearly everyone agrees, is that children ought to be reading authentic texts, and children's literature is authentic text. Put another way, children learn to do "real" reading when they are reading "real" books. Since this authentic text is literature, it seems fair to suggest that authentic actions with this material are literary. But what constitutes being literary with children's literature? What does it mean to be authentically literary in a literature-based classroom?

Being truly literary in the classroom must involve more than kits of activities. Methods of teaching with literature must involve not only what teachers do but also the perspectives teachers have toward what they are doing. Being literary consists of ways of looking at literature and how literature can be read, of ways of viewing children as readers of books, and of ways of looking at classrooms as places where children and teachers read and share books.

While working with student teachers in the EPIC program at Ohio State University, I had the opportunity to observe and talk with many master teachers in literature-based classrooms. Through my studies at Ohio State I came to know the classroom-based research of Janet Hickman (1984), Susan Hepler (1982), Barbara Kiefer (1983), Fred Burton (1985), Amy McClure (1985), and Nan Platt (1989). Then my own dissertation took me into the classroom of a

From "Being Literary in a Literature-based Classroom" by D. D. Hade, 1991, *Children's Literature in Education, 22,* pp. 1–17. Copyright © 1991 by Human Sciences Press. Reprinted with permission.

master literature-based teacher to study her literature program. It is from these sources—master teachers, promising student teachers, previous classroom-based research, and my own research—that I suggest the following as critical aspects of "literary" literature-based classrooms.

IN LITERARY CLASSROOMS READING LITERATURE IS PLAY

In literary classrooms reading literature is a form of play. Play is the way children grow. Play is the process by which children make what is new and strange part of themselves. It is, as Margaret Meek (1988) says, assimilative.

If we are to believe such scholars as Jerome Bruner (1986), Frank Smith (1985), and Anne Haas Dyson (1987), then we must acknowledge that a primary mode of human thought is the creation of "possible worlds." Some of these possible worlds are worlds of reality, while others are imaginary, "worlds of actors, objects, and actions that exist through words and through illustrations" (Dyson, 1987, p. 398). It is in the constructing of these imaginative worlds that children play with possibilities, either in their worlds of symbolic play or in their experiences with the worlds of literature.

Playing with literature involves at least two aspects. The first is a passionate adventure with the language of story. If nothing else, literature is language, and it is with these literary forms of language that children play. They take delight in words, phrases, and even entire genres. I've read *Jump, Frog, Jump* by Robert Kalan to scores of children and I've yet to have a reading where the audience didn't join in repeating the chorus. Poetry is also literary language which invites passionate adventures. I have my undergraduate children's literature students read Eloise Greenfield's *Honey I Love*. Their skepticism and tension over reading poetry is obvious. But when they hear Greenfield's poetry read with the jazz-like rhythms of the language, the tension on their faces

evaporates and smiles begin to form. Toes begin to tap and some of them will even begin to sway. Finally, someone will say, "I really like this, and I think kids will like this, too." And they are right. Because perhaps for the first time since they were young children, they've delighted in the sounds and rhythms of language. They've used poetic language for playing just as they used to do as children with playground rhymes and chants.

Illustrations are also part of the language of literature, and children also play with them. Certain books present themselves as puzzles such as Martin Handford's *Where's Waldo?* And any book by Mitsumasa Anno presents all manner of visual intrigue. Books may invite the child to play a kind of "I Spy." Readers playing "I Spy" with the illustrations in Maurice Sendak's *Where the Wild Things Are* may notice Max's drawing of a monster or the similarities between the tent he had made at home and the one he sits in in the land of the Wild Things. Many readers have been playing with Ed Young's illustrations in *Lon Po Po*, noticing the head of a wolf outlined in the landscape of several of the pages. Anthony Browne's books are almost always rewarding to the "I Spy" player. Children hunt for the jokes hidden in his *Gorilla* and the hints of witchiness in his *Hansel and Gretel*.

Literary language comes in a variety of forms, and our modern authors and illustrators continue to challenge our conventions. Books like *Stringbean's Trip to the Shining Sea* by Jennifer and Vera Williams, David Macaulay's *Black and White* and Mitsumasa Anno's *Anno's Aesop* seem to be about the act of reading as much as they are books to be read. When Chris Van Allsburg's *The Z was Zapped* first appeared, I confess I did not like it. It violated some of the basic conventions of a good ABC book. Instead of using objects, Van Allsburg used actions: no zebras, "zapping" instead. Then he didn't put the text on the page opposite the illustration. You saw the illustration first and then you had to turn the page to read the appropriate text. This seemed like a prescription for confusion. It took two second-graders to show me how narrow-minded I was. To these two children this was an ABC book which could be read in different ways. First, they went through the book looking only at the illustration, naming the actions, and talking about what they saw. When they came to the end of the book, they decided to read it again, this time in a different way. On the second reading they raced past the illustrations to turn the page and read the words. For thirty minutes they went back and forth between these styles of reading. They were obviously playing with the form of that book, seeing in it more possibilities than I previously had.

Playing with literary forms is how children come to learn them (Meek, 1988). A couple of years ago I went to my shelf to get my copy of the Ahlbergs' *Jolly Postman.* I was not too pleased to find that my then three-year-old daughter had stuffed scribbled pieces of paper in the envelope pockets. When I asked her about this, she told me she had written letters and was mailing them. She was forming some pretty good ideas about what letters were. Moreover, she was also getting a grasp on how that particular book worked, and that is clearly a valuable reading lesson.

Fred Burton's work (1989) in exploring his students' writing in relationship to the children's literature they were reading and Amy McClure's work (1985) on children's responses to poetry provide further examples of children playing with literary language. Both researchers described how children were able to compose their own stories, informational pieces, and poetry in literary forms similar to those of the literature they had read and heard. This may be a more sophisticated kind of literary play. Through their readings of a variety of forms of literature and through their writings in those forms, these children were having passionate adventures with the language of literature.

The second aspect of reading as a form of play is that literature offers a secondary world for children to play in not unlike the imaginary worlds children create in their symbolic play. Often children combine the two. Teachers of younger children have noticed their students playing their stories on the playground. Playground equipment become bridges and children become billy goats and trolls. Scores of primary teachers have had children make monster masks and puppets and then stage their own rumpuses based upon their reading of *Where the Wild Things Are.* This playing of one's stories is not confined to the very young either. When I taught fifth grade in a small Iowa town, I read Jean George's *My Side of the Mountain* to my students. After I finished the book, two boys spent the next several recesses building caves in the mounds of snow on the edge of the playground. They were trying to build a house of snow, they said, similar to the one Sam Gribley had built in the hollow of a tree.

Playing with a story involves entering the story world. I read the story of the "Three Little Pigs" once to a kindergarten class. The version I read was based on the original Joseph Jacobs version, where the wolf comes down the chimney, lands in the pot of boiling water, and is cooked and eaten by the third pig. When I finished, there was that silent pause that occurs so often when a group of listeners has been engaged in a story. Then one of the children said, "You know, I've never had wolf. I hear it's pretty good." That child was playing with the story. She had entered into that brick house of the third pig. I wouldn't be the least surprised if she knows what boiled wolf smells like. This child took what she had heard and connected it with what she already knew. She was assimilating that story, making the strange (eating wolf) familiar. I would argue that that is a more reader-like behavior than anything found on a worksheet or in a study packet which could have accompanied that story.

When readers enter the imaginative world of their stories, they play with the possibilities the story has to offer. These plays can be full of frivolity. Children take delight in the antics of the Stupid family, the trickery of Flossie as she outsmarts the fox, and the incredible pronouncements of the fools of Chelm. But literary play can also be profound and serious. Literature is about the whole range of human ideas and emotions, not only laughter, satisfaction, and delight, but also injustice, evil, loneliness, and death (Beck, 1989).

The classroom I studied was comprised of second- and third-graders. One day their teacher read to them *Ira Sleeps Over* by Bernard Waber. In this story Ira has been invited by his friend Reggie to spend the night. Ira has never slept over at a friend's house and is quite excited. He also has a problem. He always sleeps with his teddy bear and he is afraid that Reggie will laugh at him if he brings it. Ira's parents encourage Ira to take his bear, but Ira's sister points out repeatedly that Reggie will probably laugh at him if he does.

As the teacher read *Ira Sleeps Over* the children interrupted several times to comment on what was happening. It is these comments which point to the delight and the seriousness these children were experiencing in their play with this story:

Teacher: (reading) "Suppose I just hate sleeping without my teddy bear. Should I take him?"

Cindy: Sneak him along.

Teacher: What do you think? Should he take him?

Cindy: Yeah.

Teacher: What do you think he should do? Mike?

Mike: If she wants to she can.

Teacher: I think Ira is a he. You think he can if he wants to. Anybody else? What would you do?

Pete: Take it.

Teacher: Take it. OK. Why do you think he's worried about not taking it? Carolyn?

(Carolyn shakes her head.)

Teacher: I mean, why do you think he shouldn't take it? Sally?

Sally: His friend might think he's a baby.

The teacher resumed reading the story and then this discussion occurred:

Teacher: (reading) "'By the way,' I [Ira] said again, 'What do you think of teddy bears?'"

Brandon: (says something the teacher cannot hear)

Teacher: What Brandon?

Brandon: Teddy bear fight.

Mike: Yeah, instead of a pillow fight you could have a teddy bear fight.

Teacher: (reading) "Suddenly Reggie was in a big hurry to go someplace. 'See you tonight,' he said. 'See you,' I said. I decided to take my teddy bear."

Timmy: He'd better.

Teacher: Why do you think he'd better, Timmy?

Timmy: The house is going to be dark.

Teacher: Huh?

Timmy: Our house don't get dark.

Teacher: Why do you think Ira should take his teddy bear?

Timmy: Because he was going to a dark, dark, dark house.

Teacher: So why would the teddy bear help?

Timmy: He wouldn't be scared.

Teacher: Jason?

Jason: They were going to tell ghost stories and he'd get scared.

Teacher: So why should he take the teddy bear?

Jason: Because it'd take care of him.

Here is a sense of the kinds of plays readers make. These children have entered into the world of Ira, a world which exists only as language. They are delighted by this world, but they are also involved with some serious issues. Sleeping over at a friend's house, avoiding embarrassment, dealing with bratty siblings, and the potential pain of being separated from the comfort and safety of one's teddy bear are profound matters to children. For children this is serious play. In their play with this story these children try on Ira's problems and consider the possible implications of his dilemma.

Several years ago a group of fifth-graders and I read *Tuck Everlasting* by Natalie Babbitt. It was the first experience each of us had had with this novel, and none of us anticipated the degree to which we would be moved by it. When we gathered to discuss it, we found we could not talk about the book. We were unable to find the right words to describe how we felt about Winnie Foster choosing death over immortality. So instead of discussing, for forty minutes we read our favorite passages to each other. The next day I found on my desk a piece of writing from Jenny, one of the members of the discussion group. She had written:

> *Life*
>
> Life is a wheel that forever turns. Everyone is part of it. The birds, the trees, the water, and people. But always different. Never the same. Always growing in mind and in soul. Moving, growing, changing, and finally resting. Always replaced by new, different ones. The wisdom of people keeps growing, but people themselves will always be part of nature. For we could not have life without death. Light without dark. Sound without silence. Or movement without stillness. The wheel of life is forever turning.

It would be difficult to call this frivolous or even delightful, but it was nonetheless play. Jenny was pondering possibilities of why death is essential to life. She was trying them out in that "third area," the area which resides between her own inner "story," the one she tells about herself, and the outer world of actions. This third area is a world of imagination less threatening than the other two, less risky, where big ideas such as one's mortality can be considered (Winnicott, 1971).

In too many classrooms children are not playing enough with their reading. When does reading cease being play? It ceases being play when the reading loses value and importance to the child. It ceases being play when adults impose a different structure on the forms of the play, forms which meet adult ends rather than children's purposes. Using books as moral lessons or as counseling aids are examples of adults ends. Phonics, skills, cloze procedures, formulaic guided reading such as the Directed Reading–Thinking Activity, and even some kinds of projects can override children's purposes in reading. Too often when basal readers are replaced by literature books, basal perspectives are not replaced by literary ones.

What does holding a view of reading as play mean for classroom teachers? It means that literary behavior is what tries on meanings and experiments with forms. It is realizing that each player is different and that each play is potentially unique. In play the end is indeterminate; it may come out all sorts of ways, and there are always more possibilities to the play. So also with reading. Meanings are never exhausted. Readers can return again and again to their books, and more possibilities can be discovered. It is this passionate adventure with language, this trying on of possibilities, that is of value to children. It is through these literary ends that I suspect children become truly literate.

IN LITERARY CLASSROOMS READERS SHARE THEIR READINGS

When readers are exploring the possibilities of meaning and playing with literary forms, they are making a response. Children are active learners—active responders. They need to work with their literature (Hickman & Cullinan, 1989). They need to discuss their books. They need to represent their responses through pictures, artifacts, and drama. And they need to consider and reconsider their readings by sharing them in some way with others. The heart of reading lies in sharing one's readings with others (Chambers, 1985).

When members of a classroom are actively working with their books, they are sharing their readings with others. There develops then a reading culture, a body of shared knowledge of responses to literature. Susan Hepler (1982) has shown us how social reading literature is—how classrooms really are communities of readers. Literary classrooms recognize that children need to respond to their books by nurturing a community of readers.

Aidan Chambers (1985) writes that literature is its own story and that that story is discovered in the story of our own and other persons' readings of it. We learn what some of the possible readings are by hearing and seeing other readers' demonstrations of their readings.

Sociolinguists such as Shirley Brice Heath (1983) have argued that learning to read involves learning ways of taking from the text and that we learn these ways of taking from others. We learn to read, says Frank Smith (1988), from the demonstrations of reading of the important people around us. Important people can be adults, but they can also be other children. The story of Annie and Alan, two second-graders in the classroom I studied show this.

During a quiet reading time, Annie read to Alan stories from Schwartz's *In a Dark, Dark Room*. She read first the story "The Night It Rained." "The Night It Rained" is a story of a man driving a car at night who picks up a hitchhiker. He appears cold, so the driver lends him his sweater. After dropping the hitchhiker off at his home, the driver realizes the hitchhiker still has his sweater. He returns to the hitchhiker's home only to learn that his passenger has been dead for a year. Driving away, he passes a cemetery, where he finds his sweater draped across the tombstone of the hitchhiker.

Annie stopped reading in the middle of the story to explain to Alan that the hitchhiker is really dead. Alan wanted to know what was going to happen. Annie replied that she was not telling and repeated that the hitchhiker is actually dead. When Annie finished reading that story, she read "The Green Ribbon." "The Green Ribbon" is a story of a man who falls in love and marries a woman who always wears a green ribbon around her neck. She never removes the ribbon and refuses to tell her husband why she always wears it. The years go by, and the now elderly woman lying on her death bed tells her husband he may remove the ribbon. He does so and the woman's head falls off.

Ricky joined Annie and Alan. As she read, Annie covered the last illustration of the story with her hand. When she finished the story, she uncovered the picture, which showed a woman's head, which had fallen off. Ricky asked, "I wonder why it fell off?" Annie replied, "Don't you know part one?" Annie explained to Alan and Ricky that there is a story which comes before this one which tells how the woman's head became separated from her body.

The following day Alan read "The Green Ribbon" to himself. As he read he covered up the final picture, just as Annie had done the day before. When he finished the last sentence of the story, he showed the picture to Timmy and Karl.

Four days later Alan and his friend Brandon talked to their teacher about doing a project with *In a Dark, Dark Room*. The boys discussed "The Green Ribbon" and informed the teacher that there is a story which occurs before it, one which explains how the woman had her head cut off.

The children were sharing how they read the stories in *In a Dark, Dark Room* and what the stories meant to them. First, Annie demonstrated a reading to Alan and Ricky. She explained to Ricky and Alan that the hitchhiker is really dead, calling their attention to that aspect of the story. She covered up the last picture of "The Green Ribbon," adding to the suspense. Then she told them that there is another story about the woman which is not part of that book. When Alan read "The Green Ribbon," he covered up the last illustration in the story just as Annie had done when she first read the story to him. Alan and Brandon insisted to their teacher that there was a story which occurred before "The Green Ribbon." Alan shared Annie's thought with Brandon that there was an earlier story which told how the woman had her head cut off, and together the boys shared that reading with their teacher.

Sharing in the community of readers can be informal, such as the talk between Annie, Alan, and Ricky. Or sharing can be more formal, as in teachers reading aloud to children, book discussion groups, or working on some kind of project. The essence of the community of readers is the sharing of responses.

LITERARY CLASSROOMS ACCEPT WHAT IS SHARED AS "HONORABLY REPORTABLE"

In literary classrooms everything shared is "honorably reportable" (Chambers, 1985). By "honorably reportable" I mean that children's responses are accepted as honest and meaningful. Everything is "honorably reportable" because children do not necessarily read stories the way adults do (Hickman, 1984). Once I read Harry Allard and James Marshall's *Miss Nelson Is Back* to a five-year-old. For adults and many children this is a story of a sweet young teacher who takes a leave to have her tonsils removed. In her absence the class behaves terribly and Miss Nelson is forced to return early, disguised as Miss Viola Swamp, the meanest substitute teacher ever. After the class is "whipped back into shape" by their "substitute," Miss Nelson returns as herself, leaving the class to wonder whatever happened to Viola Swamp. The five-year-old had an astonishing answer for this. Viola Swamp was in another part of the school putting kids into cages. I told the child that I thought not even Viola Swamp would do such a terrible thing. The child disagreed and her logic was unassailable. The kids in the book had called Viola Swamp a "real witch," and this five-year-old knew from "Hansel and Gretel" that "real witches" put kids into cages. This was a very interesting and a rather profound reading of that book, one that was certainly playful. The question for adults is: Is this child entitled to her response or is it our duty to set her straight?

There is in every sharing of a story a "class text," an official response. We can all remember English classes where we had to figure what sense of the story, poem, or play the teacher had made and then to reproduce it on a test. There was, in a sense, one correct reading, and that was the teacher's. The teacher was the sole contributor to the class text. Class texts are shaped by social matters such as: Who has shared their readings of the story? What kinds of questions have been asked? For what purposes have the children been reading? Whose readings count, and whose do not? Can children make contributions to this text, or can only the teacher or the published teacher's guide make the class text? Is it appropriate for an adult to require children to come to an adult understanding of books? The "Miss Nelson" story illustrates these matters. Should the five-year-old be left to her reading, or should the adult show her that she is wrong and that there is a better reading of that story? Can children's readings and interpretations count in the forming of the "class text"? Are children's personal plays with books acceptable as honest plays? Enjoyment and play begin with the reader. Readings will be shared only if readers feel comfortable and their readings are accepted.

Brad, a second-grader, helped me understand the importance of feeling comfortable and accepted as a reader. He was probably one of the poorer readers in his class. He rarely chose to read books by himself. He never read to other children. He did not participate in book discussion groups. He wrote very little, and what he did write usually came as a result of his teacher's being very firm with him. He never shared his writing with others. He did little artwork about the books he did read. I should point out that none of this was any fault of his teacher. She tried in the most loving and caring ways possible to get him to read and write more.

When I interviewed Brad, he told me that when he was in first grade he had shared some of his writing and other children had laughed at him. He also said he never used paints in school because in first grade he had once made a mess of paints and again children had laughed at him. What I think Brad was telling me was that he was afraid to share his work because he was afraid it would not be accepted by others in the classroom.

What Brad did like to do was to have Patrick read to him. When Patrick read, Brad would make comments about the story and about the illustrations. He would ask Patrick to read the same stories over and over again.

Brad avoided any public display of his reading that was risky, that would entail the possibility that someone might laugh at him. But Patrick was his friend, and Brad felt comfortable enough around Patrick to share his thoughts about stories.

In literary classrooms children's responses are accepted as honest. Children will not share their honest responses if their responses are not accepted.

LITERARY TEACHERS PUSH FOR RIGOR

But what then is the teacher's role in this? Are teachers just to leave children alone, trusting in the power of literature alone to help them become readers? While accepting children's responses as honorable, literary teachers also push for rigor in their children's readings. They ask their children to consider other possibilities and to sharpen, clarify, or justify their thinking.

The following is an excerpt of a book discussion of Lynn Ward's *The Biggest Bear*. The children were third-graders:

Patrick: He [the bear] ate mash for the chickens, and after the neighbors had left, Johnny's father explained to Johnny that the bear would have to go back to the woods.

Donny: Yeah, then he kept on taking him back to the woods and the next day it came back. He even took it across the lake and it came back.

Teacher: And the bear came back?

Donny: Yep. They took him as far as they could, and after that he came back again and they decided to put him in the zoo.

Patrick: No, he was taking him out to shoot him and then he stole maple sugar.

Teacher: What in the book makes you think that they were taking him out to shoot him?

Patrick: Because it says in the book.

Mike: No.

Patrick: Yeah, it does.

Mike: It just says he never decided (inaudible) and Johnny said he would do it.

Teacher: What does that mean?

Mike: (pointing at the picture) It means that he would do it 'cause he has his gun.

The students shared their readings of *The Biggest Bear* with each other throughout this discussion. Donny seemed not to have noticed that Johnny intended to shoot his bear. Patrick said that the book said Johnny was going to shoot the bear, while Mike disagreed, arguing that all the book showed was a picture of Johnny with his gun. The teacher's role in this discussion was to accept the answers the children gave and then push for further rigor by asking them to justify their statements with something they had read in the book or to explain themselves further. Her role appears to be a subtle one, yet she was helping the children move from their first readings to reconsidering what the text might mean and to clarify their own thinking.

LITERARY CLASSROOMS PROVIDE CHILDREN WITH OPPORTUNITIES TO READ AND RESPOND

For teachers and children to be literary they must have the opportunity to read and respond to literature. There must be time for children to read and to respond. In setting up schedules principals and teachers need to plan times during the day in which children can read books, hear books being read, talk about books, and work on projects related to their reading.

The rules of the classroom need to accommodate readers. Readers need to be able to read to and talk with other readers. Keeping children at their desks potentially isolates them from the other readers in the classroom. Readers' sharing their readings with other readers is critical to the development of a literary classroom.

Children need access to books. Their classrooms need to be filled with books. They need school libraries which are well stocked and well staffed.

The teachers I have observed schedule frequent daily encounters with literature. They do not keep children confined to desks but allow them to move about the room, thus facilitating children's sharing what they know about books with each other. These teachers maintain permanent classroom collections of books and temporary collections of books checked out from area public libraries. Their schools are committed to building and maintaining well-stocked school libraries.

CHILDREN IN LITERARY CLASSROOMS HAVE PERSONAL CHOICES

In literary classrooms children can exercise personal choice in their reading. In this age of cultural literacy, and I note that there is now a cultural literacy dictionary for children, and of states and school districts prescribing reading lists of children's books, it needs to be said again that there is no list of books which all children should read.

Regardless of how well meaning such lists are, they are in the end self-defeating. I've talked to children in a school where the curriculum supervisor and teachers chose what children would read and discuss. Children were divided into groups by the teacher, and each group was given a different book to read. Some children told me they really wished they could read the book the other group was assigned, but it was not available to them. It seems misguided for any publisher, curriculum supervisor, or teacher to suggest exactly what children should be reading in their classrooms. One of the reasons for the casting off of the basal reader is that it returns curriculum decisions properly to the classroom teacher. Another, equally important reason is that it returns properly to the reader the choice of what the reader will read. Being rigidly prescriptive in what children read defeats one of the advantages of using literature.

The master teachers I've observed give their children time each day to read books of their own choosing, including the choice to reread favorite books again and again. If they are conducting book discussion groups, they offer several books as possibilities and let the children choose which one they want to read and discuss. If the children are doing projects on some book, the children may make decisions about what that project will be and what form it will take. Master teachers let children make some choices about with whom the children can read and work. These are all choices we readily allow adults to make. Children deserve the same.

Adults do not have to be apologists for pulp fiction, but if we cannot show some degree of respect for the reading choices children make, how can we be sure children will respect the choices we make for them? While many of us may not think of series books and books based upon cartoon characters as being literary, respect for readers and their choices and responses is a literary attitude.

That does not mean that teachers must resign themselves only to the popular, mass-market books. The master teachers I have observed are not passive. They fill their classrooms with good books, so that children may select from a stock of books. They share books with their children which they enjoy and feel are good examples of the best which children's literature can offer. If children are having difficulty making choices, they know how to limit the possibilities to a more manageable set. Only in extreme circumstances do these teachers limit children's choices to one.

LITERARY CLASSROOMS HAVE VARIETY

It seems a bit trite, but it is worth restating that children are different from each other. Not every child enjoys the same play. Not every child wishes to play the same play day after day, even if it is a favorite. In literary classrooms there is variety. In literary classrooms children have many different kinds of opportunities to read and respond to literature. Janet Hickman (1984), Barbara Kiefer (1983), and Susan Hepler (1982) have argued that the rich responses they observed children making in the classrooms they studied were products of a rich environment. The classroom I studied was also rich in the varieties of opportunities the children had to read and respond to literature. Children had daily opportunities to read books of their own choosing and to share their reading with other children. Their teacher read aloud to them every day, sometimes twice a day. Most read-alouds were followed with a class discussion of the book. The children kept reading logs, recording what books they read and writing a few sentences each week about one of their favorite books. Their teacher read their responses and often wrote back to them. There were book discussion groups where small groups of children met with their teacher to talk about a book they had read in common. The children had opportunities through their artwork, through their writing, and through drama to respond to the books they had been reading.

Each of these opportunities was different from the other in the manner in which the children read and responded to literature. Each was an opportunity to do something a little different with literature. What seemed significant to me was that certain children enjoyed some events more than others and all of them had some kind of frequent opportunity to enjoy books in a manner in which they were comfortable. Recall Brad. Imagine what his experiences with books would have been like had he had no opportunity to read with Patrick during school. Even in the midst of a good literature-based classroom, without this opportunity he would have found reading total drudgery.

It is from our perspectives and purposes in reading that we make meaning from the books we read. In literary classrooms literature is looked at from a variety of perspectives. In the classroom I studied I observed the children and the teacher looking at literature from these perspectives: The children and their teacher looked at their books aesthetically, expressing their feelings such as delight, disgust, and fear about the work of literature. They considered the work from inside the story world, talking about plot, characters, and theme. They looked at literature morally, commenting upon the appropriateness of characters' actions and what lessons they could learn from the books. They connected what they read to their own personal experiences. They looked at what they read as models for their own writing. Their books held a number of interpretive possibilities, and the teacher and the children made these possibilities known through sharing their readings of books through the variety of opportunities the classroom offered.

In literary classrooms a variety of literature is available and shared. Picture books, folk tales, chapter books, poetry, information books, and plays belong in every classroom, and children in literary classrooms have opportunities to read and respond to each genre.

LITERATURE IS WHAT READERS DO

Literature is the total of its public demonstrations. Each reader is an embodiment of what a reader can be. What children see and hear other readers (including teachers) doing, saying, and reading is what reading literature becomes. How is literature read in classrooms? What can and do children and teachers say about it? What material is available for children to read? The answers a classroom provides to these questions are that classroom's working definition of literature.

This list of what is authentic literary behavior is not exactly a list which tells teachers what to do on Monday. But then teachers have never lacked for that kind of advice. Just look at the advertisements in any issue of *The Reading Teacher* or browse the Heinemann catalog. And those materials are a small fraction of what is available. I agree with Frank Smith (1985) that what teachers really need is understanding. It is from a base of understanding literature, children, classrooms, and reading that teachers can make informed professional decisions about which advice to accept and try out in their classrooms and which to reject.

This list is offered in the spirit of searching to understand what happens in successful literature-based classrooms. These themes I've discussed are not easily packaged in guidebooks or book discussion packets. More likely these are developed by teachers over extended periods of reflection and study of their own teaching and of what children are doing in their classrooms. The master teachers I have observed tell me that they continue to learn about their own teaching with literature from their students, their colleagues, their student teachers, and the authors and illustrators of the children's books they use.

Other lists of what is literary may be different from mine. If they are, then please share them with others. Literature-based teaching is too good an idea to let become another fad which will fade when too many well-intentioned people who don't understand it, try it, and fail. The only way we can keep literature-based teaching healthy and vibrant is to understand better what it is and what it is not. This is not as easy as it seems. But if master classroom teachers will share what they know and if researchers will go into their classrooms for extended observations, perhaps we can understand better what is potentially so powerful: teaching children with beautifully written and illustrated books.

REFERENCES

Altwerger, B., Edelsky, C., and Flores, B. M., "Whole language: What's new?" *The Reading Teacher*, 1987, 41, 144–154.

Anderson, R. C., Hiebert, E. H., Scott, J. A., and Wilkinson, I. A. G., *Becoming a Nation of Readers: The Report of the Commission on Reading*. Washington, DC: The National Institute of Education, 1985.

Beck, F., "What should our children read?" *The Lion and the Unicorn*, 1989, 13, 151–157.

Bruner, J., *Actual Minds, Possible Worlds*. Cambridge: Harvard University Press, 1986.

Burton, F. R., *The Reading-Writing Connection: A One-Year Teacher-as-Researcher Study of Third-Fourth Grade Writers and Their Literary Experiences*. Unpublished doctoral dissertation, Ohio State University, Columbus, 1985.

Burton, F. R., "Writing what they read: Reflections on literature and child writers," in *Stories to Grow On: Demonstrations of Language Learning in K–8 Classrooms*, J. M. Jensen, ed., pp. 97–116. Portsmouth, NH: Heinemann, 1989.

Chambers, A., *Booktalk: Occasional Writing on Literature and Children*. New York: Harper & Row, 1985.

Dyson, A. H., "The value of 'time off task': Young children's spontaneous talk and deliberate text," *Harvard Educational Review,* 1987, 42, 217–231.

Hade, D. D., *Stances and Events as Foundations of Children's Responses to Literature: An Ethnographic Study of a Second and Third Grade Literature-Based Reading Classroom.* Unpublished doctoral dissertation, Ohio State University, Columbus, 1989.

Heath, S. B., *Ways with Words: Language, Life and Work in Classrooms and Communities.* London: Cambridge University Press, 1983.

Hepler, S. I., *Patterns of Response to Literature: A One-Year Study of a Fifth and Sixth Grade Classroom.* Unpublished doctoral dissertation, Ohio State University, Columbus, 1982.

Hickman, J. G., *Response to Literature in a School Environment: Grades K–5.* Unpublished doctoral dissertation, Ohio State University, Columbus, 1979.

Hickman, J., "Research currents: Researching children's response to literature," *Language Arts,* 1984, 61, 278–284.

Hickman, J., and Cullinan, B. E., "A point of view on literature and learning," in *Children's Literature in the Classroom: Weaving Charlotte's Web.* J. Hickman and B. Cullinan, eds., pp. 3–12. Needham Heights, MA: Christopher-Gordon, Inc., 1989.

Kiefer, B., "The responses of children in a combination first/second grade classroom to picture books in a variety of artistic styles," *Journal of Research and Development in Education,* 1983, 16, 14–20.

Langer, S., *Feeling and Form: A Theory of Art.* New York: Scribners, 1953.

McClure, A., *Children's Responses to Poetry in a Supportive Literary Context.* Unpublished doctoral dissertation, Ohio State University, Columbus, 1985.

Meek, M., "Prolegomena for a study of children's literature," in *Approaches to Research in Children's Literature,* M. Benton, ed., pp. 29–39. Southampton, England: University of Southampton, 1980.

Meek, M., *How Texts Teach What Readers Learn.* Lockwood, Great Britain: Thimble Press, 1988.

Pearson, P. D., "Commentary: Reading the whole-language movement," *The Elementary School Journal,* 1989, 90, 231–241.

Platt, N. G., "What teachers and children do in a language rich classroom," in *Teachers and Research: Language Learning in the Classroom,* G. S. Pinnell and M. L. Matlin, eds., pp. 8–22. Newark, DE: International Reading Association, 1989.

Smith, F., "A metaphor for literacy: Creating worlds or shunting information?" in *Literacy, Language, and Learning,* D. R. Olson, N. Torrance, and A. Hildyard, eds., pp. 195–212. Cambridge: Cambridge University Press, 1985.

Smith, F., *Reading without Nonsense,* 2nd ed. New York: Teacher's College Press, 1985.

Smith, F., *Joining the Literacy Club: Further Essays into Education.* Portsmouth, NH: Heinemann, 1988.

Winnicott, D. W., *Playing and Reality.* London: Tavistock Press, 1971.

CHILDREN'S BOOKS CITED

Ahlberg, Janet, and Ahlberg, Allan, *The Jolly Postman.* Boston: Little, Brown, 1986.

Allard, Harry, and Marshall, James, *Miss Nelson Is Back.* Boston: Houghton Mifflin, 1982.

Allard, Harry, and Marshall, James, *The Stupids Have a Ball.* Boston: Houghton Mifflin, 1978.

Anno, Mitsumasa, *Anno's Aesop.* New York: Orchard, 1989.

Babbitt, Natalie, *Tuck Everlasting.* New York: Farrar, Straus, & Giroux, 1975.

Blegrad, Erik, *The Three Little Pigs.* New York: Atheneum, 1980.

Browne, Anthony, *Hansel and Gretel.* New York: Knopf, 1981.

Browne, Anthony, *Gorilla.* New York: Knopf, 1983.

George, Jean, *My Side of the Mountain.* New York: Dutton, 1959.

Greenfield, Eloise, *Honey I Love.* New York: Thomas Y. Crowell, 1978.

Handford, Martin, *Where's Waldo?* Boston: Little, Brown, 1987.

Kalan, Robert, *Jump Frog Jump.* New York: Greenwillow, 1981.

Macaulay, David, *Black and White.* Boston: Houghton, Mifflin, 1990.

McKissack, Patricia C., *Flossie and the Fox.* New York: Dial, 1986.

Schwartz, Alvin, *In a Dark, Dark Room.* New York: Harper & Row, 1984.

Sendak, Maurice, *Where the Wild Things Are.* New York: Harper & Row, 1963.

Singer, Isaac Bashevis, *Stories for Children.* New York: Farrar, Straus, & Giroux, 1984.

Waber, Bernard, *Ira Sleeps Over.* Boston: Houghton Mifflin, 1972.

Ward, Lynn, *The Biggest Bear.* Boston: Houghton Mifflin, 1952.

Williams, Jennifer, and Williams, Vera, *Stringbean's Trip to the Shining Sea.* New York: Greenwillow, 1988.

Young, Ed, *Lon Po Po.* New York: Philonel, 1989.

Daniel D. Hade is a faculty member at Pennsylvania State University.

Literature-Based Theme Units

Maribeth Henney

With the current emphasis on whole language, the use of children's literature as the basis for reading instruction is widespread. Goodman (1986) recommended that teachers develop literature-based theme units to provide stimulating learning opportunities for children. But how does a teacher use literature other than simply turning the children loose to read whatever they choose? Is this really instruction or simply recreational reading?

WHAT IS A LITERATURE-BASED THEME UNIT?

A unit is not a peripheral of the curriculum but, rather, can be the core of what children do in school. It is an indepth study, incorporating many subject areas over a long period of time. Since children become frustrated if they begin to get involved in a topic and then have to quit, time must be allowed for the unit to unfold and develop. It is impossible to predict exactly how long a unit will run, but 6 to 8 weeks is common, depending upon the unit focus. Children become immersed in the theme, explore its many facets, experience a wide variety of literature, and become experts in some aspect of the unit in which they are personally interested (Gamberg, Kwak, Hutchings, & Altheim, 1988).

The theme selected for study must be of interest to the children and be broad enough to be divided into many smaller subtopics. The relationship of the subtopics to the overall topic should remain clear, however. Flexibility needs to be built in so that children may study any aspect of the topic in which they are interested (Gamberg et. al., 1988). The topic should lend itself to comparing and contrasting ideas. Extensive investigation of concrete situations, materials, and resources should be possible. This includes use of the community as well as resources normally found inside the school. Parental involvement is welcomed (Gamberg et al., 1988).

Unit study breaks down barriers between subjects, a false separation which occurs in many classrooms. It is truly a cross-disciplinary program that allows for problem solving and discovery as children pursue answers to their own questions about a topic. It involves children in authentic, relevant activities. Edelsky, Altwerger, and Flores (1991) distinguished theme units from theme cycles, the latter being more child-centered and inquiry based. In a theme cycle, a chain of activities grows out of questions raised by the students, all tied to some initiating question or focus which arose from students' experiences. Skills are used to serve the content, to do real things. The content is not contrived in order to teach skills, as may be done in a teacher-planned collection of activities all about one topic in order to impose interest on skills work. Meaningful theme cycles involve "honest" pure activities, learned through use as persons in specialized fields would do. Students pursue questions they are interested in, set problems, find resources, and organize their own study. They work with raw data, figure out how to make sense of it, generate hypotheses and test them, decide how to rule out competing interpretations, and draw conclusions. Such units emerge as teachers learn what is really on children's minds and provide opportunities for them to explore personally meaningful areas of life.

The whole language approach emphasizes process more than product. In other words,

From "Literature-Based Theme Units" by M. Henney, 1992, *Kansas Journal of Reading, 8,* pp. 36–41. Reprinted by permission of Dr. Maribeth Henney, Professor, Curriculum and Instruction Department, Iowa State University, Ames, Iowa.

the most valuable time for a teacher to help a child is while he or she is working at something, not after it is completed. Evaluating final products may show what the children did not know, but it does nothing to help them learn and develop. In a process approach, instruction is pertinent to the skills children need in order to do what they want to do. Help with problems is given immediately so that they can get on with the task of learning. Skills are learned because they are necessary tools for achieving a purpose. A caution, however! We should be careful not to go too far in using literature for teaching skills. If we do, children may think that books are to be used only for the teacher's purposes (Hickman & Cullinan, 1989).

Theme units facilitate process learning, but in order for process to occur, there must also be content. We study about something; we don't just study. In theme units, neither content nor process is ignored. Meaning is central. All learning is undertaken for purposes related to the content, and children decide to study the content because it is important to them.

TYPES OF LITERATURE-BASED UNITS

Literature based units may be organized in a variety of ways. The following are types of units that a teacher may choose to use. A balance of types of units should be used throughout the year.

Topic Units

A specific topic of interest to the class may be chosen, based upon a previous survey of the children's interests. For example, topics such as the circus, flight, health, music, pets, the family, weather, sports, or holidays may be the focus of study. A topic unit may also be used to study a certain country or a specific period in history. Topic units work well not only for whole class study, but also for interest grouping in which children sign up for topics they wish to investigate. Several such interest groups may be running concurrently. Children of all reading abilities may be in each group, since the focus is on the topic, not ability. There are ways in which each child can contribute to the unit study, regardless of ability.

Genre Units

A unit may center on a specific genre of literature (form of writing), such as tall tales, Greek myths, folktales, legends, fables, biography, mysteries, poetry, or plays. Types of writing found in newspapers, such as editorials, news stories, classified ads, and feature stories may also be loosely labeled genre. Distinguishing between narrative and expository writing is also appropriate. Comparing different versions of the same story is an enjoyable activity for this type of unit.

Author Units

Favorite authors of children's literature may be studied. Good readers select books according to their authors (Lamme, 1989), and all children may learn to do so. Children often enjoy learning about authors, where they come from, how they began writing, and on what they based their writing. They are then much more aware of the authors of books and begin to choose books by author rather than topic. This is one step in helping children develop the concept of "author." After studying other authors and then sharing their own writing processes, children realize that they are authors, too.

Illustrators can also be studied in a like manner, for many books have such lovely illustrations. Children can be helped to recognize the importance of the illustrations to the book and begin to select books on that basis as well.

Literary Devices Units

Units in which literary devices are studied are most appropriate for intermediate grade, or older, students. After reading and discussing many books which employ devices such as foreshadowing, flashback, irony, parody, character trait development, point of view, development of themes, or common motif patterns, students will understand the use of such devices and be able to employ them in their own writing. The elements of story grammar may also be studied to determine how narrative writing follows a pattern of development (introduction, setting, characters, conflict or problem, developmental events, obstacles, attempts to overcome the problem and reach a goal, climax, resolution, conclusion). Expository writing patterns (description, sequence, cause and effect, problem and solution, enumeration, comparison and contrast) can be studied in various sources and then students can attempt to use those patterns in their own writing. Developing language awareness is another possibility for a unit. How do authors use language in description, dialogue, and explanation?

Language Study Units

Units which enable children to explore language, play with words, and learn about a variety of types of words will interest children at any grade level. Where did our alphabet come from? How did writing come to be? Where did paper come from? How and why was printing done? How are books published? Where do our words come from? Why is spelling so inconsistent? What are eponyms, spoonerisms, malopropisms, homographs, homophones, and coined words? How do such words make writing interesting? What are alliteration, connotation, and figurative language? How do hink pinks, word mazes, crossword puzzles, tongue twisters, riddles, and pattern puzzles help us learn about words? How can we communicate without using words? What children's books about language are available? There are many possibilities for language study units.

One Book Units

Children, as a whole class or as a smaller literature group, can read a whole text, discuss it, and do related activities. All of the aspects of the units described above, such as expanding on the basic topic of the book, reading related sources, studying the author and illustrator, discussing the genre characteristics, and looking at literary devices and vocabulary used, can be incorporated. The theme that the author intended to communicate can be discussed. Then other books exemplifying that theme may be found by children and read. Other books on a related topic may also be used for extension of this basic source.

Basal Extension Units

If basals are used in the classroom, literature study can be used to extend reading and writing beyond the units of content in the texts. Library books related to the same topic, or other books by an author whose selection was in the basal, may be used. A selection from the basal may be compared to the original book, with the students noting differences in style of writing, vocabulary used, parts omitted, illustrations, and even story line. Children may read a whole book after reading a part of a book included in a basal. Time should be provided daily for some personal recreational reading during USSR (Uninterrupted Sustained Silent Reading) or DEAR (Drop Everything and Read). The importance of giving children an opportunity to lose themselves in reading literature can not be overemphasized. Through such experiences, they may be helped to discover the joy of reading and to develop habits of independent reading that will remain with them throughout their lives.

PLANNING THE UNIT

A variety of resources and materials can be incorporated into unit study. The teacher first needs to consider the content he or she wishes to convey and the type of unit to be taught and then plan appropriate activities to achieve the unit goals. As the teacher plans ideas for the unit, a literature web may reveal some possibilities. The unit focus is placed at the center of the web and spokes running out from the center are labeled with possible categories of subtopics for study, activities, related books, and other resources (Baskwill, 1988).

Books form the basis for study in a literature unit, so the teacher should gather as many books that focus on what is being taught as possible. A minimum of at least two books per child is recommended. The material collected may include not only books, but also magazines, brochures, catalogs, reference sets, posters, hands-on materials, films and filmstrips, slides, pictures, community resources, and people. Poetry, audiovisual materials, drama scripts, and vocabulary study activities are all appropriate and add variation to reading books. Everything is a possible source of learning. Include both narrative and expository literature and things written for adults as well as children. Students can often glean bits of information from a source even if they cannot read it thoroughly. Materials should be displayed attractively in order to motivate children to want to become involved in the unit (Pappas, Kiefer, & Levstik, 1990).

For a topic unit, find books about that topic. In teaching about a genre, many books demonstrating the use of that genre are required. For an author or illustrator unit, provide as many books as possible produced by that person, as well as autobiographical and biographical sources about the person. For the study of literary devices, it is essential that books be carefully selected to insure that they clearly and explicitly exemplify what is to be taught. If students cannot easily see a device being demonstrated, the book will be more confusing than helpful and should not be included. For studying about language and words, there are many interesting books written at a child's level of understanding.

COMPONENTS OF A UNIT

Each unit type described above will have certain activities which are most appropriate, but all units have some characteristics in common.

First, an inviting display should be designed, and *a motivating introduction to the unit* should be given. The teacher may discuss with the children what they already know about the theme of the unit. The children may present some questions that they have about the area of study and suggest some activities they would like to carry out to learn more about it. The teacher should explain that there are many possibilities for learning about the theme and may help the children build a web or a categorized list of ideas to show graphically what the group may want to study. The unit plans should remain flexible, allowing for changes and additions to be made as the unit progresses (Pappas et al., 1990).

Purposeful learning activities can be planned cooperatively by the teacher and the students. At the beginning of the unit, engage all the children in several activities in order to build common knowledge and experiences. One book may be read by the teacher to the class. Then students may select books from a list to read individually or in literature groups. Learning centers may be used for both assigned and independent study. All books and other resources are related to the central area of study. Children must have a clear understanding of activities and other expectations (Pappas et al., 1990).

Discussing and recording what is learned are important parts of the learning activities. Children must be guided to glean from their reading the important ideas on which the unit is focused. For instance, in studying a genre such as myths, it is essential that children understand the characteristics of that genre. How would one recognize a myth? How does that type of writing differ from some other genre? If the children are studying an author, they may discuss books written by that author. What are some recognizable patterns or devices used by the author which distinguishes his or her work from that of other authors? How do those patterns relate to what was learned about the author's background? Why do the children like to read books written by that author? For a unit about literary devices, discussion sessions will allow the students to verbalize their understanding of the devices being used, read aloud examples of their use in the books studied, tell how the author develops them within the context of the whole selection, note what significance they play to the overall understanding of the piece, and discover how the same literary device may be used somewhat differently by different authors.

Whatever the focus of the unit, children must usually be guided to study writing techniques, since they have been more accustomed to attending to content only. This type of study requires that they go beyond basic comprehension and look at what they have read from a writer's perspective. It may be difficult for some children to step beyond the story content and to study it from the author's perspective. Why were certain writing techniques used? How did the author build characterization? What genre characteristics does the piece of writing have? What is the effect of using description instead of dialogue to convey ideas? The teacher needs to model for students the thinking required for this type of literature study. Careful use of questioning will eventually lead students to analyze literature not only as readers but also as authors.

Related activities may be done as a whole class, in small groups, or individually. There should be many possibilities available, some designed by the teacher and others based on children's ideas. Children should be allowed to follow their own interests, branching off from something read. Language arts activities may be incorporated, including such things as sharing a book or one's own writing through puppetry, readers' theater, scripting a play, debates, expressing ideas through music or dance, giving speeches, and reading aloud. Learning centers present potential activities, materials to be used, additional resources to read, computers for recording ideas, tapes and tape recorders, writing materials, book binding materials, games, and art and craft ideas.

All children should be encouraged to include writing activities among their independent work. Depending on the focus of the unit, children should be expected to apply what they have learned to their own writing. For instance, during a topic unit, children may write about the topic, sharing what they have learned through the unit study or perhaps writing a poem or story related to that topic. For a genre unit, children may attempt to write a selection in the genre, using the characteristics identified earlier through reading and discussion. In an author unit, children may attempt to write as the author does, incorporating the characteristics of that person's writing in their own words. After studying various literary devices, students may attempt to write selections using such devices. For vocabulary study, children may write stories or poems using some of the new types of words they have learned. As such writing is done, further discussion may be necessary to ensure the child is conscious of the process being used. Peer response groups may be used to let children share what they have written and to get feedback from others. The goal here is not to produce a perfect piece of writing, but to experience what writers think, feel, and do as they write for a particular purpose.

If students wish to polish their writing to share it with the whole class or some other audience, they should be encouraged to do so. They may decide to do that through making a personal book, contributing to a bulletin board, taping an oral reading of their writing, making posters or charts, reading to another class, or sending their writing to a children's magazine which publishes children's work.

As a final step in the unit, a *culminating activity* of some sort should be planned cooperatively by the teacher and the children. Possibilities include a discussion of the major things that were learned and accomplished through the unit or presentations of completed projects by the children. A special program for parents could also be planned.

THE BENEFITS OF UNIT STUDY

What are children learning from participating in units other than the content focused upon? Of course, reading and writing are primary activities and are therefore strengthened through meaningful application. Because all content areas are integrated, children see a purpose for their use and enjoy studying such information much more than when it is fragmented into separate subjects. Involvement in art, music, movement, talk, and drama makes learning more interesting.

Since units are a form of guided research, children learn how to plan and organize their study; recognize possible problems and form questions and hypotheses; observe, predict, and interpret; find needed resources; compare information from various sources; analyze and question; think critically; and synthesize and present new learnings. They consider alternatives and make their own decisions based on reasons they can explain and justify.

Children experience independence in learning. They become responsible for their own learning and are active participants in the learning process, making decisions about what to read, what to write, what activities can best help them learn, and how to schedule their time to accomplish what they want to do. They learn to cooperate with peers and be supportive of each other. They find they can be useful contributors to a group. Self-confidence increases due to frequently experienced success.

CONCLUDING REMARKS

Literature-based theme units are a way to immerse children in reading and in interesting, meaningful activities related to that reading. Planning such units takes time, but once they are implemented, the benefits to children can be seen quickly. They are a natural way to bring children and literature together—a basic goal of whole language.

REFERENCES

Baskwill, J. (1988). Themestorming. *Teaching K–8, 17,* 80–82.
Edelsky, C., Altwerger, B., & Flores, B. (1991). *Whole language: What's the difference?* Portsmouth, NH: Heinemann.
Gamberg, R., Kwak, W., Hutchings, M., & Altheim, J. (1988). *Learning and loving it: Theme studies in the classroom.* Portsmouth, NH: Heinemann.
Goodman, K. (1986). *What's whole in whole language?* Ontario, Canada: Scholastic.
Hickman, J., & Cullinan, B. (Eds.) (1989). *Children's literature in the classroom: Weaving Charlotte's Web.* Needham Heights, MA: Christopher-Gordon.
Lamme, L. L. (1989). Authorship: A key facet of whole language. *The Reading Teacher, 42,* 704–710.
Pappas, C. C., Kiefer, B. Z., & Levstik, L. S. (1990). *An integrated language perspective in the elementary school: Theory into action.* White Plains, NY: Longman.

Maribeth Henney is a professor in the Elementary Education Department at Iowa State University.

Literature—S.O.S.!

Louise M. Rosenblatt

"Literature-based language arts"; "the use of literature for literacy instruction"; "the contribution of the aesthetic in the teaching of mathematics"; "aesthetic response in content area studies." Such phrases are increasingly encountered in our journals. In the past, literature and the aesthetic have been neglected in our schools; now, finally, their importance is being recognized. Surely, this is a matter for rejoicing. Alas, the contrary is true: There are signs that the very efforts to rescue literature, though often excellent, may become self-defeating.

No one seems to think it necessary to explain what is meant by *literature*, or *the aesthetic*.

If one analyzes the use of these terms in their contexts, a variety of tacit assumptions seems to operate. Sometimes, all that is required is that a text already has been designated as "literature." Sometimes, the presence of story, of a narrative, is the clue. Sometimes, the presence of rhymed words, or of verse rhythms, or of metaphoric language seems sufficient to justify the claim that "literature," or at least "the aesthetic," has been operating. Sometimes, the aesthetic is attributed to the presence of emotion, as when students become excited about scientific information.

All of these elements can indeed be found in texts read as literature. Yet none of these, either singly or all together, can insure the presence of "literature." The fact is that any text, even if it contains such elements, can be the occasion for *either* a "literary" *or* a "nonliterary" reading.

After all, narrative (story) is found not only in novels but also in scientific accounts of geological change or historical accounts of political events or social life. When we speak of the "arm" of a chair, we are using a metaphor. The physicist who uses "wave" in his theory of light is using a metaphor. As for the term *literature*—I recently received a phone call offering me "literature" about a retirement home!

The term *literature*, when it is used in contrast, say, to scientific exposition, refers to a particular mode of experience. It requires a particular kind of relation between reader and text. It requires a particular kind of reading process.

TWO WAYS OF READING

Take, for example, the couplet:

> In fourteen hundred and ninety-two
> Columbus crossed the ocean blue.

Why are we reluctant to accept:

> In fourteen hundred and ninety-three
> Columbus crossed the dark blue sea.

The point, of course, is that we want to use the verse and rhyme as a mnemonic device for the date of Columbus' arrival in America. In other words, we read the couplet in the way we read an expository essay. We pay some attention to the sound and rhythm, but our predominant interest is in acquiring information that we wish to retain after the reading has ended. I use the term efferent (from the Latin for "carry away") to refer to this nonliterary kind of reading.

Still, we can, if we wish, shift gears and pay attention mainly to what we are thinking and feeling as we read or speak the couplet. We can disregard the inaccuracy of the date in the second couplet and decide that it is, from an aesthetic point of view, preferable (e.g., we feel more comfortable with the order of words in "the dark blue sea"). We should then be adopt-

From "Literature—S.O.S.!" by L. M. Rosenblatt, 1991, *Language Arts, 68,* pp. 444–448. Copyright © 1991 by the National Council of Teachers of English. Reprinted with permission.

ing an aesthetic stance toward the text—reading it with attention, of course, to what the words refer to, but *mainly* to what we are experiencing, thinking, and feeling *during* the reading.

Obviously, these verses about Columbus do not provide much reward for the aesthetic stance. Yet they share with even the most valued poetry—say, Shakespeare's *Macbeth*—the potential for being read either aesthetically or efferently.

I was once asked to classify the metaphors in Shakespeare's plays. (This was supposed to reveal biographical information.) That would have meant approaching each play efferently, with my attention focused on how each metaphor should be classified—e.g., as nature, law, animal, etc. It would simply have been irrelevant to pay attention to what states of mind the metaphors were arousing in me. *That* kind of attention to what the metaphors were stirring up—associations, ideas, attitudes, sensations, or feelings—would have had to be reserved for the kind of reading that I call *aesthetic* reading.

Consider the following metaphor:

I am the captain of my soul.

If my purpose is to select the class of metaphors to which this might belong, an efferent reading of this line would be required. My mind would be carrying on an analytic, reasoning activity, in which "captain of a ship" would be seen as implied in the metaphor. Of course, I would have to reason, for someone else "captain" might produce an association with the army. I might have to classify it as naval *or* military.

In an aesthetic reading, on the other hand, I would be registering the effect on me, the states of mind produced by the idea or image of a ship's captain. If interrupted and questioned, I might report a feeling of strength, of independence, of mastery over "my soul." I would probably not explicitly analyze this feeling as resulting from the comparison implied in the metaphoric use of "captain." If asked, I could shift my attention away from the metaphoric effect and recognize this.

ADOPTING A PREDOMINANT STANCE

It's the either–or habit of thinking that has caused the trouble. True, there are two primary ways of looking at the world. We may experience it, feel it, sense it, hear it, and have emotions about it in all its immediacy. Or we may abstract generalizations about it, analyze it, manipulate it, and theorize about it. These are not contradictory activities, however. We cannot, for example, identify the efferent with cognition and the aesthetic, or literary, with emotion.

Instead of thinking of the *text* as either literary or informational, efferent or aesthetic, we should think of it as written for a particular *predominant* attitude or stance, efferent or aesthetic, on the part of the reader. We have ignored the fact that our reading is not all-of-one-piece. We read for information, but we are also conscious of emotions about it and feel pleasure when the words we call up arouse vivid images and are rhythmic to the inner ear. Or we experience a poem but are conscious of acquiring some information about, say, Greek warfare. To confuse matters even further, we can switch stances while reading. And we can read aesthetically something written mainly to inform or read efferently something written mainly to communicate experience. Our present purpose and past experiences, as well as the text, are factors in our choice of stance.

Teachers need constantly to remind themselves that reading is always a particular event involving a particular reader at a particular time under particular circumstances. Hence, we may make different meanings when transacting with the same text at different times. And different readers may make different defensible interpretations of the same text. We need think only of the text of the Constitution or the text of *Hamlet* to document this (Rosenblatt, 1978).

The reader brings to the text a reservoir of past experiences with language and the world. If the signs on the page are linked to elements in that reservoir, these linkages rise into consciousness. The reader recognizes them as words in a language; the child is often slowly making such connections. All readers must draw on past experiences to make the new meanings produced in the transaction with the text. This experience then flows into the reservoir brought to the next reading event.

Psychologists (e.g., Bates, 1979) have pointed out that these connections between verbal signs and what they signify involve both what the words are understood to refer to (their public, dictionary meaning) and the feelings, ideas, and attitudes (their private associations) that have become linked with them through past reading or life experiences. A mixture of such public and private elements is present in all linguistic events. The differences among them result from the individual's focus of attention.

A reading event during which attention is given *primarily* to the public aspect, I call, as indicated above, *efferent* reading. If the reader focuses attention *primarily* on the private elements, I term it *aesthetic*. But each case involves both public and private aspects of meaning.

Actually, we have been talking about a continuum, not an opposition. In a sequence from 1 to 10, for example, these two numbers are not opposites or contraries but simply the end points of a continuum. In the continuum from efferent to aesthetic, these terms are end points in a changing proportion, or "mix," of elements. In any reading, at any point in the continuum, there are both cognitive and affective, publicly referential and privately associational, and abstract and concrete elements (see Figure 1). The place where any reading event falls on the continuum reflects the proportion of what, for brevity, we can call the public and private elements. In the predominantly efferent half of the continuum, the area of attention to the public elements will be greater than the area of the private. Some readings may lean more heavily on the private aspects than others and will be closer to the middle of the continuum. A book about a foreign country read for information, for example, could entail mainly concentration on abstract generalizations (Figure 1, A) or involve much attention to experiential aspects of descriptions (Figure 1, B).

Similarly, aesthetic readings will result when the reader's attention is focused mainly on the private, experiential aspects. But some aesthetic readings pay more attention to the public, referential, and cognitive aspects than do others. An aesthetic reading of *Encyclopedia Brown and the Case of the Mysterious Handprints* (Sobol, 1986), which invites the reader to solve a problem, will probably fall closer to the efferent side of the continuum (Figure 1, C) than will an aesthetic reading of a story such as *Charlotte's Web* (White, 1952) (Figure 1, D).

Precisely because all readings tend to have such a "mix," it becomes important for readers (and writers) to keep their main purposes clear. Beautiful and moving as the words urging us to vote for a candidate may be, it's important that we keep clear that our purpose is to get accurate information. And if we want to experience a text as a poem or a story, we need to learn to evoke experiential meaning from the text and to focus attention on that, rather than simply "the message" or "the facts." Readings that fall near the middle of the continuum especially need to keep the primary purpose, the primary focus of attention, clear.

CLARIFYING A SENSE OF PURPOSE

Confusion about the purpose of reading has in the past contributed to failure to teach effectively both efferent reading and aesthetic reading. Why not help youngsters early to understand that there are two ways of reading? We do not want to give them theoretical explana-

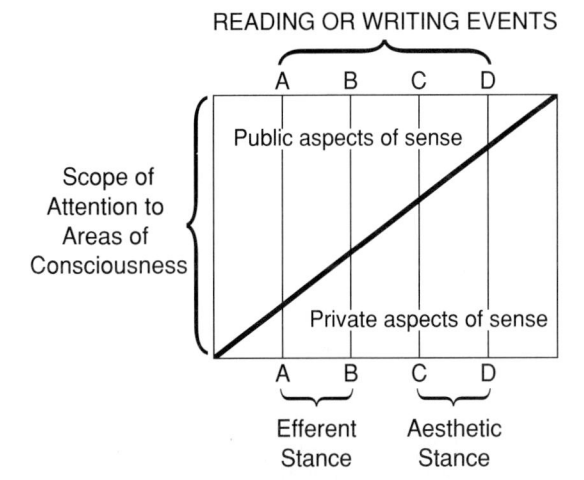

FIGURE 1
THE EFFERENT/AESTHETIC CONTINUUM.
Any linguistic activity has both public (lexical, analytic, abstracting) and private (experiential, affective, associational) components. Stance is determined by the proportion of each admitted into the scope of selective attention. The efferent stance draws mainly on the public aspect of sense. The aesthetic stance includes proportionately more of the experiential, private aspect.

Reading or writing events (A) and (B) fall into the efferent part of the continuum, with (B) admitting more private elements.

Reading or writing events (C) and (D) both represent the aesthetic stance, with (C) according a higher proportion of attention to the public aspects of sense. (Adapted from Rosenblatt, 1989)

---

tions, nor do we need to. We communicate such understandings by what we do, by the atmosphere and the activities we associate with the two kinds of reading, and by the kinds of questions we ask and the kinds of tests we give. Children who know that the teacher usually quizzes them on factual aspects of a reading, even if it is called "a poem" or "a story," will adopt the efferent stance and will read to register the facts that will be required after the reading. They know that they will be successful and rewarded if they recall the color of the horse or where the bunny hid, rather than if they linger over the experiences and feelings encountered. (Actually, that kind of fragmented questioning doesn't much improve efferent reading, either!)

With younger children, perhaps the best evidence of aesthetic experience is their demand to hear the story or poem again. Or they may wish to draw a picture or retell the story. Some may be moved to comment on it. I think of the 3-year-old who exclaimed, "She's a mean lady!" when hearing the nursery rhyme about a certain old lady who spanked her many children "all round" and put them to bed. Certainly, evidence of "comprehension" can be gained in such indirect ways from readers of all ages.

Aesthetic reading happens if students have repeatedly found that, in approaching a text called a "poem" or a "story," they can assume that they are free to pay attention to what the words call to consciousness. They can savor the images, the sounds, the smells, the actions, the associations, and the feelings that the words point to. Textbooks' and teachers' questions too often hurry the students away from the lived-through experience. After the reading, the experience should be recaptured, reflected on. It can be the subject of further aesthetic activities—drawing, dancing, miming, talking, writing, role-playing, or oral interpretation. It can be discussed and analyzed efferently. Or it can yield information. But first, if it is indeed to be "literature" for these students, it must be experienced (Rosenblatt, 1983).

It is teachers who need to be clear theoretically about efferent and aesthetic reading. As they commendably seek to present more "literature" in their language arts curricula, they need to be careful not to "use" the appeal of such texts simply or mainly for the efferent purposes of teaching grammar or "skills." Also, as teachers plan to include aesthetic elements in the work in social or natural science or to utilize the interest of story in the teaching of mathematics, they need to realize that they have a responsibility not to create confusion about primary stances appropriate to different purposes.

The different purposes lead to different modes of reading and to different criteria of evaluation of the "meanings" evoked. If the emphasis is on verifiable information or practical application, not only does the mode of reading need to be efferent, but also the interpretation of the text needs to involve some public criteria of evaluation. If the purpose is literary, the important thing is that readers relate to the text, and to one another, the different experiences produced during their transactions with it.

I am decidedly in sympathy with those who, under the rubric of "whole language," speak of the importance of meaning. But I hope that they will not confuse students by using "literary works" in such a way that students read them efferently, for the primary purpose, let us say, of learning historical data. If American history is being studied, a novel about colonial life will be valuable, but only as primarily an aesthetic experience, a sharing of what it would have been like to live in those days. If the story has been read with a primarily aesthetic emphasis, one can later, of course, ask students to recall incidental information about, for example, methods of transportation. But it would often be helpful to suggest that the author of the poem or novel had acquired that information through verified historical sources.

The distinctions in purpose and stance can be incorporated into actual classroom practice without dwelling on theoretical distinctions. Even nursery school youngsters can sense the difference between looking at a picture book in order to learn the names of birds and looking at it because there is comfort in hearing a story about finding a home—e.g., in sharing a duck family's experience of finding a place to nest. Hickman (1981) tells about the boy who complained that his teacher had brought him only "story books about dinosaurs," whereas he really wanted to *know* about them.

Obviously, what is at stake is each child's total school experience—in speech, reading, and writing—with what is termed "literature," or "the aesthetic." No one episode, whether in kindergarten or in high school, will be decisive. But it will either reinforce or weaken the student's sense of the diverse possibilities of texts—and of the world. We need to look at the whole sweep of our language arts curricula, at our use of texts across the curriculum, and especially at our methods of evaluation. We need to make sure that students are cumulatively developing, in their transactions with texts, the ability to adopt the stance on the continuum appropriate to their particular personal purposes and to the situation—in short, the ability to read both efferently and aesthetically.

REFERENCES

Bates, E. (1979). *The emergence of symbols.* New York: Academic Press.

Hickman, J. (1981) A new perspective on response to literature. *Research in the Teaching of English, 15,* 293–309.

Rosenblatt, L. M. (1978). *The reader, the text, the poem: The transactional theory of the literary work.* Carbondale, IL: Southern Illinois University Press.

Rosenblatt, L. M. (1980). "What facts does this poem teach you?" *Language Arts, 57,* 386–394.

Rosenblatt, L. M. (1983). *Literature as exploration.* (4th ed.). New York: Modern Language Association.

Rosenblatt, L. M. (1989). Writing and reading: The transactional theory. In J. M. Mason (Ed.), *Reading and writing connections* (pp. 153–176). Boston: Allyn and Bacon.

Sobol, D. (1986). *Encyclopedia Brown and the case of the mysterious handprints.* New York: Bantam/Skylark.

White, E. B. (1952). *Charlotte's Web.* New York: Harper.

Louise M. Rosenblatt is Professor Emerita of English Education at New York University.

Give Us Books! . . . But Also . . . Give Us Wings!

Nancy Larrick

The Year of the Young Child had its slogan "Give Us Books! Give Us Wings!" repeated countless times and accepted, I fear, with little thought of its true significance today. It comes, of course, from a slim little volume published by *The Horn Book* in 1944: *Books, Children and Men* by an eminent French scholar, Paul Hazard. It remains an inspired revelation of the role of adults who have, he says, "oppressed children" by "robbing imagination of its rightful place and declaring war on dreams."

And how have they done this? Paul Hazard explains:

> They have offered books that oozed boredom, that were likely to make him detest wisdom forever, silly books and empty books . . . by tens and by hundreds, falling like hail on springtime. The sooner they stifled a young heart, the sooner they effaced from a young spirit the sense of freedom and pleasure in play . . . the more men were pleased with themselves for having raised children without delay to their own state of supreme perfection. (p. 3)

Surely among the "books that oozed boredom . . . silly books by tens and hundreds" are those we have given children for their first experience with reading. These are the books produced by the process Kenneth Goodman, in the Winter 1988 issue of *The New Advocate*, called "basalization"—referring to the widespread practice of simplifying and pasteurizing selections from children's literature for inclusion in the basal readers. Thus, Judy Blume, as Goodman demonstrates, was reduced to the colorless level of Dick and Jane, if you can imagine that.

Now, in the name of whole language and the literature-based reading program, whole books, uncut and uncensored, are being used for the teaching of reading. Enthusiastic reports of children's increased skill and love of reading are coming in from all quarters. The growing use of a literature-based reading program is cause for rejoicing by teachers who were students of such pioneers as Roma Gans and Alvina Burrows years ago. We've used whole books, unaltered books, and we know that children devour them.

Today in many classrooms children are learning to read with whole books—"real books" as children often refer to the non-textbooks, called "trade books" in the publishing industry. Instead of reading watered-down snippets, patched together to make a basal reader, children in the class have their own "real book," often ones they have chosen, not necessarily the same book being read by others in the class.

Now young readers are meeting the real Pippi Longstocking, the real Ramona Quimby, the real Bingo Brown. They hear them speak the English language instead of basal-reader language, which is unfamiliar, awkward, and imprecise.

Nowadays it is easy to become euphoric when visiting the book exhibits of an education conference where hundreds of trade books for children are on display. Teachers are standing in long lines to have their books autographed by such authors as Jane Yolen, Richard Peck, Lois Lowry, and Steve Kellogg. (I never heard of anyone standing in line to have a basal reader autographed!) Tote bags are bulging with new children's books plus posters to take back to school. "Pretty exciting!" I say to myself.

But wait! I find that a satellite publishing industry is growing up to provide teachers guides for these exciting trade books for children—guides modeled directly on those for the basal readers—with diagrams for recording new vocabulary words, questions with space for writing the answers, lists of words for filling in the blanks, and so on.

I gather samples and begin to realize that in some quarters the great "Reading Initiative"[1]—as California calls it—is being distorted by procedures patterned on the old teacher's guides for the basal readers.

Most of these new teacher's guides run 50 to 70 pages, which is considerably longer than some of the children's books. The price for a teacher's guide dealing with a single book may run as high as $19.95 while the paperback edition of a child's book costs approximately $2.50.

The typical teacher's guide begins with a fairly detailed summary of the children's book—somehow suggesting that this is the equivalent of reading the whole book. But what a contrast! The summaries are bland, lifeless, with none of the tug-at-the-heartstrings of a good book. The teacher who reads only the summary never meets the subtleties of character and mood and the emotional climate which make the book unique.

Like the teacher's guides for the basal readers, the new guides for trade books provide workbook pages for each student to complete. Some are advertised as reproducible, much like the dittoed activity sheets of the past. Here, too, there are word lists: "Draw a line from each word to the picture it names." Or, "Match each word with the phrase that explains it." "Use words from this list to fill the blanks in sentences below."

The new guide-makers seem to have an addiction for what they call graphics. There are Conflict Maps, Decision Grids, Cause-and-Effect Maps, Circle Charts (one showing 32 circles), Character Maps, Mood Charts, Attribute Webs, T-Comparisons, Venn Diagrams, and more. One guide reproduces several paragraphs of a children's book, omitting 15 or 20 words. Students are to fill in their own word for each space and then compare their versions with the original book.

I have found no guide that provides a justification for word games of this sort. Why are they introduced in the name of literature? Is it to test the child's memory? Or is it to see whether the child's vocabulary is equal to—or better than the author's?

Many of the guides I have seen include questions for which children are to write answers. Often the "correct" answer is given for the teacher and the assurance that in some cases "Answers may vary."

Many of these questions fit into the DRTA method, acronym for Directed Reading Thinking Activity. This calls for a specific procedure: "Turn to the first chapter or section and predict what will happen in this section. Now read the chapter. Stop to note whether your prediction was correct. Predict what will happen in the next chapter. Read. Stop to check. Predict. Read. Stop. Check on your prediction" . . . and on and on.

This may be an effective regimen for some books in certain situations. But how could it add to the child's understanding or pleasure in reading *Sam, Bangs, and Moonshine* by Evaline Ness for which it is recommended? This is a book I remember warmly from its early days so I pulled it off the shelf for another read with the DRTA suggestions before me.

It is a charmingly illustrated book of only 32 pages with no chapter or section divisions—a tiny story of suspense, with touches of humor and tragedy as well. This is a breathless book, a tender book. But it seems to me all of that is destroyed by the DRTA mandates to stop and start, stop and start.

Then I turned to another favorite that I had not read in many years: *The Summer of the Swans* by Betsy Byars. On this latest reading, I found it just as stirring as I had remembered it, with suspense building incident by incident. I found myself suffering anew from Sarah's frustrations and the pathetic ways of Charlie, her retarded younger brother. When Charlie disappeared, I read on breathlessly, ignoring the DRTA stop-and-go lights.

Isn't it one of the joys of reading to become so involved that we want to read on and on, transported to another scene and wearing the shoes of those we read about? Why interrupt such involvement?

Directions on the reproducible pages are clear and precise so the young reader will have no trouble following to the letter. For example,

> "Combine these twelve syllables into six words."
> "Rewrite the title using exactly ten words." (Example given: Scott O' Dell's *Black Pearl* becomes *An Ebony Jewel Residing in the Shell of an Oyster*.)
> "Fill in the Cause-and-Effect Map."

Rewriting is frequently suggested too. For example,

> "Copy two sentences, leaving out the vowels for your partner to fill in."
> "Rewrite the last sentence eliminating any word beginning with the letter A. Have your partner fill in replacement words."

For what is called free-writing (limited in one case to five to ten minutes), the directions are equally explicit:

> "Write a poem in at least six lines." (This is to relate to *Julie of the Wolves*.)
> "Translate the last paragraph into a poem."
> "Write a new ending for the book."
> "Tell what the book is about in an ABC of 26 words." (This is for *The Summer of the Swans*.)
> "Write a poem in which Charlie (of *The Summer of the Swans*) talks about how he feels." (Remember that Charlie is the retarded younger brother who is unable to speak.)

As I read such directions, I get the feeling that these activities are planned for the classroom where the teacher does all the talking and children are expected to follow without question. Here and there I found a suggestion for brainstorming, carefully defined as "a nonjudgmental divergent thinking activity." However, the guides offer little opening for brainstorming, given these very specific questions, the answers to be accepted as correct, and the time limitations.

I have found no suggestions in these guides that children meet in small groups to make a list of important questions. Or that they debate their various reactions. No hint that they consult parents and neighbors to gather information about their experiences to supplement those children find in their reading.

Think, for example, of *Sarah, Plain and Tall*, by Patricia MacLachlan, a story which takes place on the prairie in the long-ago time of horse-drawn wagons and oil lamps. Can several children bring in first-hand reports of what life was like in the country without cars and electricity? Surely that would add more than writing a new title in ten words!

And wouldn't it be a delight for one group of children to hunt up the music for Sarah's ancient song, "Sumer is icumen en," and then all sing it? And for another group to collect the flowers that are so dear to Sarah? But this, I realize is not the stuff of teacher's guides.

And nowhere do I detect the suggestion that the children in one class might be reading different books—all at the same time. Yet, in any group there will surely be varied interests and levels of reading ability. Some may read easily and quickly and want to springboard to another book on the same topic.

I have found only one teacher's guide that suggests further reading of books or magazine articles on the same subject. Yet the pleasure from reading one book can readily build interest in another and another. It can be the lead to magazine articles as well as letters and news clippings from the public library archives.

The commercial publishers of these new teacher's guides to trade books for children are not the only ones producing goose-step guidelines for a literature-based reading program. Teachers are doing it, too, often in the name of "integrating the language arts."

An article in the May, 1990, issue of *The Reading Teacher* explains how one teacher uses children's literature to enhance phonics instruction. It lists popular picture books which illustrate specific vowel sounds: *The Cat in the Hat* and *Angus and the Cat* for short *a*; *The Little Red Hen* and *Hester the Jester* for short *e*, and so on. Directions are given for introducing "a whole quality literature selection" (such as *The Cat in the Hat*) and then specific drill on examples of the short *a* in that book.

At a recent conference of reading teachers, one 90-minute session was devoted to a demonstration of what was called "integration" of children's literature, specifically poetry, with the curriculum. Each of the five presenters explained how to use selected poems to teach word attack skills (initial and final consonants, blends and digraphs, affixes, and homonyms) and comprehension skills (sequencing, problem solving, cause-and-effect, making predictions before, during, and after reading.)

The poems shown with an overhead projector were among the most appealing from such distinguished poets as John Ciardi, Carl Sandburg, David McCord, Eve Merriam, and Aileen Fisher. But the poems were being used to teach parts of speech, punctuation, -ing words, and sight vocabulary. It was what one presenter called "using poetry as a data retrieval mechanism."

There was nothing about the music of the poems, the emotional pull, the fun or pathos tucked away in poetic lines. Nothing to stir the imagination or touch the heart. Everything to kill the special joy of reading, it seemed to me.

It was the vivisection of poetry in the name of reading.

I rejoice when I hear that teachers are bringing quality poetry to their pupils. Then I know they are heeding the first of the children's cries: "Give us books!" Real books, not watered-down, patchwork books.

I must confess that I once assumed that such books of poetry and prose, of fiction and nonfiction, would, through their natural sparkle and distinctive beauty, give children the incentive and the means for acquiring greater satisfaction and wisdom, greater freedom to create and dream.

"If we give them books, real books," I have reasoned, "those books, through their unique qualities, will give them wings."

Now I am fearful that we are clipping those wings by asking children to workbook their way through gripping stories, and to use poetry as a source of digraphs and homonyms. Instead of encouraging further reading and questioning, these teacher's guides provide stop-watch plans: "Read. Stop. Review. Read. Stop. Goose-step. Read for ten minutes. Write a poem in six lines. Rewrite the ending for *The Great Gilly Hopkins.* Expand the title to ten words. Copy the paragraph omitting all words that begin with the letter *a.*" All are to keep in step although it may mean an unthinking conformity.

In the name of whole language and the literature-based reading program, we are heeding the first cry of the children: "Give us books!" But we are moving dangerously close to disaster, when we introduce those books in such a way as to destroy their beauty, their significance, and thus deny the children's plea: "Give us wings!"

NOTES

1. The Fall, 1988 (Vol. 1, No. 4) issue of *The New Advocate* included three articles on The California Reading Initiative: Bill Honig's, "The California Reading Initiative," Yvonne S. Freeman's, "The California Reading Initiative: Revolution or Merely Revision," and Mary Gardner's "An Educator's Concerns About The California Reading Initiative."

Nancy Larrick has written and edited numerous trade books for the delight and enjoyment of children's literature by children, teachers, and parents.

CHAPTER DISCUSSIONS AND ACTIVITIES

1. An elementary school teacher describes himself as a "whole-language teacher." He makes the following comment:

   In a whole-language classroom, the comprehension of children using trade books must be thoroughly checked. I have the children work independently with some worksheets I have prepared.

   Pair off with a classmate and discuss your reaction to his statement.
2. Identify and discuss three activities that a teacher can use in the classroom that can help to make literature-based reading instruction work well.
3. In a small class group discuss the following questions:
   a. What is your personal definition of the term "children's literature"?
   b. List three trade books you remember from your childhood.
   c. Were you read to as a child? If yes, by whom?
   d. What children's books have you read within the past year?
   e. Can you name three authors of children's books?
4. From your college library or Instructional Materials Center, select a literature-based basal-reading series for a particular grade level. Review the teacher's manual and the text. While doing this, examine the children's literature books in the basal reader. Identify one children's literature book used in the series and compare the story to the original book. What differences do you find? Write a brief narrative stating why you would or would not recommend this program for literature-based reading instruction. Be prepared to share your findings with the class.
5. Henney, in her article, identifies various types of literature-based units. Select one and for a particular grade or age level prepare an outline identifying the name of the unit and ten children's literature books that you would use in the classroom. Discuss how you would integrate this unit into the various areas of the curriculum.
6. Define and discuss the meanings of *literature* and *aesthetic* as noted in the article by Rosenblatt. With a small group of classmates, describe how these terms relate to the philosophy of whole language.
7. Pair off with a classmate and select a historical fiction book that both of you feel would be appropriate for a particular grade level. Identify and describe the efferent and aesthetic stances in this book.
8. Find a published teacher's guide for a particular trade book. Review this guide, comparing and contrasting your findings to the points discussed by Larrick in her article. Share your findings with a small group of classmates.
9. If possible, visit a classroom in which the teacher is using whole language. From your observations, write a brief description of how children's literature was used in the class. Pair off with a classmate and share your findings.

CHAPTER 5

The Writing Connection

Basic to the whole-language philosophy is the infusion of writing in concert with reading as children learn in a holistic environment. Edelsky, Altwerger, and Flores (1991), when discussing the similarities of reading and writing through the eyes of whole-language educators, note that reading and writing are "in the same theoretical category—language" (p. 73). In a whole-language classroom, teachers introduce children to literacy by allowing them to be writers as well as readers. The connection between reading and writing is not just limited to the whole-language classroom. In *Becoming a Nation of Readers* (1985), the authors conclude that "students who write frequently and discuss their writing with others approach reading with what has been termed the 'eye of the writer' " (Anderson, Hiebert, Scott, & Wilkinson, 1985, p. 79). According to Smith (1983)

> Schools should be the place where children are initiated into the club of writers as soon as possible, with full rights and privileges even as apprentices. They will read like writers, and acquire full status in the club, if they are not denied admission at the threshold. (p. 567)

In this chapter, we will be observing the close association between reading and writing that exists in literacy instruction. We will also view the role of the computer and its place in the writing process within a whole-language classroom.

THE WRITING PROCESS

Historically, the emphasis on writing in the elementary schools focused on creative writing. The student was usually assigned a written topic that stemmed from an activity that the teacher initiated, and a composition was written by the student in a specific class-time period. Although the teacher encouraged the child to be creative, there was little or no emphasis on writing form or mechanical skills. Evaluation by the teacher of the written work was performed after the composition was completed. Thus, in this approach, only the finished product was considered important (Hoskisson & Tompkins, 1987).

In education today, writing is viewed as a process. Proett and Gill (1986) describe writing as "a complex intellectual–linguistic process involving the recursive application of a wide range of thinking skills and language abilities" (p. 1). In the writing-process approach, "children learn to understand and use the phrases and tools of authorship" (Reutzel & Cooter, 1992, p. 417). The writing process as defined by Graves (1981) is "a series of operations leading to the solution to a problem. The process begins when the writer consciously or unconsciously starts a topic and is finished when the written piece is published" (p. 4).

The various stages or activities through which children progress are discussed and described by various writing-process researchers (Britton, 1978; Murray, 1980; Graves, 1983; Daniels & Zemelman, 1985; Calkins, 1986; and Proett & Gill, 1986). According to Murray (1980), the act of writing involves a complex mixture of (1) collecting observations, (2) connecting them to our past experiences, (3) writing them out, and (4) reading them back objectively. He further points out that within these stages of writing, the writer rehearses or "prewrites" what she or he wants to say, prepares drafts or "tentative writing," and revises or rewrites the material based on her or his own critiques. Daniels and Zemelman (1985) agree, noting that the writing-process model centers around prewriting, writing, and revising. Proett and Gill (1986) carry this notion a step further by identifying three productive stages wherein teachers should directly involve students in the writing process—before they write, while they write, and after they write. Although the names assigned to the stages vary depending on the author or researcher, they fall largely into five categories: prewriting, drafting, revising, editing, and sharing.

In the prewriting stage, the student is encouraged to explore and discover. Through many useful strategies such as brainstorming, reading, observing, mapping, outlining, imagining, researching, gathering information, or listing and categorizing, they are able to focus on what they want to write about. Glatthorn (1982) as well as Fitzgerald and Markham (1987) discovered that the unskilled, poorer writers spend less time or have little interest in this stage of writing.

In the drafting or writing stage, the writer encounters some different limitations. Proett and Gill (1986) state:

> The writing stage needs to be viewed in two different ways. Seen in one way, it is the flowing of words onto the page, easily, naturally, rapidly. But it is also a time of making decisions, of choosing what to tell and what to leave out, or thinking about who is speaking and who is listening, or determining what order, what structure, what word works best. In some ways these functions even seem contradictory; the first needs to be fluid and fast while the other calls for deliberation and reason. (p. 11)

While working on the first draft, the writer must be aware of the audience, the purpose and the form that she or he wishes to reach. As noted by Bromley (1992), "Drafting is not a smooth and steady process; rather it happens in fits and bursts" (p. 343).

In the revising stage, the writer should be encouraged to scrutinize the first draft and obtain responses from peer editing groups and from conferencing with the teacher. Glatthorn (1982) states that "skilled writers either revise very little or revise extensively.... Unskilled writers either revise very little or revise only at the surface and word levels" (p. 723).

In the editing stage, the writer is placing the written material into its final form. Through proofreading, the writer can check the mechanics of writing and spelling. Because proofreading is not the same as "regular" reading, it "requires word-by-word reading and attention to form—letters, spelling, capital letters, and punctuation marks—rather than to meaning" (Hoskisson & Tompkins, 1987, p. 175).

In the last stage, sharing, the student presents her or his finished work to an appreciative audience. This can be accomplished in a variety of ways: by publishing and placing it in the library of the school or classroom, displaying it on the bulletin board, printing it in the school newspaper, or reading it aloud to the class with invited parents present. "The chance to share one's work in its finished form for others to see, touch, hear, read, and reread has a special appeal and provides the incentive for many students to write" (Bromley, 1992, p. 372).

Throughout the writing process, these stages or elements tend to occur in cycles. Sometimes the student recognizes the need for additional data; new ideas may pop up while editing; the writer may simply decide that further drafting is necessary. As with all revisions, such changes should be accompanied by considerable support from peers and from the teacher.

Flowers (1981) likens the roles of the writer to the following cast of characters:

- *Madman:* full of ideas, writing crazily and sloppily.
- *Architect:* selecting, choosing chunks to rearrange in a plan.
- *Carpenter:* fastens ideas together in a logical sequence, essay is smooth and watertight.
- *Judge:* inspecting, examining, objective, interested in details. (pp. 834–835)

She carefully warns that the writer does not play these roles in any sequential order but alternates from one role to another as need arises in the process of writing.

As they guide their children through the writing process, teachers should keep in mind sound principles of writing instruction. Students should not only be given the opportunity to write daily, but should also write material that is of interest for various audiences. In the ongoing process of writing, the teacher should provide positive reinforcement for the work of the students, doing so with genuine interest and enthusiasm. And as the students develop as writers, the teacher should be able to recognize the writing stages the students progress through and informally direct the students to self-assess their progress (Block, 1993).

Most authorities feel that strategies for teaching writing must be modified and modernized to meet the changing needs of today's young writers. For example, in the "Writing Workshop" described by Atwell (1987), students can develop their abilities as writers by starting on the first day to write about topics of their own choice. This workshop focuses on four practices: the use of the mini-lesson, the writing workshop proper, the group share meeting and the last component, the status-of-the-class conference taking place on the next day. Once the students become accustomed to this procedure, "writing class follows a predictable pattern of five-minute lesson, quick status-of-the-class check, at least half an hour for the workshop's main business of writing and conferring, and five or ten minutes for the concluding whole-class share session" (Atwell, 1987, p. 77).

> **Looking Ahead**
>
> The articles selected for this chapter, Lamme (1989), Grindler and Stratton (1991), and Fulps and Young (1991), discuss the strong bond that exists between reading and writing in the whole-language classroom.

THE USE OF COMPUTERS IN THE WHOLE-LANGUAGE CLASSROOM

Because of the increased interest in educational technology in the schools, educators are taking a closer look at the use of computers in the classroom. Computers can assist students in expanding on the reading and writing aspects of whole language. While broadening the world of reading and writing, a computer can assist a child with various strategies, such as sentence combining and story schema (Gunn, 1990). Through the use of the computer, students can write letters to each other through electronic mail, write journals, as well as execute free and chain writing (Doyle, 1988). Donald Graves, in an interview with Ellis (1991), depicts the place of the computer in the writing process by commenting:

> The miracle of the computer is the word processing. You can change things. You get a clear visual image of the word. You can put space in. You can add information in the right place so you don't have to copy it all over.
>
> For children who have motor problems, they get a magnificent machine text. You can print multiple copies. You can go to instant publication. You can use modems for children to communicate with each other. Heavens, we don't remotely know the limits yet. It's going to rely on our professional literacy and how we use it—just like everything else. (pp. 130–131)

Gollasch (1991) maintains that as primary grade teachers set out to use computers in the whole-language classroom, they need to consider the following: language-learning principles should be understood, computers should be integrated into the classroom, the computer should be viewed as a tool, the teacher's role should be perceived as that of a facilitator, the environment in the classroom should nurture literacy development, software should be carefully selected, and mindful planning should be encouraged.

Looking Ahead

DeGroff (1990), in the last article included in this chapter, provides a comprehensive description of how the computer can be used in the whole-language classroom.

During the reading of the various articles related to whole language and the writing process, you may want to reflect on some of the following questions:

- Why is it important for a whole-language teacher to have the children become involved with the use of the "Author's Chair?" Is this an activity used only in a whole-language classroom?
- What strategies should a teacher use that encourage the children to become directly involved in the writing process?
- How does a teacher "publish" children's writing?
- What are "young author conferences?" Should they be used in the school?
- What does the term "emergent literacy" mean?
- What are the advantages and disadvantages of using reading–response journals? Why is the teacher's role so important?
- What are the ways in which the use of the computer facilitates reading and writing development of students?

REFERENCES

Anderson, R. C., Hiebert, E. H., Scott, J. A., & Wilkinson, I. A. G. (1985). *Becoming a nation of readers.* Washington, D.C.: The National Institute of Education, U.S. Department of Education.

Atwell, N. (1987). *In the middle: Writing, reading and learning with adolescents.* Portsmouth, NH: Heinemann.

Block, C. C. (1993). *Teaching the language arts: Expanding thinking through student-centered instruction.* Boston: Allyn and Bacon.

Britton, J. (1978). The composing processes and the functions of writing. In C. R. Cooper & L. Odell (Eds.), *Research on composing: Points of departure* (pp. 13–28). Urbana, IL: National Council of Teachers of English.

Bromley, K. D. (1992). *Language arts: Exploring connections.* Boston: Allyn and Bacon.

Calkins, L. M. (1986). *The art of teaching writing.* Portsmouth, NH: Heinemann.

Daniels, H., & Zemelman, S. (1985). *A writing project: Training teachers of composition from kindergarten to college.* Portsmouth, NH: Heinemann.

DeGroff, L. (1990). Is there a place for computers in whole language classrooms? *The Reading Teacher, 43*(8), 568–572.

Doyle, C. (1988). Creative applications of computers assisted reading and writing instruction. *Journal of Reading, 32*(3), 236–239.

Edelsky, C., Altwerger, B., & Flores, B. (1991). *Whole language: What's the difference?* Portsmouth, NH: Heinemann.

Ellis, D. W. (1991). Thoughts on writing: An interview [with Donald Graves]. In K. S. Goodman, L. B. Bird, & Y. M. Goodman (Eds.), *The whole language catalog* (pp. 130–131). Santa Rosa, CA: American School Publishers.

Fitzgerald, J., & Markham, L. (1987). Teaching children about revision in writing. *Cognition and Instruction, 4*(1), 3–24.

Flowers, B. S. (1981). Madman, architect, carpenter, judge: Roles and the writing process. *Language Arts, 58*(7), 834–836.

Fulps, J. S., & Young, T. A. (1991). The what, why, when and how of reading response journals. *Reading Horizons, 32*(2), 109–116.

Glatthorn, A. A. (1982). Demystifying the teaching of writing. *Language Arts, 59*(7), 722–725.

Gollasch, F. (1991). Micro-computers in the whole language classroom. In K. S. Goodman, L. B. Bird, & Y. M. Goodman (Eds.), *The whole language catalog* (p. 138). Santa Rosa, CA: American School Publishers.

Graves, D. (1981). *A case study observing the development of primary children's composing, spelling, and motor behaviors during the writing process.* (Final Report, September 2, 1978–August 31, 1981, NIE Grant No. G-78-0174). Durham, NH: University of New Hampshire. (ERIC Document Reproduction Service No. ED 218 653)

Graves, D. M. (1983). *Writing: Teachers and children at work.* Portsmouth, NH: Heinemann.

Grindler, M., & Stratton, B. (1991). The reading/writing connection in whole language. *Ohio Reading Teacher, 25*(1), 11–14.

Gunn, C. (1990). Computers in a whole language classroom. *The Writing Notebook, 7*(3), 6–8.

Hoskisson, K., & Tompkins, G. E. (1987). *Language arts: Content and teaching strategies.* Columbus, OH: Merrill.

Lamme, L. L. (1989). Authorship: A key facet of whole language. *The Reading Teacher, 42*(9), 704–710.

Murray, D. M. (1980). Writing as process: How writing finds its own meaning. In T. R. Donovan & B. W. McClelland (Eds.), *Eight approaches to teaching composition* (pp. 3–20). Urbana, IL: National Council of Teachers of English.

Proett, J., & Gill, K. (1986). *The writing process in action: A handbook for teachers.* Urbana, IL: National Council of Teachers of English.

Reutzel, D. R., & Cooter, Jr., R. T. (1992). *Teaching children to read: From basals to books.* New York: Merrill/Macmillan.

Smith, F. (1983). Reading like a writer. *Language Arts, 60*(5), 558–567.

FOR FURTHER STUDY

Anderson, J. (1993). Journal writing: The promise and the reality. *Journal of Reading, 36*(4), 304–309.

Bayliss, V. A. (1994). Fluency in children's writing. *Reading Horizons, 34*(3), 247–256.

Butler, S. (1991). The writing connection. In V. Froese (Ed.), *Whole-language: Practice and theory* (pp. 97–147). Boston: Allyn and Bacon.

Chomsky, C. (1971). Write first, read later. *Childhood Education, 47*(6), 296–299.

Cooper, E. (Producer), & Klotz, N. (Director). (1993). *Integrating thinking, reading, and writing across the curriculum* [Videotape]. Princeton, NJ: Films for the Humanities and Sciences.

Cullinan, B. E. (Ed.). (1993). *Pen in hand: Children become writers.* Newark, DE: International Reading Association.

De Ford, D. E. (1981). Literacy: Reading, writing, and other essentials. *Language Arts, 58*(6), 652–658.

Donsky, B. V. B. (1984). Trends in elementary writing instruction. *Language Arts, 61*(8), 795–803.

Fitzgerald, J. (1993). Teachers' knowing about knowledge: Its significance for classroom writing instruction. *Language Arts, 70*(4), 282–289.

Franklin, E. A. (1992). Learning to read and write the natural way. *Teaching Exceptional Children, 24*(3), 45–48.
Goodman, K. S., & Goodman, Y. M. (1983). Reading and writing relationships: Pragmatic functions. *Language Arts, 60*(5), 590–599.
Graves, D., & Hansen, J. (1983). The Author's Chair. *Language Arts, 60*(2), 176–183.
Grejda, G. F., & Hannafin, M. J. (1991). The influence of word processing on the revisions of fifth graders. *Computers In the Schools, 8*(4), 89–102.
Groff, P. (1986). The implications of developmental spelling research: A dissenting view. *The Elementary School Journal, 86*(3), 317–323.
Gunderson, L., & Shapiro, J. (1988). Whole language instruction: Writing in 1st grade. *The Reading Teacher, 41*(4), 430–437.
Hairston, M. (1982). The winds of change: Thomas Kuhn and the revolution in the teaching of writing. *College Composition and Communication, 33*(1), 76–88.
Houston, G., Goolrick, F., & Tate, R. (1991). Storytelling as a stage in process writing: A whole language model. *Teaching Exceptional Children, 23*(2), 40–43.
Kahn, J., & Freyd, P. (1990). Online: A whole language perspective on keyboarding. *Language Arts, 67*(1), 84–90.
Knipping, N. Y. (1993). Let drama help young authors "re-see" their stories. *Language Arts, 70*(1), 45–50.
Lensmire, T. (1994). *When children write.* New York: Teachers College Press.
Mamchur, C. (1994). Don't you dare say "fart." *Language Arts, 71*(2), 95–100.
McAuliffe, S. (1993/1994). Toward understanding one another: Second graders' use of gendered language and story styles. *The Reading Teacher, 47*(4), 302–310.
McCoy, L. J., & Hammett, V. (1992). Predictable books in a middle school class writing program. *Reading Horizons, 32*(3), 230–234.
Montague, M. (1990). Computers and writing process instruction. *Computers in the Schools, 7*(3), 5–20.
Morgan, M. (1991). Using computers in the language arts. *Language Arts, 68*(1), 74–77.
Musthafa, B. (1994). Literary response: A way of integrating reading-writing activities. *Reading Improvement, 31*(1), 52–58.
Norton, D. E. (1993). *The effective teaching of language arts* (4th ed.). New York: Merrill/Macmillan.
Petty, W. T., Petty, D. C., & Satzer, R. T. (1994). *Experiences in language* (6th ed.). Boston: Allyn and Bacon.
Reinking, D. (Ed.). (1987). *Reading and computers: Issues for theory and practice.* New York: Teachers College Press.
Shanahan, T. (1988). The teaching–writing relationship: Seven instructional principles. *The Reading Teacher, 41*(7), 636–647.
Strickland, D. S., Feeley, J. T., & Wepner, S. B. (1987). *Using computers in the teaching of reading.* New York: Teachers College Press.
Sudol, D., & Sudol, P. (1991). Another story: Putting Graves, Calkins, and Atwell into practice and perspective. *Language Arts, 68*(4), 292–300.
TV Ontario Production Company (Producer), & Novak, A. (Director). (1992). *Beginning to read and write* [Videotape]. Princeton, NJ: Films for the Humanities and Sciences.
Wepner, S. B. (1990). Holistic computer applications in literature-based classrooms. *The Reading Teacher, 44*(1), 12–19.
Whitney, J., & Hubbard, R. (Producers). (1986). *Time and choice: Key elements for process teaching* [Videotape]. Portsmouth, NH: Heinemann.
Wood, M. (1994). *Essentials of classroom teaching: Elementary language arts.* Boston: Allyn and Bacon.

Authorship: A Key Facet of Whole Language

Linda Leonard Lamme

With a Whole Language philosophy becoming popular in American schools, the question is often asked, just what do we teach? Teachers realize that basic skills are no longer the focus of study, but with what content are basic skills replaced? The goal of Whole Language instruction is to help children become avid readers and writers. How is that accomplished in the elementary school classroom?

One of the key facets of Whole Language instruction is authorship. Emergent literacy studies indicate that an important aspect of children's natural acquisition of literacy is their attachment to favorite book authors and their sense of ownership for pieces they have written. This article traces the importance of this concept in literacy development and shows how authorship can become one focus of a Whole Language classroom.

A CLASS OF AUTHORS

Some teachers introduce themselves as authors at the beginning of the year, sharing something they have written and indicating that they know a classroom full of authors. As children learn to view themselves as authors, they become more aware of what authorship means. They bring to their reading and writing experiences a real purpose and a human dimension that is not there when children merely respond to classroom assignments.

Some young children think of books as mystical objects, rather like they view milk as coming from bottles instead of cows. Children need to learn that books are the creation of individual human beings. According to Hall (1987), "children may see the writing and reading of stories as a more reasonable activity if they understand it to be a distinctly human activity" (p. 33).

Children learn to view themselves as authors when they have opportunities to visit other classrooms to read aloud stories they have written. In one school, children leave space at the end of their published books for comments by readers (Huck and Kirstetter, 1987). This practice reinforces pride in authorship and the anticipation that one's works will be read.

Conferring with others helps children use the class as an audience, to make choices and revise their writings (Calkins, 1985). In teacher–child conferences, teachers are tempted to give advice about children's writing. This takes authorship away from the child.

Good teacher–child conferences encourage both parties to discuss the piece and try out ideas, but the teacher is careful to ask questions instead of recommending changes. During content conferences, the teacher's main role is to listen and to repeat the child's story in a way that lets the child know the teacher is interested in hearing what s/he has written.

Calkins describes process conferences as a further step in using an audience in the writing process. After children learn to confer with the teacher and their peers, they naturally evolve into asking themselves questions which were once asked by others. Children confer with themselves, but their questions to themselves are not about the subject at all, but about writing strategies.

From "Authorship: A Key Facet of Whole Language" by L. L. Lamme, 1989, *The Reading Teacher, 42*, pp. 704–710. Copyright © 1989 by the International Reading Association. Reprinted with permission of Linda L. Lamme and the International Reading Association.

This use of audience during the writing process helps children refine their creativity and skills as authors naturally.

AUTHOR STUDIES

Good readers select books by authors. When they read a book they enjoy, they find other books written by that person.

Children at all age levels enjoy writing to authors, but when they are assigned to write, the letters become merely schoolwork. On the other hand, when a child has read as many of an author's books as s/he can find and wants to write a fan letter or ask questions about the books, writing to an author is a logical, meaningful, and personal activity.

One teacher reports that "Writing letters to children's authors has been a rewarding experience. Since [the children] considered themselves to be readers and writers they wrote with confidence about questions with which they had struggled. They wrote with pride about their own accomplishments because they too had published books" (Whitin, 1984).

Authors writing to authors is one activity that thoroughly integrates the reading–writing process.

One of the reading related activities most requested by children is meeting an author, yet few children have that opportunity. A 1st grade teacher writes about the tradition in Highland Park School, Columbus, Ohio, where each year an author visits the school (Huck & Kirstetter, 1987). She tells how one author visit was supported financially from selling old textbooks and a book fair. Prior to Pat Hutchins's visit, children throughout the school read her works and participated in reading related activities.

"On the day of Pat Hutchins's visit the children were exploding with ideas and questions. The walls and tables were covered with books. Pat spent the morning traveling from one class to another to view the displays and talk with the children. She ate lunch in the cafeteria, met with small groups, talked at an assembly, and autographed books... What an exciting way to make authors seem like real people to children..." (p. 38).

In a similar experience, Chapman (1985) reports what children learned after spending two days with poet Arnold Adoff. Chapman summarizes that they learned that authors are real people, "that authors try many drafts, and that one way to become a better writer is to experiment with words, with meanings, with shapes." In short, in a community of poets, they learned how to be poets.

If a school cannot raise the money to bring in a well known author, local authors are often available. Next best to having a live author or illustrator visit the classroom is showing a film or videotape. Many children's book authors and illustrators are featured on educational films.

One school exposes the children to an author's works throughout the year in a variety of ways. The children list questions they would like to ask the author. In the spring, during a 30 minute telephone conference, the questions are answered (Adams, 1984). Personal contact allows authors to become role models for children, who then become aspiring authors during the writing program.

Milz (1985) tells of a 1st grader's reaction to receiving a book from Santa Claus at a shopping mall. As Santa handed Maleeaka a book about himself, she requested that he autograph it for her. Clearly Maleeaka knows many people who write books (including herself and other students in her classroom) and that authors are often asked to autograph their work.

A SENSE OF AUDIENCE

In some classrooms children write only to the teacher as an audience. It doesn't take much ingenuity to discover that the teacher is somewhat less than enthusiastic about having to grade 30 papers. Writing in a Whole Language classroom takes on an entirely different perspective once children realize that the teacher is only one person in the audience and typically not the most important one.

Writing for publication emphasizes the process of writing which encourages revision, taking into consideration the audience for the piece. Children who haven't published write not for an audience but for critical readers whose intent is to correct and criticize their work. No wonder children in classrooms not exposed to process writing do little self generated writing.

Each child can play the role of both author and audience to other children's pieces, and this double role influences their writing. They write, and because they understand their own work, they at first assume that other readers—the audience—will receive it with the same understanding. This is called assumptive writing. Not until they change roles and become an audience do they understand that each person listens from his or her own perspective and background.

Children as authors use the ideas of their audience when revising their writing, and in turn, see their ideas used by other children in their revised pieces. By shifting from author to audience and back again, children learn to be perceptive readers and writers (Hubbard, 1985).

The following description of a child writing shows clearly the impact of audience. "Eight year old Greg is working industriously on a long story at his desk. He seems oblivious to the classroom noises and activity going on around him as he writes, rereads and edits. An observer would think him to be an outstanding student. In reality he is not always such a hard worker. Why then this dedication to a story? Greg knows that he has an audience for what he writes" (Boehm, 1986).

You can tell when children move from writing for the teacher to writing for their peers as an audience. Instead of asking the teacher, they begin to question each other. Graves and Hansen (1983) describe three stages in the developing understanding of authorship among 1st graders.

In the "replication phase" children conceive of authors as people who write books. At this stage they invent and imitate versions of writing.

In the "transition phase" children think of themselves as authors as their books are published and displayed alongside those of professionals.

And in the "option awareness phase," children perceive themselves as authors with the responsibility of making choices and decisions about their writing. This last phase is a direct result of author's chair, where children see a variety of opinions expressed as they share their own pieces.

It is vital that children confer with each other as they write and that much time and care be given to the sharing and display of children's writing. Some time should be set aside daily for children to read orally what they have written or are in the process of writing.

Polished writing can be shared in other classrooms. Children also enjoy reading a fine piece of their writing to the school principal. One principal called a child out of a classroom to read his excellent essay aloud to me, a visitor. After the boy read his piece, which was about his grandfather's terminal illness, the principal (whose mother was terminally ill) and the child talked about this difficult situation for another 10 minutes. How refreshing it was to see the adult and child talk as equals about a serious issue of concern to them both.

AUTHOR'S CHAIR

An integral part of the writing process is author's chair. "As writers, children struggle to put their thoughts on paper, and they talk about these thoughts with other writers. As readers, they compose messages and ask questions about published books. They play, they invent, they mimic, when they compose in reading and writing and sitting on the Author's Chair" (Graves & Hansen, 1983).

Author's chair plays a key role in the revision process by: (a) giving children feedback on their writing, (b) modeling content conferencing, and (c) developing a "community of authors" (Graves & Hansen, 1983).

Children come to author's chair with questions about their own writing. They typically sign up for turns at author's chair, and the audience treats the writer and the writing seriously. Children know that their ideas are valued because many of their ideas later turn up in the work of the authors they have helped.

Children learn how to be helpful responders in author's chair. They learn how to discover good qualities of a piece and to ask good questions about the content.

Since author's chair takes a lot of time, many teachers have children confer with each other about their writings. The advantage of author's chair is that the child receives many opinions and ideas from many children, whereas during individual conferences the author receives the comments of only one person. It is interesting, however, to watch children adapt author's chair questions to their individual revision process.

The classroom atmosphere is a powerful determinant of the amount and kinds of writing attempted there. Children need to feel one another's support in order to take the kinds of risks involved in the process of producing good writing. Author's chair, when conducted in a supportive manner, creates that kind of cooperative classroom atmosphere. Children become eager to write and share their writing. The class becomes a real "community of authors."

RESPONDING TO LITERATURE

Children who merely read basals and answer worksheet questions don't get the link between reading and writing; they don't face the issue of authorship by recognizing that what they read has been written by a person who is trying to entertain or inform them. Children who read but have no opportunities to share their reading with others, similarly have few opportunities to delve into the concept of authorship. But children who read and discuss what they read, and who have opportunities to recommend books to each other, frequently focus upon their favorite authors for these discussions.

There are many ways to organize literature response programs in a classroom. In literature logs, children can make written responses to what they read, recording a response daily or weekly. Responses can either be open ended personal reactions or structured responses to questions that later can be discussed with others.

Other written responses make nice displays, such as advertisements for books, posters related to books, and book reviews that can be kept on file in the media center.

Responses can be oral. Sharing time first thing in the morning allows young children to share the books that were read to them at home and then to trade books.

Book discussions take a variety of forms. Children can be asked to find a short passage to read to their literature share group, after which the other children ask questions about the book. Discussions can focus on issues or themes, especially if all the children are reading books of the same literary type.

In responding to literature, children often turn to the author as a person. They wonder why the author wrote the book, where the author came up with the ideas presented, how long it took to write, and where it was written. If they are writers themselves, they wonder how the book was written—on a computer, by hand, or by typewriter—and how many drafts and revisions were needed. And children wonder about the person who wrote the book. What is s/he like? Where does s/he live? Does s/he have children or pets?

One teacher invited her students to make a list of their thoughts about Molly Bang after reading a number of her books. The children's responses revealed the fact that they had not only read and enjoyed her books, they had begun to view Molly Bang as a person. Here are some of their predictions:

"I think Molly Bang likes strawberries" (from *The Grey Lady and the Strawberry Snatcher*).

"I think Molly Bang likes cats" (from *The Grey Lady* and *Ten Nine Eight*).

"I think Molly Bang has lived in other countries and likes to travel" (from *Tye May and the Magic Brush*, and other folktales).

"I think Molly Bang makes quilts" (from a quilt in virtually every Molly Bang book).

"I think Molly Bang likes to tell stories" (from the many stories and folktales she has told).

"I think Molly Bang has a little girl" (from *Ten, Nine, Eight*).

"I think Molly Bang likes the sea" (from *Dawn*, a seashell mobile in *Ten, Nine, Eight*, and a horseshoe crab on the wall of the home in *The Grey Lady and the Strawberry Snatcher*).

"I think Molly Bang lives up North" (from snow in the window in *Ten, Nine, Eight*).

Children who are themselves authors have experienced the fact that knowing an author well explains a lot about a story. To learn more about children's book authors, teachers can consult one of the many sources in the reference section of a library. School media center staff can purchase reference books about children's book authors as a way to support a Whole Language curriculum.

Hansen (1983) says young authors need to respond to other authors if they are to make the important connection between reading and writing. "Authors who share their own writing and who ask other authors questions experience connections between reading and writing," claims Hansen.

She describes four different response situations: (1) Response to unfinished pieces (as in author's chair), (2) response to an author's published piece, (3) response to other students' published books, and (4) response to books written by professional authors. All four of these situations should occur in the classroom to help children develop a sense of authorship.

Smith (1983) comments that children who are writers read differently from other children. The student authors read stories, poems, and letters as though they themselves could produce these writings. They write vicariously with the authors.

Smith believes that "School should be a place where children are initiated into the club of writers as soon as possible, with full rights and privileges even as apprentices. They will read like writers, and acquire full status in the club (of writers), if they are not denied admission at the threshold."

PUBLISHING CHILDREN'S WRITING

Children enjoy having their writings published as books. If we want children to write, we need to treat them as writers. "That means treating students to that final and ultimate writerly pleasure of finding their words come alive in the faces of their listeners and their readers" (Willinsky, 1985).

In some schools, parent volunteers set up a "publishing house" to assist teachers. A binding machine is a worthwhile investment, for it saves an enormous amount of time for both teacher and child, creating bindings out of cardboard and Contac paper or fabric. We need to make it as easy as possible for children to publish their writing and for teachers to help child authors come to publication with their writing.

Individual child authored books that are nicely bound make wonderful holiday gifts after most of the children in the class have read them as a part of the classroom collection. Books can contain one illustrated story with a bit of text written on each page, or they can be a collection of the child's best writings.

If teachers can get a volunteer or secretary to do the typing, books have a more polished appearance. By 5th grade children should have the opportunity to master word processing skills so that they can type their own books. On the other hand, parents of young children enjoy reading their children's own handwriting.

Collections of children's writings make wonderful class reading. Not every child in the class needs to be represented in each collection book. In fact, publishing poor writing makes a mockery of process writing. Some collections are like literary magazines—just collections of children's best writings in all different forms and on all different topics.

Other collection books focus on a topic. Some of these might come spontaneously from writing workshop, where, when one child writes about a pet, another gets the same idea and you end up with a spate of pet stories or He Man stories or scary stories at Halloween.

Others can be written by design. Children learn science and social studies content far better when they write about what they are studying, in a sense publishing their own textbooks.

These books need to be carefully bound and laminated so that they can withstand heavy classroom use. Some can be taken apart and the pages sent home with the children at the end of the year.

YOUNG AUTHOR CONFERENCES

Some schools or school districts run writing competitions. The author of the best homemade book in each classroom gets to attend a young author conference.

Other schools follow a better policy of arranging for all of the children in the school to attend the conference (Harste, Short, & Burke, 1988). At the conference a published children's book author gives a talk and there are workshops on writing where the children confer with each other about being authors. The children's books are displayed, then put in their school libraries for others to read.

There is no doubt that "a program that encourages youngsters to write and publish their own books improves the writing and storytelling abilities of the youngsters" (Wetzel, Davis, & Jamsa, 1983). Children benefit from book formatting and binding activities. Some handwrite their books; others type them. Some illustrate their own stories; others have them illustrated. Some enjoy creating elaborate and creative bindings; others use a binding machine. The actual binding process adds value to the child's composition.

Some people question the need or value of writing competitions. After all, the rewards for becoming an author are publication and the internal satisfaction that comes from sharing one's ideas. Yet public acknowledgment of good writing helps build an awareness of the importance of writing. Just as there is value in awards for athletic or musical accomplishments, writing awards serve to reward hard effort.

Local businesses support young author conferences by bringing an adult author to town and by providing lunch for participants. Business sponsorship is another similarity to athletic award programs.

Probably the main contribution of young author conferences to the process writing curriculum is that they generate excitement about writing and promote more writing in classrooms.

COMMUNITY OF AUTHORS

The concept of authorship brings a vital dimension to reading and writing. Readers who are writers read in qualitatively different ways, and readily recognize the authors of books that they read. Writers view themselves as authors and value the interaction with their audience in the process of writing.

The most powerful influence of authorship to a process writing program is the "community of authors" feeling—the writers' club—to which everyone in the class belongs. The cooperative, caring classroom environment in which conferencing and author's chair occur and where children share and respond to literature is a supportive environment where children's reading and writing can flourish.

REFERENCES

Adams, Jane T. "Connecting with a Children's Author." *The Reading Teacher,* vol. 37 (April 1984), pp. 722–23.

Boehm, N. "Opening a Publishing House in Your Classroom." *Early Years: Teaching K–8,* vol. 16 (April 1986), p. 57.

Calkins, Lucy. "Learning to Think through Writing." In *Observing the Language Learner,* edited by Angela Jaggar and M. Trika Smith-Burke. Newark, DE: International Reading Association, 1985.

Chapman, Diane. "Poet to Poet: An Author Responds to Child-Writers." *Language Arts,* vol. 62 (March 1985), pp. 235–42.

Graves, Donald, and Jane Hansen. "The Author's Chair." *Language Arts,* vol. 60 (February 1983), pp. 176–83.

Hall, Nigel. *The Emergence of Literacy.* Portsmouth, NH: Heinemann, 1987.

Hansen, Jane. "Authors Respond to Authors." *Language Arts,* vol. 60 (November/December 1983) pp. 970–76.

Harste, Jerome C., Kathy G. Short, and Carolyn Burke. *Creating Classrooms for Authors.* Portsmouth, NH: Heinemann, 1988.

Hubbard, Ruth. "Second Graders Answer the Question, 'Why Publish?' " *The Reading Teacher,* vol. 38 (March 1985), pp. 658–62.

Huck, Charlotte S., and Kristen Jeffers Kirstetter. "Developing Readers." In *Children's Literature in the Reading Program,* edited by Bernice E. Cullinan. Newark, DE: International Reading Association, 1987.

Milz, Vera. "First Graders' Uses for Writing." In *Observing the Language Learner,* by Angela Jaggar and M. Trika Smith-Burke. Newark, DE: International Reading Association, 1985.

Smith, Frank. "Reading like a Writer." *Language Arts,* vol. 60 (May 1983), pp. 558–67.

Wetzel, Norman R., Lorri Davis, and Elizabeth Jamsa. "Young Authors Conference." *The Reading Teacher,* vol. 36 (February 1983), pp. 530–32.

Whitin, David J. "Children and Children's Authors." *Language Arts,* vol. 61 (December 1984), pp. 813–21.

Willinsky, John. "To Publish and Publish and Publish." *Language Arts,* vol. 62 (October 1985), pp. 619–23.

Linda Leonard Lamme is a faculty member in the Department of Curriculum and Instruction at the University of Florida in Gainesville.

The Reading/Writing Connection in Whole Language

Martha Grindler
Beverly Stratton

A report based on the National Assessment of Educational Progress, "Who Reads Best?" (Applebee, Langer and Mullis, 1988) states that "Recommendations for good teaching include moving from an overwhelming emphasis on basal readers and workbooks, toward a greater emphasis on comprehension strategies, a wider range of high quality reading materials, more independent reading for children and more opportunities for combining reading and writing activities" (pp. 5–6).

A great deal of space in reading and language arts journals and a large number of presentations at national conferences are devoted to discussions of whole language approaches. What is whole language teaching and what is its function in language development? Is whole language just another educational "buzzword" that will run its course and fade out in the next decade?

The focus of this article is to identify, in general, the whole language movement and in particular the part reading and writing play in this approach.

WHOLE LANGUAGE

Whole language instruction has been gaining a foothold in schools over the past five years (Shanklin & Rhodes, 1988). It is a philosophy that suggests that children learn language skills by following the natural learning behavior that governs the way they learn to talk (Ferguson, 1988). Children are immersed in language through reading, writing, and listening to stories while reading behavior emerges naturally.

Based on research by Michael Halliday, Kenneth Goodman, and Donald Graves, whole language teaching does away with basal readers and traditional teaching methods by keeping language whole. Emphasis is on the natural purpose of language which is communicating meaning. It allows for functional and purposeful language in meeting children's needs. Language is learned more easily when it is whole, functional, and meaningful (Goodman, 1986).

Weir and Benegar (1985) reported on a whole language approach in a transitional first grade at Stein Elementary School in Jefferson County, Colorado. A language experience approach for teaching beginning reading was used. The children learned to read from stories they composed together. Reading skills to be taught were derived from their stories, not from isolated workbook pages and skill sheets. The teachers discovered that as the year ended, there was a high quality of emotional commitment to writing and to reading. Writing and reading were connected; learning to write and learning to read were natural evolutionary processes which grew out of the students' need to express important ideas.

READING AND WRITING IN WHOLE LANGUAGE

Emergent literacy is a belief that a child's literacy develops very early in life and that reading and writing develop concurrently and interrelatedly rather than sequentially (Kline, 1988). Parents and early childhood educators note that even very young children read and write.

From "The Reading/Writing Connection in Whole Language" by M. Grindler and B. Stratton, 1991, *Ohio Reading Teacher*, 25, pp. 11–14. Permission granted by the *Ohio Reading Teacher*.

Among educators it is generally accepted that there is an important relationship between reading and writing. Despite much research in this area, Jaggar, Carrara and Weiss (1986) state that the nature of the relationship is unclear. They conclude that most research on the reading–writing relationship has been correlational and experimental in nature and has ignored the instructional context. As a result, it provides little information about what children learn from their reading that influences their writing and what they learn from their writing that influences their reading.

Even though common sense suggests some connecting links between reading and writing, what has happened in the classroom over the last thirty years does not attend to that connection. Reading typically dominates the scene in the language arts program with an emphasis on teaching discrete, isolated subskills. Children spend more time on workbook pages and skill sheets than on actual reading. And there is often no relationship between the story read in the basal and the activities which accompany the story.

Within the last decade, researchers and teachers are beginning to question traditional approaches in the classroom and to realize that reading and writing are closely linked. Beginning in kindergarten, children compose stories and learn to read from their writing and from shared writings of classmates. This Language Experience Approach (LEA) builds bridges to reading and written composition in a whole language activity. Children begin to see reading as simply "talk written down," a technique that suggests children do learn to read by writing.

Writing To Read, an innovative beginning to read program, also supports the reading/writing connection. Combining reading, writing, and computers, this approach has now reached an estimated 400,000 students worldwide, according to John Henry Martin (1986), the program's developer. While national statistics show less than 25 percent of children in kindergarten can write their own names, two-thirds of kindergartners using Writing to Read are producing whole written passages. Martin describes this IBM marketed program as representing a departure from traditional notions about learning to read. Instead, children learn at five separate stations in a multisensory environment using computers, tape recorders with headsets, as well as paper and pencil.

READING/WRITING CONNECTION

What is the connection between reading and writing? Charles Chew (1985) contends that both processes are similar and complementary:

- Reading and writing are expressions of oral language.
- Reading and writing are processes.
- Reading and writing are based on whole pieces of text.
- The reader and the writer bring meaning to the text.
- The errors of readers and writers have meaning.

Lesley Morrow (1989) sees a strong relationship between reading and writing:

- Writers construct meanings by constructing texts; readers reconstruct texts by constructing anticipated meanings.
- Children teach themselves to write in much the same way they teach themselves to read: experimentally. By experimenting with writing, children construct and refine the kind of knowledge about written language that makes reading possible.
- As children write, they integrate knowledge of reading with knowledge of writing.

Children's rereading of their own writing becomes an important step in developing their reading skills. In this way, children shift back and forth from reader to writer and vice versa. An integral part of this process is the author's chair. Children come to the author's chair to share their writing with the class. Questions about their own writing arise and many opinions and ideas from a real audience are received. If the teacher encourages a supportive environment children are eager to share their writing in this cooperative atmosphere. Since children serve as both author and audience, the dual role influences their reading and writing.

Smith (1983) comments that the children who are writers read differently from other children. The student authors read stories, poems, and letters as though they themselves could produce these writings. They write vicariously with the authors. As literate adults, how often do we read a children's book, a novel, or an article in our professional journals and exclaim, "I could have written this!"

WHAT NEEDS TO BE DONE?

For reading and writing to provide a functional approach to language development, a number of considerations should be addressed. The following recommendations should offer a beginning for teachers:

- Children know a lot about oral language, reading and writing. Start with what they already know. Include them in the responsibility of learning.
- Set time aside regularly for children to experiment with writing. Time must be available for reading their work with classmates and with you.
- Respond to children's writing in a positive way. Talk about content first, then work towards proper form, spelling, grammar, and punctuation.
- Make writing part of the teacher's day as well as the students'. Model writing by writing yourself. Share your work with the children on an overhead projector and show them where you had trouble in the process.
- If children work from points of familiarity such as fairy tales, poems, nursery rhymes, and well known stories, they will feel more confident and secure in their own writing.
- Allow time for reflection or "incubation" in which children can mull over and think about what they have written. Often children consider writing a one-step process from start to finish. Show them your edited rewrites.
- Teach children that you are not their only audience but only one person in that audience. It is important that children confer with each other and care should be given to sharing their writing. The collaboration which occurs in the reading/writing classroom encourages a cooperative spirit.
- Begin to write to authors as a class. This personal experience works best after reading a number of the published author's works.
- Be a risk taker and encourage risk taking in your classroom. Mistakes will occur not only as a part of your students' natural growth and development but yours as well.
- For teachers who cannot totally eliminate the basal readers or for those who feel strongly about keeping the basal in their classroom, don't feel guilty. Try an integrated approach; combine aspects of whole language with traditional approaches to fit your own personal needs and those of your students.
- Be patient. Ferguson (1988) suggests that adapting whole language requires at least five years. Begin by incorporating into your classroom those elements of whole language which you support the most. Keep an open mind and an open door—let parents, administrators and other teachers join you in your quest for an environment that is conducive to language development.

REFERENCES

Applebee, A. N. Langer, J. A., & Mullis, I. S. (1988). *Who reads best?* Princeton, NJ: Educational Testing Service.

Chew, C. (1985). Instruction can link reading and writing in the elementary school. In J. Hansen, T. Newkirk & D. Graves (Eds.), *Breaking ground: Teachers relate reading and writing in the elementary school* (pp. 169–173). Portsmouth, NH: Heinemann Educational Books, Inc.

Ferguson, P. (1988). Whole language: A global approach to learning. *Instructor, 97,* 24–27.

Goodman, K. S. (1986). Basal readers: A call for action. *Language Arts, 63,* 358–363.

Jaggar, A. M., Carrara D. H., & Weiss, S. E. (1986). Research currents: The influence of reading on children's narrative writing (and vice versa). *Language Arts, 63,* 292–300.

Kline, L. W. (June, 1988). Reading: Whole language development. Renewed focus on literature spurs change. *ASCD Curriculum Update.*

Martin, J. H., & Friedberg, A. (1986). *Writing to read.* New York: Warner Books.

Morrow, L. M. (1989). *Literacy development in the early years.* Englewood Cliffs, NJ: Prentice Hall.

Shanklin, N. L., & Rhodes, L. K. (1988). Transforming literacy instruction. *Educational Leadership, 46,* 59–63.

Smith, F. (1983). Reading like a writer. *Language Arts, 60,* 558–567.

Weir, L., & Benegar, C. (1985). Using a whole language approach in a transitional first grade. *Early Years, 15,* 52–54.

Martha Grindler and Beverly Stratton are both faculty members of the Department of Early Childhood and Reading at Georgia State.

The What, Why, When and How of Reading Response Journals

Julia Shinneman Fulps
Terrell A. Young

Today much student time is spent in preparation for mandated reading and writing tests. Consequently, students rarely get a chance to generate their own meanings as they read and compose from their own thoughts as they write. Ruth (1987) points out the need to present opportunities for students to ask and answer real questions of their own about reading and writing. Reading response journals provide students with an opportunity to respond and interpret their reading personally.

Reading response journals are informal, written communications between two or more people about something one person has read about. These journals can include personal reactions to, questions about, and reflections on what has been read (Parsons, 1990). Students can respond to what they've read, or, to what has been read to them. Even kindergarten and first grade students can respond to a story using illustrations, scribbles, random letters, and invented spellings (Farris, 1989; Hipple, 1985).

WHY USE READING RESPONSE JOURNALS?

All students can experience success in responding to literature regardless of reading ability. One of the primary benefits of reading response journals is increased comprehension. Reading response journals enable students to grow as readers and writers by requiring them to use their own background knowledge to construct personal meaning (Wollman-Bonilla,

From "The What, Why, When and How of Reading Response Journals" by J. S. Fulps and T. A. Young, 1991, *Reading Horizons, 32,* pp. 109–116. Copyright © 1991 by Western Michigan University. Reprinted by permission.

1989) and by encouraging, in writing, the integration of new experiences with past ones. Besides transforming feelings and thoughts about what they've read into words (Strackbein & Tillman, 1987), responses allow students to make the personal connection to texts (Simpson, 1986). In addition, Kelly (1990) reported that her third grade students displayed increased fluency and greater detail as a result of responding in journals. Besides developing children's understanding of reading strategies, comprehension, knowledge of literature and their ability to communicate and refine ideas, often the most striking development is students' growth in confidence, and motivation to read. Furthermore, reading response journals are an excellent means of recording how students' writing has changed and matured, and a valuable means of catching up on new literature that the students are reading (Strackbein & Tillman, 1987).

Reading response journals are not only for responding to independent reading and reading in the language arts block. They can also be used during shared reading time. In this manner, listening skills are sharpened. However, Parsons (1990) cautions that too much writing can strangle a read aloud program. When used in other content areas, response journals pay off with increased learning (Fulwiler, 1987; Smith, 1988). Smith cites several research studies which have favored written responses over reading alone as a study technique. As readers put what was read into their own words, they take ownership of what was read. The ownership and increased understanding result in better test results.

WHAT DO THE JOURNALS LOOK LIKE?

There is no one physical appearance for reading response journals. Likewise, content can vary, as can the format that these responses take. Below are some suggestions for design, content, and format of reading response journals. Teachers should look to see which of these will best fit their needs and the needs of their students. The suggestions can be adapted in order to make journals fit the needs of the class.

Design

Reading response journals can be as simple as a few pages stapled together. Some teachers choose to fold $8\frac{1}{2}'' \times 11''$ sheets in half and sew them down the middle, while others prefer a spiral notebook. Teachers who have tried both homemade and spiral notebooks report that in addition to saving time and materials, the spiral notebooks make the journals seem more like the "real thing" to students (Harste, Short, & Burke, 1988). For younger students who are responding to their reading through illustrations and writing, blank artist's spirals are an ideal solution. Whatever style of journal is used, students should be encouraged to decorate their reading response journals to make them their own. Brewster (1988) encourages students to use colored ink pens or scented markers when writing their entries. This further encourages students to be creative and frees them from what is usually done in the classroom with standard writing instruments.

Format

Often the format for a response will depend on the response that the teacher is requesting. Reed (1988) suggests that the teacher encourage students to think and write as they read. Besides the traditional paragraph format, some teachers prefer that their student react to their reading in a letter format (Atwell, 1987; Five, 1988). These letters can be addressed to the author, a character in their reading, or the teacher. Another format is a half-page entry. The students divide their sheets in half (length-wise). On one half they write a sentence or phrase that they liked from the book. Then on the other half they react to what they've written—how they felt when they read the passage, why they like it, or why they decided to write that phrase down. In order to help sustain motivation, the teacher can vary the format every couple of weeks (Brewster, 1988).

There are a variety of formats that readers may choose to use when responding to their reading texts. The list in Figure 1 was compiled from several sources (Atwell, 1990; Tompkins, 1990b; Tschudi & Tschudi, 1983).

Content

Regardless of the different types of content within reading response journals, three items should appear on each page: the date, the title, and the author of the book. Title and author are needed so that students and teacher can refer to the book later (Parsons, 1990). The content of a reading response journal can be decided by the teacher or left up to the students to decide. Initially the teacher might suggest the students react to the reading in a specific way: from a different point-of-view, by altering the time and setting of the story, alternating knowledge and opinion entries, by using drawings instead of words, or relating what they've read to an experience they've had that was similar. After several weeks (and a variety of reactions) teachers should allow the students to decide how they will respond to their reading (Strackbein & Tillman, 1987). As students become more independent and begin to accept their autonomy in the reading process, they should be guided away from a reliance on prompts (Parsons, 1990). It is important for teachers to remember that response journals allow for different interpretations of text depending on what the readers bring to the reading. If the teachers opt to use questions or prompts to direct students' responses, they should be broad and open-ended (Kelly, 1990); thus the questions should encourage students to develop their own meaning rather than teachers' desired interpretation (Wollman-Bonilla, 1989).

WHAT IS THE TEACHER'S ROLE?

Much of the success (and failure) of reading response journals lies with the teacher and the

ABC books	ads/commercials	"All About ____" books
anecdotes	biographies	book reviews
brainstormed list	calendars	cartoons/comics
catalogs	charts	diagrams
clusters	coloring books	comparisons
five senses clusters	five senses poems	games
greeting cards	interviews	journals—simulated
letters—business	letters—friendly	letters—simulated
lifelines/time lines	maps	newspapers
newspapers	oral histories	poetry
predictions	RAFTs (Dueck, 1986)	raps
resumes	riddles	songs
telegrams	word searches	wordless picture books

FIGURE 1

RMATS FOR READER RESPONSES

teacher's responses to what the students have written. Wollman-Bonilla (1989) reports that children invest more interest and energy in journal writing when their teacher writes back to them. When responding to what students have written in their reading response journals, it is best to comment informally as one might comment in dialogue journals (Kelly, 1990). And these should be responses—not a smiley face, a "GREAT!" or an "I agree." Strackbein and Tillman (1987) believe three or four sentences that respond positively and specifically to the writer's content will encourage the students to share their ideas and questions far more than a smiley face will. Wollman-Bonilla (1989) further suggests that the teacher affirm ideas and feelings, provide information, request information related to students' responses, model elaboration, and guide students to examine their ideas as they discover new insights.

It is important that the teacher's responses be focused on the depth of thinking, rather than the mechanics of writing (Simpson, 1986; Strackbein, 1987). Otherwise there is no real request for reflection, but instead the journal becomes a vehicle to display the student's mechanical knowledge. Ruth (1987) points out that if the teacher's response is only to the mechanics and failures to approximate adult models of writing, then children's real accomplishments in relation to their purposes and intentions may be overlooked. Teachers may model correct usage in their responses, but they should *not* correct the students' actual entries.

Naturally, teachers should also write in a journal (whenever the students are asked to write in class). This shows students that journal writing is valued by teachers. Ideally, journals would be collected and responded to on a daily basis. This is often not practical, however, and teachers should schedule a way to respond on a regular basis. Keeping the reading response journals in a box or in one location makes them easier to manage (Simpson, 1986).

HOW DOES ONE BEGIN?

When beginning to use reading response journals, the first task is to encourage students to go beyond simple retrieval of information, and instead, to take risks when interpreting what they read. This can be accomplished most effectively by beginning with a group entry. Teachers first encourage the students to *respond* to rather than summarize some text that all of the students have experienced through reading or listening (Tompkins, 1990a). Then, teachers can solicit oral responses. The oral responses allow the students to hear each other's thoughts about the story and also provide the teacher with the opportunity to model that all responses are valid. Predictably, students at first will say what they think the teacher wants to hear. As students become convinced that there are no right or wrong answers, they will begin commenting and predicting because they have the assurance that their *ideas* are important (Simpson, 1986). Finally, this oral presentation provides a framework and practice for future opportunities to respond to literature (Kelly, 1990). Once the class has made the move to written responses, students should still be given the opportunity to share with the class their written responses orally.

WRAPPING IT ALL UP

Reading response journals provide a teacher with a means of looking inside students' minds to view their understanding of what was read. In addition, these journals foster students' ability to connect literature with their own lives and therefore increase comprehension. With a carefully modeled introduction, management, and thoughtful teacher responses, reading response journals can work in any classroom. The rewards for students will more than make up for the time and effort of their teachers.

REFERENCES

Atwell, N. (1987). *In the middle: Writing, reading, and learning with adolescents.* Portsmouth NH: Boynton Cook.

Atwell, N. (1990). *Coming to know: Writing to learn in the intermediate grades.* Portsmouth NH: Heinemann.

Brewster, M. (1988). Ten ways to revive tired learning logs. *English Journal, 77,* 57.

Dueck, K. (1986). RAFT: Writing. *Kappa Delta Pi Record, 22,* 64.

Farris, P. (1989). Story time and story journals: Linking literature and writing. *The New Advocate, 2,* 179–185.

Five, C. L. (1988). From workbook to workshop: Increasing children's involvement in the reading process. *The New Advocate, 1,* 103–113.

Fulwiler, T. (Ed.). (1987). Guidelines for using journals in school settings. *The journal book.* Portsmouth NH: Boynton/Cook.

Harste, J., Short, K., & Burke, C. (1988). *Creating classrooms for authors.* Portsmouth NH: Heinemann.

Hipple, M. (1985). Journal writing in kindergarten. *Language Arts, 62,* 255–261.

Kelly, P. (1990). Guiding young students' response to literature. *The Reading Teacher, 43,* 464–470.

Parsons, L. (1990). *Response journals.* Portsmouth NH: Heinemann.

Reed, S. D. (1988). Logs: Keeping an open mind. *English Journal, 77,* 52–56.

Ruth, L. (1987). Reading children's writing. *The Reading Teacher, 40,* 756–760.

Simpson, M. K. (1986). A teacher's gift: Oral reading and the reading response journal. *Journal of Reading, 28,* 45–50.

Smith, C. B. (1988). Does it help to write about your reading? *Journal of Reading, 30,* 276–277.

Strackbein, D., & Tillman, M. (1987). The joy of journals—with reservations. *Journal of Reading, 29,* 28–31.

Tompkins, G. E. (1990a). The literature connection: How one teacher puts reading and writing together. In T. Shanahan (Ed.), *Reading and writing together: New perspectives for the classroom,* 201–223. Norwood MA: Christopher-Gordon.

Tompkins, G. E. (1990b). *Writing: Balancing process and product.* Columbus OH: Merrill.

Tschudi, S. N., & Tschudi, S. J. (1983). *Teaching writing in the content areas: Elementary.* Washington DC: National Education Association.

Wollman-Bonilla, J. E. (1989). Reading journals: Invitations to participate in literature. *The Reading Teacher, 43,* 112–120.

Julia Shinneman Fulps is an elementary school teacher in the Arlington Independent School District in Arlington, Texas. Terrell A. Young is a faculty member in the Department of Literacy Education at Washington State University in Richland, Washington.

Is There a Place for Computers in Whole Language Classrooms?

Linda DeGroff

Are you a whole language teacher? Or are you interested in adopting whole language practices in your classroom? If so, you may have wondered how computers can facilitate teaching and learning in ways that are consistent with your existing beliefs and goals.

For whole language teachers, as for other good teachers, it is the teacher's beliefs about curriculum and instruction rather than technology that will determine the role of the computer in the classroom. With that in mind, I have selected six points of belief commonly held by whole language teachers and considered how computers can facilitate teaching and learning in ways that are consistent with those points of belief.

From "Is There a Place for Computers in Whole Language Classrooms?" by L. DeGroff, 1990, *The Reading Teacher, 43,* pp. 568–572. Copyright © 1990 by the International Reading Association. Reprinted with permission of Linda DeGroff and the International Reading Association.

SOCIAL INTERACTION

Whole language theories and practices have been greatly influenced by the work of Vygotsky (1962), who explained how children's language learning begins with social interaction. If whole language teachers believe that children must interact with each other and with more capable adults in order to learn to read, write, speak, and listen, then teachers will want to know how computers can facilitate such interaction.

Recent investigations have illustrated the rich social interactions that occur when children use computers (Cochran-Smith, Kahn, & Paris, 1988; Daiute, 1983). Interaction around computers happens in diverse instructional contexts. Children talk to each other during language arts lessons (Dickinson, 1986) and during Logo (IBM) programming lessons (Genishi, 1988). The nature and frequency of interaction depends less on the software being used than on the ways in which teachers encourage or allow children to work with computers.

Forming new participant structures with pairs of children working together at one computer is one way to increase interaction (Mehan, 1989). Sometimes pairs are necessary when access to computers is limited; at other times, pairs are voluntary and self-selected. In either case, when children work in pairs at the computer, learning through interaction seems inevitable.

The upright, larger-than-paper, and sometimes colorful computer screen also has been shown to stimulate interaction (Silvern, 1988). As Cochran-Smith et al. (1988) explain, "The public screen is apparently irresistible" (p. 64). As children and teachers pass by the screen or wait for turns, they talk spontaneously about writing and graphics displayed on computer screens (Bruce, Michaels, & Watson-Gegeo, 1985). Public printer terminals also provide similar opportunities for learning through interaction.

WHOLE AND MEANINGFUL TEXTS

We all know how good computers can be at spitting out multiple choice questions, informing us in microseconds of our errors, branching us to remedial instruction, then giving us a second chance to respond correctly, and finally rewarding us with a beep or a blink when we get the answer right. This image of the computer may not appeal to whole language teachers, but this is not all that computers offer.

Computers also can be a medium for reading and writing whole and meaningful texts. At the computer, children read instructions and messages (Genishi, McCollum, & Strand, 1985), follow directions to games (Costanzo, 1985), or read stories and informational literature (Leu, 1988). Children also can write anything at the computer that they can write with pencil and paper. Even the youngest children have been successful at using word processors for writing personal narratives and imaginative stories (Phenix & Hannan, 1984). And word processing software is available for writers of all ages: for example, FirstWriter (Houghton Mifflin) for primary grade students; Bank Street Writer (Broderbund) for intermediate grade students.

In other whole language classrooms, Newman (1989) explains how children have organized notes and data for writing reports with database software such as Appleworks (South-Western). And Bruce et al. (1985) have shown how children share stories and newsletters when computers in different classrooms and schools are linked by networks or electronic mail systems such as QUILL (D.C. Heath). When teachers use these reports, stories, and newsletters as reading materials, children make connections between reading and writing.

REAL PURPOSES AND AUDIENCES

In the world outside of school, we seldom read to answer comprehension questions or copy other writers' sentences in order to practice punctuating. Instead we read to have our emotions stirred, to be entertained, to learn about other people and how they live, or to acquire information. We write to express our thoughts and organize our lives, or we write to communicate, entertain, and inform friends, colleagues, or distant readers. In whole language classrooms, reading and writing are done for these real-world purposes and audiences.

Computers facilitate reading and writing for real purposes when they involve whole and meaningful texts. In addition to opportunities for purposeful reading and writing, the experience of learning how to use computers provides opportunities for using purposeful oral language with real audiences.

Genishi (1988) observed pairs of kindergarten children as they learned Logo, a programming language. She found that children's talk focused on their tasks. The audiences for their talk were each other rather than the computer or the teacher. And their talk was cooperative rather than argumentative.

If teachers believe that actively using language in purposeful situations is important for language development, then using computers may help teachers reach their goals.

PROCESS APPROACHES

The idea of a process approach to teaching and learning has been most prominent in writing instruction (Graves, 1983). In process-approach classrooms, children learn to write by actively engaging in writing whole and meaningful texts. Children select their own topics, write drafts, interact in conferences, revise, edit, and publish their work for real audiences.

Word processors offer many functions that have the power to facilitate writing processes. With word processors, writers can easily revise and edit their drafts. Whole sections of writing can be moved for large-scale reorganization, and other sections can be added or deleted. Wording, spelling, and punctuation, for example, are easily edited. Saving a sequence of drafts as separate files makes it possible to compare drafts in conferences. The ability to mail or print copies of drafts gives writers the opportunity to receive responses to their work that may aid revision. Mailing and printing options also facilitate publishing.

At present, we understand very little about the effects of using these word processing functions on individual elementary school children's writing processes. A larger, more important understanding, however, is becoming increasingly clear: It is teachers' beliefs about writing and writing with computers, rather than the technology itself, that makes a difference in how instruction proceeds.

Mehan (1989) examined how computers were used in four classrooms from Grades 2 to 6. Before the research began, the teachers were already teaching writing as a process. When computers were made available to the teachers to use in their classrooms, the teachers used the computers to help them reach existing goals for their writing process classrooms. The teachers taught writing, not computing, and they taught in ways that were consistent with their established beliefs about teaching and learning to write.

In another study of the ways that computers were used in writing instruction, Cochran-Smith et al. (1988) observed writing with word processors in nine classrooms from kindergarten to fourth grade. The researchers concluded that teachers taught writing with word processors in ways that were consistent with how they generally taught writing. When teachers had an understanding of the recursive nature of writing processes, this understanding was reflected in how they taught writing with word processors. Children wrote with word processors, moving between drafting, conferring, and revising, based on their needs rather than on a step-by-step schedule set by either the teacher or the computer.

The findings of these studies should be good news for teachers who are already emphasizing processes in their writing instruction. For these teachers, the most important elements for good instruction are already in place. Writing-process teachers' beliefs will guide their practices; computers help them achieve their goals.

TIME AND CHOICE

For years, researchers have observed children learning to speak and comprehend their native languages (Genishi & Dyson, 1984). From these observations, we now know that children learn language at varying rates. We also know that the sequence of language learning is similar but not identical for all children. Children construct understandings of their native languages by choosing what to learn and working on it at their own paces. They do this without instruction and without adults (or machines) telling them what to learn next or how quickly they should work.

Whole language teachers understand children's need for time and choice in language learning. If whole language teachers are to use computers in their classrooms, they need assurances that it will be the children, rather than the computer, who will be controlling time and choice.

Notice that the software mentioned so far in this article has not been the drill and practice variety that in the worst cases can take control of time and choice away from children. Instead, most of the software mentioned has been from the group of software usually referred to as "tools"—word processing software, database software, networking systems, and electronic mailing software.

When we give children computer tools for language learning, the children determine what to read and write, and they set their own paces. For example, when children write with word processors, the machine sits as patiently as a pile of blank sheets of paper. The child determines what to write on the paper and how quickly to write and rewrite. When children use database software, the computer resembles a vast empty file cabinet, waiting for the child to fill it with information. When the child is ready, he or she returns to reorganize or to retrieve only that information that is important to current work. Networking systems and electronic mail programs serve the way telephones and the postal system do. Children choose what to read or write and do so for as often or as long as is necessary.

This is not to say that time is never a constraint when children use computers. At a recent workshop on using computers in whole language classrooms, I asked teachers if they were using computers and if not, why not? A chorus of voices replied, "We don't have enough access to computers." When access to computers is limited, children do not have ample time for language learning with computers.

The 1986 report of the National Assessment of Educational Progress states that only 25% of third-grade students have *ever* used a computer in reading and language arts (LaPointe & Martinez, 1988). The report concludes that access to computers is a serious problem in our schools. What can whole language teachers do to give children time for language learning with computers when access is limited?

One temporary solution is to cluster time at the computer. By clustering time into a few weeks or months, children can depend on the availability of word processors or databases. And how do teachers get clusters of time? They bargain for it. If a teacher or a group of teachers within a school would normally get a computer for the classroom one day a week, the teachers each would have the computer for one fifth of the school year. The teachers bargain to have the computer for 8 weeks in a row rather than 40 Fridays throughout the year.

But clustering time is only a temporary solution. We must use evidence of demonstrated successes with computers in whole language classrooms to bargain for more computers. The goal should be a level of access that assures all students of time for learning throughout the year.

RISK TAKING

Observations of young children have also shown us that risk taking is essential to language learning (Goodman, 1986). Children learn by trying out their developing understandings of how language works. When they stretch to reach new levels of competence, they learn from both their successes and errors. This is also true of language learning in classrooms. If elementary school children are to grow as language users, they must be encouraged and supported as risk takers (Allen & Mason, 1989).

Much of the drill and practice software available for elementary classrooms is designed to identify children's errors. But this is not the case with the software tools. For example, when children write with word processors, the computer accepts their invented spellings or less-than-conventional punctuation. The children, not the computer, identify aspects of writing that are within their capacity to change. When the children understand that change is easy with the word processor, they are more willing to take chances with their writing (Phenix & Hannan, 1984). Taking chances and making changes are no longer synonymous with the dreaded recopying of an entire piece of writing.

CONCLUSION

Is there a place for computers in whole language classrooms? Yes. And that place is best defined by whole language teachers' beliefs and practices. When teachers plan to use computers in their reading and writing programs, they begin with their sound understandings of how children learn and how to teach. From there, teachers select software that supports their goals and facilitates teaching and learning. Teachers teach, children learn, and the computer serves as a tool for teaching and learning.

REFERENCES

Allen, J., & Mason, J. (Eds.) (1989). *Risk makers, risk takers, risk breakers: Reducing the risks for young literacy learners.* Portsmouth, NH: Heinemann.

Bruce, B., Michaels. S., & Watson-Gegeo. K. (1985). How computers can change the writing process. *Language Arts, 62*(2), 143–149.

Cochran-Smith, M., Kahn, J., & Paris, C. L. (1986). When word processors come into the classroom. In J. L. Hoot & S. B. Silvern (Eds.), *Writing with computers in the early grades* (pp. 43–74). New York: Teachers College Press.

Costanzo, W. (1985). Language, thinking and the culture of computers. *Language Arts, 62*(5), 517–523.

Daiute, C. (1983). Writing, creativity, and change. *Childhood Education, 59,* 227–231.

Dickinson, D. K. (1986). Cooperation, collaboration, and a computer: Integrating a computer into a first–second grade writing program. *Research in the Teaching of English, 20*(4), 357–378.

Genishi, C. (1988). Kindergartners and computers: A case study of six children. *The Elementary School Journal, 89*(2), 185–201.

Genishi, C., & Dyson, A. H. (1984). *Language assessment In the early years.* Norwood, NJ: Ablex.

Genishi, C., McCollum, P., & Strand, E. (1985). Research currents: The interactional richness of children's computer use. *Language Arts, 62*(5), 526–532.

Goodman, K. (1986). *What's whole in whole language?* Portsmouth, NH: Heinemann.

Graves, D. H. (1983). *Writing: Teachers and children at work.* Exeter, NH: Heinemann.

LaPointe. A. E., & Martinez, M. E. (1988). Aims, equity, and access in computer education. *Phi Delta Kappan, 70*(1), 59–61.

Leu, D. J. (1988, May). *Using children's literature in speech-based software to teach reading comprehension.* Paper presented at the Thirty-third Annual Convention of the International Reading Association, Toronto, Ontario.

Mehan, H. (1989). Microcomputers in classrooms: Educational technology or social practice? *Anthropology and Education Quarterly, 20*(1), 4–22.

Newman, J. M. (1989). Online: Dealing with Information. *Language Arts, 66*(1), 58–64.

Phenix, J., & Hannan, E. (1984). Word processing in the grade one classroom. *Language Arts, 61,*(8), 804–812.

Silvern. S. B. (1988). Word processing in the writing process. In J. L. Hoot & S. B. Silvern (Eds.), *Writing with computers in the early grades* (pp. 23–39). New York: Teachers College Press.

Vygotsky, L, (1962). *Thought and language.* Cambridge, MA: MIT Press.

Linda DeGroff teaches language arts and children's literature at the University of Georgia in Athens.

CHAPTER DISCUSSIONS AND ACTIVITIES

1. Pair off with a classmate and discuss the classroom procedures that you would like to use in teaching the writing process for a particular grade level. Share your procedures with the class.
2. Keep a reading-response journal for some of the articles contained in this chapter. Exchange journals with a classmate, and respond to the other person's journal. When finished, exchange ideas and feelings about this experience.
3. With three or four classmates, list some of the experiences and activities that you believe would be effective in encouraging children to become involved with "authorship."
4. If possible, visit an elementary school classroom and observe the writing process. Compare what you observed in the classroom to what was discussed in this chapter about the writing process. What similarities or differences do you perceive?
5. A variety of computer software materials related to the writing process on the elementary school level is published by numerous companies. In fact, DeGroff refers to some in her article. Contact some of the publishers and ask for their brochures. If possible, ask them for the name of a local school district that is using the material, so that you can visit a classroom or observe children using the software. Perhaps your university library has some of the material available for you to review. By visiting the elementary school or looking at the library materials, you will be able to determine if this material fits the criteria for the writing process and whole language discussed in this chapter.
6. Prepare an annotated bibliography of computer software related to the writing process. You may select material for either the Apple II, Macintosh, IBM, or any computer of your choice. Prepare a list of criteria by which each program may be evaluated and share your findings with the class.

CHAPTER 6

Whole Language in the Multicultural Classroom

Educators in the United States have long been concerned with developing a quality educational system for all students. But today, teachers face "a challenge of extraordinary dimensions because their students are amazingly diverse" (Tiedt, 1992, p. 13). Over the years, our feelings toward such diversity have changed; no longer are immigrants expected to immediately adopt the language and culture of the majority of Americans and no longer are students with disabilities required to experience the isolation and humiliation of an insensitive system. The idea of multicultural education is a response to these new attitudes regarding diversity. According to Banks and Banks (1993):

> Multicultural education is an idea, an educational reform movement, and a process whose major goal is to change the structure of educational institutions so that male and female students, exceptional students, and students who are members of diverse racial, ethnic, and cultural groups will have an equal chance to achieve academically in school. (p. 1)

As stated by the National Council for Accreditation of Teacher Education (1986):

> A multicultural perspective is a recognition of: (1) the social, political, and economic realities that individuals experience in culturally diverse and complex human encounters; and (2) the importance of culture, race, sex, ethnicity, religion, socio-economic status, and exceptionalities in the education process. (p. 47)

In this chapter, we will be looking at the place of whole language with culturally and linguistically diverse students, as well as with exceptional students. Exceptional or special-needs students, for this discussion, will include the learning disabled and the remedial readers, mainstreamed students, and gifted youngsters.

CULTURALLY AND LINGUISTICALLY DIVERSE STUDENTS

The cultural and linguistic diversity of students is evident in many classrooms in urban settings, as well as in rural communities throughout the country. The student population is shifting dramatically, with an increase of students from non-European-American backgrounds (Kennedy, 1991). Bennett (1990) speaks to this point in stating, "Today approximately 25 percent of this society's school-age children are ethnic minorities" (p. 14). She goes on to note that, "It is estimated that by the year 2000 over 30 percent of our school-age population will be children of color" (p. 15).

Recognizing that the nature of the student body is undergoing a wholesale transformation, Baruth and Manning (1992) believe that:

> The increasing cultural diversity of the United States challenges elementary and secondary educators to understand different values, customs, and traditions, and to provide responsive multicultural experiences for all learners. The melting pot, once thought to be a means of erasing cultural differences, obviously did not assimilate differences, and, in light of the richness brought to a nation by diversity, should not be viewed as a means of achieving a just, equal, and accepting society. (p. 2)

Teachers have an obligation not only to teach their students effectively but, most important, to perceive, accept, and address the students' differences (Barry, 1990). In order to succeed in this undertaking, teachers must understand certain relevant terms used in the professional literature. These include:

- *bilingual education:* The use of two languages as mediums of instruction. In our society, one of the two languages will be English, and the second language of instruction is the language used in the student's home.
- *English-as-a-second-language (ESL):* Refers to the education of those students who acquire English while maintaining knowledge of their native language. *L1*—designates the first language that the individual learns, while *L2*—refers to the second language that the individual learns.
- *limited English proficiency (LEP):* Refers to students who have not mastered English.
- *potentially English proficient (PEP):* A less pejorative term, used in place of LEP.

In addition to the relevant terminology, teachers need to understand the students' problems with language development and language usage. Crawford (1993) maintains that such students "need to develop high-level language and literacy competencies to live and work as equals in a multicultural society"

(p. xv). Thonis (1990) points out that bilingual students are very diverse with regard to language usage and literacy. She strongly maintains that reading teachers making instructional plans for these students should focus on the following relevant questions:

- How well does the student understand and speak the home language?
- Can the student read and write the home language?
- How well does the student understand and speak English?
- Can the student read and write English?
- Is the student's achievement in either or both languages appropriate for the age and grade placement? (p. 8)

In the past, skills orientation was "the" method used in teaching reading to these students. Fillmore (1986) in examining the type of instruction afforded the LEP student notes: "I came to realize that what these LEP children generally get in school does not add up to a real education for all. Much of what they are being taught can be described as 'basic skills' rather than as 'content' " (p. 478).

In most traditional ESL programs, the various language modes—reading, writing, speaking, and listening—were separated. In the whole-language class, all four modes are integrated and every student has the "opportunity to zero in on the aspect of language they most need help with" (Rigg, 1991, p. 526). MacGowan-Gilhooly (1991) specifies that "research on L2 literacy development . . . points to the desirability of a whole language approach, with an emphasis on integrative skills rather than grammar, memorization, and repetitive exercises" (p. 77).

It has been suggested by Freeman and Freeman (1989) that language is best learned when it is: learner-centered; kept whole; keyed to listening, speaking, reading, and writing; meaningful and functional; learned through social interaction; and learned when teachers have faith in learners. They recommend that in classrooms for second-language learners, these whole-language principles be employed. It would appear that the integration of language with the teaching of reading and writing in whole language can be readily incorporated in the instruction of bilingual and ESL students.

In order to implement multicultural education in the schools, Tiedt and Tiedt (1990) recommend that teaching should be student-centered rather than teacher-dominated. An effective way to directly involve students is through the use of broad themes or units, focusing on literature or trade books rather than textbooks for instruction in all subject areas. This "humanizes the curriculum and lends a vitality to learning that has not heretofore been present" (p. 334).

Looking Ahead

Abramson, Seda, and Johnson (1990), in their article offer the reader some ideas on how to expand the literary development of LEP kindergarten children. Lim and Watson (1993) discuss and describe a content-rich, whole-language curriculum for an ESL class. In the article by Arthur (1991), the author recounts her personal experiences working with junior high ESL students.

LEARNING DISABLED AND REMEDIAL READING STUDENTS

Although numerous definitions of the term "learning disabilities" appear in the literature, there is no one, universally agreed-upon definition (Heward & Orlansky, 1992). For a child to be identified as learning disabled, he/she must: "(1) have a severe discrepancy between potential or ability and actual achievement; (2) have learning problems that cannot be attributed to other handicapping conditions, such as blindness or mental retardation; and (3) need special education services to succeed in school" (p. 181).

The term "reading problem" is also defined in many different ways by authorities in the field. Rubin (1993) states that "a disabled reader may be any student who is reading below his or her ability level; a disabled reader is one who is underachieving" (p. 421). The remedial reader is considered to be "a reader whose reading achievement is two or more years behind reading expectancy" (Burns, Roe, & Ross, 1992, p. 688). The poor reader is described as "one who has difficulty learning to read" (Burns, Roe, & Ross, 1992, p. 643).

The difficulty of coming to terms with the differences between reading disabilities and learning disabilities cannot be clearly decided. Bartel (1990) aptly notes the ongoing confusion:

> Students with reading problems are often labeled as "developmental," "corrective," "retarded," or "remedial." Sometimes more complicated and threatening labels are attached—"strephosymbolic," "dyslexic," "brain injured," and so on. The list could go on *ad nauseum*. It should be pointed out that these words have no precise (i.e., no generally accepted) meaning among professionals working in the field. For example, "developmental" may refer to a class (or to a student) taught using regular class methods: sometimes the use of the term is limited to students who are performing at a level commensurate with their ability; sometimes it is used with students who are working far behind their expectancy, but are still being taught by regular class methods. A "corrective" class may be one in which the students are functioning below expectancy but do not appear to have any associated learning problems (brain damage, specific learning disabilities, etc.); "corrective" may also refer to any student who is one to two years behind expectancy regardless of the presence or absence of any associated learning problems. To some professionals, "remedial" students have associated learning problems; to others, the term is applied to all students who are more than two years behind expectancy in reading. (p. 111)

Even though we lack consensus concerning the definition of these terms, as educators our major priority should be to help these students succeed by providing appropriate literacy instruction. In the past, most instruction was based on drill and practice with emphasis focusing on the student's apparent weaknesses (Rhodes & Dudley-Marling, 1988; Goodman, 1986). The shift toward focusing on the children's strengths rather than on weaknesses is evident in the more holistic models of reading and writing (O'Donnell & Wood, 1992). In moving toward the goal of having students become "learning able" rather than learning disabled students, Routman (1991) observes that "students no longer *practice* skills through exercises and drill. With guidance, they learn how and when to apply skills strategically as they *use* them in authentic contexts"

(p. 402). When using whole language with such students, Zucker (1993) found that the children viewed "themselves as readers and writers, rather than as failures" (p. 669). In accomplishing this, the students gained a positive attitude toward learning independently and they became more sociable and communicative.

> ### Looking Ahead
> The article by Farris and Andersen (1990) describes the experiences of a learning-disabilities teacher moving toward the adoption of whole language. Mather (1992) identifies some of the dangers and provides some safeguards for using whole language with learning-disabled students.

MAINSTREAMED STUDENTS

The proliferation of terms for this student population is confusing, even for the seasoned educator. Writers and researchers use such phrases as "mentally retarded," "mildly mentally handicapped" (MMH), "slow learner," "educable mentally retarded" and other, even more pejorative terms. In 1992, the American Association on Mental Retardation (AAMR) Ad Hoc Committee on Terminology and Classification revised the organization's ten-year-old definition to reflect the way in which people with mental retardation are viewed today:

> Mental retardation refers to substantial limitations in present functioning. It is characterized by significantly subaverage intellectual functioning, existing concurrently with related limitations in two or more of the following applicable adaptive skill areas: communication, self-care, home living, social skills, community use, self-direction, health and safety, functional academics, leisure, and work. Mental retardation manifests before age 18. (Luckasson et al., p. 1)

For the purposes of this section, we will limit our discussions to those students who exhibit the characteristics listed by Buttery and Mason (1979):

- Generally they do not read up to their mental age levels, but come closer when instructed in regular classrooms.
- Reading comprehension tends to be the difficult skill to master. It is even more difficult than reading orally.
- When compared to normal children who are their equivalents in mental age, the MMH children are inferior in comprehension, in locating relevant facts, in recognizing main ideas, and in drawing inferences and conclusions.
- In oral reading, the MMH children . . . [rank below] children who are their mental age equivalents. In word attack skills, they make more vowel errors and omissions of sounds. They make significantly fewer errors by adding sounds and by repetitions, and they require more words to be pronounced for them. They also tend to be inferior in the use of context clues.

- Research has failed to substantiate that any one method of teaching MMH children is universally superior to another.
- The teacher seems to be the most important variable in the reading success of MMH children. Superior teachers tend to find the best methods for particular children. (pp. 334–335)

Traditionally, children with mild retardation were educated in self-contained classrooms in the public schools. Today, such children are being educated in the regular classroom with assistance provided by special education teachers. When needed the children are given additional help in the resource room setting (Heward & Orlansky, 1992)

The importance of the teacher is also strongly emphasized by Polloway and Smith (1992) who state that "the teacher virtually determines student success; the instructor's ability to teach so that a student learns to read takes precedence over any approach, material, or program." They conclude that there is a great deal to learn about the teaching of reading and "that all teachers must continue to be learners" (p. 265).

Looking Ahead

The authors in the next article discuss the use of whole language with mainstreamed mildly handicapped students. Tunnell, Calder, Justen, and Waldrop (1988) offer some practical ideas on how to do this, based on their personal experiences.

GIFTED STUDENTS

There are numerous definitions of the term "gifted," but none is acceptable to everyone. In 1978, the U.S. Congress adopted the following definition:

> The term "gifted and talented children" means children and, whenever applicable, youth, who are identified at the preschool, elementary, or secondary level as possessing demonstrated or potential abilities that give evidence of high performance capability in areas such as intellectual, creative, specific academic, or leadership ability, or in the performing and visual arts, and who by reason thereof, require services or activities not ordinarily provided by the school. (P.L. 95-561, Title IX, Part A, Section 902)

Renzulli (1977) has proposed that gifted children be defined as those who have demonstrated high ability, high creativity, and high task commitment. His definition is frequently portrayed by a three-ring Venn diagram, the overlapping sections of which represent the gifted population. Hallahan and Kauffman (1978, p. 440) modified Renzulli's definition by stating that a child should be superior to 85 percent of peers on all three criteria and superior to 98 percent on at least one. They estimate that between 2 and 5 percent of all school-aged children may be considered gifted.

Although most gifted children learn to read with ease prior to attendance in school, they are often subjected to unnecessary drill and repetition. Shafer (1985) maintains that gifted youngsters are often "marking time in basic readers" (p. 84).

They should not be expected to learn on their own nor should they be required to do more classwork than the other children. In summing up the various studies on teaching reading to gifted children, Carr (1984) found that "gifted students differ from the average students in cognitive processes related to reading, and therefore require an instructional program that is different in content, method, and pacing" (p. 145). Because they have a wide range of interests, their teacher should afford them the opportunity to pursue what they like in depth (Rubin, 1993). For the gifted pupils who have limited interests, the teachers and the librarians should provide supplemental activities that broaden their experiences and balance their reading (Witty, 1985; Labuda, 1985).

Though intellectually superior, gifted children can also have learning disabilities in reading and writing. In some instances, these problems are masked because they can compensate for the deficiencies (Wallace & McLoughlin, 1988). These children have been characterized as having:

1. High reasoning and verbal abilities.
2. Often a special talent area.
3. Discrepant verbal and performance abilities on an intelligence test.
4. Visual perceptual/fine-motor difficulties.
5. Attention-deficit disorders.
6. Slow response/reaction time.
7. Difficulty shifting activities.
8. Lack of organizational skills.
9. Deficit or uneven academic skills.
10. Perfectionism and low self-esteem.
11. Easily discouraged, quickly upset.
12. Vulnerability to social relationships.

(Cordell & Cannon, 1985, p. 144)

Teachers need to be constantly vigilant and aware of the possibility that a gifted student may be learning disabled and require individual instruction or special accommodations.

Looking Ahead

In the last article in this chapter, Ganopole (1988) provides practical suggestions and strategies for the application of the whole-language philosophy with the gifted.

The purpose of this chapter is to address the place of whole language in a multicultural framework. While reading these articles, you may want to direct your attention to the following questions:

- What are some of the strategies that kindergarten teachers of ESL students can use in expanding language development? How do they relate to whole language?
- How can reading, writing, and language experiences be integrated in a whole-language classroom for PEP students?

- What are the advantages of using whole language with ESL junior high school reading students? What are the disadvantages?
- How would a teacher move from using a basal-reader program to using whole language with learning-disabled students? What are some of the important considerations that need to be addressed?
- What are some of the major concerns regarding the use of whole language with learning-disabled students?
- Should skills be taught to learning-disabled and mainstreamed children? If so, how? If not, why not?
- How does literature-based reading instruction improve the teaching of reading for mainstreamed students?
- In what ways can whole language aid the development of reading and writing abilities for the gifted student?

REFERENCES

Abramson, S., Seda, I., & Johnson, C. (1990). Literacy development in a multilingual kindergarten classroom. *Childhood Education, 67*(2), 68–72.

Arthur, B. M. (1991). Working with new ESL students in a junior high school reading class. *Journal of Reading, 34*(8), 628–631.

Banks, J. A., & Banks, C. A. M. (1993). *Multicultural education: Issues and perspectives* (2nd ed.). Boston: Allyn and Bacon.

Barry, A. L. (1990). Teaching reading in a multicultural framework. *Reading Horizons, 31*(1), 39–48.

Bartel, N. R. (1990). Teaching students who have reading problems. In D. D. Hammill and N. R. Bartel (Eds.), *Teaching students with learning and behavior problems* (pp. 97–178). Boston: Allyn and Bacon.

Baruth, L. G., & Manning, M. L. (1992). *Multicultural education of children and adolescents*. Boston: Allyn and Bacon.

Bennett, C. I. (1990). *Comprehensive multicultural education* (2nd ed.). Boston: Allyn and Bacon.

Burns, P. C., Roe, B. D., & Ross, E. P. (1992). *Teaching reading in today's elementary schools* (5th ed.). Boston: Houghton Mifflin.

Buttery, T. J., & Mason, G. E. (1979). Reading improvement for mainstreamed children who are mildly mentally handicapped. *Reading Improvement, 16*(4), 334–337.

Carr, K. S. (1984). What gifted readers need from reading instruction. *The Reading Teacher, 38*(2), 144–146.

Cordell, A., & Cannon, T. (1985). Gifted kids can't always spell. *Academic Therapy, 21*(2), 143–152.

Crawford, L. W. (1993). *Language and literacy learning in multicultural classrooms*. Boston: Allyn and Bacon.

Farris, P. J., & Andersen, C. (1990). Adopting a whole language program for learning disabled students: A case study. *Reading Horizons, 31*(1), 5–13.

Fillmore, L. W. (1986). Research currents: Equity or excellence? *Language Arts, 63*(5), 474–481.

Freeman, Y. S., & Freeman, D. E. (1989). Whole language approaches to writing with secondary students of English as a second language. In D. M. Johnson & D. H. Roen (Eds.), *Richness in writing: Empowering ESL students* (pp. 177–192). New York: Longman.

Ganopole, S. J. (1988). Reading and writing for the gifted: A whole language perspective. *Roper Review, 11*(2), 88–92.

Goodman, K. S. (1986). Basal readers: A call for action. *Language Arts, 63*(4), 358–363.
Hallahan, D. P., & Kauffman, J. M. (1978). *Exceptional children: Introduction to special education.* Englewood Cliffs, NJ: Prentice-Hall.
Heward, W. L., & Orlansky, M. D. (1992). *Exceptional children.* New York: Merrill/Macmillan.
Kennedy, M. (1991). Policy issues in teacher education. *Phi Delta Kappan, 72*(9), 659–665.
Labuda M. (1985). Gifted creative pupils: Reasons for concern. In M. Labuda (Ed.), *Creative reading for gifted learners* (pp. 2–7). Newark, DE: International Reading Association.
Lim, H. L., & Watson, D. J. (1993). Whole language content classes for second-language learners. *The Reading Teacher, 46*(5), 384–393.
Luckasson, R., Coulter, D. L., Polloway, E., Reiss, S., Schalock, R. L., Snell, M. E., Spitalnik, D. M., & Stark, J. A. (1992). *Mental retardation: Definition, classification, and systems of supports.* Washington, D.C.: American Association on Mental Retardation.
MacGowan-Gilhooly, A. (1991). Fluency first: Reversing the traditional ESL sequence. *Journal of Basic Writing, 10*(1), 73–87.
Mather, N. (1992). Whole language reading instruction for students with learning disabilities: Caught in the cross fire. *Learning Disabilities Research and Practice, 7*(2), 87–95.
National Council for Accreditation of Teacher Education. (1986). *Standards, procedures and policies for accreditation of professional teacher education units.* Washington, DC: National Council for Accreditation of Teacher Education.
O'Donnell, M. P., & Wood, M. (1992). *Becoming a reader: A developmental approach to reading instruction.* Boston: Allyn and Bacon.
Polloway, E. A., & Smith, T. E. C. (1992). *Language instuction for students with disabilities* (2nd ed.). Denver, CO: Love Publishing.
Public Law 95–561. Financial Assistance to Local Educational Agencies (Education amendments of 1978—Gifted and Talented Children's Education Act). (Title IX, Part A, section 902)
Renzulli, J. S. (1977). *The enrichment triad model: A guide for developing defensible programs for the gifted and talented.* Wethersfield, CT: Creative Learning Press.
Rhodes, L. K., & Dudley-Marling, C. (1988). *Readers and writers with a difference.* Portsmouth, NH: Heinemann.
Rigg, P. (1991). Whole language in TESOL. *TESOL Quarterly, 25*(3), 521–542.
Routman, R. (1991). *Invitations: Changing as teachers and learners K–12.* Portsmouth, NH: Heinemann.
Rubin, D. (1993). *A practical approach to teaching reading* (2nd ed.). Boston: Allyn and Bacon.
Shafer, R. E. (1985). Fostering creative reading at the intermediate level. In M. Labuda (Ed.), *Creative Reading for gifted learners: A design for excellence* (pp. 80–96). Newark, DE: International Reading Association.
Thonis, E. W. (1990, *February/March*). Teaching English as a second language. *Reading Today,* p. 8.
Tiedt, P. L. (1992). Embracing multicultural teaching. *Kappa Delta Pi Record, 29*(1), 13.
Tiedt, P. L., & Tiedt, I. M. (1990). *Multicultural teaching: A handbook of activities, information and resources* (3rd ed.). Boston: Allyn and Bacon.
Tunnell, M. O., Calder, J. E., Justen III, J. E., & Waldrop, P. B. (1988). An affective approach to reading: Effectively teaching reading to mainstreamed handicapped children. *The Pointer, 32*(3), 38–40.
Wallace, G., & McLoughlin, J. A. (1988). *Learning disabilities: Concepts and characteristics.* Columbus, OH: Merrill.
Witty, P. A. (1985). Rationale for fostering creative reading in the gifted and the creative. In M. Labuda (Ed.), *Creative reading for gifted learners: A design for excellence* (pp. 8–25). Newark, DE: International Reading Association.
Zucker, C. (1993). Using whole language with students who have language and learning disabilities. *The Reading Teacher, 46*(8), 660–670.

FOR FURTHER STUDY

Allen, J., Michalove, B., Shockley, B., & West, M. (1991). "I'm really worried about Joseph": Reducing the risks of literacy learning. *The Reading Teacher, 44*(7), 458–472.

Brand, S. (1989). Learning through meaning. *Academic Therapy, 24*(3), 305–314.

Clay, M. (1987). Implementing Reading Recovery: Systemic adaptations to an educational innovation. *New Zealand Journal of Educational Studies, 22*(1), 35–58.

Clay, M. (1987). Learning to be learning disabled. *New Zealand Journal of Educational Studies, 22*(2), 155–173.

Danielson, K. E., & Tighe, P. (1994). Generating response to literature with at-risk third grade students. *Reading Horizons, 34*(3), 257–278.

Dooley, C. (1993). The challenge: Meeting the needs of gifted readers. *The Reading Teacher, 46*(7), 546–551.

Fradd, S. H., & Bermudez, A. B. (1991). Power: A process for meeting the instructional needs of handicapped language-minority students. *Teacher Education and Special Education, 41*(1), 19–24.

Freeman, D. E., & Freeman, Y. S. (1993). Strategies for promoting the primary languages of all students. *The Reading Teacher, 46*(7), 552–558.

Fitzgerald, J. (1993). Literacy and students who are learning English as a second language. *The Reading Teacher, 46*(8), 638–647.

Gaskins, I. W. (1982). Let's end the reading disabilities/learning disabilities debate. *Journal of Learning Disabilities, 15*(2), 81–83.

Gersten, R., & Dimino, J. (1990). *Visions and revisions: A perspective on the whole language controversy* (Report No. CS 010–464). Paper presented at the Annual Meeting of the National Reading Conference, November 27–December 1, 1990. Washington, DC: Office of Special Education and Rehabilitative Services. (ERIC Document Reproduction Service No ED 329 913)

Gersten, R., & Jiménez, R. T. (1994). A delicate balance: Enhancing literature instruction for students of English as a second language. *The Reading Teacher, 47*(6), 438–449.

Heymsfeld, C. R. (1992). The remedial child in the whole-language cooperative classroom. *Reading and Writing Quarterly, 8*(3), 257–271.

King, D. F., & Goodman, K. S. (1990). Whole language: Cherishing learners and their language. *Language, Speech, and Hearing Services in Schools, 21*(4), 221–227.

Marlow, L., & Reese, D. (1992). Strategies for using literature with at-risk readers. *Reading Improvement, 29*(2), 130–132.

Miller-Lachmann, L. (1994). Multicultural publishing: The folktale flood. *School Library Journal, 40*(2), 35–36.

Morgan, N. B. (Producer and Director). (1991). *Whole language the bilingual way.* [Videotape]. Evanston, IL: Universal Dimensions.

Morrow, L. M. (1992). The impact of a literature-based program on literacy achievement, use of literature, and attitudes of children from minority backgrounds. *Reading Research Quarterly, 27*(3), 251–275.

Pinnell, G. S. (1989). Reading recovery: Helping at-risk children learn to read. *The Elementary School Journal, 90*(2), 161–183.

Rasinski, T. V., & Padak, N. D. (1990). Multicultural learning through children's literature. *Language Arts, 67*(6), 576–580.

Renick, P. R. (1992). A whole language approach in an L.D. classroom. *The Clearing House, 65*(4), 206–208.

Reyes, M. D., Laliberty, E. A., & Orbanosky, J. M. (1993). Emerging biliteracy and cross-cultural sensitivity in a language arts classroom. *Language Arts, 70*(8), 659–668.

Robb, L. (1993). A cause for celebration: Reading and writing with at-risk students. *The New Advocate, 6*(1), 25–40.

Sawyer, D. J. (1991). Whole language in context: Insights into the current great debate. *Topics in Language Disorders, 11*(3), 1–13.

Scala, M. A. (1993). What whole language in the mainstream means for children with learning disabilities. *The Reading Teacher, 47*(3), 222–229.

Sears, S., Carpenter, C., & Burstein, N. (1994). Meaningful reading instruction for learners with special needs. *The Reading Teacher, 47*(8), 632–638.

Smith-Burke, M. T., Deegan, D., & Jaggar, A. M. (1991). Whole language: A viable alternative for special and remedial education? *Topics in Language Disorders, 11*(3), 58–68.

Taylor, B. M., Short, R. A., Frye, B. J., & Shearer, B. A. (1992). Classroom teachers prevent reading failure among low-achieving first-grade students. *The Reading Teacher, 45*(8), 592–597.

Wade, B. (1992). Reading Recovery: Myth and reality. *British Journal of Special Education, 19*(2), 48–51.

Weaver, C. (1991). Whole language and its potential for developing readers. *Topics in Language Disorders, 11*(3), 28–44.

Young, T. A. (1990). The dialogue journal: Empowering ESL students. *The Writing Notebook, 8*(1), 16–17.

Literacy Development in a Multilingual Kindergarten Classroom

Shareen Abramson
Ileana Seda
Candy Johnson

Bilingual and English-as-a-Second-Language (ESL) teachers possess special expertise in teaching limited English-proficient (LEP) students, but their availability is limited. This is especially true of those who speak the many languages found in classrooms today. Primary instruction for most LEP students now occurs outside LEP classrooms. Moreover, teachers can achieve a sufficient grasp of principles of second language acquisition needed to teach LEP students successfully, including strategies for enhancing English language and literacy development.

To a great degree, second language acquisition follows the same patterns and stages as first language acquisition (McLaughlin, 1984). In mastering a second language, learners repeat the stages of first language acquisition, moving from a silent period of receptive language development to one-word then two-word utterances, phrases and sentences. As in learning first language, words and concepts arise from action and experience, not the reverse (Genishi, 1988). Although developmental and ability levels of individual children vary, by recognizing similarities between learning a first and a second language, early childhood educators can apply basic strategies for language development with all children in the classroom, regardless of their linguistic background.

From "Literacy Development in a Multilingual Kindergarten Classroom" by S. Abramson, I. Seda, & C. Johnson, 1990, *Childhood Education, 67*, pp. 68–72. Reprinted by permission of Shareen Abramson, Ileana Seda, Candy Johnson and the Association for Childhood Education International, 11141 Georgia Avenue, Suite 200, Wheaton, MD. Copyright © 1990 by the Association.

ESL INSTRUCTIONAL METHODS

Until recently, ESL methods of teaching had a strong behavioristic, skills orientation. Instruction for LEP students typically involved direct teaching of English vocabulary and syntax, using rote learning techniques such as drill and practice. A major cornerstone of this approach was that English oral language skills must be sufficiently developed before written forms of English language can be introduced (Hudelson, 1984). In addition, the first language was seen as interfering with acquisition of English and its use therefore was discouraged. The same accumulating body of research leading to more holistic methods of literacy instruction, however, is affecting ESL instructional beliefs and practices. Current ESL literature identifies attainment of communicative competence as the goal of instruction (Enright & McCloskey, 1985; Krashen & Terrell, 1983; McLaughlin, 1985; Richard-Amato, 1988).

Congruent with a whole literacy approach, a communicative model of second language teaching rests on the following key assumptions: (a) children learn language by communicating rather than studying language as a curriculum subject; (b) because oral and written communication involve both a sender and a receiver, listening, speaking, reading and writing are interrelated activities that are best developed simultaneously; (c) children learn language through purposeful interaction within an environment that furnishes many opportunities to practice language in a variety of contexts; (d) communication is most likely to occur when it is meaningful, interesting and connected to concrete experiences and children's background knowledge; (e) language use is encouraged by focusing on meaning rather than correctness of form, regarding errors as part of the learning process (Enright & McCloskey, 1985, pp. 434–436). Moreover, a child's first language is viewed positively as a means for supporting and mediating second language growth.

As a result of this new outlook, instructional approaches that integrate language, reading and writing skills have gained increasing favor among bilingual and ESL educators. Research suggests that whole language activities may be helpful in furthering both oral and written English language development of LEP students. Enright and McCloskey (1985) stressed the importance of oral collaboration among students during literacy instruction. Edelsky (1986), Peyton (1986), Urzua (1987) and Flores and Hernandez (1988) found that writing, in the form of stories or interactive journals, helped LEP students acquire English language and literacy skills. Edelsky observed that 2nd- and 3rd-grade children in a bilingual program wrote stories in English with invented spellings similar to those of native English-proficient children. Based on recent studies, Hudelson (1984) found that language experience activities, environmental print and reading materials appropriate for the students' cultural background encourage second language growth. She also found that some LEP students become aware of English print and can read and write in English before expressing themselves orally.

To learn the extent to which these approaches might assist English literacy development of young children, we conducted a year-long observational study in a kindergarten classroom within a school serving a multilingual population that included Hmong, Latino, Laotian and Cambodian students. Twenty of the 30 students in the kindergarten were classified as LEP. The curriculum included language experiences, literature, thematic studies and interactive journal writing.

TEACHING CONSIDERATIONS AND LANGUAGE DEVELOPMENT

In *Classroom Discourse,* a study of language use in the classroom based on her experiences as a primary grade teacher and researcher, Courtney Cazden (1988) makes a detailed analysis of language use in classroom settings. Drawing from her work, a number of teaching strategies for promoting language development of first and second language learners are recommended: (a) context-specific instruction, (b) scaffolding, (c) caretaker speech, (d) wait-time, (e) peer interaction and (f) cultural relating. Let's examine how these strategies may be applied.

Context-Specific Instruction

When teachers and students experience an activity together, such as finding caterpillars or making and flying kites, they share a context for developing concepts and vocabulary. Field trips broaden the context of learning beyond school walls. For example, in the classroom observed, literacy activities arose after a field trip to the zoo, such as talking about zoo animals, reading stories, singing songs and writing stories about zoo animals. Vang, a Hmong student who spoke no English at the beginning of the school year, was delighted with his visit to the zoo. Several days later in his journal he drew and verbally labeled an elephant. He wrote (written right to left):

After drawing another, smaller elephant in his journal, the following interaction ensued:

Vang: Teacher, look. I made baby. Baby elfant.

Teacher: A baby elephant. Oh, that's great. Can you write "baby elephant"?

Vang: Sure!

Then he wrote the following:

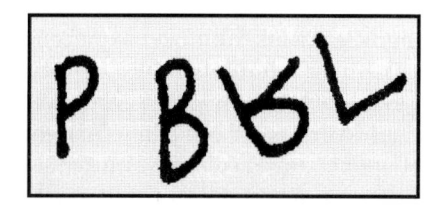

Vang's literacy behaviors were closely linked with the visual experience of seeing large, adult elephants and small, elephant calves firsthand and the many reminders of this experience in the classroom—books, charts and pictures.

Scaffolding

Adults mediate children's learning by carefully structuring literacy events to lead them from limited skills to independent performance (Cazden, 1988). Scaffolding involves organization as well as content of instruction. Contextual organization found in certain literacy activities such as journal writing may afford a scaffold for language development.

In the classroom observed, the writing center was located in an area where students could interact without being distracted by other activities. It consisted of a semicircular table with chairs around it, an organization conducive to verbal exchanges among students. The writing center was in close physical proximity to charts, class library, alphabet strip and chalkboard. This type of print-rich environment spurs early literacy development (Sulzby, 1986). The journal-writing activity itself was a predictable, daily activity consistently carried out. Such routines as taking out journals and pencils, asking children, "What are you going to write about today?" gave clues about the task and the types of literacy behaviors required. These kinds of repetitions provided scaffolding for beginning writing.

To begin journal writing, students were asked to draw pictures in their journals and talk about their pictures. At other times, the teacher would model writing to the whole group by composing language experience stories with them, demonstrating to students how the skill was performed. As awareness of letters and words grew out of a variety of literacy activities in the classroom, students began to copy environmental print and book print and to use invented spellings in their journals. After having students "read" their stories, the teacher offered assistance with writing by encouraging them to make letter–sound correspondences. Children often left the writing table momentarily to consult books and charts, occasionally bringing books back to the table for reference. As children's skills developed, the teacher began to "dialogue" in students' journals, responding to their ideas in writing while saying her dialogue out loud as they watched. Frequently her dialogue consisted of questions to stimulate more discussion, reading and writing. These intermediary steps moved students along a continuum until they were able to write independently.

The early stages of English writing development that have been identified in native speakers, from scribbling to invented spelling (Henderson, 1981; Hoffman & Knipping, 1988; Kamii, Long, Manning & Manning, 1987), were also observed in LEP students' writing progress (Seda & Abramson, 1990). Without looking at names, it was difficult to distinguish which journals belonged to LEP students and which to native, English-proficient students.

Caretaker Speech

Caretaker speech refers to communication patterns between parents and children related to enhancing language development. Research has documented ways in which parents modify their speech to communicate with their infants and encourage verbal expression (Cazden, 1988). Types of caretaker speech include labeling, talking on behalf of the preverbal infant and repetition, elaboration and expansion of the toddler's first utterances. Parents rarely correct young children's speech, no matter how ungrammatical, rewarding their efforts instead. Teachers can also employ some aspects of caretaker speech.

With an LEP student at the receptive stage of English language development, the teacher was observed talking about the student's highly detailed picture of airplanes:

Teacher: Tell me about what you drew, Souksavanh.

Souksavanh: (Points to his drawing while speaking in Lao)

Teacher: Is that an airplane? . . . Are the airplanes fighting?

As the interaction progressed, Souksavanh observed the teacher, nodded and continued to verbalize in Lao and the teacher continued in English. There were no signs of frustration on the part of either participant as they engaged in this clearly communicative exchange.

In other instances, a teacher may offer expanded description after an LEP student's one-word story. For example, when Maria told her story, "Store," the teacher elaborated: "You went to the store. That must have been fun. What did you buy?"

Wait-Time

Students must be given time to frame verbal and written comments. Often teachers supply answers without giving students time to think through possibilities. Wait-time, a strategy suggested by Rowe (1986), is especially crucial for LEP students who must find the words in their second language. Teachers need to exercise patience in waiting for student responses to their queries. Wait-time should at least constitute counting to 10 after asking a question (Rowe, 1986). Teachers should also take some wait-time to reflect on children's comments and questions. Immediate replies are not often the best replies.

During sharing time, LEP students are often eager to share but may have difficulty communicating. Sharing time represents a significant occasion for developing language (Cazden, 1988). A sensitive teacher allows students the time they need by creating a relaxed atmosphere that supports the process of sharing, rather than focusing on what is shared or how many children share. In the classroom observed, the teacher warmly received an LEP student's sharing contribution: he stood up and, after a few moments had passed, grinned and said, "Shirt!" as he turned and displayed his brightly colored tee shirt to the other children.

Peer Interaction

Peer interaction significantly enhances language development (Cazden, 1988). The more students interact, the more they learn. Peer interaction is most productive when students of varying abilities and backgrounds work together. Multilingual groupings are appropriate for literacy activities. Children with similar and dissimilar language backgrounds and varying levels of ability can collaborate as they begin to explore reading and writing. In this way, monolingual students, including those who speak only English, talk to other monolingual children, as well as practice a new language with bilingual students proficient in English and a native language. At the same time, bilingual students build skills in both languages. Bilingual students can also assist the teacher in working with monolingual, non-English speaking students by acting as translators. This communication strategy provides the teacher with important insights about LEP students' developing literacy awareness.

An instance of valuable peer interaction was observed when a bilingual Hmong child, Kao, spoke to Vang in English about his journal writing. This peer interaction centered on conventions of English print, supplying information on correct appearance of writing. Vang was copying letters that were upside down. To our surprise, Kao appeared to modify her English when addressing Vang; using Hmong intonation, Kao said, "It's backwards." Vang looked puzzled and repeated questioningly, "Backwards?" Kao went on to say, "Just turn it over," while demonstrating by turning her journal around and pointing in a left-to-right progression.

Cultural Relating

Cultural relating maximizes students' language development by creating continuity between students' cultural background and the classroom. Effective teachers learn about cultures represented in their classroom, appreciate their students' heritages, relate students' cultures to the curriculum and are sensitive to cultural differences, particularly as they affect communication and learning styles. By learning more about students' cultures, teachers are able to develop another type of shared context for literacy instruction. For example:

- In studying about elephants, the teacher included a song in Lao. Laotian students were very enthusiastic and took an immediate leadership role in teaching others the words of the song, printed in Lao on a chart and posted near the writing center (a Laotian parent prepared the chart).
- During journal writing, the teacher would ask the bilingual children how to say a word in Spanish, Hmong or Lao, "so I can learn how to say it." She also encouraged LEP students to discuss their story ideas among themselves in their first language.
- Children delighted in learning words in the language of their peers also. As part of the morning routine, the day of the week and the attendance count were done in one of the languages of the classroom—Lao, Hmong, Spanish or English.

In each instance, literacy became culturally relevant.

Literacy in a Multilingual Classroom

The relationship between oral and written language appears to be interactional (Dyson, 1985; Sulzby, 1986). This also seems to be the case for second language learning. Verbal and written interactions serve as mediating events that assist students in their understanding of concepts and literacy performance. Learners talk about words, writing, reading, ideas and common experiences as they engage in journal writing and other literacy events.

Whole language activities promote English literacy development of LEP young children. It is our contention that appropriate, well-planned teacher stagings of literacy events are essential. Teachers need to organize the learning environment and structure literacy activities to encourage meaningful communication. By creating shared contexts, mediating students' learning through ongoing literacy activities, providing vocabulary, modeling language and literacy behaviors such as reading and writing, encouraging peer interactions, relating to students' cultural background and according high status to LEP students' first language, teachers can successfully develop language and literacy skills in multilingual classrooms.

REFERENCES

Cazden, C. B. (1988). *Classroom discourse*. Portsmouth, NH: Heinemann.

Dyson, A. H. (1985). Individual differences in emerging writing. In M. Farr (Ed.), *Advances in writing research: Vol. 1. Children's early writing development* (pp. 59–125). Norwood, NJ: Ablex.

Edelsky, C. (1986). *Writing in a bilingual program: Habia una vez*. Norwood, NJ: Ablex.

Enright, D. S., & McCloskey, M. L. (1985). Yes, talking! Organizing the classroom to promote second language acquisition. *TESOL Quarterly, 15*, 431–453.

Flores, B., & Hernandez, E. (1988, December). A bilingual kindergartner's sociopsychogenesis of literacy and biliteracy. *Dialogue, 5*, 2–3.

Genishi, C. (1988). Children's language: Learning words from experience. *Young Children, 43*(1), 16–23.

Henderson, E. H. (1981). *Learning to read and spell: The child's knowledge of words*. DeKalb, IL: Northern Illinois University Press.

Hoffman, S., & Knipping, N. (1988). Spelling revisited: The child's way. *Childhood Education, 64*, 284–287.

Hudelson, S. (1984). Kan yu ret an rayt en Ingles: Children become literate in English as a second language. *TESOL Quarterly, 18*, 221–238.

Kamii, C., Long, R., Manning, M., & Manning, G. (1987, April). *Spelling in kindergarten: A constructivist analysis comparing Spanish and English-speaking children*. Paper presented at the meeting of the American Educational Research Association, Washington, DC. (ERIC Document Reproduction Service No. ED 285 396)

Krashen, S. D., & Terrell, T. D. (1983). *The natural approach*. Hayward, CA: Alemany.

McLaughlin, B. (1984). *Second language acquisition in childhood: Volume 1. Preschool children* (2nd ed.). Hillsdale, NJ: Lawrence Erlbaum.

McLaughlin, B. (1985). *Second language acquisition in childhood: Volume 2. School-age children* (2nd ed.). Hillsdale, NJ: Lawrence Erlbaum.

Peyton, J. K. (1986, September). Interactive journal writing: Making writing meaningful for language minority students. *NABE News, 10*(1), 19–21.

Richard-Amato, P. A. (1988). *Making it happen: Interaction in the second language classroom*. White Plains, NY: Longman.

Rowe, M. B. (1986). Wait time: Slowing down may be a way of speeding up! *Journal of Teacher Education, 37*, 43–50.

Seda, I., & Abramson, S. (1990). English writing development of young, linguistically different learners. *Early Childhood Research Quarterly, 5*, 379–391.

Sulzby, E. (1986). Writing and reading: Signs of oral and written language organization in the young child. In W. H. Teale & E. Sulzby (Eds.), *Emergent literacy: Writing and reading* (pp. 50–89). Norwood, NJ: Ablex.

Urzua, C. (1987). "You stopped too soon": Second language children composing and revising. *TESOL Quarterly, 21*, 279–303.

Shareen Abramson is a professor in the Department of Literacy and Early Education at California State University-Fresno. Ileana Seda is an assistant professor in the Division of Curriculum and Instruction at The Pennsylvania State University. Candy Johnson is a teacher, Hidalgo School in Fresno, California.

Whole Language Content Classes for Second-Language Learners

Hwa-Ja Lee Lim
Dorothy J. Watson

For many English-as-a-second-language (ESL) learners, the classroom is a major source for the development of academic and social language proficiency (Cummins, 1984). It is our position that ESL teachers can help youngsters reach their potential English proficiency by shifting the focus of instruction from direct teaching of language to using classroom strategies in which language is naturally and functionally learned. This can happen when students are engaged with each other in compelling and intellectually stimulating content areas.

The acronym PEP will be used to identify the potentially English proficient students we are describing. Freeman and Freeman (1992) propose that labels such as limited English proficiency (LEP) promote negative attitudes toward learners. Hamayan (1989) suggests PEP, while Rigg and Allen (1989) prefer REAL, Readers and writers of English as Another Language. For the sake of brevity and positive identification, we will use PEP.

Research involving second-language learners indicates that content-rich language arts programs are as appropriate for PEP students as they are for native English-speaking children (Chamot & O'Malley, 1987; Crandell, 1987; Early, 1990a, 1990b; Freeman & Freeman, 1989; Hudelson, 1989). Second-language learners, just as native speakers, learn naturally how to read and write by reading and writing about something of substance. Halliday (1980) postulated that a child learns language and subject matter through the process of constructing meaning from meaningful content (learning content by using language). A child understands the nature and function of language itself in the same manner (learning about language by using language). Halliday's notions hold true for PEP students as well.

The idea that young children learn language forms, language uses, and content through transacting with others (Jaggar, 1991) supports the use of real, functional language in content-rich, socially based programs. In other words, learners develop second-language fluency by using language authentically for purposeful tasks necessary in learning meaning-filled content. Chamot and O'Malley's (1987) Cognitive Academic Language Learning Approach (CALLA) was designed on the premise that second-language development will progress most effectively when learners can use their second language on the materials for which they are expected to demonstrate academic competence.

Another instructional program that actualizes integration of language learning with cognitive or academic development is Sheltered English, which teaches language through content dealing with real subject matter that is important and relevant to the students' lives (Freeman, Freeman, & Gonzales, 1987; Krashen, 1985; Lapkin & Cummins, 1984). For a review of CALLA and Sheltered English from a whole language perspective, see Freeman and Freeman's (1992) *Whole Language for Second Language Learners*.

The benefits of the content-rich curriculum depend on how successfully teachers utilize effective language-learning principles. Educators such as Freeman and Freeman (1989),

---

From "Whole Language Content Classes for Second-Language Learners" by H. L. Lim and D. J. Watson, 1993, *The Reading Teacher, 46*, pp. 384–393. Copyright © 1993 by the International Reading Association. Reprinted with permission of Hwa-Ja Lee Lim and the International Reading Association.

Hudelson (1989), Rigg and Allen (1989), and Early (1990a, 1990b) draw upon whole language theory and practice in suggesting principles of language learning and learning in general as a starting point for PEP teachers and students. When a content-rich curriculum is implemented within a whole language philosophy of learning and teaching, the classroom becomes an optimal environment for second-language learners. Students who are involved in natural, authentic, and content-rich settings will develop the language and concepts of the content while developing literacy and oracy skills. In order to learn about content, children are invited to participate in field trips, television and video viewing, creating and studying works of art, lectures by guest speakers, and reading and writing articles and books.

All these meaning-filled experiences are combined with reflective instructional practices. Reflective instruction includes both indirect and transactive instruction of concepts that are immediately applicable, concise, and important to the learner. Reflective instruction involves both the teacher and student as critical learners.

Because whole language content classes necessitate meaning-focused, learner-centered experiences, they look different from traditional classes, which provide more skills-focused, teacher-centered instruction. In this article, we describe one whole language content classroom, highlighting experiences that were successful in facilitating literacy development.

A CONTENT-RICH WHOLE LANGUAGE PEP CLASSROOM

To present a content-rich whole language curriculum, a summer school ESL class in Columbia, Missouri, will be described. The class was made up of 10 second- and third-grade children who had been in the United States from 1 month to 2 years and whose English proficiencies varied greatly. Five children's native language was Cambodian, one was Korean, two were Chinese, one was Taiwanese, and one was Arabic.

Betty Belcher, the classroom teacher, was familiar with whole language philosophical premises and experiences and thus was able to generate learning engagements that reflected whole language principles. Belcher and her students decided to study caves, which involved reading books and articles that provided relevant information; writing for a variety of purposes, including what the children knew, were learning, and wanted to learn about caves; field trips; presentations by guest speakers; playing games; cooking; and creating and viewing cave art. All through the class activities, the teacher used content-area language naturally and helped the children develop concepts about topics within the theme.

The classroom was filled with print materials and activities: messages on the chalkboard, brainstorming charts, daily schedules, a class calendar, personal information charts, newspapers, magazines, labels on artifacts, resource books, individual writings, and pieces written by the class using a Language Experience Approach (LEA). (For an in-depth description and suggestions for using LEA with English-as-second-language learners, see Rigg, 1989.)

WHOLE LANGUAGE CONTENT AND LITERACY EXPERIENCES

Every classroom experience in the summer program was an invitation to the children to become more proficient in their reading and writing by using content materials, and to learn content by reading and writing about that content. Oral and written language were vehicles to content and second-language learning. The teacher invited the children to read, write, and talk about whatever was appealing, available, and related to their chosen theme.

Reading Experiences

The students were routinely engaged in reading activities such as reading a meaningful morning message, an overview of a day's plan, and individually written stories or group-dictated LEA texts. Together Belcher and the students shared articles from magazines and newspapers, letters from cave offices, and a variety of brochures on the topics of caves and bats. All print thematic materials provided by students and the teacher were shared and valued in class. This sharing motivated the children, generated interest, and expanded concepts.

Even though the children were beginning English-language readers, the teacher selected reading materials on the basis of relevance and interest rather than on readability formulas. When brochures and articles contained a great deal of unfamiliar vocabulary and complex syntax, Belcher initiated a discussion, often beginning with comments about the title and pictures included in the text. Through talk and writing, the children became acquainted with concepts and vocabulary included in their reading. With this immediate help, the readers then risked guessing meanings based on the available cues within the written text. The teacher's stance on reading instruction was reflected in one student's view of the reading process. The child (C) wanted to take home one of the brochures on bats to read to her mother. She was asked by a visitor (V):

V: Are you going to read this to your mom? . . . and talk about what you learned today?

C: Yeah.

V: Your mom will be glad to hear about bats because I learned a lot about bats from your class. Can you read what this brochure says?

C: Yeah. I can read titles . . . big letters . . . and words I know. I can say to my mom about bat because I can figure out.

This child regarded reading as a meaning-making process in which she used all available cues to "figure out" text.

The children's view of written text was influenced by their teacher's whole language view of language, learning, and teaching. Belcher never isolated sentences, words, and sounds when making specific linguistic features salient for the children. She constantly encouraged the students to read for meaning, making use of all the information available within the text and within the context of their lives. She sometimes verbalized reading strategies. When one child asked for help with the unfamiliar word *membrane,* she encouraged the reader to refer to the entire text, the illustrations, a previous discussion of the term, and to the beginning and ending letters and sounds. Reading instruction moved from whole to part by presenting phonetic cues within a context that supported their meaningful and effective use. The focus of reading was on how to make sense of the text; *whole* language was utilized.

Writing Experiences

Betty Belcher involved the children in various writing experiences that included expressive writing, journal writing, letter writing, and expository writing.

Expressive writing. Expressive, personal writing allows children to reflect on their own experiences; to write about something they know better than anyone else, their feelings and ideas; and, if they choose, to share with friends, teachers, and family.

Even though the summer curriculum was focused on a content-based theme, the teacher made use of "this is me" literacy activities. After the Fourth of July, Belcher invited the children to share their holiday activities through talking and writing. While most of the children chatted about picnics and fireworks, one child listened quietly. Later she wrote a personal narrative that showed concern about her family. This child was distressed about her personal problems, and from the depths of her concern, she wrote a painfully poignant story (see Figure 1). Her limited knowledge of English did not hinder the meaning-making process once she had a voice and ownership. The illustration reflects her emotional turmoil: family "photos" of Dad with bags about to leave, and Mom and herself standing separately.

The piece exemplifies a personal matter with spontaneous self-expression, without the author worrying about the mechanics of grammar, spelling, and punctuation. If the teacher had focused on writing conventions instead of meaning-filled expression, the child also would

At home

My dad is moving away from me because my mom Don give him a mony my dad say go get mony and my mom go get mony my dad talk all the miny dad I say if you my mom talk all the mom mony don got no mony and He say no one Kind.

FIGURE 1
EXPRESSIVE WRITING COMPLEMENTED CONTENT INSTRUCTION

have focused on the surface features of language, at the expense of a personal and important story—a story that might never have been written or drawn.

Daily personal journals. Journal writing, a daily activity for the students and teacher, usually involved anecdotal descriptions of some curricular experience that was intellectually significant to the children. The journals showed that the students wanted to express what they were learning and that they could use their working and growing knowledge of orthography, vocabulary, and grammar to do so.

Even though the teacher did not suggest topics for daily journal entries, the children developed similar topics and patterns of writing. On one day, 6 of the 10 students wrote about the bats brought by the conservation officer. Two examples are shown in Figure 2. The common and compelling content was expressed regardless of the varied English proficiency of the children. This observation supports the finding that second-language learners can be engaged in creating meaning, using whatever knowledge they possess of both their native and second language (Edelsky, 1986; Hudelson, 1984).

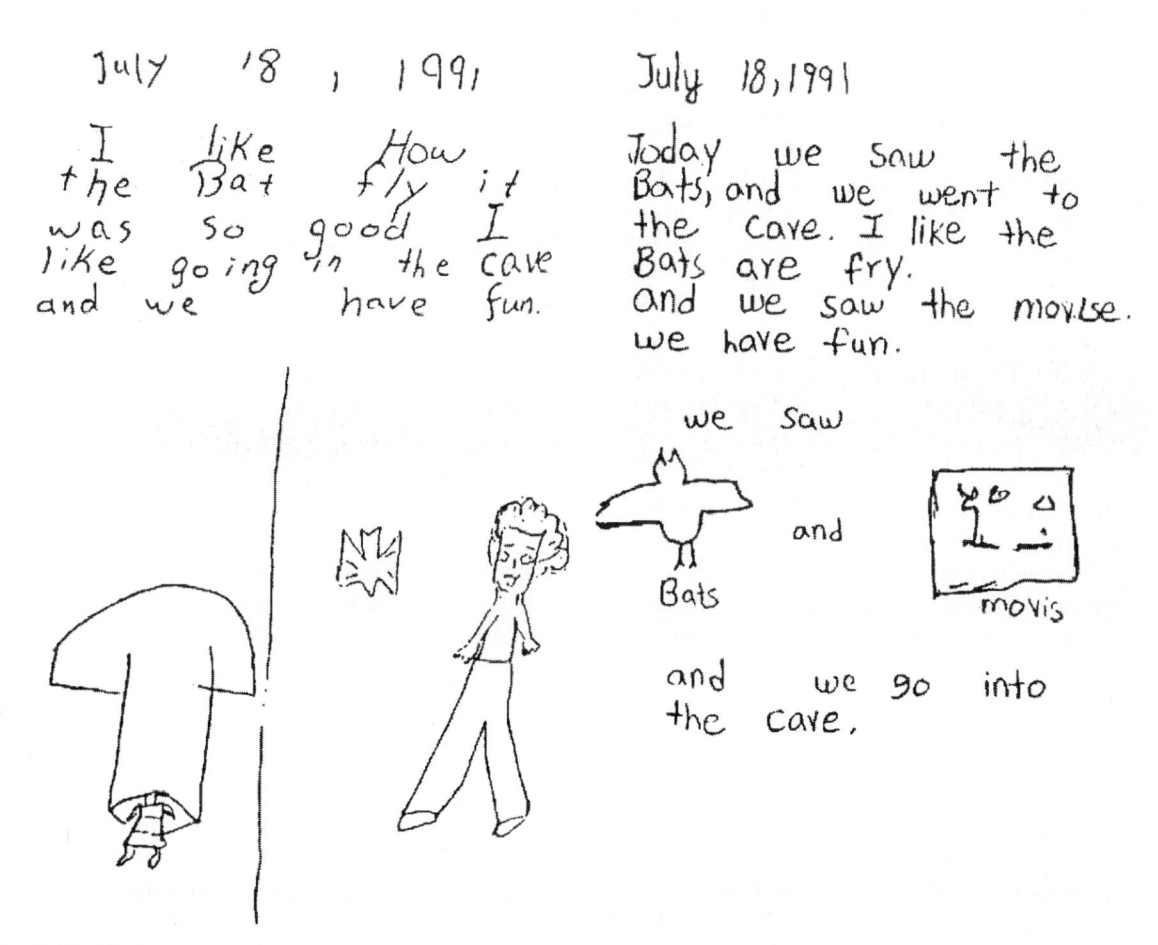

**FIGURE 2
JOURNAL WRITING OFTEN INVOLVED RESPONSES TO CLASS ACTIVITIES**

Writing letters. Writing letters was an important real-life curricular experience that enhanced awareness of audience, purpose, ownership, and authenticity. Each child was invited to choose one cave in Missouri and to write to the cave office requesting some information about it. The children received a reply from the office of each selected cave. They shared their letters with classmates and made use of the information received. Through reading, writing, and talking about their letters, the learners were involved in an authentic experience that evidenced the function of written and oral language as communication.

The second letter-writing experience involved thank-you notes to guest speakers. The children made explicit attempts to establish personal relationships with each addressee. This observation of the children's writing behaviors adds evidence to the finding that "young children are sensitive to the needs of their audience and to the demands of different types of texts and context" (Edelsky, 1986, p. 172). For example, Jiunn wrote:

> Dear Steve,
> Thank you for talling for your cave. I lik your liht. Which cave do you like? You tall us lots things. I lik it.
>
> Jiunn

Through letter writing, children were willingly engaged in important writing while they were seeking clues to conventions (such as spelling and letter formation) by asking other learners and by using reference books, their own earlier writings, and print around the classroom.

Expository writing. The study of content provided a way to move children easily toward expository or informational writing. Through talk and shared readings, the children were given many invitations to investigate specific topics related to the cave theme. Interestingly, the teacher involved the children in expository writing by inviting them to write imaginatively, for example, by asking them to respond to questions such as, "What would you do if you were a bat?" and "What is it like to be a bat?" Belcher purposefully led the class discussion to focus on the imaginary experience of being bats, and the children's pieces resulted in a combination of personal and informational writing, a style the teacher considered to be challenging and creative.

The examples in Figure 3 demonstrate that beginning PEP students can produce recognizable writing that organizes and synthesizes knowledge of content. Each piece includes key language with supplementary vocabulary to express important concepts. The analysis of the expository writings supports the belief that, if they are encouraged and motivated, students labeled low English proficiency are able to work on academic tasks that are usually postponed until their communicative English is well underway (Early, 1990b).

TALK EMERGING FROM WHOLE LANGUAGE CONTENT EXPERIENCES

Talk occurring during the learning experiences was important, facilitated reading and writing, and was almost constant. To ensure optimal language learning, Belcher guided transactions in which the children often took the lead, or she scaffolded collaborative discourse. These talk experiences were built on the notion that scaffolding and topic initiation on the part of learners result in collaborative meaning construction (Palincsar, 1986; Wells, 1985).

Talk and Reading

As a morning routine, Belcher and the children read the class schedule and the chalkboard messages, and they talked about what might happen in class that day. The intention of this activity was to make the children aware of the function of written language and, at the same time, to get the class organized for the

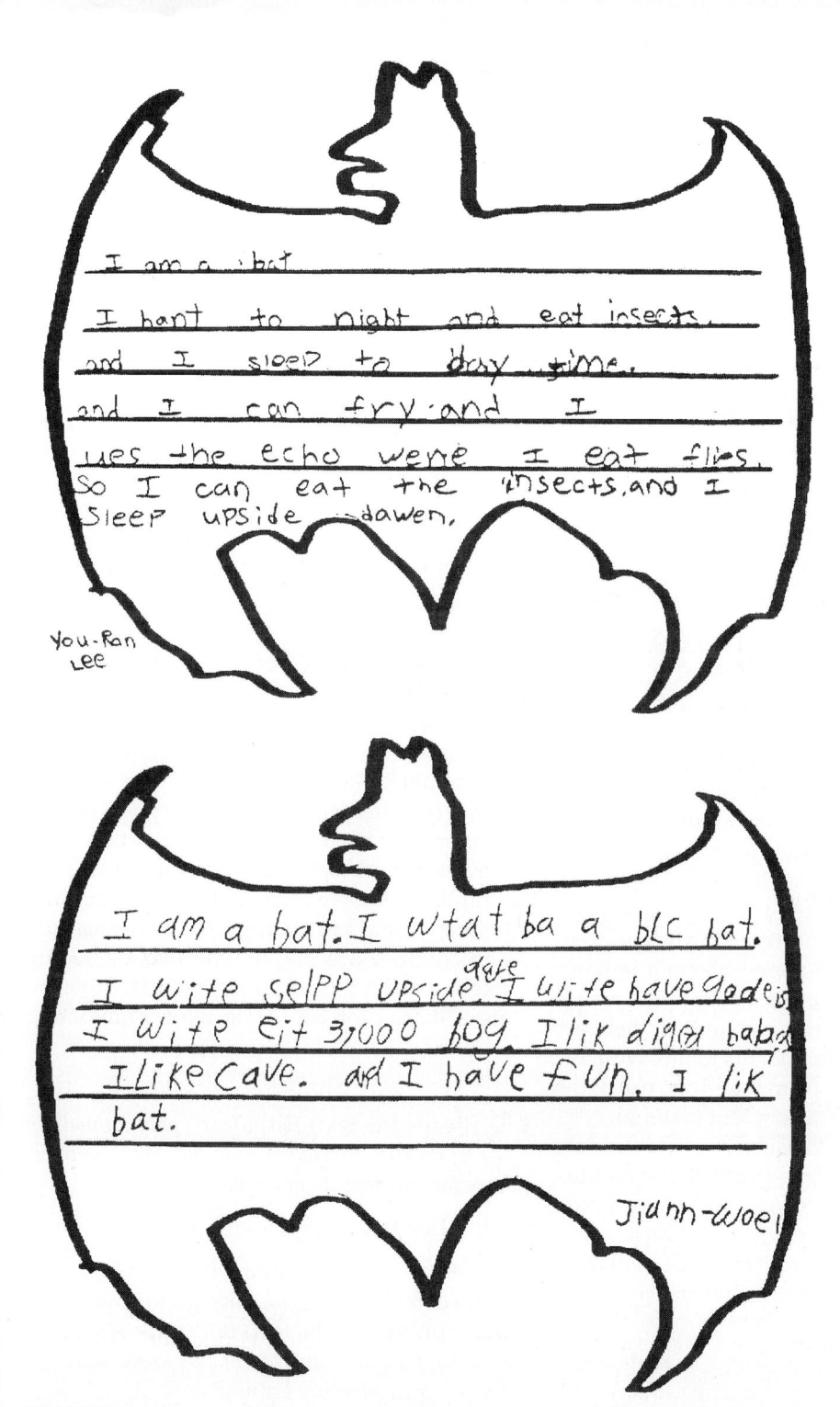

I am a bat.
I hant to night and eat insects.
and I sleep to day time.
and I can fry. and I
ues the echo wene I eat flies.
So I can eat the insects, and I
sleep upside dawen.

You-Ran Lee

I am a bat. I wtat ba a blc bat.
I wite selpp upside dae. I wite have godeis.
I wite eit 3,000 fog. I lik digo baby.
I like cave. and I have fun. I lik bat.

Jiann-Woe

FIGURE 3
EXPOSITORY WRITING WAS PROMPTED BY ASKING CHILDREN TO RESPOND TO IMAGINATIVE QUESTIONS SUCH AS "WHAT IS IT LIKE TO BE A BAT?"

day. The following dialogue occurred one morning as the children attempted to read the chalkboard message: *Practice a game for Friday.*

Child (C): We will puh . . . I can't read.

Teacher (T): Yes, you can. Labna, what would you do next?

C: (Keeps reading) and a game for Friday.

T: O.K. Can you think of what I said? About what we are going to do tomorrow.

C: Oh! Practice the game.

T: Right. If you don't know the word, keep going and figure it out. Sometimes you can know what the word is by figuring out.

In this episode, Belcher did not seek to guide the child's responses with formal directions. When the child pronounced the initial consonant of the word *practice,* Belcher might have given more specific phonetic cuing. Instead, she supported the reader through encouragement and by suggesting meaningful cues.

The pattern of content lessons in conventional classes tends to be that of teacher domination through the use of "closed" questions (Ellis, 1988). When the teacher always occupies the role of information-giver and initiator of a dialogue and the students are the recipients of information and responders, there are few opportunities for students to talk with one another and to learn from their own use of the second language or the content material.

Belcher organized instruction to allow for greater interdependence and flexibility on the part of the students. Even though she adopted questioning as a means to initiate transactions, her questions were mostly open questions that permitted a number of possible answers:

T: (Reads the text) *A bat's wings are made of thin skin. This membrane, or thin skin, stretches between the bones of the fingers and the legs.* Membrane is thin skin. What is thin? Show me with your hands.

C1: I got it.

C2: This is thin (showing a book).

T: Come here, Sophea. She is thin.

C3: You are thin.

T: I'm not thin.

C4: Mrs. B. is big.

T: Right, I'm big. Look at your skin. Where is a piece of thin skin on you?

C1: Here on leg, ear, nose.

C2: Hands.

T: What about this skin on your eyes?

C: That's thin.

C5: That's membrane.

The teacher referred to the children's physical appearance—the "here-and-now" classroom context—to make the concept of *membrane* comprehensible. The purpose of the reading was not to transfer information from the teacher's head to the class but to use the written text as a resource to invite the children to interact and learn, supported by the teacher. The children did not assume that their only role was to be listeners. They were free to initiate a discussion any time while transacting with text:

T: (Reads the text) *Bats are the only animals in the world that have wings and fur. Many animals have fur, but they do not have wings.*

C4: Birds have wings and fur, too.

T: Oh! A good question. Birds have something soft on their skin. Let's go to page 2 and find out. (Reads the text) *Birds have wings, but they have feathers instead of fur.* Does that answer your question, Labna?

C4: Feathers?

C2: Maybe, that's a different kind of fur.

T: Sophea is right. There is some difference between birds and bats. Birds have feathers and bats have fur.

C2: Bats are mammal.

T: Thank you, Sophea, for saying that. Bats are mammal and birds are oviparous. Do you remember we talked about oviparity?

C4: Yeah. So, only bats have wings and fur.

Child 4's understanding was built on peer responses and teacher support through scaffolding. Belcher was not a "transmission" teacher but an "interpretation" teacher in Barnes's (1990) terms. To help the child clarify the differences between bats and birds, she made use of Child 2's ideas and helped link that information to new knowledge. This is an example of reflective teaching in which both text information and student information are utilized. Belcher was adroit in involving the children in a three-way conversation that involved negotiating meaning, scaffolding information, initiating topics, utilizing a here-and-now principle, and activating previous knowledge.

Talk and Writing

Even though the process of writing is personal and much like a monologue in that the writer "interacts" with an assumed reader, Belcher understood the social nature of writing. She encouraged the children to use talk as a means to learn how to write. The task involved not only teacher–child transactions but also child–child transactions.

After reading, the children were invited to write in their learning logs. As they began their work, Belcher urged the children, "You guys help each other write." She then addressed Chantu, who held back: "Don't you want to write?"

Chantu (C): I can't write.

Teacher (T): Yes, you can. Ask Sophea.

Sophea (S): I don't know nothing.

C: Don't take a marker.

S: I got it first.

C: Give me the red one.

T: Instead of a marker, let's find a pencil.

C: (to the teacher) How do you spell *mammal*?

T: Could you find a mammal in the book?

C: I don't know how to spell.

S: I'll help you. M . . .

C: (writes *M*). Ma . . . Mal (writes another *M*).

S: No. Write *A*. Here . . . here I found it.

The teacher gradually withdrew her assistance and left the task to be solved by the children themselves.

Writing letters necessitated talk about organization of a task, conventions of a letter, content of a letter, and social amenities:

T: Take a yellow sheet if you want to write to Ara and a pink sheet if it goes to Amy. And a blue sheet to Steve. We'll make a card. Fold your paper. Let's make "To Ara" or "To Amy" (writes on the chalkboard). When you write, what do we put on the top?

C1: Date.

T: (Writes) *July 19, 1991.* How are we going to start?

C2: *Dear boys and girls.* It's on the blackboard (points to the written message on the chalkboard).

T: Dear Amy, Dear Steve, or Dear Ara.

C3: May I cut this paper like a bat?

T: Sure! It would be fun for a bat lady to get a bat-shaped card.

C6: May I color, too?

T: Yes. And tell me when you come up with an idea how to start.

C1: Thank you for coming.

C2: Thank you for telling about a bat.

C6: Give me the yellow marker.

C7: Bats are black. You color with a black marker.

C6: But I want to make a beautiful bat.

To make the class instantly responsive to the organizational requirement, the teacher used directives in the imperative form. Since directives require a here-and-now response, and because of the social nature of the experience, even a student who had been in the country for only 1 month fully comprehended the assignments and immediately went to work. Because of the content of the experience, one child requested permission to transmediate her knowledge, that is, to cut the notepaper into the shape of a bat. The socialization of the task is evident throughout, including the talk about coloring the bat. This experience needed the teacher only as an organizer.

Talk and Cooking

The children chose to make food for a spelunker. The talk associated with this task was on making "gorp," not on gaining linguistic knowledge. This experience provided opportunities for the children to act as initiators and to negotiate meaning with each other and their teacher:

C1: What are the things you have?

T: Roen. Come here. Tell us what is in this sack. You can smell and feel with your fingers.

C2: Let me try.

C3: Let me try.

C4: I can see what it is.

C1: Be quiet.

T: Yang, do you want to find out what it is?

C5: (Shakes her head.)

T: O.K. I'll give you one little piece of this to taste it?

C5: I don't want it.

T: What's wrong? Do you feel all right?

C5: I just don't want it.

C1: It taste like apple.

T: Yes. It's dried apple chips. We say in America that an apple a day keeps your doctor away. That means—

C2: Apple is good for your heart and teeth.

T: Thank you, Shanto. Apple has vitamins to keep your body healthy.

Although not the primary purpose, the activity itself generated use of many linguistic facilitative features. Since real-life objects such as food, bowls, and napkins were brought to the classroom, the students were eager to express their knowledge and interests through talk.

EFFECTS OF THE PROGRAM

Every instructional experience in the content-rich classroom held to the premise that reading, writing, and talking were tools that enabled PEP students to learn intellectually interesting content while increasing their language proficiency. The students and teacher moved collaboratively into each child's achievable zone of next development (Vygotsky, 1978), with gradual withdrawal of teacher support. Talk that emerged from the whole language content experiences had the characteristics of talk as a means of learning rather than talk as a target of learning. Through talk, Belcher engaged the children in real explorations, thoughtful experiences, and genuine exploring, thinking, and learning about content. The focus was not on interactions of explaining, comparing, and practicing specific language items isolated from the context of meaning and use. The children were invited to control their learning through the use of language as a means of asking questions, offering suggestions, and thinking.

The children (a) were involved in language to make sense of written and spoken texts from the first hour of class—all at the risk of making errors; (b) maintained interpersonal relations with the teacher and other learners by initiating talk instead of always playing the role of respondent in planning, decision-making, performing, and sharing; and (c) willingly engaged in purposeful experiences such as reading and writing a wide variety of texts. These whole language practices, originally developed for native language speakers, were equally beneficial for second-language learners. The reading and writing behaviors demonstrated by these linguistically diverse students indicated that they were risk takers, using their developing English for exploration and expression of meaning within a central theme. The need and constant invitation to communicate with each other helped them seek ways of making sense of real content and of expressing themselves regardless of the linguistic demands and the possibility of making errors. Their teacher knew that such deviations from the standard form were indicators of second-language growth (Edge, 1989; Stern, 1990).

CONCLUSION

Combining authentic and natural language experiences with content-rich classroom practices leads to optimal language learning and optimal subject matter learning. When the instructional focus moves away from language as an object and away from content as facts to a content-rich, usable language, second-language learners will gain confidence in themselves, and their knowledge of both language and content will flourish. Effective language learning, either native or second language, depends not on the direct teaching of identified skills, but rather on a sound philosophy of learning and teaching, underlying a meaning-filled curriculum.

REFERENCES

Barnes, D. (1990). Oral language and learning. In S. Hynds & D. Rubew (Eds.), *Perspectives on talking and learning* (pp. 41–54). Urbana, IL: National Council of Teachers of English.

Chamot, A. U., & O'Malley, J. M. (1987). The cognitive academic language learning approach: A bridge to the mainstream. *TESOL Quarterly, 21*, 227–249.

Crandell, J. (Ed.). (1987). *ESL through content-area instruction.* Englewood Cliffs, NJ: Prentice-Hall.

Cummins, J. (1984). *Bilingualism and special education: Issues in assessment and pedagogy.* Clevedon, England: Multilingual Matters.

Early, M. (1990a). ESL beginning literacy: A content-based approach. *TESL Canada Journal, 7*(2), 82–93.

Early, M. (1990b). Enabling first and second language learners in the classroom. *Language Arts, 67*, 567–575.

Edelsky, C. (1986). *Writing in a bilingual program.* Norwood, NJ: Ablex.

Edge, J. (1989). *Mistakes and correction.* New York: Longman.

Ellis, R. (1988). *Classroom second language development.* New York: Prentice-Hall.

Freeman, Y. S., & Freeman, D. (1989). Whole language approaches to write with secondary students of English as a second language. In D. M. Johnson & D. H. Roen (Eds.), *Richness in writing* (pp. 177–192). New York: Longman.

Freeman, Y. S., & Freeman, D. (1992). *Whole language for second language learners.* Portsmouth, NH: Heinemann.

Freeman, D., Freeman, Y. S., & Gonzales, R. D. (1987). Success for LEP students: The sunnyside sheltered English program. *TESOL Quarterly, 21*, 361–367.

Halliday, M. A. K. (1980). Three aspects of children's language development: Learning language, learning through language, learning about language. In Y. Goodman, M. Haussler, & D. Strickland (Eds.), *Oral and written language development research: Impact on the schools* (pp. 7–20). Urbana, IL: National Council of Teachers of English.

Hamayan, E. (1989). *Teach your children well.* Plenary address, 12th Annual Illinois Conference for Teachers of Limited English Proficiency Students, Oak Brook, IL.

Hudelson, S. (1984). Kan yu ret an rayt en ingles: Children become literate in English as a second language. *TESOL Quarterly 18*, 221–237.

Hudelson, S. (1989). Teaching English through content-area activities. In P. Rigg & V. G. Allen (Eds.), *When they don't all speak English: Integrating ESL students into the regular classroom* (pp. 139–152). Urbana, IL: National Council of Teachers of English.

Jaggar, A. (1991, August). *Talking to learn across curriculum.* Paper presented at the second annual meeting of the Whole Language Umbrella, Cassette, WL-BO5, Phoenix, AZ.

Krashen, S. (1985). *Inquiries and insights.* Hayward, CA: Alemany Press.

Lapkin, S., & Cummins, J. (1984). Canadian French immersion education: Current administrative and instructional practices. In S. Lapkin & J. Cummins (Eds.), *Studies on immersion education* (pp. 58–86). Sacramento, CA: California State Department of Education.

Palincsar, A. S. (1986). The role of dialogue in providing scaffolded instruction. *Educational Psychologist, 21,* 73–98.

Rigg, P. (1989). Language experience approach: Reading naturally. In P. Rigg & V. G. Allen (Eds.), *When they don't all speak English: Integrating the ESL student into the regular classroom* (p. 65–76). Urbana, IL: National Council of Teachers of English.

Rigg, P., & Allen, V. G. (Eds.). (1989). *When they don't all speak English: Integrating the ESL student into the regular classroom.* Urbana, IL: National Council of Teachers of English.

Stern, H. H. (1990). Analysis and experience as variables in second language pedagogy. In B. Harley, P. Allen, J. Cummins, & M. Swain (Eds.), *The development of second language proficiency* (pp. 93–109). New York: Cambridge University Press.

Vygotsky, L. S. (1978). *Mind in society: The development of higher psychological processes* (M. Cole, V. John-Steiner, S. Scribner, & E. Souberman, Eds. & Trans.). Cambridge, MA: Harvard University Press.

Wells, G. (1985). *Language development in pre-school years.* Cambridge, MA: Cambridge University Press.

Hwa-Ja Lee Lim is an assistant professor in the English Department of Suncheon National University in Suncheon City, Korea. Dorothy J. Watson is a professor in the Department of Curriculum and Instruction at the University of Missouri-Columbia.

Working with New ESL Students in a Junior High School Reading Class

Beth M. Arthur

You teach reading. You get a new student. A common event in the life of a teacher. But this student does not speak your language. Your anxiety level rises as you realize that you do not speak the student's language, either. Yet you are expected to teach the student to read. What do you do?

I've faced that problem, and this article presents some of my solutions. I'll be speaking from the perspective of my work as an English-speaking teacher in a developmental reading classroom where the adolescent students came from a mixture of cultures.

First of all, don't panic. The same basic activities used to teach primary children to read will also be helpful in teaching English as a second language (ESL) students. You even have advantages over the teacher of beginning readers who do speak English.

Often, new ESL students already read another language. That is an advantage because they know that print is talk written down and they understand that the purpose of reading is to gain meaning. In addition, ESL students are often highly motivated to learn to read in order to adjust to their new life, culture, and language. Although your job of teaching students with little English proficiency to read might

From "Working with New ESL Students in a Junior High School Reading Class" by B. M. Arthur, 1991, *Journal of Reading,* 34, pp. 628–631. Copyright © 1991 by the International Reading Association. Reprinted with permission of Beth M. Arthur and the International Reading Association.

look difficult at the onset, a workable program of instruction can be established.

The basic plan I used in the junior high school for teaching reading to non-English-speaking students was the same one I had used in other years with beginning English-speaking readers. I did everything I could to get them to use all of the language arts. I had them write as much as possible, read as much as possible, listen as much as possible, speak as much as possible, and think as much as possible in doing all of the other activities. I attempted to set up a natural language environment in which oral and written expression were perceived as communication tools (Nurss, 1980).

Furthermore, I found that some of the same materials, techniques, and strategies worked for both ESL students and native speaking beginning readers. I have attempted to categorize the activities, which all required thinking, to illustrate that all the language arts could be addressed.

WRITING

I have been told by the parents or guardians of at least half of the ESL students with whom I have worked that communication logs were the most helpful technique I used to help them learn to read. I found steno notebooks worked very well as logs. When they were not available, I made logs using lined composition paper and construction paper.

In the beginning, I made the first entry in the communication log. In it I asked my students questions which I thought could be easily read and answered. I also explained my hope was that through this log we could become better acquainted. They were to ask me questions and I would respond honestly. They were to do the same.

An example of a first entry from me might be something like the following:

> I like having students from different countries. I like to write to my students from different countries in a book like this one. In this book, I ask my students questions about their countries and about them. They ask me questions also. We get acquainted by writing to each other
>
> There are many things I would like to know about you.
>
> What do you like here?
>
> What do you miss about your country?
>
> What do you like to eat in America?
>
> What do you want to know about me?

These few questions seemed to be as many as the students could handle in one night. Usually my adolescent students arrived with dictionaries in their backpacks which included entries for both their language to English and English to their language. They set to work on the questions in their logs as soon as they received them. If they did not have dictionaries with them, they had them at home because they were so necessary for survival in a new country. They brought their dictionaries daily after they knew they would be using them in my class.

Almost all of the ESL students with whom I worked had at least one person in the home who spoke English in addition to the native language so my students could seek personal help beyond their dictionaries. ESL students with English speakers at home and with dictionaries might be unique to the university community where I live. However, because of the support they had at home, my experience was that my students returned with responses in their logs soon after I distributed them.

Often, students did not generate many questions for me at first. Responses varied from one word to longer dialogue. It did not take long for the students to become interested and determined to get quick responses from me. Frequently, my ESL students brought their logs in to me before school so that I could respond to them during my planning or lunch hour and they could take them home every night.

I think perhaps the main motivation for students to use the communication logs was that they had many questions about their new situation but some shyness about asking questions. My students did not have to ask me orally, but they could get the answers to puzzling questions when they needed them. As their comfort level with me increased, the number of queries also increased.

Writers Kreeft, Staton, and Gutstein (1984) delineated conditions for dialogue journal writing in general. These conditions ideally fit the circumstances of ESL students.

1. There is an intrinsic purpose or goal for communicating and the participants communicate about real issues that are important to them.
2. Both parties are engaged equally in the interaction, providing and seeking information.
3. There is freedom for both participants to choose topics as the topics become important, without fear of censure or reproach.
4. The communication is frequent and continuous, between the same two parties, over an extended period of time.
5. The focus is on meaning and understanding rather than on form.
6. The communication is private, not subject to public scrutiny.
7. There is time for rereading and reflection before response.
8. The exchange takes place in some tangible form or context, which is available to both parties and can be reviewed at any time.

In summary, the teacher's responses provided a good model for the ESL student and thus the student's writing improved. When ESL students used communication logs, they learned to read and write English in a natural, purposeful way.

Computers provided another excellent way to promote writing with ESL students. I used a computer program named *Walt Disney Comic Strip Maker* (Balcer, Benton, Casolaro, Haldeman, & Snider, 1986) which had Disney cartoons in which the characters did not have speech. Other programs are also available in

---

Tenets for evaluating approaches and materials for ESL students

There are many materials, techniques, and strategies for teaching students with little English proficiency when teachers do not speak their language. The following tenets will help teachers to evaluate whether materials and strategies will support a holistic approach to language learning (Fountas & Hannigan, 1989). These tenets are as appropriate for use with ESL students as with English speakers. Use them to evaluate ideas and materials you are considering for use with ESL students.

Does the material, technique, or strategy in question encourage the following?

1. Learners are empowered as language users.
2. Oral language assumes greater prominence.
3. Reading is considered a thinking process.
4. The use of whole text is emphasized.
5. Classical literature experiences a revival.
6. Writing is taught as a process.
7. Skills are taught within the context of reading and writing.
8. Connections between reading and writing are fostered.
9. Curriculum becomes integrated.
10. The teacher's role is of great importance.

which the student must generate conversation to go into the conversation balloons.

This activity seemed to appeal to the technical sophistication that many of my ESL students possessed. They seemed to like working on the computer and being regarded as capable with the equipment. In this way, they had an opportunity to express their frequently well-developed senses of humor through cartoon conversations.

Another means I used to get ESL students to write was to provide them with wordless stories or books. Their task was to write stories to go with the pictures. Often these were put into an attractive book with colored pictures.

I found that my ESL students were almost compulsive about producing perfect books. Usually they wrote a story and then gave it to me for correction. After editing, they copied their story into a book. If errors slipped by, I wrote corrections on self-sticking notes and attached them at the sites of the errors. Students used correction fluid so their books could appear nearly perfect.

READING/LISTENING

ESL students must practice reading in order to become more proficient at reading, but usually their content area texts were much too difficult for them to read. In fact, even the books used in my special reading class were too difficult for them.

I found that the predictable books recommended for use with beginning readers worked very well with my junior high ESL students. I asked my students if they were offended by using books written for younger children. The unanimous response was that they did not mind them at all. They wanted to learn to read and they recognized the need to start with easy materials.

I read the predictable books aloud and recorded my reading. That way the ESL students could listen to the book over and over and see the words as they were being read. This provided an activity for ESL students to do independently as I worked with the rest of the class. I normally made worksheets to accompany the stories that focused on both literal and inferential comprehension as well as figurative language. The worksheets allowed me to check their understanding and provided another place for them to practice their writing.

Commercially prepared books on tape are also available and I used them successfully with my ESL students also. At my school and library, the books available were too difficult for my students to read initially. But after becoming somewhat proficient at reading the predictable books, they progressed to the more difficult commercially recorded books.

Some sets of books with cassettes that I found particularly useful with the junior high ESL students were Bill Martin's *The Little Nature Series* (1975), *The Little Woodland Series* (1979), and *The Little Seashore Series* (1985). These little science books with simple language contained limited text but were not conceptually juvenile. They were available with cassette recordings for repeated listening.

SPEAKING

Even though speaking is very difficult for beginning ESL students, it should not be ignored in the instructional program. Until my students became comfortable with their surroundings, their junior high classmates, and me, they were often hesitant to talk.

I used Richard Scarry's *Best Word Book Ever* (1974) with them. The colorful book was arranged topically. Pictures of everyday items were labeled and in context, which provided subject matter for discussion between the ESL student and me. For example, a two-page spread might include forms of transportation or items found in a kitchen. The fact that the words were presented logically provided context and helped fix them in the students' minds. We talked about the pictures, the use of the objects in them, and whether the student had seen those things, and conversed in other appropriate ways about the pictures.

Beginning conversations about pictures in this book might have included things like "Show me something that carries many people" and "Tell me about ____ ." Our roles soon reversed and the students began asking me to explain the workings or purposes of pictured items.

I also used catalogs and newspaper advertisements for discussion with my ESL students. I glued items from grocery ads on index cards with their English words. Some students wrote their language's equivalents on the cards as well. The ads seemed to be a good source of vocabulary for discussion. Students developed word banks of words they knew and those they were learning. Usually these were alphabetically organized in a box by the student, which reinforced their familiarity with the English alphabet. I selected a small number of words from one of the banks and asked the student to use them in sentences or to tell me a story using the selected words. If I was occupied with other members of the class, I had them use words selected from their word banks in meaningful writing activities.

The language experience approach and modifications of it were very useful in promoting language related activities with the ESL junior high students. DeFord (1981) indicated that beginning readers learn language through concrete experiences in functional, ongoing language settings. This is a powerful instructional imperative also within the ESL classroom. Shared experiences are the best source of language experience stories for ESL students, although the complication of having ESL students in a classroom with non-ESL remedial readers may prevent shared experiences due to multiple demands on the teacher's time.

Although shared experiences were preferable, I made alterations. I sometimes had the ESL students dictate to me stories they generated about anything they chose. Sometimes, their stories were simply about a reading class, their new school, their new home, or pictures from the Scarry book or other books or pictures. I wrote or typed the dictated stories and then had the students read them to me. If their English was extremely limited, we did little more than label pictures and write sentences about the pictures. As their English improved, sentence expansion was used to increase their vocabularies and their facility with the syntax.

SUPPORT AND MEANINGFUL ACTIVITIES

The emphasis of teaching students who are learning English should be the same as when young students learn to read their native language. A supportive environment in which abilities develop within a context of meaningful reading and writing should be the focus.

Thinking and using all of the language arts was effective for my students and certainly preferable to rote learning of words. It represented the whole language approach which had materials and philosophy that worked well with my students whose literacy was emerging in English but who were already literate in their native languages.

REFERENCES

Balcer, M. S., Benton, R., Casolaro, N., Haldeman, M., & Snider, C. (1986). *Walt Disney comic strip maker.* New York: Bantam Electronic Publishing.

DeFord, D. E. (1981). Literacy: Reading, writing, and other essentials. *Language Arts, 58,* 652–658.

Fountas, I. C., & Hannigan, I. L. (1989). Making sense of whole language: The pursuit of informed teaching. *Childhood Education, 65*(3), 133–137.

Kreeft, J., Staton, J., & Gutstein, S. (1984). What is dialogue? *Dialogue: The Newsletter about Dialogue Journals, II*(1), 1–2.

Martin, B. (1975). *Little nature series.* Chicago, IL: Encyclopedia Britannica.

Martin, B. (1985). *Little seashore series*. Chicago, IL: Encyclopedia Britannica.

Martin, B. (1979). *Little woodland series*. Chicago, IL: Encyclopedia Britannica.

Nurss, J. (1980). Linguistic awareness and learning to read. *Young Children, 35*, 57–66.

Scarry, R. (1974). *Best word book ever*. New York: Golden.

Beth M. Arthur is Coordinator, Clinical Reading Services, in the Clinical Center at Southern Illinois University at Carbondale.

Adopting a Whole Language Program for Learning Disabled Students: A Case Study

Pamela J. Farris
Carol Andersen

The study of how children learn has moved from examining the accumulation of isolated pieces of knowledge to the current research position that it is appropriate to study children's acquisition of complex subject matter and development of learning strategies. Resnick and Klopfer (1989) believe that "[k]nowledge is acquired not from information communicated and memorized but from information that students elaborate, question, and use." As researchers become concerned with how students develop and utilize learning strategies, Resnick (Brandt, 1989) warns that "strategies will not be effective unless there is also attention to self-monitoring and motivation."

Classroom instruction for many children is dictated by teachers and school districts depending upon textbooks as guides. Wilkerson (1988) cautioned against such reliance upon textbooks in her response to *Becoming a Nation of Readers*, stating that "... continuity and quality control through textbooks, and accountability based on tests that have been denounced as inadequate, do not help us accomplish our goal in excellence in literacy education." Unfortunately, the desire for control over the sequence and accountability of learning often continues to have priority over the student's role in learning when the emphasis remains upon the product rather than the process of learning.

The whole language approach is a contrast to the teacher and curriculum centered educational view in that the students and their needs become the heart of schooling (Reutzel & Hollingsworth, 1988). Reading strategy instruction, building upon students' prior knowledge and language strengths, is a part of this meaning centered curriculum as students are taught to integrate learning and become flexible in their application of efficient and effective reading strategies (Slaughter, 1988).

This article is a case study of a learning disabilities teacher who struggled with the traditional instructional approaches and who adopted a literature-based, whole language program. Her reflective comments are presented along with references from the literature of whole language researchers and theorists.

From "Adopting a Whole Language Program for Learning Disabled Students: A Case Study" by P. J. Farris and C. Andersen, 1990, *Reading Horizons, 31*, pp. 5–13. Copyright © 1990 by Western Michigan University. Reprinted by permission.

RATIONALE

As a teacher of learning disabled junior high school students, I have seen many students who have had difficulty in learning to read, comprehending what they read, and having no desire to read. Over the years, I have experienced a growing dissatisfaction with the behavioral approaches in which much of my training and educational background have emphasized almost to the exclusion of any other methods. The philosophy of the whole language approach is one which is diametrically opposed, but which holds the promises of all new approaches—fresh excitement and a possible solution.

In special education, students' problems with reading have been assumed to be due to a deficiency in previous skills necessary for reading, and remediation has included the use of precise teaching methods in specific skill areas. The basic premise has been that once students know the parts, they will be able to combine the parts to form a whole. In my experience, there has been little transfer from isolated drills to actual reading, where skills must be integrated.

The predominant reading instructional technique in regular classrooms has been the skills-oriented and teacher-centered basal reader. In special education for many years, students' reading problems have been met with rigid, structured methods to insure that the students acquire and master the missing skills or pieces of knowledge that are essential for comprehension to occur. However, Reutzel and Hollingsworth (1988) recently stressed in an article that "[t]he solution to the problem for many learning disabled children is to put language together again for the LD learner[s] and help [them] rediscover the meaningful relationships that exist in our language."

Basal readers contain a wide range of selections written by well-known children's authors; however, due to the need to control the length of the selections, the majority of the selections are reduced or modified to meet publishers' specifications. This results in shortened sentences and a limited vocabulary as less frequently used words are exchanged for those more commonly used. According to Ken Goodman (1988), "In the process of controlling the vocabulary and syntax, the style and wit of the original is lost and the language becomes much less natural and thus less predictable." He goes on to state that, "[w]hat we now know is that authentic, sensible, and functional language is the easiest to read and to learn to read. When we tamper with narrative language, try to control the vocabulary, or tinker with texts to lower their readability levels, we make them less predictable, less cohesive, and less interesting. And that makes them harder to read."

Literature-based reading programs have been found to be successful when compared with basal reader and/or mastery learning programs. In Tunnell and Jacobs' (1989) review of the research in this area, they found that " . . . even older children who have experienced years of failure with reading and writing have been exposed to literature-based, whole language programs with notable success."

The change from a basal reading program to a literature-based approach can help to break the cycle of failure experienced by most, if not all, remedial and learning disabled students. Students with reading problems often are given reading materials which are less interesting, and therefore less motivating to read, than those given to good readers. In addition, the materials provided for the learning disabled students are often written for younger students. A change to a literature-based reading program can result in the improvement of self-esteem and a positive attitude towards reading. Literature can revitalize and enrich their experiences. A paperback copy can excite them and challenge them. My students hated carrying around a "babyish looking" reading book last year. There are no complaints about being seen with a real book.

In Holdaway's (1980) view, "[i]t is difficult to provide natural motivation for reading in an environment where books are things you work through rather than things you come to depend on for special pleasure and enlightenment." In a literature-based approach, rather than being asked to read material two to three grade levels below their grade placement, students are allowed to read high interest materials which have excellent language models. Instead of being embarrassed about their reading level, they aspire to read more challenging materials.

READING ALOUD

A characteristic of literature-based reading programs is that teachers regularly spend more time reading aloud to their students. This was my entry point into a period of change in my teaching methods and philosophy. In the summer of 1988, while browsing in a bookstore, I came across a copy of *The Read Aloud Handbook* by Jim Trelease (1985), and bought it for my summer improvement reading. Over the years my program had become so fragmented with students coming and going from my resource room, I had stopped reading aloud to my students. Even though I was now teaching junior high, I decided to incorporate read aloud time on a daily basis in my classroom. Much time during the rest of the summer was spent in locating appropriate books and reading them to myself. I rediscovered the sheer enjoyment of reading children's literature.

It took a while for my students to get into the swing of things, but I soon began to notice little changes. They asked to borrow books from my collection. They noticed authors and brought up their names in class. I also learned something important about my students' strengths in reading that were usually overlooked in the push to learn more basic skills. The "worst" reader had the strongest skills in prediction, in story sense, in analyzing and synthesizing information orally. He was hooked on listening!

Trelease (1985) urges adults to, "[r]ead aloud to children to awaken their sleeping imaginations and improve their deteriorating language skills." Children with reading problems often can listen and comprehend at levels above their own reading level. According to Chambers (1983), "Listening to books read aloud bridges that gap, making available to children books they are mature enough to appreciate but which they cannot yet read with ease themselves."

SELF SELECTION OF READING MATERIALS

I read an article by Henke (1988) who reported that the West Des Moines Schools use whole class reading because they believe that a learning community is built on shared experiences. I began in January of 1989 with a similar structure in one of my reading classes. The class selected several books from an educational book club. I ordered the books, and they have become a major component of our reading class. I felt this was important in order to get a handle on how my LD students would react to reading real books, and to have a common ground to begin working on reading strategies. Independent reading of books of their own choosing has also become a part of the class. Letting students select their own reading materials is advocated by Atwell (1987) and Calkins (1986). Atwell believes that students should have complete choice and read independently in class; Calkins supports having students read from a thematic web or common genre, with each student selecting a personal book.

WRITTEN AND ORAL RESPONSES TO LITERATURE

Students responded to the books they were reading using reading journals, spiral bound notebooks in which they recorded all written responses. They included self-selected vocabulary as used in context, with their interpretation of the meaning of the word; diary entries written from the point of view of a character; character descriptions, traits, comparisons and contrasts; their personal reactions to the book at various points in the story, including why they thought the way they did; as well as any other written responses they wished to record. Effective instruction research indicates that active learning time is an important variable in student achievement (Levin & Long, 1981). Writing in a response journal cannot guarantee that the student will be actively engaged in learning, but this type of activity makes it difficult for the student to be passive (Fulwiler, 1980).

The writing process causes the student to be actively engaged in discovering and stating relationships between newly acquired and old information (Van Nostrand, 1979). Manipulation of the random flow of thoughts one has during response writing allows the individual to discover meaning by creating connections and verifying or rejecting knowledge and information already possessed. Acting as a memory prompt, such writing facilitates reflection upon the ramifications of an idea and allows for evaluating a particular stance or viewpoint (Moffet, 1984). Atwell (1987) states, "[w]ritten dialogues about literature can work to open up texts to young readers and compel reflection."

Typically, learning disabled students have been taught primarily through teacher directed activities. Because they are so conscious about giving the "correct" answer, they tend to be hesitant about speaking in student directed group discussions. It is as though the students have been trained to let others do their thinking and talking for them (Koeller, 1988). In addition to their reading journals, students participated in group discussions at points throughout the book. I guided their discussions by focusing on higher level thinking skills and away from literal questioning. They were encouraged to look back into the book for support of their opinions. I found that after a few discussions they automatically went back to the book, even if they were talking among themselves. The students also demonstrated much better recall of literal information than I expected. They were constantly surprising me with their insights.

SUSTAINED SILENT READING (SSR)

Sustained silent reading is a time provided for students and teachers to read materials of their own selection without interruption. Everyone in the classroom, including the teacher, reads for a set duration of time (McCracken and McCracken, 1978). I incorporated time for sustained silent reading during class with the current trade book students were reading as a group. Students were given 15–20 minutes each day to read the book at their own pace. If they had finished reading their group book, they read a book of their own choice during this time.

CONCLUSION

Throughout my years of teaching learning disabled students, I have done my share of looking for the "magic" solutions that would allow my students to "catch up" and join the mainstream. Unfortunately, I never found the cure. A literature-based reading program may not be the answer for all students, but it is a desirable alternative. The research is still continuing to be gathered in comparing traditional with whole language programs. Motivation to read seems to favor the whole language program. Whether or not students will become lifelong users of the learning strategies they develop in a whole language program remains to be seen.

REFERENCES

Atwell, N. (1987). *In the middle: Writing, reading, and learning with adolescents.* Portsmouth NH: Heinemann.

Brandt, R. (1989). On learning research: A conversation with Lauren Resnick. *Educational Leadership, 46,* 12–16.

Calkins, L. M. (1986). *The art of teaching writing.* Portsmouth NH: Heinemann.

Chambers, A. (1983). *Introducing books to children.* Boston MA: Horn Books.

Fulwiler, T. (1980). Journals across the disciplines. *English Journal, 69,* 14–19.
Goodman, K. (1988). Look what they've done to Judy Blume! The "basalization" of children's literature. *The New Advocate, 1,* 29–41.
Henke, L. (1988). Beyond basal reading: A district's commitment to change. *The New Advocate, 1,* 42–51.
Holdaway, D. (1980). *Independence in reading.* Gosford, New South Wales: Ashton Scholastic.
Koeller, S. A. (1988). The child's voice: Literature conversations. *Children's Literature in Education, 19,* 3–16.
Levin, T., & Long, R. (1981). *Effective instruction.* Alexandria VA: Association for Supervision and Curriculum Development.
McCracken, R., & McCracken, M. (1978). Modeling is the key to sustained silent reading. *The Reading Teacher, 31,* 406–408.
Moffett, J. (1984). Reading and writing as mediation. In J. M. Jensen (Ed.), *Composing and comprehending.* Urbana IL: ERIC Clearinghouse.
Resnick, L. B., & Klopfer, L. E. (1989). Toward rethinking the curriculum. In L. B. Resnick & L. E. Klopfer (Eds.), *Toward rethinking the Curriculum.* Arlington VA: Association for Supervision & Curriculum Development.
Reutzel, D. R., & Hollingsworth, P. M. (1988). Whole language and the practitioner. *Academic Therapy, 23,* 405–416.
Slaughter, H. B. (1988). Indirect and direct teaching in a whole language program. *The Reading Teacher, 4,* 30–34.
Trelease, J. (1985). *The read-aloud handbook.* New York NY: Penguin.
Tunnell, M. O., & Jacobs, J. S. (1989). Using "real" books: Research findings on literature-based reading instruction. *The Reading Teacher, 42,* 470–477.
Van Nostrand, A. D. (1979). Writing and the generation of knowledge. *Social Education. 43,* 178–180.
Wilkerson, B. (1988). A principal's perspective. In J. Davidson (Ed.), *Counterpoint and beyond.* Urbana IL: National Council of Teachers of English.

Pamela J. Farris is a faculty member in the Department of Curriculum and Instruction at Northern Illinois University in DeKalb, Illinois. Carol Andersen is a special education teacher at Eastland Junior High School in Lanark, Illinois.

Whole Language Reading Instruction for Students with Learning Disabilities: Caught in the Cross Fire

Nancy Mather

Upon entering the first-grade classroom, a visitor notices a sign informing the children of the clues to use for deciphering unknown words when reading. The list includes: (a) make up a word that makes sense, (b) read ahead, (c) guess, or (d) skip it. A parent, observing the poster, wonders: Why aren't the students being advised to try and "sound out" the word? Shouldn't students also be encouraged to take advantage of the available graphophonic information? When the parent asks the teacher about this omission, the teacher responds that basic reading skills are not a focal point of instruction in her classroom. The parent, who may remember being taught to read with a phonics approach, is puzzled. After all, knowledge of phonics helps children identify words.

Teachers, spurred by a philosophic orientation that is often referred to as the whole language movement, are changing the nature of reading and writing instruction in our schools.

From "Whole Language Reading Instruction for Students with Learning Disabilities: Caught in the Cross Fire" by N. Mather, 1992, *Learning Disabilities Research and Practice, 7,* pp. 87–95. Copyright © 1992 by the Division for Learning Disabilities. Reprinted with permission of the Division for Learning Disabilities/Council for Exceptional Children.

Although most of the changes are positive, some have produced controversy, particularly in relationship to beginning reading instruction.

WHOLE LANGUAGE VERSUS CODE-EMPHASIS APPROACHES

In analyzing beginning reading programs, two seemingly diverse methodological orientations emerge: basic skill or code-emphasis (Chall, 1967) versus whole language or meaning-based approaches. Whole language is not one reading method, but rather a coherent philosophy of language, curriculum, learning, and teaching (Goodman, 1989). It is a set of beliefs about the world and people (King & Goodman, 1990). Within a whole language classroom, many reading methods are possible to promote natural learning. The key distinction that emerges between whole language theorists and traditional educators involves the role of explicit, skill-by-skill decoding instruction in the teaching of reading (McKenna, Robinson, & Miller, 1990a, 1990b). Whole language theorists feel that decontextualized instruction disrupts the reading process, whereas code-emphasis methodologists believe that specific instruction in word structure in decontextualized frameworks is often necessary and facilitates reading acquisition. Many whole language theorists oppose direct instruction in decoding and object to teaching practices that fragment the language arts into hierarchies of discrete skills (Goodman, 1986). Focus on the subsystems of language results in useless, time-wasting, and confusing instruction (King & Goodman, 1990). Purists insist that you cannot have both a whole language and a basic skills approach because they contradict each other (Heymsfeld, 1989). Carefully controlled vocabulary and decontextualized phonics instruction are incompatible with meaningful, authentic texts (Goodman, 1989). Within a whole language orientation, meaning-making is the focus of reading and writing; whole, meaningful texts are used, not isolated words, sounds, or vocabulary-controlled stories (Edelsky, Draper, & Smith, 1983). The underlying belief is that children will learn language rules without explicit instruction (King & Goodman, 1990).

Although most whole language teachers provide some basic skill instruction, they take their cues from instruction from their students and teach necessary strategies within the greater context of language (Goodman, Crites, & Whitmore, 1991). The teacher teaches phonics but not as something separate from actual reading; for example, when a child is writing, a teacher may give the child a phonic hint to help the child spell a particular word (Newman & Church, 1990).

Practitioners are questioning how this paradigmatic shift affects students with learning disabilities. Historically, these students, who were identified as word-blind or dyslexic, required specialized techniques to learn to read. Can these students with severe reading disabilities learn to read in a whole language, mainstream classroom? Before addressing this question, a few illustrations of the contemporary conflict, followed by a brief historic perspective, are presented.

The Battlefield

The rift and struggles between whole language theorists and code-emphasis methodologists have been brought to the public's attention. A recent article in *Newsweek* entitled "The Reading Wars" (Kantrowitz, 1990) reviewed the controversy between phonic and whole language advocates for beginning reading instruction. At times, the interactions among members of these differing philosophic orientations resemble a war and, subsequently, contribute to discordance, tension, and poor teaching. Out on the battlefield, disbelievers in the prevailing camp may be seen as traitors, the enemy. The outcasts are forced to resort to diversionary tactics to accomplish their goals. The following examples are true scenarios:

A second-grade teacher in a whole-language-oriented school admits to sneaking into the copy room after hours to prepare phonic dittos for her three non-readers. She states that she cannot get caught teaching phonics, so if anyone questions her subversive approach, she will call the worksheets "spelling awareness activities."

A first-grade teacher in a school that has adopted a systematic phonics curriculum wants to change to a language experience approach. He is informed that if he does not follow the board-approved method, he will have to resign.

A large school system adopts a literature-based reading series. The teachers are told to exchange their linguistic readers for the new series. When asked if they are allowed to keep a few copies to use, the administrative answer is a resounding "no." Several teachers hide copies in the bottom drawer of their desks, because they know the readers were effective with some children.

The Debate

All of these individuals are caught in a philosophic conundrum: Does one try to teach all children or abide by educational trends? Often, caustic exchanges occur, both within the schools and the research literature. As an example, McKenna, Robinson, and Miller (1990a) recently proposed several suggestions for research in the next decade to help resolve the current rift in perspective between whole language and traditional language arts instructors. They explain the need for a variety of designs, improved instrumentation, and collaborative investigations.

In a critical reply, Edelsky (1990) asserted that they missed whole language by a mile: "They use incorrect discourse for whole language, identify the wrong issues and problems for it, presume to have the right to speak for all parties, assume common goals while overlooking contradictory ones, implicitly pretend to a nonexistent eclecticism that their skills assumptions betray, impose a supposedly impasse-ending research agenda that violates everything whole language stands for, and then disingenuously expect whole language to be a party to what would be its own undoing" (p. 7). In a reply, McKenna et al. (1990b) note that Edelsky's militant tenor represents an extreme camp and that others within the whole language community are more receptive to collaborative efforts.

This type of debate is not new. Conflicts among reading theorists have been raging for over a century. With each decade, the artillery and the weapons change, new generals emerge, but the fundamental disputes are never resolved. The proponents of both sides remain fiercely committed to their positions, and at times, adamant and unyielding about their stance. They build fortresses around their kingdoms (not necessarily supported by research) and position themselves strategically on the battlefield to ward off the oncoming attackers. Each side sings praises of their approach for beginning reading instruction and each side suffers casualties among their students. The exact number of losses, however, is rarely reported. In the interim, the peacemakers embrace whatever is usable and integrate new ideas and materials into an eclectic approach.

HISTORIC PERSPECTIVE

The history of reading instruction in our country is characterized by movement from one extreme to another. The main controversy centers around the emphasis placed on phonics instruction in beginning reading programs. In the 1930s and 1940s, basal reading materials dominated instruction. Teachers were advised that if nothing else helped the child learn to read, they could then try phonics (Chall, 1967; Groff & Seymour, 1987). In 1955, Flesch published a controversial book, *Why Johnny Can't Read*, that redirected parents and teachers to the importance of early phonics training for the development of reading skill. Flesch (1955) commented that by using the sight method to teach reading, we ignore the alphabetic system and teach learning to read English as if it were Chinese. In discussing the deadly warfare between the entrenched "experts" and the advocates of common sense in reading, Flesch commented that "today the phonetic system of teaching reading is kept out of our schools as effectively as if we had a dictatorship with an all-powerful Ministry of Education" (p. 18). He continued by reporting that the application of sight methods had done untold harm to the reading performance of the younger generation. These methods are gradually destroying democracy in our country because children who come from educated, book-reading homes have a tremendous advantage that allows them to learn the fundamental facts about the English language. As a solution to the nation's reading woes, Flesch recommended the *Remedial Reading Drills* (Hegge, Kirk, & Kirk, 1936), a structured phonics approach. By teaching a student structured phonics, Fiesch asserted that a child's emotional problems will "disappear like snow in the sun."

Kirk and Kirk (1956) disapproved of Flesch's recommendation to teach phonics to all children and countered that he advocated an extreme use of phonics and exaggerated the opposing point of view. They explained that the reading drills were designed for the limited group of children who need help in learning to recognize details in words, not the majority of children who acquire this ability naturally and independently of direct instruction.

After a careful, extensive review of research conducted on beginning reading instruction, Chall (1967) recommended a change in beginning reading methods from meaning-emphasis programs to code-emphasis programs. Chall also advocated eclecticism in approaches. She described the pendulum effect that occurs when firm allegiance is given to one or another approach for teaching beginning reading. New criticism is directed at the approach that "wins out" for the moment. When students receive too much or unnecessary training in systematic phonics, another reaction occurs. A new best seller will angrily denounce the prevailing trend to emphasize a linguistic or a phonics approach. The suggested "cure" will be the natural approach, one that emphasizes whole-word instruction, meaning, and appreciation of literature for teaching beginning reading (Chall, 1967).

In reviewing Chall's work, Smith, Goodman, and Meredith (1970) indicated that both approaches described were designed to teach children decoding skills. What Chall described as a code-emphasis approach relates to phonics programs and what she described as a meaning-emphasis approach relates to sight word programs. They indicated that neither of these programs is sufficient for beginning reading instruction because reading is a psycholinguistic process whereby the reader uses his experiential and conceptual knowledge to reconstruct the writer's message. Reading is a psycholinguistic guessing game that involves partial use of available minimal language cues that are selected from perceptual input based upon the reader's expectation (Goodman, 1967). Goodman explained: "Efficient reading does not result from precise perception and identification of all elements, but from skill in selecting the fewest, most productive cues necessary to produce guesses which are right the first time" (p. 127). Goodman advised that insistence on precise word identification may cause the reader to use only graphic information. In fact, teaching with lists and phonic charts may actually impede development. Consequently, reading teachers should abandon their preoccupation with letters and words and focus on reading as communication (Smith, Goodman, & Meredith, 1970).

More recently, after a further review of pertinent studies, Chall (1983) concluded that research support for the effectiveness of initial phonics instruction appears to be even stronger than it was in 1967. Several recent publications have provided further support that students have an advantage in learning to read if they are taught using well-designed phonics instruction (Anderson, Hiebert, Scott, & Wilkinson, 1985; Finn, 1986; Samuels, 1986).

When whole language/language experience approaches are compared to basal reading approaches, one methodology does not appear superior to another. Stahl and Miller (1989) conducted an extensive review of research that compared basal reading approaches to whole language or language experiences approaches for beginning reading instruction. They concluded that the approaches are approximately equal to their effects with a few exceptions. Whole language/language experience approaches appeared to be most effective in kindergarten to help students develop concepts regarding language and print, whereas basal reading approaches appeared more effective in first grade for helping students acquire word recognition skills.

LEARNING TO READ IS NATURAL?

Fortunately, most students learn to read regardless of the selected approach or despite ineffective instruction. Liberman, Shankweiler, and Liberman (1989) describe the lucky 75% of the students who master the alphabetic code without explicit instruction. These students, who possess strengths in the phonological domain, intuitively discover the relationships between spoken and written words and learn to read with any method. For these students, reading instruction should be meaning-based with the goal of expanding the student's linguistic and conceptual knowledge.

Some students, however, do not intuitively develop knowledge of the alphabetic principle and may require more explicit instruction in the letter–sound relationships of the English language. For these students, Liberman et al. explain that meaning-based reading methods, such as whole language and language experience approaches, are likely to be disastrous. Unless provided with additional assistance in phonological structure, the students remain locked into a sight–word stage of reading. Liberman et al. predicted that these children "are likely to join the ranks of the millions of functional illiterates in our country who stumble along, guessing at the printed message from their inadequate store of memorized words, unable to decipher a new word they have never seen before" (p. 24). Similarly, in the *Newsweek* interview (Kantrowitz, 1990), Chall suggests that a whole-language method works against poor children, immigrants, and students with learning disabilities.

Samuels (1986) provided an illustration that supports Chall's conclusion. He reviewed the work of Feitelson (1973), who demonstrated why children from Israeli middle-class homes did better in school than children from lower-class homes. Because the Hebrew language has a high degree of sound–symbol correspondence, it lends itself to the teaching of phonics in beginning reading instruction. During the 1940s, a whole word child's center of interest method was the only permissible method to use in schools. In the 1950s, with mass immigration from Arab countries, there was an alarming increase in reading failure. A study was conducted to identify the reasons for reading successes and failures in schools attended by lower-class children. The findings indicated that, in classes with successful readers, teachers were violating the officially designated method and secretly teaching phonics and other word recognition skills. Additional investigation revealed that the reason the whole word method had worked prior to the mass immigration was that middle-class parents taught children the skills that they failed to acquire in school at home, whereas lower-class parents often did not provide the necessary home tutoring. Middle-class parents help their children acquire the skills needed for school success (Taylor, Harris, & Pearson, 1988).

READING METHODOLOGIES FOR STUDENTS WITH LEARNING DISABILITIES

For students with language and learning disabilities, some of the assumptions of whole language may be incorrect (Westby, 1990). For whole-language approaches to be successful, students must retain words that they have encountered and develop understanding of the structural relationship between spoken and written language. Although whole language does not mean the whole word (look–say, sight word) approach (Smith, Goodman, & Meredith, 1970; Watson, 1989), success in this method requires retention of words and natural acquisition of letter–sound relationships. These methods assume that children have the basic concepts that sounds in combination match to letters in combination and that certain sound and/or symbol combinations carry meaning.

With non-phonic approaches, first-grade students tend to rely more on visual cues for word recognition, such as distinctive letters patterns, than upon sound–symbol relations (Juel & Roper-Schneider, 1985). This may place some students with learning disabilities at a serious disadvantage as they have extreme difficulty acquiring a sight vocabulary and learning to apply graphophonic analysis to unfamiliar words. To enhance retention and increase graphophonic skill, these students require specific methods that employ systematic, direct teaching. Although meaning-based approaches are intuitively appealing, they do not provide enough repetition or explicit, sequential instruction for students to develop the necessary competency in word recognition. Consequently, without explicit instruction, these students do not learn to "crack the code," and remain deficient in phonological knowledge and, as a consequence, reading vocabulary.

As we are caught up in the momentum of the swinging pendulum, we often fail to consider and integrate our knowledge from the past. We hop on a bandwagon (defined as a party or faction that attracts adherents and amasses power with its timeliness, showmanship, and momentum) and don't look back. For the past century, phonic and multisensory methods have been used effectively to teach reading and writing to students with learning disabilities. A review of clinical history affirms the value of these methods for teaching reading.

Historic Perspective

In discussing the education of students with word blindness, Orton (1925) noted that a sight reading method would place these students under an unnecessary and unjust handicap. He described a case of a third-grade girl who failed to learn to read for 3 years by the sight method, but was finally successful when trained by her mother using the "old fashioned" methods of repetitive phonics drill. Orton recommended that the logical training for students with word blindness would be extremely thorough repetitive drill on the fundamentals of phonic associations with letter forms, both visually presented and reproduced in writing.

Several years later, Orton (1937) reiterated that the main reason for reading failure in children with dyslexia was the whole-word method currently in vogue. He noted that these students needed to study words in more detail to learn them. The alphabetic approach helps the child eliminate guessing and establish the concept that words are built out of phonetic units and are not primarily ideograms to be remembered as wholes.

Structured Phonics Methods

In an extensive study of 415 children with reading disabilities, Monroe (1932) found that a sound-tracing method with several variations was effective for improving reading performance. Instruction emphasized developing the recognition of words from their sound components. Special drills in sound blending were often needed. She recognized that the methods that were found helpful for remedial readers are not necessary or advisable for ordinary instruction.

The success of structured phonic techniques for helping students with learning disabilities acquire successful word identification skills is well-documented in the literature. These approaches are designed for students who have difficulty recalling word units, either heard or seen (Gillingham & Stillman, 1973). Approaches, such as Orton-Gillingham and Slingerland, help students compensate for weaknesses with retrieval, organization, and generalization (Enfield & Greene, 1981). Eventually, through repetitious practice and usage, a child's ability to perceive and unlock words becomes automatic and words are instantly recognized (Slingerland, 1978).

Research has also supported the effectiveness of a direct instruction model for teaching reading to students with low decoding skill or disadvantaged backgrounds (Becker, 1977; Becker & Gersten, 1982; Carnine, Silbert, & Kameenui, 1990; L. E. Stein & Goldman, 1980). *Reading Mastery* (Englemann, Bruner, Hanner, Osborn, Osborn, & Zoref, 1983–1984), formerly known as DISTAR, and *Corrective Reading* (Englemann, Johnson, Hanner, Carnine, Meyers, Osborn et al., 1988) are highly structured, skill-oriented programs that are designed to increase academic engaged time. The teaching techniques vary according to the skill levels of the students (Becker & Carnine, 1981). Delpit (1988) observed that no one criticizes the instructional efficacy of DISTAR, only the explicit teacher control of material.

Fernald Method

Another remedial approach, the Fernald method, does not emphasize direct phonics instruction. In this method, tracing and pronouncing a word are performed simultaneously, thus helping increase awareness of phonemic structure and recognition of word parts. This multisensory, modified language experience approach emphasizes meaning: Students learn words as they compose their own stories. Research has documented the effectiveness of this technique. For example, Fernald (1943) found that in treating 93 students with moderate to severe reading disabilities, the kinesthetic method resulted in normal or superior reading for all but one student. More recently, in a series of 14 experiments, Hulme (1981) demonstrated that subjects with reading disabilities remembered words better when they were allowed to trace them. He concluded that tracing aids visual–verbal paired associative learning by helping students with reading disabilities learn to associate and retain written and spoken forms. He also observed that many students with reading disabilities were unable to segment words into their constituent phonemes and to recognize similarities in sound among words.

PHONOLOGICAL AWARENESS AND READING ACHIEVEMENT

Research results suggest that children with dyslexia do not have available phoneme segmentation skills or phonological memory codes at a time when these skills are required for learning to read (Snowling, 1987). As a result, they are unable to decode unfamiliar words in their reading. Some students come to school without the expected and required oral language proficiency (Westby, 1990) and, consequently, have difficulty acquiring reading skills. As Liberman, Shankweiler, and Liberman (1989) noted, the students who learn to read by any method are the ones who when tested in kindergarten have strengths in the phonological domain.

Predictor of Reading Achievement

The phonemic awareness of children entering school may be the single most powerful determinant of reading success or failure (Adams, 1990; Stahl, Osborn, & Lehr, 1990). Results from a longitudinal study of 543 children indicated that phonological processing tasks were one of the best predictors of reading achievement at the end of kindergarten and first grade (Share, Jorm, Maclean, & Matthews, 1984). Additionally, a strong, highly specific relationship exists between knowledge of nursery rhymes and development of phonological skills (Maclean, Bryant, & Bradley, 1987). These findings suggest that individual differences in phonological awareness prior to school entry are highly related to and predictive of the ability to learn to read in first grade. In fact, the low decoding skill observed in poor readers may be primarily attributed to a lack of phonological awareness that impairs ability to segment, analyze, and synthesize speech sounds (Stanovich 1982a, 1982b). Findings also indicate that simple phonological skills are significantly related to reading and spelling performance through high school; poor readers at all grades having failed to master these skills (Calfee, Lindamood, & Lindamood, 1973). In a longitudinal study, Juel (1988) found that 9 out of 10 students who entered first grade with low phonemic awareness were in the bottom quartile on decoding and comprehension measures 4 years later.

Training in Phonological Awareness

Fortunately, considerable evidence demonstrates that phonological awareness can be developed and that training produces improved performance in reading and spelling. In a longitudinal study, Vellutino and Scanlon (1987) found that direct instruction in phonemic segmentation of second- and sixth-graders improved word identification skill. They concluded that ability to analyze world structure phonemically is essential for building a sizable reading vocabulary and that reading success depends on an individual's ability to store and retrieve phonological associations.

In another longitudinal study, Bradley and Bryant (1983) tested 400 children on phonemic awareness prior to learning to read. Sixty-five students who were low in phonemic awareness were divided into two groups, a control group and a group that received phonemic awareness training. The students who received the training scored significantly higher when in first, second, and fifth grades than the controls in reading and spelling. Phonological awareness training in preschool has a facilitating effect on reading and spelling acquisition (Lundberg, Frost, & Petersen, 1988).

When providing instruction, a metacognitive approach to phonemic awareness training may be most effective. First-grade children who received training in blending and segmentation and reflected upon and discussed the value, application, and purpose of these skills outperformed students who only received skill and drill instruction (Cunningham, 1989). This finding suggests that it is important to help children understand how phonemic knowledge is related to learning to read.

To summarize, the evidence suggests that a deficiency in phonological skill can directly affect the development of decoding skills. Some students will acquire these skills through reading because a reciprocal relationship exists between phonemic knowledge and learning to read. Acquisition of orthographic principles through reading enables the discovery of parallel phonemic principles (Perfetti, Beck, Bell, & Hughes, 1987). Other children will need to develop a conscious awareness of the linguistic components of speech and how these components relate to word identification. Appreciation of the alphabetic principle depends upon phonemic awareness (Adams, 1990; Stahl, Osborn, & Lehr, 1990). When phonemic skills do not develop naturally or children come to school with limited language backgrounds, systematic instruction is often required. Understanding that words have an internal structure is, in fact, a necessary achievement for use and understanding of an alphabetic script (Liberman & Liberman, 1990).

BALANCE THE LANGUAGE SYSTEMS

In providing reading instruction, a teacher tries to facilitate balance of the language systems: to help the student use graphophonic, syntactic, and semantic knowledge to aid in word recognition and, consequently, reconstruction of meaning. When a student cannot grasp the meaning with higher-level strategies, he or she can engage a lower-level strategy, such as knowledge of letter–sound associations (Clay, 1985). Good readers use both top–down (conceptually derived) and bottom–up (phonemically derived) mental processing when reading (Idol, 1988), whereas poor readers operate on a narrow range of strategies (Clay, 1985).

Interactive-Compensatory Model

In contrast to a conceptually-driven view of the reading process, Stanovich (1980) suggested that top–down information combines with bottom–up information in an interactive-compensatory model. A deficit in any particular process results in greater reliance on the other processes. In other words, readers use contextual constraints in a compensatory manner: When decoding skill is not automatic and the reader struggles to identify words, context facilitates processing; when decoding skill is automatic and words are rapidly identified, context has no effect on word identification skill. Unskilled readers make greater use of context than skilled readers to compensate for their difficulties in decoding (Pring & Snowling, 1986).

Eye Movements

Studies of the eye movements of good and poor readers also provide support for Stanovich's model of the reading process. Good readers do not skip over words, whereas poor readers sample the print, guessing at words they are unable to identify (Rayner & Pollatsek, 1987). Rayner and Pollatsek observed that words that are predictable from context receive shorter fixations and are more likely to be skipped than less frequent or less predictable words. When a word is not readily identified, attention to graphophonic information is often necessary (McConkie & Zola, 1987). Considering these findings, one must question the wisdom of encouraging students who are having marked difficulty with word recognition to skip or guess at unknown words. It is only after a child learns to read that miscues, which do not distort meaning, are of minor importance (Heilman, 1985). Students must be provided with all of the elements and language codes for constructing meaning (Anderson, Hiebert, Scott, & Wilkinson, 1985). Given that a text is at an appropriate instructional level, a student should not be encouraged to skip words, but rather to study a word and then reread the sentence in which it appears (Adams, 1990; Stahl, Osborn, & Lehr, 1990).

Automaticity

Psycholinguistic theory is derived from observations of efficient readers. A potentially dangerous generalization is that whereas skilled readers do not appear to use letter–sound cues, children learning how to read do not need to be taught letter–sound relationships (Heilman, 1985). Students need to develop some understanding of letter–sound relationships in the beginning reading stage. Fast, accurate word identification results when readers are so familiar with letter–sound relationships that words are identified automatically (Anderson, Hiebert, Scott, & Wilkinson, 1985). In fact, context-free word recognition is the most apparent characteristic of reading ability (Perfetti, 1985). To obtain automaticity in word recognition, some children require extremely high levels of overlearning and practice (Felton & Wood, 1989).

THE NEED FOR EXPLICIT INSTRUCTION

This article has focused on the need for explicit instruction in word recognition for the students with learning disabilities who do not develop these skills easily and naturally. As this is the focal point of disagreement between whole language and code-emphasis advocates, students who are members of a whole language classroom may be deprived of the necessary instruction in basic reading skills and as a result, enter the third-grade classroom with poor decoding abilities. The intent is not to suggest that students with learning disabilities be subjected to meaningless drills or an endless series of workbook pages. The optimum amount of instruction in letter–sound relationships for any child is the *minimum* amount that child needs to become an independent reader (Heilman, 1985). Children with learning disabilities should be immersed in literature, be active classroom participants, be in a language-rich environment, and most importantly, be taught to read.

MATCHING MATERIALS TO INSTRUCTIONAL LEVELS

One final caveat regarding the use of literature-based readers in a classroom of heterogeneous students: A teacher must provide texts at appropriate instructional levels for the students. For students with limited (or accelerated) oral language proficiency, the teacher must make a match between the students' present pragmatic, semantic, syntactic, and graphophonic skills and the language level of the materials that they are using (Westby, 1990). Effective language learning requires that the input is comprehensible to the student and only one step above the child's present language abilities (Krashen, 1982).

Ladas (1980) presents two crucial facts for education and psychology related to instructional planning: (a) students have differences in learning rate, and (b) a wide span of student ability exists in any grade. Under optimal instructional conditions, students need a different amount of time to learn; consequently, procedures designed to treat students as equal are ineffective for students in either the lower or upper ranges or both (Carroll, 1963). As Betts (1946) observed: "No one can justify ordering thirty similar third-grade workbooks for the thirty dissimilar third-grade pupils found in any classroom in the country" (p. 525). After appraising the status of high school reading in 1965, Muskopf and Robinson (1966) asserted that each day in the United States 3 million children are given literature textbooks that they cannot read. Hopefully, the count would be lower today, one hopes.

CONCLUSION

As noted in the *Newsweek* article, good teachers are committed to balanced, eclectic approaches; they provide whatever a child needs to achieve optimal growth in language and reading development. As new practices emerge, veteran teachers adapt these methods to fit their notion of what works with the students they teach (Pearson, 1989). One worries, however, about new teachers, particularly those who have been indoctrinated by college training programs into one camp. With whole language indoctrination, how many years does it take teachers to realize that some students will require explicit instruction in the alphabetic code? Will a whole language orientation result in teachers ignoring the alphabetic principle on which our language is based (MacGinite, 1991)? With phonics or direct skill instruction indoctrination, how many years does it take teachers to discover that most children do not require extensive instruction in the alphabetic code to learn to read and, consequently, the students' valuable time, time that could be spent reading literature, is being wasted? In the interim, while the teachers are learning through the discovery method, what happens to the reading development of the children? A negative outcome of the revolutionary spirit of the whole language movement may be that many children are trapped in poor programs produced in the heat of intense ideological debates (Pearson, 1989). As MacGinite (1991) noted, the sad result is that children receive the best and worse of each new educational trend.

Understanding of the reading process would be hastened if the reading paradigm wars were ended and investigators agreed to coexist peacefully (Stanovich, 1990). The pendulum effect holds reading instruction hostage and suppresses significant modifications in strategy (Heilman, 1985). Teachers become hesitant to modify or alter the "accepted" instructional method. The dichotomy between phonics and meaning-based instruction that has dominated the field of reading is false (Anderson, Hiebert, Scott, & Wilkinson, 1985). After all, most theorists and practitioners agree that: (a) the purpose of reading is reconstructing meaning; (b) teachers and students should be active participants in literary acquisition; (c) students should be provided with integrative learning experiences and engage in meaningful reading and writing activities; (d) students should be intrinsically motivated, acquire skill in self-monitoring, and develop responsibility for their own learning; and, (e) children's literature is valuable and belongs in reading programs.

A more descriptive metaphor than a pendulum to describe the historic zigzag movement of acceptance of reading approaches is the tacks made by a sailing ship as it traverses its course. Although at certain points the ship turns with the wind and sails in the opposite direction, the movement is always forward. For remedial reading instruction, new approaches emerge that are child-centered and provide explicit skill instruction in contextualized formats. One example is *Reading Recovery* (Clay, 1985), an early intervention program that has been highly successful in teaching children with reading difficulties how to use a variety of strategies to comprehend text. With this method, first- or second-grade students receive one-to-one instruction from a trained teacher for thirty minutes daily for twelve to fifteen weeks. Even with this intensive, tutorial program, however, 1–2% of the participants continue to require special interventions to learn to read (Watson, 1991).

The major objective of all reading instruction is to enhance ability to derive meaning from text. For some children, however, poor decoding is a major impediment to comprehension. As Glass (1973) noted: "Thus we can state what at first only seems a contradiction: decoding is at once a least important aspect of reading, and at the same time the most crucial aspect of reading. If one does not learn to decode efficiently and effectively, one will never be allowed the opportunity to read, i.e,. deal with and react to meaning via the printed word" (pp. 4–5). A reading approach that emphasizes decoding is not at odds with one that emphasizes comprehension (Shankweiler, 1989). In discussing the nature of reading difficulties, Shankweiler indicated that "a genuine concern with what limits reading comprehension leads us back to decoding difficulties and their causes" (p. 64). As Monroe (1932) noted, even though their remedial methodology stressed the mechanics of word recognition, this was not an end in itself, but rather a means for accomplishing the final goal, the construction of meaning. Skillful word reading depends uncompromisingly upon a deep and thorough acquisition of sound–symbol relationships (Adams, 1990; Stahl, Osborn, & Lehr, 1990). Students who develop good word recognition abilities are better prepared to read quality literature with enjoyment and understanding (Stahl & Miller, 1989).

For students who learn to read easily, it seems sensible and advisable to use a natural approach to beginning reading instruction: an approach that is meaning-based, promotes interest, and emphasizes language comprehension and literature. Most children do not require special, intensive methodologies to learn to read. For children who do not learn to read easily and have difficulty in forming associations between sounds and printed symbols, special methods are required (Goldberg, Shiffman, & Bender, 1983). These methods may involve teaching letter–sound associations in contextualized formats, or if necessary, decontextualized formats.

One best method does not exist for teaching reading to children. A study of the history of reading instruction shows that almost every conceivable technique has been used to teach children to read (Fernald, 1943). No program can do all things for all children, nor be all things for all teachers (Chall, 1967). Two facts, however, remain: (a) all children do not learn to read by the same method, and (b) different children require different reading methods at different times in their development.

When asked what is the right method for teaching children to read, one should answer: The right method is the method or combination of methods that helps the child learn to read (Goldberg, Schiffman, & Bender, 1983). Written language is like a safe-deposit box: more than one key is needed to unlock it (Heymsfeld, 1989). As teachers of students with learning disabilities, we may incorporate the spirit and theoretical orientation of the whole language movement, while we continue to provide appropriate instruction by selecting the most efficacious routes for helping students become proficient, lifelong readers. Students with severe reading disabilities may learn to read in a whole language, mainstream classroom, as long as appropriate, explicit instruction is provided, a variety of instructional techniques are employed, and the intensity and duration of the provided services are based on the individual's needs.

A final true scenario . . . A special education teacher recounted the story of her visit to a third-grade classroom. Students were engaged in a round-robin reading activity. Larry, who was wide-eyed and listening intently to his classmates read, suddenly turned to his teacher and queried: "Hey, when is somebody going to teach me to read?" We can only respond: "One hopes, soon."

REFERENCES

Adams, M. J. (1990). *Beginning to read: Thinking and learning about print*. Cambridge, MA: MIT Press.

Anderson, R. C., Hiebert. E. H., Scott. J. A., & Wilkinson, I. A. G. (1985). *Becoming a nation of readers: The report of the Commission on Reading*. Washington, DC: U.S. Department of Education.

Austin, M. C., & Morrison, C. (1963). *The first R: The Harvard report on reading in elementary schools*. New York: Macmillan.

Becker, W. C. (1977). Teaching reading and language to the disadvantaged—What we learned from field research. *Harvard Educational Review*, 44, 518–543.

Becker, W. C., & Carnine, D. W. (1981). Direct Instruction: A behavior theory model for comprehensive educational intervention with the disadvantaged. In S. W. Bijou & R. Ruiz (Eds.), *Behavior modification: Contributions to education* (pp. 145–210). Hillsdale, NJ: Erlbaum.

Becker, W. C., & Gersten, R. (1982). A follow-up on Follow Through: The later effects of the direct instruction model on children in fifth and sixth grades. *American Education Research Journal*, 19, 75–92.

Betts, E. A. (1946). *Foundations of reading instruction*. New York: American Book Company.

Bradley, L., & Bryant, P. E. (1983). Categorizing sounds and learning to read: A causal connection. *Nature*, 301, 419–421.

Calfee, R. C., Lindamood, P., & Lindamood, C. (1973). Acoustic–phonic skills in reading: Kindergarten through twelfth grade. *Journal of Educational Psychology*, 64, 293–298.

Carnine, D. W., Silbert, J., & Kameenui, E. (1990). *Direct instruction reading* (2nd ed.). Columbus, OH: Merrill.

Carroll, J. (1963). A model of school learning. *Teachers College Record, 64*, 723–733.

Chall, J. S. (1967; 1983). *Learning to read: The great debate.* New York: McGraw-Hill.

Clay, M. M. (1985). *The early detection of reading difficulties* (3rd ed.). Auckland, New Zealand: Heinemann.

Cunningham, A. E. (1989). Outstanding dissertation award 1987–1988. Phonemic awareness: The development of early reading competency. *Reading Research Quarterly, 24*, 471–472.

Delpit, L. D. (1988). The silenced dialogue: Power and pedagogy in educating other people's children. *Harvard Educational Review, 58*, 280–298.

Edelsky, C., Draper, K., & Smith, K. (1983). Hookin' 'Em in at the start of school in a 'whole language' classroom. *Anthropology and Education Quarterly, 14*, 257–281.

Edelsky, C. (1990). Whose agenda is this anyway? A response to McKenna, Robinson, and Miller. *Educational Researcher, 19*(8), 7–11.

Enfield, M. L., & Greene, V. E. (1981). There is a skeleton in every closet. *Bulletin of the Orion Society, 31*, 189–198.

Englemann, S., Bruner, E. C., Hannet, S., Osborn, J., Osborn, S., & Zoref, L. (1983—1984). Reading mastery. Chicago: Science Research Associates.

Englemann, S., Johnson, G., Harmer, S., Carnine, D., Meyers, L., Osborn, S., Haddox, P., Becker, W., Osborn, J., & Becker, J. (1988). *Corrective reading*, Chicago: Science Research Associates.

Feitelson, D. (1973). Israel. In J. Downing (Ed.), *Comparative reading* (pp. 426–439). New York: Macmillan.

Felton, R. H., & Wood, F. B. (1989). Cognitive deficits in reading disability and attention deficit disorder. *Journal of Learning Disabilities, 22*, 3–13, 22.

Fernald, G. M. (1943). *Remedial techniques in basic school subjects.* New York: McGraw-Hill.

Finn, C. E. (1986). *What works: Research about teaching and learning.* Washington, DC: U.S. Department of Education.

Flesch, R. (1955). *Why Johnny can't read.* New York: Harper Brothers.

Gillingham, A., & Stillman, B. W. (1973). *Remedial training for children with specific disability in reading, spelling, and penmanship.* Cambridge, MA: Educators Publishing Service.

Glass, G. G. (1973). *Teaching decoding as separate from reading.* New York: Adelphi University.

Goldberg, H. K., Shiffman, G. B., & Bender, M. (1983). *Dyslexia: Interdisciplinary approaches to reading disabilities.* New York: Grune & Stratton.

Goodman, K. S. (1967). Reading: A psycholinguistic guessing game. *Journal of the Reading Specialist, 6*, 126–135.

Goodman, K. S. (1986). *What's whole in whole language?* Portsmouth, NH: Heinemann.

Goodman, K. S. (1989). Whole language is whole: A response to Heymsfeld. *Educational Leadership. 46*(6), 69–70.

Goodman, Y. M., Crites, A., & Whitmore, K. F. (1991). Teaching skills in whole language classrooms. In K. S. Goodman, L. B. Bird, & Y. M. Godman (Eds.). *The whole language catalogue* (p. 308). Santa Rosa, CA: American School Publishers.

Groff, P., & Seymour, D. Z. (1987). *Word recognition: The why and the how.* Springfield, IL: Charles C. Thomas.

Hegge. T., Kirk, S. A., & Kirk, W. (1936). *Remedial reading drills.* Ann Arbour, MI: George Wahr.

Heilman, A. W. (1985). *Phonics in proper perspective* (5th ed.). Columbus, OH: Merrill.

Heymsfeld, C. R. (1989). Filling the hole in whole language. *Educational Leadership, 46*(6), 65–68.

Hulme, C. (1981). *Reading retardation and multi-sensory teaching.* London: Routledge & Kegan Paul.

Idol, L. (1988). Johnny can't read: Does the fault lie with the book, the teacher, or Johnny? *Remedial and Special Education, 9*(l), 8–25, 35.

Juel, C. (1988, April). *Learning to read and write: A longitudinal study of fifty-four children from first through fourth grade.* Paper presented at the meeting of the American Educational Research Association, New Orleans, LA.

Juel, C., & Roper-Schneider, D. (1985). The influence of basal readers on first grade reading. *Reading Research Quarterly, 20*, 134–152.

Kantrowitz, B. (1990, Fall/Winter). The reading wars. *Newsweek* (Special Edition), 8–9, 12, 14.

King, D. F., & Goodman, K. S. (1990). Whole language: Cherishing learning and their language. *Language, Speech, and Hearing Services in Schools, 21*, 221–227.

Kirk, S. A., & Kirk, W. D. (1956). How Johnny learns to read. *Exceptional Children, 22*, 158–160.

Krashen, S. (1982). *Principles and practice in second language acquisition.* New York: Pergamon Press.

Ladas, H. S. (1980). A handbook of irreducible facts for teaching and learning. *Phi Delta Kappan, 61*, 606–607.

L. 'E. Stein, C., & Goldman, J. (1980). Beginning reading instruction for children with minimal brain dysfunction. *Journal of Learning Disabilities, 13*, 219–222.

Liberman, I. Y., & Liberman, A. M. (1990). Whole language vs. code emphasis: Underlying assumptions and their implications for reading instruction. *Annals of Dyslexia, 40*, 51–76.

Liberman, I. Y., Shankweiler, D., & Liberman, A. M. (1989). The alphabetic principle and learning to read. In D. Shankweiler and I. Y. Liberman (Eds.), *Phonology and reading disability: Solving the reading puzzle.* (pp. 1–33). Ann Arbor: University of Michigan.

Lundberg. I., Frost, J., & Petersen, O. (1988). Effects of an extensive program for stimulating phonological awareness in preschool children. *Reading Research Quarterly, 23*, 263–284.

Maclean, M., Bryant, P., & Bradley, L. (1987). Rhymes, nursery rhymes, and reading in early childhood. *Merrill-Palmer Quarterly, 33*, 255–281.

McConkie, G. W., & Zola, D. (1987). Visual attention during eye fixations while reading. In M. Coltheart (Ed.), *Attention and performance XII: The psychology of reading* (pp. 385–401). London: Erlbaum.

MacGinite, W. H. (1991). Reading instruction: Plus ca change. *Educational Leadership, 48*, 55–58.

McKenna, M. C., Robinson, R. D., & Miller, J. W. (1990a). Whole language: A research agenda for the nineties. *Educational Researcher, 19*(8), 3–6.

McKenna, M. C., Robinson, R. D., & Miller, J. W. (1990b). Whole language and the need for open inquiry: A rejoinder to Edelsky. *Educational Researcher, 19*(8), 12–13.

Monroe, M. (1932). *Children who cannot read.* Chicago: University of Chicago Press.

Muskopf, A., & Robinson, A. (1966). High school reading, 1965. *Journal of Reading, 10*, 75–87.

Newman, J. M., & Church, S. M. (1990). Myths of whole language. *Reading Teacher, 44*(1), 20–26.

Orton, S. T. (1925). Word-blindness in school children. *Archives of Neurology and Psychiatry, 14*, 581–615.

Orton, S. T. (1937). *Reading, writing, and speech problems in children.* New York: W.W. Norton.

Pearson, P. D. (1989). Commentary: Reading the whole-language movement. *Elementary School Journal, 90*, 231–241.

Perfetti, C. A. (1985). *Reading ability.* New York, NY: Oxford.

Perfetti, C. A., Beck, I., Bell, L. C., & Hughes, C. (1987). Phonemic knowledge and learning to read are reciprocal: A longitudinal study of first grade children. *Merrill-Palmer Quarterly, 33*, 283–319.

Pring, L., & Snowling, M. (1986). Developmental changes in word recognition: An information processing account. *Quarterly Journal of Experimental Psychology, 38A*, 395–518.

Rayner, K., & Pollatsek, A. (1987). Eye movements in reading: A tutorial review. In M. Coltheart (Ed.), *Attention and performance XII: The psychology of reading* (pp. 327–362). London: Erlbaum.

Samuels, S. J. (1996). Why children fail to learn and what to do about it. *Exceptional Children, 53*, 7–16.

Shankweiler, D. (1989). Problems of comprehension related to decoding. In D. Shankweiler and I. Y. Liberman (Eds.), *Phonology and reading disability: Solving the reading puzzle* (pp. 35–68). Ann Arbor: University of Michigan.

Share, D. L., Jorm, A. F., Maclean, R., & Matthews, R. (1984). Sources of individual differences in reading acquisition. *Journal of Educational Psychology, 76*, 1309–1324.

Slingerland, B. H. (1978). *Why wait for a criterion of failure.* Cambridge, MA: Educators Publishing Service.

Smith, E. B., Goodman, K. S., & Meredith, R. (1970). *Language and thinking in the elementary school.* New York: Holt, Rinehart, and Winston.

Snowling, M. (1987). *Dyslexia: A cognitive developmental perspective.* Oxford: Basil Blackwell.

Stahl, S. A., & Miller, P. D. (1989). Whole language and language experience approaches for beginning reading: A quantitative research synthesis. *Review of Educational Research, 59*, 87–116.

Stahl, S. A., Osborn, J., & Lehr, F. (1990). *Beginning to read: Thinking and learning about print—A summary.* Urbana-Champaign: University of Illinois Center for the Study of Reading.

Stanovich, K. E. (1980). Toward an interactive compensatory model of individual differences in the development of reading fluency. *Reading Research Quarterly, 16*, 32–71.

Stanovich, K. E. (1982a). Individual differences in the cognitive processes of reading: I. Word decoding. *Journal of Learning Disabilities, 15*, 485–493.

Stanovich, K. E. (1982b). Individual differences in the cognitive processes of reading: II. Text-level processes. *Journal of Learning Disabilities, 15*, 549–554.

Stanovich, K. E. (1990). A call for an end to the paradigm wars in reading research. *Journal of Reading Behavior, 22*, 221–231.

Taylor, B., Harris, L. A., & Pearson, P. D. (1988). *Reading difficulties: Instruction and assessment.* New York: Random House.

Vellutino, F. R., & Scanlon, D. M. (1987). Phonological coding, phonological awareness and reading ability: Evidence from a longitudinal and experimental study. *Merrill-Palmer Quarterly, 33*, 321–363.

Watson, B. (1991, January). Reading recovery colloquium. Presentation at the University of Arizona, Tucson.

Watson, D. J. (1989). Defining and describing whole language. *Elementary School Journal, 90*, 129–141.

Westby, C. (1990). The role of the speech-language pathologist in whole language. *Language, Speech, and Hearing Services in Schools, 21*, 228–237.

Nancy Mather is a faculty member in the College of Education, Division of Special Education and Rehabilitation at the University of Arizona in Tucson.

An Affective Approach to Reading: Effectively Teaching Reading to Mainstreamed Handicapped Children

Michael O. Tunnell
James E. Calder
Joseph E. Justen III
Phillip B. Waldrop

Bill was a thirteen-year-old second-grade reader in an inner city school. Literacy did not seem to be part of his future until his junior high school initiated an affective approach to reading instruction. One day, project consultant Daniel Fader noticed Bill intensely reading the adult novel *Jaws*. He asked Bill if the book was good, and the boy responded with an enthusiastic "Yeah!" "But isn't it hard?" Fader asked. "Sure it's hard," Bill answered, "but it's worth it!" (Fader, Duggins, & McNiel, 1976, p. 236).

Bill was and is proof of a successful program designed to make readers of all children, including the mildly handicapped learner. However, in order to initiate a literature-based, affective reading curriculum, teachers and administrators must alter a widespread mind-set concerning the troublesome nature of language development.

We believe that language development is a fairly natural process. Most of us learn to speak with little effort, and reading should also be a natural act—at least more so than the way it is traditionally taught in the schools.

Unfortunately, basal readers, skill cards, and phonics lessons are all too often the total reading program. Reading aloud or silent reading time is ignored or sandwiched in during a few extra minutes in an already crowded day. The process of reading has been broken down into a thousand intricate parts that are then taught to children in hope that they will weave them all back together into the act we call reading. Reading instruction in many schools is artificial—workbooks, exercise sheets, basal readers, texts, and other materials seldom read outside of school. In short, students are seldom involved in "real reading."

Despite the prevalence of the skills emphasis approach, there is some evidence to suggest that this is not the best method to teach reading. Gibson and Levin (1975, p. 324), for example, have determined that "when teaching a complex task (reading) it is preferable to start training on the task itself, or a close approximation to it, rather than giving training on each component skill independently and then integrating them." Research has also shown that an enriched school program with no formal introduction to reading in first grade can prove to be more successful than conventional instruction (Shepherd & Ragan, 1982). Perhaps most convincing was a recent study conducted at Brigham Young University that involved 1,200 children from four Utah school districts. Eldredge and Butterfield (1986) discovered that second graders made startlingly significant progress in reading achievement when taught with children's trade books (children's

---

From "An Affective Approach to Reading: Effectively Teaching Reading to Mainstreamed Handicapped Children" by M. O. Tunnell, J. E. Calder, J. E. Justen III and P. B. Waldrop, *The Pointer, 32*(3), pp. 38–40, Spring 1988. Published by Heldref Publications, 1319 Eighteenth Street, N.W., Washington, D.C. 20036–1802. Copyright © 1988. Reprinted by permission.

literature) as compared with other instructional methods and materials.

We are certainly not advocating total abandonment of skills training. Skills have their place. But often they are overemphasized to the detriment of children's reading progress. Ironically, Trelease (1985) has pointed out that it is the poorest readers who receive the heaviest doses of skills instruction and therefore spend the least amount of time on the objective itself—reading. We propose a procedure for teaching reading to mildly handicapped children that calls for a radical shift away from skills instruction in favor of oral and silent reading of children's literature. The rationale is simply that reading improves when more words pass before your eyes. The cycle is designed to work as follows: you practice, you get better, you like it better because you are better at doing it, you practice some more, and so on.

The goal of affective reading instruction is to improve attitudes towards reading, thereby increasing time spent in personal reading activities. This leads to an increase in reading abilities and skills. We suggest that such activities will have similar positive effects on mildly handicapped learners (learning-disabled, educable mentally retarded, and behaviorally disordered children).

The objectives of an affective reading program for handicapped learners differ little from those used with regular education students. The most basic objective is that students will develop a positive attitude toward books and reading. Others include students self-selecting reading materials, reading outside of class, achieving 30 minutes of sustained silent reading during school hours, and listening daily with interest to at least 15 minutes of oral reading by their teachers from trade books.

In order to implement an affective approach to reading, there are several steps that teachers will need to take. First, teachers will need to familiarize themselves with children's books and their authors. Familiarity with these books will enable the teacher to model a genuine appreciation and enthusiasm for personal reading while developing a knowledge of the materials that make a literature approach possible. One basic source for book selection is *Adventuring with Books*, published by the National Council of Teachers of English (Monson, 1985). This familiarization will allow the teacher to build a classroom library of children's trade books, generally paperbacks. This library should include books on a wide range of interest and reading levels and will serve as the basic resource for implementing this approach to reading.

After establishing the classroom library, the teacher will need to identify and develop affective reading activities that must include sustained silent reading (ideally 30 minutes daily), the teacher reading aloud (15 to 30 minutes daily), and independent reading at home (5 hours weekly). Other activities might include writing to authors, creating personal books, writing and printing a school book review newsletter, purchasing books through book clubs, literature-oriented art projects, and booksharing activities.

In addition, the teacher may wish to identify and organize a skill program that can be efficiently presented within a 15- to 30-minute time period. We are not against skill training per se, just the overuse of this approach. In order to further reinforce reading activities, the teacher might devise a plan to integrate literature with other content areas. For example, historical fiction and biography can be used to supplement lessons in social studies.

In implementing the program, teachers must orient students to the goals and procedures of the literature-based approach to reading instruction, with emphasis on generating enthusiasm among the children. Also, to improve carry-over, parents should be oriented to the literature approach and trained to use supportive activities in the home. For example, parents can keep a log of the number of hours children read at home, encourage a reduction in television viewing, provide a role model (e.g., family reading time each evening), and encourage book ownership (e.g., giving books as gifts). Parent involvement is highly desirable, but it is not essential for the success of this approach.

Although the basic strategies described above should be sufficient for most situations, there will be times when some modifications will be required. For instance, teachers must serve as surrogate parents for those children who have little if any parental involvement in their reading program. Extra time and effort must be provided for helping these children select books, establish book ownership, and build positive attitudes and enthusiasm toward reading, as well as for modeling proper personal reading habits.

Also, resource teachers are encouraged to seek active support and involvement from regular classroom teachers in implementing this approach. However, in cases where regular classroom teachers are resistant, resource teachers may still implement this program with necessary modifications. These modifications might include reducing amounts of time spent in sustained silent reading and reading aloud, designating certain days for skills training and others for silent reading and reading aloud, and scheduling fewer yet more select reading-related activities.

Last, although this approach is designed to capitalize on the intrinsic rewards of reading, consider the initial use of extrinsic rewards with some children. This is especially crucial with children who have a previous history of difficulty with reading. In doing this, one can ensure that the learner continues to participate in the instruction until he/she is functioning at an intrinsic level of reward.

As accountability is becoming more of an issue in education, it would be wise for teachers to develop an evaluation plan in order to demonstrate that their reading approach is working. The following are some suggestions for developing such a plan:

1. Use a pretest/posttest measure to assess changes in reading attitudes. Suggested instruments include the San Diego County Inventory of Reading Attitudes (1961) or the Attitudes Toward Reading Scale (1975).
2. Keep track of the number of pages of students' personal reading using log books, wall charts, and so on.
3. Keep track of time spent by students on personal reading outside of school.
4. Use a pretest/posttest measure to assess changes in reading comprehension. Suggested instruments include the reading comprehension section of your district's standardized achievement test or the Peabody Individual Achievement Test (Dunn & Markwardt, 1970).
5. Keep anecdotal records on each child as he/she discusses completed books with the instructor during interview sessions. Records will include information about books read, the child's response to his/her reading, and attitudinal comments made by the child.

In addition to program evaluation, it will be necessary for teachers to evaluate students. For this purpose, the teacher should devise a grading technique based on the number of pages read, the number of hours reading outside class, performance and/or participation in affective reading activities, and reading skills mastery.

The literature approach to reading instruction advocated here was field tested in a regular classroom, the population of which included several mildly handicapped children. The treatment was administered to 28 fifth-grade students. Results of the pretest/posttest attitude survey showed that all students, including the mildly handicapped, had significantly improved their attitudes toward books and reading. Though individual scores were not carefully examined, the fact that negative responses virtually disappeared indicated that all students were positively influenced.

An anonymous parent survey with a return rate of 86% indicated that parents were pleased by the positive changes in their children's reading behavior and attitudes. At least 75% of the responses for each item fell in the positive category. Most items received a positive response rate of near or above 90%. Though the questionnaire used a five-point Likert scale, it also solicited written comments that unquestionably indicated support for the program.

Students attending resource and Chapter One classes showed particular progress both in attitude and reading ability. Anecdotal records showed that most of these students began to speak positively about reading to their teachers and to their peers. The students also showed significant increases in the amount and frequency of personal reading. Of the eight students receiving resource or Chapter One instruction, six progressed from reading nearly nothing to having read 1,000 pages or better per term in personally selected materials. These same eight students achieved an average growth of one year and three months on the reading section of the SRA achievement test, which was two months higher than the class average. Their growth in reading comprehension exceeded their total reading achievement as measured on the SRA.

If you decide to implement this approach in your classroom, we have one last parting suggestion. Plan a party at the end of the first year to celebrate the success of your programs. Give books as prizes!

REFERENCES

Dunn, L., & Markwardt, F. (1970). *Peabody Individual Achievement Test.* Circle Pines, MN: American Guidance Service.

Eldredge, J. L., & Butterfield, D. (1986). Alternatives to traditional reading instruction. *The Reading Teacher,* 40(1), 32–37.

Fader, D., Duggins, J., & McNiel, E. (1976). *The new hooked on books.* New York: Berkeley.

Gibson, E., & Levin, H. (1975). *The psychology of reading.* Cambridge, MA: MIT Press.

Monson, D. (Ed.). (1985). *Adventuring with books.* Urbana, IL: NCTE.

Pennsylvania State Department of Education. (1975). *Attitudes toward reading scale.* Harrisburg, PA: Bureau of Curriculum Services. (ERIC Document Reproduction Service No. ED 117647)

San Diego County, California Department of Education. (1961). *An inventory of reading attitude.* San Diego, CA: Superintendent of Schools, Department of Education.

Shepherd, G., & Ragan, W. (1982). *Modern elementary curriculum* (6th ed.). New York: Holt, Rinehart and Winston.

Trelease, J. (1985). *The read-aloud handbook.* New York: Penguin.

Michael O. Tunnell is an assistant professor of elementary education in the Department of Curriculum and Instruction at Northern Illinois University in DeKalb. James E. Calder, Joseph E. Justen III, and Phillip B. Waldrop are, respectively, associate professor of special education, professor of special education, and chairperson, all in the Department of Special Education and Speech Pathology at Arkansas State University.

Reading and Writing for the Gifted: A Whole Language Perspective

Selina J. Ganopole

Over the past two decades, research in a variety of fields. including cognitive psychology, neurobiology, linguistics, and sociology, along with research in composition and literacy, have provided us with dramatic insights into how people learn and how language and literacy are acquired. Rooted in this research is a curricular approach to language development that has come to be referred to as "whole language" (Edelsky, 1986; Goodman, 1986; Goodman & Goodman, 1981; Newman, 1985), the characteristics of which are briefly summarized below:

1. A view of learning as an active constructive process in which prior knowledge, interests, and self-motivated purposes play a major role.
2. A view of language as central to learning.
3. Acknowledgment of the important role social interaction plays in the learning process.
4. A functional view of language learning that suggests that language is learned through actual use in efforts to accomplish relevant purposes.
5. A view of reading as a meaning-making process in which meaning is constructed by building associations between the text and what is already known and believed.
6. A view of writing as a meaning-making process in which writers make their own connections and construct their own meanings.

In spite of the recent proliferation of articles on whole language theory, little attention has been given to its implications for the gifted. Yet, gifted students have much to gain from a curriculum which reflects this theoretical perspective. This paper presents some practical suggestions and strategies for translating current theory into practice in developing reading and writing curricula capable of fostering the language and cognitive development of gifted learners.

IMPLICATIONS FOR THE READING PROGRAM

Current theory and research on learning and language development emphasize the importance of approaching reading instruction from an active, meaning-making stance. Equally emphatic is the current stance that "reading, like all language, only develops easily and well in the context of its use" (Goodman et al., 1988). Over the past two decades, sufficient research and theory have accumulated to support making changes with respect to the following: the nature of the reading materials which comprise the reading program; the way comprehension is taught and evaluated; the nature of the questions teachers ask students about the text as well as the nature of the responses they should expect (and encourage); and who should control what students read. In the following section, each of these changes is discussed in turn. An additional change that deals with the relationship between reading and writing and its implications for instruction will be discussed in a separate section later in the paper.

From "Reading and Writing for the Gifted: A Whole Language Perspective" by S. J. Ganopole, 1988, *Roeper Review, 11*, pp. 88–92. Copyright © 1988 by Roeper City and Country School. Reprinted by permission of Selina J. Ganopole and the *Roeper Review*, P.O. Box 329, Bloomfield Hills, MI 48303.

An Emphasis on Authentic Materials

In light of what we now know about learning and language development, reading instruction based on reductionist models of language learning—those which reflect the notion that reading is learned from the smallest unit to the largest, one skill at a time—can no longer be viewed as valid. We have also come to realize that instruction which ignores students' prior knowledge, interests, or their existing capabilities, does little to foster learning (Goodman, 1986; Goodman et al., 1988). Similarly, instruction which affords learners little opportunity for choice or control over their own reading fails to support the development of reading ability or learning.

Yet, nowhere are these elements more evident than in the basal readers which continue to be a mainstay of reading instruction in today's schools. While the use of basals may have been justified years ago when books and school libraries were at a premium, and basals provided easy access to a collection of stories, such justification no longer exists (Watson & Weaver, 1988). The abundance of readily available, quality literature for children and adolescents makes it possible for all teachers to provide students with authentic materials and programs.

The implications for instructional materials should thus be clear. There is no place for skills drills and workbooks that provide practice on isolated skills presented in decontextualized settings. Sequenced skills programs and materials which fragment language learning should be shelved along with the controlled-vocabulary basal texts. What should replace these materials? Appropriate replacements include the vast array of real world materials that are whole, meaningful, and related to a context that has purpose. Such materials include literature—books representing the various genres, and reflecting a wide range of complexity and interest; topical materials which reflect content from across the curriculum as well as the special interests of students; adult reference books; and such real world resources as magazines, newspapers, and tradebooks. The importance of providing students with authentic materials was recently underscored by the Commission on Reading in their 1985 publication, Becoming a Nation of Readers:

> The most logical place for instruction in most reading and thinking strategies is in social studies and science rather than in separate lessons about reading. The reason is that the strategies are useful mainly when the student is grappling with important but unfamiliar content. (p. 73)

For gifted students, who tend to learn new skills quickly, often without direct instruction and certainly with no need for the endless drill required by most basal reading series, the current perspective offers a "release" from the unnatural control over learning exerted by traditional reading programs. In its place, the current perspective provides students with the opportunity to assume ownership and control over their own reading and learning.

A Modified Approach to the Use of Basals

Since (for a variety of reasons) basal reading programs continue to be a fact of school life in many classrooms, at the very least, their use should be open to modification in order to accommodate the abilities and interests of individual students. Following are several suggestions teachers may wish to consider in efforts to enhance the utility of these materials for their gifted students.

1. Break out of the lock-step sequence presented in the basal program. Instead, select stories on the basis of student interest (even allowing students to self-select stories), and teach skills on the basis of need.
2. Modify the instructional strategies to reflect recent research on comprehension,

for example: (a) focus on meaning as opposed to strategies which focus on isolated skills; (b) help students fit new material into personal experience—one of the most important findings to emerge from recent research is the extent to which a learner's prior knowledge of a topic influences comprehension; (c) encourage students to set their own purposes for reading—encourage them to formulate their own questions about the material rather than always requiring them to respond to the questions and purposes of "others"; (d) encourage divergent thinking and responses as opposed to strategies which suggest there is but one single right answer to any given question; and (e) foster creative reading ability. As Torrance (1985) notes:

> When a person reads creatively, he is sensitive to problems and possibilities in whatever he reads. He makes himself aware of the gaps in knowledge, the unsolved problems, the missing elements, things that are incomplete or out of focus. To resolve this tension, so important in the creative thinking process, the creative reader sees new relationships, creates new combinations, synthesizes relatively unrelated elements into a coherent whole, redefines or transforms certain pieces of information to discover new uses, and builds onto what is known. (Torrance in Witty, 1985, pp. 16–17)

3. Provide enrichment through "collateral reading," a term which refers to reading material related to the main topic or theme being studied. Such materials are used to support, enrich or broaden the experience of the reader (Tonjes & Zintz, 1981). When textbooks are used in this way, they can "become elements in resource kits to provide more specific focus on single concepts or depth treatment of groups of related concepts" (Goodman, 1976, p. 486).

Reconceptualizing the Teaching and Evaluation of Comprehension

A constructivist view of learning suggests that readers take a far more active role in their own comprehension, integrating new knowledge from the text with previous knowledge. Consequently, teachers must reconsider where meaning "resides." As Pearson (1985) argues, meaning does not reside principally in the text itself; rather, it provides cues that enable readers to construct their own meaning. Since individuals bring different kinds of knowledge and prior experience to the learning situation, it should be expected that different perceptions will produce different interpretations. As such, the text itself can no longer be viewed as the single criterion for determining the extent of an individual's comprehension. Instead it must be taken along with other factors such as the student's prior knowledge, strategies, and the context of the task itself, "as one facet in the complex array we call comprehension" (Pearson, 1985, p. 726).

This view not only advises against the practice of assessing comprehension solely on the basis of how closely readers' responses approximate the text being read, it underscores the fact that divergent responses are to be expected. This has particular significance for the instruction of gifted students who, with their voracious curiosity, tendency to read extensively, and ability to see relationships between diverse issues, often respond to questions about a particular reading selection in unexpected ways.

Questions Which Encourage Divergent Responses

In contrast with the traditional instructional paradigm which discourages divergent responses, dismissing them as inappropriate, irrelevant, or otherwise unacceptable, a common sense imperative emerges from the current perspective on reading comprehension: divergent responses should not only be expected, they should be encouraged. Thus, questions should be structured so they invite different responses. Questions such as "What else could this character have done in this situation?" or "What other solutions do you see for this problem?" are open ended and invite divergent responses.

Students might also be asked to respond to a particular question from different perspectives. For example, depending on the nature of the problem or issue presented in the literature, students could be asked to speculate about how children or adults from different countries and cultures might respond. Although given free reign to speculate, students would nevertheless be expected to back up their responses with plausible explanations.

In this way, the discussions about what was read would require far more than the regurgitation of known facts. Instead, such discussions would require students to interpret meanings, give their opinions, compare and contrast ideas, and synthesize facts to form general opinions or conclusions.

In speaking about divergent responses, it should be remembered that ideas can also be reflected in a variety of formats: through a drawing or painting, a sculpture, a poem, a story, or through interpretive dance movements. It is generally agreed that creativity involves the ability to restructure ideas in new ways. By encouraging students to present ideas through a variety of media, teachers can effectively use literature to spark creativity in art, music, movement and writing.

However, accepting divergent responses does not mean giving students carte blanche, allowing them to believe that anything goes. What it means is that teachers are willing to accept responses even if they are not the ones they anticipated. It also means that students must accept responsibility for developing their ideas and making them clear enough for others to understand.

For students to respond freely and creatively, however, they must first believe that what they have to say will be treated with respect. Only in an accepting environment will students feel free enough to speculate, guess, and try new things. Such an environment is vital if we are to encourage what Bruner (1960) describes as the most valuable coin of the thinker at work: the shrewd guess, the fertile hypothesis, and the courageous leap to a tentative conclusion.

Allowing Opportunities for Self-Selection of Books

At the heart of the current perspective on learning and language development is recognition of the importance of interest and self-initiated purpose in the learning process. As such, students need to be given greater opportunity to self-select topics for study and materials to read that reflect their personal interests (Renzulli, 1977).

Although self-selection is advocated, this is not meant to suggest that teachers abdicate their responsibility for guiding the reading selections of their gifted students. As with other students, the gifted often need to be guided toward appropriate materials. Take for example, the gifted student who tends to read extensively on a topic of particular interest. While wide reading in a particular area can lead to valuable comparative reading activities, such students often need to be guided toward exploring other areas as well. And, since the concept of readability has little meaning when it comes to gifted readers, teachers can feel free to guide them toward exploring as broad a variety of reading materials as possible.

A Cautionary Note

Much as independent reading should be encouraged, alone it does not constitute a comprehensive reading program. In spite of their prodigious abilities to learn new skills quickly and gain abstract concepts with ease, it must not be assumed that gifted readers automatically know how to deal effectively with the demands of different kinds of written materials or know how to utilize various reference materials. Gifted students, like all other students, need guidance and instruction in order to gain essential skills that will enhance their versatility to handle the diversity of materials that characterize communication in the real world. Their skills need to be assessed and appropriate instruction provided.

IMPLICATIONS FOR THE WRITING PROGRAM

As with reading, implications for the writing program stem from (a) an active view of learning as a meaning-making process and (b) recognition of the fact that writing, like other aspects of language, develops through actual use in meaningful contexts. With increased understanding of the writing process, we have come to view writing not merely as a "product," but as a valuable tool for learning as well.

The premise that writing serves as a tool for learning hinges on certain concepts and assumptions. First, it requires an understanding that in the process of writing the learner is actively involved in building connections between new information and what is already known. Second, in the process of writing we often discover what it is we have to say. And third, in the process of interacting with our own thoughts, new ideas are born, suggesting that "writing not only reflects our knowing . . . but . . . also causes our knowing" (Dillon, 1985, p. 9).

It also assumes that the writing requires the writer to make purposeful decisions about how to express whatever is being learned. Such nonwriting activities as filling in the blanks on exercise sheets or activities which require minimal language choices, such as answering questions by parroting the teacher or the text, do little to promote learning. Thus, an effective writing program could be characterized as one which emphasizes writing as a way of learning about oneself as well as about the world, with the expectation that in the process of using writing to learn other things, writing skills develop. With this as a basic premise, the following suggestions are provided to assist teachers in planning appropriate writing experiences for their students.

Use Writing as a Tool for Learning in All Content Areas

Writing can no longer be viewed as the sole province of the language arts curriculum, but rather must be acknowledged as an appropriate tool for learning in all subject areas; its use integrated within and throughout the curriculum. However, as important as it is to encourage students to write, equally important is the kind of writing they do. Britton et al. (1975) describe writing according to three function categories: transactional, expressive, and poetic. Transactional writing, according to Britton, uses language to get things done; to inform, instruct and persuade. Expressive writing, on the other hand, is described as thinking and speculating on paper; writing usually done for oneself. In poetic writing, language is viewed as an art medium in which the writer uses language for creative expression; in this respect, it may be said that language is to the writer what paint is to the artist and clay is to the sculptor.

What kind of writing is emphasized in schools today? Although the current trend toward writing across the curriculum may be prompting an increase in the amount of expressive writing occurring in classrooms today, the research continues to show that transactional writing receives, by far, the greatest emphasis (Applebee, 1981; Britton, 1975; Emig, 1977; Freisinger, 1982). Findings such as these prompted Britton to conclude that the small amount of speculative (expressive) writing done in today's schools indicates that curricular aims do not include the fostering of writing that reflects or promotes independent thinking. Expressive writing, according to Britton (1975), is the language closest to thought and "may be at any stage the kind of writing best adapted to exploration and discovery. It is the language that externalizes our first stages in tackling a problem or coming to grips with an experience" (p. 165).

On the other hand, transactional writing, according to Emig (1971) is:

> ... other-directed—in fact, it is other-centered. The concern is with sending a message, a communication out into the world for the edification, the enlightenment, and ultimately the evaluation of another. Too often, the other is a teacher, interested chiefly in a product he can criticize rather than in a process he can help initiate through imagination and sustain through empathy and support. (p. 97)

We have come to see that the transactional function of language does not engage students in the kinds of thinking that promote open-ended exploration. As Freisinger (1982) notes, the excessive reliance on transactional writing in today's schools seemingly reflects our educational system's neglect of the discovery function of writing.

The time has come for teachers to take a closer look at the writing activities they provide their students. While some forms of student writing need to be evaluated, there is general agreement among researchers that the current practice of emphasizing transactional, product-oriented writing has a negative effect on the writing and learning abilities of students. Greater emphasis needs to be given to expressive writing—writing which encourages exploration, speculation, and personal inquiry. (Strategies for encouraging such writing will be discussed later in the paper.)

Emphasize Function before Form

As in reading, the emphasis in writing should be on meaning. This is not meant to suggest that clarity, organization, grammar, spelling, or the conventions of capitalization and punctuation be overlooked. Instead, what is being suggested is a shift in emphasis, that is, a shift as to when and how appropriate attention will be given to these skills.

The current view of language development stresses the functional use of language, suggesting that individuals learn the forms of language through its functional use (Crafton, 1983). In following the belief that function precedes form, the emphasis is then appropriately placed on the creative aspect of language which enables people to cope with novel ideas and situations (Mayher et al., 1983).

Thus, teachers are urged to lift the constraints of "correctness" from first drafts. Students should be encouraged to focus on constructing the "message," concentrating on the expression of ideas. Once the message has been constructed, attention can then turn to the "refining" process. It is usually only after writers have engaged in the process of committing to paper what it is they want to say that they are inclined to attend to the conventions of writing in order to clarify their message (Graves, 1984; Hartwell, 1985; Mayher, 1983).

When attention is finally directed to the conventions, the instruction provided should occur within the context of the writing produced by the writer. Instructional planning must thus be guided by the writing that students produce and not by the curriculum guide. In other words, instruction should focus on particular problems that are evidenced in the papers of particular students. In this way, students are more likely to attend to the instruction provided since it is perceived as purposeful and necessary.

Allow Flexibility in Topic Choice

If we accept the notion that writing develops through use in purposeful situations, then it follows that the writing experiences provided must be perceived as relevant to the writer. Although the notion itself is hard to fault, its translation into practice has often been less than appropriate. Telling students to "write about anything that interests you" may not be the ideal assignments some teachers think they are. While such assignments may be appropriate for some of the students some of the time, their lack of context often produces less than desirable results. A more effective strategy may be to provide what Mayher et al. (1983) refers to as "freedom in context." What this means is that students and teachers negotiate choices within the context of a particular assignment. For example, students may be given a wide variety of choices with respect to voice, purpose, and audience. Or, they may be given a variety of choices with respect to which aspects of a particular topic they would like to devote their learning/writing efforts. Giving students choices such as these allows them to gain ownership of topics they may not have originally selected. By providing freedom in context, students' interests are taken into account, inventiveness often stimulated, and the efforts that went into curriculum planning are not ignored. However, the present state of the art reminds us that flexibility must be built into curricular plans. As such, they are capable of guiding the teaching/learning experiences provided, but with the expectation that modifications will be made to accommodate the interests and abilities of individual students.

Provide Sufficient Time for Students to Engage in the Writing Process

Students need sufficient time to engage in the various stages of the writing process: time to explore the topic they will write about; time for information gathering which may occur in a variety of ways, including observation, reading, and interviewing others; time for composing the first draft, a stage during which students put their ideas down on paper, changing and shaping as they go, receiving input from teachers and peers in the process; and time to engage in the revision and editing of their work. There must also be time allotted for teachers to demonstrate "solutions" to problems, provide writing models, and model appropriate revision strategies.

Provide Opportunities for Sharing What Students Write

Not to be overlooked is the important role that writing can play in the development of creative products, a component frequently emphasized in programs for the gifted. Here the product can take the form of a book, a play, a brochure, or an article written for the class, school or community newspaper. While the benefits which derive from engaging in the creative process itself are of primary interest to teachers, for the students—the gifted as well as other students—the primary motivation for persisting with a particular writing task often lies in the knowledge that their efforts will be shared with others.

Publication provides children with recognition and credit for the thought, care, and effort that went into the written product they created. For gifted students, the benefits which may be derived from such recognition may be especially important in light of the fact that their high level performance and creativity are often taken for granted by teachers. Thus, publication often provides recognition and feedback about the quality of their work that are sometimes denied them.

Provide Activities That Emphasize the Reading, Writing, Learning Connection

There is considerable agreement among authorities that reading and writing involve analogous skills, knowledge, cognitive processes and strategies (Aulls, 1985; Kucer, 1985; Tierney & Leys, 1986; Tierney & Pearson, 1983). While this should not be interpreted to mean that reading and writing are so closely related that students need instruction in only one or the other, there is ample evidence to suggest that their curricular combination can foster the development of each (Shanahan, 1980; Stotsky, 1983). As such, it makes good instructional sense to engage students in a variety of writing experiences which allow them to develop, examine, reinforce, and extend their understandings about what they have read.

For example, in the conversational format of dialogue journals, students can be encouraged to respond to aspects of the text (expository or narrative) which concern them or in some way touch them. In this way, students are encouraged to reflect on what they have read. They are free to ask questions about what they don't understand, speculate about alternative answers, argue points they disagree with, describe their reactions to characters and events, and, in general, express their personal feelings. In essence, students are encouraged to think in written language. Since these are "dialogue" journals, the teacher writes a personal response in return, directing her message to the content of the student's writing—not to its form or style. Although the teacher may pose some probing questions, the responses, essentially, are natural extensions of the students' thinking about issues and experiences.

An alternative to the dialogue journal is the personal journal. Here, students write only for themselves. Although they may choose to share excerpts from time to time, the perceived sense of freedom provided by this kind of writing often encourages more creative and reflective thinking about ideas encountered in text. In general, however, journal writing allows students to set the pace and the direction of the extended thinking they will do about issues and ideas encountered in text.

More structured responses can be elicited by asking students to respond in ways such as the following: write an example from personal experience that illustrates a particular point made in the book; present an argument against a particular idea, issue, or point; consider alternative ways to apply ideas presented in the text; compare different treatments of the same topic as presented by different authors. Asking students to respond in this way presents a significantly different approach from the traditional "read the passage and answer the single-answer questions" pedagogy typical of traditional reading programs.

Inviting students to "edit" their textbook provides a novel approach to the development of critical thinking and language development in conjunction with content area learning. In describing this strategy, Bonnie Armbruster (1984) suggests that questions such as the following be used as evaluative criteria in the "editing" process: What did the author intend for me to learn? Is there something "inconsiderate" about the way the text is presented? What could be done to make the text "considerate" (i.e.. more comprehensible)? How are these ideas really related? What would be a better title? Not only do students engage in critical reading and thinking skills, but as Armbruster notes, they begin to realize that textbooks aren't sacred, that authors make mistakes, and that all texts should be read with a critical eye.

Teachers sometimes wonder if gifted students really need to be involved in the writing program. The answer to this question should be considered in light of the following. Although many gifted students can and do write, it cannot be assumed that their advanced cognitive or verbal abilities automatically signal ability to write effectively in a variety of forms. Indeed, as Kaplan (1979) points out, the advanced logical ability which often characterizes gifted learners is not always evident in their ability to produce well-organized writing. Neither is it unusual to find that in spite of their ability to reach high-level abstractions quickly, gifted students often require guidance in discovering the logic behind their ideas. And, although they are often creative thinkers, they frequently require guidance in putting their ideas on paper in such a way that what was conceptualized in their own mind will materialize in the mind of the reader. Activities such as those described in this paper not only place the instruction of reading and writing in meaningful (and often stimulating contexts), they also place gifted learners where they rightfully belong: at the center of their own learning.

REFERENCES

Anderson. R., Hiebert. E., Scott, J., & Wilkinson, I. (Eds.). (1985). *Becoming a nation of readers.* The report of the commission on reading. (Contract No. 400-83-0057). Washington, DC: National Institute of Education.

Applebee, A. (1981). Writing in the secondary school. *English and the content areas.* Urbana, IL: NCTE.

Armbruster, B. (1984). The problem of "inconsiderate text." In G. G. Duffy, L. R. Roehler, & J. Mason (Eds.). *Comprehension instruction.* New York: Longman.

Aulls, M. (1985). Understanding the relationship between reading and writing. *Educational Horizons, 64,* 39–44.

Britton, J., Burgess, T., Martin, N., McLeod, A., Rosen, H. (1975). *The development of writing abilities,* London: Macmillan.

Bruner, J. (1960). *The Process of Education.* Cambridge, Mass.: Harvard University Press.

Crafton, L. (1983). Oral and written language: Related processes of a sociopsycholinguistic nature. In U. H. Hardt (Ed.), *Teaching reading with the other language arts.* Delaware: International Reading Association.

Dillon, D. (1985). Editorial. *Language Arts, 62,* 9.

Edelsky, C. (May, 1986). *Whole language—Theory and practice.* Paper presented at the 7th Transmountain Regional Conference of the International Reading Association, Vancouver, BC.

Emig, J. (1977). Writing as a mode of learning. *College Composition and Communication, 28,* 122–127.

Emig, J. (1971). *The Composing Processes of Twelfth Graders.* Urbana, Ill.: NCTE, 97.

Freisinger, R. (1982). Cross-disciplinary writing programs: Beginnings. In T. Fulwiler & A. Young (Eds.). *Language Connections: Writing and reading across the curriculum.* Urbana, Ill.: NCTE.

Goodman, K. (1986). *What's whole in whole language?* Exeter, N.H.: Heinemann Books.

Goodman, K., & Goodman, Y. (1981). *A whole language comprehension-centered view of reading development.* Occasional Paper no. 1. Program in Language and Literacy, University of Arizona, Tucson, AZ.

Goodman, K. (1976). Behind the eye: What happens in reading? Theoretical models and process of reading. In H. Singer and R. Ruddell (ed.). *Theoretical models and process of reading.* Newark, Del.: International Reading Association.

Goodman, K., Shannon, P., Freeman, Y., & Murphy, S. (1988). *Report Card on Basal Readers.* New York: Richard C. Owen Publishers.

Graves, D. (1984). *Writing: Teachers and children at work.* New Hampshire: Heinemann Educational Books.

Hartwell, P. (1985). Grammar, grammars, and the teaching of grammar. *College English, 47,* 120–127.

Kaplan, S. (1979). Language arts and social studies curriculum in the elementary school. In A. H. Passow (Ed.). *The gifted and the talented: Their education and development.* 78th Yearbook of the National Society for the Study of Education. Chicago: The University of Chicago Press.

Kucer, S. (1985). The making of meaning: Reading and writing as parallel processes. *Written Communication, 2,* 317–36.

Mayher, J., Lester, N., Pradl, G. (1983). *Learning to write/writing to learn.* Upper Montclair, N.J.: Boynton-Cook.

Newman, J. (Ed.)., (1985). *Whole language theory in use.* Portsmouth, N.H.: Heinemann Books.

Pearson, D. (1985). Changing the face of reading comprehension. *The Reading Teacher, 38,* 724–738.

Renzulli, J. (1977). *The enrichment triad model: A guide for developing defensible programs for the gifted.* Mansfield Center, CT: Creative Learning Press.

Shanahan, T. (1980). The impact of writing instruction on learning to read. *Reading World, 19,* 357–68.

Stotsky, S. (1983). Research on reading/writing relationships: A synthesis and suggested directions. *Language Arts, 60,* 627–43.

Tierney, R., & Leys, M. (1986). What is the value of connecting reading and writing? In B. Peterson (ed.), *Convergences: Transactions in reading and writing.* Urbana, IL: National Council of Teachers of English.

Tierney, R., & Pearson, P. (1983). Toward a composing model of reading. *Language Arts, 60,* 568–80.

Tonjes, M., & Zintz, M. (1987). *Teaching reading thinking study skills in content classroom.* Dubuque, IA: Brown Publishers.

Watson, D., & Weaver, C. (1988). Basals: Report on the Reading Commission Study. *Teachers Networking, The Whole Language Newsletter.* Richard Owens Publishing, Inc.

Witty, P. (1985). Rationale for fostering creative reading in the gifted and the creative. In M. Labuda (Ed.). *Creative Reading for the Gifted Learners.* Newark, DE: International Reading Association.

Selina J. Ganopole is an assistant professor in the Department of Curriculum and Instruction, University of Hawaii, Honolulu.

CHAPTER DISCUSSIONS AND ACTIVITIES

1. Pair off with a classmate and discuss the similarities and differences between the way whole language is used with multicultural primary grade children and junior high students.
2. Two terms, *limited English proficiency* (LEP) and *potentially English proficient* (PEP) are used in the literature concerning multicultural students. Which term would your prefer to use if you were a teacher of such students and why?
3. Name and describe the strategies primary grade teachers can use in fostering language development for LEP students as discussed in the article by Abramson, Seda, and Johnson. How are these six strategies directly related to the goals of whole language and in what specific ways?
4. Identify and review the published materials for LEP or PEP students found in your college library or Instructional Materials Center. Which of these are related to language development and reading instruction? Are these materials skills oriented or whole-language based? Discuss your findings with a small group of classmates; as a group, develop a list of those materials that are appropriate for use in a whole-language classroom. Share and discuss your findings with the whole class.
5. With three or four classmates, prepare an informal questionnaire that you would like to use for an interview with an ESL teacher. Make sure your questions include references to language and reading instruction.
6. The following comment was made by a classroom teacher with mainstreamed children:

   > I don't see how I can possibly use children's literature books for reading instruction with all the children in my class. Their range of differences is so vast. The less capable students need a great deal of drill on the basic skills in reading. If they don't know the difference between a short "a" from a long "a" how are they going to read trade book material?

   How would you respond to this teacher? Compare your answer to the points discussed in the article by Tunnell, Calder, Justen, III, and Waldrop.
7. Be prepared to discuss several student-centered, whole-language activities that you feel could be used effectively with learning-disabled students.
8. If possible, interview a teacher of students with learning disabilities. Discuss with the teacher how language, reading, and writing are integrated in the classroom. Ask the teacher what advantages and what disadvantages she/he finds with the instruction being used. How does this compare to the points discussed by Mather in her article?
9. A teacher of gifted students was heard to make the following comment:

   > I have decided to abandon the basal reader with my class and use whole language. These students are such bright, capable, independent readers that they do not need much direction from me.

   Respond to this comment, keeping in mind the suggestions discussed in the article by Ganopole.

CHAPTER 7

Content Areas and Whole Language

The content areas are an important part of the curriculum, usually starting in the intermediate grades. The use of reading in the content area has been defined by Bean and Readance (1989) as "the process of guiding students' comprehension in history, English, science or other subject areas" (p. 14). In these subjects, children are expected to read with ease and independence, understand important concepts, retain primary and pivotal information, draw inferences and make decisions. In this chapter, we will be viewing the differences between narrative and expository reading, comparing the disparities between basal readers and content-area texts and, most important, applying the whole-language philosophy to content-area learning.

NARRATIVE AND EXPOSITORY READING

In the primary grades, children are learning to read, and much of what they are exposed to is narrative in style; the stories used, even the excerpts from basal readers are drawn from children's literature (McGee and Richgels, 1985). When reading narrative material, children depend on the book to tell them a story. However, after the third grade, students are expected to learn by reading expository as well as narrative materials. Expository material has the fundamental purpose of explaining and is usually found in content-area textbooks. Durkin (1993) notes that "Inherent in expository text is the reason to read: to acquire information" (p. 316).

Most teachers expect that once youngsters master the fundamental aspects of the art of reading, they can easily make the shift from learning to read to being able to read in order to learn. Unfortunately, this is not what usually happens—especially within the content areas. Over the years, numerous references have been made to the difficulties that youngsters encounter. Chall (1983) refers to these difficulties as the "fourth grade slump," which results from changes in the child, changes in the curriculum and changes in instructional materials (p. 67). Heilman, Blair, and Rupley (1994) note that:

> One of the major problems in reading is the gap between students' store of meanings and the demands of the content reading matter. In addition, content reading contains many idiomatic expressions, abstract and figurative terms, and new connotations for familiar words. (p. 352)

CONTENT-AREA TEXTS COMPARED TO BASAL READERS

When reading in the content areas, students often find the texts too difficult to comprehend and the material very dry and boring. In many cases, the factual information is presented too rapidly for the students to digest. This is not surprising, as mentioned by The Commission on Reading in *Becoming a Nation of Readers* (Anderson, Hiebert, Scott, & Wilkinson, 1985), "Subject matter textbooks pose the biggest challenge for young readers being weaned from a diet of simple stories" (p. 67).

The obvious differences between content-area texts and basal reader texts are seen when they are compared.

Content Area Texts	*Basal Reader Texts*
1. Text is written in expository style.	1. Text is written in narrative style.
2. Each sentence and paragraph presents information that needs to be understood in order to comprehend future passages or chapters.	2. Usually, each story is complete in itself and unrelated to any other story.
3. Children read the text for information, rarely for enjoyment.	3. Stories are selected on the basis of their entertainment qualities and are read primarily for enjoyment.
4. The various new concepts, coupled with technical vocabulary terms, are introduced in rapid fashion with little opportunity provided for repetition or reinforcement.	4. Text contains a controlled vocabulary with carefully planned repetition for the reinforcement of key words and phrases.
5. Students need to learn specialized vocabularies for each of the content areas. Much of the vocabulary contains abstract meanings and some common words known in one context are given technical meanings unfamiliar to the child (e.g., "The President talked to the *Cabinet*").	5. Very little technical vocabulary is introduced. Even new words as they are introduced fall within the confines of the child's background and experience.

6. Because many graphic aids (i.e., charts, maps, tables, figures, etc.) are included in the text, children need much assistance in interpreting them.
7. Illustrations aid the student in understanding and conceptualizing key concepts.
8. Most texts are organizationally arranged with bold typographical headings. These help the student with outlining, semantic mapping, and finding the main idea of the chapters.
9. Questions for the students to answer individually or in small groups are provided at the end of each chapter in the text.
10. The readability by grade level is not carefully identified. With many texts, either the reading level is above the grade level for which the book is intended or the reading level fluctuates throughout the text.

6. Little or no graphic aids are included in the text.

7. Illustrations are mostly used to interest the child in reading and understanding the story plot.

8. Usually, the only bold typographical heading is the title of the story itself.

9. Some comprehension questions are provided in the teacher's manual for the teacher to ask before and after silent reading.

10. Readability of each text in a series is usually related to the grade level for which the book is intended. The identification of the grade level for each book is usually noted in the teacher's manual.

CONTENT AREAS AND WHOLE LANGUAGE

While literature is a valuable resource for teaching reading and English, it can also be used throughout the curriculum. Vacca and Vacca (1993), in discussing instruction in the content areas, state that "The promise of literature is that it has the potential to provide students with intense involvement in a subject and the power to develop in-depth understandings in ways that textbooks aren't designed to do" (p. 297).

In a whole-language classroom, teachers do not have to depend solely on the use of textbooks, but can use "authentic" materials. For example, in social studies, periodicals, and historical documents can be read by the students. In doing this, the teacher will rely less on lectures and worksheets and more on the direct involvement of the students in the learning process (Freeman & Freeman, 1991). Through the reading of biographies and historical fiction, American history can be made interesting and exciting for students (Brown & Abel, 1982). Literature can also help youngsters understand basic science concepts through the use of information or science-fiction books (Dole & Johnson, 1981).

The use of literature in the content-area classroom does not necessarily mean a complete abandonment of the textbook. Teachers can effectively combine textbooks with literature in order to enrich and expand the curriculum. Brozo and Tomlinson (1986) in discussing this joining of reading resources, point out that "thus, the storybook becomes the students' *terra firma* on their journey into the uncharted sea of exposition" (p. 289). Alfonso (1987) suggests that teachers use literature, especially information books, biographies, and historical fiction to assist students in understanding the wealth of knowledge in the various content areas. She notes that "a history textbook becomes what it should be—a reference book, one source of information rather than 'the' source" (p. 682). The textbook, joined with literature, provides the unfolding of relevant information that will be more readily retained—with the added benefits of the integration of all the language arts.

Looking Ahead

Moss (1991), Spiegel (1987), and Brown (1991) describe how teachers can infuse whole language into the various content areas. Hiebert and Fisher (1990) discuss three concerns directly and indirectly related to content-area instruction in the whole-language classroom.

The articles in this chapter recount the various ways in which teachers can effectively use literature in the content areas of social studies, science, and math. Some of the issues that will be addressed include:

- What are some of the strategies that teachers can use with literature in social studies and science?
- Where should content-area textbooks be in a whole-language classroom?
- In what ways can teachers use the genre of information books in a whole-language classroom?
- What fundamental curriculum changes need to be addressed when thinking about adopting whole-concept mathematics?
- What significances exist with regard to the exclusive use of narrative texts in the content areas?
- What problems are thought to exist in many whole-language classrooms with regard to the integration of subject matter areas?
- Why is the use of a variety of grouping strategies an important consideration in the content areas?

REFERENCES

Alfonso, S. R. (1987). Modules for teaching about people's literature—Module 6: Informational books. *Journal of Reading, 30*(8), 682–686.

Anderson, R. C., Hiebert, E. H., Scott, J. A., & Wilkinson, I. A. G. (1985). *Becoming a nation of readers: The report of the Commission on Reading.* Washington, DC: The National Institute of Education, U.S. Department of Education.

Bean, T. W., & Readance, J. (1989). Content area reading: Current state of the art. In D. Lapp, J. Flood, & N. Farnan (Eds.), *Content area reading and learning: Instructional strategies* (pp. 14–24). Englewood Cliffs, NJ: Prentice-Hall.

Brown, C. L. (1991). Whole concept mathematics: A whole language application. *Educational Horizons, 69*(3), 159–163.

Brown, J. E., & Abel, F. J. (1982). Revitalizing American history: Literature in the classroom. *The Social Studies, 73*(6), 279–283.

Brozo, W. G., & Tomlinson, C. M. (1986). Literature: The key to lively content courses. *The Reading Teacher, 40*(3), 288–293.

Chall, J. S. (1983). *Stages of reading development.* New York: McGraw-Hill.

Dole, J. S., & Johnson, V. R. (1981). Beyond the textbook: Science literature for young children. *Journal of Reading, 24*(7), 579–582.

Durkin, D. (1993). *Teaching them to read* (6th ed.). Boston: Allyn and Bacon.

Freeman, D. E., & Freeman, Y. S. (1991). "Doing" social studies: Whole language lessons to promote social action. *Social Education, 55*(1), 29–32, 66.

Heilman, A. W., Blair, T. R., & Rupley, W. H. (1994). *Principles and practices of teaching reading* (8th ed.). New York: Merrill/Macmillan.

Hiebert, E. H., & Fisher, C. W. (1990). Whole language: Three themes for the future. *Educational Leadership, 47*(6), 62–64.

McGee, L. M., & Richgels, D. J. (1985). Teaching expository text structure to elementary students. *The Reading Teacher, 38*(8), 739–748.

Moss, B. (1991). Children's nonfiction trade books: A complement to content area texts. *The Reading Teacher, 45*(1), 26–32.

Spiegel, D. L. (1987). Using adolescent literature in social studies and science. *Educational Horizons, 65*(4), 162–164.

Vacca, R. T., & Vacca, J. L. (1993). *Content area reading* (4th ed.). New York: HarperCollins.

FOR FURTHER STUDY

Alvermann, D. E. (1992). Educational reform initiatives and the move to more student-centered textbook instruction. In E. K. Dishner, T. W. Bean, J. E. Readence, & D. W. Moore (Eds.), *Reading in the content areas: Improving classroom instruction* (pp. 142–154). Dubuque, IA: Kendall-Hunt.

Baker, D., Semple, C., & Stead, T. (1990). *How big is the moon?: Whole maths in action.* Portsmouth, NH: Heinemann.

Baker, J., & Baker, A. (1991). *Raps and rhymes in math.* Portsmouth, NH: Heinemann.

Bickmore-Brand, J. (1993). *Language in mathematics.* Portsmouth, NH: Heinemann.

Bohning, G., & Radencich, M. (1989). Informational action books: A curriculum resource for science and social studies. *Journal of Reading, 32*(5), 434–439.

Borasi, R., Sheedy, J. R., & Siegel, M. (1990). The power of stories in learning mathematics. *Language Arts, 67*(2), 174–189.

Burns, M. (1992). *Math and literature.* Portsmouth, NH: Heinemann.

Fortner, R. W. (1990). How to combine language arts and science in the classroom. *Science Activities, 27*(4), 34–37.

Gordon, C. J., & MacInnis, D. (1993). Using journals as a window on students' thinking in mathematics. *Language Arts, 70*(1), 37–43.

Guzzetti, B. J., Kowalinski, B. J., & McGowan, T. (1992). Using a literature-based approach to teaching social studies. *Journal of Reading, 36*(2), 114–122.

Heacock, G. A. (1990). The we-search process: Using the whole language model of writing to learn social studies content and civic competence. *Social Studies and the Young Learner*, 2(3), 9–11.
McClure, A. A., & Zitlow, C. S. (1991). Not just the facts: Aesthetic response to elementary content area studies. *Language Arts, 68*(1), 27–33.
McKenna, M. C., & Robinson, R. D. (1993). *Teaching through text: A content literacy approach to content area reading.* New York: Longman.
Olson, M. W., & Gee, T. C. (1991). Content reading instruction in the primary grades: Perceptions and strategies. *The Reading Teacher, 45*(4), 298–307.
Pappas, C. C., Kiefer, B. Z., & Levstik, L. S. (1990). *An integrated language perspective in the elementary school: Theory into action.* New York: Longman.
Richards, L. (1990). "Measuring things in words": Language for learning mathematics. *Language Arts, 67*(1), 14–25.
Sanacore, J. (1990). Creating the lifetime reading habit in social studies. *Journal of Reading, 33*(6), 414–418.
Scott, J. (Ed.). (1993). *Science and language links.* Portsmouth, NH: Heinemann.
Sinatra, R. (1991). Integrating whole language with the learning of text structure. *Journal of Reading, 34*(6), 424–433.
Towery, R. W. (1991). Integrating literature in social studies instruction: Getting started. *Reading Improvement, 28*(4), 277–282.
Wood, K. D. (1992). Fostering collaborative reading and writing experiences in mathematics. *Journal of Reading, 36*(2), 96–103.

Children's Nonfiction Trade Books: A Complement to Content Area Texts

Barbara Moss

Nonfiction books for children are suddenly in vogue. David Macaulay's (1988) *The Way Things Work* topped the best seller list for 6 weeks. Russell Freedman's (1987) *Lincoln: A Photobiography* won the coveted Newbery Medal for 1988—the first children's nonfiction book in 12 years to be so honored. Lillian N. Gerhard (1989), editor-in-chief of the *School Library Journal,* referred to nonfiction as the "hot topic in book selection for the young" (p. 34).

This interest in children's nonfiction, a term usually referring to information books and biographies, comes at a time when elementary and middle grade teachers are gradually replacing basal reader programs with children's literature. Moreover, teachers are finding such literature-based programs effective.

As teachers implement literature-based programs across the curriculum, they see the advantages of children's nonfiction as a vehicle for helping students learn subjects such as social studies, science, and health. In addition, they discover how nonfiction trade books compensate for many of the weaknesses of content area textbooks. The purpose of this article is to explain how nonfiction trade books, when used

---

From "Children's Nonfiction Trade Books: A Complement to Content Area Texts" by B. Moss, 1991, *The Reading Teacher, 45,* pp. 26–32. Copyright © 1991 by the International Reading Association. Reprinted with permission of Barbara Moss and the International Reading Association.

in tandem with content area textbooks, can enrich content area learning experiences. First, I will identify the limitations of content area textbooks and the advantages of nonfiction trade books. Then, I will suggest criteria for selecting nonfiction books and organizing the content area classroom to incorporate their use.

LIMITATIONS OF CONTENT AREA TEXTBOOKS

There are many valid reasons for using textbooks in content area instruction. Textbooks systematically introduce information to students, and they help teachers plan by specifying and sequencing content in advance. They also provide a framework for teaching students a myriad of facts and generalizations about a given topic of study (Moore, Moore, Cunningham, & Cunningham, 1986). However, the use of nonfiction trade books as an accompaniment to content area texts is inviting when we consider the limitations of content area textbooks. Five such limitations have been discussed in the literature.

First, content area textbooks are often written above the level for which they were intended (Hillerich, 1987); moreover, the abstract, technical vocabulary found in content area textbooks contributes to the level of difficulty. This is especially evident in science textbooks (Hurd, Robinson, McConnell, & Ross, 1981; Yager, 1983).

Second, content area textbooks are often unappealing; in fact, the content is often boring. Textbook publishers, in appeasing special interest groups, have created texts that succeed in avoiding controversy, but fail to arouse student interest (Elliott, 1990; Tyson-Bernstein, 1988).

Third, textbooks often teach children about many topics in a general way, but provide little opportunity for extensive study of a particular subject (Fielding, Wilson, & Anderson, 1984; Tyson & Woodward, 1989). Hence, students have superficial knowledge about many topics, but lack real understanding of any (Tyson-Bernstein, 1988).

Fourth, content area textbooks are inconsiderate—i.e., they are not written using an organization and style students readily understand (Kantor, Anderson, & Armbruster, 1983). Most textbooks are written in a descriptive mode, making retention of material more difficult than with other modes of expression (Englert & Hiebert, 1984). In addition, content area texts seldom use generally accepted organizational patterns such as cause–effect, temporal sequence, or comparison contrast (Fielding, Wilson, & Anderson, 1984). Furthermore, transition words are often implied rather than stated (Irwin, 1986), making relationships between ideas less evident to children.

Finally, content area textbooks are often dated. Many districts can't afford to update such texts more frequently than every 5 to 10 years, resulting in textbooks that lack current information in a given subject area. Moreover, textbook publishers are often slow to incorporate current information into their texts (Tyson & Woodward, 1989).

Despite the aforementioned shortcomings, textbooks are the "bread and butter" of the content area classroom, providing the framework for instruction in 75 to 90% of American classrooms (Tyson & Woodward, 1989). Textbook content typically reflects the curriculum prescribed by states or communities. Nevertheless, despite the problems inherent in textbooks, children must comprehend such material if they are to become fluent, flexible readers. By using nonfiction trade books concomitantly with textbooks, teachers can provide children with meaningful encounters with print in a multiplicity of materials.

ADVANTAGES OF NONFICTION TRADE BOOKS

Children's nonfiction books, when used effectively, have many advantages over content area texts. I elaborate on five such advantages in this section.

First, teachers can more readily individualize content area reading instruction through the use of nonfiction trade books. By choosing from the abundance of children's nonfiction books in print, teachers can provide students with materials which are closer to their individual reading levels (Hillerich, 1987; Shanahan, 1989).

Second, nonfiction trade books have both content and visual appeal (Kobrin, 1988). Primary and upper grade children often prefer nonfiction books to other types of trade books (Greenlaw, 1983; Purves & Monson, 1984). In addition, such books often have interesting cover designs, attractive graphics, and effective illustrations, features that influence children's choices (Huck, Hepler, & Hickman, 1987). Books such as *To Space and Back* (Ride & Okie, 1986), *Exploring the Titanic* (Ballard, 1988), and *The Human Body* (Miller, 1983) are particularly noteworthy in this area.

Third, nonfiction trade books provide in-depth information on particular content area topics ranging from people, to places, to scientific processes. Exploration of a topic through trade books allows children to discover how knowledge in particular domains is organized, used, and related (Pappas, Kiefer, & Levstik, 1990); it provides them with a rich context for understanding many aspects of some real time, place, or phenomenon, thus enhancing their schemata. Moreover, through wide reading on a particular content area topic, children will learn the concepts and terms associated with that topic.

Fourth, nonfiction trade books often contain information arranged more logically and coherently than it is in content area textbooks. Fielding, Wilson, and Anderson (1984) elaborate upon this point noting that unlike textbooks which are often "baskets of facts," nonfiction trade books usually contain coherently organized content.

Finally, nonfiction trade books, since they are published every year, are more current than content area textbooks, which are usually revised every 5 to 10 years. Hence new trade books reflect the latest developments in science as well as recent world events. Moreover, these new books are readily accessible to teachers through libraries and other sources.

SELECTING NONFICTION BOOKS FOR THE CLASSROOM

In this section I will elaborate upon two important aspects of selecting nonfiction trade books—criteria for selection and resources.

Criteria for Selection

What criteria should teachers use when selecting children's nonfiction for classroom use? Cullinan (1989) has identified criteria for selecting children's nonfiction based upon three essential considerations: the integrity of the author, the tone of the book, and the content of the work. Below, I discuss each criterion and discuss briefly nonfiction trade books that exemplify each criterion.

Cullinan suggests that authors exhibit integrity in writing nonfiction when they "are honest with their readers. They reveal their point of view and let their reader know how their interest in the topic motivates them. They inculcate a questioning attitude in their readers and reveal the sources of their own research" (p. 529).

In *To Be a Slave* (1968), a Newbery Honor book, Julius Lester represents a superb example of an author who exhibits integrity in his writing. From the opening pages of this book, the reader is made aware of Lester's stance regarding slavery and the source of his abiding interest in the topic—the fact that both his maternal and paternal grandparents were slaves.

Cullinan further suggests that the truly honest writer clearly distinguishes between facts and theories and explicitly labels such information appropriately. Moreover, the author with integrity presents different viewpoints about particular subjects and supports generalizations with facts. Finally, superior nonfiction authors possess the necessary qualifications to write on a given topic or acknowledge those who have helped them.

Consideration of tone represents a second criterion for judging a nonfiction book. One aspect of tone is the presence of the author. For children to feel that a real person is behind the information provided in a book, they must hear the writer's voice, as projected in the following paragraph from *Lincoln: A Photobiography* by Russell Freedman (1987):

> Lincoln was the most photographed man of his time, but his friends insisted that no photo ever did him justice. It's no wonder. Back then cameras required long exposures. The person being photographed had to "freeze" as the seconds ticked by. If he blinked an eye, the picture would be blurred. That's why Lincoln looks so stiff and formal in his photos. We never see him laughing or joking. (p. 2)

Through Freedman's informal yet informative tone, readers gain a sense of the author as someone who is communicating with them, not as someone who is simply transmitting information.

Cullinan's third consideration in evaluating nonfiction is content. Two major concerns are paramount here: (a) the comprehensibility of the text, and (b) the extent to which the book appeals to children. Material in nonfiction books should be well organized; ideas should be presented logically and coherently. The presence of subject and/or author indices, bibliographies, appendices, reference notes, glossaries, and other reference materials enhances the credibility of the text. Pages should be well designed with attractive layouts, and illustrations should help to illuminate the information provided in the text. Gail Gibbons's *Sunken Treasure* (1988), a nonfiction picture book detailing the story of the discovery of the Spanish treasure ship *The Atocha*, exemplifies excellence in terms of clearly organized content and reference materials specifically geared toward children ages 6 to 10.

An ever-increasing number of books that meet Cullinan's criteria are published every year; moreover, the breadth of topics covered by these books makes them ideal for classroom use. Children's nonfiction books encompass such topics of study as the arts, animals, mathematics, sex, the life cycle, man-made objects, and language (Stewig, 1988). Subjects for children's biographies range from historical characters such as Paul Revere and Pocahontas to recent figures such as Anwar Sadat and Martin Luther King, Jr.

Resources

A variety of resources can aid teachers in selecting nonfiction books for use in content area instruction. Beverly Kobrin's *Eyeopeners* (1988) provides annotations of 500 children's nonfiction books and suggestions for classroom use for many of the titles. Each year the Children's Book Council works with the National Science Teachers Association and the National Council for the Social Studies, respectively, to compile annotated bibliographies of "Outstanding Science Trade Books for Children" and "Notable Children's Trade Books in the Field of Social Studies." *The Horn Book Magazine* annually honors a small number of nonfiction books for excellence in production and graphics as part of their Graphic Gallery competition. The books chosen represent the most well designed nonfiction books published each year, the majority of which can be used in teaching the content areas. Finally, *The Reading Teacher*'s own "Children's Books" department routinely annotates nonfiction trade books themed according to content disciplines like science or social studies.

Once teachers have selected nonfiction books for classroom use, how can they acquire them? How can schools and teachers with limited budgets find the resources necessary to bring trade books into the classroom? First, they can contact their school or community librarian; many libraries are willing to purchase multiple copies of particular books for classroom use. Second, teachers can frequent garage sales, bookstores that sell used books, and book sales where books can be obtained at low cost. Third, teachers can involve their students in book clubs such as Scholastic and Trumpet. These clubs provide teachers with many opportunities to get free, high quality paperback books. Fourth, many teachers have obtained small grants from foundations, corporations, or parent–teacher organizations to fund the purchase of classroom trade books. Finally, many schools are deferring the purchase of new textbooks and using those funds to buy trade books. Although this practice requires children and teachers to use the same text for a few more years, it results in an influx of a variety of new reading materials to build up their selection of classroom trade books.

ORGANIZING INSTRUCTION

Zarrillo's (1989) recent research identified three formats associated with successful literature-based programs: (a) the use of a single trade book (or core book) read by all children; (b) the use of literature units; and (c) the use of an individualized reading program. In the first pattern the teacher selects the book to be shared, but children determine the form of their response to the book that may include such activities as dramatization through Readers Theatre, writing poetry, journals, or advertisements, or independent reading of related books. The second pattern involves use of a variety of books related to the unit theme. Some books are read aloud to the entire group; other titles pertinent to the topic are read in small groups based upon ability, gender, and interest. Students participate in both large group and self-selected response activities. The third instructional pattern allows each child to select a different book, based upon individual interest. Children read their books silently at their own pace and confer with the teacher periodically; they may participate in skills instruction and share their books with peers in some way (Veatch, 1958, 1978).

The aforementioned organizational patterns can be used separately or simultaneously, but can easily provide a framework for the use of nonfiction children's books in the content areas. Moreover, they can be used along with study of the textbook. Below, I provide examples of how teachers can use the three organizational patterns to integrate textbook-based instruction with the use of nonfiction trade books.

Use of a Single Trade Book

An example of the first organizational pattern would be to have fifth graders follow up their textbook study of volcanoes by reading and reacting to the book *Volcano* (Lauber, 1986). This exquisite book, illustrated with photographs, gives children accurate information about the eruption and subsequent renewal of Mount St. Helens. Following their reading, children could work in research groups to read about, explore, and compare information about other volcanoes such as Vesuvius, Krakatau, and Kilauea. By using a variety of materials, children not only examine the scientific principles associated with the eruption of volcanoes, but also develop an understanding of the effect of such disasters upon the environment and the people of a given region, thus going well beyond the type of information typically provided by a science text.

Use of a Literature Unit

An example of the second organizational pattern would involve the use of a literature unit. In a given year, a teacher might select one or two important topics of study around which to develop such in-depth units. During a middle grade social studies unit on the American Revolution, the teacher might read aloud *The Secret Soldier* (McGovern, 1975). Small interest or ability groups might participate in response activities related to that era. Titles such as *Can't You Make Them Behave, King George?* (Fritz, 1977), *Ben and Me* (Lawson, 1951), and *George Washington and the Birth of Our Nation* (Meltzer, 1986) would provide different perspectives on that time in American history. Children could conduct imaginary interviews with these characters from the past, create time lines based upon their lives, or write plays or dramatizations illustrating important historical events in which each was involved. Through these readings, students would not only learn about King George, Benjamin Franklin, and George Washington, but would develop an enhanced schema for understanding the people, places, and events associated with the American Revolution. Another literature unit might focus exclusively on one historical figure such as Abraham Lincoln. By reading the differing accounts of Lincoln's life provided by *Lincoln: A Photobiography* (Freedman, 1987), *Me and Willie and Pa* (Monjo, 1973), and *Abraham Lincoln* (I. D'Aulaire & E.P. D'Aulaire, 1957), children would learn to appreciate various authors' perceptions of this complex historical figure. Students might examine each author's treatment of Lincoln through a chart comparing the scope of each book, the narrator's point of view, and the life incidents included or omitted in each book. They could then discuss why the authors chose to present Lincoln in the way they did. Students could also consider how their view of Lincoln was influenced by the author's presentation.

Use of an Individualized Reading Program

An example of the third organizational pattern would be to develop an individualized reading program for a particular content area. To do this, a wide array of nonfiction titles must be available from the school or classroom library. The resources mentioned earlier in this article provide ideas for book selection. Students could be encouraged to read widely on given topics or about particular areas of interest. The use of sustained silent reading time, wherein students read silently for approximately 15–20 minutes each day, would help promote such a program. Two students might read the same book and then confer with each other through dialogue journals, wherein they engage in written conversations detailing their responses to the book read. These conversations might include discussions of why people presented in the book behaved in certain ways, what students would have done if they were the subject of the book, what they learned from their reading, questions they would like to ask the author, or ways they think the book might have been improved.

CONCLUSION

Reading to learn is necessary to academic success. How, then, can we best teach children about content area subjects such as science, social studies, and health? How can we tap children's natural curiosity about today's world and worlds of the past and future?

By using children's nonfiction trade books in concert with content area textbooks, teachers can make information exciting to children. According to Sebesta (1989), "Trade books serendipitous to a curricular topic can make the difference between a passive reader who quits when the bell rings and an active, lifelong, self-motivated reader/learner" (p. 114). If we are to have an informed citizenry in this country, we must have students who are knowledgeable about content area subjects. Moreover, if we are to develop "a nation of readers," we must motivate children to read long after the bell rings. Through judicious selection of nonfiction books and effective incorporation of such titles into content area instruction, both of these goals can be achieved. Teachers can capitalize upon children's natural curiosity and help ensure that today's children will not become tomorrow's illiterate or aliterate adults.

REFERENCES

Cullinan, B. E. (1989). *Literature and the child* (2nd ed.). New York: Harcourt, Brace, Jovanovich.

Elliott, D. L. (1990). Textbooks and the curriculum in the postwar era: 1950–1980. In D. Elliott & A. Woodward (Eds.), *Textbooks and schooling in the United States: NSSE yearbook* (pp. 42–55). Chicago: The National Society for the Study of Education.

Englert, C. S., & Hiebert, E. H. (1984). Children's developing awareness of text structure in expository materials. *Journal of Educational Psychology, 76*, 65–74.

Fielding, L. G., Wilson, P. T., & Anderson, R. C. (1984). A new focus on free reading: The role of trade books in reading instruction. In T. Raphael (Ed.), *The contexts of school-based literacy* (pp. 149–162). New York: Random House.

Gerhard, L. (1989). Publishers' nonfiction forecast for 1990. *School Library Journal, 35*, 34.

Greenlaw, M. J. (1983). Reading interest research and children's choices. In N. Roser & M. Frith (Eds.), *Children's choices: Teaching with books children like* (pp. 90–92). Newark, DE: International Reading Association.

Hillerich, R. (1987). Those content areas. *Teaching K–8, 17*, 31–33.

Huck, C., Hepler, S., & Hickman, J. (1987). *Children's literature in the elementary school* (4th ed.). New York: Holt, Rinehart & Winston.

Hurd, P., Robinson, J. T., McConnell, M. C., & Ross, N. M., Jr. (1981). *The status of middle and junior high science, Vol. 1; summary report, Vol. 2* (Technical report, edited by R. E. Yager.) Louisville, CO: Center for Educational Research and Evaluation/Biological Science Curriculum Study.

Irwin, J. (1986). *Understanding and teaching cohesion comprehension*. Newark, DE: International Reading Association.

Kantor, R. N., Anderson, T. H., & Armbruster, B. B. (1983). How inconsiderate are children's textbooks? *Journal of Curriculum Studies, 15*, 61–72.

Kobrin, B. (1988). *Eyeopeners*. New York: Viking Penguin.

Moore, D., Moore, S. A., Cunningham, P., & Cunningham, J. (1986). *Developing readers and writers in the content areas*. New York: Longman.

Pappas, C. C., Kiefer, B. Z., & Levstik, L. S. (1990). *An integrated language perspective in the elementary school*. White Plains, NY: Longman.

Purves, A. M., & Monson, D. L. (1984). *Experiencing children's literature*. Glenview, IL: Scott, Foresman.

Sebesta, S. L. (1989). Literature across the curriculum. In J. W. Stewig & S. L. Sebesta (Eds.), *Using literature in the elementary classroom* (pp. 110–128). Urbana, IL: National Council of Teachers of English.

Shanahan, T. (1989). Nine good reasons for using children's literature across the curriculum. In *Distant shores teacher's resource package level N* (pp. 19–22). New York: McGraw-Hill School Division.

Stewig, J. W. (1988). *Children and literature* (2nd ed.). Boston: Houghton Mifflin.

Tyson, H., & Woodward, A. (1989). Why students aren't learning very much from textbooks. *Educational Leadership, 47*, 14–17.

Tyson-Bernstein, H. (1988). *America's textbook fiasco: A conspiracy of good intentions*. Washington, DC: The Council for Basic Education.

Veatch, J. (Ed.). (1958). *Individualizing your reading program: Self-selection in action*. New York: G. P. Putnam's Sons.

Veatch, J. (1978). *Reading in the elementary school* (2nd ed.). New York: John Wiley & Sons.

Yager, R. (1983). The importance of terminology in teaching K–12 science. *Journal of Research in Science Teaching, 19*, 577–588.

Zarrillo, J. (1989). Teachers' interpretations of literature-based reading. *The Reading Teacher, 43*, 22–28.

TRADE BOOK SELECTION RESOURCES CITED

The Horn Book Magazine. Boston: The Horn Book Inc. 14 Beacon Street, Boston, MA 02108.

Kobrin, B. (1988). *Eyeopeners*. New York: Viking Penguin.

Outstanding science trade books for children and *Notable children's trade books in the field of social studies*. Children's Book Council, 67 Irving Place, P.O. Box 706, New York, NY 10216, USA.

The Reading Teacher. The International Reading Association, 800 Barksdale Road, Newark, DE 19714-8139, USA.

RECOMMENDED NONFICTION TRADE BOOKS FOR THE CONTENT AREA CLASSROOM

Animal books

Bonners, S. (1978). *Panda*. New York: Dell.

Bonners, S. (1981). *A penguin year*. New York: Dell.

National Geographic Society. (1987). *Creatures of the desert world*. Washington, DC: National Geographic Society.

National Geographic Society. (1987). *Strange animals of the sea*. Washington, DC: National Geographic Society.

Selsam, M. (1966). *How to be a nature detective.* New York: Harper & Row.

Biographies
D'Aulaire, I., & D'Aulaire, E. P. (1957). *Abraham Lincoln* (rev. ed.). New York: Doubleday.
Freedman, R. (1987). *Lincoln: A photobiography.* New York: Clarion Books.
Fritz, J. (1973). *And then what happened, Paul Revere?* New York: Coward, McCann & Geoghegan.
Fritz, J. (1975). *Where was Patrick Henry on the 29th of May?* New York: Putnam.
Fritz, J. (1977). *Can't you make them behave, King George?* New York: Coward, McCann & Geoghegan.
Lauder, P. (1988). *Lost star.* New York: Scholastic.
Lawson, R. (1951). *Ben and me.* Boston: Little, Brown.
Marrin, A. (1987). *Hitler.* New York: Viking Kestral.
McGovern, A. (1975). *The secret soldier: The story of Deborah Sampson.* New York: Scholastic.
Meltzer, M. (1986). *George Washington and the birth of our nation.* New York: Watts.
Monjo, F. N. (1973). *Me and Willie and Pa.* New York: Simon & Schuster.

Discovery and exploration
Ballard, R. (1988). *Exploring the Titanic.* New York: Scholastic.
Barton, B. (1988). *I want to be an astronaut.* New York: Scholastic.
Gibbons, G. (1988). *Sunken treasure.* New York: Crowell.
Macaulay, D. (1988). *The way things work.* Boston: Houghton Mifflin.
Ride, S., & Okie, S. (1986). *To space and back.* New York: Lothrop, Lee & Shepard.
Simon, S. (1988). *Mars.* New York: Crowell.

Geography
Kuskin, K. (1987). *Jerusalem, shining still.* New York: Harper & Row.
Lauber, P. (1986). *Volcano: The eruption and healing of Mount St. Helens.* New York: Dell.
Siebert, D. (1988). *Mojave.* New York: Crowell.

Life in the past
Freedman, R. (1983). *Children of the wild west.* New York: Clarion.
Lester, J. (1968). *To be a slave.* New York: Dial.
Macaulay, D. (1977). *Castle.* Boston: Houghton Mifflin.

The human body
Cole, J. (1989). *The magic schoolbus inside the human body.* New York: Scholastic.
Miller, J. (1983). *The human body.* New York: Viking.
Silverstein, A., & Silverstein, V. (1983). *Heartbeats: Your body, your heart.* New York: Lippincott.

Barbara Moss is an assistant professor at The University of Akron.

Using Adolescent Literature in Social Studies and Science

Dixie Lee Spiegel

Literature is a valuable resource for teaching social studies and science concepts to adolescents. By integrating literature with other subjects, students develop their reading skills and learn more about specific content areas. A relationship is fostered in which the student's total growth is more than the sum of the individual parts.

This article will explore several reasons for integrating literature into content areas and suggest activities that will promote this integration. The article is directed at students in grades five through eight.

From "Using Adolescent Literature in Social Studies and Science" by D. L. Spiegel (1987), *Educational Horizons*, 65, pp. 162–164. Copyright © 1987 by Pi Lambda Theta. Reprinted with permission from *Educational Horizons*, quarterly journal of Pi Lambda Theta, International Honor and Professional Association in Education, 4101 E. Third Street, Bloomington, IN 47407–6626.

WHY SHOULD STUDENTS CHOOSE READING?

Although there is some evidence that we are doing a better job of teaching children how to read, we have yet to develop adolescents who select reading as a leisure-time activity.[1] This is unfortunate because reading is an excellent way to learn about the world, both current and past. Furthermore, reading expands students' vocabulary and allows them to practice their reading skills in a non-threatening, self-selected environment, at their chosen level of difficulty. For all of these reasons, we want students to choose to read as well as watch television, participate in sports, and work at part-time jobs.

WHY SHOULD STUDENTS BE AWARE OF INFORMATION IN LITERATURE?

When students are assigned to read a social studies text or when they go to the library to seek information for a science class, they see the informational value of nonfiction. But, they also need to develop a conscious awareness that literature can broaden their knowledge of the world.

Think about a book you have read recently for pleasure. (Of course you've read something recently!) While detecting with Agatha Christie's Miss Marple, did you learn about life in sleepy English villages in post-war Great Britain? While trudging along the prehistoric tundra with Jean Auel's Ayla in *The Valley of the Horses*, did you add to your information on biomes and wilderness survival? While chuckling through Bill Cosby's *Fatherhood*, did you gain a little insight into why your own children and students act (and react) as they do?

How can we as teachers develop in adolescents an awareness of the rich store of information available in literature? The following five activities can help achieve that goal.

1. *Find time for Sustained Silent Reading (SSR) in your content area classes at least twice a week.* During SSR everyone (you too!) reads silently for 10–20 minutes something he or she has chosen. After each SSR period, take a minute or two to describe what you have learned about the world from your book. Vary the kinds of information you share. For example, one day you might talk about the kind of food that Pakistanis eat. The next day you might relate what you learned about how different people deal with envy or another specific emotion. Make this a time of joyful discovery for the class, not one of odious compulsory recitation. Encourage students to pause and reflect as they read and to expand their view of the world and its people.

2. *Provide "What I Learned" cards that students can fill in voluntarily after reading a selection of literature.* The cards should have space for bibliographic information and the student's name. Sections labeled "About People," "About Places," "About Events," "About Nature," and "About Myself" should be included on the card. Having to think about these kinds of information rehearses the information and commits it to long-term memory, thereby expanding the reader's information base. The cards can be used for student–teacher conferences, bulletin boards, sharing periods, book talks, or reference files.

3. *Have students make bulletin boards that center on "What We Have Learned about X and Y and Where We Learned These Facts."* Divide the board into several areas, each on one topic. As the students find interesting information, they will tack information cards onto the bulletin board. The information might take the form of questions with the answers hidden under a flap: Why did colonial Americans bathe very little? or, What happens if you mix acid with water? If students discover a

conflict in posted information, the rest of the class can be challenged to help resolve the conflict.
4. *Have the class compare a textbook description of a person or place with a literature description.* For example, an American history class might compile all of the descriptions of Benjamin Franklin in their social studies text and prepare a class chart of information about Franklin's accomplishments and character. Then members of the class could read a variety of biographies about Franklin and add to the information they learned from their text.[2]
5. *Have trivia contests in which students post trivia questions and the literature sources of the answers.*[3]

LITERATURE ADDS DEPTH AND MEANING TO CONCEPTS

Literature can become a natural means of teaching social studies and science content so that it is relevant and memorable. In social studies, literature can help students acquire a feeling for a way of life in another time or place and develop empathy vicariously with other cultures. Literature captures the mood of a time or event, not just the facts; it transplants us. In science, literature can suggest real-life uses and abuses of scientific knowledge and can draw readers into the drama of scientific exploration, frustration, and discovery. (Remember Watson's account of the discovery of DNA in *The Double Helix?*) As the excerpts from *Pilgrim at Tinker Creek* and *The Matchlock Gun*)(below) illustrate, literature can also provide detail that might be didactic in a text but comes alive through literature.

Artley emphasizes the reciprocal relationship between the content areas and literature:

> The content being studied is clarified, enriched, and dramatized through literature. In turn, good reading is motivated and becomes functional as it relates to content being studied.[4]

Literature provides examples to broaden concepts by providing specific instances that flesh out cognitive networks of information (schemata) about particular topics. For example,

---

All these drifting animals [plankton] multiply in sundry bizarre fashions, eat tiny plants or each other, die, and drop to the pond bottom. Many of them have quite refined means of locomotion—they whirl, paddle, swim, slog, whip, and sinuate—but since they are so small, they are no match against even the least current in the water. Even such a sober limnologist as Robert E. Coker characterizes the movement of plankton as "milling around."
—Annie Dillard,
Pilgrim at Tinker Creek

She wondered whether Teunis would get back that night. She wondered whether he had any more news of the French and Indians. There never was any definite word of them until the raid was over. Not even when they had burned Schenectady in 1690 had any word of the raid reached Albany until Simon Schemmerhoorn had ridden into town early the next morning. She felt afraid. Their fields were so small in all these woods. An Indian might walk onto the stoop before they were aware of his presence on the farm, if they were indoors at the time. She made up her mind abruptly to keep outside as much as she could all day.
—Walter D. Edmonds,
The Matchlock Gun

if our only knowledge of pirates came from one or two paragraphs in a social studies text about the Barbary pirates in northern Africa, we would have an impoverished schema about pirates. But as we read literary accounts of Long John Silver, Bluebeard, and even Captain Hook, we develop a more complete picture of pirates. As educators, we know that the best concept development comes through the use of multiple examples, and literature provides these.

Several activities can be used to tap literature's store of information.

1. *When you read aloud to your students (of course you read to your students!), stop after each chapter or so and add to a chart of "What we know about X."* It may be more efficient to learn just the facts, but literature places facts in context and makes them more memorable. For example, from the first three short chapters of Forbes's *Johnny Tremain*, students can gain several insights about colonial America: the apprenticeship system, the vast class differences in ways of life (even for children), and the pervasive influence of religion in everyone's daily life.
2. *Have students compare several interpretations of the same broad topic.* For example, in a unit on immigration, students might choose to read such works as Cohen's *Molly's Pilgrim*, Sachs's *Call Me Ruth*, Siegel's *Sam Ellis's Island*, Ashabranner's *The New Americans*, and Day's *The New Immigrants*. After they finish the books, the class can compile a list of information about immigration in the early twentieth century. Such an activity provides natural and motivating opportunities to practice critical reading, because instances of conflicting information will arise from the different sources. In addition, this activity allows students at different reading levels to contribute because each piece of literature is unique.
3. *For both social studies and science, read with the students fictionalized accounts of historic events and people.* Such accounts as Monjo's *King George's Head Was Made of Lead*, Round's *The Morning the Sun Refused to Rise: An Original Paul Bunyan Tale*, Bulla's *Charlie's House*, or Ruckman's *Night of the Twisters* provide important content in a dramatic and personalized manner.

LITERATURE STIMULATES TRANSFER, GENERALIZATION, AND APPLICATION OF CONCEPTS

In addition to teaching the specific facts found in a social studies or science text, we also teach broad generalizations and approaches to issues in each area. A broad information base and relevant examples improve the transfer of information and application of the concepts. Hennings expands on this by stating that readers of literature have to process concepts more deeply because

> the messages in story form are generally implied rather than stated explicitly. This means that the youngsters must think through relationships and formulate conclusions that go beyond the text—a skill particularly important in social studies.[5]

To enhance the transfer value of literature, consider the following teaching methods.

1. *Use an example from literature and have students extend it by following patterns established in the story line.* The students can strengthen their understanding of the material because they must transfer it to a new example. For example, Sheer and Bileck's *Rain Makes Applesauce*, a children's picture book, could be used as a model for any cycle in nature. In this book, wild fantasy pictures and extremely ridiculous statements are accompanied by tiny pictures of two children saying "And rain makes applesauce." These two kibbitzers appear on nearly every page. But as readers investigate the tiny pictures, they see that indeed rain does make applesauce! The little

pictures start with the two children dropping an apple seed into the ground. Next come the rains, the sprouting of the seed, the growth of the tree (more rain), the blossoms (and rain), the apples, the harvest, and the cooking of the applesauce. Even older adolescents might enjoy creating books on "Trees Make Rain," "Sand Makes Pearls," or "People + Plants = Oxygen."
2. *Have the students create alternative endings to stories.* After reading Lawson's *Mr. Revere and I,* the story of events leading up to the American Revolution as told by Paul Revere's horse, have the class identify all the places in the last ride where disaster could have struck. Have each student choose one of these situations, propose a real disaster, and predict how the outcome of history might have been changed.
3. *Have the students develop additional chapters or sequels consistent with the story.* The students could add new survival problems to Heyerdahl's *Kon-Tiki: A True Adventure of Survival at Sea.* During an ecology unit, the class could read Dr. Seuss's *The Lorax* and provide two sequels—one that revitalizes the planet and one that continues down the path toward ecological disaster.

LITERATURE PROVIDES MULTIPLE EXAMPLES FOR CRITICAL INTERPRETATION

An important obstacle to critical reading is the reliance on a single source of information, usually the assigned textbook. As far as students are concerned, the text is "truth," to be accepted without question. But Huck emphasizes that when literature selections are also used, conflict of information is inevitable.

> ... [C]hildren should be encouraged to verify, extend, or contradict the presentation of their textbook by contrasting it with facts found in other books.[6]

She reminds us that history, by its very nature, requires interpretation. Keeping this in mind, try using literature to help students develop critical reading and thinking skills.

1. *Discuss social issues.* For example, "Should there be mandatory drug testing of athletes?" or "What should be done about illegal immigration into the U.S.?" Have teams research these questions and compare information that conflicts by genre, date of information, and quality of source. Huck points out that literature may contain the most current information, because trade books take less time to produce and disseminate than textbooks.[7]
2. *At the end of a unit of study in which literature and the content area have been integrated, have the class compare what they have learned from their studies with information from an encyclopedia.* It is likely that they will find that the encyclopedia gives only minimal data.
3. *Encourage students to rewrite history (including scientific history) by reporting the events from another point of view.* Good models for this include Lawson's *Ben and Me* (the life of Benjamin Franklin as told by his mouse companion and mentor), Speare's *The Sign of the Beaver* (a native American view of the conflicts with white settlers at the end of the eighteenth century), and Morpurgo's *War Horse* (World War I from the point of view of a British Cavalry Horse).

LITERATURE PROVIDES A CHANGE OF PACE, STIMULATES IMAGINATION AND CREATIVITY

Just as integrating literature with social studies and science can enhance interest in reading, such an approach also works in reverse. Students who tend to view social studies and science as dry and dull may find their interest piqued and their view dramatically changed. Goodman and Melcher suggest that literature promotes active rather than passive learning because students must reach their own conclusions rather than just accept "the answers."[8] They become involved interpreters rather than passive receivers because the content becomes even more alive and more memorable.

NOTES

1. National Assessment of Educational Progress, *Reading, Thinking, and Writing* (Denver, CO: Education Commission of the States, 1981).
2. See Robert Lawson, *Ben and Me* (Boston: Little, Brown, and Co., 1939); Ingri and Edgar Parin d'Aulaire, *Benjamin Franklin* (Garden City, NY: Doubleday and Co., 1950); James Daugherty, *Poor Richard* (New York: Viking Press, 1970); Eve Merriam, *The Story of Benjamin Franklin* (New York: Four Winds Press, 1965); Clara Ingram Judson, *Benjamin Franklin* (Chicago: Follett, 1957).
3. Kathleen C. Stevens, "Trivia Contest Stimulates Enthusiastic Reading," *The Reading Teacher* 33 (1980): 466–467.
4. A. Sterl Artley, "Literature in the Language Arts Program," in *Readings on Contemporary English in the Elementary School*, Iris M. Tiedt and Sidney W. Tiedt, eds. (Englewood Cliffs, NJ: Prentice-Hall, 1967), pp. 214–219.
5. Dorothy C. Hennings, "Reading Picture Storybooks in the Social Studies," *The Reading Teacher* 36 (1982): 284–288.
6. Charlotte S. Huck, "Planning the Literature Program for the Elementary School," in *Readings on Contemporary English*, Tiedt, pp. 205–213.
7. Ibid.
8. Jesse Goodman and Kate Melcher, "Culture at a Distance: An Anthroliterary Approach to Cross-cultural Education," *Journal of Reading* 28 (1984): 200–207.

Dixie Lee Spiegel is a Professor of Reading and Language Arts and Assistant Dean for Students in the School of Education at the University of North Carolina at Chapel Hill.

Whole Concept Mathematics: A Whole Language Application

Cheryl L. Brown

The scenario is all too familiar: elementary students, perhaps third-graders, begin to study fractions, but many never master the concept. Each year that follows, they work on a sequence of exercises covering various fraction topics, always repeating study from the past year. Year after year, they are *exposed* to the same exercises and information. Usually there are no real-life situations in which they can perceive, through practice, how important fractions really are, nor do they study fractions in depth over a period of time or have an opportunity to see "the big picture" in order to solve everyday problems. Instead, they plug along year after year doing rote exercises, being bored with worksheets and workbooks, grading

From "Whole Concept Mathematics: A Whole Language Application" by C. L. Brown, 1991, *Educational Horizons, 69*, pp. 159–163. Copyright © 1991 by Pi Lambda Theta. Reprinted with permission from *Educational Horizons*, quarterly journal of Pi Lambda Theta, International Honor and Professional Association in Education, 4101 E. Third Street, Bloomington, IN 47407–6626.

homework, watching the teacher do examples of the next day's assignment, then working on assignments. Disinterest soon sets in, leading to anxiety and dread about math, followed by bewilderment on the part of the teacher when he or she discovers that the students still do not understand fractions!

Paralleling these frustrations is the professional realization that traditional mathematics teaching has been founded on societal myths, as borne out in a recent report on school mathematics by the Wisconsin Center of Education Research.[1] Such myths as rote learning and dividing classes into ability groups go unchallenged and become fundamental principles that many educators accept as verifiable truths. Yet, emphasizing rote learning suggests that students are not capable of grasping holistic mathematical concepts, and ability grouping ignores the benefits of students interacting with one another.

THREE INSTRUCTIONAL MYTHS

Three of the most powerful instructional myths involve thinking skills, the right answer, and educational stages. The thinking skills myth purports that thinking is composed of discrete cognitive skills or sequential steps, implying that all thinking should be linear in nature. An additional assumption is that once thinking is separated into isolated pieces, the steps can later be reassembled without damage or difficulty. However, if a student has learned a skill, he or she has done just that and nothing more. There is no indication that that particular skill will result in or be used in thinking, since skills and strategies are independent from content.[2] The acquisition of skills does not necessarily lead to the understanding of content, the latter being tied directly to the application, but not the rote learning, of mathematics.

The myth of the right answer encourages students to focus on rote memorization rather than thoughtful analysis. Rote learning is rooted in drill and practice, which need not reflect understanding or integration of new knowledge with assimilated knowledge. Students need to organize knowledge prior to attempting to remember it by understanding how it all fits together, connecting new knowledge with old knowledge, and acknowledging connections and interrelationships. This is the type of thought that contributes to the problem-solving process.

The last critical myth addresses how acceptance of Jean Piaget's stages can have negative effects on expectations regarding a student's ability to learn. Research suggests that task-relevant knowledge, rather that chronological age, determines readiness to learn.[3] Current research is now focusing on how youth organize what they already know so that instruction can be matched to their existing mental schemata.

WHOLE CONCEPT MATHEMATICS

A new approach to mathematics instruction, whole concept mathematics, eliminates these and other barriers that have existed in mathematics education. In the whole concept approach, students can see the whole picture, not just an aggregation of separate skills. They realize why they are learning mathematics, have an idea of where they are headed, and see how it all fits together. Connections and relevancy become obvious to everyone, not just to students who have a knack for independently understanding mathematical interrelationships. The whole concept approach emphasizes problem-solving situations that are real and significant, enabling students truly to master what they have learned.

Whole concept mathematics is an adaptation of the whole language approach to learning that emphasizes clear and functional communication, both verbal and written, addressing real-life situations in a natural way. As an educational innovation, whole language represents a significant progression in current instructional thought, providing an encompassing and holistic philosophy that ties together a variety of innovative ideas within a theoretical framework where the ideas can be evaluated.

Because the phrase *whole language* suggests that a language component would be incorporated into a mathematics curriculum, alternative terminology is needed to accurately transfer a whole language perspective to mathematics. Thus, the phrase *whole language* should be replaced with that of *whole concept* in an attempt to place the proper emphasis on the development of concepts in a meaningful, relevant, and holistic manner.

REVISIONING METHODOLOGY

Consistent with whole language theory, students have demonstrated that they are able to create new knowledge. Therefore, they should be provided with active, direct experiences with the deep structures of situations. The Wisconsin Center indicates that the traditional emphasis on teaching computations and procedures should be replaced with a) didactic situations in which structures are reinvented; b) diversity of expression involving various representational notations; c) dialogue allowing students to process learning; d) diagnosis as a means of ascertaining obstacles; e) delegation of duties so that students are in control of their learning; and f) dissimilarity rather than homogeneity in the composition of classes, so that all students participate and are recognized as contributors to learning.[4]

In view of this research, it seems appropriate that stylized word problems should be replaced with posed problematic situations that are realistic and complex enough to challenge students. Patterns should be emphasized, as well as the ability to express concepts in mathematical notation. These research-based ideas for teaching mathematics are an integral part of the framework of whole concept mathematics.

Cooperative learning activities provide a structured forum in which students can express mathematical concepts in their own words and build upon an exchange of ideas. Similarly, writing can be used as a method of individually clarifying concepts. Daily logs and math journals provide continuous opportunities both to express ideas and restate logical principles. Learning logs promote mastery of knowledge, recognize individual learning styles in math settings, provide a forum for unanswered questions, and improve student attitudes.[5] Cooperative learning experiences in group settings and logs for individual use make mathematics more humanistic, adding an affective dimension to study. These strategies are key components of whole concept mathematics.

The use of logs and cooperative learning exercises also encourages metacognitive exploration, since students include statements that identify points of frustration as well as the type of assistance that has helped to clarify concepts. In addition, such insights lead to the identification of learning preferences. Type theory is based on the premise that individuals perceive differently, thus indicating the need for each student to communicate his or her particular interpretation and providing a means to direct each interpretation toward the formulation of verified concepts.

Various types of writing can be used to synthesize mathematical concepts. Daily summaries, formulations of student word problems, explanations of procedures and concepts, and reflections on each day's study material all can be used to promote thought about mathematics. Just the act of verbalization itself can improve a student's ability to recall and organize information.[6] Communicating about mathematics is doing mathematics, and that is the purpose of whole concept mathematics.

REFORMULATING THE CURRICULUM

Whole concept mathematics not only requires revision in methodology, but also an entire reformulation of the content structure inherent in the current mathematics curriculum. Elliot Eisner offers a summary of curriculum orientations, three of which are compatible with a whole language approach as applied to mathematics: cognitive processes, personal relevance, and social reconstruction.[7] A cognitive processes design emphasizes universal concepts and the process of learning how to learn. In personal relevance the focus is on learning through personal meaning, and in social reconstruction standard social norms are challenged and analyzed. The fact that any of these three can be adapted to use with this approach indicates its flexibility in a teaching situation.

Whole concept mathematics means that the focus of mathematics is on the *natural* use of mathematics. Mathematical skills are learned when they are needed in order to solve meaningful, real problems. This represents a reordering of the teaching sequence. Currently schools teach separate skills, which constitutes the major focus of mathematics work. Then students are expected, though never instructed, to integrate these skills independently so that applications to stylized word problems can be achieved. In whole concept mathematics, study begins with a problematic situation; students can assist even in determining what situation to examine. A necessary part of the approach is the assessment, through observation and student identification, of the mathematics knowledge that students have to work with in exploring and eventually solving the problematic situation. If students do not know the necessary skills, then instruction is provided to bring the operating knowledge base up to the appropriate level. Students then have a reason to learn additional mathematics and will use it immediately in solving the identified problem. This is a "user friendly" approach to mathematics.

Inherent in the whole concept approach is an orientation of concentrated, in-depth study. Students are not able to apply knowledge until they have achieved a thorough understanding of the concepts. Cognitive retention is a step that precedes the application of knowledge.[8] In-depth study is consistent with a theme or problem-solving approach to whole concept mathematics and requires a curriculum based upon extensive study of concepts, followed by complex applications at each level. Most mathematics curricula offered in today's public schools are dependent on textbooks, teach isolated skills, and only *expose* students to mathematics. Students do not study mathematics topics in depth, analyze mathematical concepts, reconstruct mathematical theory, or struggle with the attributes of various problem-solving approaches. Rather, students are exposed briefly to individual skills and rote drill is encouraged as a means of remembering them.

Therefore, a whole concept mathematics curriculum necessitates a number of changes. First, mathematics is studied in depth. No longer are students briefly exposed to the same mathematical concepts year after year; each year they contemplate a few major concepts from a variety of perspectives, constantly working with these concepts in practical situations. Second, since mathematics is a tool, it becomes part of an integrated curriculum. The theme approach at the elementary level offers an ideal application for whole language philosophy and can easily offer opportunities for the use of problematic situations involving whole numbers, fractions, decimals, percents, etc. Elementary programs like "Mathematics Their Way" and "Box It or Bag It" offer conceptual approaches focusing on pattern development and communication skills, but lack the full philosophical foundations of whole concept mathematics.

Students also can solve everyday problems in whole concept mathematics. For instance, to celebrate her birthday, Rita wants to bring popsicles for each student in her third-grade class. Popsicles are packaged in boxes of one dozen each, and there are thirty students in the class. The class helps Rita figure out how many boxes to purchase and how many popsicles to leave at home. To provide another example, students in upper elementary grades could examine safety at school crossings, studying how many feet are required to stop when cars travel at various speeds and suggesting appropriate areas near their school for reduced speeds.

At the secondary level, math/science blocks offer a feasible approach. Higher level mathematics also can be approached using problematic situations in which students learn processes and notational skills as they are needed. Algebra students can learn addition of positive and negative numbers by studying temperatures, weight gain and loss, and bookkeeping/checking account practices. As students' mathematical concepts become more advanced, learners can examine, using exponential functions, the safety of chemical and nuclear waste dumps in their city or state.

The problem-solving approach to teaching mathematics as well as the theme approach are familiar methodologies. One other pedagogy that correlates with whole concept mathematics is the *The 4MAT System*.[9] Four learning styles—concrete experience, reflective observation, abstract conceptualization, and active experimentation—are combined with left- and right-brain thinking modes to form a learning cycle that addresses each of these styles. Since one concept is studied with eight different approaches in order to address each student's learning mode, students have a variety of experiences with the same concept. Such an approach allows all students to master the material.

J. Ronald Gentile presents Benjamin Bloom's work on mastery learning as well as additional research demonstrating that 90 percent of all learners can master material if allowed to study it at least eight different times with a different approach each time.[10] Following a final component that focuses on over-learning in order to complete the cycle of mastery, both "fast" and "slow" learners have the same retention. As Gentile puts it:

> We shall have to stop thinking of teaching as "covering the material," and begin thinking of mastering it. If that implies that only a small proportion of students master what is now considered an entire course, so be it. It is likely that only a few are doing so anyhow. For the rest, it is better that they master a small proportion of curricular objectives than to "be exposed to" a large number and master none.[11]

Mastery learning is fostered in the *The 4MAT System* through a sequence of steps designed to encourage thorough analysis and examination of a concept. The student's first step is to experience a problematic situation or one representative of a concept and then reflect on and analyze this experience. Learners integrate this reflective analysis into a concept. Skills are developed to further explore the concept or situation. Students then practice these skills and add something of their own construction. Students move to analyzing the application for relevance and usefulness and end by applying it to a more complex experience.

GETTING LEARNERS INVOLVED

The benefits of the whole concept approach are obvious. Students are involved and interested. They actually use mathematics and understand the practicality of what they are studying. They construct their own mathematical systems and then attempt to verify them. They become involved *learners*, not bored *recipients*. Because they are applying mathematics, they are retaining it. Recognizing these benefits can be helpful in evaluating whole concept mathematics.

For evaluation purposes, students should be observed in order to provide regular feedback to the teacher. Behaviors and goals to look for include examples of independent thinking, a willingness to take risks and hypothesize, the ability to communicate mathematical thought in personal language, a positive attitude toward mathematics, the amount and quality of class participation, the absence of math anxiety, etc. These criteria are representative of active, involved learning that has meaning for students.

Whole concept mathematics represents a learner-centered approach to mathematics that treats each student with respect. Although it is challenging, by its very nature it is also meaningful and useful. In adapting whole language to an objective subject such as mathematics, fundamental curriculum changes are required, but these changes lead to a philosophy that ties together various methodologies that have had growing appeal. Whole concept mathematics emphasizes the meaningful use of mathematics, conceptual learning, verbal and written communication, and the integration of disciplines while being learner-centered, holistic, and natural in its environment and approach. It utilizes real-life situations, manipulative and concrete experiences, mastery or in-depth study, knowledge of learning styles, variety, and cooperative learning techniques. It is consistent with learning theory and yields teaching methodologies emphasizing themes and problem solving. Because it is a philosophy, it is flexible in its application while consistent in its nature. It offers a well-developed alternative to the study of mathematics by utilizing the tenets of whole language.

NOTES

1. Catherine Combleth, Thomas Romberg and Deborah Stewart, "The Monitoring of School Mathematics" (Teaching and Future Directions Program Report 87-3, Wisconsin Center for Education Research, Madison, WI, 1987), 30-39.
2. Ibid., 32.
3. Ibid., 36-37.
4. Norman Webb et al., *The Urban Mathematics Project: Report to the Ford Foundation of the 1986-87 School Year* (Wisconsin Center for Education Research, Madison, WI, 1988).
5. Mary Linn, "Effects of Journal Writing on Thinking Skills of High School Geometry Students" (Masters of Education Project, University of North Florida, Jacksonville, August 1987).
6. Dorothy Goldberg, "Integrating Writing into the Mathematics Curriculum," *College Mathematics Journal* 14 (November 1983): 421-24.
7. Elliot Eisner, *The Educational Imagination* (New York: Macmillan, 1979), 61-85.
8. J. Ronald Gentile, "Recent Retention Research: What Educators Should Know," *The High School Journal* 70 (December/January 1987): 77-85.
9. Bernice McCarthy, *The 4MAT System* (Barrington, IL: Excel, Inc., 1986).
10. Gentile, "Recent Retention Research," 80.
11. Ibid., 84.

Cheryl L. Brown is Assistant Director of Educational Support Programs and Coordinator of the Learning Assistance Center, Northern Arizona University at Flagstaff, Arizona.

Whole Language: Three Themes for the Future

Elfrieda H. Hiebert
Charles W. Fisher

America is witnessing a revolution in classroom teaching and learning. In the new paradigm, knowledge is internal and subjective, learning is constructing meaning, and teaching is a dynamic combination of coaching and facilitating. While many ideas underlying this new paradigm have been around for decades and even centuries (see, e.g., von Glasersfeld 1983), their current incarnation as constructivism is increasingly influencing instructional practices.

Encouraging movements in this direction are evident within several subject matter areas. However, the whole-language or literature-based[1] movement in literacy instruction is far and away the most advanced in its development and use in schools. Since whole language represents the vanguard of a broader set of influences on education, the experiences of students, teachers, and others as they encounter it can either support a transformation or constitute yet another short-lived pendulum swing in educational practice. In its vision of literacy as a thoughtful and active process, whole language offers a promising alternative for the future. Our concern is that its initial success may be so great as to create potential problems. In other words, as new practices associated with whole language gain in popularity, new participants may assume that all of them are appropriate in all situations and that all the old skills-oriented practices are suddenly inappropriate.

In a recent study, we compared literacy tasks in classes implementing whole language and skills-oriented instruction (Fisher and Hiebert, in press). We examined 180 literacy tasks in 40 days of instruction in eight grade 2 and 6 classes. While the whole-language movement is by no means monolithic, the practices we observed were congruent with the underlying philosophy. We found that students in whole-language classes spent more time on literacy tasks, especially writing tasks and, more importantly, that their literacy tasks were larger and more cognitively complex when compared to tasks in the skills-oriented classes. In addition, students in whole-language classes had more influence in determining what literacy task to work on and what the task goal would be. Although whole-language classes had clear advantages, we identified three themes that require attention: balance between narrative and expository text, integration of subject matter areas, and variety in instructional grouping strategies.

BALANCE BETWEEN NARRATIVE AND EXPOSITORY TEXT

Our observations of reading and writing tasks in whole-language classrooms revealed that virtually all lessons and materials read or written by students used narrative text. We also found an emphasis on student self-selection of reading materials and topics for writing. A preponderance of self-selected narrative text is an understandable reaction to the overconcentration on the prescribed materials and specific skills of past years. However, if these practices become exclusive, the benefits could quickly become detriments and, in the long run, do little to alleviate American children's problems with reading and writing expository text (Applebee et al. 1988).

From "Whole Language: Three Themes for the Future" by E. H. Hiebert and C. W. Fisher, 1990, *Educational Leadership*, 47, pp. 62–64. Copyright © 1990 by ASCD. All rights reserved. Reprinted with permission of the Association for Supervision and Curriculum Development.

Therefore, we must examine the question of balance between narrative and expository text and between self-selection and prescription for particular students, for particular aspects of literacy use, and at particular times in literacy development. As children are acquiring fluency in reading, extensive use of narrative text, with its more familiar structures and themes, may be most appropriate. Similarly, self-expressive writing may be appropriate for gaining fluency in writing (Graves 1983). As children attain the desired fluency, however, the use of expository text should increase.

This does not mean that narrative materials that interest children or serve meaningful functions for them should be discontinued. Topics in content areas can often be treated thoughtfully and effectively through narrative text (Levstik 1986). The challenge for whole-language proponents is to progressively increase students' use of expository material as they acquire fluency in reading, thereby providing more diverse contexts for problem solving and critical thinking, while providing autonomy for students to experience joy and creativity in reading and writing.

INTEGRATION OF SUBJECT MATTER AREAS

Second, we believe that teachers need to break through subject matter boundaries in their application of whole-language principles. Our observations of classroom practices over entire school days, for example, found the dramatic differences between whole-language and skills-oriented classrooms to be restricted to reading and writing periods. Even after teachers had participated in whole-language practices for several years, mathematics, science, and social studies instruction in their classrooms remained, for the most part, unaffected. Even when the same person taught all subjects, we found relatively crisp subject matter boundaries.

This situation presents two challenges to whole language, and to educational reform generally: (1) active promotion of analogous principles in other subject areas and (2) support of interdisciplinary tasks. At the very least, school tasks can be integrated through common reading and writing processes that cross subject matter lines. Interdisciplinary themes that provide opportunities to grapple with interpretations, understand others' perspectives, and solve problems require the content of social studies, science, and mathematics, not just of literature.

At first, teachers' attempts to break through subject matter boundaries may produce somewhat artificial connections. For example, reading *Charlotte's Web* may be accompanied by units on spiders or farm states. While this kind of curricular juxtaposition may begin to build some interdisciplinary bridges, it maintains the centrality of content-based knowledge.

What schools need is an infusion of authentic tasks. That is, students need to participate in activities that occur in action-oriented social contexts and that, when completed, make a difference in their day-to-day lives (Brown et al. 1989). For example, children in a Colorado school wrote reports and letters to the city council to lobby for a pedestrian walk light on a street adjacent to the school (*Boulder Daily Camera* 1988). Authentic tasks such as this one are possible when students are presented with a real problem that has tangible consequences for them. This particular context provided many opportunities for reading, writing, science, mathematics, and social studies tasks, where subject matter knowledge boundaries were secondary to the problem itself.

STRATEGIES FOR INSTRUCTIONAL GROUPING

Grouping patterns in whole-language classrooms showed a clear break from the rigid three-group structure that earned the epitaph "once a bluebird, always a bluebird." Students in whole-language classrooms, as compared to those in skills-oriented ones, spent more time in whole-class instruction and approximately the same amount of time working as individuals. However, our observations revealed no occasions when students in whole-language classrooms met with their teachers in small groups, as did students in skills-oriented classes.

Whole-class, cooperative groups, individual activities, and conferencing of teachers with individual students are the "new" organizational formats for classroom literacy experiences (see, e.g., the recommendations in California's *English-Language Arts Framework* 1987). But teacher-led small groups, regardless of the grouping criteria or substance of the activities, are conspicuously missing in guidelines for practice and in practice itself. This situation may reflect deep dissatisfaction with the three-group plan that has dominated reading instruction for so long. For the record, however, it is not ability grouping per se that constitutes the problem, but *long-term* ability grouping (see, e.g., Allington 1983, Hiebert 1983).

Teacher-led small groups based on criteria other than generic reading ability are in danger of being a baby thrown out with the bathwater. Just as overreliance on ability groups created problems in the past, overreliance on whole-class instruction and peer interaction can be expected to provide less than optimal learning environments for students over the long run. Thus, teachers need to give more attention to appropriate uses of teacher- and peer-led small groups within their classrooms.

A PROMISING ALTERNATIVE

As the whole-language movement expands its influence to more schools, educators must make choices that have extraordinary importance not only for the survival of the movement but also for reform in education. To lead literacy instruction, and instruction in general, into a new era, we must give serious consideration to the three areas discussed here: balance between narrative and expository text, integration of subject matter areas, and instructional grouping strategies. If left unheeded, overreaction to past practices may lead to another pendulum swing and our strong commitment to high-quality literature and authentic tasks will suffer. No one wants that to happen.

[1] For purposes of the current discussion, we use the term "whole language" to characterize literacy instruction that is heavily influenced by constructivist ideas about the nature of knowledge, teaching, and learning.

REFERENCES

Allington, R. L. (1983). "The Reading Instruction Provided Readers of Differing Abilities." *Elementary School Journal* 83: 548–559.

Applebee, A. N., J. A. Langer, and I. V. A. Mullis. (1988). *Who Reads Best? Factors Related to Reading Achievement in Grades 3, 7, and 11.* Princeton, NJ.: NAEP and ETS.

Boulder Daily Camera. (December 2, 1987). "Students Give City Council Results of Intersection Study," C–1.

Brown, J. S., A. Collins, and P. Duguid. (1989). "Situated Cognition and the Culture of Learning." *Educational Researcher* 18: 32–42.

California Department of Education. (1987). *English-Language Arts Framework for California Public Schools: Kindergarten Through Grade Twelve.* Sacramento: California Department of Education.

Fisher, C. W., and E. H. Hiebert. (In press). "Characteristics of Tasks in Two Approaches to Literacy Instruction." *Elementary School Journal.*

Graves, D. (1983). *Writing: Teachers and Children at Work.* Exeter, N.H.: Heinemann.

Hiebert, E. H. (1983). "An Examination of Ability Grouping for Reading Instruction." *Reading Research Quarterly* 18: 231–255.

Levstik, L. S. (1986). "The Relationship Between Historical Response and Narrative in a Sixth-Grade Classroom." *Theory and Research in Social Education* 14: 1–15.

von Glasersfeld, E. (1983). "Learning as a Constructive Activity." In *Proceedings of the Fifth Annual Meeting of the North American Chapter of the International Group for the Psychology of Mathematics Education,* Vol. 1, pp. 42–69, edited by J. C. Bergeron and N. Herscovics. Montreal: Universite de Montreal, Faculte de Sciences de l'Education.

Elfrieda H. Hiebert is an associate professor at the University of Colorado at Boulder. Charles W. Fisher is an associate professor at the University of Northern Colorado in Greeley.

CHAPTER DISCUSSIONS AND ACTIVITIES

1. Select a particular grade level and identify five children's literature books appropriate for that age and grade level. Describe how you would use these books in integrating social studies, science, and math.
2. For a particular grade level, obtain a social studies, a science, and a math textbook. Identify the major themes you might select for that grade level and describe how you would integrate major topics in the content areas centered around those particular themes with the use of literature.
3. An eighth-grade science teacher was heard to remark, "I teach science. Some of these students can't read the text. I don't have time to teach them how to read." Pair off with a classmate and discuss how you would respond to this comment.
4. With a small group of classmates, prepare a comparison chart between content-area textbooks and nonfiction genre books. Discuss how they are alike and how they are different.
5. A fifth-grade teacher, in responding to the use of whole language across the grades, made the following statement, "I am skeptical about using literature to teach mathematics. The whole-language advocates have gone too far. It is one thing to enrich mathematics through the use of literature, but to do the whole thing! Nothing can replace the practice and drill necessary to achieve basic mathematic competency." In a small group, please comment on this remark.

CHAPTER 8

Assessment

Educators have long been concerned with the assessment of the students entrusted to their care. The progress of students is not only a major consideration for teachers, but also is of prime significance for administrators, parents, and especially the children themselves. In this chapter, we will view how assessment has been conducted in the past, how assessment is defined, and how it is handled in the whole-language classroom.

ASSESSMENT IN THE TRADITIONAL CLASSROOM

Prior to World War I, students were tested with time-consuming essay examinations and in many instances with oral exams. As Popham (1993) notes, it was during World War I, through the development of the "Army Alpha Examination," that the "use of multiple-choice questions profoundly altered the subsequent nature of educational testing in this country and abroad" (p. 471).

Over the years, achievement tests emerged that were modeled closely on the "Alpha's" multiple-choice-type questions. Their use snowballed and by the 1970s, legislative requirements for testing emerged, with test results "being used to hold students back and to indicate educators' effectiveness" (Popham, 1993, p. 471). The use of multiple-choice, norm-referenced and criterion-referenced standardized tests not only narrowed the curriculum, but measured only low-level knowledge and skills (Madaus & Kellaghan, 1993). The effects of the use of such testing on education is further noted by Popham (1993):

> The accountability-forced achievement tests of the Seventies and Eighties, even though they had been conceived as devices to monitor educators' accomplishments,

had turned into *curricular magnets*. Because students' test performances began to have such important ramifications, what was tested became what was taught. Measurement-driven instruction was upon us. (p. 471)

Although there have been revisions and improvements of standardized tests, Cox and Zarrillo (1993) believe that "the best a standardized reading test can offer is a broad view of how well someone reads" (p. 377). They also note that standardized tests do not afford the type of information that a teacher can use to make accurate assessments of students; they do not reveal the child's ability to read orally with fluency and style; and they do not recount what books a child has read.

Alternative methods of assessment have evolved because of the changing views of reading and writing. We are moving away from the traditional ways of assessing the progress of children through the employment of multiple-choice questions found in standardized tests (Gunning, 1992). Although such tests have been used for evaluation purposes for many years, "they are viewed as too narrow or confining to explain many of the complexities of written language development" (Wiseman, 1992, p. 266). Anderson, Hiebert, Scott, and Wilkinson, the authors of the influential book *Becoming a Nation of Readers: The Report of the Commission on Reading*, (1985), state:

> A more valid assessment of basic reading proficiency than that provided by standardized tests could be obtained by ascertaining whether students can and will do the following: Read aloud unfamiliar but grade-appropriate material with acceptable fluency; write satisfactory summaries of unfamiliar selections from grade-appropriate social studies and science textbooks; explain the plots and motivations of the characters in unfamiliar, grade-appropriate fiction; read extensively from books, magazines and newspapers during leisure time. (p. 99)

ASSESSMENT DEFINED

When discussing assessment it is important to review the many ways in which the term has been discussed in the literature. Harris and Hodges (1981) define assessment as:

> The act or process of gathering data in order to better understand some topics or area of knowledge, as through observation, testing, interviews, etc.; especially, the gathering of data to include strengths and weaknesses in learning. (p. 22)

According to Cox and Zarrillo (1993), "Assessment must be viewed as an ongoing process. It involves gathering, analyzing, and sharing information. The process should begin the first day of school and continue through the year" (p. 365). Froese (1991) states that the purpose of assessment includes: diagnosis by the teacher and feedback for the student; the monitoring of progress for an individual over a time period; and supplying a grade or anecdotal record for parents.

With assessment, two different kinds have been identified, *external* and *internal*. Standardized tests are the main source of assessment that is considered to be external, while in recent years, interest in assessment is focusing more on internal means. Through the use of portfolios, dated audiotapes, anecdotal records of literacy behaviors, writing samples, reading response journals and interest inventories, teachers are using other means to assess student growth (Bean, 1989; Wepner & Feeley, 1993).

Assessment is also perceived as being: continuous—not just relying on end-of-the-year evaluation; multidimensional—not just depending on one measure or index; collaborative—not just using the exclusive judgment of the teacher; knowledge-based—not just solely using the source of information from others; and authentic—not just emphasizing extrinsic values. It is involved with what teachers and students do to measure progress rather than being viewed "as a series of paper and pencil tests imposed on teachers and students by those in position of authority—those concerned with accountability" (Valencia, McGinley & Pearson, 1990, p. 125).

ASSESSMENT IN THE WHOLE-LANGUAGE CLASSROOM

According to Kenneth Goodman (1989), whole-language teachers have railed against traditional evaluation techniques. They find standardized tests to be "synthetic, contrived, confining, and controlling, out of touch with modern theory and research" (p. xi). Evaluation in whole language is viewed as an integral part of the curriculum and is not perceived as a separate aspect of education. "It cannot be divorced from classroom organization, from the relationship between teachers and students, from continuous learning experiences and activities" (Y. Goodman, 1989, p. 4).

For whole-language teachers, evaluation in the classroom evolves from observation, interaction, and analysis. Observation can be informal as the teacher moves around the classroom noticing the youngsters' behavior in small groups or individually. Formal observation occurs when the teacher keeps anecdotal records of the various activities of the children throughout the day. With interaction, the teacher and the student are both directly involved in the evaluation process whether conversing or conferencing. It is the children who question what they are thinking and doing. Interaction is informally evident in daily conversations and discussions of the children. Formal interaction occurs during strategy lessons, such as the use of the cloze procedure, journal writing, or learning logs. Analysis also includes direct involvement of the students in the evaluation of their progress. The use of portfolios provides the teacher and the students with records of the reading and writing materials prepared by the students (Y. Goodman, 1989).

Looking Ahead

Gutknecht (1992) in his article, discusses the differences between assessment in the traditional classroom and the informal assessment procedures in the whole-language classroom.

An important and growing portion of the assessment puzzle is the portfolio. Traditionally, artists, actors, photographers, and models have used the portfolio to showcase their achievements and capabilities. As noted by Pikulski (1989):

> One of the most dynamic assessment concepts currently being discussed in our field is that of a *portfolio approach* to the assessment of reading and literacy. Since there are *no* tests or test materials that are specifically associated with this approach, it has the potential for placing teachers and students—not tests and test scores—at the very center of the assessment process. (p. 81)

A portfolio is a systematic collection of materials, made by the student as well as the teacher, which indicates the effort and processes attained by the student in reading and writing. Through use of portfolios, teachers are able to monitor the reading and writing progress of students; collect continuing information of the child's progress; engage students in assessing their progress and accomplishments in an ongoing fashion; support student self-evaluation and motivation; direct improvement, effort, and achievement; yield feedback about instruction; and connect assessment and teaching to learning (Tierney, Carter & Desai, 1991; Wiseman, 1992).

According to Gomez, Graue, and Block (1991), portfolios afford teachers an excellent opportunity "to reconsider their teaching practice by making a tight connection between instruction and assessment. The reality of portfolio assessment, however, tells us that the responsibility of making this restructured assessment work falls squarely on the shoulders of already burdened teachers" (p. 628).

Looking Ahead

In the article about portfolio assessment by Valencia (1990), the need for such assessment is discussed, the physical appearance of a portfolio is described and aspects of the organizational framework are addressed. Hansen (1992) discusses Literacy Portfolios, which show the direct involvement of students in the assessment process. Bembridge (1992) describes a particular assessment instrument developed by one school district. In the last article, Linek (1991) discusses other grading and evaluation techniques that whole-language teachers can use in the classroom.

Although portfolios furnish an excellent means of assembling a broad range of assessment information, there are some essential questions for reflective teachers. Specifically, what should be placed in a portfolio? Which work samples should be included? Should the items be tracked or grouped? Who decides what to keep, the teacher or the student? How are the results of observations handled? Are all the contents of the portfolio shared with parents during conference time? What is the relationship between the information provided in the portfolio and the report card? These are just a few of the concerns that teachers need to ponder. Johns (1991) issues the following warning:

One of the real dangers of using portfolios is that they can become an unfocused collection of many pieces of information. Such an unorganized accumulation of bits and pieces will reduce their usefulness. To promote usefulness, you will need to think carefully about the purposes of the portfolio as they apply to your curricular and instructional priorities. (p. 5)

The five articles focus on the various assessment strategies that are used in the whole-language classroom. Some of the questions that will be addressed include the following:

- What are the specific differences between traditional, formal assessment and assessment in the whole-language classroom?
- Why is "kidwatching" considered an assessment procedure for whole-language teachers?
- How can student conferences be used by teachers as an assessment procedure?
- What are some of the advantages in employing literary journals for student assessment?
- How can portfolios be used effectively in an elementary school classroom?
- What are the different kinds of portfolios that can be used on various grade levels?
- In what ways do portfolios keep pace with students' progress in reading and writing?
- What options does a whole-language teacher have with regard to formal assessment?
- What are the different kinds of assessment techniques that teachers can use to track the progress of students in reading and writing?
- How is grading handled in a whole-language classroom?

REFERENCES

Anderson, R. C., Hiebert, E. H., Scott, J. A., & Wilkinson, I. A. G. (1985). *Becoming a nation of readers: The report of the Commission on Reading.* Washington, DC: The National Institute of Education, U.S. Department of Education.

Bean, R. M. (1989). Effective reading program development. In S. B. Wepner, J. T. Feeley, & D. S. Strickland (Eds.), *The administration and supervision of reading programs* (pp. 3–21). New York: Teachers College Press.

Bembridge, T. (1992). A MAP for reading assessment. *Educational Leadership, 49*(8), 46–48.

Cox, C. & Zarrillo, J. (1993). *Teaching reading with children's literature.* New York: Merrill/Macmillan.

Froese, V. (1991). Assessment: Form and function. In V. Froese (Ed.), *Whole language: Practice and theory* (pp. 283–311). Boston: Allyn and Bacon.

Gomez, M. L., Graue, M. E., & Block, M. N. (1991). Reassessing portfolio assessment: Rhetoric and reality. *Language Arts, 68*(8), 620–628.

Goodman, K. S. (1989). Preface. In K. S. Goodman, Y. M. Goodman, & W. J. Hood (Eds.), *The whole language evaluation book* (pp. xi–xv). Portsmouth, NH: Heinemann.

Goodman, Y. M. (1989). Evaluation of students: Evaluation of teachers. In K. S. Goodman, Y. M. Goodman, & W. J. Hood (Eds.), *The whole language evaluation book* (pp. 3–14). Portsmouth, NH: Heinemann.

Gunning, T. G. (1992). *Creating reading instruction for all children.* Boston: Allyn and Bacon.

Gutknecht, B. (1992). Learning about language learners: The case for informal assessment in the whole language classroom. *Reading Improvement, 29*(4), 210–219.

Hansen, J. (1992). Literacy Portfolios: Helping students know themselves. *Educational Leadership, 49*(8), 66–68.

Harris, T. L., & Hodges, R. E. (Eds.). (1981). *A dictionary of reading.* Newark, DE: International Reading Association.

Johns, J. L. (1991). Literacy portfolios: A primer. *Illinois Reading Council Journal, 19,* 4–10.

Linek, W. M. (1991). Grading and evaluation techniques for whole language teachers. *Language Arts, 68*(2), 125–132.

Madaus, G. F., & Kellaghan, T. (1993). The British experience with 'authentic' testing. *Phi Delta Kappan, 74*(6), 458–469.

Pikulski, J. J. (1989). The assessment of reading: A time for change? *The Reading Teacher, 43*(1), 80–81.

Popham, W. J. (1993). Circumventing the high costs of authentic assessment. *Phi Delta Kappan, 74*(6), 470–473.

Tierney, R. J., Carter, M. A., & Desai, L. E. (1991). *Portfolio assessment in the reading–writing classroom.* Norwood, MA: Christopher-Gordon.

Valencia, S. (1990). A portfolio approach to classroom reading assessment: The whys, whats, and hows. *The Reading Teacher, 43*(4), 338–340.

Valencia, S. W., McGinley, W., & Pearson, P. D. (1990). Assessing reading and writing. In G. G. Duffy (Ed.), *Reading in the middle school* (pp. 124–153). Newark, DE: International Reading Association.

Wepner, S. B., & Feeley, J. T. (1993). *Moving forward with literature: Basals, books and beyond.* New York: Merrill/Macmillan.

Wiseman, D. L (1992). *Learning to read with literature.* Boston: Allyn and Bacon.

FOR FURTHER STUDY

Afflerbach, P. (1993). Report cards and reading. *The Reading Teacher, 46*(6), 458–465.

Au, K. H., Scheu, J. A., Kawakami, A. J., & Herman, P. A. (1990). Assessment and accountability in a whole literacy curriculum. *The Reading Teacher, 43*(8), 574–578.

Belanoff, P., & Dickson, M. (1991). *Portfolios process and product.* Portsmouth, NH: Boynton/Cook.

Farr, R. (1992). Putting it all together: Solving the reading assessment puzzle. *The Reading Teacher, 46*(1), 26–37.

Grady, E. (1992). *The portfolio approach to assessment: Fastback 341.* Bloomington, IL: Phi Delta Kappa Educational Foundation.

Goodman, Y. M., Hood, W. J., & Goodman, K. S. (Eds.). *Organizing for whole language.* (1991). Portsmouth, NH: Heinemann.

Grindler, M. C., & Stratton, B. D. (1992). Whole language assessment. *Reading Improvement, 29*(4), 262–264.

Herman, J. L. (1992). What research tells us about good assessment. *Educational Leadership, 49*(8), 74–78.

Hetterscheidt, J., Pott, L., Russell, K. R., & Tchang, J. (1992). Using the computer as a reading portfolio. *Educational Leadership, 49*(8), 73.

Lamme, L. L., & Hysmith, C. (1991). One school's adventure into portfolio assessment. *Language Arts, 68*(8), 629–640.

Marzano, R. J., Pickering, D., & McTighe, J. (1993). *Assessing student outcomes: Performance assessment using the dimensions learning model.* Alexandria, VA: Association for Supervision and Curriculum Development.

Rhodes, L. K., & Nathenson-Mejia, S. (1992). Anecdotal records: A powerful tool for ongoing literacy assessment. *The Reading Teacher, 45*(7), 502–509.

Rowell, C. G. (1993). *Assessment and correction in elementary language arts.* Boston: Allyn and Bacon.

Valencia, S. W., Hiebert, E. H., & Afflerbach, P. P. (1994). *Authentic reading assessment.* Newark, DE: International Reading Association.

Wiggins, G. (1993). *Assessing student performance: Exploring the purpose and limits of testing.* San Francisco, CA: Jossey-Bass.

Wiggins, G. (1993). Assessment: Authenticity, context, and validity. *Phi Delta Kappan, 75*(3), 200–214.

Winograd, P., Paris, S., & Bridge, C. (1991). Improving the assessment of literacy. *The Reading Teacher, 45*(2), 108–116.

Learning about Language Learners: The Case for Informal Assessment in the Whole Language Classroom

Bruce Gutknecht

INTRODUCTION

For the last twenty years or so, during the back-to-basics accountability-driven era in education, teachers, were not expected or encouraged to be instructional decision-makers. Teachers were considered managers, as defined by Bennis and Naus (1985), who do things right, rather than leaders, who identify the right things to do. Good teaching was defined as *doing things right* rather than identifying and acting on the *right things to do*. Of course, doing things right usually meant doing things the way they have always been done.

State legislators and boards of education, school system administrators and principals, and even parents put great stock in formal paper-and-pencil measurement of children's reading abilities. In most cases, this meant total reliance on standardized tests. According to Valencia and Pearson (1987), this led to a false sense of security when proficient reading was equated with standardized test scores.

Informal assessment was suspect because of its subjectivity, resulting in the view of administrators, principals, and even teachers that standardized test data were more trustworthy. So these data were used in making promotion decisions, selecting children for remedial or gifted placements, comparing one student to another and one school to another and one state to another and America to other

From "Learning about Language Learners: The Case for Informal Assessment in the Whole Language Classroom" by B. Gutknecht, 1992, *Reading Improvement, 29,* pp. 210–219. Copyright © 1992 by Project Innovation of Mobile. Reprinted by permission.

countries and even one teacher to another. Standardized tests worked OK for some of these purposes, since their goal is providing data for classification, accountability, and progress monitoring (Johnston, 1987). And for teachers, who were not expected to be decision-makers, standardized test data were used for instructional planning purposes.

Teachers and parents were both misled. The parent whose third grade child scored GE 6–3 in reading comprehension on a standardized test assumed that the child was a candidate for a gifted program. The teacher acting on the same information provided sixth grade level reading materials for the student. Or, if the same third grade child scored at the GE 1–5 level in phonetic analysis, the teacher provided more phonetic analysis drill and practice so the child could make up the measured deficiency. Neither of these actions was appropriate since they were based on measurement instruments whose design and function serve administrative purposes; not instructional purposes.

Under the current banners of restructuring or school improvement or education reform and accountability, expectations for teachers are undergoing considerable change. In addition to helping students think and to model the verbal and higher order thinking skills children need to use information effectively, to serve as guides and resource consultants, to use technology to enrich and enlarge both the content and process of knowledge, to let technology serve as the primary information-giver while spending their time as learning facilitators, coaches, and guides, and to work together in teams which can provide a continuing supporting environment in which teachers, staff, students, and parents work toward superior school-wide outcomes, teachers are now being encouraged and expected to be *decision-makers*. At the same time reading instruction is moving from a skills acquisition to a whole language model with readers bringing meaning to the text, so it's time to review *informal* assessment procedures which can provide teachers with those data necessary for making sound instructional decisions.

In this paper, the current changes in reading instruction are described, traditional formal assessment is reviewed, and informal assessment procedures are suggested, all leading toward the goal of learning about language learners and planning appropriate instruction for them in the whole language classroom.

CHANGES IN READING INSTRUCTION

For the last twenty years or so, elementary school reading instruction was carried on in the following manner: (a) each child's performance level on a prespecified set of reading skills was measured, (b) each child was placed on the appropriate level in a skill development program, (c) each child's progress was monitored through each sequential step of the program, (d) the performance level of each child was measured during program implementation and following program completion, and (e) the skill acquisition competence of each child was certified, based on extensive record-keeping. Today this pattern is being challenged because while skills acquisition instruction has led to high levels of skills acquisition— mostly word recognition, these aren't the skills required in the reading-to-learn world of science, social studies, literature, and other content areas; and the real world out-of-school tasks requiring at least functional levels of literacy (Gutknecht, 1991). In other words, at the direction of local school administrators, curriculum specialists, and school boards who approved the adoption of required reading instructional materials; state departments of education; and even legislatures; teachers worked hard to do things right, rather than identifying and implementing the right things to do.

Some of the changes now going on in reading instruction are shown below:

From:	To:
Skills-acquisition model	Instruction using whole, natural language
Starting emphasis on word recognition skills	Starting emphasis on meaning and understanding
Skills as an end in themselves	Skills as a means to learning
Oral reading emphasis	More silent reading to learn
Often-unreal, basal-reader stories	Quality children's literature and real-world print materials
Emphasis on activities *after* reading story	Much activity *before* reading story
Over-reliance on formal evaluation—test results	Informal evaluation using teacher judgment—portfolio and other informal data
Traditional three reading groups	Flexible groups to fit instructional needs
"Lock-step" progress through reading program and materials	Flexible progress with self-selection and alternatives
"Special" placements for those having difficulty	Instruction for all in regular classroom
Telling kids what they've done wrong	Self-monitoring by students, "Does it sound right?" and "Does it make sense?"

These changes, and others, are being implemented in classrooms across the country. Where they are going on, teachers are acting as leaders—instructional decision-makers who are identifying and acting on the right things to do, rather than managers who are still trying to do the right things better.

TRADITIONAL FORMAL ASSESSMENT

Traditional formal assessment of reading abilities in the form of standardized norm referenced or criterion referenced tests is not relevant for administrative purposes or instructional planning purposes in whole language classrooms or schools. Standardized tests are not congruent with current research-based beliefs about language learning. They are skill, not process oriented, they are used to sort and classify children rather than provide direction for instructional planning, they are incomplete in that they don't ask all the questions necessary to gather information about whole language learning, and they have a mistaken aura of objectivity (Heald-Taylor, 1989). They have become so institutionalized at school, district, state, and federal levels that to question them is almost blasphemous.

Many teachers experience great difficulty in applying the current measurement-based approach to assessment in the whole language classroom. Their uneasiness is reported by Cambourne and Turbill (1990, p. 338) who were told such things as, "I can't understand why my principal forces me to take half of every Friday to stop teaching and give all these weekly tests," "I'm unhappy about basing my assessment on the reading test we use or on a one-draft piece of writing done under pressure... neither tells me very much about the processes involved," and "These tests have no relationship to the goals and expectations that I have in language."

While both language curricula and evaluation of instructional effectiveness have been test-driven, the focus here is on the problems encountered when traditional standardized test assessment procedures are used in the whole language classroom. First, standardized tests are not reflective of current conceptualizations of the reading process. They reflect the behavioral research of thirty years ago and based on the assumption that language is learned through the acquisition of isolated, sequentially-organized skills, mastered one at a time (Valencia & Pearson, 1987).

Second, these tests contain a number of subtests of specific, decontextualized skills that do not require students to demonstrate the full range of their ability (Goodman, 1986; Weaver, 1989). They are an incomplete measure of language learning because they focus mainly on reading and ignore other language processes—speaking, listening, and writing.

Not only do standardized reading tests focus on abstract, isolated skills, they focus mainly on word recognition skills and vocabulary skills—sight words and their meanings outside of a natural, real language context. Comprehension is measured with passages so brief that whole language students are unable to apply the metacognitive meaning-seeking strategies (Does it sound right? Does it make sense?) they are learning.

These tests ignore very important aspects of the language learning process, such as children's background experiences and how these experiences were conceptualized into idea and thoughts, the oral syntactic and semantic language systems, print awareness developed through early involvement with environmental print, attitude toward and interest in learning to read, familiarity with characters and events in stories resulting from listening to stories being read to them, and meaning seeking strategies employed in listening and reading.

Finally, the quantitative, multiple choice, one right answer approach to the measurement of language ability required in standardized testing, leaves little, if any, room for the most important ingredient in language learning—the child her/himself. This approach focuses on what children take away from the their language learning experiences in school—skills, rather than on what they bring—meaning. Any language instruction that stops short of meaning—the communication of a message from speaker or writer to listener or reader, isn't effective instruction at all, no matter what prestige is accorded it by standardized tests.

While there are other reasons for questioning the measurement of reading abilities of whole language learners with standardized tests, the concerns presented above should alert whole language teachers and other school personnel responsible for whole language instruction to the gap between current instructional approaches and the instruments and methods available for evaluation of their effectiveness.

ASSESSMENT IN THE WHOLE LANGUAGE CLASSROOM

Whole language learning cannot be assessed with traditional assessment methods. Assessment/evaluation procedures must be consistent with whole language philosophy. Standardized tests are not congruent with whole language philosophy because they are *skill*, not *process* oriented. Whole language is based on current knowledge about language learning that suggests that language is learned through a thinking, social, participatory, interactive process as children are immersed in rich literary experiences involving all of the language processes—speaking, listening, writing, and reading (Harste, Woodward & Burke, 1984; Smith, 1983). So, process knowledge—what language-users do—as well as skills knowledge must be included in whole language assessment.

Children, according to Smith (1985), are highly skilled and experienced learners. Learning to read requires no learning skills that haven't already been developed by children before they arrive at school. The oral language facility developed by most children themselves, without interference from parents or teachers, demonstrates their competence in learning to learn. This same competence, developed by children because of their need to communicate, needs to be evaluated by teachers and become the basis for writing and reading instruction. In addition, children have been learning to read environmental print by themselves long before they are confused in school by reading instruction. Goodman (1986) suggests that children are *driven* to become language learners by their need to communicate. This built-in motivation needs to be captured by teachers as formal reading and writing instruction begins.

Purpose

The purpose of assessment in the whole language classroom is to measure children's underlying language learning competence. The results of this assessment then provide teachers with the *information needed for planning effective language instruction*. Formal standardized norm or criterion referenced tests do not serve this purpose. Informal assessment can.

Teachers link assessment to instruction when they interact with students as they engage in reading and writing, intervening to provide support or make suggestions. Assessment identifies strategies and behaviors in which children take part as their language grows and develops and which suggest to teachers the development of appropriate instructional situations to promote continuous growth.

The focus of informal assessment is on what kids *can* do, not on what they *can't*; on what *they're doing* while learning language, not on what *they've done*.

Kid-Watching

Goodman (1986) calls such assessment kid-watching. He says:

...one can learn much more about pupils by carefully watching then by formal testing. Whole language teachers are constant kid-watchers. Informally, in the course of watching a child write, listening to a group of children discuss or plan together, or having a casual conversation, teachers evaluate. It even happens while children are playing. It happens more formally in one-to-one conferences with pupils about their reading and writing, as teachers make anecdotal records of what they observe. It may involve instruments like the *Reading Miscue Inventory* [(Goodman, Watson & Burke, 1987)] or a writing observation form. The key is that it happens in the course of ongoing classroom activities. (p. 41)

Suggestions from the Literature

"Teachers now have at their disposal an array of assessment techniques based upon a strategic view of the reading process" (Ridley, 1990, p. 645).

Heald-Taylor (1989) suggests several data collection formats-anecdotal records and checklists which focus on speaking, listening, writing, and reading behaviors rather than on isolated word recognition skills, log books and writing logs which, along with work samples (tapes of oral language, dictated stories, and writing samples), document language growth; and a series of whole language behavior inventories which show characteristics of language growth.

Cambourne and Turbill in "Assessment in Whole-Language Classrooms: Theory into Practice" (1990) propose a "natural" theory of language assessment called *responsive evaluation* which involves observing, reacting, intervening, and participating in many of the language learning activities in which children are engaged each day. Qualitative data gathered through such student–teacher interaction are as trustworthy and more useful than the numbers generated by tests. Several examples and guides are provided in the article's appendices.

Forms of evaluation that are consistent with whole language principles are addressed by classroom teachers from a variety of school settings and levels in *The Whole Language Evaluation Book* (Goodman, Goodman & Hood, 1989). The focus of this book is on how evaluation can help whole language teachers learn more about their students in incidental, informal, and formal ways resulting in the planning of effective language teaching and learning. Self-evaluation by teachers and students, evaluation of students by teachers, and evaluation of teachers by students is presented along with suggestions to be used in reporting to parents, other teachers, and administrators.

LEARNING ABOUT LANGUAGE LEARNERS: SEVERAL SUGGESTIONS

Three Important Questions

Consideration of the answers to the following questions raised by Gutknecht, Johnson and Chapman (1987) forms the basis for assessment in the whole language classroom. First, *where is the student now?* This question focuses on the present in terms of the student's grade placement, type of language learning instructional program, ability level, resource placements, experiential background, interests, and attitudes. Next, *where has the student been,* in terms of the number of schools attended, type of language learning instructional programs experienced, resource placements, ability level, what's worked, and what hasn't in the past. Finally, *where is the student going?* This question addresses the language requirements faced by the student next term or next year—more oral or silent reading, research writing, and/or emphasis on comprehension of specific content materials.

Information can be gathered in a variety of ways as a means to answering these questions. Introspective techniques/instruments, such as interest inventories, attitude inventories, student conferences, and reading records provide teachers with a great deal of information useful in planning effective language learning. The retrospective device of the reading autobiography and the use of a literacy journal are also very valuable in learning about language learners. A number of these techniques/instruments can be found in *Planning Effective Reading Instruction* (Gutknecht, Johnson & Chapman, 1987).

Student Conferences

Student conferences can provide insight into student interests, attitudes, motivation, goals, and ambitions. Stimulus questions might include:

1. How do you feel about what we've been doing in reading (language, science, social studies) so far this term? Are you enjoying it?
2. What one thing do you like most about reading (language, science, social studies)? What one thing do you like least? What one thing would you change if you were the teacher?
3. Do you feel comfortable with the materials, activities, assignments and homework, pace of instruction, tests, and grading in reading (language, science, social studies)?
4. What do you do when you have trouble understanding the meaning of words in the textbooks? What do you do when you don't understand text materials while you're reading and/or when you've finished reading?
5. Are you satisfied with your learning so far this term? Do you have any questions about your grades or comments on your papers? Would you like to go over something that was difficult for you to learn?

Literacy Journals

Literacy journals are not summaries, but reactions to literacy events—books/stories read, written assignments, dramatizations, oral reports, interviews with other students. Stimulus items for entries might include:

1. Literacy event (name of book/story, written assignment, oral language activity).
2. What did you like most about the event? Least? Why?
3. Who was you favorite character? Why? Describe the character. If you were this character, what would you do differently?
4. Which character didn't you like? Why? Describe the character. If you were this character, what would you do differently?
5. What's your favorite event in the story? Why?
6. What one thing did you know after the event that you didn't know before?
7. What would you do/say to get someone else interested in the event?

More Formal Informal Assessment

Whole language teachers can learn more about language learners by using qualitative instruments such as DeSanti's *Cloze Reading Inventory* (1986). It combines the cloze procedure with an informal reading inventory format, which can be group-administered, employing qualitative analysis to focus on reader's abilities to comprehend and to use language structures. The CRI results in determination of the student's functional reading levels, based not on oral reading errors, but on analysis of the reader's word choices to fill the deletions in cloze passages.

Oral reading substitutions, omissions, and insertions can be analyzed using Gutknecht's (1987) qualitative analysis worksheet. To use the worksheet, **ER** (expected response)/**OR** (observed response) pairs are recorded for about *twenty-five miscues*. For substitutions, the responses to seven questions are coded about each pair using a +/0/– marking system:

1. Graphic Similarity: How much does the ER look like the OR?
2. Phonemic Similarity: How much does the ER sound like the OR?
3. Grammatical Function: Is the grammatical function of the OR the same as that of the ER?
4. Syntactic Acceptability: Does the OR occur in a grammatically acceptable structure?
5. Meaning Acceptability: Does the OR occur in a semantically acceptable structure?
6. Meaning Change: Does the OR result in a change of meaning?
7. Correction Behavior: Is the OR corrected?

For omissions and insertions, only questions 3 through 7 are used. After each miscue is coded, the percentages of +/0/– codes are calculated for each column, yielding information about the reader's use of grapho-phonic, syntactic, and semantic reading strategies.

Folders and Portfolios

Folders in which teachers collect samples of children's writing have been used for some time. Whole language teachers can expand on this idea through the development of a portfolio with each child. Johnston (1992) suggests that writing folders are a place where children store all their bits and pieces of writing—a working file, while the portfolio is a public demonstration of the child's development as a literate person and as a learner. The portfolio contains the examples of a child's work that s/he sees fit to display and talk about to others in much the same way an artist or architect keeps a collection of works.

Folders can provide a paper trail of a child's writing development and history as a learner. They describe and document development that is instructionally useful, they can increase the time spent learning and the quality of learning, provide teachers with a means to evaluate their own instructional effectiveness, furnish something tangible for discussion among the teaching/learning stakeholders—students, teachers, administrators, and parents, and facilitate personal, individualized contact among them.

A directory of materials in the folder can include a checklist used to keep track of the status of pieces of writing. Checkpoints might include planning, lead, draft or draft number, review, revise, confer, edit, and publish. Teach-

QUALITATIVE ANALYSIS WORKSHEET

ER	OR	GS	PS	GF	SA	MA	MC	CB
% +								
% 0								
% −								

ER: EXPECTED RESPONSE
GS: GRAPHIC SIMILARITY
GF: GRAMMATICAL FUNCTION
MA: MEANING ACCEPTABILITY
CB: CORRECTION BEHAVIOR

OR: OBSERVED RESPONSE
PS: PHONEMIC SIMILARITY
SA: SYNTACTIC ACCEPTABILITY
MC: MEANING CHANGE

GS, PS, SA, MA: + = HIGH DEGREE, 0 = SOME DEGREE/PARTIAL − = NO DEGREE
GF: + = SAME, 0 = INDETERMINATE, − = DIFFERENT
MC: + = NO, 0 = MINIMAL, − = MAJOR
CB: − = CORRECTED, 0 = UNSUCCESSFUL ATTEMPT, − = NO ATTEMPT

ers can begin each class with a "status of the class" conference during which each student indicates what s/he will be working on that day (Atwell, 1987). Such conferences can help children set their own goals and can serve as verbal contracts with the teacher.

Bird, in her article, "Anatomy of a Student Portfolio," (1991) suggests that a portfolio should contain a variety of holistic evaluative measures, including: semimonthly anecdotal records, quarterly writing samples, retellings of stories read, evaluation of invented spelling development (pretend writing, prephonetic, phonetic, and conventional), environmental print awareness, listing of books/stories read, and qualitative analysis information. In addition, teachers can include data obtained from one or more of the informal techniques/instruments described above.

Written records for students can be kept at three levels (Johnston, 1992). The first level is the working folder of writing with various drafts and revisions, a checklist of the status of work in progress, and might include a journal containing a learning log and/or a personal response journal which keeps track of day-to-day writing, reading, and the learning taking place. At the second level, the student from time to time might put together a portfolio containing pieces s/he considers her/his best work of the term, a piece taken from draft to final form, a list (perhaps annotated) of books read, a character extension, and/or a book review. Also included could be an introspective self-evaluation in which the student addresses what has changed about her/his reading (writing), possible reasons for this change, changes s/he would like to see, plans for making these changes, and/or a comment about the most difficult part of writing (reading).

It's important that students select materials for inclusion in the portfolio. If the portfolio is to serve a means of communication between school and home, teachers, with the student's agreement, might include information or materials to further illustrate the student's learning.

The third level of record might be comprised of copies of end-of-year portfolios along with narrative descriptions by teachers. These could become part of cumulative records and provide both the student and the school with an instructional history.

SUMMARY

This paper set out to present the case for informal assessment in the whole language classroom. Today's changes in reading instruction from a skills acquisition to a whole language model require a change in assessment from the traditional formal standardized paper and pencil test approach to a focus on the use of informal techniques/instruments and qualitative analysis. Whole language teachers who understand and use the techniques/instruments presented will collect a variety of data that will not only enable them to plan effective reading instruction, but confidently communicate with parents, other teachers, and administrators what they've learned about the language learners in their classroom.

REFERENCES

Atwell, N. (1987). *In the middle: Writing, reading and teaming with adolescents.* Portsmouth, NH: Heinemann/Boynton-Cook.

Bennis, W. & Naus, B. (1985). *Leaders: The strategies for taking charge.* New York, NY: Harper & Row.

Bird, L. (1991). Anatomy of a student portfolio. In K. Goodman, L. Bird & Y. Goodman (Eds.), *The whole language catalog* (p. 262). Santa Rosa, CA: American School Publishers.

Cambourne, B. & Turbill, J. (1990, January). Assessment in whole language classrooms: Theory into practice. *The Elementary School Journal, 90*(3), 337–349.

DeSanti, R. (1986). *The DeSanti cloze reading inventory.* Boston, MA: Allyn and Bacon.

Goodman, K. (1986). *What's whole in whole language?* Portsmouth, NH: Heinemann.

Goodman, K., Goodman, Y. & Hood, W. (1989). *The whole language evaluation book.* Portsmouth, NH: Heinemann.

Goodman, Y., Watson, D. & Burke, C. (1987). *Reading miscue inventory: Alternative procedures.* New York, NY: Owen.

Gutknecht, B. (1991, March). Transition in reading instruction: From a skills acquisition to a whole language model. *Journal of Instructional Psychology, 18*(1), 3–9.

Gutknecht, B., Johnson, G. & Chapman, D. (1987). *Planning effective reading instruction.* Dubuque, IA: Kendall/Hunt.

Harste, J., Woodward, V., & Burke, C. (1984). *Language stories and literacy lessons.* Portsmouth, NH: Heineman.

Heald-Taylor, G. (1989). *The administrator's guide to whole language.* Katonah, NY: Owen.

Johnston, P. (1992). *Constructive evaluation of literate activity.* New York, NY: Longman.

Johnston, P. (1987, April). Teachers as evaluation experts. *The Reading Teacher, 40*(8), 741–743.

Ridley, L. (1990, May). Enacting change in elementary school programs: Implementing a whole language perspective. *The Reading Teacher, 43*(9), 640–646.

Smith, F. (1993). *Essays into literacy.* Exeter, NH: Heineman.

Smith, F. (1985). *Reading without nonsense.* New York, NY: Teachers College Press.

Valencia, S. & Pearson, D. (1987, April). Reading assessment: Time for a change. *The Reading Teacher, 40*(8), 726.

Weaver, C. (1989). The basalization of America: A cause for concern. In *Two reactions to the "Report card on basal readers"* (pp. 4–7, 14–22, 31–37). Bloomington, IN: ERIC Clearinghouse on Reading and Communication Skills.

Bruce Gutknecht is a professor at the University of North Florida in Jacksonville.

A Portfolio Approach to Classroom Reading Assessment: The Whys, Whats, and Hows

Sheila Valencia

WHY DO WE NEED PORTFOLIOS?

Developing artists rely on portfolios to demonstrate their skills and achievements. Within the portfolio, they include samples of their work that exemplify the depth and breadth of their expertise. They may include many different indicators: work in a variety of media to demonstrate their versatility, several works on one particular subject to demonstrate their refined skill and sophistication, and work collected over time to exemplify their growth as artists. With such rich sources of information, it is easier for the critics and the teachers, and most importantly, artists themselves, to understand the development of expertise and to plan the experiences that will encourage additional progress and showcase achievements. A portfolio approach to the assessment of reading assumes the position that developing readers deserve no less.

A portfolio approach to reading assessment has great intuitive appeal: It resonates with our desire to capture and capitalize on the best each student has to offer; it encourages us to use many different ways to evaluate learning; and it has an integrity and validity that no other type of assessment offers. In addition to its intuitive appeal, there are theoretical and pragmatic reasons for a portfolio approach to reading assessment that are summarized in four guiding principles drawn from both research and instructional practices.

1. Sound assessment is anchored in authenticity—authenticity of tasks, texts, and contexts. Good assessment should grow out of authentic reading instruction and reading tasks. Students read a variety of authentic texts in class and in life; thus, they should be presented with that same diversity of texts during assessment. Students read for a variety of purposes; therefore, they should be presented with various purposes for reading during assessment. Reading assessment must mirror our understanding of reading as an interactive process. Any assessment must consider not only how the reader, the text, and the context influence reading but how they interact and impact the construction of meaning.

    Further, because the assessment activities resemble actual classroom and life reading tasks, they can be integrated into ongoing classroom life and instruction. Teachers and students do not have to take time away from real reading for assessment. Real reading is *used* as an assessment opportunity.

    Finally, the principle of authenticity insures that we assess the orchestration, integration, and application of skills in meaningful contexts. We cannot become lost in the mire of subskill assessment because assessment of such isolated skills would not resemble authentic reading.

2. Assessment must be a continuous, ongoing process; it must chronicle development. This is the difference between simply assessing the outcome of learning (the product) and assessing the process

of learning over time. When we are positioned to observe and collect information continuously, we send a message to students, parents, and administrators that learning is never completed; instead, it is always evolving, growing, and changing.
3. Because reading is a complex and multifaceted process, valid reading assessment must be multidimensional—committed to sampling a wide range of cognitive processes, affective responses, and literacy activities. In addition to assessing across a range of texts and purposes, we need to consider other important dimensions of reading such as interest and motivation, voluntary reading, and metacognitive knowledge and strategies. If we simply model our assessments on existing reading tests, we accept a constrained definition of reading and ignore many of the aspects that we value and teach.
4. Assessment must provide for active, collaborative reflection by both teacher and student. Historically, teachers and students have viewed assessment as something that must be done to appease others, something to be done for them rather than something to be done for ourselves. Instead, assessment must be viewed as a process within our control that helps us evaluate how well we have learned and what we need to learn next.

As teachers, assessment helps us evaluate our own teaching effectiveness and helps us with our instructional decisions. Similarly, assessment activities in which students are engaged in evaluating their own learning help them reflect on and understand their own strengths and needs, and it instills responsibility for their own learning. It is when students and teachers are collaboratively involved in assessment that the greatest benefit is achieved. Collaborative assessment strengthens the bond between student and teacher and establishes them as partners in learning. Collaboration precipitates meaningful dialogue about the criteria and process we use in evaluation and provides an important model for students as they become self-evaluators.

These four guiding principles provide a powerful rationale for proposing a portfolio approach. No single test, single observation, or single piece of student work could possibly capture the authentic, continuous, multidimensional, interactive requirement of sound assessment.

WHAT DO PORTFOLIOS LOOK LIKE?

Our rationale for portfolios helps us construct a picture of what such an approach to assessment might look like. Physically, it is larger and more elaborate than a report card. Practically, it must be smaller and more focused than a steamer trunk filled with accumulated artifacts. It is more like a large expandable file folder that holds (a) samples of the student's work selected by the teacher or the student, (b) the teacher's observational notes, (c) the student's own periodic self-evaluations, and (d) progress notes contributed by the student and teacher collaboratively. The range of items to include in a portfolio is almost limitless but may include written responses to reading, reading logs, selected daily work, pieces of writing at various stages of completion, classroom tests, checklists, unit projects, and audio or video tapes, to name a few. The key is to ensure a *variety* of types of indicators of learning so that teachers, parents, students, and administrators can build a complete picture of the student's development.

Logically, portfolios should be kept in a spot in the classroom that is easily accessible to students and teachers. Unlike the secretive grade book or the untouchable permanent records stored in the office, these are working folders. Their location must invite students and teachers to contribute to them on an ongoing basis and to reflect on their contents to plan the next learning steps.

HOW IS A PORTFOLIO ORGANIZED?

There is little doubt that portfolios can be messy business. However, many teachers and school districts committed to more valid and useful assessment procedures are beginning to give portfolios a try. Because the exact nature of the portfolio will vary depending on the curriculum goals and the students, it is difficult to prescribe exactly what should be included and how and when it should be evaluated. But it *is* possible to think of some organizational strategies that might make a portfolio more useful and more manageable.

Planning for a portfolio. First, it is important to be *selective* about what should be included in the portfolio. Since the decision about what to assess must grow out of curricular and instructional priorities, the critical step is to determine, as a school, grade level, district, or state, the key goals of instruction. Goals of instruction are broad, not overly specific-isolated skills or individual lesson objectives. For example, goals might involve understanding the author's message, learning new information from expository texts, summarizing the plot of a story, using word identification skills flexibly to construct meaning, reading fluently, or exhibiting an interest and desire to read. If the goals of instruction are not specified, portfolios have the potential to become unfocused holding files for odds and ends, or worse, a place to collect more isolated skills tests.

Second, it is helpful to think about what you do *instructionally* to help students progress toward those goals and how you and the students determine progress. This step will help you to identify some of the content and format of the assessment activities. One way to approach this task is to examine existing evaluation strategies and to decide the areas that are being assessed adequately and those that need to be added, adapted, or expanded. There is no need to start from scratch because many good instructional activities currently used in classrooms would be appropriate for portfolios. For example, many teachers use story maps as part of their instruction on understanding story structure. The very same technique could be used to assess students' plot knowledge after they have completed a story. No special test would be required; no special text or passage would be assigned; yet, we would assess an important goal of instruction.

What goes into a portfolio. After planning the focus of the portfolio, it is helpful to organize the contents in two layers: (a) the actual evidence, or raw data, that is included in the portfolio, and (b) a summary sheet or organizing framework to help synthesize that information. Including the first layer enables teachers to examine students' actual work and progress notes rather than relying simply on a number or grade. Including the summary sheet forces teachers to synthesize the information in a way that helps them make decisions and communicate with parents and administrators.

Managing the contents of a portfolio. In many ways, a portfolio approach to assessment mirrors what good teachers have been doing intuitively for years. The difference is that now we acknowledge the importance and value of alternative forms of assessment. However, if we are not careful, portfolio information will remain only in the classroom, failing to inform others who are involved with decision making. That is why we must deliberately plan to make portfolio assessments accessible to administrators and parents.

While the flexibility of the portfolio is one of its greatest assets, it may also be one of its greatest problems. One reason this type of classroom assessment has not been more popular is the concern about unreliability, inconsistency, and inequity across classrooms, schools, and districts. However there are several mechanisms to protect against this criticism. First, by engaging in discussions about the goals and priorities for instruction and assessment, we can build a common understanding of expectations and criteria. Second, by assessing in an ongoing way, we collect several indicators for any particular goal; generally, the more measures one has, the greater the reliability of the conclusions or decisions one makes.

A third way to attend to consistency is to include two levels of assessment evidence—required evidence and supporting evidence. The required evidence enables us to look systematically across students as well as within each student. This provides the kind of evidence that administrators desire and expect, thus enhancing the likelihood that they will use the portfolio in *their* decision making. These assessments might be particular activities, checklists, or projects (or a list from which to choose), which are tied to identified goals and included in the portfolios of all students at a grade level. They might be fairly structured (e.g., an emergent literacy checklist; a reading log) or more flexible (e.g., students select their best piece of writing to include every six weeks; an audio tape of a student reading a favorite passage recorded at the beginning and end of the school year).

Supporting evidence is additional documentation of learning to include in the portfolio. The evidence may be selected independently or collaboratively by the student and the teacher. It may be the result of a spontaneous activity (e.g., a letter to an author of a favorite book), or it may be carefully planned (e.g., a semantic map completed before and after reading an informational selection). Supporting evidence is critical to building a *complete* picture of a student's literacy abilities because it adds the depth and variety typically missing in traditional assessments. It provides the opportunity for teachers and students to take advantage of the uniqueness of each classroom and each student by encouraging the inclusion of a variety of indicators of learning.

Using the portfolio for classroom decision making.
A portfolio can be used at planning time for periodic review and reflection of its contents. The teacher and student might plan to collaboratively visit the portfolio every several weeks; in addition, the students might plan to visit it at other times individually or with a friend. During the collaborative visits, the teacher and student might discuss progress, add written notes, and plan for the inclusion of other pieces. At the end of the school year, they might collectively decide which pieces will remain in the portfolio for the next year and which are ready to go home. In addition, portfolios are a valuable source of information during conferences with parents and administrators. While parents might be interested in the raw data, the actual evidence of learning, principals or superintendents might be interested in the condensed information found on the summary sheet. In either case, the assessments would reflect more authentic, continuous information than ever before available.

The intrapersonal and interpersonal dialogue that results from visits to the portfolio is a critical component of both assessment and instruction. And as a way of encouraging and monitoring the use of the portfolio, everyone might be asked to initial and date each visit. This is a sure way to remind us that portfolio evaluation is intended to be used.

SUMMARY

In the coming months and years, there are sure to be many very different, perhaps conflicting, iterations of a portfolio approach to reading assessment. The real value of a portfolio does not lie in its physical appearance, location, or organization; rather, it is in the mindset that it instills in students and teachers. Portfolios represent a philosophy that demands that we view assessment as an integral part of our instruction, providing a process for teachers and students to use to guide learning. It is an expanded definition of assessment in which a wide variety of indicators of learning are gathered across many situations before, during, and after instruction. It is a philosophy that honors both the process and the products of learning as well as the active participation of the teacher and the students in their own evaluation and growth.

For additional information on portfolios see the following:

Au, K. H., Scheu, J. A., Kawakami, A. J., & Herman, P. A. (1990). Assessment and accountability in a whole literacy curriculum. *The Reading Teacher, 43*(8), 574–578.

Lucas, C. K. (1988). Toward ecological evaluation, part one and part two. *The Quarterly of the National Writing Project and the Center for the Study of Writing, 10*(1), 1–7; *10*(2), 4–10.

Valencia, S. W., McGinley, W., & Pearson, P. D. (1990). Assessing reading and writing: Building a more complete picture. In G. Duffy (Ed.), *Reading in the middle school.* (pp. 124–146) Newark, DE: International Reading Association.

Wolf, D. P. (1989). Portfolio assessment: Sampling student work. *Educational Leadership, 46*(7), 4–10.

Sheila Valencia is a faculty member at the University of Washington.

Literacy Portfolios: Helping Students Know Themselves

Jane Hansen

Scott is a 4th grade student at an inner-city school in Manchester, New Hampshire. He is telling Karen Harris, his resource room teacher, why he chose the items he included in his Literacy Portfolio:

- A drawing. "This shows that I can draw pictures, because before I couldn't draw. I'll always remember this. At home my mother used to give me paper and pencil, and I broke the pencils and crossed my arms. Now I write."
- A draft of a piece of writing he had published as a book in the resource room the previous year. "This is the first book I wrote. I can write books."
- A piece of writing from the current year. "Before I couldn't write that good, and now I can. Now I can write better and read better."
- A list of books he can read. "This says that I'm a reader, that I can read these books."
- A book, *The Little Engine That Could.* "This is one of my favorite books. My mom used to read it to me."
- His report card from 3rd grade. "This was the best report card I ever had." The school gives grades of S (satisfactory), W (working on), and N (needs improvement). Previously, Scott had gotten mostly Ns, but last year he got mostly Ws.
- A photo of his father. "I miss my father. He's part of my life. He has to stay in jail for about 12 years."
- A photo of his grandparents. "I love my grandparents. They bring me up to see my father."

Scott is a member of a group of students and adults involved in a Literacy Portfolios Project in Manchester (Hansen 1991). The adults are students and teachers from the University of New Hampshire, teachers from five elementary and secondary public schools in the inner city, and two administrators. The students

From "Literacy Portfolios: Helping Students Know Themselves" by J. Hansen, 1992, *Educational Leadership, 49,* pp. 66–68. Copyright © 1992 by ASCD. All rights reserved. Reprinted by permission of the Association for Supervision and Curriculum Development.

are from a 1st grade classroom, an elementary school resource room, a self-contained 6th grade, and junior and senior high English classes. As many as 79 percent of the elementary school children receive free lunch, and the dropout rate in the high school is one-third.

Every adult and student in the project has created a Literacy Portfolio. Whether or not we know ourselves better than anyone else does, our portfolios give us the opportunity to get to know ourselves better. Our literacy is who we are (Neilsen 1989). Many of the students in these inner-city schools think, "I'm nobody." Later, with a self-created Literacy Portfolio in hand, they say, "This is me. I exist."

A NONSCHOOL IDENTITY

We get to know Scott when we see the items in his Literacy Portfolio and hear his reasons for selecting them. We may be surprised to see family photos in Scott's portfolio, but we've learned the significance of "real" life to our academic selves.

At one of our first research team meetings, Andrea Luna, a university student and research assistant, wrote about Kevin, a high school student who spent most of a period staring at his desk, hunched over his paper, not writing. When she asked to see his work, he dragged his book bag overflowing with books onto the desk. When Andrea commented that he had a lot of stuff in there, Kevin told her that he had only two books in it; the other books didn't count because they were Dungeons and Dragons books. He used those D&D materials outside of school. Andrea wrote about this young man for our meeting and ended her paper this way: "Kevin seemed to recognize borders that separate what is important to him from what happens in school."

From this, we learned that a student's portfolio must contain items from beyond school if it's to be called a Literacy Portfolio. Students' most significant involvement with literacy may be outside of school (Heath 1983, Hill 1989).

Similarly, resource teacher Karen Harris interviewed a 6th grade girl referred to her resource room (Harris 1991). A statement in the girl's records labeled her "illiterate." In her interview with the girl, Karen learned that the girl "reads a great deal at home and has a high interest in reading rock magazines. In fact, she and her friend write their own fantasy interviews with each other." Again, her Literacy Portfolio would be inaccurate if it did not include items from beyond school.

WHAT STUDENTS VALUE

When students select items for their portfolios, they weigh each item's significance. They determine the relevance of an item in terms of these questions: "Who am I?" "Who am I as a reader–writer?" "How does this item show my growth?" The focus of the Literacy Portfolios is on self-evaluation (Rief 1990, Asher 1991).

First grade teacher Brenda Ross thought long and hard about how her students could start to gain a sense of their literacy. Her principal and the university researcher in her classroom shared their portfolios with the children. Then Brenda asked her students to find something to use as a portfolio. Some of them folded large sheets of paper in half and stapled them along the edges to create large pockets. Others brought folders, binders, and shoe boxes from home. Shawn used a Raisin Bran cereal box. In it he included a book, *The Hungry Thing Returns*. "I'm putting in this book because I have trouble talking, like him," Shawn explained. The boy in the book has a speech problem and so does Shawn. Karla, another 1st grader, used a book cover as her portfolio. One of her items was a comic of the bird Shoe saying, "Who? What? Where? When?" Karla explained, "All the time when I read a book I wish there was a part two. Like when you read a book and you want more information you ask, "Who? What? Where? When?"

These students' portfolio selections and their reasons for their choices show their awareness of their literacy and their unique viewpoint (Hindley 1990, Graves and Sunstein, 1992). At the end of the first year of the Literacy Portfolios project, Brenda said, "The children taught me what was important to them. I assumed I'd be able to predict what they'd choose to put in, but I would have chosen incorrectly. They showed me they truly could self-evaluate."

TOWARD MORE COMPREHENSIVE EVALUATIONS

Because of the students' portfolio choices, the system we use to evaluate students can become not only more accurate, but more comprehensive. The student becomes more than a number or a letter grade.

Eric, a 6th grader, has many items in his portfolio, including a ribbon from an athletic event, several drawings, a book of poems by Edgar Allan Poe that his father gave him, several poems he has written, and two treasured comic books. Eric is a poet, an artist, an athlete, and an avid reader of comic books. He also has good grades and high standardized test scores; but do those numbers and letters give an adequate picture of who Eric is? Maybe the students are right when they say that we don't care who they are, but we can change that. A list of the items in a student's portfolio—information that comes from the students themselves—may belong in the school records as well as test scores and grades.

SHARING PORTFOLIOS

At the end of the marking periods, Karen Boettcher's 6th graders shared their portfolios with her and with other students. Then they took them home. The class talked about how they must arrange a time with someone at home to sit down and explain each item. In the back of each student's portfolio was a sheet labeled Portfolio Comments. Whenever a student shared a portfolio with someone in school, that person wrote a comment. At home, someone was asked to do the same.

Each of the portfolios came back with a comment. Something about these Literacy Portfolios was important, and the students had conveyed the significance to their families. Someone in each household had found time to listen.

Because the students consider the portfolio items valuable, sharing them can make a difference. David was relatively new to his school and Jody Coughlin's junior high English class, and he had only two items in his portfolio. The first was a piece of writing about a rock concert that he'd put in his portfolio because, "My older brother took me and that made my mom feel good." The other students interested in the concert asked David about it, and he told them about the event. Their interest impressed him, as we shall see.

His second item was a response to a book. "In this book the boy steals a jeep and has to go to one of those places like a camp. While he's there he decides to straighten out. I decided if the kid in the book can, then I can. I've changed." David's comment piqued the students' curiosity. He had come to this school because he'd been kicked out of his previous school, and, with successive questions, he told his story.

Then someone asked what he might put in next. He didn't know, but he might put in something about his uncle, who's paralyzed from the neck down because of a diving accident. The students had questions again.

During the following week, the university researcher in his classroom, Dan-Ling Fu, interviewed David. He'd added a picture of his uncle and intended to write about him. He'd also added a Valentine from his mother, with whom he wishes he could live. Dan-Ling asked, "What have you learned about yourself through putting your portfolio together?" David responded, "I thought nobody liked me, and nobody wanted to be with me. But after I put my portfolio together, I found people do like me and want me to be around them. They want me to do good. . . ."

CREATING GOALS

David has set a specific goal for his Literacy Portfolio. He plans to write about his uncle. The goals the students set for their portfolios show they can shed their passive school posture. They no longer sit and wait for the teacher to give the next assignment and then grudgingly do it—or not. They make their own plans. The teacher's task is to help the students become better writers at their self-assigned tasks (Hansen 1987).

This fall, as the second year of the project began, Karen Harris, the resource room teacher, shared her portfolio with her students on the first day of school. The last item in it was her list of goals for herself. She then asked her students to write their own goals. Each listed what he or she wanted to learn in reading and writing. Some wanted to read specific books, some wanted to learn to use quotation marks in their writing, and some set broader goals, such as, "I want to read harder books." These goal statements became the first item in their portfolios, and as they accomplish their goals, they put in artifacts to show their growth. Sometimes the items they add are from home. As the year unfolds, they make new goals or revise old ones.

Literacy Portfolios enable students to plan a relevant curriculum for themselves. As we learn what each student values, we look for ways to honor the student's concerns and interests within the school (Krogness 1991). Maybe students will stay in a school in which they find authentic work.

According to the high school students, their portfolios have started to influence their writing and reading. One student wrote, "By making a portfolio, I found, even though my teachers often tell me this, that I am too much of a one-dimensional reader and that I should broaden my horizons to more than sports. I may have trouble doing so, but I am willing to try."

REFERENCES

Asher, C. (Spring 1991). "Writing on Your Own: It's Lighter on You." *The Quarterly of the National Writing Project and the Center for the Study of Writing and Literacy* 13, 2: 3–9.

Graves, D., and B. Sunstein, eds. (1992). *Portfolio Portraits*. Portsmouth, NH: Heinemann.

Hansen, J. (1987). *When Writers Read*. Portsmouth, NH: Heinemann.

Hansen, J. (Winter 1991). Evaluation: "My Portfolio Shows Who I Am." *The Quarterly of the National Writing Project and the Center for the Study of Writing and Literacy* 14, 1: 5–9.

Harris, K. (1991). In *Teachers as Readers, Writers, and Researchers: Creating Supportive Classroom Environments for Students with Learning Difficulties*, edited by W. Wansart. Durham, NH: The Writing Lab, University of New Hampshire.

Heath, S. B. (1983). *Ways with Words: Language, Life, and Work in Communities and Classrooms*. Cambridge: Cambridge University Press.

Hill, M. W. (1989). *Home: Where Reading and Writing Begin*. Portsmouth, NH: Heinemann.

Hindley, J. M. (1990). "Books in the Classroom." *The Horn Book* 66, 5: 579–586.

Krogness, M. M. (1991). "A Question of Values." *English Journal* 80, 6: 28–33.

Neilsen, L. (1989). *Literacy and Living: The Literate Lives of Three Adults*. Portsmouth, NH: Heinemann.

Rief, L. (1990). "Finding the Value in Evaluation: Self-Assessment in a Middle School Classroom." *Educational Leadership* 47, 6: 24–29.

Jane Hansen is an associate professor at the University of New Hampshire in Durham.

A MAP for Reading Assessment

Teri Bembridge

Eight-year-old Jenny sits on a cushion in the library corner of her grade 2 and 3 classroom flipping pages of a colorful book. Around the room at desks and tables, her classmates are busy with books, papers, and pencils. Posters, poems, and child-published materials cover the classroom walls. Into this activity-oriented class walks the resource teacher. The classroom teacher has requested an assessment because Jenny hasn't been reading the same types of books as her classmates or engaging in book discussions, although she participates enthusiastically in other oral activities.

A few years ago, the resource teacher would have whisked Jenny off to a little office. There Jenny would have been tested using some form of a "read-this-paragraph, fill-in-these-blanks, what-does-this-word-say" test created by experts, published by a large corporation, and packaged in bright shiny boxes containing reproducible pages. The classroom teacher and Jenny's parents would have then received a report listing the number of sight words Jenny read; the grade equivalent level in years and months at which Jenny was performing; and perhaps a listing of phonetic blends she had not yet mastered.

SEARCHING FOR A BETTER INSTRUMENT

Resource teachers in the St. Vital School Division in Winnipeg, Canada, began to question the purpose, validity, and reliability of an assessment practice that was so different from classroom practice. Our students learn in activity-based, literature-oriented, and child-centered classrooms. Our provincial Language Arts Curriculum promotes integration of subject matter in activity-based settings, and many thematic units have been developed and shared locally. Our graded, multi-age classrooms boast large libraries of carefully selected quality literature. Many of our teachers have spent countless hours voluntarily learning about language and how to help students learn language. Many have studied with specialists like Ken Goodman, Dorothy Watson, Carolyn Burke, and Frank Smith, to name but a few.

As our knowledge about children's language learning grew, so did our frustration. We could hardly be called in to assist in assessment when the methods we were using were so out of touch with the learning environment of the students. As resource teachers, we had kept up to date with assessment information. We were using Informal Reading Inventories and, in fact, had developed a local inventory.

We decided to purchase an assessment tool in keeping with our instructional methodologies. Through our monthly meetings and with leadership from our consultant and assistant superintendent, we formed a committee to search for a published test that could be administered to individual students in their classrooms. Our ideal test would:

- contain materials similar to those found in classrooms, that is, real books, not reproduced paragraphs written with a controlled vocabulary;
- be observational and interactive but still provide data in the form of scores for comparison and reporting purposes;
- have easy-to-follow procedures that allow for observation of the child's reading behavior by either resource or classroom teachers;

From "A MAP for Reading Assessment" by T. Bembridge, 1992, *Educational Leadership, 49*, 46–48. Copyright © 1992 by ASCD. All rights reserved. Reprinted with permission of the Association for Supervision and Curriculum Development.

- be diagnostic in order to give us a picture of the child's reading strengths and weaknesses, or suggest when a more in-depth assessment, such as a Miscue Analysis (Goodman et al. 1987), is needed.

Our committee met monthly and shared readings, experiences, and information about assessment of children's reading. Finally, we realized that a commercial instrument that would meet our criteria and be adaptable to rapidly changing times did not exist. By this time, we'd come to believe enough in our professional knowledge and judgments to create our own assessment package.

DEVELOPING OUR OWN ASSESSMENT TOOL

Assembled over a five-year period, the Multi-Layered Assessment Package (MAP) is a set of procedures accompanied by suggested books, transcripts, and retelling and recording forms. The books, which are examples of narrative literature typically found in particular grades, are a great convenience, but teachers can implement the procedures using any other book they choose. In this sense, the MAP is a generic, flexible assessment tool.

The title's mention of "layers" acknowledges the complexity of child development, which cannot be measured with pinpoint accuracy. Countless variables about children and their reading must be considered before an evaluation statement and a plan of action can be formulated. One set of layers are the four strands of literacy: reading, speaking, writing, and listening. Currently, the MAP assesses only reading (oral and silent) and listening.

Another set of layers identified by Goodman, Burke, and Watson (1987) are the four cuing systems used when reading: graphophonics, semantics, syntax, and pragmatics. Meaning cannot be separated from grammar like cream from milk. The cuing systems have differing properties but are part of the text and must be assessed in such a manner.

Other layers may include physical and emotional health, interest in stories, motivation to read, and other variables perceived by teachers as relevant.

USING OUR ASSESSMENT PACKAGE

Using the MAP to assess Jenny's oral reading, the resource teacher today joins her on the cushions, shows her two or three books, and asks her to select one to read aloud. During the reading, the teacher listens to and watches Jenny, noting her reading behaviors on a double-spaced typed transcript copy of the book. After reading, Jenny tells her teacher about the story she just read. Her responses, which may be prompted by the teacher, are written on a retelling form. (To avoid writing while listening, the teacher can tape-record Jenny's reading and retelling.) Before leaving, the teacher shares with Jenny some of his or her observations. For example, Jenny used her finger to follow the print, corrected several of her mistakes, or figured out a troublesome word. Or they might discuss Jenny's interests or perhaps read another book.

Later, the resource teacher analyzes Jenny's reading behaviors and calculates three scores:

1. The *word accuracy* score is a percentage reflecting the number of words the student read correctly. It is important that the words were read in the context of a story and not from a list of words that 3rd graders are supposed to know.
2. The *sentence comprehending* score is a percentage of the number of sentences read by the student that are meaningful within the context of the story. Here the student's changes to the text are analyzed and, if they make sense within the story, are allowed. This score was adapted from Goodman, Watson, and Burke (1987), who

examined the roles of the four cuing systems and self-correction in reading. Determining this score requires professional judgment, yet in training teachers to use the MAP, we've found they've been remarkably consistent in discerning acceptable sentences.
3. The *retelling* score is a percentage of the number of story elements the student can talk about, perhaps with some prompting, after reading. This score reflects comprehension in a much broader manner than does asking a set of predetermined questions. Morrow (1985) originally conceived the retelling form to quantify a child's open-ended responses to a story. The MAP provides a retelling form tailored for each of the suggested books, as well as blank forms for use with other books.

These three scores satisfy our need for accountability and, when accompanied by professional observations, provide us a useful profile of a student from which to develop action plans to enhance the student's reading practices.

The classroom teacher and Jenny's parents then meet with the resource teacher to learn about the nature of Jenny's reading with books typically found in a 2nd–3rd grade classroom. It must be noted that the books are not labeled on the basis of any type of readability formula (Zakaluk and Samuels 1989). They are grouped into levels according to the kinds usually read by students in certain grades in the St. Vital School Division. We selected the books through a lengthy process that included sorting, categorizing, and field-testing. They represent local norms by which we can compare students within our area only.

Next, an action plan is developed to assist Jenny based on strategies consistent with her reading patterns. Many strategies have been collected and shared among our resource teachers for distribution to classroom teachers and parents.

This type of assessment is quite different from, and we believe more useful than, saying that Jenny is reading at a grade equivalent of 1.8.

EVERYONE LEARNING TOGETHER

We agree with Chittenden (1991) that assessment must be interactive, open-ended, cumulative, and based on theory that matches the instructional practices in local classrooms. The Multi-Layered Assessment Package is an attempt by resource teachers to create an authentic tool for elementary reading assessment. Using the MAP, everyone is a learner: adults learn about a child's interaction with print, and the child learns about his or her own reading and thinking.

Even though we now have a set of procedures and materials, the assessment process is not at an end. Our committee continues, with new and returning members, to train teachers to use the package and to revise it as needed. Our present project is assessment of student writing, and a future goal is the development of reading assessment tools using expository texts.

By developing the MAP, we have shown that teachers can be agents of change. Perhaps other local groups of teachers or even commercial firms will continue such efforts so that assessment will be an integral, meaningful part of teaching.

REFERENCES

Chittenden, E. (1991). "Authentic Assessment, Evaluation, and Documentation." In *Expanding Student Assessment,* edited by V. Perrone, pp. 22–31. Alexandria, Va.: Association for Supervision and Curriculum Development.

Goodman, K., Y. Goodman, and W. J. Hood. eds. (1989). *The Whole Language Evaluation Book.* Toronto: Irwin Publishing Co.

Goodman, Y., C. Burke, and D. Watson. (1987). *Reading Miscue Inventory Alternative Procedures.* New York: Richard Owen Publishers Inc.

Morrow, C. (1985). "Retelling Stories as a Diagnostic Tool." In *Re-examining Reading Diagnosis,* edited by S. Glazer, L. Searfoss, and L. Gentile. Newark, Del.: International Reading Association.

Zakaluk, B., and S. Samuels, eds. (1989). *Readability: Its Past, Present, and Future.* Newark, Del.: International Reading Association.

Teri Bembridge is Chair, MAP Committee 1991–1992, and a resource teacher at the Darwin School, 175 Darwin Street, Winnipeg, Manitoba, Canada.

Grading and Evaluation Techniques for Whole Language Teachers

Wayne M. Linek

Teaching from a whole language perspective means teaching children to use the tools of communication (reading, writing, speaking, and listening) in a purposeful, meaningful, and integrated manner. It means valuing what children already know and immersing them in all aspects of communication—they learn by doing. But how do you survive as a whole language teacher when you are held accountable for skills measured by standardized tests? How do you determine grades that are required on report cards?

You may want to implement whole language learning but hesitate because it doesn't fit district grading requirements. You may use whole language strategies but still base your grades on a few assignments that can be graded objectively. Or you may use whole language approaches but feel uncomfortable with all the subjective judgments you have to make about grades.

You are not alone. Many teachers and administrators see grading and accountability as stumbling blocks to making whole language work. Inconsistencies between current knowledge of reading/writing processes and existing school, district, or state policies cause these stumbling blocks. Until the inconsistencies are resolved, compromises on assessment, grading, and evaluation have to be worked out.

As you know, whole language does not focus on teaching skills in isolation with workbooks, worksheets, and mechanics drills. Whole language teaches students to think critically, value themselves as readers and writers, value others as readers and writers, and value their literacy products. Kids listen, speak, write, and read to learn about reading; they read, listen, speak, and write to learn about writing. Their desire to communicate, coupled with a model that is caring, goal-oriented, and professional, helps them move toward expected standards (Goodman, K., 1986). So how do you evaluate and what do you grade when you focus on student interaction and cooperative learning to develop communication skills?

Let me give you my view, that of an elementary principal who sees the integration of reading and language arts finally possible through whole language. I've found two major issues that cause problems and questions. Those two issues are: philosophy/policy and record keeping.

From "Grading and Evaluation Techniques for Whole Language Teachers" by W. M. Linek, 1991, *Language Arts, 68,* pp. 125–132. Copyright © 1991 by the National Council of Teachers of English. Reprinted with permission.

PHILOSOPHY/POLICY

First, consider each of the following questions about your district's philosophy and policy; then consider each suggestion and choose the processes that work for you:

> *Question 1:* Are individual needs and growth in learning stressed in policy and philosophy?
> *Suggestion 1:* Compare the individual to himself/herself.
> *Question 2:* Is norm-referenced achievement the basis of education philosophy and policy?
> *Suggestion 2:* Compare the individual to a group or class.
> *Question 3:* Are criterion-referenced achievement objectives set in philosophy and policy?
> *Suggestion 3:* Compare students to established criteria.
> *Question 4:* Are individual needs and growth stressed in philosophy while standardized testing, inflexible grading guidelines, evaluative comparisons, and skills-based criteria are stressed in policy?
> *Suggestion 4:* Try using a combination of all the processes suggested below while actively working to bring the inconsistencies to light.

Individual Comparison Process

With individual comparison children work for self-improvement by building on their strengths. No comparison is made to any standard or any other student. Present performance is compared to previous performance. For example, when writing folders are kept for process writing, pieces of writing can be reviewed with the student to note progress and growth patterns. By using a curriculum guide or teacher-developed list of general writing goals, individual goals and objectives can be mutually determined at the beginning of each grading period. Contracts can then be established with specific quality and quantity requirements for specific grades.

Once individual goals and objectives are set, teaching and learning can focus on the process during class time. At the end of each grading period, you can conference with students on how much was accomplished, using their writing folders as evidence. Grades can then be mutually determined according to how well the quantity and quality requirements were met (E. Pryor, personal communication, October 10, 1989).

Group Comparison Process

With group comparison a student's work is compared to the work of other students in the class or group. Students must be aware of the criteria for grading prior to doing the work. Students should also select which completed piece they would like to submit for grading.

For example, at the beginning of a week you might tell students that the class will be working on writing descriptions. Mini-lessons for the whole class that week focus on description using similes and metaphors. Students are directed to include similes and metaphors in their writing. At the end of the week each student selects one piece of writing completed during that week to polish and have graded for description. After reading through all the papers once, you begin to compare and separate the papers into five piles corresponding to letter grades (E. Pryor, personal communication, October 10, 1989).

The failing stack may be reserved for those students who hand in nothing or show no evidence of using the descriptive techniques discussed. Few students will end up failing if you conduct individual conferences throughout the week. Those who compare poorly to their classmates may be identified for small group mini-lessons. These students can be given the options of trying again or showing evidence of improvement in this area on their next graded paper.

Criteria Comparison Process

Often clear-cut criteria are spelled out for mastery in courses of study. Criteria grading and evaluation can be accomplished using five-point scales that compare student work to these criteria. Once again, students must be aware of the criteria for grading prior to doing the work, and they should be permitted to select which completed piece they would like to submit for grading.

For example, if the course of study states, "Students will correctly use apostrophes to show missing letters in contractions with at least seventy-five percent accuracy," you could use a scale as follows:

5 Consistently writes contractions where possible without spelling or apostrophe placement errors.
4 Consistently writes contractions where possible with some apostrophe placement errors or inconsistently writes contractions where possible without apostrophe placement errors.
3 Inconsistently writes contractions where possible with some apostrophe placement errors.
2 Consistently or inconsistently writes contractions where possible with many apostrophe placement errors.
1 Does not write contractions or use apostrophes appropriately.

At the beginning of the week you can tell students that the focus will be on using contractions in their writing. Mini-lessons incorporated into the process-writing class during the week focus on identifying words that could be made into contractions and using the apostrophe when deleting letters. Students are directed to include contractions in their writing for the week. At the end of the week each student selects one piece of writing completed during that week to polish and have graded for using contractions. You then assign a score of 5, 4, 3, 2, or 1 to each paper. Traditional checklists and tally lists work equally well (more later).

RECORD KEEPING

Data to Be Kept

Data collection includes documentation of student attitudes, behaviors, achievements, improvements, thinking, and reflective self-evaluation. Attitudes are noted to show that whole language gets kids to read and write because they want to, not because they have to. Student behaviors are recorded to show increasing sophistication as a communicator. Achievements are noted to develop a sense of self-worth and personal pride in students. Improvements are noted to give students, parents, administrators, and you a sense of progress and accomplishment. Thinking processes are documented to give you an idea of mental growth and to make students metacognitively aware. Finally, student self-evaluation is incorporated to encourage a feeling of ownership and to develop children's metacognitive awareness, thereby fostering a self-improving system. It helps student to think objectively, think critically, know their strengths and weaknesses, value the process, value their products, and value themselves.

Documentation validates your approach. It provides proof to administrators, parents, students, and skeptics that you are a knowledgeable professional. It proves that students are learning.

Recording

Collection is ongoing. Data may be documented and evaluated through questionnaires, surveys, anecdotal records, observational journals, miscue analysis, conferences, interviews, student journals, checklists, tally lists, files, portfolios, albums, audio tapes, and video tapes.

Questionnaires and Surveys. Questionnaires that ask "how to" questions about reading and writing may be used to document metacognition and use of strategies. For example, Atwell's writing survey asks "How do people learn to write?" and "What do you think a good writer needs to do in order to write well?" (Atwell, 1987, pp. 270–271). Padak and Pryor's reading questionnaire asks "What do you do if you don't understand what you read? What do you do to try to figure it out? What do you do if that doesn't work?" (Padak & Pryor, 1988).

Reading and writing surveys that ask affective questions may be used to record attitudes. McKenna and Kear's Elementary Reading Attitude Survey (1990), for example, is an easily administered quantitative instrument that gives norms for attitude toward recreational reading, academic reading, and total reading. Heathington's Primary and Intermediate Scales (Alexander & Filler, 1976) are two more resources that can be easily administered to entire classes for diagnosis of six areas of reading attitude. Questionnaires and surveys complement qualitative data and may be used at the beginning, middle, and end of the year to document progress and changes.

Miscue Analysis. A miscue analysis of any reading passage or a miscue analysis of a student's own language experience stories (Jacobsen, 1989) may be used to document reading behaviors, achievements, and improvements. Students can tape themselves while reading, or you can tape them during an oral reading time. Analyses may be done at the beginning, middle, and end of the year to document progress and changes.

Taping also allows students to use a retrospective miscue analysis or RMA (Marek, 1989). This strategy involves readers in instructive self-evaluation of their own reading. Marek (1989) states:

In a typical RMA session a reader is asked to read a self-selected text, unaided by the teacher, into a tape recorder. . . . Following a retelling of and discussion about the text, miscues from the tape recording . . . are analyzed by the reader. . . . The following questions are asked by the teacher during the RMA session in order to guide the reader in evaluating the quality of the miscues. . . . :

1. Does the miscue make sense?
2. Was the miscue corrected? Should it have been? . . .
3. Does the miscue look like what was on the page?
4. Does the miscue sound like what was on the page? . . .
5. Why do you think you made this miscue?
6. Did that miscue affect your understanding of the text? (pp. 159–160)

When students take a reflective position encouraged by the RMA as they listen to themselves read, they focus on meaning instead of pronunciation. This changed focus helps students to revalue their own strengths while creating a more aware and objective viewpoint for self-evaluation (Bird, 1989).

Files, Portfolios, and Albums. An album (Pearson, 1988), portfolio (Wolf, 1989), or file (Atwell, 1987) combines many kinds of data for thorough documentation. A file includes rough drafts and finished products to document achievements and improvements. The album or portfolio may also include written comments on the student's processes and products by teachers, principals, adult helpers, parents, peers, or the students themselves. Examples of comments might include: impressions about the student's attitude (willingness to read and enthusiasm for books), responses to books (listening attentively to certain stories and identifying with characters or events), notations about reading behavior and strategies employed (cues relied upon and style displayed while reading or writing), and comments about oral contributions that help to build a profile of the child's language development (Pearson, 1988). Parents can make entries on student papers or on peel-and-stick labels when papers are sent home—on a weekly basis, during conferences, or when something worth noting is observed.

Inclusion of video or audio tapes allows students, parents, and teachers to compare reading and writing together. Tapes document reading miscues, fluency development, reading rate, use of strategies, and use of time so that development of processes and products can be reviewed during conferences. A file, portfolio, or album provides the stimulus necessary for cooperative reflection and evaluation.

Observations, Conferences, Dialogue Journals, and Interviews. Teacher observations document reading and writing attitudes, behaviors, achievements, and improvements. Conferences or interviews with parents and students document attitudes and thinking. Student dialogue journals document thinking and self-evaluation (Galindo, 1989). The three easiest ways to keep track of this information are anecdotal records, checklists, and tally lists.

Anecdotal records are observations written down. They may be expanded to include conference notes, interview notes, goals, objectives, and parental perceptions. Anecdotal records may also include notes on student thinking and metacognition from dialogue journals.

Checklists may be used to record book handling, skills, and interactions. Checklists can be simple adaptations of curriculum guides, objectives, or developmental skills lists combined with student rosters (N. D. Padak, personal communication, October 26, 1989). The simplest method of keeping track is to:

1. Leave a box on the checklist blank if there is not evidence of the skill,
2. Place a diagonal line in the box once the skill starts to develop, and
3. Complete the "X" when the student consistently uses the skill.

Gradebooks or loose sheets on clipboards are easily used.

Checklists may also be used to record where students are at the moment in reading (Huck & Kerstetter, 1987). A checklist for this purpose might focus on:

1. Concepts of print (concept of letter, concept of word, function of space, directionality, uses of punctuation, etc. [e.g., Clay, 1979])
2. Letter/sound identification in context
3. Types of oral reading miscues (substitution, omission, insertion, etc.)
4. Cues used to make self-corrections (visual, meaning, or structural)
5. Books children read in school
6. Books children share in school

Tally lists are a quick and easy way to record the frequency of projects begun, projects completed, types of peer interactions, questions asked, and strategies employed. At the end of a day, week, or grading period, tally marks may be totaled for individual, group, or criteria evaluation (Dalrymple, 1989). For example, as depicted in Figure 1 on page 314, you could tally first graders' use of the five types of "language structures" (Rynkofs, 1988) one time per week. During the first grading period make tally marks in black. During the second grading period make tally marks in blue. During the third grading period make tally marks in red. You can then use these colored marks for individual or criteria comparison.

Caution. Do not plan to do all of these recording techniques at the same time or continuously. You'll soon become disillusioned with whole language and the amount of record keeping. One purpose of whole language is to free you for interaction with students. Pick and choose recording techniques according to your needs (Graves, 1983). You may, for example, use tally lists to document student interaction only three times during the year. The professional choice is yours.

Language Structure	One- or Two-Word Labeling	Pre-sentence	Simple Sentence	More Complex Sentence	Pre-Paragraph
John	IIII + +	II + + + + **	****		
Marco	II +	IIII + + + + *	+ *****		
Aisha			IIIII + +	I + + + *****	*
Melissa	IIIII + + + + +	+ ***			

First Grading Period: I
Second Grading Period: +
Third Grading Period: *

FIGURE 1
"LANGUAGE STRUCTURES" TALLY LIST FOR FIRST GRADE

In our school we found that questionnaires and surveys are most helpful at the beginning of the year to gain insight into the attitudes and strategic awareness of individuals and the class as a whole. This gives initial direction to planning and focus to observations. We also try to get a miscue analysis of each student early in the year by recording on pages copied from classroom texts that students read aloud. The above information, coupled with standardized testing information, gives a quick and easy basis on which you can form cooperative learning groups. It also gives the ability to see who would benefit most from RMA activities.

Observations, anecdotal records, checklists, tally lists, and taping are used the entire year but are used selectively and intermittently as the learning focus and student needs change. Dialogue journals are kept by students the entire year. Sometimes teachers respond and sometimes peers respond, depending on the purpose and content. As long as students know who will be responding to their journal entry before writing it, few take exception; and you don't get bogged down with too many journals. When peers respond, we give students the option of pointing out significant or special entries.

We have also found that sending work home on a weekly basis for parent comments really keeps lines of communication open while boosting student cooperation in the classroom. After commenting, parents return the work, and teachers file it in the portfolio. Getting copies of a few crucial pieces (initial writing samples) before sending them home is a good idea until parents and students get used to the routine.

A second round of questionnaires, surveys, and miscue analyses midyear, coupled with the other information gathered, gives you a real sense of whether you're accomplishing what you set out to do or whether you need to change direction. Repeating this process at the end of the year provides concrete evidence of individual and class growth, development, and learning. The portfolio and other records also provide the ideal basis for conferencing and grading.

We have found that implementing these procedures over a period of years works best. Portfolios, surveys, and simple checklists come first, followed by tally lists, journals, and anecdotal records. Once again, do what works best for you, but don't overdo it when you are just getting started.

Evaluating

Consider giving the processes of reading and writing as much weight as the products during evaluation. Analyzing records on speaking, questioning, peer interaction, and improvement will balance the process/product scale (Goodman, Y., 1989).

When evaluating products, inform students of your criteria for grading and allow *them* to choose which pieces will be graded. An example of evaluation criteria for third-grade writing might be:

1. *Fluency:* How much was written? Was it easy or a struggle?
2. *Semantics:* Does it make sense?
3. *Message quality:* Is there a sense of audience? Is there a beginning, middle, and end? (Howe-Tompkins, 1989).
4. *Specific objectives:* What skills are used? What individual objectives have been met?

From December on you might also have students rework pieces of writing from early in the school year. It is important to choose pieces on student-selected topics produced with limited teacher intervention so that individual strengths as writers can be revealed. When you give pieces of writing back to the same students later in the year and allow them to revise and expand, you get a clear and measurable picture of growth (Hull, 1989). You can compare and contrast the present product to previous ones when evaluating progress on individual or class goals and objectives.

Evaluation may be shared by all people who play a part in the child's language, reading, and writing development (Wortman & Haussler, 1989). Allowing students to reflect on their work creates an awareness of how they have improved, as well as where they need further improvement. For example, students could listen to tapes of their own oral reading from different times in the year or compare their early pieces of writing to later pieces of writing.

Parental perceptions on improvement may help document changes that you don't notice in the context of school or just one school year. For example, a student may only have been able to read picture books at the end of second grade but through practice during the summer is able to read chapter books at the beginning of third grade. Other students may never have picked up a book for pleasure reading at home or asked their parents to take them to the library. When these significant events occur for the first time, you may miss them without parental collaboration.

A running list of objectives (mutually decided upon by the teacher, parents, and the student) may be kept as a yardstick for measurement. Credit may be given for: improved fluency, speed, pacing, risk-taking, personal involvement, recognizing good writing and what authors do, making use of prior knowledge, predicting, critiquing, revising, editing, establishing criteria for selecting and abandoning, and so on.

Grading

Holistic scores of 5, 4, 3, 2, or 1 may be assigned on a weekly basis for reading and writing: 5 reflects a high level of performance, and 1 reflects unacceptable performance. "The holistic scores are based on the degree to which the children have completed the task they set out to do, their effectiveness in expressing themselves, and any growth or development that the writing [or reading] demonstrates" (Woodley & Woodley, 1989, p. 73). These scores are similar to traditional grades (A, B, C, D, F), the 4.00 system, and can easily be converted to percentages. Holistic scores have fewer negative associations and eliminate the problems caused by zeros or very low scores when working with percentages.

Holistic grading can be converted to percentages to satisfy your district's policy requirements (Woodley & Woodley, 1989). If 90 to 100 is an A, a holistic score of 5 is given a value of 95 percent. A holistic score of 4 is assigned a value of 85 percent, and so on. The student motivation and attitude problems caused by low percentage grades (0% + 85% + 85% = 57% average; grade = F) is lessened because a holistic score of 1 may be given a value of 55 percent (1 [55%] + 4 [85%] + 4 [85%] = 75% average; grade = C). Using this system, a student who does poorly on one assignment does not lose hope of ever being able to bring up a grade. A holistic score of 0 (0%) may be reserved for students who refuse to turn in work.

If your grading scale is not 90–80–70–60, take the percentage score that is midway between the cutoff points for converting the holistic scores. For example, if 94 to 100 is an A, a holistic score of 5 would be equal to 97 percent. If 86 to 94 is a B, a holistic score of 4 would be 90 percent, and so on. Once you convert in your gradebook, arriving at a percentage score for each grading period is plain old averaging.

Checklists and tally lists are more objective. Checklists document skills, interactions, use of processes, and behaviors, whether they are consistently present, developing, or not present. Expectations may be set on how many skills are developing or are to be mastered for particular grades. How many times a particular strategy is used may be considered for particular levels of performance. Color coding by grading period can make this list viable for an entire school year.

Tally lists document how often skills, interactions, processes, and behaviors are used or occur. You may want to set some expectations for how many times a skill or strategy must be used to achieve a particular grade or level of performance. Holistic scoring, checklists, and tally lists work well with any of the three comparison processes you choose based on philosophy/policy.

EMPOWER YOURSELF AND YOUR STUDENTS

With compromise, you *can* be a whole language teacher *now*—even though school district policies may not make it easy. Many of the evaluation and grading techniques explained here are familiar; some are new. Select those that suit your needs or develop your own. If you step back, evaluate, reflect on, and evolve your own system of grading and evaluation, you'll be able to focus on significant interactions with learning. This focus will help both you and your students to reflect and make the critical judgments necessary for grading.

These same reflections and judgments promote student growth, teacher growth, and provide useful information to others (Jacobsen, 1989). The key factor is making certain that your grading system reflects the expectations that you communicate to your students (Atwell, 1987). The process you use will be a unique combination of policy requirements, professional knowledge, and personal choice. "The goal is that teachers think of themselves as practitioners of intellectual life who teach, not as technicians moving ahead an assembly line of topics imposed on them by district or state curricula" (Taylor, 1988, p. 19).

Reading research from the 1960s told us that the methods we use to teach are not as significant when it comes to student achievement as we are (Bond & Dykstra, 1967; Dykstra, 1968). Your attitude and your approach influences students' attitudes and approaches. So if you sincerely believe in whole language, *use it* and you *will* make a difference! Just develop record-keeping techniques that meet district requirements, and you'll survive as a whole language teacher until your system catches up.

REFERENCES

Alexander, J. E., & Filler R. (Eds.). (1976). *Attitudes and reading*. Newark, DE: International Reading Association.

Atwell, N. (1987). *In the middle*. Upper Montclair, NJ: Boynton/Cook.

Bird, L. (1989). The art of teaching: Evaluation and revision. In K. Goodman, Y. Goodman, & W. Hood (Eds.), *The whole language evaluation book* (pp. 15–24). Portsmouth, NH: Heinemann.

Bond, G., & Dykstra, R. (1967). The cooperative research program in first-grade reading instruction. *Reading Research Quarterly, 2*, 5–142.

Clay, M. (1979). *The early detection of reading difficulties* (3rd ed.). Portsmouth, NH: Heinemann.

Dalrymple, K. (1989). "Well, what about his skill?" Evaluation of whole language in the middle school. In K. Goodman, Y. Goodman, & W. Hood (Eds.), *The whole language evaluation book* (pp. 111–130). Portsmouth, NH: Heinemann.

Dykstra, R. (1968). Summary of the second grade phase of the Cooperative Research Program in primary reading instruction. *Reading Research Quarterly, 4*, 49–70.

Galindo, R. (1989). "Asi no se pone si" (That's not how to write "si"). In K. Goodman, Y. Goodman, & W. Hood (Eds.), *The whole language evaluation book* (pp. 55–67). Portsmouth, NH: Heinemann.

Goodman, K. (1986). *What's whole in whole language?* Portsmouth, NH: Heinemann.

Goodman, Y. (1989). Evaluation of students: Evaluation of teachers. In K. Goodman, Y. Goodman, & W. Hood (Eds.), *The whole language evaluation book* (pp. 3–14). Portsmouth, NH: Heinemann.

Graves, D. (1983). *Writing: Teachers and children at work*. Portsmouth, NH: Heinemann.

Howe-Tompkins, S. (1989). ". . . Of flying to the stars and looking at the dipr": Whole language evaluation on the Navajo reservation. In K. Goodman, Y. Goodman, & W. Hood (Eds.), *The whole language evaluation book* (pp. 167–175). Portsmouth, NH: Heinemann.

Huck, C., & Kerstetter, K. (1987). Developing readers. In B. Cullinan (Ed.), *Children's literature in the reading program* (pp. 30–40). Newark, DE: International Reading Association.

Hull, O. (1989). Evaluation: The conventions of writing. In K. Goodman, Y. Goodman, & W. Hood (Eds.), *The whole language evaluation book* (pp. 77–83). Portsmouth, NH: Heinemann.

Jacobsen, D. (1989). The evaluation process—in process. In K. Goodman, Y. Goodman, & W. Hood (Eds.), *The whole language evaluation book* (pp. 177–188). Portsmouth, NH: Heinemann.

Marek, A. (1989). Using evaluation as an instructional strategy. In K. Goodman, Y. Goodman, & W. Hood (Eds.), *The whole language evaluation book* (pp. 157–164). Portsmouth, NH: Heinemann.

McKenna, M., & Kear, D. (1990). Measuring attitude toward reading: A new tool for teachers. *The Reading Teacher, 43*, 626–639.

Padak, N., & Pryor, F. (1988, April). *First graders' perceptions of themselves as authors*. Paper presented at the meeting of the American Educational Research Association, New Orleans, LA.

Pearson, H. (1988). The assessment of reading through observation. *Reading, 22*, 158–164.

Rynkofs, J. (1988). Send your writing folders home. In T. Newkirk & N. Atwell (Eds.), *Understanding writing* (pp. 226–235). Portsmouth, NH: Heinemann.

Taylor, P. (1988). None of us is smarter than all of us: The reform in California's curriculum. *English Journal, 77*, 14–19.

Wolf, D. (1989). Portfolio assessment: Sampling student work. *Educational Leadership, 46*, 35–39.

Woodley, J., & Woodley, C. (1989). Whole language, Texas style. In K. Goodman, Y. Goodman, & W. Hood (Eds.), *The whole language evaluation book* (pp. 69–75). Portsmouth, NH: Heinemann.

Wortman, R., & Haussler, M. (1989). Evaluation in a classroom environment designed for whole language. In K. Goodman, Y. Goodman, & W. Hood (Eds.), *The whole language evaluation book* (pp. 45–54). Portsmouth, NH: Heinemann.

Wayne M. Linek is an adjunct instructor at Kent State University, on leave from his permanent position as an elementary school principal in the Jefferson Area Local School District in Jefferson, Ohio.

CHAPTER DISCUSSIONS AND ACTIVITIES

1. Compare and contrast the differences between traditional assessment and whole-language assessment. How are they alike and how are they different?
2. Define the term "responsive evaluation." How would you explain this term to fellow teachers?
3. Pair off with a classmate and, using a children's book, plan a student–teacher conference. What are some of the questions that the teacher might ask about this book? What are some of the questions that the student might ask?
4. For a particular grade level, select a children's book and prepare a literacy journal for that book.
5. Select a particular grade level and discuss the products you would want included in a portfolio for assessment.
6. Hansen provided an in-depth description of Literacy Portfolios in her article. Over a two-month period, develop a Literacy Portfolio about yourself. At the end of that time period, share your portfolio with a classmate and write a summary of what you learned about one another.
7. Take a fellow student's written report and grade this paper using holistic scoring of 5, 4, 3, 2, and 1. How can you compare this scoring with traditional grades and with percentiles?

CHAPTER 9

Teachers and Parents with Whole Language

When whole language is discussed, attention needs to be directed to key elements in its development and incorporation in the school. Central to the inclusion of whole language in a classroom are the roles of the teachers, school administrators, and parents. In this chapter, we will examine ways in which educators and parents affect and are affected by the transition to whole language.

THE SCHOOL STAFF AND WHOLE LANGUAGE

Experienced teachers, beginning teachers, and teachers-in-training view whole language with varying degrees of interest. Some teachers are highly motivated, some perceive the change simply as additional work and some, although drawn to the underlying philosophy of whole language, are hesitant because of the uncertainty of the implementation. Whatever their attitudes, teachers should remain open-minded about the possible need for training in whole language in order to help them refocus and reshape their teaching styles.

In the traditional classroom, the teacher depended upon already prepared commercial materials for classroom instruction and for curriculum design. When discussing the teaching of reading, Shannon (1989) calls this "the deskilling of teachers" (p. 78). When there is strong use of commercially prepared materials, the importance of the teacher is lessened. He further notes that when teachers use basal readers and textbooks, they are not directly involved in making instructional decisions. Instead, they are following the path laid out by the publishers.

In the whole-language classroom, the role of the teacher is critical and the teacher is considered to be a "meaning-making facilitator" (Ruddell, 1992, p. 617), that is, an influential teacher—one identified by former students as someone who has affected them personally and academically. Such a teacher is further described as an individual who is:

> First, . . . sensitive to individual student needs, motivations and aptitudes. . . .
> Second, . . . strategy-oriented . . . has a clear instructional plan based on his or her beliefs and teaching knowledge that provides cohesion, direction, and feedback during instruction. . . .
> Third, . . . holds high expectations for his or her students, and responsibility for learning is shared with the student. The teacher helps students in monitoring and evaluating their own learning. (Ruddell, 1992, pp. 617–618)

The shift in the roles of teachers in the whole-language classroom is a professional change that the teachers create themselves. This new role has been depicted as of one who is an initiator, a mediator, a kidwatcher, a liberator, and a curriculum maker (Goodman, 1992). It is also necessary for the whole-language teacher to become a risk taker, as well as a deductive, divergent, and systematic thinker (Pahl & Monson, 1992). Pace (1991) states that "a whole language teacher is a co-learner and an active participant in the learning endeavor" (p. 15).

The different kinds of patterns (or roles) that such teachers use in instructional situations are described by Yatvin (1992). She notes that in the *presentation pattern*, new material is formally presented through assimilation, practice, and application (e.g., the task of addressing an envelope). In the *exploratory pattern*, children investigate activities and strategies that are unfamiliar (e.g., publishing a class newspaper). And in the *generative pattern*, by using knowledge and skills that they already possess, children can produce something (e.g., keeping a journal). Yatvin also discusses the last role of the teacher as that of a manager—in the interplay with the children, the teacher balances and combines all the previous patterns and plans, teaches, and assesses the students' needs using personal discretion. The whole-language teacher does not depend on a manual or a guide for direction, but uses subjective judgment.

As Whitmore and Goodman (1992) point out, "whole language teachers respect their students as learners. Whole language administrators must value teachers in the same manner" (p. 26). Superintendents and principals need to have a true understanding of whole language, realizing that teachers cannot change overnight to a whole-language classroom, but that professional training needs to be provided with direct input from the teachers. There are other considerations that administrators need to address. They must modify their opinions about the teaching of reading and writing and keep an open mind in working with the teachers in the curriculum changes. They should understand that children are actively involved in the learning process and the classrooms may not look like classrooms did before the changeover—there may be more activity and more noise. They need to appraise the materials used in the classrooms, expand the classroom libraries, and allocate funds for the shift in needed materials. They should afford opportunities for the teachers to meet and discuss their progress and concerns. Most important, teachers need continuous support and encouragement from administrators. Monson (1992) sums up a description of how whole language has been integrated into his school district by commenting that: "Whole language demands both top–down facilitation from superintendents and bottom–up commitment from teachers if long-term, internalized, and systemic improvement in literacy education is to occur in America's public schools" (p. 23).

> ### Looking Ahead
> Some of the problems facing the school staff and some alternate strategies for implementing whole language are discussed in the articles by Burk and Melton-Pagés (1991); Monson and Pahl (1991); and Walmsley and Adams (1993).

PARENTS AND WHOLE LANGUAGE

Parents, too, need to be directly involved in the education of their children. In *Becoming a Nation of Readers*, the Commission on Reading (1985) states that, "Throughout the school years, parents continue to influence children's reading through monitoring of school performance, support for homework, and, most important, continued personal involvement with their children's growth as readers" (Anderson, Hiebert, Scott, & Wilkinson, p. 26). In a survey of parents of school-age children from urban, rural, and suburban communities, Rasinski and Fredericks (1989) found there was less than complete agreement on how the children should be taught and there were mixed feelings about whether or not the schools were doing an adequate job. But they found that parents really were concerned with classroom reading instruction. The authors recommend that educators should encourage greater parent involvement with the reading program used in the school.

Unfortunately, there are also parents who choose to be disinterested and uninvolved in the school's reading program. Fredericks and Rasinski (1990) offer some techniques that educators can employ in order to alleviate this problem. Their proposals are presented below, summarized and adapted for this volume:

1. Over the school year, furnish the parents continuously with written and visual informational material.
2. Have parental involvement become a schoolwide endeavor, not limited solely to a particular class or grade level.
3. Afford recognition to the parents and students who demonstrate a commitment to reading instruction.
4. Involve students directly in the recruitment of parents by having them prepare invitations and awards.
5. Foster the interest of the entire family in participating in various activities, so that reading becomes a family project.

6. Try not to limit the school involvement only to parents of school-age children, but include the community as a whole, such as senior citizens, business people, and government representatives.
7. Establish the school and the classroom as a comfortable environment for the parents to visit. For some parents, a visit to the school presents a formidable experience and they would prefer to meet at their own home or another community location.
8. Use the telephone as a means of conveying good news to the parents and not just communicating bad news.
9. Attempt to find out why some parents are distancing themselves from the school programs. Sometimes this goal can be accomplished through phone calls or home visits.
10. Provide a flexible schedule for various school activities; alternate them in morning, afternoon, evenings, and weekend time periods. This may allow the parents to participate at times that are convenient for them.
11. Establish a parent hotline through the parent–teacher association in the district in order to keep parents current and informed throughout the year.
12. Through community, business, and government leaders solicit endorsements for your reading program.
13. If possible, prepare videotapes of special events and programs and have them available for the parents.
14. Whenever a special event is held in the school, consider offering babysitting or driving services so that the parents may find it easier to attend.

Just as parents have demonstrated diverse attitudes and concerns regarding reading instruction in general, in the same way, they have shown a variety of feelings and perceptions about whole language. Some are encouraged by the advantages that whole language can afford their children; others label this change as being merely experimental; and, again, still others show limited interest in the literacy development of their children.

Because most parents were taught to read with basal readers, it is not surprising that some harbor a host of questions directly related to their children's instruction. A few of their concerns include the lack of workbooks, the indirect teaching of specific skills, the absence of ability-based reading groups, and the acceptance of invented spelling. Educators must describe more precisely just what whole language is and explain how and why it is being used in the education of their children.

Looking Ahead

The articles that follow by Fields (1988), Bruneau, Rasinski and Shehan (1991), and Vassallo (1992) discuss the various ways in which educators have familiarized parents with whole language.

Because the articles will discuss the ways in which teachers, administrators, and parents are directly and indirectly affected by the inclusion of whole language in the literacy curriculum, the following questions will be addressed:

- What are the distinct roles of the whole-language teacher?
- How is the teacher a decision-maker in the whole-language classroom?
- Why is it necessary for a whole-language teacher to be a "kidwatcher"?
- What effect does the philosophy of whole language have on the teaching–learning process?
- What are some of the problems that teachers face in assuming the role of a whole-language teacher?
- What are the changing roles of the whole-language administrator?
- How can teachers and administrators actively and effectively implement whole language in the schools?
- How and where do teachers acquire the knowledge necessary to implement and manage whole language?
- What are some of the major concerns that whole-language teachers have in using whole language in the classroom?
- How does whole language affect the parent's view of the educational process?
- What are some of the most effective procedures that a teacher can use in opening up the lines of communication with parents concerning the shift in literacy development?
- What are some of the key terms that parents should understand in order to assess the merits of whole language?

REFERENCES

Anderson, R. C., Hiebert, E. H., Scott, J. A., & Wilkinson, I. A. G. (1985). *Becoming a nation of readers: The report on the Commission on Reading*. Washington, DC: National Institute of Education, U.S. Department of Education.

Bruneau, B., Rasinski, T., & Shehan, M. (1991). Parent communication in a whole language kindergarten: What we learned from a busy first year. *Reading Horizons, 32*(2), 117–127.

Burk, J., & Melton-Pagés, J. (1991). From recipe reader to reading professional: Extending the roles of the teacher through whole language. *Contemporary Education, 62*(2), 96–101.

Fields, M. V. (1988). Talking and writing: Explaining the whole language approach to parents. *The Reading Teacher, 41*(9), 898–903.

Fredericks, A. D., & Rasinski, T. V. (1990). Involving the uninvolved: How to. *The Reading Teacher, 43*(6), 424–425.

Goodman, K. S. (1992). Why whole language is today's agenda in education. *Language Arts, 69*(5), 354–363.

Monson, R. J. (1992). Bringing whole language. *The School Administrator, 49*(5), 22–23.

Monson, R. J., & Pahl, M. M. (1991). Charting a new course with whole language. *Educational Leadership, 48*(6), 51–53.

Pace, G. (1991). When teachers use literature for literacy instruction: Ways that constrain, ways that free. *Language Arts, 68*(1), 12–25.

Pahl, M. M., & Monson, R. J. (1992). In search of whole language: Transforming curriculum and instruction. *Journal of Reading, 35*(7), 518–524.
Rasinski, T. V., & Fredericks, A. D. (1989). What do parents think about reading in the schools. *The Reading Teacher, 43*(3), 262–263.
Ruddell, R. B. (1992). A whole language and literature perspective: Creating a meaning-making instructional environment. *Language Arts, 69*(8), 612–620.
Shannon, P. (1989). *Broken promises: Reading instruction in twentieth-century America.* New York: Bergin and Garvey.
Vassallo, P. (1992). Putting children before grown-ups. *The American School Board Journal, 179*(3), 42–44.
Walmsley, S. A., & Adams, E. L. (1993). Realities of "whole language." *Language Arts, 70*(4), 272–280.
Whitmore, K. F., & Goodman, Y. M. (1992). Inside the whole language classroom. *The School Administrator, 49*(5), 20–26.
Yatvin, J. (1992). *Developing a whole language program for a whole school.* Midlothian, VA: Virginia State Reading Association.

FOR FURTHER STUDY

Allen, J., Combs, J., Hendricks, M., Nash, P., & Wilson, S. (1988). Studying change: Teachers who become researchers. *Language Arts, 65*(4), 379–387.
France, M. G., & Hager, J. M. (1993). Recruit, respect, respond: A model for working with low-income families and their preschoolers. *The Reading Teacher, 46*(7), 568–572.
Fredericks, A. D., & Rasinski, T. V. (1990). Whole language and parents: National partners. *The Reading Teacher, 43*(9), 692–694.
Garan, E. M. (1994). Who's in control? Is there enough "empowerment" to go around? *Language Arts, 71*(3), 192–199.
Hiebert, E. H., & Fisher, C. W. (1990). Whole language: Three themes for the future. *Educational Leadership, 47*(6), 62–64.
Moss, B. (1992). Planning effective whole language staff development programs: A guide for staff developers. *Reading Horizons, 32*(4), 299–315.
Prenn, M. C., & Scanlon, P. A. (1991). Teaching as we are taught: A model for whole language inservice. *Reading Horizons, 31*(3), 189–198.
Raskinski, T. V., & Fredericks, A. D. (1988). Sharing literacy: Guiding principles and practices for parent involvement. *The Reading Teacher, 41*(6), 508–512.
Salzer, R. T. (1991). TAWL teachers reach for self-help. *Educational Leadership, 49*(3), 66–67.
Shapiro, J., & Kilbey, D. (1990). Closing the gap between theory and practice: Teacher beliefs, instructional discussion and critical thinking. *Reading Horizons, 31*(1), 59–73.
Strickland, D. S. (1988). The teacher as researcher: Toward the extended professional. *Language Arts, 65*(8), 754–764.
Sumara, D., & Walker, L. (1991). The teacher's role in whole language. *Language Arts, 68*(4), 276–285.
Wollman-Bonilla, J. E. (1991). Shouting from the tops of buildings: Teachers as learners and change in schools. *Language Arts, 68*(2), 114–120.
Watson, D. J. (1994). Whole language: Why bother? *The Reading Teacher, 47*(8), 600–607.

From Recipe Reader to Reading Professional: Extending the Roles of the Teacher through Whole Language

Jill Burk
Joyce Melton-Pagés

In recent years society has watched the role of teacher change from information giver to caretaker, counselor, social worker, baby-sitter, and nurse. The roles of reading teachers have also changed over the years. In the past the teacher of reading was a follower of directions, technician, corrector of errors, grader of worksheets, and checker of oral reading. Reading was taught during "reading time" and children learned to read when they came to school. The teacher was responsible for filling the empty vessel. In contrast theory, research, and practice in recent years have shown us a great deal about how children learn language. Research on children's natural language learning processes supports the creation of whole language classrooms. As a result, the roles of the reading teacher have been redefined and extended.

The purpose of this paper is to describe the many and varied roles of the reading professional in schools and to discuss the implications of those roles for administrators and teacher educators. In order to provide the context for this discussion, a description of a whole language classroom will be given.

THE WHOLE LANGUAGE CLASSROOM

Whole language does not lend itself to a narrow definition. It is not a kit, an activity, a method, or an approach. Goodman (1986) explains whole language as "a way of bringing together a view of language, a view of learning, and a view of people, in particular two special groups of people: kids and teachers" (p. 5). Just what are these views or beliefs that whole language teachers hold? Whole language teachers believe that language is learned best and easiest when it is whole and in natural context. Language is learned by actually using it, not by practicing its separate parts. Whole language teachers believe that schools should complement the way children are learning language effectively and naturally at home. They value the language and varied life experiences that children bring to school. They focus on learners' strengths and watch for growth. Whole language teachers believe that all children can learn, that learning is a social experience, and that the teacher should also be a learner. Whole language is a framework of beliefs that shapes practice.

A whole language classroom, then, is one with a whole language teacher. Each teacher may use different activities and materials, but their individual practices are tied to the previously stated beliefs. Thus, whole language classrooms, while diverse, have commonalities. Watson (1986) identifies the following components that are present daily in whole language classrooms.

From "From Recipe Reader to Reading Professional: Extending the Roles of the Teacher through Whole Language" by J. Burke and J. Melton-Pagés, 1991, *Contemporary Education, 62*, pp. 96–101. Copyright © 1991 by Jill Burk and Joyce Melton-Pagés and Contemporary Education. Reprinted by permission.

1. Students are read to or told stories every day; they need to be involved with language.
2. Students have time to read and write independently every day; they need to practice oral and written language.
3. The world of the student is brought into the classroom every day; this helps students to make connections between their outside lives and school and to know that they are valued.
4. Reading and writing are brought to conscious awareness every day; this helps students to develop and enhance effective strategies for reading and writing.

In a whole language classroom, real reading and writing are taking place. Language is considered a tool for learning and the classroom is learner-centered. Through the establishment of a community of learners, teachers provide children with opportunities to use language, read literature, use integrated language processes across the curriculum, and grow as language users through risk-taking.

ROLES OF THE WHOLE LANGUAGE TEACHER

Instead of reading a script from the teacher's manual for reading class, the whole language teacher makes appropriate instructional decisions that are informed by the teacher's theory and classroom transactions. The whole language teacher is not a technician, but a decision-maker who is teaching students rather than teaching programs.

In line with the role of decision-maker, many teachers are now seeing themselves as researchers. Current literature contains many descriptions of research by in-service teachers (Allen, Combs, Hendricks, Nash, & Wilson, 1988; Atwell, 1982; Patterson, 1985; Strickland, 1988). Teacher/researchers are interested in using their research to improve students' learning. They ask questions, seek answers, and are potential contributors to education theory and practice. They may work alone or collaboratively. They are teachers who learn from students and their classrooms become "learning workshops" (Bissex, 1986, p. 484).

Kidwatchers discover the development of their students by watching them. The learners' processes are important to kidwatchers. They understand that valuable information can be gained from learners' errors and they recognize the influence of context on learning. Instead of delivering a lesson, kidwatchers continually evaluate and refine instruction based on the response of their students. When teachers are researchers they are kidwatchers (Goodman, 1986). As a result, they sharpen and value their observation skills and provide appropriate instruction tied to that observation.

Whole language teachers are readers and writers. As a result of a teacher/researcher stance, whole language teachers are reading and writing professionally and sharing their research, reading, writing, and thinking with others. They read and write for many purposes as they explore their own literacy and learn more about their own cognitive processes. Graves (1990) encourages teachers to read and write *with* children. In the classroom this means that whole language teachers let their students see that they like to read and write, that they *play* with language, and that they struggle with putting their ideas into words. In relation to resolving writing dilemmas, teachers also need responses. Response and sharing are key elements for all writers. As a result of being visible language learners in the classroom, teachers do what Routman (1988) suggests. She proposes that as teachers, "we must personally demonstrate that we hold 'knowledge' —the product we work so hard to promote and produce—in the highest regard" (p. 221). In taking charge of their own personal literacy, whole language teachers demonstrate literacy to their students.

As whole language teachers grow as kidwatchers, questioners, theorists, researchers, and decision-makers, they discover that other roles surface. In addition to developing a more global perspective of who they are as educators, they discover a new relationship to parents of their students.

Whole language teachers may be confronted by parents who expect their children to be taught the same way they were taught (Fields, 1988). They expect children to move systematically through a basal reading program, completing worksheets, reading in ability-based reading groups, and practicing their oral reading every day. Further, they expect columns of copied words from spelling books, pages of penmanship practice, and red-inked corrections on writing. Since whole language teachers teach reading, writing, speaking, and listening through meaningful learning experiences across the curriculum, many of the products of traditional reading instruction are not available for parents' examination.

Whole language teachers respect the role of the parent in the child's language learning. As a result, whole language teachers communicate to parents what they are doing in the classroom, why they are doing what they are doing, what products parents can expect to see coming home, and what parents can do to support their child's language learning at home. As teachers work to harness the energy and commitment of the natural ally that parents are, they establish routines which broaden their role as teacher (Melton, 1985).

Misconceptions about whole language can sometimes pose problems for whole language teachers (Newman & Church 1990). They are often questioned by colleagues and administrators about their instructional practices. As a result, whole language teachers often must explain their instructional strategies, management of the classroom for instruction, utilization of materials, evaluation practices, and documentation procedures to their peers. Further, these teachers must often walk a tightrope as they reconcile their theoretical orientation with state-mandated curricula, materials, assessment procedures, and teacher appraisal instruments.

In addition, whole language teachers often find themselves functioning as change agents in the school environment. As a whole language teacher's instruction gains respect and recognition in a school, administrators and teachers may request assistance from the teacher to make program improvements. This role of facilitating change may involve the whole language teacher in serving on the district curriculum committee, ordering materials for the school professional library, conducting in-service workshops for other teachers, inviting other teachers into their classrooms to view instruction, or mentoring another teacher in relation to whole language instruction. The teacher as change agent is a significant role in most settings for the whole language teacher.

In addition to being a change agent in the school, whole language teachers sometimes find that they must become politically involved in district and state education issues. Whole language teachers sometimes find that policymakers, politicians, bureaucrats, and journalists have the same notions about language learning that parents have. In order to guard against mandated reductionism and behaviorism in the form of standardized curricula, instructional materials, assessment measures, documentation procedures, report cards, subject/time allocations, and teacher evaluation, these teachers must articulate their views in persuasive ways. They must be politically savvy public relations experts as they deal with school board members, community groups, legislators, and members of the media. They must work for a supportive environment that will free them to make professional decisions for their students.

ROLES OF ADMINISTRATORS

The ability of knowledgeable, motivated whole language teachers to meet the needs of their students is largely dependent on school administrators' attitudes toward whole language instruction. In many settings, principals and central office personnel make most of the decisions about the utilization of materials, management of student behavior, report card format, utilization of the school library, acceptability of classroom libraries, the organization of the classroom for instruction, the availability of funds for additional support materials, the organization of the curriculum guide, and the nature of instruction to be provided. Administrators who are not informed about whole language are frequently unable to provide the institutional support which teachers require to meet the needs of their students. The following recommendations are proposed for administrators who hope to support the provision of whole language instruction in their schools.

1. Administrators must broaden their view of reading instruction. They must understand that reading is not a separate subject, but instead a process which strengthens learning across the curriculum. Reading, writing, speaking, and listening are at the heart of the lifelong learners that students ultimately become.
2. When administrators understand the role of schooling in the creation of lifelong learners, they must acknowledge their role in the reading program. They must enroll in appropriate reading courses, attend conferences, and read professionally in reading journals. A major complaint of whole language teachers is that principals' knowledge of reading instruction is not current (Melton-Pagés & Burk, 1990).
3. These administrators must then use their understanding of whole language instruction to provide institutional support for whole language instruction. They attempt to break down the barriers between subjects in the daily schedule. They free teachers to make informed decisions in the classroom related to materials to be used, strategies to be implemented, routines to be established, and grouping strategies to be employed. In addition, they give teachers as much access to the school library, book-making materials/equipment, and monetary resources as possible. Further, they define procedures for lesson plans, grades, and pupil progress reporting which are more theoretically consistent with language learning processes. Finally, they make teacher evaluation instruments conform to instruction which supports student language learning instead of forcing teachers to "stand and deliver" a lesson which conforms to the evaluation instrument.
4. Administrators who understand whole language instruction know that they must provide children with opportunities to see adults as readers, writers, and learners. They free teachers to share their reading and writing experiences with students. In addition, they demonstrate for students that they, too, are readers and writers. They read books to students, join in reading/writing workshop sharing time, and respond to students' stories and letters.
5. Whole language administrators feed the intellectual development of their teachers. They provide professional libraries, encourage teachers to join professional organizations, provide teachers with opportunities to visit other classrooms/ schools, encourage teachers to network with teachers in other schools/ districts, and allow teachers to attend professional conferences. They encourage questioning, thinking, and risk-taking in the professional development of teachers. They understand that an environment which fosters teacher learning and curiosity will, likewise, foster student learning. They encourage teachers to conduct research, work with university personnel on projects, present at conferences/ workshops, and write professionally. Further, they give teachers opportuni-

ties to share what they're doing, what works, what doesn't work, and what they're learning. They allow teachers time to support each other's professional development. In short, they support the ongoing learning of teachers and children (Teale, 1989).

6. Administrators who respect their teachers as professionals work with the teachers and other district personnel to set direction for the instructional program. They do not dictate which materials and programs will be used to teach reading (Harste, 1989). They focus more on building teacher competence and confidence and less on mandating basal reading instruction (Goodman, Shannon, Freeman, & Murphy, 1988). They recognize teachers as learners and support their professional right to try to improve the status of literacy instruction (Harste, 1989).

7. In relation to program development, administrators of effective programs of change work under the assumption that curriculum and curriculum development take time and are enhanced with partnership. Such programs facilitate and encourage collaboration between educators in college and educators in classrooms as they actively engage in the pursuit of practical theory (Harste, 1989).

8. Finally, administrators enlist the aid of the community at large in supporting the school language arts program [e.g., recruiting volunteer aides, developing business contracts, finding ways for citizens to serve as resource persons in the classroom, compiling a directory of places where teachers can take children to learn outside the school (Teale, 1989)]. In addition, they treat parents as participants and partners in learning who are permitted options, choices, involvement, and information about the instructional alternatives available to students (Harste, 1980).

ROLES OF TEACHER EDUCATORS

Whole language teachers face many pressures in the public school setting. They must be able to meet the needs of all learners. In addition, they must be able to respond to the questions of parents, colleagues, administrators, school board members, legislators, and state department of education officials. They must be problem-solvers, self-starters, and change agents. Quality whole language instruction is largely dependent on the quality of the teacher's preparation for teaching. This preparatory period at the undergraduate level is the beginning of the teacher's active theory development about the teaching and learning of language. Certainly the teacher's personal experiences as a learner are influential, but teacher educators have a significant responsibility to encourage theory development which may differ from the preservice teachers' own school experiences. The following recommendations are proposed for teacher educators who wish to support the development of whole language instruction.

1. Teacher educators should refocus teacher education on preparing informed professionals rather than basal technicians (Goodman et al., 1988). There is no recipe for whole language instruction. The teacher's ability to provide strong whole language instruction is dependent on his or her ability to reason out instructional goals, establish a learning environment which is consistent with those goals, and explore instructional options in relation to those goals. The teacher must be constantly examining his/her thinking for contradictions and fallacies in reasoning. In order to stimulate this kind of thinking, the teacher education program must encourage students to examine who they are as language learners/users, question beliefs about language learning, discuss

ideas and issues, and analyze instructional practices for underlying theoretical assumptions.

The intellectually rigorous teacher preparation program instills in students a respect for the degree which they are earning, an understanding of who they are as learners, and a sense of who they can be as teachers.

2. Teacher educators should help preservice teachers become effective, confident language users and learners. They should give students many opportunities to read, write, and use language in meaningful ways. They should inspire a love of learning in their preservice teachers. They should endeavor to reflect language learning principles in their courses and program organization. For example, they should integrate language-related courses, rather than enrolling students in separate courses for reading methods, language arts methods, and children's literature (Teale, 1989).

3. At the heart of the teacher education program is the field experience component. Teacher educators must build into the program as many field experiences as possible. Preservice teachers should work with students in a variety of settings. Opportunities to work in school/classroom publishing centers, tutor individual students, observe in classrooms, conference with students, conduct mini-lessons, and implement thematic units help strengthen the development of the preservice teachers. It is through these experiences that they test assumptions, develop a personal theory, explore options, ask questions, refine definitions, and examine themselves as developing professionals. Further, in concert with other teacher education experiences, field experiences can equip future teachers to adopt a reflective practitioner perspective (i.e., teacher researcher perspective) on students' learning and their own teaching (Teale, 1989).

Teacher educators must negotiate with elementary school personnel the methods for achieving teacher education goals so that future teachers receive support from both the college or university and the cooperating teacher in their student teaching experience. In addition, the selected cooperating teachers must be the finest possible classroom models for preservice teachers (Teale, 1989).

4. Teacher educators must develop in future teachers a sense of purpose, belief, and commitment to the profession that will serve as a rationale for their behavior (Teale, 1989). Teacher educators should encourage preservice teachers to join professional organizations, afford them opportunities to read professional journals, encourage attendance at professional conferences, provide them with opportunities to conduct classroom research (Melton-Pagés, Burk, & Burgess, 1990), and involve them in professional presentations.

5. Teacher educators must establish a relationship with preservice teachers which encourages a strong future school–university relationship. Their relationship should support the learning for developing teachers, should promote school involvement for teacher educators (Teale, 1989), and should encourage collaborative research between teacher educators and classroom teachers (Teale, 1989).

6. Teacher educators will make provision for school administrators to continue to grow in relation to language learning. Through courses, workshops, and consultations, teacher educators can strengthen administrators' attempts to support the instruction of whole language teachers.

CONCLUSIONS

Teachers must accept responsibility for the learning of their students. As a result, all teachers have one initial decision to make: "Am I going to provide instruction that someone else prescribes?" OR "Am I going to make my own instructional decisions for my students?" If teachers perceive themselves as decision-makers and have the courage to effect those decisions, then they accept a multitude of roles. These roles must be acknowledged and supported by teacher educators in preparation programs and school administrators in the field. The extent to which this support exists ultimately determines the success of the whole language teacher who is trying to make a difference in the lives of children.

REFERENCES

Allen, J., Combs, J., Hendricks, M., Nash, P., & Wilson, S. (1988). Studying change: Teachers who become researchers. *Language Arts, 65,* 377–389.

Bissex, G. (1986). On becoming teacher experts: What's a teacher-researcher? *Language Arts, 63,* 482–484.

Fields, M. V. (1988). Talking and writing: Explaining the whole language approach to parents. *The Reading Teacher, 41,* 898–903.

Goodman, K. (1986). *What's whole in whole language?* Portsmouth, NH: Heinemann.

Goodman, K., Shannon, P., Freeman, Y., & Murphy, S. (1988). *Report card on basal readers.* Katonah, NY: Richard C. Owen Publishers, Inc.

Graves, D. H. (1990). *Discover your own literacy.* Portsmouth, NH: Heinemann.

Harste, J. C. (1989). *New policy guidelines for reading.* Urbana, IL: National Council of Teachers of English.

Melton, J. M. (1985) *A qualitative analysis of the effects of the parent–teacher relationship on parent educative behavior.* Unpublished doctoral dissertation, Indiana University, Bloomington, IN.

Melton-Pagés, J., Burk, J., & Burgess, D. (1990). *Preparing preservice teachers to be classroom researchers.* Paper presented at the National Reading Conference, Miami, FL.

Melton-Pagés, J., & Burk, J. (1990). *A survey of whole language teachers' descriptions of administrative support.* Unpublished manuscript.

Newman, J., & Church, S. (1990). Myths of whole language. *The Reading Teacher, 44,* 20–26.

Patterson, L. A. (1987). *Responses to socio-psycholinguistic composition instruction in a secondary classroom: Toward a transactional stance for teacher researchers.* Unpublished doctoral dissertation, Texas A&M University, College Station.

Routman, R. (1988). *Transitions from literature to literacy.* Portsmouth, NH: Heinemann Educational Books.

Strickland, D. S. (1988). The teacher as researcher: Toward the extended professional. *Language Arts, 65,* 754–766.

Teale, W. H. (1989). Language arts for the 21st century. In J. M. Jenson (Ed.), *Stories to grow on: Demonstrations of language learning in K–8 classrooms* (pp. 1–34). Portsmouth, NH: Heinemann Educational Books.

Watson, D. (1986). *Whole language classrooms.* Paper presented at meeting of Teachers Applying Whole Language, Columbia, MO.

Jill Burk is an assistant professor of education at Tarleton State University, Stephenville, Texas. Joyce Melton-Pagés is the director of the Reading Specialist Certification Program at Tarleton State University.

Charting a New Course with Whole Language

Robert J. Monson
Michele M. Pahl

In the past 20 years, no proposed change in the craft of teaching has generated as high a level of emotion within the profession as the current debate over reading/writing instruction. By virtually limiting the discussion of the issue to "Phonics vs. Whole Language,"[1] practitioners have entrenched themselves in two opposing pedagogical camps, making it increasingly difficult to establish common ground. Despite all the heated commentary and rhetoric, literacy educators and educational reformers on both sides are so focused on the phonics battle that the true cause of the war has eluded them. In this article, we enlarge the debate by conducting it within the broader context of our beliefs about the teaching/learning process.

In doing so, we focus not on the issue of phonics instruction, but on the evolving role of the classroom teacher. Whole language involves a fundamental change in a teacher's belief system about the culture of the classroom; this reconceptualization is at the core of the controversy surrounding the teaching of reading and writing. If the whole language philosophy is to be successfully implemented, it requires a complex shift in emphasis from the historical model of teaching, in which teachers dispense knowledge to students, to an approach through which students actively construct meaning. We have characterized this change as a paradigm shift from *transmission*—teachers transmitting knowledge to students—to *transaction*—students engaging in a transaction between what is known and what is unknown (see Figure 1). Such a view of the teaching/learning process encompasses considerably more than the issue of phonics instruction; it has direct impact on the role of the professional—it forces a teacher to chart a new course.

LEARNING FROM THE PAST

If we accept that instructional practice ought to be based on what we know about learning, we should consider the historical origins of the present role and the cognitive assumptions that supported its development. Nineteenth century America demanded that its system of public schooling develop an efficient, cost-effective way of providing large numbers of children with basic skills. The industrial efficiency model, which worked so well in factories, was transplanted to schools using Ebbinghaus' (1885) "drill and practice" theory, thereby enabling teachers to effectively cover material in the time allotted. Skills in reading, writing, and arithmetic were acquired with the pragmatics of the workplace in mind. Thus, by the late 1880's, the culture of the schools closely resembled the culture of the factory (Callahan 1962). As teachers developed into "assembly line workers with a quota to attain in a certain time period" (Hall 1986), the transmission model became synonymous with this perception of their role.

PHONICS IN PROPER PERSPECTIVE

Much of what is defended as "proven practice" in literacy education today is built on early learning theories that have undergone considerable revision in more recent times. The basic assumptions underlying a synthetic/basal reader approach to phonics instruction are firmly embedded in the belief structure that

---

From "Charting a New Course with Whole Language" by R. J. Monson and M. M. Pahl, 1991, *Educational Leadership, 48*, pp. 51–53. Copyright © 1991 by ASCD. All rights reserved. Reprinted by permission of the Association for Supervision and Curriculum Development.

TRANSMISSION MODEL		TRANSACTION MODEL
	What Is Learned	
Defining what we know	*Objective*	Interacting with the unknown
Acquisition of knowledge	*Purpose*	Construction of meaning
Fact-orientation	*Outcome*	Thinking process
	How It Is Learned	
Teacher-centered instruction		Student-centered learning
Part to whole	*Strategy*	Whole to part
Skills-based	*Content*	Concept-based
One dimensional	*Context*	Multi-dimensional
Dissemination of information	*Teacher role*	Catalyst for problem solving
Passive learning	*Learner role*	Active learning
Mastery	*Assessment*	Demonstrated competence

FIGURE 1
PARADIGM SHIFT REQUIRED OF THE WHOLE LANGUAGE PHILOSOPHY

supports the transmission model; namely, "that reading must be taught in an explicit way, that reading is learned from parts to whole through a carefully worked-out sequential hierarchy of skills, and that each skill must be taught, positively reinforced, mastered, and tested before the next appropriate skill in the hierarchy is presented" (Goodman et al. 1987). This drill and practice, part-to-whole philosophy of phonics proponents, which is being passionately defended today, rests upon the theoretical assumptions posited by our 19th century ancestors; far too few of the advocates of this approach, we believe, recall the historical genesis of the transmission model. Most, we suspect, would retreat if they realized that the belief system behind the transmission paradigm is based upon an industrial model.

In contrast, the holistic view of the reading process defended by advocates of whole language rests upon more current developmental, psycholinguistic, and sociolinguistic research.[2] Although their point is rarely heard (and less frequently comprehended) above the noise of battle, proponents of whole language do not deny that phonics plays a role in an integrated model of reading instruction. Rather, they promote the belief that the construction of meaning is at the center of a semantic language system, surrounded and supported by syntactic and graphophonic surface features (Goodman et al. 1987). When the phonics dispute is placed in perspective, the changing role of the teacher in a whole language classroom emerges as a critical issue in the overall debate.

THE TEACHER'S ROLE AND THE PARADIGM SHIFT

Whole language is creating a ruckus because it is pushing against 100-year-old assumptions about teaching; whole language requires a new set of assumptions about learning. This set of assumptions comprises the transaction model, a model in which the teacher designs learning experiences that foster active engagement with the known for the purposes of understanding the unknown. The transaction model is based upon the belief that learning is a process of meaning making and problem-solving; the acquisition of specific facts and skills are peripheral to this central process. The transaction model not only suggests that *what* is learned is different from our historical understandings, it also suggests that *how* it is learned is different.

Transactional learning rests upon the assumption that learning, in large part, is self-directed. The prior knowledge brought to each new learning situation varies from child to child; subsequently, the meaning taken from the learning situation is equally diverse. Students build upon their knowledge base by using it as a framework for interpretation. Through the process of negotiating new understandings into the existing framework, the student constructs meaning, internalizes patterns, makes connections, and responds emotionally. As a result of this negotiation, the learner is confronted with questions, feelings, discrepancies, and inconsistencies; in an ongoing attempt to resolve these, the process becomes recursive. Although transactional learners never completely master the learning process, they demonstrate their competence as active participants. Because the process is unique to each individual, it does not come about as a result of teacher-centered instruction.

If learning is viewed as a one-dimensional activity in which the teacher is the sole source of information and the student's only role is to accumulate as much information as possible in a given amount of time, then we have reduced the process to information storage and retrieval. In contrast, the whole language approach and the transaction model demonstrate respect for the idiosyncratic and complex nature of the learning process. Synthetic phonics and/or basal reading approaches, used exclusively, do not demonstrate the same respect for the inquiring minds of individuals.

Although the definition of transaction may seem to suggest a primary focus on process, we are not contending that content should be discarded. Students must develop a knowledge base; facts must be learned and skills acquired. In order for readers to effectively use graphophonic surface structures to construct meaning from text, for instance, a firm foundation in sound/symbol relationships ("phonics") is necessary. This foundation is built, however, upon active engagement with text through which generalizations can gradually be internalized, tested, and solidified. The building of such a foundation cannot be communicated to the learner; it must be experienced by the learner.

EFFECTING THE PARADIGM SHIFT

This brings us to the core of why the whole language philosophy inspires such strong opposition and emotional resistance. It suggests, indeed, *requires,* that the context for learning be radically altered. As schooling moves from teacher-centered instruction to student-centered learning, classroom norms and patterns of interaction will undergo important changes. The process of transactional learning requires that traditional roles for teachers and learners be reconfigured. In the transmission model, the teacher is the authority and disseminator of knowledge; in the transaction model, the teacher facilitates the learning process by acting as a catalyst for problem solving. The changing role of the teacher directly influences the role of the learner. No longer seen as merely receptive—a "blank slate" or an "empty vessel"—the learner interacts with peers and teachers in a cooperative fashion and shares the responsibility for learning. In a community of learners, teaching is a shared endeavor.

A paradigm shift of this magnitude is no easy feat, particularly if one has experienced success with the transmission belief system and practices. For practitioners, it means breaking down the prevailing norms of isolation and control and replacing them with the new norms of collaboration and responsibility. For a district attempting to implement whole language, it means shifting the focus of staff development from a traditional "corrective orientation" to a more developmental "growth orientation" (Krupp 1989). Teachers, too, are transactional learners. Our practices in staff development should reflect and be consistent with what we believe about the learning process in general. This means, in effect, changing our emphasis in staff development from transmission to transaction.

CONTRIBUTING TO THE PARADIGM WARS?

Whole language is one of several movements that are focusing our attention on the need for a new way of conceptualizing the role of the classroom teacher. Echoes of the transaction model are seen in the recently developed standards of the National Council of the Teachers of Mathematics, in the ARTS PROPEL concept espoused by Howard Gardner that is being piloted in the Pittsburgh Public Schools, and in the "Pathways" approach to education at Harvard Medical School. In each of these initiatives, practitioners are pushing at the borders of the traditional role of teachers. As this transition takes place, it does not have to be as a battle between opposing forces. In the words of N. L. Gage (1989), "paradigm differences do not require paradigm conflict."

Although we believe that the transaction model will be more effective in helping learners become creative problem solvers and strategic thinkers, it is not the final model. Like any paradigm, it is a conceptualization limited by what is presently known. In the final analysis, those of us in the education profession must sustain and encourage a transaction between effective practice and the knowledge that is yet to be discovered.

NOTES

1. For a more complete discussion of the debate, see M. Carbo, (1988), "Debunking the Great Phonics Myth," *Phi Delta Kappan* 70: 226–240; J. S. Chall, (1967), *Learning to Read: The Great Debate* (New York: McGraw Hill); J. S. Chall, (1989), "Learning to Read: The Great Debate Twenty Years Later. A Response to 'Debunking the Great Phonics Myth,'" *Phi Delta Kappan* 71: 521–538; and M. J. Adams, (1990), *Beginning to Read: Thinking and Learning About Print* (Cambridge, Mass.: MIT Press).
2. For a comprehensive analysis of the research base see M. M. Clay, (1972), *Reading: The Patterning of Complex Behavior* (Auckland, New Zealand: Heinemann); Y. Goodman, (1990), *How Children Construct Literacy: Piagetian Perspectives* (Newark, Del.: International Reading Association); J. C. Harste, V. A. Woodard, and C. L. Burke, (1984), *Language Stories and Literacy Lessons* (Portsmouth, N.H.: Heinemann); E. B. Huey, (1908, 1968), *The Psychology and Pedagogy of Reading* (Cambridge, Mass.: MIT Press); F. Smith, (1973), *Psycholinguistics and Reading* (New York: Holt, Rinehart, and Winston); C. Weaver, (1988), *Reading Process and Practice: From Socio-Psycholinguistics to Whole Language* (Portsmouth, N.H.: Heinemann); and L. Vygotsky, (1986), *Thought and Language* (Cambridge, Mass.: MIT Press).

REFERENCES

Callahan, R. E. (1962). *Education and the Cult of Efficiency*, Chicago: The University of Chicago Press.
Ebbinghaus, H. (1885). *Memory*. Leipzig: Dunker and Humboldt.
Gage, N. L. (1989). "The Paradigm Wars and Their Aftermath: A 'Historical' Sketch of Research on Teaching Since 1989," *Teachers College Record* 91, 2: 135–150.
Goodman, Y. M., D. J. Watson, and C. L. Burke. (1987). *Reading Miscue Inventory: Alternative Procedures*. New York: Richard C. Owen.
Hall, M. (1986). "Teaching and Language Centered Programs." In *Roles in Literacy Learning: A New Perspective*, edited by D. Tovey and J. Kerber. Newark, Del.: International Reading Association.
Krupp, J. A. (1989). "Staff Development and the Individual." In *Staff Development: A Handbook of Effective Practices*, edited by S. J. Caldwell. Oxford, Ohio: National Staff Development Council.

Robert J. Monson is Superintendent and Michele M. Pahl is Reading Specialist/Staff Developer in the Westwood Public Schools, 660 High Street, Westwood, MA 02090.

Realities of "Whole Language"

Sean A. Walmsley
Ellen L. Adams

> I don't think that whole language will ever be understood by a great majority of teachers.... I see teachers who are in the early stages of whole language who are misconstruing some of it. They think they are doing whole language, but they really aren't. I don't think that it will ever be truly understood, but I think that people who do understand it and really follow it will teach their student teachers to do it. I think there will be a small group who will continue it. It's a philosophy, but it's also a style...a style that fits some teachers. The student teachers are now coming out of colleges that are really promoting whole language.... They come well prepared, and they love it.... Those of us who are still doing whole language may sometimes go into hiding.... I think that whole language will continue, but it will be a very small movement; and I think that the majority of teachers in the United States will never know what it is, much less learn to do it. (Grade 4 teacher)

For the past several years, large numbers of elementary school teachers have taken on the challenge of what is called a "whole language" approach to literacy instruction. As they do so, they are finding that making the transition from traditional to whole language instruction isn't quite as easy or trouble-free as they thought it might be. In many of the whole language conferences, and in much of the whole language literature, it seems that the struggles, concerns, and doubts of individual teachers are sometimes caught in the eddies of the fast-flowing whole language movement. In this article, we focus less on the ecstasy of whole language and more on the realities of becoming a whole language teacher and sustaining a whole language classroom.

To investigate the issues that teachers confront as they make the transition to whole language and attempt to sustain it, we conducted a series of confidential interviews, mostly at a whole language conference with 71 teachers in elementary and middle schools drawn from rural, urban, and suburban school districts (public and private) in upstate New York. Although we did not employ a rigorous sampling technique, the sample of teachers we interviewed represent a cross section of age and teaching experience, but they all viewed themselves as teachers with a whole language orientation. We asked how long they had been whole language teachers, how they became whole language teachers, how they defined whole language, what problems they encountered in their transition to this approach, concerns they had about sustaining it, and what they thought about the future of the whole language movement. All the interviews were tape recorded and transcribed. The data were analyzed using a contrastive analysis technique, in which repeated readings of the transcripts were made and generalizations were generated, then reverified in the transcripts.

What emerges from these educators' stories about their experiences are several concerns that relate to the amount of work involved in whole language instruction; relations with other faculty members, administrators, and parents; organization of instruction; defining what whole language is; evaluating student progress in a whole language classroom; and where respondents see themselves and the whole language movement in the next few years. From an analysis of the interviews, some generalizations about the realities of implementing whole language can be identified.

From "Realities of 'Whole Language' " by S. A. Walmsley and E. L. Adams, 1993, *Language Arts, 70*, pp. 272–280. Copyright © 1993 by the National Council of Teachers of English. Reprinted with permission.

WHOLE LANGUAGE INSTRUCTION IS VERY DEMANDING

The teachers were unanimous in their view that whole language instruction is tremendously demanding, greatly more so than traditional basal reading instruction. For the majority, even those who had been using a whole language approach for some time (but especially among beginners), the work wasn't getting any easier—in fact, many described it as "intensive," "exhausting," or "overwhelming":

> I feel overwhelmed. I don't know where to start, and I don't know where to go. It's too much all at once. (Grade 2)
> Starting out in whole language, I used to think: Oh, it won't take me long to make those materials, so I'll just save some money and do it myself . . . but it was hard to keep up. . . . I was exhausted. . . . Sometimes I would stay until 9:00 at night . . . or come in on Saturday or Sunday. (Grade 1)

Teachers were not only disheartened by how much there was to do (e.g., building up a library of tradebooks, individualizing instruction, building thematic units, locating or making materials) but also about how much they still had to learn:

> I'm so overwhelmed with everything that I have learned. . . . I feel like a sponge that has absorbed so much information, and now I'm just dripping. . . . I'm wet with information. (Grade 3)

These feelings, however, are counterbalanced for most teachers by a growing sense of comfort and confidence in themselves and their program, and a greater degree of reflectiveness in their teaching:

> Well, actually I'm very comfortable with it. It's a lot of work, but actually I'm much happier. I feel like I've come into my own in the past years, and now I am really comfortable. (Grade 4)
> The more I become involved in whole language, the more I realize how much I have to learn and do. I find it very tough. There is always something else to do or learn . . . and yet through all of this, I find myself more at peace with myself when I think about what I do with kids. (Grade 2)

Unlike the whole language teachers interviewed by Manning, Manning, and Long (1989), who seemed to have quickly overcome their initial difficulties making the transition to whole language, our respondents appeared to have difficulties implementing their whole language program that had yet to be resolved, even after several years of teaching from this perspective. From the almost unanimous agreement among our respondents on this issue, we are convinced that whole language advocates have underestimated the demanding nature of making the transition to whole language.

WHOLE LANGUAGE ALIENATES AND DIVIDES

We were struck by the number of respondents who felt vulnerable, isolated, alienated, or ostracized as a consequence of adopting a whole language philosophy. For some teachers, being in the minority was particularly troublesome:

> I jumped into my classroom and expected it to happen overnight, and I really became very, very depressed . . . and I was alone . . . I needed someone to talk to. . . . I had been taught a different way, and I was making a 180-degree turn . . . and my principal didn't even really know what I was doing . . . so I certainly didn't have any backing. (Grade 3)

More unsettling to the teachers than isolation was the polarizing effect of their adopting whole language, which separates teachers into educational camps representing stereotypes of traditional (i.e., teacher-dominated instruction; children sitting passively in rows;

doing dittos; being drilled, not taught; working on mindless basal stories and exercises) versus whole language (i.e., child-centered, individualized instruction; warm, colorful rooms; authentic reading of self-selected literature; journal writing; singing and chanting; project work):

> The first time I attended a whole language workshop I was told to expect daggers from other teachers.... To be someone different who is not using workbooks can be very threatening to other teachers. (Grade 2)
>
> There are these young teachers in our school ... and I'm at the 15th-year point now ... and they make me feel guilty for not just jumping on the bandwagon.... I'm more comfortable just being me, and that's what whole language advocates—let your kids be themselves ... but yet they don't respect me.... They should let me do whole language in my own way.... They are philosophizing a philosophy without practicing it. (Grade 1)
>
> In our school, there are about 30 teachers, and 5 of us are whole language teachers. The principal likes to march visitors into the whole language classroom but not into the traditional ones. This causes a lot of hard feelings because the traditional teachers feel that they don't have anything to share or show. (Grade 3)

Many of the teachers prefer not to use the term "whole language," fearful of the negative feelings it elicits:

> If you go in and say, "Oh, I'm a whole language teacher," then right away we are putting this wall around ourselves.... It's the label.... In my district you don't want to use the label because it's like a porcupine getting his bristles out.... They hear "whole language," and boom! the needles come out. (Grade 2)
>
> I don't like the term "whole language" because there is a stigma attached. It's like waving a red flag in front of a bull for some teachers. (Grade 5)

Several of the teachers commented on how vulnerable they felt as they left the security of traditional basal materials and ventured into the unsure waters of whole language:

> Sometimes it's kind of scary to walk into my classroom not knowing how the day is going to go.... The students determine this.... You just can't sit back and look through your lesson plans to see what worksheets come next. (Grade 1)
>
> I know that some of my kids are going to end up in traditional classrooms, and their teachers will say, "What did she do with them?" It's a worry that I have. (Grade 1)

These uncertainties also reveal themselves in teachers' comments about parents. Many parents, like fellow teachers, are either wedded to traditional notions about the elementary curriculum, or they simply do not understand what a whole language philosophy is about. Their criticisms of whole language classrooms tend to focus on the issues of grouping practices, spelling, phonics, and worksheets; and they clearly unsettle some of the teachers we interviewed:

> It's hard with the parents because they don't see all these papers coming home.... (Grade 1)
>
> One day a parent came in and said, "What is this total language? What's this whole group teaching?" So I said, "Well, you must mean whole language." The parent then wanted to know why her daughter wasn't in the top group. When I told her that we didn't have any grouping, she said, "Well, I'm going to the administration.... My daughter is gifted ... she belongs in a top group." (Grade 1)

That whole language teachers feel isolated, alienated, or even ostracized is hardly surprising, given the challenge that whole language represents to traditional classroom practice. Whole language is not merely a new set of teaching routines that can be added to existing practices: It directly confronts and opposes practices that most teachers have become wedded to over the past 20 years. For example, it emphasizes child-centered versus teacher-dominated instruction; it strongly opposes direct teaching of isolated reading and editing "skills"; it advocates replacing the basal program with tradebooks. And it promotes these practices without providing teachers with an alternate set of materials and guides they can simply purchase and follow. What these teachers have discovered is that they are very much on their own with respect to building their new literacy programs (and it's hard work to build a program from scratch). Further, they have to contend with the political problem of how their programs will coexist with traditional ones in the same building. The very act of their adopting a whole language philosophy sets a number of opposing forces in motion. Some teachers are made to feel that they are not "progressive" if they don't join the movement, and they resent the implication that they are somehow not "with it." Other teachers who reject whole language as "soft" and lacking in "standards" and "skills coverage" are sometimes openly critical of the whole language teachers. And if they are not openly critical, there's a constant "undertow" of criticism that can be felt throughout the building. So the whole language teachers, far from being greeted as pioneers of innovative literacy instruction, unexpectedly find themselves not only the targets of resentment and hostility but also partially responsible for an atmosphere of disharmony among colleagues. Given how difficult it is to make the transition into whole language, the intolerant atmosphere simply exacerbates their feeling of uncertainty and vulnerability. There are more consequences of adopting whole language than they ever anticipated, and these extend well beyond the classroom.

IT'S HARD TO MANAGE WHOLE LANGUAGE INSTRUCTION

There is little doubt that managing whole language instruction was a major issue facing whole language teachers in our study. One of the reasons why teachers find it challenging is because whole language is an instructional philosophy that does not come bundled with a set of packaged materials, teacher manuals, and student workbooks. There are many routines and activities typically associated with whole language instruction (e.g., Big Books, chanting, independent reading time, reading and writing conferences, project work), but teachers are generally left on their own to figure out how to implement these activities and what they are expected to accomplish through them. Many of the teachers seemed to be still working through this issue of translating philosophy into practice:

> People are throwing out traditional materials without knowing what to do to replace them. Whole language is starting to be thrown at everyone. People are lost because they don't have the background of people like [John] Dewey and [Frank] Smith. (Remedial Reading Teacher, Primary Grades)
>
> Because whole language is not a formula for teaching, you tend to get in the middle of a project, and you don't know exactly where to go with it. . . . You don't have that book to open up like a recipe for teaching, which we would all love to fall back on in the way we were taught as students . . . and trained as teachers. We may resort to (teacher-dominated methods) again, but then you feel bad the next day . . . so you just take two aspirin and try it again! (Grade 6)

A second issue faced by these whole language teachers stems directly from the philosophy that a whole language curriculum should be child-centered, not teacher-dominated. Many teachers have struggled (and still are struggling) with this concept, and the consequences of adopting it (e.g., increased noise and movement, changes in classroom behavior):

> I had a hard time letting go and not being in charge . . . because I wanted to be the dictator of

the class. . . . I didn't want to trust the children's decisions. . . . I even need to let go a little more. . . . (Grade 4)

The teachers have to learn how to handle the freedom, and the kids have to learn how to handle the freedom. (Grade 1)

That whole concept of inquiry is an important part [of whole language]. . . . Now I find as a teacher that I have a lot more questions than I have answers. I had to get to a point where I realized that it was OK. . . . That's really where I wanted to be. I kept thinking that I had to be the old model of a teacher where I knew all the answers. It changes the teacher's role entirely. (Grade 1)

Well, this may sound a little crazy, but I still have a traditional frame of mind in a whole language classroom. . . . I miss having a neat room . . . everything gets so messy. . . . Also, the room gets so noisy, and I can't seem to quiet the kids down. It's so unsettling. (Grade 2)

When you're doing traditional things like workbook pages all together, you can take comfort in the fact that everybody is doing the same thing at the same time. You know that kids aren't wasting time, and if anybody walks into your classroom, everyone is busy at work. . . . It's scary to some people letting the control go to the kids. . . . What if they all sit around wasting time? (Grade 4)

A third issue concerns the day-to-day business of planning, organizing, and running a whole language classroom. Teachers found it difficult to find (and fund) appropriate materials and supplies; to plan for and schedule the day's activities; and to set up the physical layout of the classroom, to allow for reading and writing areas:

You just can't give kids dittos for busy work while you sit with reading groups. . . . So much planning has to take place now. (Grade 1)

You can't plan a week ahead because you don't know how the kids are going to react. . . . You may plan something and have it bomb. Then you have to stop and take the direction where the kids want the lesson to go. (Grade 5)

Another problem is gathering the supplies. I have found this to be very difficult . . . just getting them and the money involved . . . and the time to go get the materials and the time to research . . . and even knowing what to get for all of the projects. (Grade 1)

Room management and time are my biggest things. I just don't know how I can possibly keep all 25 of my kindergartners writing at the same time—I'm afraid I'll wear myself out. (Kindergarten)

Finally, teachers face the challenge of covering aspects of the traditional curriculum that either they or their school insist be taught (e.g., phonics, spelling and grammar rules, isolated reading skills such as "main idea" and "sequencing" and vocabulary lists) or skills they think students need to have mastered before they go to the next grade:

"I've always worried about what my kids are learning. . . . Their test scores aren't tons better or anything . . . but I'm scared about when they go on. . . . At least I can say that they've learned to be writers and readers. (Grade 2)

We have a generalized vocabulary list for schoolwide assessment. You hate to have those things . . . but you must meet people halfway. . . . (Grade 4)

When you are into whole language and you're getting away from the textbook idea, all of a sudden you reach a point in the calendar year when you say: Oh, my God, the tests are coming up. What am I going to do? I want my kids to be prepared for the test. Then a good part of my teaching ceases, and I begin to get the kids ready for the tests. (Grade 3)

I did something that was kind of taking half a step backward. . . . I found that my kids did poorly in some of the end-of-year skills tests last year, so I'm having this year's kids work in a language arts workbook . . . for only about 15 minutes per week. . . . Then at least I can say, Here it is. It was done. (Grade 6)

A common thread running through the teachers' statements about managing their whole language programs is their need for more knowledge about how to implement a whole language philosophy, either on its own or in concert with existing literacy instruction. One of the problems teachers face is that instead of having instructional materials do the bulk of the teaching, a whole language approach places the burden of teaching on the teacher's shoulders—the program comes from her head rather than from the materials. Given the full range of language arts activities, this is an enormous task; and it clearly daunts even the experienced whole language teachers. But teachers face other challenges in translating whole language philosophy to practice. Letting go some or all of the traditional teacher's control of the classroom's activities and behaviors does not come easily to teachers, even if they subscribe to a child-centered philosophy. And the consequences of liberating oneself from traditional practice are often not easy to accept. Many of the teachers are finding it hard to adjust to a changed classroom environment, even though few of them have serious doubts about the instructional philosophy they have newly embraced. The rewards apparently outweigh the frustrations.

ADMINISTRATORS SEND MIXED MESSAGES ABOUT WHOLE LANGUAGE

If whole language teachers have concerns about how their programs are viewed by their colleagues, they also worry about the mixed messages being sent to them from some of their administrators. These mixed messages take a variety of forms. In some cases, administrators insist that teachers use both whole language and approaches that are philosophically incompatible with whole language:

> I was supposed to teach Distar and process writing. I had to. I was told to use the same program as the other first-grade teachers because this is what the parents expected.... It was really hard. ... It happened for 2 years.... So I taught Distar—the whole thing—in 4 weeks. (Grade 1)

> In our district what is difficult is that we are getting mixed messages.... They asked me to do a whole language workshop for the teachers, but they won't let go of Madeline Hunter. (Grade 4)

> I was teaching in a Madeline Hunter stronghold where everyone had to be put through the course.... I'm not a political pioneer.... I tried to do whole language, but the principal came in with his Madeline Hunter checklist to evaluate me. (Grade 4)

In other cases, administrators supported whole language in principle but did not follow through when came time to fund or support the program:

> Don't worry, there'll be plenty of money ... but $50,000 was spent on basals, and there was only $10,000 left for our district to get the children's literature. Here they spent $50,000 for basals, and they want me to do a whole language workshop in the fall. I don't understand where they are coming from. (Grade 2)

> We got a lot of support from our principal. He had enough confidence in us as teachers, and he said: "In September, you can leave the basal and use the money that is normally spent on workbooks to buy your tradebooks...." That's how we got started. A stumbling block was that our reading coordinator left, and someone new came. He didn't really want the two of us to be doing something different from the rest of the staff. We were told to go back to the basal and told that we could do whole language as something "extra." This daunted our enthusiasm because we had to do two reading programs at one time. (Grade 2)

Finally, some teachers were concerned that their administrators simply did not understand what they were doing:

> The publishers are trying to push whole language basals.... Every time I opened my mouth when I was on the language arts committee, my administrator would give me this "Oh no, here she goes again" look. (Grade 4)

> I'm supposed to be testing kids on things I'm not teaching, and this seems to fly over my administrator's head. (Grade 2)

The mixed messages that our teachers reported receiving from their administrators may seem to them to be indicators of an inconsistent policy on curriculum reform, but perhaps we should not be surprised that a movement which advocates teacher and student empowerment is eventually bound to clash with the traditional "top–down" model of elementary school administration. Administrators often support the introduction of whole language simply as a set of new teaching techniques, unaware of the fundamental challenges that whole language poses to traditional ways of teaching, assessing, and organizing language arts. In many ways, the administrators face the same uncertainties about whole language as teachers do, and their "mixed messages" convey the same underlying uncertainties as those expressed by the teachers. Just as whole language teachers face the challenge of traditional colleagues, administrators—even if they wholeheartedly support whole language—face the pressures and challenge of traditional assessment and accountability mandated by the district or the state. As Glickman (1989) points out, administrators are caught between telling teachers to comply with district and state requirements and insisting that they do what they think is professionally appropriate for their students.

WHOLE LANGUAGE IS NOT COMPATIBLE WITH TRADITIONAL FORMS OF ASSESSMENT

Teachers were almost unanimous in their criticism of traditional standardized measures of reading and writing, mostly because of the mismatch between what's covered in the tests and what's valued in the classroom:

> What's horrible is to watch your kids taking all of these standardized tests, using this wonderful logic and getting the answers wrong.... (Grade 2)
> I feel frustrated having to give the dumb end-of-the-year tests that really emphasize phonics. ... Our end-of-the-book tests have 100 phonics questions and only 8 on comprehension. Reading is for meaning, and it's a shame that somehow our district can't establish another way of testing.... (Grade 2)
> Every year I sweat through those standardized tests.... I don't value them, but I know that a lot of other people do.... I don't want someone coming to my classroom saying, "You can't teach this way" based on a lousy test score; so I just hope that my kids are going to do O.K. (Grade 3)

What we did not hear from these teachers was what they considered to be valid alternatives to traditional forms of assessment. Indeed, several teachers admitted to having difficulty assessing their students' growth in a whole language environment:

> I know that my students are learning, but I'm not always comfortable with the terms that I'm using to define their growth. (Grade 2)
> In the Teacher's Manual it says that if you teach all of these skills, then you will have done a good job teaching sixth-grade English ... but then (after I adopted a whole language approach), I had to determine where I wanted my kids to be at the end of the year; and that was a responsibility that I never had to handle before. It was scary, and it still is. (Grade 4)

We were struck by how uncomfortable these teachers were, talking about assessment in their whole language classrooms. While they forcefully opposed traditional measures, they seemed equally frustrated by alternative assessment techniques and were not straining at the leash to tell us about new and exciting approaches they use. We sensed an air of resignation in teachers' comments about traditional assessments—they didn't like them, yet hoped their students would do well on them; and they tolerated their use as measures of their students' growth. In contrast to their exuberance about their teaching techniques, the teachers had very little to say about how they thought children's progress should be measured in a whole language program. Given the rash of recent literature on alternative techniques for assessment (Brown & Cambourne, 1987; Clay, 1985; Johnston, 1992; Tierney, Carter, & Desai, 1991), we might have expected the experienced teachers in our sample to be using some of these in their classrooms and enthusiastically endorsing them. It would seem that the teachers we interviewed are far less comfortable with these assessment techniques than those who are promoting them.

WHOLE LANGUAGE IS HARD TO DEFINE

We asked teachers to tell us about what counted as whole language instruction (and what didn't), and their responses reveal just how difficult it is to define the term whole language. Teachers talked about whole language in terms of attributes or features present in their classrooms, such as its having "an abundance of books"; "lots of print"; "children making choices about what they read and write"; "children having freedom to move about the room"; "the room looking colorful, inviting, and comfortable"; "tolerating a mess"; "using literature throughout the curriculum"; and "teaching on the rug." Process reading and process writing, invented(ive) spelling, lack of worksheets, independent reading of self-selected books, shared reading of Big Books, cooperative learning, and making school enjoyable and interesting seemed to these teachers essential characteristics of a whole language classroom. Teachers focused on the practical, daily routines of whole language. What we heard was a potpourri of ideas about the classroom, not a set of instructional activities derived from a coherent pedagogy, although, as Hargreaves (1989) points out, teachers rarely articulate underlying teaching philosophies. We were unsure whether teachers had simply picked up a set of new teaching methods but were unable to articulate how these methods

fit an instructional philosophy, or whether they had a sense of the philosophy but were still working through its practical application. In either case, we had the feeling that most of the teachers were still grappling with a concept that they did not fully understand (they seemed more certain about why traditional methods were not appropriate than why whole language was); and yet they enthusiastically embraced many of its practices (e.g., letting children decide, using literature throughout the curriculum). Certainly, many of the teachers' responses revealed a belief in the existence of a "true" whole language approach, even if they themselves hadn't yet found it:

> Right now I wonder if I am truly a whole language teacher because even though I do a lot of reading and writing, and I do a lot of projects, I still sometimes use textbooks in science and social studies. (Grade 5)

We also learned that these teachers were not "purist" whole language teachers, in the sense that they religiously eschew the basal; textbooks for science and social studies; direct instruction of skills; workbooks; and formal, standardized testing. To one degree or another, most of the teachers compromise, either tacking on whole language activities to an existing traditional program or supplementing their whole language program with traditional materials. And yet, most of these teachers still regard themselves as whole language teachers.

> Some teachers say they are whole language teachers, but they still pull out their basals. . . . (Grade 2)
>
> I still use a basal, so if you talk to the whole language people, they would not accept me even though I supplement my basals tremendously with the morning newspaper, literature, and response logs. (Grade 3)

The difficulty these teachers have defining whole language parallels the debate in the professional literature, in which whole language is variously defined as "a set of beliefs about language development, language learning, and language instruction" (Altwerger, Edelsky, & Flores, 1987); a set of "conditions" for "natural learning" (Cambourne, 1988); and an educational movement that stands *for* some things (e.g., authentic reading and writing) and *against* others (e.g., basal readers, skills in isolation). We should not be surprised that teachers have difficulty defining the concept when so many different instructional practices are covered by the whole language umbrella. Further, there are many theoretical, philosophical, and practical issues surrounding whole language that have yet to be resolved (McCaslin, 1989; Watson, 1989; Willinsky, 1990).

WHOLE LANGUAGE WILL SURVIVE, BUT AMONG THE DEDICATED FEW

Finally, we asked teachers to look ahead and forecast what they saw as the future of the whole language movement. Paradoxically, their responses reflect both pessimism and optimism for the future of whole language. They are pessimistic about the extent to which whole language will gain widespread acceptance in schools, but they are personally optimistic about their own development as whole language teachers.

Their pessimism focuses on a number of factors that inhibit the growth of whole language, including: the validity of teachers having different (even traditional) ideas about how to teach; lack of collegial, parental, district, even state support for whole language; the widespread misconceptions about whole language held even by teachers professing to practice it; the draining, time-consuming nature of preparing and managing a whole language program; the reluctance of schools to make systemic changes in their programs; the inability of whole language to guarantee satisfactory results in traditional assessments (or at least the perception that it cannot guarantee results); and finally, the threat posed by a conservative and traditional view of schooling that singles out whole language as one more reason to "get back to basics."

Their optimism focuses on the profound changes these teachers have made in their own teaching philosophy and practice, changes which they regard as irreversible, despite the hard work and the ever-present controversy that surrounds them. This optimism extends to the movement as a whole but acknowledges that whole language will always be the philosophy of a dedicated few, rather than the orthodoxy of a entire school, district, or state. In other words, whole language will survive, but it will not dominate American public education.

I think that it's easy for the people involved in whole language to get so caught up in it that they don't see the bigger picture. A lot of people think that it's the answer to everyone's prayers ... but I see a lot of people that aren't comfortable with it because they are not well read. I don't think that the majority of teachers will ever be confident enough to be whole language teachers because of the way we have all been taught. We've been taught to follow manuals. (Grade 4)

Whole language really hasn't had a bigger impact than some earlier philosophies such as the Language Experience Approach; it has just had more exposure. (Grade 2)

Because your goals are very different from the traditional classrooms, people like guidance counselors, building principals, and parents, and even the kids in your classroom begin to ask some real serious questions about why things are so different. We need to be able to articulate this.... I think whole language is going to be coming head-to-head with very traditional values about education. It's going to be scary. (Grade 2)

Yes, I do think whole language will survive because those of us who are doing it won't let it go. (Grade 1)

CONCLUSION

In this paper, we have tried to articulate some of the realities of becoming and sustaining oneself as a teacher with a whole language philosophy. From lengthy interviews with about 70 practicing whole language teachers drawn from a variety of school settings, grade levels, and teaching experience, we have uncovered a number of issues that whole language teachers rarely articulate but are deeply concerned about. These issues send some important messages to educators who are thinking about whole language as a viable option for reform.

One message is that whole language is not for everyone and is inappropriate for teachers who do not hold its basic instructional philosophy or have the mindset needed to run a child-centered classroom. Adopting a whole language approach involves making fundamental changes in the way teachers view children and themselves, and many teachers simply are unable or unwilling to contemplate these changes, especially without support. Another is that it may demand more of them than they are willing or able to give: It is clear from these interviews that preparing for and running a whole language classroom consumes enormous amounts of time and energy. Whole language teachers insist that it is worth the expenditure of effort and time, but they think that newcomers should not underestimate what is involved. Newcomers should also be prepared for unanticipated consequences beyond their classroom. As has been pointed out by Goodman (1988), the politics of whole language is as difficult as its practice and involves a number of issues such as being resented by traditional teachers, questioned by parents and administrators, and worrying about whether the students will do well on traditional tests or how successful students will be in the next grade. Whole language teachers will almost certainly be in a "glass bubble" (as one teacher described it), under the constant scrutiny of colleagues, parents, and administrators; they need to have confidence in their own abilities to handle these pressures. They can also expect, if our respondents' experiences are typical, occasionally to have feelings of self-doubt ("Am I really doing the right thing?") that will make them wonder if it was all worth the effort, prompting them, if only momentarily, to consider a retreat.

Another message is that educational change is a long, drawn-out process, and given the challenge of whole language to the "existing regularities" of the elementary language arts curriculum (Sarason, 1982), whole language reform will take a very long time. It is clear from accounts of teachers and programs in transition (e.g., Routman, 1991; Walmsley & Walp, 1990) that it takes not only time but also intensive support to bring about these changes. We wondered, from these interviews, whether teachers or administrators had sufficient staying power to build their whole language reforms into the school's infrastructure, not just tack them on as innovations. Also, administrators and staff need to work through the conflicts between whole language instruction and traditional assessment so that instruction and assessment are philosophically congruent, and between whole language teachers and traditional teachers in such a way that neither are devalued, ostracized, or resented. Despite its commitment to the notion of empowerment, the whole language reform movement is not particularly mindful of the importance of taking into account the legitimately different needs, expectations, philosophies, and teaching approaches of the various stakeholders in education (i.e., teachers, administrators, parents, communities); but neither are its opponents. A particularly troublesome issue is that the general thrust of federal and state reforms is in the direction of mastery of externally defined subject matter (e.g., "U.S. students will be first in the world in science and mathematics") and a focus on results as opposed to process—all of which seem to be reaffirming traditional goals (e.g., mastery of "readiness skills" before formal schooling, competency in subject areas) and traditional methods to attain them (e.g., direct teaching of a fixed rather than developmental curriculum). Despite the magnitude of the challenges facing whole language, we are encouraged by the perseverance and optimism of the teachers we interviewed. We are concerned, however, that if the issues they raise—uncomfortable as they may be to whole language advocates—are ignored, progress toward whole language may well be at risk. A better understanding of the concerns of practitioners as they make their transition to whole language will surely help ease the transition and ultimately strengthen the whole language movement.

REFERENCES

Altwerger, B., Edelsky, C., & Flores, B. M. (1987). Whole language: What's new? *Reading Teacher, 41*, 144–154.

Brown, H., & Cambourne, B. (1987). *Read and retell.* North Ryde, NSW (Australia): Methuen.

Cambourne, B. (1988). *The whole story: Natural learning and the acquisition of literacy in the classroom.* New York: Scholastic.

Clay, M. M. (1985). *The early detection of reading difficulties: A diagnostic survey with recovering procedures.* Exeter, NH: Heinemann.

Glickman, C. D. (1989). Has Sam and Samantha's time come at last? *Educational Leadership, 47,* 4–9.

Goodman, K. (1988). Do teachers have to suffer to become whole language teachers? Unpublished manuscript, University of Arizona, Tucson.

Hargreaves, A. (1989). *Curriculum and assessment reform.* Bristol, U.K.: Open University Press.

Johnston, P. (1992). *Constructive evaluation of literate activity.* New York: Longman.

Manning, G., Manning, M., & Long, R. (1989). In the process of becoming process teachers. In G. Manning & M. Manning (Eds.), *Whole language: Beliefs and practices, K–8* (pp. 235–240). New York: National Education Association.

McCaslin, M. M. (1989). Whole language: Theory, instruction, and future implementation. *Elementary School Journal, 90,* 223–229.

Routman, R. (1991). *Invitations.* Portsmouth, NH: Heinemann Educational Books.

Sarason, S. B. (1982). *The culture of the school and problem of change.* Boston, MA: Allyn and Bacon.

Tierney, R. J., Carter, M. A., & Desai, L. E. (1991). *Portfolio assessment in the reading–writing classroom.* Norwood, MA: Christopher Gordon Publishers.

Walmsley, S. A., & Walp, T. P. (1990). Integrating literature and composing into the language arts curriculum: Philosophy and practice. *Elementary School Journal, 90,* 251–274.

Watson, D. (1989). Defining and describing whole language. *Elementary School Journal, 90,* 129–141.

Willinsky, J. (1990). *The new literacy: Redefining reading and writing in the schools.* New York: Routledge.

Sean Walmsley is an associate professor in the Department of Reading, State University of New York at Albany. Ellen Adams is currently on leave from her second-grade teaching position in Mechanicville, New York, and is pursuing doctoral studies in the Department of Reading at SUNY Albany.

Talking and Writing: Explaining the Whole Language Approach to Parents

Marjorie V. Fields

Teachers using whole language and writing project approaches to reading and writing instruction may be confronted with parents who are uncomfortable with these ideas. How can teachers of young children guide parents to accept the natural approach to literacy which current research supports (Farr, 1985)? How can we reassure parents that our literate society fosters literacy just as our verbal society fosters speech (Goodman, 1985)? How can we help parents realize that their children will become literate at their own uniquely appropriate rate just as they walked and talked on their own schedule?

Oral language/written language comparison studies tell us that reading and writing abilities develop similarly to listening and speaking abilities (Nelson, 1981; Snow, 1983), but this research is fairly abstract. In an attempt to more fully understand the commonalities of oral language and written language development, I created a chart comparing stages of writing with stages of talking (see Table 1). I have found that this chart is useful in helping parents understand the process of their child's emerging literacy. It documents the observable, the form of output, in the two language modes.

If teachers also maintain cumulative files of each child's writing during a school year, they will provide tangible evidence of the child's growth and will make this comparison chart personally relevant for parents. Maximum benefit can be obtained from this approach only if teachers ensure parents' understanding that reading and writing develop together and are interdependent (Sulzby and Teale, 1985; Dyson, 1982).

Parents know from their own recent experience that children go through these stages of oral language development. They have observed the natural progression from babbling to understandable speech; furthermore, they saw it happen without drill or other directed instruction. When parents understand how written language development is comparable

TABLE 1
COMPARABLE ORAL AND WRITTEN STAGES IN LANGUAGE DEVELOPMENT

Oral Language Stages	Written Language Stages	Level of Understanding
Babbling and cooing	Scribbling	Exploration of medium
Language intonation	Linear/repetitive drawing	Refining the form
Native language sounds	Letterlike forms	Cultural relevance
Words	Letters and early word–symbol relationships	Conventions of language
Creative grammar	Invented spelling	Overgeneralization of "rule" hypotheses
Adult speech	Standard spelling	Formal structure

From "Talking and Writing: Explaining the Whole Language Approach to Parents" by M. V. Fields, 1988, *The Reading Teacher, 41*, pp. 898–903. Copyright © 1988 by the International Reading Association. Reprinted with permission of Marjorie V. Fields and the International Reading Association.

to oral language development, they can more readily accept written language instruction which uses the same types of teaching that facilitated oral language development.

EXPLORING THE MEDIUM

The chart can stimulate parents' memories of the random babbling and cooing of their child's earliest verbalizations. Parents also will be familiar with the random marks on paper which youngsters sometimes label "writing" (see Figure 1).

Early childhood teachers can assist parents in viewing both babbling and scribbling as equally important first explorations of a language medium. Both show youngsters' interest in the language around them and their eagerness to participate in it. Both babbling and scribbling deserve similar kinds of encouragement—the kind that comes so naturally to parents responding to a cooing baby. The proven effectiveness of spontaneous adult assistance in children's oral language learning (deVilliers and deVilliers, 1979) can be transferred to written language learning.

**FIGURE 1
SCRIBBLE STAGE**

REFINING THE FORM

Parents will also readily remember when their baby began to string sounds together with the rising and falling intonations of adult language. They probably listened intently, trying to hear what these "sentences" were saying, only gradually realizing that there were no recognizable words in these sophisticated sounding utterances.

Samples of children's writing from the linear/repetitive stage will assist parents in understanding the similarity between this stage of writing and the language intonation stage of talking (see Figure 2). In each case, the child is demonstrating knowledge of the broad characteristics of the language medium: how it generally looks or sounds. In each case, essential concepts are being formed as a result of the child's self imposed practice.

CULTURAL RELEVANCE

Listening to infants tells us that babbling gradually limits itself to the sounds of the language the child hears. Parents have seen babies succeed at the incredibly complicated process of sorting out the significant differences between accidental clicks and grunts and purposeful variations of timing in voiced and unvoiced sounds. Babies do this through exposure to language as people talk to them, and through practice as they play with oral language and attempt to use it purposefully.

As teachers show parents samples of young children's writing with letterlike forms, parents can be led to see how this too represents a gradual sorting out of the various shapes which we use as a code to represent our language. Again, children must sort out the significant from the insignificant differences: a curl on the top of the *t* makes it an *f* and yet either a curl or a straight line on the *a* still makes an *a*.

This comparison reassures parents of their child's competency in the task of mastering

FIGURE 2
LINEAR/REPETITIVE STAGE

written language and frees parents to allow children the necessary time to explore for understanding (see Figure 3).

CONVENTIONS OF LANGUAGE

All parents remember the excitement of their child's first word. They eagerly accepted whatever variations and simplifications their youngster used in the treasured first words. They learned to understand the many sound substitutions and omissions of this early speech so that they could respond appropriately to it. They accepted "ba" for "ball" and "guck" for "truck" without even knowing the reasons for these common patterns. Parents don't criticize or correct imprecise beginning speech; they offer praise and encouragement.

Comparison between first words and first writing with actual letters reveals remarkable similarities. As children begin to note and attempt to replicate sound–symbol relationships in writing, they simplify and omit letters in much the same way they did in early spoken words. Thus, whole words are often written with just one letter and all letters are assumed to have the sound of the letter name. This knowledge enables us to read and value writing such as that in Figure 4 on page 350.

OVERGENERALIZATIONS

Much of the charm of young children's language is a result of their unique grammatical constructions such as "I wented to the store" or "My feets are cold." Parents can remember similar examples from their own children's

FIGURE 3
LETTERLIKE FORMS

FIGURE 4
BEGINNING INVENTED SPELLING

speech and can be sure those language patterns were not learned from adults. They can be helped to understand that such sentences are a result of their child's efforts to make sense of language rules.

The errors made represent overgeneralizations of common usage patterns; it is logical that a child learning English would assume all past tense verbs end in *ed* and that all plurals are formed with an *s*. These errors are a demonstration of the child's method of building understanding.

When the teacher shows parents examples of children's invented spelling and explains the overgeneralizations of phonics rules, parents can come to understand the role of invented spelling in their child's understanding of phonics principles (see Example). When parents realize that the grammatical overgeneralizations disappear with continued practice and exposure to standard speech, they can be convinced that invented spelling will give way to standard spelling in the same manner.

Advanced invented spelling

my brthda i wonend to go to mecdonod.s my mommy sid no i crid meme ters rold doun my chec i got vare mad at my mommy i sed to my mommy poo poo i went en to my wom and crid wun ter rold daon my hec my mommy cam en my rom and sed to me you can go to mecdonalld.
the end by ashley capps
4 22

Parents who respond uncritically to the communication intent of children's incorrect oral language can become equally supportive of children's incorrect written language efforts.

PARENTS BECOME ALLIES

When teachers are successful in explaining the common patterns in the form of children's oral and written language production, they can make parents their allies in supporting children's natural striving to become literate. Parents' confidence in their child's own drive to crack the code of written language will free them from the anxiety that can hamper their effectiveness in helping their youngsters. Parents' understanding of how children construct their knowledge of language from their experiences with it will guide them in creating the print-rich home environments which foster growth in literacy.

Teachers can help parents realize they are teaching reading and writing when they read and write for their own purposes, when they read to their children, when they encourage children's free exploration of print, when they write to children, and when they write children's words for them. These informed parents will be able to teach children to read as well as they taught them to talk.

REFERENCES

deVilliers, Peter A., and Jill G. deVilliers. *Early Language.* Cambridge, MA: Harvard University Press, 1979.

Dyson, Anne Haas. "Reading, Writing and Language: Young Children Solving the Written Language Puzzle." *Language Arts,* vol. 59 (November/December 1982), pp. 829–39.

Farr, Marcia, ed. *Advances in Writing Research, Volume One: Children's Early Writing Development.* Norwood, NJ: Ablex, 1985.

Goodman, Yetta M. "Developing Writing in a Literate Society." *Educational Horizons,* vol. 64 (January 1985), pp. 17–21.

Nelson, K. "Individual Differences in Language Development: Implications for Development and Language." *Developmental Psychology,* vol. 17 (March 1981), pp. 170–87.

Snow, Catherine E. "Literacy and Language: Relationships during the Preschool Years." *Harvard Education Review,* vol. 53 (May 1993), pp. 165–89.

Sulzby, Elizabeth, and William H. Teale. "Writing Development in Early Childhood." *Educational Horizons,* vol. 64 (May 1985), pp. 8–12.

Marjorie V. Fields is Professor of Education at the University of Alaska Southeast in Juneau.

Parent Communication in a Whole Language Kindergarten: What We Learned from a Busy First Year

Beverly Bruneau
Timothy Rasinski
Martha Shehan

Among recent developments in literacy research and practice is the increased recognition of the critical roles that parents play in the education of their children (Rasinski and Fredericks, 1989). For example, in her review of research on parental involvement in educational programs and student achievement, Henderson (1988) found that parents have a highly positive impact on the achievement of their children and that "involving parents when their children are young has beneficial effects that persist throughout the child's academic career" (p. 15). Durkin's (1966) seminal work on early literacy learning found that parents played the key role in the literacy development of children who learned to read prior to formal school-based instruction. In a more recent study, Taylor and Dorsey-Gaines (1988) described the rich literate home environments which initiated and supported the successful

From "Parent Communication in a Whole Language Kindergarten: What We Learned from a Busy First Year" by B. Bruneau, T. Rasinski, and M. Shehan, 1991, *Reading Horizons, 32,* pp. 117–127. Copyright © 1991 by Western Michigan University. Reprinted by permission.

early literacy development of inner city children whose SES environments would not predict great achievement in reading. Clearly, parents do play one of the most important roles in the development of their children as young readers.

Involving parents in their child's literacy learning is particularly important for kindergarten teachers. The kindergarten literacy curriculum should build upon what children have begun to learn at home, and, continue to involve parents in supporting their child's literacy development. Communicating with parents on how they can continue to give active support to their children's literacy learning is an important task for kindergarten teachers.

Although teachers may be eager to inform parents about their whole language literacy program, communicating with parents about how children develop literacy may be difficult. This difficulty may occur because a whole language approach may bear little resemblance to traditional readiness programs which the parents or their older children have received in school. In an interview study to determine parents' perceptions of how reading and writing develop in kindergarten children Bruneau, Rasinski, and Ambrose (1990) found that many parents believed that reading develops through check-point, systematic skills-based instruction; e.g., learning letter names and sounds and practicing the reading of simple words in isolation. Although the interviewed parents were pleased with their children's excitement and the enthusiasm for books which was emphasized in their child's whole language kindergarten, they also expressed concern for what they perceived as a lack of attention to necessary systematic skill development. Thus potential exists for miscommunication, because parents expectations may not match the description of a whole language program provided by the kindergarten teacher.

A parent education program concerning whole language instruction appears to be necessary to inform parents about recent research on early literacy development and how this is translated to sound classroom practice and also to advise them about ways they can continue to be actively involved in their child's literacy learning. Following is a description of what we learned when a classroom teacher not only initiated a whole language program, but also attempted to inform parents about the program.

PARENT COMMUNICATION IN ONE CLASSROOM

A newly hired kindergarten teacher in a university-based child development center planned and initiated a whole language literacy program, a significant change from the skills-based program which had previously been in place. Twenty-five children were enrolled in the kindergarten classroom. The children were primarily of middle SES families, families highly concerned about their children's early success in reading development. Although initially the kindergarten teacher's attention and energy were channeled into building her new program and getting to know her students, she also realized she would have to explain this new program fully to the parents. She decided to begin this communication through the traditional parent orientation session held in early October.

Parent Orientation Meeting

At this meeting the teacher focused almost entirely on the new literacy curriculum. She emphasized three important components of her reading program: surrounding the children with a print-rich environment, using children's literature and experience stories as a means of involving children in reading meaningful text, and facilitating children's writing development through engaging children in invented spelling. She explained that children learn to read and write when they are placed in environments that encourage them to experiment with literacy and where they can use their literacy abilities in functional tasks such as writing notes to and reading notes from others, creating and listening to stories, using recipes, and charting results from science experiments. She illustrated her talk with examples of experience charts already constructed with the children, described and displayed her well-stocked and attractive library corner, and talked about children's work in the writing center. Although the teacher had expected "hard questions" from the parents, there were none. Individual parents talked with the teacher about their child's enthusiasm for kindergarten. The teacher felt the evening had been successful because she had communicated the important goals for her program and the parents' responses to the program had not reflected concern or criticism.

With the parent orientation completed, the teacher again focused primarily on the children and their learning. Literacy experiences were subsumed within content areas. For example, the children predicted and charted results of science experiments such as listing objects which would sink or float. They prepared for a Thanksgiving feast by listing individual job responsibilities, things to remember to do, and recipes for their food preparation. Favorite songs and fingerplays were written into a class music book. Each week a different author was highlighted. Soon the children began to bring in library books from home written by favorite authors. The classroom teacher wrote regularly to parents describing these activities. However, as she wrote, she focused on content, the science or social studies unit, rather than on the development of reading ability. This seemed congruent with basing literacy activities in a functional print-rich environment.

Parent Conferences

The second major opportunity for the teacher to talk with parents about literacy occurred through individual conferences held at the close of the first semester in December. The teacher had developed individual portfolios of each child's writing. These portfolios were shared with the parents and became a basis for talking about the development of invented spelling. The teacher was able to show parents where children had attempted to spell words on their own and to suggest encouragement for such risk taking.

During these conferences, some parents expressed their concerns. For example, one mother reported that her child who had been a "writing maniac" was becoming frustrated. She reported her daughter would say, "I don't like writing because the teacher won't tell me how to spell the words." The mother then described how at home the child had been told how to spell words correctly. The child was getting mixed messages from home and school. As part of the conference the teacher was able to help clarify how both home and school could work together. The parents could help the child begin to listen for sounds and the teacher could work on developing the child's confidence. The mother reported that as a result of the conference her daughter became less frustrated and more enthusiastic toward early writing.

The teacher reported answering many specific questions within these individual conferences. As the school year progressed, more parents appeared concerned about literacy instruction and would often "drop in for an informal chat." After such a conference one mother suggested to the teacher that it would be helpful to have specific information on literacy development written in a letter. The teacher decided this would be a good idea. In this way she could reach all of the parents, explain her approach to literacy instruction and address concerns that many parents seemed to share.

The Literacy Letter

In early spring the teacher wrote a letter to the parents in which she described how she read stories to the children, encouraged children to read on their own, facilitated their use of invented spelling, and offered suggestions for extending literacy activities at home. The teacher was pleased with the letter because she was able to articulate her belief that there was no one correct way to help a child, but that a number of strategies could be used depending on the child and the situation. (A copy of this letter is included in Appendix A.)

Several parents reported they found the letter helpful in not only understanding literacy instruction at school, but in also supporting their child's enthusiasm and growth for literacy at home. They mentioned that the letter allayed many of their concerns and they appreciated the permanent nature of the letter. They could refer back to the letter when a question about instruction in literacy arose. A few parents commented that they wished they had the information earlier in the year and suggested that the letter could have been presented in shorter segments throughout the year. Some parents mentioned that the length of the letter did not make it conducive to a thorough reading.

The First Year's Experience: What We Learned

This paper describes one kindergarten teacher's attempt to establish communication with parents during a very busy year in which she was very much engrossed in developing a whole language curriculum. For the most part, the teacher's initiative was successful.

Initially the teacher had hoped that the orientation session combined with parent–teacher conferences would suffice to inform parents and gain their involvement. However, we learned these limited and verbal communications were not enough. Although parents appeared to have accepted the initial message, as time passed other questions and concerns were raised. The teacher wisely responded to the parents' concerns and followed one parent's suggestion to give the information in writing. The letter was received by the parents as valuable in content, but several stated the letter would have been more valuable earlier in the year. In retrospect, it seems that frequent communication, in which segments of the letter would be presented, would make the most sense. Using this format, the teacher would be able to communicate with parents about the kinds of strategies she was using with children in the classroom.

Parent communications need to be a continuous part of a holistic literacy curriculum. In the case described here, it took a follow-up letter in the spring to complete communication with the parents. An ideal situation, perhaps, would have been to send information contained within the letter at more frequent intervals in which the information could be presented in readable chunks that reinforce and build on one another. For example, one letter could deal with reading instruction and home extensions, a second with writing and others dealing with supporting invented spelling, and connecting the content areas with literacy. A final letter might focus on vacation literacy activities. Although the teacher did write monthly newsletters, these emphasized content activities. Highlighting how the children used reading and writing during these activities as well as perhaps including information on how the teacher was helping children engage in their own writing would be helpful. When parents are kept informed of what is happening in the classroom, they are more likely to identify with and support the teacher's/school's curriculum.

Not all parents read the written communications and not all parents attend conferences. The use of a variety of communication vehicles (e.g., group presentations, personal conferences, frequent newsletters, informal chats both in person and through the telephone) helps insure that parents are kept informed of classroom developments. Gaining parental involvement in ways that are congruent with the whole language curriculum can be achieved only through an aggressive approach to parental communication. We have learned the importance of maintaining a constant flow of communication to parents and providing variety in the media that are used to carry the communication.

REFERENCES

Bruneau, B., Rasinski, T., & Ambrose, R. (1990). Parents' perceptions of children's reading and writing development in a whole language kindergarten program. In S. McCormick & J. Zutell (Eds.), *Literacy theory and research: Analyses from multiple paradigms*. Thirty-ninth yearbook of the National Reading Conference, 209–16. Chicago IL: National Reading Conference.

Durkin, D. (1966). *Children who read early*. New York NY: Teachers' College Press.

Henderson, A. T. (1988). Parents are a school's best friends. *Phi Delta Kappan*, 148–53.

Rasinski, T., & Fredericks, A. D. (1989). Parents can make a difference. *The Reading Teacher, 41*, 508–12.

Taylor, D., & Dorsey-Gaines, C. (1988). *Growing up literate: Learning from inner city families*. Portsmouth NH: Heinemann.

APPENDIX A

Text of Teacher's Letter to Parents

Dear Parents,

Many of you have asked me to describe how I've been teaching and encouraging the children to read and write. The foundation of my literacy program was developed in the fall. The children were immersed in a print-rich environment from the first day of kindergarten. As we made group charts and stories, they began to understand that what they say can be written down and read back to them. From these charts and stories we discovered the many purposes of writing. Together we wrote not only stories, but letters and recipes; we put labels on objects all around the room; we wrote up our classroom rules and jobs; and we made many kinds of charts: lists of ways to describe our feelings, lists of words to describe foods that we used our senses to examine, lists of things we needed to do before parties and field trips, sequencing events from a story, steps of a science experiment, directions for a recipe, and making predictions and charting the results.

The children are continually allowed the opportunity to write for themselves. A variety of paper, markers, crayons and pencils are always made available to the children. Some of the writing they have done includes making up their own stories, writing notes and letters to me and to each other, making signs for the buildings and forts they create in the block corner, and in the dramatic play area writing checks and bills in their "office" and taking orders in their "restaurant."

The children enjoy keeping journals as their own personal books. Some like to try to write their own words for their pictures, and others prefer to ask me for help. Most children do a mixture of both. Either way is wonderful. They are interested in writing, seeing their words written down and hearing them read back to them. At least once a day we do a writing activity in their journals, on a chart, on the computer, or in a class group story.

Reading to the children is another important aspect of my program. There are two bookshelves in the kindergarten packed with all kinds of books: fairy tales, legends, myths, picture dictionaries, children's encyclopedias, poetry, fiction and non-fiction books and wordless picture books. I read quality literature to the children at least once a day. They often ask to have their favorites read over and over again. They like to read the books back to me from memory, or by looking at the pictures and making up their own words.

The shelves also contain "easy" readers, which are also available at the library! These are beginning "I Can Read" books with limited vocabulary, few words to a page and lots of repetition. The children have a lot of success with these books, especially if I read it once through first to them. They are so proud to be able to read a "real" book, as they see it.

During our morning center time, I am able to spend individual time with the children reading books together and writing in their journals. There are different approaches I use when reading depending on the child's needs and interests on that particular day.

- I read the whole story to the child without stopping
- I read a page, pointing to the words as they are read, and the child repeats the page after me
- I read most of the sentence, but stop and let the child read a word that I know he or she can read
- They'll read the whole story to me, only paying attention to the pictures and making up their own words
- They'll read the story to me, sometimes without any help at all

When they are reading to me and get stuck on a word, there are different things I may do:

- I wait a second to see what the child does
- If they are trying to sound it out, I may encourage it as long as they are not becoming frustrated
- I'll tell them to skip the word and read the rest of the sentence. Then they'll go back and figure out what word would make sense there
- They'll stop and look at the picture and try to find the word through what is happening on that page

Most times I will just tell them the words they don't know so as not to disrupt the continuity of reading and risk losing the meaning of what was already read. I don't believe that there is one right or wrong way to approach such a situation. What's most important, I feel, is to keep it positive! I want the children to think of reading as fun, not as a difficult chore.

When writing with the children I use a lot of the same approaches as described, but applied to pen and paper:

- I may write the whole story from dictation, writing down the child's exact words
- I may write most of it, but pass the pen over to the child to write a word or two that I know they can write
- Sometimes they want to write the whole thing and just have me there for support and encouragement

Even when I am doing all of the writing, I keep the children involved verbally. If they dictate to me, "Dear Mom," I may say something like, " 'Dear'—what do you think that begins with?" By using this strategy I am encouraging the children to think about sounds in words, and putting their knowledge of letters and sounds into actual use as children write their very own words.

The most exciting thing happening in the kindergarten right now is children reading to each other and helping each other read and write. They love bringing in books from home that they can read and being able to sit in front of the room and share that book with the whole class, or individually with a friend or with me.

Here are some ideas I have for you to continue working with your child at home and all summer long:

- Keep going to the library and allowing your child to browse and choose books.
- Show your child how to research topics in the library: if you're getting a new pet, look up information on how to take care of it; if you see a shooting star, read to find out more about them; if you are going on a trip, look in an Atlas to find out where the place is located.
- Put simple notes and pictures in your child's lunchbox or under their pillow. Writing notes on the bathroom mirror with lipstick is always fun!

- Read to your child daily (poetry, too!)
- Do simple follow-up activities together after you read a story. If it is a story about plants, visit a greenhouse or plant some seeds; if it is a story about airplanes, make a paper or model airplane, or go to the library and research about the first airplane; if it's about friends, write a letter to a friend.
- Set an example: have a family reading time every night when you read a good book, too.
- Be aware of print wherever you go. Discuss signs on buildings, along roads and in the supermarket. Talk about why those words are important and needed at the particular place.
- When they are reading to you, KEEP IT FUN! Give them the words that they don't know and praise them for the ones that they do know.
- Write stories together, taking turns making up the adventure that the character goes through.
- When reading, talk about the author, the illustrator, the dedication, the publisher, and the title page. Discuss the illustrations and find other books by the same illustrator to compare and find similarities in pictures and style.
- Make labels for things around the house.
- Write a story yourself and let your child be the illustrator, and you illustrate one of your child's stories.
- Tape record a story while riding in the car and transcribe it later to be illustrated.
- When taking dictation, keep them involved, writing a word or at least a beginning letter or two per page.
- Write for a variety of different purposes; write letters to friend and relatives, invitations to a party or sleep over.

This has been a wonderful year. The children have shown enthusiasm and an "I can do it" attitude toward reading and writing. Please let me know if you have any further questions.

Sincerely,
Martha Shehan

Beverly Bruneau is a faculty member in Early Childhood Education at Kent State University in Kent, Ohio. Timothy V. Rasinski is a faculty member in the Department of Elementary Education at Kent State University. Martha Shehan is a teacher with the McLean County Unit District #5 school system in Normal, Illinois.

Putting Children before Grown-Ups

Philip Vassallo

It's easy enough to identify the qualities that distinguish a good school: Teachers are professional and caring. The instructional program is demanding but appropriate to the age of the children. And, most important of all, students are learning.

But how many schools actually embody those qualities? And how can parents know if their child's school is one of them? As a parent, I've found that all too often, communication between the school and the home is insufficient. And that means even the best schools might go unappreciated.

One school where that doesn't happen is the Children's School, a pilot project at P.S. 257 in the South Bronx. In this New York City school, a unique program for kindergarten to third-grade students features "whole language" instruction (which incorporates reading, writing, speaking, and listening into classroom activities). This philosophy puts children first and provides an environment that gives children exciting and varied choices for learning. The school also makes sure parents understand the school's philosophy and operations.

The story of the Children's School—and what led me to discover it—might be instructive to board members and school administrators who are seeking not just to put children first but also to make sure parents know it.

IS THIS ALL THERE IS?

I first learned of the Children's School in 1986, soon after one of my daughters entered a kindergarten elsewhere. I was a concerned father who wanted to know everything about her schooling, but as the weeks went by, I grew disturbed by the lack of information I was receiving from the teacher.

Sure, I had the 10 minutes allotted me during the parent–teacher conference (which the teacher explained, without my asking, was required of her by the union contract). But beyond this meeting, at which little more than introductions could be exchanged, I was left in the dark about my daughter's education. No messages about the material being covered in lessons. No descriptions of how a typical school day was structured. No notes suggesting activities we could do at home to complement what was being done in the classroom.

The teacher was gracious enough to give me her home telephone number, but the first time I called, she said, "Your daughter didn't get into trouble. Don't worry, I'll call you if she causes any problems."

"Is this what I can expect from my daughter's teachers throughout her school years?" I wondered. "Is this typical of today's schools?"

To answer that question, I sought the counsel of an old mentor, Robert Delisle, professor of education at Lehman College in the Bronx. I hadn't seen Delisle for years. but I knew he served as professor-in-residence for a pilot project in New York City's Bronx School District 10. When I asked Delisle's advice, he said, "Meet me at the Children's School and see for yourself." And then he added cryptically, "It's a unique school: We're child-centered, not teacher-centered."

In his college lectures, I'd many times heard Delisle emphasize the importance of "putting children first," but I'd always cynically assumed he was out of touch with the realities of demanding class loads, difficult scheduling and discipline problems, and demoralizing budget constraints. Yet here he was talking of a school that *does* put children first. I decided to accept his invitation and see for myself.

A DIFFERENT KIND OF SCHOOL

District 10 is the most densely populated school district in New York City, serving 32,000 elementary and junior high school children in 32 schools. Most of the students are black and Hispanic, and most come from low-income families.

Many of the schools in District 10—as elsewhere in New York City—are multilevel brick structures dating to before World War II. From the outside, the Children's School looked no different. It was a grim, gray building surrounded by the ruins of the South Bronx—a landscape of abandoned tenements littered with household refuse and graffiti.

Inside, however, I discovered a clean and cheerful learning environment. I also discovered that the Children's School occupies only a small part of P.S. 257. Originally designed as an overflow facility for kindergartners only, the Children's School served kindergartners and first-graders at the time of my visit. (The school now enrolls 90 students in kindergarten through grade three.) The Children's School continues to serve an overflow function: Unlike many pilot projects, the school does not handpick students to ensure success. Instead, students are bused in from several overcrowded schools in the district, with the overcrowded schools deciding whom to send.

Conceived as a joint venture between Lehman College and District 10—neither of which allocates any extra money to the project—the Children's School was the brainchild of Delisle and school Principal Carolyn Jones, whose philosophy for the school was clear. "Children are empowered, trusted, and encouraged to [take risks]."

"That all sounds fine," I said. "But how do you manage that in practice?"

The answer came to me as I toured the school. One important means of encouraging learning among children is a specially designed environment. Classrooms are organized into centers of interest. A few bookshelves form a library. A table and chairs serve as an area for silent reading, while a corner serves as an area where the teacher reads to students. Another area is set aside for children to play with blocks and manipulable toys. Each of these areas is designed to invite children to explore, make choices, and learn and work independently.

In addition, instructional practices make good use of this environment. For example, in one classroom of 20 students, I saw three learning activities take place simultaneously. In one corner, a teacher whispered a tale from a book to half the children. In another corner, more children sat on the floor thumbing through picture books. And in another corner, three children were retelling a story to a teacher's aide.

Another important element of the school's success is the emphasis on allowing children to learn in many different ways. In one classroom, for example, the teacher immersed the children in literature: Storybook posters brightened the walls, and bookcases brimmed with children's books. Following the whole-language instructional approach, the teacher began by reading a story to her class. Afterward, the children wrote their own versions of the story by dictating them to the teacher or an aide. Then students read back their sentences to the class, and finally, they bound what they had written into a book to store in the classroom library.

A SCHOOL FOR CHILDREN

What impressed me most was that the children I observed were totally engaged in their work. They were bright-eyed, eager children, equally at ease working individually, in small groups, or with the entire class. I was also impressed by how quietly the teachers and aides spoke to the children—none used the authoritarian tone of voice I remembered from my own school days.

"Why don't teachers speak to the children in a normal pitch?" I asked.

"This is a school for children, not teachers," Jones answered. "Teachers are observers, facilitators, interactors, and extenders of growth in children." In fact, she added, the teachers and aides serve as role models by engaging in the same listening, storytelling, and reading activities as the children.

Another noteworthy element of the Children's School is the professionalism of the staff—due in no small part to an emphasis on staff development. Delisle reviews current literature on education research and, during a weekly, two-hour training session, suggests practical applications. He says he sees himself as an agent for change in a great experiment.

"I and other teachers at the school will see something that looks interesting—an instructional technique or a child-based theory on curriculum, for instance—and if it looks right for our children, we'll say, 'Let's give it a try,'" Delisle told me.

Before my visit came to an end, Delisle presented me with a parent's handbook and a children's handbook—publications designed to introduce these two groups of readers to the school, its rules, and its activities. The handbooks were invaluable guides, and I thought, "That's what my daughter's school is missing. Concrete communication that children and parents can understand." I decided to pass the handbooks on to the principal at my daughter's school as a way to promote good relations between the school and home.

A lot has happened since then. The Children's School has expanded to include second and third-grade students, as well as special education students of the same age group. The ideas of Delisle, who still serves as professor-in-residence at the school, have been chronicled in many publications and adopted by schools across the nation. What's more, my youngest daughter entered kindergarten not long ago. And on the first day of school, she came home with an attractive little children's handbook about her new school.

Philip Vassallo is an adjunct professor of writing at Middlesex County College in Edison, New Jersey, and Cornell University.

CHAPTER DISCUSSIONS AND ACTIVITIES

1. Compare and contrast the roles of teachers in basal-reader programs and in whole language. Pair off with another classmate and prepare a chart outlining the differences.
2. A group of elementary school teachers, working in an inner-city school with limited materials are excited and enthusiastic about moving towards complete adoption of whole language in their school. The principal is more interested in purchasing a new basal-reader series. What factors must be considered and what steps should be taken to resolve this conflict?
3. You are a fourth grade, whole-language teacher. It is the middle of the school year and a new student has arrived. She is having a difficult time adjusting to her new surroundings. Much of the problem stems from the fact that the youngster came from a traditional school in which basal readers were used. The parents are very upset with the way in which their child is being taught. What do you do?

4. In groups of three or four people, define the following terms:

   kidwatching   empowerment   transmissional learning
   TAWL   invented spelling   transactional learning

   Report your definitions to the class and discuss your reactions to the various definitions provided.
5. If possible, interview a whole-language teacher and discuss with her or him the problems experienced by this teacher. Compare and contrast these findings to those discussed in the article by Walmsley and Adams.

CHAPTER 10

Research Signposts

The term "signpost" is defined by Webster (1990) as "a post bearing a sign that gives information or guidance" (p. 842). In this chapter, we will be viewing the ways in which research enhances the field of reading by providing information and guidance about whole language for teachers, administrators, and parents. Such research provides us with "signposts" that alert us to the wealth of available knowledge that offers us ways of critically evaluating how we should or should not view the reading process. While the emergence of research pertaining to whole language is a relatively new phenomenon, the interest in studying the literacy of youngsters spans many decades. Before looking at specific research findings, we need to view how the structure and function of research are perceived in education.

EDUCATIONAL RESEARCH

There are varying opinions and views about the value of educational research. Finn (1988) believes that such research has produced few findings that have been used in the past or can be used presently to improve schools. On the other hand, Shavelson (1988) claims that research has made an important contribution, not in producing immediate change, but in "constructing, challenging, or changing the way policymakers and practitioners think about problems" (p. 4). As noted by Slavin (1992):

> Results of educational research cannot be used by themselves to guide educational decisions; our common sense, values, and laws must also be involved. However,

> only research can provide the kind of objective information needed to intelligently make educational decisions on which so much depends. (p. 2)

The National Academy of Education also strongly emphasizes the importance of research in education by pointing out that "current efforts to implement broad-based school reforms without adequate research to guide the directions of change will fail" (James, 1991 p. 19).

Before discussing the implications of research strategies in the whole-language classroom, we need to look at two broad categories of research: *quantitative* and *qualitative*. In quantitative research, the researcher collects numerical data either from individuals or groups and by using statistical analyses attempts to determine the extent to which relationships exist. In such research, hypotheses are usually stated and, through the data collected in the study, the hypotheses are supported or refuted. Experimental or correlational studies are usually considered to be quantitative.

With qualitative research, on the other hand, the emphasis is on a highly detailed description of a particular setting without the formulation of stated hypotheses at the onset; hypotheses can develop informally as the researcher proceeds with the study. Often, in the literature, qualitative research is referred to as ethnographic or naturalistic research (Slavin, 1992; Bogdan and Biklen, 1992). And while there are significant differences between the two methods, one finds that many times they complement one another. "Indeed, all good quantitative researchers gather qualitative data in their studies so as to better understand what they are studying, and qualitative researchers often use counts and tabulations to reduce their data to meaningful proportions" (Krathwohl, 1993, p. 354).

In educational research, an intense dispute has arisen over the relative merits of quantitative and qualitative research. Howe (1988) concludes that:

> Although few researchers can be expected to master and pursue both quantitative and qualitative methods, they need at least a rudimentary understanding of what alternative approaches can provide and, accordingly, they should bring a collaborative (rather than paradigm-clique) attitude to research. (p. 15)

This adversarial dialogue is equally alive and flourishing in the field of reading research. Stanovich (1990) argues that even though these "paradigm wars" have existed in the general educational community for the last decade, he strongly believes that this should not continue in reading research. He calls for an end to this debate, noting that "we have much to lose from a divisive zero-sum game that separates the efforts of researchers. We have much to gain from searching for convergences among research perspectives, a possible benefit that can only derive if we reject the incompatibility thesis" (p. 229).

RESEARCH IN WHOLE LANGUAGE

The attitudes of whole-language proponents and traditionalists differ widely and strongly. McKenna, Robinson, and Miller (1990a) suggest that:

Qualitative research designs should be used in tandem with quantitative approaches. In conducting such research, which is still regarded skeptically by many, it will be vital to adhere to credibility procedures such as referential adequacy checks, triangulation, and negative case analysis. In addition, the informal measures developed by whole language proponents (e.g. Clay, 1990; Shanklin & Rhodes, 1989) should be used as one basis for group comparisons. (p. 5)

Edelsky (1990) in responding to this article by McKenna, Robinson, and Miller raises the question, "Whose agenda is this anyway?" Expanding on her concerns about their proposed research agenda, she points out that:

Whole language also objects to relative effectiveness studies because, with their typical reliance on test score data, they promote test-driven curricula. Such curricula and such studies weaken teachers and students and subvert whole language goals; that is, they feed into mechanisms for stratifying society (e.g., test score-based teaching). (p. 9)

In reply, McKenna, Robinson, and Miller (1990b) answer her question by noting that it is everyone's agenda. They caution that "the stakes for young children are too high to tolerate an avoidance of critical issues of instructional methodology" (p. 13).

As interest in whole language has increased over the last decade, researchers dissatisfied with experimental research have come to explore qualitative research. Ethnography and naturalistic approaches using observations of children have become of keen interest to some classroom teachers; the idea of the teacher as researcher is gaining prominence throughout education. As McFarland and Stansell (1993) point out, "this 'new' idea is not new at all" (p. 13). Historically, interest in teacher research can be traced back to Aristole, Comenius, Rousseau, Pestalozzi, Herbart, and Montessori. In different ways, all were interested in the teacher observing the learner. In the United States, the work of Parker, Dewey, Mayhew and Edwards, Mitchell, and Lewin did much to nurture and further develop observational research by classroom teachers. Lewin, in fact, coined the term "action research" and made an explicit differentiation between quantitative and qualitative research (McFarland & Stansell, 1993).

According to Bissex (1987), "A teacher–researcher may start out not with a hypothesis to test, but with a 'wondering' to pursue" (p. 3). For those teachers, the major aspects of research center around: the importance of asking questions; the development of personal theory building; the value of sharing such research with others; and most important, allowing teachers the opportunity to grow and control their own professional lives (Patterson, Stansell, & Lee, 1991).

Although teacher research does not follow the academic rigor applied by experimental researchers, Lincoln and Guba (1985), in discussing naturalistic inquiry, provide us with the following standards: credibility—the study report should not only be believable but also accurate; transferability—the reader of the study should be able to apply the study to her own situation; dependability—the decisions of the researcher should be reliable and trustworthy; and confirmability—the results and conclusions of the study should be upheld by the careful recorded notes of the researcher.

Smith (1993) contends that although we have seen increased interest and status with teacher research, there is a definite challenge facing teachers:

> To meet this challenge, teachers will have to ensure that they remain open to negotiation, criticism, and new ways of thinking lest the dynamic process of teacher research become stagnant and contradict the processes of reflecting, inquiring, and acting—the very activities that give impetus to this genre of research. (pp. 40–41)

Although some teachers are directly involved with research in the classroom, there are still others who are disinterested or completely uninformed about research in education. Jongsma (1992) questioned teachers as to why they do not read abstracts or reviews of research studies. Their responses were quite revealing:

> The materials are not accessible.... Their schools don't have such materials.... University libraries are far from their schools and homes.... The costs of professional materials was so exorbitant that classroom teachers cannot and will not subscribe to professional journals.... They were too busy grading papers and dealing with daily problems to devote time to professional reading.... Research studies are too theoretical to have practical and immediate transfer to the classroom. A last category of responses suggested that teachers don't regularly read such materials because they don't know of their existence. (p. 548)

Unfortunately, those teachers who carefully read the research and are knowledgeable about what is happening in reading instruction, are unable to directly apply the suggested practices in their classrooms because of pressure from colleagues, administrators, and parents (Jongsma, 1993). Harste (1988) advises that:

> The agenda ahead for educators of all kinds is to develop a research methodology for their discipline. They must begin by not being afraid to acknowledge who they are, and by conducting and reporting real educational inquiries in real instructional settings.
>
> To further accomplish this new agenda, teachers must become researchers, and researchers teachers. (p. 11)

Looking Ahead

Goodman (1989) offers the reader a great deal of information about the foundations and development of whole-language research. In the article by Tunnell and Jacobs (1989) the research findings about literature based reading instruction are discussed, while Farris and Hancock (1991) provide a description of a survey that investigates the use of literature in and outside of school and its connection to reading achievement. Varble (1990) offers the results of an analysis of writing samples of students taught by teachers, using whole language and traditional approaches. In the last article, Hamman (1992) describes a study that centered around teachers' awareness of reading terms.

While reading these articles about research and whole language, you may want to consider the following questions:

- According to Goodman (1989), what is the research base for whole language?
- What are some of the potential areas for research in the whole-language classroom and what are some of the research methods that might be used?
- What does research say about the effectiveness of using trade books for reading instruction?
- In what manner does the use of literature in the classroom influence reading success?
- How does whole language have an effect on the writing ability of students?
- How knowledgeable are classroom teachers with regard to current terms related to reading instruction?

REFERENCES

Bissex, G. L. (1987). What is a teacher-researcher? In G. L. Bissex & R. H. Bullock (Eds.), *Seeing for ourselves: Case study research by teachers of writing* (pp. 3–6). Portsmouth, NH: Heinemann.

Bogdan, R. C., & Biklen, S. K. (1992). *Qualitative research for education* (2nd ed.). Boston: Allyn and Bacon.

Clay, M. M. (1990). Research currents: What is and what might be in evaluation. *Language Arts, 67*(3), 288–298.

Edelsky, C. (1990). Whose agenda is this anyway? A response to McKenna, Robinson, and Miller. *Educational Researcher, 19*(8), 7–11.

Farris, P. J., & Hancock, M. R. (1991). The role of literature in reading achievement. *The Clearing House, 65*(2), 114–117.

Finn, C. E., Jr. (1988). What ails educational research? *Educational Researcher, 17*(1), 5–8.

Goodman, K. S. (1989). Whole-language research: Foundations and development. *The Elementary School Journal, 90*(2), 207–221.

Hamman, V. E. (1992). Teachers' awareness of reading terms. *Reading Improvement, 29*(3), 174–178.

Harste, J. C. (1988). Tomorrow's readers today: Becoming a profession of collaborative learners. In J. E. Readence, & R. S. Baldwin (Eds.), *Dialogues in literacy research: Thirty-seventh Yearbook of The National Reading Conference* (pp. 3–13). Chicago: The National Reading Conference.

Howe, K. R. (1988). Against the quantitative-qualitative incompatibility thesis of dogmas die hard. *Educational Researcher, 17*(8), 10–16.

James, T. (1991). Research and the renewal of education: Executive summary and recommendations. *Educational Researcher, 20*(6), 19–22.

Jongsma, K. S. (1993). Continuing concerns. *The Reading Teacher, 46*(8), 704–706.

Jongsma, K. S. (1992). Just say know! *The Reading Teacher, 45*(7), 546–548.

Krathwohl, D. R. (1993). *Methods of educational and social science research: An integrated approach*. New York: Longman.

Lincoln, Y. S., & Guba, E. G. (1985). *Naturalistic inquiry*. Newbury Park, CA: Sage.

McFarland, D. P., & Stansell, J. C. (1993). Historical perspectives. In L. Patterson, C. M. Santa, D. G. Short, & K. Smith (Eds.), *Teachers are researchers: Reflection and action* (pp. 12–18). Newark, DE: International Reading Association.

McKenna, M. C., Robinson, R. D., & Miller, J. W. (1990a). Whole language: A research agenda for the nineties. *Educational Researcher, 19*(8), 3–6.

McKenna, M. C., Robinson, R. D., & Miller, J. W. (1990b). Whole language and the need for open inquiry: A rejoinder to Edelsky. *Educational Researcher, 19*(8), 12–13.

Patterson, L., Stansell, J. C., & Lee, S. (1991). *Teacher research: From promise to power.* Katonah, NY: Richard C. Owen.

Shavelson, R. J. (1988). Contributions of educational research to policy and practice: Constructing challenging, changing cognition. *Educational Researcher, 17*(7), 4–11, 22.

Slavin, R. E. (1992). *Research methods in education* (2nd ed.). Boston: Allyn and Bacon.

Smith, K. (1993). Meeting the challenge of research in the elementary classroom. In L. Patterson, C. M. Santa, K. G. Short, & K. Smith (Eds.), *Teachers are researchers: Reflection and action* (pp. 37–41). Newark, DE: International Reading Association.

Stanovich, K. E. (1990). A call for an end to the paradigm wars in reading research. *Journal of Reading Behavior, 22*(3), 221–231.

Tunnell, M. O., & Jacobs, J. S. (1989). Using "real" books: Research findings on literature based reading instruction. *The Reading Teacher, 42*(7), 470–477.

Shanklin, N. L., & Rhodes, L. K. (1989). Transforming literacy instruction. *Educational Leadership, 46*(6), 59–63.

Varble, M. E. (1990). Analysis of writing samples of students taught by teachers using whole language and traditional approaches. *Journal of Educational Research, 83*(5), 245–251.

Webster's desk dictionary of the English language. (1990). New York: Portland House.

FOR FURTHER STUDY

Bader, L. A., Veatch, J., & Eldredge, J. L. (1987). Trade books or basal readers? *Reading Improvement, 24*(1), 62–67.

Bullock, R. J. (1987). A quiet revolution: The power of teacher research. In G. L. Bissex & R. H. Bullock (Eds.), *Seeing for ourselves: Case study research by teachers of writing* (pp. 21–27). Portsmouth, NH: Heinemann.

Fetterman, D. M. (1988). Qualitative approaches to evaluating education. *Educational Researcher, 17*(8), 17–23.

Gage, N. L. (1989). The paradigm wars and their aftermath: A "historical" sketch of research on teaching since 1989. *Educational Researcher, 18*(7), 4–10.

Holland, K. W., & Hall, L. E. (1989). Reading achievement in the first grade classroom: A comparison of basal and whole language approaches. *Reading Improvement, 26*(4), 323–329.

Hollingsworth, P. M., Reutzel, D. R., & Weeks, E. (1990). Whole language practices in first grade reading instruction. *Reading Research and Instruction, 29*(3), 14–26.

Klesius, J. P., Griffith, P. L., & Zielonka, P. (1991). A whole language and traditional instruction comparison: Overall effectiveness and development of the alphabetic principle. *Reading Research and Instruction, 30*(2), 47–61.

Milligan, J. L., & Berg, H. (1992). The effect of whole language on the comprehending ability of first grade children. *Reading Improvement, 29*(3), 146–154.

Reutzel, D. R., & Cooter, R. B. (1990). Whole language: Comparative effects on first-grade reading achievement. *Journal of Educational Research, 83*(5), 252–257.

Shapiro, J. (1990). Sex-role appropriateness of reading and reading instruction. *Reading Psychology, 11*(3), 241–269.

Stahl, S. A., & Miller, P. D. (1989). Whole language and language experience approaches for beginning reading: A quantitative research synthesis. *Review of Educational Research, 59*(1), 87–116.

Whole-Language Research: Foundations and Development

Kenneth S. Goodman

The practice of whole language is solidly rooted in scientific research and theory. While it owes much to positive, child-centered educational movements from the past, it goes beyond them in integrating scientific concepts and theories of language processes, learning and cognitive development, teaching, and curriculum into a practical philosophy to guide classroom decision making (see Y. Goodman, 1989, in this issue).

In a very real sense, whole language represents a coming of age of educational practice, a new era in which practitioners are informed professionals acting on the basis of an integrated and articulated theory that is consistent with the best scientific research and the theories in which it is grounded. The consistencies among the articles in this issue and indeed the consistencies of practice across whole-language classrooms come from this shared scientific theory. The differences in whole-language classrooms come about because teachers are not relying on gurus and experts to tell them what to do. They make their own decisions and build their own implementations based on their own understandings.

There is a tradition for educational research to be atheoretical, particularly as it deals with classroom practice. A trial-and-error kind of experiment has been popular in which the acceptability of school practice is studied by contrasting an experimental instructional methodology or set of materials with an alternative considered to be a control. Most often gain scores on a test, usually a published standardized test, are used to judge the effectiveness of the "treatment." It has become common to argue in support of methods, materials, or techniques by citing evidence from such studies that they "work" (i.e., produce better gain scores than the control treatment), though it is difficult to draw conclusions from such research that could provide useful knowledge about *why something "works."*

It is not the intention of this article to review or criticize the large body of such experimental research. But often whole-language teachers and advocates are asked for evidence that whole language "works." This demand reflects the common acceptance of this trial-and-error research. Appropriate research to judge whole language, because it has a base in research and theory, can deal with much more important and productive questions. It can examine the extent to which whole-language practice is consistent with its scientific base; it can study what happens to learners and teachers when the philosophy is implemented. And whole-language classrooms can provide authentic settings for studying some basic research concerns, such as how cognitive and language processes develop. Research in whole-language classrooms can test the underlying theory and contribute to its development.

Any research designed to examine whole language must start by considering what whole language is, the goals of whole-language teachers, and how whole language can be studied without destroying or distorting it in the research design. As Rich, (1983, p. 165) says, "Whole language . . . goes beyond the simple delineation of a series of teaching strategies to describe a shift in the way in which teachers think about and practice their art."

Whole language starts with the premise that the whole is more than the sum of its parts; it cannot be studied or evaluated by reducing what happens in whole-language classrooms to what also happens to skill-based classrooms. Controlled studies that compare whole-language to traditional classrooms by using scores on standardized tests do just that. They reduce whole language to posttest skills gains. Whole-language teachers are trying to do more than that.

I begin this article with a simple summary of what whole language is about, where is comes from, and what teachers and pupils in whole-language classrooms do. In doing this, the theoretical views of learners, teachers, language, and curriculum that whole language incorporates are explicated. Then I discuss the strong research base for whole language. Finally, I suggest some of the rich research whole-language classrooms make possible.

KEY CHARACTERISTICS OF WHOLE LANGUAGE

Whole language is a dynamic, evolving grass-roots movement. For that reason there is considerable variability among views of whole language held by its advocates and among whole-language classrooms. Furthermore, most whole-language teachers and advocates are themselves in transition from more conventional subject and skill paradigms. So traditions hang on in their minds and actions. A further complexity is that, particularly in the United States, whole-language teachers often find themselves limited by unsympathetic administrators, inflexible and restrictive policies and decision making, and mandated inappropriate materials.

Whole-language teachers, as I indicated above, operate from an examined theory of how language, thought, and knowledge develop holistically and in support of each other. These teachers regularly use this theory to make teaching decisions. They are constantly collecting a wide range of data from their classrooms to make their decisions and examine and develop their operational theory. Whole-language teachers do not attribute the learning of their pupils to published programs, prescribed behaviors, and preset outcomes. They believe that they play key mediating roles in facilitating the learning of their pupils. Most adherents of whole language recognize the key tenets that follow (K. Goodman, 1986; Newman, 1985).

A Positive View of Human Learners

Whole language takes seriously Dewey's statement about starting where the learner is. It views learners as strong, capable, and eager to learn. It is child centered in that is accepts the responsibility for helping every child to grow as much as possible in whatever directions are most useful (Dewey & Bentley, 1949). At the same time that whole language sees common strengths and universals in human learning, it expects and recognizes differences among learners in culture, value systems, experience, needs, interests, and language. Some of these differences are personal, reflecting human variability, and some of them are social, reflecting the ethnic, cultural, and belief systems of the social groups pupils represent.

Thus teachers in whole-language programs value differences among learners as they come to school and differences in objectives and outcomes as students progress through school. They view the goals of education as expansion on the learners' strengths and maximum growth, not conformity and uniformity. In whole-language classrooms learners are empowered. They are invited to take ownership over their learning and given maximum support in developing their own objectives and fulfilling them.

Redefining the Teacher's Role

Vygotsky (1978) offered a view of teachers as mediators who facilitate learners' transactions with the world. Whole-language teachers accept that view of their role. They are professionals who know children, learning, and teaching. They support learning but they do not see themselves as controlling learning. They reject the definition of teachers as technicians administering a fixed technology to learners (Goodman, Shannon, Freeman, & Murphy, 1988). Whole-language teachers accept responsibility for facilitating growth in their pupils but they also expect power and authority to plan, organize, and choose resources.

Whole-language classrooms are communities of learners. Teachers learn with and from their pupils. Teachers share what they know with their pupils but collaborate with them in defining and solving problems and seeking answers to questions. Whole-language teachers reject restrictive models of effective teaching because they view teaching as much more complex and comprehensive than do these models.

Language as Central to Learning

Language exists for two reasons. First, humans are capable of symbolic thought, that is, they let things represent other things—they can create semiotic systems. The second reason for language is that humans are social beings, dependent at birth and interdependent throughout their lives. Social communication among people is necessary. So language is central to human communication and human thought. Language, as Halliday (1978) describes it, is a social semiotic. It is also the medium of human learning and makes human learning quite different from the learning of other species. Humans can share their experiences and insights through language and thus pool their intelligence.

Vygotsky (1978) has shown that people internalize language from social interactions. Halliday (1975) calls language learning "learning how to mean" because in the process of learning language people learn the social meanings language represents. Halliday (1984) describes three kinds of language learning that happen simultaneously: learning language, learning *through* language, and learning *about* language.

In school and out of school, both oral and written language are learned best and most easily in authentic speech acts and literacy events that serve real functions. So whole-language programs reject part-to-whole views of literacy development, insisting on *real* reading and *real* writing from the very beginning. Whole language builds on the base of print awareness that children growing up in a literate society bring to school. Ferreiro and Teberosky (1982), Piagetians, have shown that even children in the barrios of Mexico City are seeking to make sense of print in their physical environment. Yetta Goodman (1984) and others have shown in their research how widespread a developing knowledge of print is among American preschoolers. So reading and writing in whole-language classrooms start where learners are and help them build their own literacy.

Miscue research by K. Goodman and Y. Goodman (1978) and many others provides an understanding of the reading process and how it develops. The work of Graves (1975, 1981) and of Britton (1977) and other researchers in England offers similar insights into writing. Whole language incorporates this knowledge into a holistic program to support and sustain written language development. Literacy is seen as a major part of the language expansion that pupils achieve during their school years.

Traditional school concerns—spelling, handwriting, grammar, and usage—are integrated in whole-language classrooms into authentic language experiences. Reading, writing, speaking, and listening are not isolated for instruction but rather are integrated.

A Dual Curriculum

Halliday (1984) concludes that we learn through language while we learn language.

The whole-language curriculum builds on this conclusion; it is a dual curriculum; every activity, experience, or unit is an opportunity for both linguistic and cognitive development. Language and thinking develop at the same time that knowledge is developed and concepts and schemas are built.

Whole-language teachers plan thematic units to provide opportunities for both curricula. They are "kid watchers" who monitor language development while pupils solve problems and pursue the answers to questions they have generated. None of this is new in education. Whole language reestablishes Dewey's (Dewey & Bentley, 1949) learning-by-doing views and the project method of William Heard Kilpatrick (1918). But it does so with a new base in theory and research. In this dual curriculum, integration, authenticity, learner choice, and collaboration are all of basic importance. The term whole language itself draws on two meanings of *whole*. It is undivided, and it is integrated and unified.

THEORY, RESEARCH, AND PRACTICE

All research requires a theoretical base, and there must be harmony between theory, research, and related practice. Since whole-language teachers operate on the basis of well-developed theory and use it to plan their teaching, one cannot usefully study or evaluate whole-language classrooms outside of the theoretical context whole language derives from. Reductionist, experimental paradigms are of limited utility in studying whole-language classrooms. It is possible to conduct experiments using traditional designs in whole-language classrooms, but researchers must fully understand the relation of what they are studying to the theoretical premises of whole language. To study *time on task,* for example, researchers would need to define *task* to fit the concepts of dual curriculum, of learner choice, and of integration around problem solving. It probably would be necessary to replace the concept of *time on task* with a term like *learner commitment and involvement.*

Research in whole-language classrooms may well require redefinition of usual research roles. Pupils and teachers in whole-language classrooms will be found in a wide range of activities, locations, and ways of relating to each other. So it will not be easy to define role structures. The researcher, too, may not be able to maintain the role of dispassionate outsider coming in to give a test or two or gather data quickly. To research the whole-language classroom adequately the researcher may need to be present and participate. Teachers and pupils may themselves need to become part of the research team.

Seeing for Ourselves, a recent compilation of case-study research by teachers, underscores this change:

> The classroom becomes a place of inquiry, where questions are explored in meaningful contexts and teacher and students collaborate to seek answers. No longer dispensers of curricula designed by "experts" from universities, textbook companies, or their school districts, these teachers become experts themselves, bringing knowledge and confidence to their teaching and showing that they are professional educators to be respected within schools and without. By becoming researchers, these teachers take control over their classrooms and professional lives in ways that confound the traditional definition of *teacher* and offer proof that education can reform itself from within. [Bissex & Bullock, 1987, p. xi]

Case study and ethnographic research fit well for the study of whole language. However, other methodologies are also appropriate. Whatever methodology is used, researchers must be able to study what happens in whole-language classrooms without restricting it, changing its nature, or isolating features from their natural contexts.

Relating Research and Practice

The relation between research and practice is never simple, never an isomorphic, one-to-one correspondence between a research finding and an application in practice. Too often researchers, particularly experimental researchers, conclude their reports with brief sections in which they recommend direct application of a particular finding in classrooms, like a shot or a pill to be administered. In any practical situation, even the most useful insights must be considered within particular contexts.

Research will be most applicable to whole-language classrooms if it draws on the same theoretical base as the whole-language practice and if it is conducted in the real world rather than in laboratories. Even then, the concepts or ideas drawn from research must be integrated within a unified theory and translated into practice.

Consider, for example, the concept of invented spelling (Read, 1971). Read's actual interest was the sense of the phonology young children have. He discovered, incidental to his intent, that children begin representing, in invented spellings, the sounds they hear in oral language. In this they show a remarkable sensitivity to actual sounds of speech, in contrast to adults, who tend to impose their adult knowledge of the phonemic system and the orthography (the spelling system) on what they perceive.

Teachers and researchers closer to the classroom recognized that this was an important developmental insight: children invent the spelling system just as they do other language systems. The concept fit well with the holistic view that language control develops in the context of its use. Furthermore, it supported the intuition of many teachers that pupils learn spelling without direct instruction if they read and write. Subsequent research by classroom teachers such as Vera Milz (1982), who studied her own first-grade pupils, and researchers such as Y. Goodman and S. Wilde (1985) went beyond Read's work to study the evolution of spelling in children's writing in school. They demonstrated the remarkable development toward conventional spelling over time that children achieve without explicit instruction. Thus theory, research, and practice come together, and whole-language teachers gain confidence in teaching spelling in the context of meaningful reading and writing.

Out of Goodman's miscue analysis came a transactional, psycholinguistic theory of the reading process (K. Goodman, 1984). A key insight is that readers predict as they read and use cues from their reading to confirm or disconfirm their predictions. For whole-language teachers, this is a more useful and powerful concept than the concept of readability, a largely atheoretical attempt to measure potential text difficulty. The problem for whole-language teachers is that readability leaves the reader totally out of the estimation. What whole-language teachers saw was that texts, any kind of coherent and cohesive reading material, were hard or easy for particular readers to the extent that they were predictable. They realized that books that beginning readers found easy to read had this characteristic of predictability. Successful writers for children, showing a sense of audience, had been creating predictable children's literature. Teachers were able to collect numerous predictable books that facilitated their pupils' reading development. In turn, they communicated this to publishers and authors, who produced more predictable books.

While contemporary psychologists were discovering that the past experiences and schemas of readers strongly influenced what they understood from what they read, insightful teachers responded, "Yes, of course. We start where the learner is." As whole-language teachers are finding their voices, the communication between researchers, theorists, and teachers is no longer one way. Academics are finding that they have much to learn from practitioners.

Interdisciplinary Research

The current period of research relating to language and literacy can best be characterized as multidisciplinary. Important research is being done in psychology, linguistics, literary criticism, semiotics, composition, rhetoric, ethnography, artificial intelligence, and education. But there is not nearly enough interdisciplinary work. The net result is that it is left to practitioners, with the support of a small number of synthesizers and disseminators, to integrate new information into practical theory and theory-based practice.

In fact, a dynamic international literature is developing to support the integration and practical implementation of new ideas. It involves Canadians, Britons, Americans, Australians, and New Zealanders. It is collaborative with groups of teachers in Nova Scotia, Manitoba, New England, the Southwest, England, Australia. It involves teachers writing for teachers.

So dynamic is the whole-language movement that innovative practice is leaping ahead of research and rapidly expanding and explicating the fine points of theory. This is as it should be. There is sound, scientifically based theory underlying whole-language practice. Teachers need not wait for research findings before innovating within their classrooms. When skeptical administrators and colleagues say to such innovative teachers, "Where is the proof that what you are doing works?" teachers have a right to answer that the proof is in their classrooms and their pupils.

In another recent compilation, *The Whole Language Evaluation Book* (K. Goodman, Y. Goodman, & Hood, 1989), a wide range of teachers report how they have gone far beyond testing in finding creative ways of evaluating learning and teaching in their classrooms. This evaluation is a part of the ongoing activity in their classrooms. It involves learners in reflective self-evaluation and makes it possible continually to improve what happens in their classrooms.

Young children, given the opportunity to read and write in holistic, authentic, and functional contexts, are learning faster and producing more than their teachers thought possible. In classroom after classroom, at a wide range of grade levels, students are far exceeding in their productivity and in the scope of their learning what schools have traditionally expected. It is up to researchers to find ways of documenting and explicating these classroom events. They can perform a useful service for teachers by helping them to understand the processes at work so that they can be used in other classrooms and so that teachers can expand on what is working. There is also much in these dynamic whole-language classrooms for researchers to learn about language learning and language teaching when neither is constrained by sequenced textbooks or narrow curricula.

Bringing Science and Humanism Together[1]

For three-quarters of a century, American education has been split between a science/technology view, on the one hand, and humanistic, child-centered view, on the other. These views have a common history. At the end of the last century, as scholarship in education began to emerge, there was a movement to replace tradition and the personal views of text writers with practice more solidly based in theory and research. In the beginning there were studies centered around understanding language and learning and school practice. There was concern for both scientific understanding and humanistic practice.

Joseph Rice, whose research spanned several decades, reported in 1893 the conclusion of his studies of the extent to which contemporary school practice reflected the best knowledge:

In schools conducted upon the principles of unification, language is regarded simply as a means of expression and not as a thing apart from ideas. Instruction in almost every branch now partakes of the nature of a language-lesson. The child being led to learn the various phases of language in large part incidentally while acquiring and expressing ideas.... And, strange as it may seem, it is nevertheless true that the results in reading and expression of ideas in writing are, at least in the primary grades, by far the best in those schools where language, in all its phases, is taught incidentally. [Rice, 1893, pp. 223, 224]

Rice's comments sound as if they could have been written today as an endorsement of whole language. Teacher education was emerging in places like Cook County Normal School under Francis Parker. Dewey was beginning to raise key philosophical concerns about the purposes and issues of education. He had started the laboratory school at the University of Chicago, which began initiating experimental programs.

However, in 1914 Rice published his second book, *Scientific Management in Education.* Key educationists and researchers had been swept up in the American fascination with the efficiency of the assembly line. They saw science as a new synonym for technology. Recognizing that teachers of the time were minimally educated, they believed that they could insure that students received the benefits of scientific learning theory if the theory were incorporated into tightly constructed materials with detailed teachers' manuals to guide teachers step by step in their use.

In a National Society for the Study of Education yearbook, William S. Gray published the "Principles of Method in Teaching Reading, as Derived from Scientific Investigation" (Gray, 1919). Gray enunciated the key criteria on which basals are still constructed. These principles, together with Thorndike's laws of learning, have dominated reading instruction through the basal reader ever since (Cuban, 1984).

Science was seen as represented by the texts and tests that proliferated over the ensuing decades. A separate movement that was humanistic, child-centered, holistic, and focused on meaningful experience was perceived as emotionally based and unscientific or even antiscientific. The humanistic tradition was represented by the new education, progressive education, open education, and in reading by such approaches as language experience and individualized reading.

Reconceptualizing Science

The dichotomizing of educational belief and practice was never valid. However, while educational research and curriculum were dominated by behavioral psychology and narrow experimental views of what constituted acceptable research, the theory and research of the humanistic movement in education were not valued. Simultaneous with the emergence of whole language, however, education has been broadening and reconceptualizing its necessary scientific base.

Research on reading and writing and related issues in the several disciplines mentioned above is producing useful knowledge. It is foundational knowledge that must be integrated to produce practical applications in classrooms. That is what whole language does. It recombines the scientific and humanistic traditions in education. It builds solidly on Dewey's epistemology, his philosophical theories of how knowledge develops, how we learn by doing what is functional and relevant. It also expands on the psychological research and theories of Piaget and Vygotsky. Whole language incorporates the concepts of language as social semiotic and language learning as "learning how to mean" from the theory and research of Halliday (1975). It builds on and contributes to the research on reading and writing from print awareness, miscue analysis, process writing, schema theory, discourse analysis, literary criticism, and artificial intelligence. It draws on ethnography and descriptive and collaborative research in building curriculum and methodology that support natural language learning.

In doing this, whole language shifts school literacy programs away from technology. It gives to teachers the power to make decisions and provides them with the knowledge necessary to do so. Thus it shifts power from teachers' manuals to teachers. The curriculum is no longer the texts and the tests. Now it becomes a network of authentic experience in which language is developed. Teachers, supported by informed administrators who see themselves as facilitators of classroom teachers, translate scientific knowledge in the context of humanistic theory. It is the teachers who bring science and humanism back together for the service of their pupils.

Whole-language teachers read broadly and deeply because they recognize that they have undertaken the responsibility for translating theory and research into practice. Nancy Atwell, an exemplary researcher, reported her own development in a presentation to the National Council of Teachers of English in November 1987:

> All the while my activity in the classroom changed, my professional activity outside was changing, too. I read all the writing theory and all the relevant research I could lay my hands on. For me, as for many other classroom teachers, "relevant" meant process-observational studies of young writers, readers and speakers.... These studies were in every way unlike the experimental design research I had read in English education courses. Context was so fully explained and explored I could understand why teachers and learners were teaching and learning.... these were explorations of principles underlying practices. [pp. 3–4]

The energy and innovations these empowered teachers are generating are producing a new base of practical knowledge for teachers and researchers to draw upon. A good deal of this development is passed from teacher to teacher in personal contacts, in teacher support groups, and in local conferences. Teachers are not only sharing their classroom innovations, they are collaborating with researchers and conducting their own research as they teach.

Atwell (1987) cites reports of a number of studies by teacher-researchers. The data in these studies are not only carefully gathered and richly described, they are supported by authentic vignettes and examples of young people reading and writing in the real world of the classroom. That is why teachers find the research so easily applicable. It is also why it is so full of insights for researchers.

Politics, Economics, and Traditions

If American education existed in a rational world, it would be clear that whole language brings together and is based in modern research in language, learning, and teaching. However, American education is being pulled by several forces that make it less than rational.

One force is the politics of fundamentalism, which underlies the back-to-basics movement. In all fields this fundamentalism tries to reduce complex phenomena to simple ones. In reading that means insisting that direct teaching of a reduced and inaccurate set of letter–sound relationships, phonics, is necessary and sufficient to develop readers. It would be easy to dismiss such a view in light of modern research on language and language learning, but this misconception has so powerful a political base that even reports by authoritative research groups find it politic to endorse early direct instruction in phonics as essential to reading development. The authors of *Becoming a Nation of Readers* (Anderson, Hiebert, Scott, & Wilkinson, 1985) proclaimed that the research literature had proven that early direct instruction in phonics is essential. That put a scientific seal of approval on simplistic phonics programs that the *Reader's Digest* and the

Reading Reform Foundation hastened to broadcast, most conspicuously in a full-page ad in the *New York Times*.

Whole language does support the learning of phonics, to the extent that phonics is the set of relations between the sound system and the orthographic system of written language. That is shown in the invented-spelling research and in the studies of developing readers. However, there is abundant research to show that direct instruction in phonics is neither necessary nor desirable to produce readers. Since the studies Rice reported in 1893, it has been clear that learning to make sense of print in reading or express sense in writing does not require learning letter–sound relations in isolation. Now researchers are providing evidence that phonic relations develop consistently and most usefully as pupils write (Y. Goodman & Wilde, 1985) and read (K. Goodman & Y. Goodman, 1978).

Another tradition interfering with the objective pursuit of truth is the remarkable status that basal texts and standardized tests have achieved. Shannon's (1983) research showed that both teachers and administrators believe that basal readers incorporate the best knowledge from research and that they should therefore be carefully and mechanically followed by all teachers and learners. It is not simply that they have a scientific base, but that everything in them is in a specific place in the sequence for scientific reasons.

Publishers succeeded so well in equating science with technology that local and state authorities require by law or edict that teachers must use basals in prescribed ways. Specific published tests are mandated by law in several states as the key basis for pupil promotion and program evaluation.

Most recently the State Board of Education in Georgia ruled that scores of kindergarten children on a mandated test must be given serious consideration in deciding whether the children may enter first grade. This decision is not based on research but on the belief that research strongly underlies both the test and the text-based phonics curriculum mandated for Georgia kindergartens. Many Georgia children will experience failure and defeat even before they enter first grade because state policymakers are convinced that the children have been scientifically shown to be inadequate.

The National Association for the Education of Young Children has gathered substantial research evidence to show that curricula and promotion criteria based on skill hierarchies are developmentally inappropriate for young children (NAEYC, 1987).

The scientific aura around basals is so strong that researchers are reluctant to suggest that dropping basals may be necessary. Duffy and Ball (1986) studied how teachers use basals: "the data suggest that teachers do not rely upon rational models to make decisions, but instead, focus on procedural concerns regarding classroom organization and management . . . which encourage teachers to follow the prescriptions of the instructional materials in a technical rather than a professional manner" (p. 173).

When Duffy, Roehler, and Putnam (1987) attempted to help teachers become substantive (make their own decisions about how to use the substance of the lessons rather than the explicit directions) in their use of basals, they achieved no long-term effects because "neither the content nor the instructional design offered much structure for decision making" (p. 360). Yet the researchers decided that "the solution does not lie with abandoning basal textbooks" (p. 362).

It will be difficult to find American school systems willing to replace textbooks completely, particularly basal readers, with trade books and resource materials so that research evidence can be accumulated to show that students can learn in whole-language classrooms without controlled and controlling textbooks. Schools spend almost 10 times as much on basal readers as they do on trade books (K. Goodman et al., 1988). Researchers need to support teachers and schools who have the courage to teach without basals. The more research there is that shows readers succeeding without basals, the less irrational will be the enforced dependence on basals in our schools.

POTENTIAL RESEARCH IN WHOLE-LANGUAGE CLASSROOMS

This article has shown that the theory and practice of whole language are solidly based in fundamental research on language, learning, literacy development, and the relation of teaching to learning. No movement in education has ever been so comprehensively based on scientific theory. Further, it has shown that there is a growing tradition of research in whole-language classrooms.

There is much to be learned in whole-language classrooms, not only in evaluating whole language in concept and practice but in studying teaching, learning, language and literacy development, curriculum, and other aspects of education. Some fundamental questions can be studied in whole-language classrooms in ways that were not possible before because of the authenticity of the language transactions and the integration around themes and problem solving. Vygotsky believed that spontaneous and scientific concepts were learned differently, but he did not consider how they might be learned similarly if schools changed. If learning in schools is more like learning outside of school, then what does that mean for the development of scientific concepts?

Dewey talked about learning by doing, but this and other concepts of progressive education never developed a grass-roots constituency comparable with the whole-language network of teachers. Research in classrooms that operationalize learning by doing can explore the potential of Dewey's concepts.

Frank Smith (1986) has argued that those who are successful in becoming literate in school become members of the "literacy club." In whole-language classrooms researchers can explore the validity of this concept. What happens in classrooms that includes or excludes pupils from this club? Here is a research concern that may profit from the comparison of whole-language and skills-based classrooms. Does whole language do a better job of making more pupils feel like members of the literacy club?

It would be interesting to explore how pupil and teacher roles change as transitions are made to whole-language from more traditional classrooms. Studies of success of pupils and teachers as it relates to the evidence of their empowerment would also be valuable.

These studies will require research methods from a wide range of disciplines. Discourse analysis, drawing on functional grammar, might look at the language teachers use in inviting students into the literacy club. Ethnography would be appropriate for studying access to and use of resource materials. Schema theory could be combined with cohesion analysis in examining children's choices of topics in their writing. Small-group methodology from social psychology would be appropriate to studying participation in literature study groups. Case studies of individuals—teachers, learners, or administrators—would help to examine the pupils' development as readers, writers, and problem solvers. Piagetian research methodology, as Ferreiro and her colleagues have developed it (Ferreiro & Teberosky, 1982), could be useful for studying transitions into literacy. In whole-language classrooms, Vygotsky's "zone of proximal development" can be studied in authentic problem-solving situations.

Just as teaching and learning have broken out of the constraints of an outmoded technology in whole-language classrooms, so educational research needs to break the behavioristic ties that bind it. That means learning how to do real-world, naturalistic research without controlling the variables in what we study so that we destroy it. It also means researchers raising their sights, broadening their perspectives, and asking new sets of questions about the potential of teaching and learning that whole-language programs make possible. Next I identify five of many such areas of focus.

Invention

Whole-language classrooms empower the learners to invent language and conceptual schema. Researchers and teachers have been aware for some time, as I indicated above, of the role of invention in children's spelling development. But invention is present in all aspects of linguistic and cognitive development. In the research on writing of Goodman and her colleagues (Y. Goodman & Wilde, 1985), for example, there was evidence of invention in narrative, in report writing, in grammar, in punctuation, and in concepts. Research could use the rich evidence of invention in whole-language classrooms to explore the process fully. More understanding is needed of how invention follows similar and different directions among groups of learners. Teachers will appreciate insights from research on how mediation supports and extends invention without stifling or misdirecting it. Studies of the social, personal, cultural, and classroom resources that pupils draw on in their inventions would also be useful. For example, in a study that was a part of the Goodman research, Bird (1987) looked at how Native American learners drew on their own life experience in their written expression.

Convention

All learners need to come to control a wide range of social conventions in order to communicate successfully. These social conventions become internalized and play a vital role in thinking and learning. Whole-language teachers share the concern of other teachers in assuring that learners come to control these conventions, but they recognize that traditional attempts to teach conventions directly distort them, often suppress invention, and do not assure that pupils will usefully internalize the conventions. There is evidence from the Piagetian research of Ferreiro and her colleagues of how the conventions of written language develop. Halliday has shown how linguistic conventions of grammar and texts develop. Whole-language teachers monitor development as they work closely with pupils. They understand that conventions are inferred as learners engage in functional, meaningful, authentic social transactions. They understand the importance of encouraging risk taking as they help pupils deal with the tension between their inventions and social convention.

Research is needed to document the development of the conventions of various oral and written language genre. How do pupils build a sense of written sentences? How do they learn the pragmatic conventions of personal and business letters? How do they develop a sense of audience in oral and written presentations? What kinds of experiences enable readers to read like writers and learn the conventions of written language to use in their own writing? Research should examine the tension between personal invention and social convention in developing reading, writing, thinking, and problem solving.

Organizing for Whole Language

Traditionally teachers have organized around the teachers' manuals of textbooks, around discrete subjects, or around specific activities. Whole language integrates language and its use in learning. Thematic units are planned to last several weeks and integrate social studies, science, language arts, mathematics, and the arts. So there is long- and medium-term planning as well as daily planning. Whole-language teachers use flexible, ad hoc grouping rather than relatively permanent ability grouping of pupils. Furthermore, different pupils and groups of pupils may be doing different things at the same time. All this makes developing facilitative organizational procedures very important. This is a very dynamic area now as whole-language teachers move away from traditional practice and create holistic alternatives. Research can help teachers while knowledge is developed about how innovative uses of time, space, materials, and social transactions facilitate teaching and learning. Practice is leading theory in this area, and both can profit from creative research.

Resources for Whole-Language Classrooms

It is relatively easy to set aside basal readers and use real children's literature to develop reading in whole-language classrooms. But what other materials do whole-language classrooms need to facilitate literacy development, problem solving, question answering, and researching for thematic units? Commercial publishers and governmental and quasi-governmental groups have developed whole-language resource materials such as big books, predictable books, writing portfolios, kits of trade books, and teaching units for use with literature sets. And the whole-language label is being used by commercial publishers on materials that appear to have little in common with the principles discussed in this article. Development of resources is another dynamic area in whole-language classrooms. Many teachers feel quite comfortable with their own ability to assemble enough authentic "real-world" resources to meet the needs of their pupils. They enlist parents in finding resources and scavenge from their homes and communities. But they often have a good sense of resources that would be useful that do not exist, such as factual resources for use by pupils of various ages, abilities, and language backgrounds.

Research on materials for supporting whole language is another broad area that could be opened up. Research might also help whole-language teachers to fight off the "basalization" of literature by superimposing skill packages on the reading of stories. Research could document for teachers their innovative use and development of unconventional resources. Teachers and administrators need research help to establish criteria for evaluation of available materials and specifications for new resources.

New Roles for Teachers and Learners

There are no teachers today who were themselves learners in whole-language classrooms. As teachers move away from the conventional, limited roles to new and broader ones, and as they open the range of roles for learners in their classrooms, they are moving into unexplored territory. Even when they become comfortable, confident, and highly effective in these new roles as kid watchers, mediators of learning, and liberators of learners, they encounter resistance, skepticism and sometimes hostility from colleagues, administrators, and the community. Besides their own careful documentation of the success of their new professionalism, they need the support of research. They need the insights that systematic research can provide to continue their innovation in desirable directions, to modify their practice to achieve their goals better, and to help doubters to understand what is happening. Teachers and learners need to be partners with researchers in these studies.

In places where whole language has become policy on national, state or provincial, and local levels, research is needed on ways of supporting teachers and learners as they make transitions from traditional to holistic schooling. Preservice and staff-development programs have been developed, particularly in New Zealand and Australia, for dissemination of whole-language philosophy and practice. As these and other programs are implemented in North America, their effects need to be carefully researched.

SUMMARY: A MESSAGE FOR TEACHERS AND A CHALLENGE FOR RESEARCHERS

I hope the message has come through to teachers from this discussion that they ought not to be defensive about their whole-language programs. There is a solid research base to whole language. Whole-language teachers incorporate this into a philosophy that they use in making instructional decisions and planned innovations. What they are attempting is different and much more ambitious than the objectives of traditional classrooms. Whole-language teachers and administrators need to document what they and their pupils are doing. Many of them do research in their classrooms themselves or with researchers. They need to resist attempts of researchers and evaluators to make them restrict or modify what they are doing to fit conventional research designs and evaluation instruments, such as standardized tests.

Whole language offers a challenge to researchers. They need to understand that whole language is a major step forward. It involves bold new innovative programs and settings for teaching and learning. The professionals participating in this grass-roots movement are eager to have research support. But it is up to the researchers to demonstrate their ability to do useful, relevant research. The practitioners will move ahead, with or without this support.

---

1. Many of the quotes and ideas in this section come from Patrick Shannon's contribution to *Report Card on Basal Readers*, which I coauthored (K. Goodman et al., 1988).

REFERENCES

Anderson, R. C., Hiebert, E. H., Scott, J. A., & Wilkinson, I. A. (1985). *Becoming a nation of readers: The report of the Commission on Reading*. Washington, DC: National Institute of Education.

Atwell, N. (1987, November). "Wonderings to pursue": The writing teacher as researcher. Paper presented to the National Council of Teachers of English, Los Angeles.

Bird, L. B. (1987). *The reflection of personal experience in the writing of Papago Indian children.* Unpublished doctoral dissertation, University of Arizona, Tucson.

Bissex, G., & Bullock, R. (Eds.). (1987). *Seeing for ourselves.* Portsmouth, NH: Heinemann.

Britton, J. (1977). Language and the nature of learning: An individual perspective. In J. R. Squire (Ed.), *The teaching of English* (76th Yearbook of the National Society for the Study of Education, Pt. 1, pp. 1–38). Chicago: University of Chicago Press.

Cuban, L. (1984). *How teachers taught.* New York: Longman.

Dewey, J., & Bentley, L. (1949). *Knowing and the known.* Boston: Beacon.

Duffy, G. G., & Ball, D. L. (1986). Instructional decision making and reading teacher effectiveness. In J. V. Hoffman (Ed.), *Effective teaching of reading: Research and practice* (pp. 163–180). Newark, DE: International Reading Association.

Duffy, G. G., Roehler, L. R., & Putnam, J. (1987). Putting the teacher in control: Basal reading textbooks and instructional decision making. *Elementary School Journal, 87,* 357–366.

Ferreiro, E., & Teberosky, A. (1982). *Literacy before schooling.* Portsmouth, NH: Heinemann.

Goodman, K. (1984). Unity in reading. In A. Purves & O. Niles (Eds.), *Becoming readers in a complex society* (pp. 79–114). Chicago: University of Chicago Press.

Goodman, K. (1986). *What's whole in whole language?* Portsmouth, NH: Heinemann.

Goodman, K., & Goodman, Y. (1978). *Reading of American children whose language is a stable rural dialect of English or a language other than English* (Final Report). Washington, DC: National Institute of Education.

Goodman, K., Goodman, Y., & Hood, W. (1989). *The whole language evaluation book.* Portsmouth, NH: Heinemann.

Goodman, K., Shannon, P., Freeman, Y., & Murphy, S. (1988). *Report card on basal readers.* Katonah, NY: Richard C. Owen.

Goodman, Y. (1984). The development of initial literacy. In H. Goelman, A. Olberg, & F. Smith (Eds.), *Awakening to literacy* (pp. 102–109). Exeter, NH: Heinemann.

Goodman, Y. (1989). Roots of the whole-language movement. *Elementary School Journal, 90,* 113–127.

Goodman, Y., & Wilde, S. (1985). *Writing development: Third and fourth grade O'odham (Papago) students* (Occasional Paper No. 14). Tucson: Program in Language and Literacy, University of Arizona.

Graves, D. (1975). An examination of the writing process of seven-year-old children. *Research in the Teaching of English, 9,* 227–241.

Graves, D. (1981). *A case study observing the development of primary children's composing, spelling, and motor behaviors during the writing process* (Project NIE-G-78-0174). Washington, DC: National Institute of Education.

Gray, W. (1919). Principles of method in teaching reading, as derived from scientific investigation. In C. Seashore

(Ed.), *Fourth report of committee on the economy of time* (18th Yearbook of National Society for the Study of Education, Pt. 2, pp. 26–51). Chicago: University of Chicago Press.

Halliday, M. A. K. (1975). *Learning how to mean*. London: Arnold.

Halliday, M. A. K. (1978). *Language as social semiotic*. London: Arnold.

Halliday, M. A. K. (1984). Three aspects of children's language development: Learning language, learning through language, and learning about language. In Y. M. Goodman, M. Haussler, & D. Strickland (Eds.), *Oral and written language development research: Impact on the schools* (pp. 165–192). Urbana, IL: National Council of Teachers of English.

Kilpatrick, W. H. (1918). The project method. *Teachers College Record, 19,* 319–35.

Milz, V. (1982). *Young children write: The beginnings* (Occasional Paper No. 5). Tucson: Program in Language and Literacy, University of Arizona.

National Association for the Education of Young Children. (1987). *Developmentally appropriate practice in early childhood programs serving children from birth through age 8* (Publication No. 24). Washington, DC: NAEYC.

Newman, J. (1985). *Whole language: Theory in use*. Portsmouth, NH: Heinemann.

Read, C. (1971). Pre-school children's knowledge of English phonology. *Harvard Educational Review, 41,* 1–34.

Rice, J. (1893). *The public-school system in the United States*. New York: Century.

Rice, J. (1914). *Scientific management in education*. New York: Hinds, Noble & Eldridge.

Rich, S. (1983). On becoming teacher experts: Teacher researchers. *Language Arts, 60,* 892–894.

Shannon, P. (1983). The use of commercial reading materials in American elementary schools. *Reading Research Quarterly, 19,* 68–85.

Smith, F. (1986). *Insult to intelligence*. New York: Arbor House.

Vygotsky, L. S. (1978). *Mind in society*. M. Cole, V. John-Steiner, S. Scribner, & E. Souberman (Eds.). Cambridge, MA: Harvard University Press.

Kenneth S. Goodman is a professor at the University of Arizona. He is well known for his extensive work in psycholinguistics and whole language.

Using "Real" Books: Research Findings on Literature-Based Reading Instruction

Michael O. Tunnell
James S. Jacobs

How should reading be taught and with what sorts of materials? Basals or trade books? Phonics or sight words or context clues? Do "real" books come later, after a child has mastered decoding skills? Or might the child start with "real" books from the library or book club and learn skills as needed in so-called "natural context?" What are the best ways of leading a child to literacy?

Advocates of basal instruction cite the logic and successful tradition of their method. Basal reading programs have dominated the classroom for decades—95 to 99% of American teachers relied on the basal in 1958 and 80 to 90% still did as of 1980 (Koeller, 1981).

Those who use literature-based reading instruction to challenge the basal tradition boast stunning levels of success with all types of students and particularly with disabled and uninterested readers. Recently the Whole Language movement, which has gained great momentum in the 1980s, has given renewed attention to individualized reading—redefining and refining the process which pri-

---

From "Using 'Real' Books: Research Findings on Literature-Based Reading Instruction" by M. O. Tunnell and J. S. Jacobs, 1989, *The Reading Teacher, 42,* pp. 470–477. Copyright © 1989 by the International Reading Association. Reprinted with permission of Michael O. Tunnell and the International Reading Association.

marily uses "real" books to teach and foster literacy.

Can reading be taught successfully without the basal? What does the literature in reading instruction indicate about both the success rate and the components of literature based, Whole Language approaches to building literacy?

A VARIETY OF STUDIES

A number of controlled studies have directly compared literature based reading with basal and mastery learning instruction while others have simply looked at growth within Whole Language classrooms employing literature based reading programs.

A landmark study by Cohen (1968) used a control group of 130 students in 2nd grade who were taught with basal readers and compared them to 155 children in an experimental group using a literature component along with regular instruction. The schools, in New York City, were selected because of academic retardation likely due to low socio-economic backgrounds of the students.

The experimental treatment consisted mainly of reading aloud to children from 50 carefully selected children's trade picture books—books without fixed vocabulary or sentence length—and then following up with meaning related activities. The children were encouraged to read the books anytime.

The experimental group showed significant increases over the control group (on Metropolitan Achievement Tests and A Free Association Vocabulary Test administered in October and June) in word knowledge ($p < .005$), reading comprehension ($p < .01$), vocabulary ($p < .05$) and quality of vocabulary ($p < .05$). When the six lowest classes were compared, the experimental group showed an even more significant increase over the control.

Cohen's study was replicated a few years later by Cullinan, Jaggar, and Strickland (1974), yielding basically the same results.

Another controlled study that warrants a closer look is one conducted by Eldredge and Butterfield (1986), whose initial study involved 1,149 children in 2nd grade in 50 Utah classrooms. They compared a traditional basal approach to 5 other experimental methods, including 2 which used variations of a literature based program.

Employing a variety of evaluative techniques (an instrument for evaluating phonics skills developed and validated by Eldredge, the Gates-MacGinitie Reading Test, and a Pictorial Self-Concept Scale), the researchers discovered that 14 of 20 significant differences among the instructional methods favored the literature approach teamed with a series of special decoding lessons (also developed by Eldredge) taking no more than 15 minutes daily.

The other literature based group also placed highly. Eldredge and Butterfield were able to conclude that "the use of children's literature to teach children to read had a positive effect upon students' achievement and attitudes toward reading—much greater than the traditional methods used." (See also Bader, Veatch, and Eldredge, 1987.)

NEW ZEALAND AND OHIO

Under the auspices of the New Zealand Department of Education, a literature based, developmental program for 1st graders called the Shared Book Experience was examined closely. Holdaway (1982) explains that "no grade or structured materials were used and all word solving skills were taught in context during real reading. This experimental group proved equal or superior to other experimental and control groups on a variety of measures including Marie Clay's *Diagnostic Survey*."

So impressed was the Department of Education that it embarked on a country-wide program of inservice in New Zealand, and subsequently, developmental programs such as Shared Book Experience have taken over on a national scale.

The influence of this New Zealand program spread. The Ohio Reading Recovery Program, reported by Boehnlein (1987) to be an American version of New Zealand's Reading Recovery Program, is specifically targeted at beginning readers who indeed have a profile that will make failure likely. Results of a controlled study match those of the New Zealand findings, which are best encapsulated in this remarkable statement: "After an average of 15 to 20 weeks, or 30 to 40 hours of instruction, 90% of the children whose pretest scores were in the lowest 20% of their class catch up to the average of their class or above and *never need remediation again.*"

The Ohio Reading Recovery program confirmed that gains are maintained, and when compared to control groups, the Reading Recovery children "not only made greater gains than the other high risk children who received no help, but they also made greater gains than the children who needed no help." (See also Pinnell, 1986.)

LIMITED ENGLISH SPEAKERS

One of the more recent experiments dealing with literature based reading and children at high risk of failure is the story of a school on New York City's west side (Larrick, 1987). Of these children, 92% came from non-English speaking homes, 96% lived below the poverty level, and 80% spoke no English when entering school. The Open Sesame program was initiated with 225 kindergarten students, providing them an opportunity to read in an unpressured, pleasurable way—using neither basals nor workbooks. Immersion in children's literature and language experience approaches to reading and writing were the major instructional thrusts, and skills were taught primarily in meaningful context as children asked for help in writing.

As the year concluded, all 225 students could read their dictated stories and many of the picture books shown in class. Some were even reading on a 2nd grade level. School officials were so impressed that they made a written commitment to extend the program gradually through 6th grade.

The following year, the spring of 1987, all 350 in 1st grade were happily reading English—60% on or above grade level. In fact, only 3 of the 350 failed to pass district comprehension tests, and those 3 had been in the United States less than 6 months.

White, Vaughan, and Rorie (1986) reported that 1st grade children from a small, economically depressed rural community responded well to reading and writing programs not using a basal. As to the methods employed, "print was something that permeated their day. . . . Books became theirs, 'in a natural way, in a real way.' "

Though quick to say that the children understood far more about the reading process than could ever be measured by a pencil and paper test, White and her colleagues were also pleased that 20 of the 25 children scored a grade equivalent of 2.0 or better on the spring standardized tests. The other 5 children had scores of 1.6, 1.7, or 1.9, and the lowest percentile ranking was 54th.

THOSE WHO HAVE FAILED

But what about children who have already failed? Chomsky (1978), in a research report aptly titled "When You Still Can't Read in Third Grade: After Decoding, What?" addresses the plight of the young "stalled" reader, who for better than 1 year has made no progress in reading.

Chomsky worked in a middle class suburban community near Boston with 5 children in 3rd grade who had average IQs and no apparent language or speech problems but who had always been remedial reading students, hated reading, and had made no progress in reading since 1st grade. Abandoning the intensive decoding program, the researcher instead asked the children to listen to tape recorded stories from "real" books, returning to the book often until the story was memorized.

The neurological impress method using natural, enjoyable text proved to be the key to eventual success. Standardized achievement test scores (MAT) after a year of treatment showed that these no-progress children were off and running. Average increase in overall reading scores was 7.5 months (grade equivalent) and in word knowledge was 6.25 months (grade equivalent), a significant increase for children whose former test scores showed no progress.

Even older children who have experienced years of failure with reading and writing have been exposed to literature based, Whole Language programs with notable success. Fader et al. (1976) flooded secondary classrooms in inner city Detroit with paperbacks, finding great success in raising reading achievement and developing the reading interests of high school students who ordinarily did not read often or well.

But the true proof of their literature based program was best put to the test with hardcore subjects—students at the W. J. Maxey Boys' Training School in Lake Whitmore, Michigan. Hundreds of paperbacks were provided for W. J. Maxey, along with the time to read them and no obligation to write the usual book reports or summaries. Another Midwestern boys' training school was used as a control group.

Though there were no significant differences to be found in control and experimental groups at the onset, by the end of the school year the boys at W. J. Maxey showed significant gains over the control on measures of self-esteem, literacy attitudes, anxiety, verbal proficiency, and reading comprehension. In some instances, the control group's scores actually decreased from the year before while the experimental group's surged ahead, even doubling the control group scores.

STALLED READERS

Stalled children also showed marked improvement in a classroom study with 5th graders. With the entire class, Tunnell (1986) employed a literature based reading/writing program adapted from the program suggested by Eldredge and Butterfield (1986). Eight of the 28 students in his classroom were reading disabled, receiving federally funded Chapter 1 or resource instruction in a pull-out program.

After 7 months of treatment, the standardized tests (SRA) were administered, and the average gain in the overall reading score was a grade equivalent of 1.1. The 8 reading disabled children, who also were virtually stalled in their reading progress, posted an average gain of 1.3 with a comprehension gain of 2.0.

Even more noteworthy was the swing in reading attitudes in all children. A 13 question reading attitude survey was administered to the class in August and again in April. Negative attitudes toward books and reading virtually disappeared as self concept in relation to literacy rose. (See also Tunnell et al., 1988.)

It is important to note that gains in reading skills using a literature based approach are not limited to students at risk. In the studies by Eldredge, Holdaway, and Tunnell, the average and above average reader made progress equal to and most often better than students in traditional programs, as measured by the typical achievement tests.

Some of the strongest evidence for the broad use of a Whole Language program involving literature comes from Ray Reutzel, an associate professor at Brigham Young University who took a 1 year leave to teach reading to 63 children in 1st grade in nearby Sage Creek Elementary. With a classroom library of 2,000 books, Reutzel taught the elements and skills of reading within the meaningful context of story books.

No basal was used, nor was the state program of worksheets and drill activities, called the Utah Benchmark Skills. The goal prescribed by the state is to have the students pass the Utah Benchmark Skills Test at an 80% level in May. Reutzel's students scored 93% in January, 13 points higher than district expectations and 4 months earlier than the normal testing time.

When the Stanford Achievement Test (SAT) was given in March, group percentiles across all reading categories—word study skills, comprehension, and total reading were uniformly in the 99th percentile for the 63 children. Individual scores were all above grade level except for 4 children who scored below 1.6. The lowest score was 1.2, and that from a boy who knew only a few letters of the alphabet when entering 1st grade. Even a girl whose IQ tested at 68 came out at grade level. There was not one nonreading 1st grader in the school (Reutzel and Fawson, 1988).

MEANINGFUL READING

Rasinski and Deford (1985) indicate why literature based reading approaches may have a profound positive effect on learners. They compared three 1st grade classrooms, each with competent teachers using different approaches to teaching reading: content centered mastery learning, traditional basal, and child centered literature based approaches. The researchers looked less at achievement than at student conceptions about reading assessed through interviews.

The responses to the basic questions "What is reading?" or "What happens when you read?" were rated by a team of raters in relation to whether they were meaning related (high score of 7) or letter–sound related (low score of 1). Mean scores showed that children from the literature based program conceived reading to be more of a meaning related activity than did the other children. The mean scores were mastery group: 3.45, basal group: 4.32, literature group: 4.91.

Conclusions indicate that good readers in all three groups tended to define reading as being concerned with meaning while poor readers saw it as a process of converting symbol to sound. Natural texts support reading as a meaning related activity.

That children in classroom situations can be taught to read from "real" books is not a new idea. Thompson (1971) examined 40 studies from 1937 through 1971 which compared the basal approach to reading instruction with the individualized approach. He noted that 24 of the studies favored individualized reading, while only 1 chose the basal as better. (The remaining studies were ties.)

Thompson concluded that "individualized reading programs can facilitate reading achievement to the extent of basal programs, and . . . more often than not . . . have facilitated higher reader achievement than basal programs in controlled studies." (See also Davis and Lucas, 1971.)

BASIC ELEMENTS OF LITERATURE BASED PROGRAMS

Though each study mentioned employed its own brand of literature based reading instruction, several basic premises are found often in the different approaches. Elements of instruction varied depending upon the age of the students, but in some way the following commonalities were overtly employed or subtly implied in all of the literature based reading programs.

Premises learned from "natural readers." Advocates of Whole Language tend to believe reading skills can be acquired in much the same manner as learning to speak (Forester, 1977; Holdaway, 1982). Durkin (1961), for example, identified 49 from a pool of 5,103 students in 1st grade who had received no formal reading instruction but entered school reading at a grade equivalent of 1.5 to 4.6.

These 49 "natural readers" had vastly different racial and socioeconomic backgrounds and IQ levels, but there were common factors in the reading models they had at home. Their families had a high regard for reading, children were read to regularly from age 2 forward, and parents answered frequent questions about words and reading.

Durkin concluded that natural readers acquire abilities through experiences with whole texts provided by strong reading models.

Both Clark (1976) and Thorndike (1973) support Durkin's conclusions. Clark's study of young readers in Scotland yielded two basic common factors in natural readers. All were read to from an early age and all had access to books at home or through libraries.

Thorndike, studying reading comprehension in 15 countries, discovered two conditions that prevailed in strong readers. All had been read to from an early age and had come from homes that respected education.

Immersion in natural text at an early age has the same effects on reading as immersion in aural and spoken language has on speech.

Hoskisson (1979) concurred by suggesting that natural readers "solve the problem of learning to read as they construct their knowledge of written language." Therefore, no formal hierarchy of reading skills should be imposed on children, because only the child can determine what can be assimilated and accommodated within that highly personal cognitive structure. Hearing written language is essential to testing these personal hypotheses about written language.

Learning to read naturally begins when parents read to young children and let them handle books, and that process is continued with the teacher reading aloud and including books naturally in the classroom.

Use of natural text. In every study examined, researchers were emphatic about using children's literature written in natural, uncontrolled language.

Goodman (1988) supports this move away from basal reading materials, especially after evaluating the ways in which such programs select, write, or alter the stories they include: "Basals have tended to isolate sounds, letters, and words from the [language] systems. And they have given little attention to the systems and how they relate in natural texts." He maintains that basal materials often produce distorted abstractions, loss of contextual meanings, and loss of grammatical function due to letter–sound relationships taught in isolation or words used out of context.

The process of controlling vocabulary and syntax also causes a loss of style and makes language less natural and less predictable. A closer look at two leading basal series showed Goodman that only about 20% of the texts reproduced were authentic renderings.

It is also interesting to note that the 104 books used with the 2nd grade children in the Eldredge and Butterfield (1986) study were not controlled for vocabulary. In fact, 91% of the books had readability scores above 3rd grade level, and 62% were at a 4th grade level. Despite the lack of vocabulary control, the students made superior progress.

Neurological impress method. In the studies that involved beginning readers, a variation of the neurological impress method was generally employed.

In Chomsky's study, children "read" in the trade book while following along with the recorded version on audio cassette. Eldredge and Butterfield used reading pairs (dyads) or groups of 3 (triads) where poor readers were teamed with average readers. They sat together and read aloud from the same book while the faster reader touched words as they were read and the slower reader repeated them. Groups changed every few days, and as proficiency was gained the slower reader began to read silently, using the better reader as a word resource.

Even the use of Big Books, as suggested by Holdaway and White, allows for a form of neurological impress. Big Books usually are trade picture books which have been reproduced in a format large enough to be seen from 20 feet away. With Big Books teachers can have their students follow their fluent reading.

Reading aloud. Another characteristic of literature based programs is that teachers regularly spend time reading aloud to their students. In all of the studies reviewed, reading aloud seemed to be a must. Daily reading aloud from enjoyable trade books has been the key that unlocked literacy growth for many disabled readers. Opportunities for modeling and neurological impress abound during read aloud time. And, of course, being read to is the essential element in the backgrounds of "natural readers."

Sustained silent reading. SSR is the time provided for students and teacher to read materials of their own choosing without interruption. Every study examined for this report included, as a part of its plan, time for children to be alone with books.

Allington (1977) suggests the more words that pass in front of the eyes, the better the reader becomes. The time children spend in independent reading "is associated with gains in reading achievement" (Anderson et al., 1985, p. 119). Opportunity to reread favorites, reread books recorded on audio tape, or to read something new is the best way to give children the practice they need to apply their newly learned skills.

Teacher modeling. Another important element usually only hinted at by the researchers listed in this article is that of teacher modeling. One of Holdaway's three basic requirements of the Shared Book Experience is that teachers need to present new books with wholehearted enjoyment.

According to the same principle, teachers themselves should read during sustained silent reading (McCracken and McCracken, 1978). A prerequisite for this sort of modeling is a teacher who values reading in his/her personal life and also knows and loves the children's books that will be read by the students.

Emphasis on changing attitudes. An affective approach to reading instruction is also a recurring element of literature based programs. Tunnell's study showed a marked improvement of student attitudes, and other researchers made comments such as that of Larrick (1987): "Best of all, they loved to read."

Fader et al., (1976, p. 236–37) illustrate an extreme shift in attitude and its benefits with the story of Bill, a 13 year old 2nd grade level reader who was watched busily reading Jaws. When Fader asked him if the book was hard, Bill answered "Sure it's hard. But it's worth it"

Self selection of reading materials. Positive attitude toward reading seems to be affected by allowing children to select their own reading materials. Every study examined had a time when students at every age level were encouraged to find and read books of their own choosing.

Though sometimes books were read together (as with Big Books), there was always a large classroom library from which children could choose their own books. Sustained silent reading is unsuccessful unless children are allowed to read books of their own choosing.

Meaning oriented with skills often taught in meaningful context. Most studies reviewed suggested teaching reading skills as they relate directly to the books and writings of the children (Holdaway, Chomsky, Larrick, Cohen, Boehnlein). Eldredge and Butterfield employed a brief decoding lesson, but they suggest moving quickly into "real" reading so that the lesson can be put into immediate practice.

Process writing and other output activities. In every instance some sort of follow-up output activity accompanied reading experiences. Often the output activities involved writing. Forester, White, Chomsky, Holdaway, Larrick, Fader, and Tunnell all mentioned writing, and usually process writing in particular. In fact, Chomsky (1978) stated that the children who progressed the most achieved in both reading and writing.

OTHER CONSIDERATIONS

Success of literature based programs is well documented. Disabled readers are brought into the world of literacy (and not just decoding) using "real" books. When children learn that reading and books are worth their time, then as Fielding, Wilson, and Anderson (1984) point out, they will spend more self-initiated time in books. Children who participate in this self-initiated practice (some children read from 10 to 20 times more than others) make more progress because frequent personal reading improves the "automaticity" of basic reading skills.

Unfortunately, in a study of 5th graders' activities after school, Fielding (1984) and her colleagues discovered that only 2% of free time is spent reading (a daily average of 9.2 minutes). Half the children read only 4 minutes or less each day, and 30% read 2 minutes or less (10% did not read at all).

It is no surprise that television watching consumed most of their after school time (an average of 136.4 minutes daily). Yet, these researchers concluded that "among all the ways children can spend their leisure time, average minutes per day reading books was the best and most consistent predictor of standardized comprehension test performance, size of vocabulary, and gains in reading achievement between 2nd and 5th grade" (Fielding, Wilson, and Anderson, 1984, p. 151).

Greaney (1980), reviewing studies concerning leisure reading, discovered that "a number of studies have reported significant relationships between amount of leisure reading and level of pupil attainment." One of the studies Greaney points to was conducted decades ago by LaBrant (1936). This longitudinal study reported that students completing a 6 year free reading program were, 25 years later, reading significantly more than most other groups to which they had been compared. (Also see Connor, 1954; Maxwell, 1977.) In fact, *Becoming a Nation of Readers* (Anderson et al., 1985, p. 82) suggests that "priority should be given to independent reading."

Fielding, Wilson, and Anderson (1984) note that reading books deepens knowledge of forms of written language. Conversely, primary grade basals have fewer plot complications, less character development, and less conflict among and within characters. They lack the richness in vocabulary, sentence structure, and literary form found in children's books. Koeller (1981) notes a study by Blom, Waite, and Zimet (1970) that "analyzed over 1300 stories in 12 basal readers and noted a regressive pull, developmentally," in the material.

Early experiences with the richness and variety of "real" reading materials seems to give children reason to read, teaching them, as Trelease (1985, p. 6) explains, not only "how to read, but to want to read." The affectivity of literature based, Whole Language programs gives meaning and pleasure to the process, thus making skills instruction at last meaningful—empowering both teachers and students. At least, it is safe to say the basal reader is not the only way to successfully teach children to read.

REFERENCES

Allington, Richard. "If They Don't Read Much, How They Ever Gonna Get Good?" *Journal of Reading*, vol. 21 (October 1977), pp. 57–61.

Anderson, Richard C., Elfrieda H. Hiebert, Judith A. Scott, and Ian A. G. Wilkinson. *Becoming a Nation of Readers: The Report of the Commission on Reading.* Washington, DC: The National Institute of Education, U.S. Department of Education, 1985.

Bader, Lois A., Jeannette Veatch, and J. Lloyd Eldredge. "Trade Books or Basal Readers?" *Reading Improvement*, vol. 24 (Spring 1987), pp. 62–67.

Blom, Gaston E., Richard R. Waite, and Sara G. Zimet. "Motivational Content Analysis of Primers." In *Basic Studies on Reading*, edited by Harry Levin and Joanna P. Williams. New York, NY: Basic Books, 1970.

Boehnlein, Mary. "Reading Intervention for High Risk First-Graders." *Educational Leadership*, vol. 44 (March 1987), pp. 32–37.

Chomsky, Carol. "When You Still Can't Read in Third Grade: After Decoding, What?" In *What Research Has to Say about Reading Instruction*, edited by S. Jay Samuels. Newark, DE: International Reading Association, 1978.

Clark, Margaret. *Young Fluent Readers*. London, England: Heinemann, 1976.

Cohen, Dorothy. "The Effect of Literature on Vocabulary and Reading Achievement" *Elementary English*, vol. 45 (February 1968), pp. 209–13, 217.

Connor, D. V. "The Relationship between Reading Achievement and Voluntary Reading of Children." *Educational Review*, vol. 6 (1953/1954), pp. 221–27.

Cullinan, Bernice, Angela Jagger, and Dorothy Strickland. "Language Expansion for Black Children in the Primary Grades: A Research Report." *Young Children*, vol. 29 (January 1974), pp. 98–112.

Davis, Floyd W., and James S. Lucas. "An Experiment in Individualized Reading." *The Reading Teacher* vol. 24 (May 1971), pp. 737–43, 747.

Durkin, Dolores. "Children Who Read before Grade One" *The Reading Teacher*, vol. 14 (January 1961), pp. 163–66.

Eldredge, J. Lloyd, and Dennie Butterfield. "Alternatives to Traditional Reading Instruction." *The Reading Teacher*, vol. 40 (October 1986), pp. 32–37.

Fader, Daniel, James Duggins, Tom Finn, and Elton McNeil. *The New Hooked on Books*. New York, NY: Berkeley, 1976.

Fielding, Linda G., Paul T. Wilson, and Richard Anderson. "A New Focus on Free Reading: The Role of Trade Books in Reading Instruction." In *The Contexts of School Based Literacy*, edited by Taffy E. Raphael. New York, NY: Random House, 1984.

Forester, Anne D. "What Teachers Can Learn from 'Natural Readers.'" *The Reading Teacher*, vol. 31 (November 1977), pp. 160–66.

Goodman, Ken. "Look What They've Done to Judy Blume!: The 'Basalization' of Children's Literature." *The New Advocate*, vol. 1 (Winter 1988), pp. 29–41.

Greaney, Vincent. "Factors Related to Amount and Type of Leisure Reading." *Reading Research Quarterly*, vol. 15, no. 3 (1980), pp. 337–57.

Holdaway, Don. "Shared Book Experience: Teaching Reading Using Favorite Books." *Theory into Practice*, vol. 21 (Fall 1982), pp. 293–300.

Hoskisson, Kenneth. "Learning to Read Naturally." *Language Arts*, vol. 56 (May 1979), pp. 489–96.

Koeller, Shirley. "25 Years Advocating Children's Literature in the Reading Program." *The Reading Teacher*, vol. 34 (February 1981), pp. 552–56.

LaBrant, Lou L. *An Evaluation of Free Reading in Grades Ten, Eleven, and Twelve*. Columbus, OH: Ohio State University Press, 1936.

Larrick, Nancy. "Illiteracy Starts Too Soon." *Phi Delta Kappan*, vol. 69 (November 1987), pp. 184–89.

Maxwell, James. *Reading Progress from 8 to 15*. Windsor, England: National Foundation for Educational Research, 1977.

McCracken, Robert, and Marlene McCracken. "Modeling Is the Key to Sustained Silent Reading." *The Reading Teacher*, vol. 31, (January 1978), pp. 406–08.

Pinnell, Gay Su. "Reading Recovery in Ohio 1985–86: Final Report." Technical Report, The Ohio State University, Columbus, OH, 1986.

Rasinski, Timothy V., and Diane E. Deford. "Learning within a Classroom Context: First Graders' Conceptions of Literacy." ED 262 393. Arlington, VA: ERIC Document Reproducing Service, 1985.

Reutzel, Ray, and Parker Fawson. "A Professor Returns to the Classroom: Implementing Whole Language." Unpublished manuscript, Brigham Young University, Provo, UT, 1988.

Thompson, Richard A. "Summarizing Research Pertaining to Individualized Reading." ED 065 836. Arlington, VA: ERIC Document Reproducing Service, 1971.

Thorndike, Robert L. "Reading Comprehension, Education in 15 Countries: An Empirical Study," vol. 3, *International Studies in Education*. New York, NY: Holsted-Wiley, 1973.

Trelease, Jim. *The Read-Aloud Handbook*. New York, NY: Viking/Penguin, 1985.

Tunnell, Michael O. "The Natural Act of Reading: An Affective Approach" *The Advocate*, vol. 5 (Winter/Spring 1986), pp. 156–64.

Tunnell, Michael O., James E. Calder, Joseph E. Justen, III, and Phillip B. Waldrop. "An Affective Approach to Reading: Effectively Teaching Reading to Mainstreamed Handicapped Children." *The Pointer*, vol. 32 (Spring 1988), pp. 38–40.

White, Jane H., Joseph L. Vaughan, and I. Laverne Rorie. "Picture of a Classroom Where Reading Is for Real." *The Reading Teacher*, vol. 40 (October 1986), pp. 84–86.

Michael O. Tunnell teaches in the Department of Curriculum and Instruction at Northern Illinois University in DeKalb, Illinois. James S. Jacobs teaches elementary education at Brigham Young University in Provo, Utah.

The Role of Literature in Reading Achievement

Pamela J. Farris
Marjorie R. Hancock

Since the report *Becoming a Nation of Readers* (Anderson et al. 1985), the relationship between the amount of time elementary school students spend reading and their level of reading achievement continues to generate interest. The findings of this report strongly suggest that school reading programs should give greater priority to time spent on actual reading throughout the school day. Equally important is the acknowledgement of a relationship between students' time spent reading outside of school and their reading achievement (Anderson, Wilson, and Fielding 1988). Time spent reading books is closely associated with the measure of a child's status as a reader. Reading books has been found to be "a cause, not merely a reflection of reading proficiency" (35).

The gradual effect of these reports has been to shift the focus of elementary reading programs away from a traditional basal reader program toward a literature-based approach, using quality children's literature as the basis of a sound reading curriculum (Cullinan 1987). In response to this research, teachers have encouraged more reading not only within their reading programs but also during free-time activity. Sustained silent reading, reading incentive programs, and reading aloud are activities that have reappeared in elementary classrooms in an attempt to influence reading habits both inside and outside of school.

REVIEW OF LITERATURE

The growing influence of literature in both the school reading program and out-of-school reading endeavors has provided a new perspective for the study of reading achievement. Recent research offers some insights into literature-based reading as an effective alternative to traditional instruction and into the relationship of time spent on reading, in and out of school, on reading achievement.

The question of whether children, using children's paperback literature books, could learn to read as well as they learn using basals was addressed by Eldredge and Butterfield (1986). Experimental approaches to beginning reading based on the use of literature with and without special decoding strategies resulted in students' significant achievement and attitudinal gains when compared to traditional programs. The findings of this study provided the impetus for teachers who desired to use children's literature books in place of traditional programs to do so without fear of loss of achievement.

A similar study comparing literature reading programs with basal reading programs (Bader, Veatch, and Eldredge 1987) suggested that a literature program with heterogeneous grouping of students offered an effective alternative to the traditional reading approach. Not only did this study provide data supporting the use of children's literature, but it also firmly disputed the effectiveness of ability-based reading groups on reading achievement.

Research support for literature-based reading instruction continues to supply momentum for the use of literature in the reading program by encouraging this alternative with children of all ages and abilities (Tunnell and Jacobs 1989). At the same time, findings of research relating time spent reading and reading achievement have further supported literature's role in reading achievement.

The amount of independent, silent reading that children do in school has been found to be related significantly to gains in reading achievement (Leinhardt, Zigmond, and Cooley 1981). The amount of reading students do out of school has also consistently been found to be related to gains in reading achievement by Anderson, Wilson, and Fielding (1988). Unfortunately, however, 50 percent of the fifth-grade students in their two studies read books four minutes a day or less. For the majority of their subjects, reading books occupied only 1 percent or less of their leisure time.

A comprehensive research study by Taylor, Frye, and Maruyama (1990) investigated the impact of time spent reading at school and at home on the reading achievement of intermediate-grade students. Statistical analysis revealed that minutes of reading per day during reading class (15.8 minutes of a 50-minute period) contributed significantly to gains in students' reading achievement. This finding provided additional research support for the theory that time engaged in silent reading at school is beneficial for intermediate-grade students. Although minutes of reading per day at home (15.0 minutes) were not found to contribute significantly to students' growth in reading achievement, it is notable that the findings did approach significance.

Fielding, Wilson, and Anderson (1986) have suggested that the amount of time devoted to reading both in and out of school is dependent on the priority the classroom teacher gives to independent reading. Through their emphasis on the importance of literature, teachers do influence the amount of time students read in their classrooms. The choice of materials in the reading program, the inclusion of additional time for independent reading, the decision to read aloud to students, the arrangement of time to check out books in the school library, and the support of students' participation in paperback book clubs illustrate the impact a teacher has on the actual time spent reading in and out of school.

The results of these studies collectively support the conventional belief that time spent reading in the classroom contributes to reading growth. This conclusion is especially important because it supports the criticism that students in the nation's elementary classrooms spend too much time on skill worksheets and too little time in silent reading, as stated in *Becoming a Nation of Readers* (Anderson et al. 1985). To a lesser degree, the results also support the implications of reading time outside of school and its relationship to reading achievement. If, in fact, the adage "practice makes perfect" is true, time spent practicing the art of reading can contribute to reading achievement. The focus of school reading programs and the methods of the classroom teacher can indeed have an impact on the role of literature in reading achievement.

PURPOSE OF THE STUDY

The purpose of this study was to investigate the use of literature in and outside of school and its relationship to reading achievement. The literature reading patterns of students were derived from three sources: type of classroom reading program, school library availability and circulation, and level of paperback book club participation. Information on these three sources of literature was gathered and examined in an effort to establish a possible relationship between reading of children's literature and reading achievement. A study of the relationship between reading achievement levels and the related use of literature in school and outside of school reading may produce insights into the reading programs and independent reading patterns of children in our nation's elementary schools.

DESIGN OF THE STUDY

A survey study was designed to provide information on the reading achievement of sixth-grade students and the role of literature in their reading. A two-page survey consisting of fifteen questions was prepared, focusing on information for the entire school and on achievement data for sixth-grade students.

Specific questions covered school enrollment, volumes in the school library, number of circulated volumes for the prior school year, percentage of teachers in the school providing the opportunity for students to purchase books through paperback book clubs, and the primary method of teaching reading. Questions on reading achievement focused on sixth graders. Information collected included sixth-grade enrollments, racial/ethnic background, and mean percentile of sixth-grade students in reading achievement.

SUBJECTS

The schools that served as subjects for the survey were randomly chosen from a list, provided by Scholastic Books, of rural elementary schools with an enrollment of less than five hundred students in areas populated by 150 inhabitants or less per square mile. Because over two-thirds of elementary schools in the United States have enrollments under five hundred students (National Center for Educational Statistics 1989) and many of these are located in rural areas, this population was appropriate for acquiring insight into the reading programs and literature practices of this large proportion of our nation's elementary schools.

Surveys were mailed to a random sampling of elementary schools in those states that were known to report reading achievement scores using the Iowa Test of Basic Skills. A total of forty-six usable surveys representing schools in thirteen states with a total student enrollment of 11,128 students and a mean school enrollment of 241.9 students supplied data for analysis.

The forty-six schools accounted for eighty-four sixth-grade classrooms enrolling 1,694 sixth-grade students. Of these students, 879 were male, and 815 were female. Sixth-grade enrollment ranged from 2 to 153 students per school. The average sixth-grade classroom contained 20.1 students with 10.5 males and 9.6 females. The racial/ethnic composition of the 1,694 sixth graders included 1,658 white/Caucasian (97.9 percent), 20 Hispanic (1.2 percent), 8 Asian/Pacific Islander (0.5 percent), and 3 African American (0.2 percent).

FINDINGS

Reading Program and Reading Achievement

The mean percentile for reading achievement for sixth graders when reported as reading comprehension on the Iowa Test of Basic Skills was the 68.7 percentile. Mean percentiles in all forty-six schools ranged from the 35th to the 80th percentile.

The survey indicated that three programs were used for the teaching of reading in the participating elementary schools. The traditional basal series program was primarily used by about one-third of the schools (sixteen schools or 34.8 percent). A total literature-based approach was reported in use by only one school. The combination approach of using both basal and literature was overwhelmingly reported by nearly two-thirds of the schools (twenty-nine schools or 63.0 percent). There was no significant difference, however, between the type of reading program used and the reading comprehension achievement of sixth graders ($t = 1.47$; $p > .05$).

Paperback Book Club Participation and Reading Achievement

Survey participants were asked to indicate the range of paperback book club participation in their schools. All but one of the 46 schools indicated 75–100 percent of their teachers participated in paperback book clubs. Purchase totals of paperback books for the 1988–1989 school year by the 46 participating schools ranged from $162.20 to $3344.65 per school. The mean amount for each school was $1023.43 with the mean amount per student being $4.23. The average amount per pupil ranged from $0.64 to $26.23. No significant differences were found, however, between the reading comprehension achievement of students who spent more than $4.00 on paperback books and those who spent less than $4.00 on paperback purchases through the book club ($t = 0.59; p > .05$).

Paperback book club participants who indicated they used a combination (literature plus basal) reading program spent $4.62 per student on paperbacks. Those schools reporting only the use of a basal series, on the other hand, spent $5.78 per student on paperbacks. Programs using real literature may purchase trade books as part of their reading program while schools using basals may encourage their students to purchase quality literature in paperback form for their own personal use.

Library Volumes, Circulation, and Reading Achievement

The library volumes in the school libraries of thirty-eight of the forty-six participating schools totaled 213,414 volumes. Twelve schools did not report total library volumes but, in many cases, indicated classroom rather than school libraries. The libraries ranged in size from 400 to 15,500 volumes. The mean number of volumes per school was 5,616. The volumes per student ranged from 5 to 129.2. The average volumes per student was 24.2. There was no significant difference in reading achievement between students in schools with greater than 25 volumes per student and students in schools with fewer than 25 volumes per student ($t = 0.64; p > .05$).

Library circulation for the 1988–89 school year was reported by twenty-seven of the participating schools at 185,194 volumes. Circulation ranged from 500 volumes to 21,600 volumes per school year. Each school averaged a circulation of 6,859 volumes. The mean for each student in those schools reporting circulations was 25.64 volumes circulated per student. The number of circulated volumes per student ranged from 1.5 to 77.7. Surveys from nineteen schools did not report circulated volumes probably because of incomplete circulation records or the existence of classroom rather than school libraries. A significant difference between sixth-grade reading achievement and circulated volumes per student was evident for students using greater than 30 volumes per year and students using less than 30 volumes per year ($t = 2.894; p < .01$).

DISCUSSION

The findings of this study did not reveal statistical differences between paperback book club purchases and reading achievement nor between availability of school library volumes and reading achievement. A significant difference was revealed, however, between library circulation and reading achievement. Because many elementary schools do not have a librarian on a full-time basis, a teacher's knowledge and encouragement of children's literature may be vital in fostering library circulation. That influence, however, may have even greater impact in the classroom where a teacher's personal reading/literature philosophy is implemented.

The results of this survey study may actually point to the key role of the classroom teacher in the use of literature for in-school and leisure reading. Further research is obviously necessary to explore the impact of the teacher in implementing literature in the reading program and assessing the effect of literature usage on reading achievement. In the meantime, however, in lieu of empirical research findings, teachers may influence reading both in and out of school by promoting literature in several ways.

To keep up with the increasing wealth of trade books, classroom teachers must be prepared and encouraged to grow in their knowledge of children's literature. Reading journal articles and perusing the latest book reviews is necessary for teachers wishing to be current about the rapidly changing world of literature. A graduate-level children's literature course or a series of inservice workshops may provide new insights into using, sharing, and responding to literature in the classroom.

Throughout the school day, elementary teachers have the power to give priority to literature within their classrooms. Everyday, teachers can portray reading as a source of pleasure by reading to their students. They can assure students' access to interesting books through the school library, public library, or classroom library. Paperback book club participation can be encouraged to spread the powerful feeling of book ownership. Each day, time can be provided for children to read books of their own choosing. Reading a book and enjoying it can be given priority in the reading program. Children need time to share books and their responses to them through discussion, writing, art, drama, and music activities that deepen their reading experience and make it memorable.

Through their knowledge of books, teachers can influence students' reading achievement. Knowing enough about books to place the right book in the hand of the right child at the right moment may have enormous impact on personal reading.

If the future of our country depends on developing a "nation of readers," then each classroom must become a small community of children and teachers who know the value of books and discover the joy of reading. (Huck, Hepler, and Hickman 1987, viii)

Rather than merely concentrating on the skills of the traditional reading program, a teacher can focus on literature in the reading program and help children explore the joys of reading as a lifelong journey.

Conventional wisdom and empirical research point to the relationship between time spent reading and reading achievement. The recent thrust toward incorporating literature into the reading program in order to spend more time on actual reading may have effects that reach beyond even reading achievement. For, in addition to the achievement scores acquired for validating research, the only true test of reading is whether students do indeed read. Incorporating literature into the classroom reading program may not only lead to improved reading scores but also to an attitude toward reading that transcends the classroom door to a lifetime of personal enrichment.

REFERENCES

Anderson, R. C., E. H. Hiebert, J. A. Scott, and I. A. Wilkinson. 1985. *Becoming a nation of readers: The report of the Commission on Reading.* Washington, DC: The National Institute of Education, U.S. Department of Education.

Anderson, R. C., P. T. Wilson, and L. G. Fielding. 1988. Growth in reading and how children spend their time outside of school. *Reading Research Quarterly* 23:285–303.

Bader, L. A., J. Veatch, and J. L. Eldredge. 1987. Trade books or basal readers? *Reading Improvement* 24:62–67.

Cullinan. B., ed. 1987. *Children's literature in the reading program.* Newark, DE: International Reading Association.

Digest of education statistics. 1989. Washington, DC: U.S. Government Printing Office.

Eldredge, J. L., and D. Butterfield. 1986. Alternatives to traditional reading instruction. *The Reading Teacher* 40:32–37.

Fielding, L. G., P. T. Wilson, and R. C. Anderson. 1986. A new focus on free reading: The role of trade books in reading instruction. In *The Contexts of School Based*

Literacy, edited by T. E. Raphael, 149–60. New York, NY: Random House.

Huck, C. S., S. Hepler, and J. Hickman. 1987. *Children's literature in the elementary school*. 4th ed. New York, NY: Holt, Rinehart and Winston.

Leinhardt, G., N. Zigmond, and W. Cooley. 1981. Reading instruction and its effects. *American Educational Research Journal* 18:343–62.

Taylor, B. M., B. J. Frye, and G. Maruyama. 1990. Time spent reading and reading growth. *American Educational Research Journal* 27:351–62.

Tunnell, M. O., and J. S. Jacobs. 1989. Using "real" books: Research findings on literature based reading instruction. *The Reading Teacher* 42:470–77.

Pamela J. Farris is an associate professor of curriculum and instruction at Northern Illinois University in DeKalb. Marjorie R. Hancock is an assistant professor of elementary education at Kansas State University in Manhattan.

Analysis of Writing Samples of Students Taught by Teachers Using Whole Language and Traditional Approaches

Mary Ellen Varble

Throughout the elementary school years, a child's writing competency receives major attention. Instruction begins during the first year in school when the child is taught to write symbols that represent the sounds of language. As the child becomes equipped to handle the mechanics of the writing task, the written language experience becomes the most important part of the writing skill.

Traditionally, the elementary school curriculum stressed the mechanics when written expression was considered. Because of the current stress on meaning and content, researchers are now questioning the emphasis on mechanics in the improvement of written expression (Calkins, 1985; Hajek, 1984; Humes, 1983; Slaughter, 1988).

BACKGROUND

For the past 2 decades, educators have been disenchanted with the quality of writing produced by public school children (Reutzel & Hollingsworth, 1998). This concern has grown recently, fueled by competency tests now given in more than 39 states (Calkins, 1985). Students spend over 40% of the school day with pencil in hand, but the bulk of that time is spent in exercises that require students to record responses without composing text (Applebee, 1984). McCaig (1982) has stated that the inability of students to compose an intelligible, coherent passage of written English is a national disgrace and a source of outrage in communities throughout the country.

In a year-long study on writing, Graves (1978) found that writing usually consists of workbook exercises, drills in penmanship, vo-

From "Analysis of Writing Samples of Students Taught by Teachers Using Whole Language and Traditional Approaches" by M. E. Varble, 1990, *Journal of Educational Research, 83*, pp. 245–251, May/June, 1990. Reprinted with permission of the Helen Dwight Reid Educational Foundation. Published by Heldref Publications, 1319 Eighteenth Street, N.W., Washington, D.C. 20036–1802. Copyright © 1990.

cabulary, spelling, punctuation, capitalization, and grammar.

To ensure that children acquire the necessary basic writing skills, researchers have identified lists of skills, taught by the teachers, and learned by children (Ruddell, 1985). These skill lists are usually accompanied by record-keeping systems and mandated testing programs. Teachers and children are so caught up in record keeping, completing work sheets, and testing that little time is left for instruction. Dissatisfaction with schools is growing anew as parents, teachers, and researchers have noticed a reduction in the time students actually spend in writing (Reutzel & Hollingsworth, 1988). Studies show that most writing time is devoted to mechanical chores. "Only 3% of the school day is actually spent on composing" (Calkins, 1985, p. 26).

Teachers using the traditional writing method and teachers using a natural writing technique approach instruction differently. The traditional writing method stresses the visible aspects of language and assumes that by isolating skills used in writing the child will learn more easily and quickly (Holdaway, 1985). The traditional approach of teaching written expression has recently come under critical observation.

Children learn to talk through social contexts rather than isolated skills (King & Rentel, 1979). One view is that the teaching of writing in the elementary school should follow the same type of natural development exhibited by children who learn to write through an exposure to written material, paper, and pencils before going to school (Holdaway, 1988; Staab & Smith, 1985).

Gunderson and Shapiro (1986) and Reutzel and Hollingsworth (1988) believe that if teachers replaced their traditional approach to teaching writing with the "whole language" approach, the quality of students' writing would improve (Gunderson & Shapiro, 1986; Reutzel & Hollingsworth, 1988). Many teachers are becoming enthusiastic about the whole language approach as an answer to the problem (Hajek, 1984). The whole language approach of teaching writing emphasizes an approach to learning that advocates teaching language as a whole, connected process.

Writing experts believe that one way to improve the quality of students' writing is to spend more time on composing and less time practicing isolated skills, that is, punctuation, capitation, grammar, spelling, and legibility (Graves, 1985).

The whole language approach to teaching writing includes the following principles (Baumann, 1985; Gunderson & Shapiro, 1986; Hajek, 1984; Reutzel & Hollingsworth, 1988; Rich, 1985; Wangberg & Reutten, 1986):

1. Students spend at least 30 min a day, 4 days a week in the composing process.
2. Children start composing sentences as soon as they can write a few consonants.
3. Students are encouraged to use invented spelling.
4. Learners are encouraged to express their thoughts, feelings, and experiences in writing.
5. Students think of themselves as authors.
6. The steps included in the writing process are prewriting, drafting, conferencing, editing, revising, and publishing.
7. Teachers use trade books as a model of quality writing.
8. Teachers and students together evaluate the assignment by looking at the composition as a whole.
9. Students and their needs are the heart of schooling.
10. Whole language writing provides students with the opportunity to express their ideas privately without fear of mistakes. Each student's writing assignment is made public only with that student's permission.
11. Students spend a large period of time writing and thus learn to write by writing.

PURPOSE

In this study I examined writing samples to assess the quality of writing of second and sixth graders who were taught by whole language and traditional writing approaches. Only the students of teachers using whole language and traditional approaches, as defined in Figure 1, were included in this study. This research was conducted at the second- and sixth-grade levels in seven schools in western Indiana.

METHOD

The initial procedure for conducting this research was to identify teachers who had used one of the two writing approaches for the entire year. The sample population used in this study was second- and sixth-grade students in selected elementary schools in the counties of Clay, Greene, Owen, and Vigo in Indiana. The total number of students participating in the study was 248. This figure included 120 second graders (62 in the whole language group and 58 in the traditional group) and 128 sixth graders (62 in the whole language group and 66 in the traditional group). Classroom teachers were asked to complete the Writing Instruction Information sheet. (See Appendix 1 for a reproduction of the one given to the teachers.) I analyzed characteristics that identified traditional and whole language approaches from the traditional and whole language definitions of teaching writing. The students of teachers who indicated on at least 8 out of 10 questions that they use the whole language approach were placed in the whole language group, and the students of teachers who indicated on at least 8 out of 10 questions that they used the traditional approach were placed in the traditional group (see Appendix 2). The students of teachers who did not use either the whole language or the traditional approach to teaching writing, as defined in Appendix 2, were not included in the study.

All the students in the study participated in a 45-min session that included 15 min for a prewriting activity and 30 min for writing. All the sessions were held at the same time of day. I was the teacher for all the students in the study. All the second graders wrote on the

Whole Language	*Traditional*
Whole to parts learning is emphasized.	Parts to whole learning is emphasized.
Process is most important.	Product is most important.
Language learning is based on experience.	Language learning is based on hierarchy of skills.
Learners use writing for personal purposes.	Learners use writing to satisfy others.
Learning begins with need and moves to skills.	Learning begins with skills and moves to need.
Need—Writing—Skills	Skills—Writing—Need
Language is learned through social context.	Language is learned through skills.
School environment is like home.	School environment is different from home.
Students choose topics.	Teacher assigns topics.
Invented spelling is encouraged.	Emphasis is on correct spelling.
Evaluation is informal.	Evaluation is formal.

**FIGURE 1
CONSTRASTING WHOLE LANGUAGE AND TRADITIONAL APPROACHES TO TEACHING WRITING**

same subject (fantasy), and all the sixth graders wrote on the same subject (mystery). (See Appendixes 3 and 4 for lesson plans.)

Collecting the Data

Samples of writing were collected in May 1988. All the subjects had been exposed to the teaching method for the same length of time. The subjective nature of original writing was regarded as a problem to be resolved through procedures of measurement. In order to establish a maximum degree of objectivity, an attempt was made to control certain variables. Those variables significant to research in composition include the writer, the assignment, the rater, and the colleague (the "between rater") (Braddock, Lloyd-Jones, & Shoer, 1963). The variables and the techniques employed to secure objective evaluations of the subjects' writing samples were as follows:

The writer variable. Each subject wrote once on the day that the researcher taught at his or her school.

The assignment variable. Each subject in the second grade wrote on the same topic (fantasy), and each subject in the sixth grade wrote on the same topic (mystery). Each student had approximately 30 min to complete his or her writing sample.

The rater variable. Writing samples were coded so that names did not appear on the papers. In an effort to control the fatigue factor, suggestions for rest periods were included as a part of the instructions for rating.

The colleague, or between-rater, variable. The most important variation to be controlled may be one that exists between raters. To meet this problem, I gave considerable time and effort to five areas: (a) the preparation of the writing samples for rating, (b) the development of criteria for evaluation, (c) the writing of instructions for rating, (d) the selection of the raters, and (e) the training of the raters. The following paragraphs discuss the details of each of these areas in the sequence of their occurrence.

Preparation of papers. Three photo copies of each writing sample were made so that the original could be returned to the writer. Each writer was assigned to a different number so that the papers were anonymous. Each of the second-grade papers was evaluated twice by each rater, and each of the sixth-grade papers was evaluated twice by each rater so that all the papers were evaluated a total of six times.

Criteria for evaluation. Two categories of criteria were defined and typed on a single page, and a copy was given to each rater. The copy read as follows:

Criteria for Evaluation

Quality of Content
- Key ideas developed with appropriate and varied details and reasoning
- Clear sense of writer's purpose
- Organized with obvious beginning and end with focus on topic
- Demonstrates sophisticated language expressions
- Writing shows a keen awareness of audience and can be understood by peers

Mastery of Mechanics
- Words spelled correctly
- Correct punctuation
- Complete sentences
- Variety of sentence structures
- Correct grammar and usage

Raters worked with one criterion measure at a time; thus, the instructions for rating were used with each of the writing samples for each of the two criteria. This procedure was designed to help the rater to be objective.

The instructions for rating. The outline of instructions that follows is a reproduction of the one used by the raters:

Instructions for Rating

1. Review the criteria for evaluation in order to focus clearly on the evaluation you will be doing at this time.
2. Read carefully the content evaluation. (See following page)
3. Read all the papers and sort them into piles: the top group, the middle group, and the low group. The criteria for these piles are: (1) this seems to follow the criterion for evaluation very well; (2) this seems to follow the criterion in some ways; (3) this doesn't follow the criterion very well.
4. Upon the second reading, separate each pile into two smaller piles. There will now be six piles containing papers from low to high.

High	Average	Low	
6 5	4 3	2 1	= Score to be written on each paper in each pile

5. Assign the proper score on score sheet for each paper. (The criterion for each score is outlined with the Criteria for Evaluation guide noted above)
6. Read carefully the mechanics evaluation. Then follow steps 3, 4, and 5 above.

Selection of the raters. The researcher selected raters from teachers in Vigo County, Indiana.

Training of the raters. Three raters were each given a copy of the Criteria for Evaluation and the Instructions for rating. The criteria were discussed orally with the typed copy of the Criteria for Evaluation used as a guide. The Instructions for Rating was also discussed. Because it is important that raters have a common understanding of the rating procedure, each rater practiced using the criteria through the sequence of instructions by evaluating sample student essays. This method of training raters to use a common set of criteria through a planned sequence of evaluation was designed to provide a substantial measure of objectivity to the process of rating subjective material. Sweedler-Brown (1985) stated:

> Studies on holistic evaluation of essay examinations indicate that training graders to use the holistic scale affects their evaluations in general and the reliability of their essay grading in particular. Most studies attempting to isolate factors which affect the reliability of essay grading conclude that the best reliability levels can be attained if graders are trained by studying descriptions and then using the scale to evaluate sample student essays. If it is properly conducted, training seem critical in establishing good reading reliability. (p. 49)

Analysis of Data

First, three reliability coefficients were calculated: (a) between Rater 1 and Rater 2, (b) between Rater 1 and Rater 3, and (c) between Rater 2 and Rater 3. A correlation of .66 or higher was considered acceptable. Reliability coefficients between ratings of the subjects' writing samples were sufficiently high to support the tests of significance between the treatments (see Tables 1 and 2 for the results). Sec-

TABLE 1
CORRELATION MATRIX OF RELIABILITY BETWEEN RATERS (QUALITY OF CONTENT CRITERIA)

Rater	Rater 1	Rater 2	Rater 3
1	1.0000		
2	.7416	1.0000	
3	.7818	.7610	1.0000

TABLE 2
CORRELATION MATRIX OF RELIABILITY BETWEEN RATERS (MASTERY OF MECHANICS CRITERIA)

Rater	Rater 1	Rater 2	Rater 3
1	1.0000		
2	.7413	1.0000	
3	.8000	.7708	1.0000

ond, analysis of variance was used to examine the difference between the two groups' scores (Mosenthal, Tamor, & Walmsley, 1983). The basic hypotheses of this study were as follows:

1. No significant difference exists between the evaluators' ratings on quality of content of writing samples of second-grade students who were taught by teachers using the whole language approach in teaching writing and of students who were taught by teachers using the traditional approach.
2. No significant difference exists between the evaluators' ratings on quality of content of writing samples of sixth-grade students who were taught by teachers using the whole language approach in teaching writing and of students who were taught by teachers using the traditional approach.
3. No significant difference exists between the evaluators' ratings on mastery of mechanics of writing samples of second-grade students who were taught by teachers using the whole language approach in teaching writing and of students who were taught by teachers using the traditional approach.
4. No significant difference exist between the evaluators' ratings on mastery of mechanics of writing samples of sixth-grade students who were taught by teachers using the whole language approach in teaching writing and of students who were taught by teachers using the traditional approach.

Significance was tested at the .05 level. At the second-grade level, 58 students taught by teachers using the traditional approach and 62 students taught by teachers using the whole language approach were evaluated on both content and mechanics. At the sixth-grade level, 66 students taught by teachers using the traditional approach and 62 students taught by teachers using the whole language approach were evaluated on both content and mechanics. Students were placed in groups according to the teaching approach of their teachers. An analysis of variance of scores from the written samples was justified as the appropriate test for this study.

RESULTS

Difference effects between the written samples of the subjects taught by the traditional approach and those taught by the whole language approach were of major importance to this study (see Table 3 on page 402 for a summary of all test results). The test results of the four hypotheses were as follows:

1. The results of the statistical test for the quality of content criterion of second graders, $F = .0260$, revealed that a significant difference existed between the evaluators' rating of students who were taught by teachers using the whole language approach in teaching writing and of students who were taught by teachers using the traditional approach.
2. The results of the statistical test for the quality of content criterion of sixth graders, $F = .3537$, revealed that no significant difference existed between the evaluators' rating of students who were taught by teachers using the whole language approach in teaching writing and of students who were taught by teachers using the traditional approach.
3. The results of the statistical test for the mastery of mechanics criterion of second graders, $F = .4295$, revealed that no significant difference existed between the evaluators' rating of students who were taught by teachers using the whole language approach in teaching writing and of students who were taught by teachers using the traditional approach.
4. The results of the statistical test for the mastery of mechanics criterion of sixth

TABLE 3
SUMMARY OF ANALYSIS OF VARIANCE TEST RESULTS

Source	Degrees of Freedom	Sums of Squares	Mean Squares	F Ratio	F Prob.
Criterion 1: Quality of content					
Grade 2					
Between groups	1	62.9518	62.9518	5.0830	.0260[a]
Within groups	118	1461.4149	12.3849		
Total	119	1524.3667			
Grade 6					
Between groups	1	8.5323	8.5323	.8667	.3537[b]
Within groups	126	1240.4599	9.8449		
Total	127	1248.9922			
Criterion 2: Mastery of mechanics					
Grade 2					
Between groups	1	5.5388	5.5388	.6284	.4295[b]
Within groups	118	1040.0528	8.8140		
Total	119	1045.5917			
Grade 6					
Between groups	1	2.4206	2.4206	.2110	.6468[b]
Within groups	126	1445.7590	11.4743		
Total	127	1448.1797			

[a] Significant; [b] not significant.

graders, $F = .6468$, revealed that no significant difference existed between the evaluators' rating of students who were taught by teachers using the whole language approach in teaching writing and of students who were taught by teachers using the traditional approach.

DISCUSSION

This study evaluated the quality of writing of second and sixth graders who were taught by two different writing instructional approaches (traditional and whole language).

In this study, second-grade students who were taught by the whole language approach produced better writing samples when evaluated on content. From the responses given by the teachers who used this writing approach, I am confident that these second graders had whole language writing instruction for 1 year. Nothing is known about the writing instruction prior to second grade. Some of the students may have had whole language instruction; some may not have had such instruction. For second graders, 1 year of emphasis on content appears to make a difference in the writing samples when evaluated on key ideas, purpose, organization, language expression, and an awareness of audience.

The sixth-grade whole language group did not show a difference in the area of quality of content. An analysis of the responses given by the teachers of the students in the whole language group indicated that the sixth-grade students included in this study were exposed to the whole language writing approach for 1 year. I do not know what type of instruction was used by the teachers of these students prior to the sixth grade. To determine whether differences occur at the sixth-grade level, researchers may need to ensure that, when testing the whole language approach, older students who are being tested have had at least several years of whole language writing instruction if a traditional emphasis was used during the primary years (K–3) of schooling. More than one year of the whole language approach may be needed before the writing samples of such students show an improvement when evaluated for ideas, purpose, organization, language expression, and awareness of audience.

No difference was found in the mastery of mechanics in any of the second-grade or sixth-grade groups of students. The teachers who used the traditional approach indicated that they stressed correct spelling and punctuation, complete sentences, variety of sentence structure, and correct grammar and usage. The students taught writing by teachers using the traditional approach, however, did not produce better writing samples when evaluated by the mastery of mechanics criteria. Those students who were taught by teachers using the whole language writing approach were as proficient as the traditional group in their mastery of mechanics.

While collecting data for this study, I made the following observations in the classrooms of the subjects:

1. The students willingly wrote the fantasy and mystery stories, although some students needed more prewriting discussion time than others to get an idea.
2. Before writing, students in every class asked if the stories would be graded. When I assured the students that the stories would not be graded, they were eager to begin writing.
3. There were some traditional-group sixth-grade students who wrote lengthy stories for the study, but, according to teacher comments, many of those students were reluctant to write during normal class time.
4. One class of traditional-group second-grade students wrote individual books for the researcher 2 days after the data were collected because of their motivation to write (as stated by the classroom teacher).
5. The students wanted reassurance that the stories would be returned so that they could share them with their classmates and parents.
6. The students seemed proud of their writing. Some comments made were: "Do you like my title?" "May I draw you a picture?" "Will you be able to read my writing?" and "Will my story be published?"

Collecting the writing samples for this study was an enjoyable experience. The students were willing to write and share their writing samples. The procedure used for the writing activity was positive.

The results of this research project are encouraging to the advocates of whole language; a study evaluating more than one writing sample from each student who has been taught for over 1 year by a teacher using the whole language approach would be beneficial.

REFERENCES

Applebee, A. N. (1984). Writing and reasoning. *Review of Educational Research, 54,* 577–596.

Baumann, J. F. (1985). *Whole language instruction and basal readers.* Ginn Occasional papers, Writings in Reading and Language Arts. No. 20. Columbus, OH: Silver, Burdett & Ginn.

Braddock, R. Lloyd-Jones, R., & Shoer, L. (1963). *Research in written composition*. Champaign: National Council of Teachers of English.

Calkins, L. M. (1985). 'I Am One Who Writes' New Approaches to Children's Writing. *American Educator, 9*, 26–29, 42, 44.

Graves, D. H. (1978). *Balance the basics: Let them write*. New York: The Ford Foundation.

Graves, D. H. (1985). All children can write. *Learning Disabilities Focus, 1*, 36–43.

Gunderson, L., & Shapiro, J. (1986). Some readings on whole language instruction. *Reading-Canada-Lecture, 5*(1), 22–26.

Hajek, E. (1984). Whole language: Sensible answers to the old problems. *Momentum, 15*, 39–40.

Holdaway, D. (1995). *Stability and change in literacy learning*. Portsmouth, NH: Heinemann Educational Books.

Humes, A. (1983). Research on the composing process. *Reviewing Educational Research, 53*, 210–216.

King, M. K., & Rentel, V. (1979). Toward a theory of early writing development. *Research in the Teaching of English, 13*, 243–253.

McCaig, R. (1992). *How to (and How not to) Conduct an Assessment of Student Writing*, (ERIC Document Reproduction No. 229 396)

Mosenthal, P., Tamor, L., & Walmsey, S. (1983). *Research on writing: Principles and methods*. New York: Longman Inc.

Reutzel, D. R., & Hollingsworth, P. M. (1988). Whole language and the practitioner. *Academic Therapy, 23*, 405–415.

Rich, S. J. (1985). Restoring power to teachers: The impact of "whole language." *Language Arts, 62*, 717–724.

Ruddell, R. B. (1985). Knowledge and attitudes toward testing: Field educators and legislators. *The Reading Teacher, 38*, 538–543.

Slaughter, H. B. (1988). Direct and indirect teaching in a whole language program. *The Reading Teacher, 42*, 30–34.

Staab, C. F., & Smith, K. (1985). Classroom perspective on teaching writing. *The Reading Teacher, 38*, 841–844.

Sweedler-Brown, C. O. (1985). The influence of training and experience on holistic essay evaluations. *English Journal, 74*, 49–55.

Wangberg, E. G., & Reutten, M. K. (1986). Whole language approaches for developing and evaluating basic writing ability. *Lifelong Learning, 9*, 13–15, 24, 25.

APPENDIX 1

Writing Instruction Information

1. What is the average amount of time per week that your students are involved in writing in completing work sheets? _____
2. What is the average amount of time per week that your students are involved in writing (other than work sheets)? _____
3. What is the average amount of time per week that your students are instructed in handwriting skills? _____
4. What type of prewriting techniques do you use? _____
5. Do your students ever publish their stories? _____
   If yes, _____ often, _____ sometimes, _____ rarely.
   If yes, in what form? _____
6. Do you encourage invented spelling? _____
7. Do you assign grades to writing assignments? _____
8. When evaluating writing assignments, do you base your evaluation more heavily on content (sentence sense, coherence, good ideas, organization, word clarity), or mechanics (capitalization, punctuation, spellings legibility)? _____
9. Do your students edit their own stories? _____
10. When assigning a writing project, do you specify a purpose? _____

APPENDIX 2

Definitions for Scoring Procedure

The following characteristics were taken to identify traditional and whole language approaches. The numbers correspond with the numbers on the Writing Instruction Information form. Students of teachers who indicated on at least 8 out of 10 questions that they use the whole language approach were placed in one group; students of teachers who indicated on 8 out of 10 questions that they used the traditional approach were placed in the other group.

Traditional	Whole Language
1. Students spend 4 or more hours a week in completing work sheets.	Students spend less than 4 hours a week in completing work sheets.
2. Students spend less than 2 hours a week in writing (other than work sheets).	Students spend 2 or more hours a week in writing (other than work sheets).
3. Students spent 2 or more hours per week instructed in handwriting skills.	Students spend less than 2 hours per week instructed in handwriting skills.
4. Teachers do not use prewriting techniques.	Teachers use brainstorming, discussion, semantic webbing, children's literature, or questioning techniques.
5. Students do not publish stories.	Students publish their stories.
6. Teachers do not encourage invented spelling.	Teachers encourage invented spelling.
7. Teachers assign grade to assignment.	Teachers do not assign grade to assignment.
8. Evaluation is based on mechanics.	Evaluation is based on content.
9. Teachers edit stories.	Students and teachers both edit stories.
10. No purpose is specified in writing project.	A purpose is specified in writing project.

APPENDIX 3

Lesson Plan (Second Grade)

Objective. To understand the meaning of the concept "fantasy" and write a short story that is fantasy.

A Common Experience. Ask the children to listen, as I read *Where the Wild Things Are* by Maurice Sendak, for all the things that could really happen (real things) and all the things that could not really happen (unreal things) so they can tell me what they are when I finish reading. (Read book)

An Oral Discussion. What are some of the real things that happened in this story? What are some of the unreal things? How many of you have read or have seen on television the story *Charlotte's Web*? What are the real and unreal things in that story? Have you read or have you seen *Mary Poppins*? Is there anything real or unreal in that story? This kind of a story, which has both real and unreal things happen, is called fantasy. Can any of you think of any story you may have read that is fantasy? What about television programs? Who is the character on television that children love to watch who is unreal but does real things? Do you understand why *Alf* is a fantasy show?

The writers of all these stories are called authors. These authors try very hard to write stories that children will enjoy reading. Today, I want you to become an author and write a story that has some real parts and some unreal parts. It may take you a few minutes to think of an idea. When you are ready, you may begin writing. It you have difficulty thinking of an idea, raise your hand, and I will try to help you think of an idea.

An Experience with Written Language. (Allow at least 30 min for the children to complete their stories.)

Collect writing samples.

Summary. Thank you all for being such good writers! I am eager to read all of your stories, and I will return them to your teacher in a few days.

APPENDIX 4

Lesson Plan (Sixth Grade)

Objective. To understand the elements of a mystery and be able to write a short mystery.

A Common Experience. Ask the students to listen while I am reading *The Case of the Hungry Hitchhiker* by Donald Sobol, to be able to tell me how many characters are included in the story. Ask the students to try to figure out the answer to the problem at the end of the mystery? (Read the story to the class.) How many main characters are in the story? Are they all necessary? Does anyone know the answer to the problem at the end of the mystery. How did Encyclopedia Brown know the hitchhiker was a member of the holdup gang? How many characters does an author need to include in a mystery? Have you read any mysteries? Which ones? Have you read any of the Hardy Boys or Nancy Drew books? How are the Hardy Boys and Nancy Drew mysteries different from Encyclopedia Brown mysteries? Have any of you seen *Murder, She Wrote* or *Moonlighting* on television? What makes these mysteries different from other types of stories, i.e., fantasy, biography, fiction, folk tale?

The people who write mysteries want others to read and watch their stories. These people are called authors. Today I want you to become an author and write a short mystery. Think about the elements necessary for a mystery and write any kind of mystery that you would like. What are some of the crimes or puzzles that you could write about? Make it interesting so that others will want to read it. It may take you a few minutes to think of an idea; you may start whenever you are ready. If you would like to write a mystery similar to Encyclopedia Brown, you may challenge me to see if I can figure out your mystery. Just write "Challenge" at the top of your paper. When you are finished, hand in your paper.

An Experience with Written Language. (Allow at least 30 min. for students to write.) Collect writing samples.

Summary. Thank you for being so cooperative today. I am eager to read your mysteries, and for those of you who challenged me, I hope I can figure out your secret. After I read your mysteries, I will return them to your teacher. I will put my answer to your challenges on a "postem" on the front of your story. Good luck in junior high!

Mary Ellen Varble is a faculty member at Eastern Illinois University.

Teachers' Awareness of Reading Terms

Vincent E. Hamman

Reading and writing instruction are two important aspects of the elementary school curriculum. Reading and writing instruction is, often, discussed with regard to two approaches. One approach has characteristics of whole language instruction. The other method relies on basal reading materials.

Many college and university reading, writing, and language arts classes for undergraduate and graduate students focus, at least in part, on the theories and strategies of the whole language philosophy (Rosberg, 1989). Newman (1985) stated, "as teachers we need to know what current research has demonstrated about many aspects of language learning in order to build curricula which can support children's language development" (p. 8). Routman (1988) declared, "teachers as a whole, are not well informed about the latest research and current educational trends" (p. 120). It seems reasonable, then, that elementary teachers have an awareness of reading terms since they are responsible for teaching reading throughout the school day and the entire school year.

PURPOSE

The purpose of this study was to identify and evaluate the existing awareness elementary classroom teachers have, if any, with basal reading terms and whole language reading terms. An additional goal of this study was to identify teachers' self-reported sources of awareness with reading terms.

INSTRUMENTATION

In order to assess elementary classroom teachers' awareness of basal reading terms and whole language reading terms a two-part self-report questionnaire was constructed.

Part A consisted of three questions covering the respondents' demographic data. Teachers were asked to indicate how long they had taught in the elementary (K–6) grades, their highest level of education, and the year their highest level of education was earned. This information was solicited to observe possible patterns, if any, which might have emerged from this study.

Part B of the survey asked teachers to indicate their level of awareness with thirty reading terms. After reading a particular item, the teacher marked one of the three categories: "Aware of term," "Minimal awareness of term," "No awareness of term." If, in fact, they were aware of a particular term, they were asked to indicate the source of this awareness from the following choices: professional organizational meeting, staff meeting, inservice meeting, university/college class, book, professional journal, colleague, or other.

The thirty reading terms were: author's chair, authentic writing, base word, book talk, conferencing, consonant blends, consonant clusters, decoding, digraph, diphthong, final consonants, focus units, grapheme, initial consonants, invented spelling, letter recognition, letter/sound association, literature circles, long vowel sounds, phonogram, process writing, reading workshop, response groups, scaffolding, semantic webbing, short vowel sounds, student-centered curriculum, syllabication, thematic units, and transaction. The terms associated with whole language reading instruction were selected because they are topics of current educational inservices, research, and university/college classes. The terms associated with basal reading instruction were arrived at by completing a hand tally of five recent basal reading series. The five basal reading series were:

1. *Ginn Reading Program.* (1987). Lexington, MA: Ginn and Company.
2. *HBJ Reading Program.* (1987). Orlando, FL: Harcourt Brace Jovanovich.
3. *Houghton-Mifflin Reading.* (1986). Boston, MA: Houghton-Mifflin.
4. *The Riverside Reading Program.* (1986). Chicago, IL: Riverside Publishing Company.
5. *Scott, Foresman Reading.* (1985). Glenview, IL: Scott, Foresman and Company.

Three different forms of the questionnaire, with the items randomly organized, were distributed. This method was employed to limit any type of order effect. When the questionnaires were mailed out the three forms of the questionnaire were distributed randomly for receipt by elementary classroom teachers.

DATA COLLECTION

A Department of Education and Cultural Affairs printout was used to identify all public and private elementary classroom teachers in South Dakota.

From this list, three hundred elementary classroom teachers were randomly selected. Questionnaires were then mailed to the random sample participants. Each questionnaire contained a letter of explanation and a stamped, self-addressed envelope. The respondents were assured that their responses would be anonymous and the questionnaire would take 10 minutes or less to complete. Teachers were asked to mail back their completed questionnaire within 2 weeks.

RESULTS

A total of 211 completed questionnaires were received (70.33%). Table 1 represents demographic information of the 211 respondents. For comparison purposes the data was interpreted two ways. First, the percentage of teachers' awareness with survey terms was examined.

TABLE 1
RESPONDENT DEMOGRAPHIC DATA

Elementary Teacher	Percent	Number
Level of Education		
Bachelor's degree	85%	180
Master's degree	15%	31
Experience		
1–10 years	41%	86
11–20 years	39%	83
21–25+ years	20%	42
Sex of Respondent		
Male	4%	9
Female	96%	202

TABLE 2
SUMMARY OF TEACHERS' AWARENESS OF SURVEY TERMS IN PERCENTAGE ORDER

Term	Percent
Letter Recognition	98%
Long Vowel Sounds	98%
Short Vowel Sounds	98%
Base Word	97%
Final Consonants	97%
Consonant Blends	94%
Initial Consonants	94%
Syllabication	94%
Decoding	92%
Letter/Sound Association	91%
Consonant Clusters	89%
Diphthongs	87%
Digraph	83%
Reading Workshop	76%
Conferencing	62%
Student-Centered Curriculum	57%
Phonograms	56%
Thematic Units	52%
Invented Spelling	47%
Book Talks	41%
Semantic Webbing	39%
Process Writing	36%
Literature Circles	35%
Focus Units	34%
Author's Chair	28%
Grapheme	28%
Transaction	27%
Response Groups	26%
Authentic Writing	22%
Scaffolding	6%

Scoring was accomplished by visual inspection and hand tallying of responses in each category. The percentage of teachers' awareness in order of percent may be found in Table 2.

DISCUSSION

As an overall group, elementary classroom teachers in South Dakota were more aware with the reading terms indicative of basal reading instruction. The thirteen terms, of the entire thirty survey items, which received the highest percentage of awareness from survey respondents were basal reading terms. The highest reported awareness with whole language reading terms was fourteenth overall of the thirty reading terms.

A secondary purpose of this study was to record teachers' self-reported sources of awareness with whole language and basal reading terms. It is worth noting that the university/college class category was reported with the highest percentage as a source awareness with each of the thirty survey terms.

The "other" category provided additional information as to source(s) of awareness of survey terms. The two teacher reported sources were: 1) elementary school education of the reporting teacher, 2) teacher's manuals.

CONCLUSIONS

There was a difference in percentages of awareness of basal reading terms and whole language reading terms. Teachers reported higher percentages of awareness on the basal reading terms. The highest reported whole language reading term was fourteenth overall of the thirty reading terms.

It appears university/college class(es) are an important source of elementary classroom teachers' awareness of reading terms. The respondents reported their colleagues as a source of awareness with survey terms.

In examining the high return rate, it would appear that the subject of this study is of interest to elementary classroom teachers. Therefore, they were willing to participate and provide information.

This inclusion of phonics in the elementary curriculum is continuing. The awareness of phonics terms provides some insight that paradigm shifts are slow in developing in the area of elementary reading instruction.

The findings of this study have importance to university/college faculty members. The highest reported source of awareness was university/college class for each of the thirty survey terms. Elementary classroom teachers, seemingly, view the university/college classroom as a primary source of information for their profession.

There appears to be some difficulty in the process from theory into practice. Since university/college courses have begun to focus attention on the whole language philosophy, it doesn't appear that most elementary classroom teachers are aware of the information.

REFERENCES

Newman, J. (1985). *Whole language: Theory and use.* Portsmouth, NH: Heinemann.

Rosberg, M. A. (1989). *The reading writing connection: Using student teachers.* Des Moines, IA: Iowa State Reading Association. (ERIC Document Reproduction Service No. ED 308 476).

Routman, R. (1988). *Transitions: From literature to literacy.* Portsmouth, NH: Heinemann.

Vincent E. Hamman is a faculty member at Creighton University in Omaha, Nebraska.

CHAPTER DISCUSSIONS AND ACTIVITIES

1. Which type of research methodology do you believe best supports the philosophy of whole language? How do your opinions compare or contrast with the views discussed in the article by Goodman?
2. In this chapter, which suggestions about research do you think would be most helpful to you as a whole-language classroom teacher, and why would you want to use them?
3. Why do some whole-language advocates reject the use of quantitative research methods in assessing or comparing the relative merits of various reading approaches? Do you agree with them? Why or why not? How do you feel such research should be conducted?
4. Ask a classmate to describe the person or persons who most motivated her or him to become an interested reader. Write down the characteristics that these models possessed and the particular aspects of their behavior that were most influential. What form of research methodology does your description most resemble? How else could you have obtained this information?

AUTHOR INDEX

Boldfaced page numbers indicate the beginning page of the author's article.

Aaron, P., 2
Abel, F., 257
Abramson, S., 193, **201**
Adams, E., 321, **336**
Adams, J., 171
Adams, M., 69, 92, 93, 95, 96, 103, 130, 234, 335, 238
Adoff, A., 171
Ahlberg, J., 136
Alexander, J., 312
Alfonso, S., 258
Allen, J., 188, 326
Allington, R., 280, 388
Altwerger, B., 9, 68, 163, 344
Andersen, C., 195, **223**
Andersen, G., 7
Anderson, R., 17, 67, 98, 100, 120, 163, 231, 235, 236, 237, 256, 284, 321, 376, 388, 389, 391, 392
Anno, M., 135
Applebee, A., 177, 249, 278, 396
Arbuthnot, M., 124
Armbruster, B., 252
Arthur, B., 193, **218**
Artley, A., 272
Asher, C., 303
Ashton-Warner, S., 51, 52, 54
Atwell, N., 166, 181, 182, 225, 226, 296, 312, 316, 326, 376
Auel, J., 268
Aukerman, R., 33
Aulls, M., 251

Babbitt, N., 138
Bader, L., 67, 383, 391
Baghban, M., 39
Balcer, M., 220
Ballard, R., 262
Bang, M., 174
Banks, C., 191

Banks, J., 191
Barnes, D., 215
Barry, A., 192
Bartel, N., 194
Baruth, L., 192
Baskwill, J., 149
Bates, E., 154
Baumann, J., 69, **72**, 397
Bean, R., 285
Bean, T., 255
Beck, F., 137
Becker, W., 233
Bembridge, R., 286, **306**
Bennett, C., 192
Bennis, W., 289
Bergeron, B., 1, 73
Bettelheim, B., 130
Betts, E., 236
Biklen, S., 364
Bird, L., 8, 296, 312, 379
Bissex, G., 30, 39, 326, 365, 372
Blair, T., 66, 67, 256
Blake, R., 55
Blanchard, J., 57, 98
Block, C., 165
Block, M., 286
Blom, G., 389
Bloom, B., 104
Boehm, N., 172
Boehnlein, M., 384
Bogdan, R., 364
Bond, G., 316
Boyd, R., 80
Braddock, R., 399
Bradley, L., 234
Brandt, R., 223
Brewster, M., 181
Bridge, C., 94
Britton, J., 129, 164, 249, 371
Bromley, K., 165

Brophy, J., 116
Brown, C., 258, **272**
Brown, H., 343
Brown, J., 116, 257, 279
Browne, A., 135
Brozo, W., 257
Bruce, B., 185
Bruneau, B., 322, **351**, 352
Bruner, J., 135, 248
Burk, J., 321, **325**
Burns, P., 66, 67, 70, 121, 194
Burton, F., 134, 136
Burrows, A., 54
Busching, B., 39
Butler, A., 40, 68, 75
Buttery, T., 195
Byars, B., 158

Caines, J., 78
Calder, J., 196, **241**
Calfee, R., 234
Calkins, L., 78, 130, 164, 170, 225, 396, 397
Callahan, R., 332
Cambourne, B., 75, 82, 291, 293, 344
Cannon, T., 197
Carbo, M., 92
Carle, E., 81
Carnine, D., 233
Carr, K., 197
Carroll, J., 236
Carter, M., 286
Cary, R., 12
Cazden, C., 202, 203, 204, 205
Chall, J., 92, 93, 228, 230, 238, 256
Chambers, A., 139, 140, 225
Chamot, A., 207
Chaney, C., 3
Chapman, D., 171
Chew, C., 178

411

Author Index

Chittenden, E., 308
Chomsky, C., 39, 384, 388
Church, S., 3, **24**
Ciardi, J., 160
Clark, L., 97
Clark, M., 387
Clay, M., 103, 104, 105, 235, 237, 313, 343, 365
Clymer, T., 96
Cochran-Smith, M., 185, 186
Cohen, D., 383
Cohen, M., 76
Combleth, C., 277
Combs, M., 36, **43**
Connor, D., 389
Coody, B., 125
Cooter, Jr., R., 164
Copperman, P., 17
Cordell, A., 197
Cosby, B., 268
Costanzo, W., 185
Cox, C., 284
Crafton, L., 250
Crandell, J., 207
Crawford, L., 192
Crook, P., 125
Cuban, L., 375
Cullinan, B., 119, 123, 125, **129,** 132, 262, 263, 383, 391
Cummins, J., 207
Cunningham, A., 234
Cunningham, C., 97

Dahl, K., 69
Daiute, C., 185
Dalrymple, K., 313
Daniels, H., 164
Daugherty, J., 272
D'Aulaire, I., 265, 272
Davis, F., 386
DeFord, D., 129, 222
DeGroff, L., 167, **184**
Delpit, L., 233
Delton, J., 76
Desai, L., 286
DeSanti, R., 295
deVilliers, P., 348
Dewey, J., 370, 372
Dickinson, D., 185
Dillard, A., 269
Dillon, D., 110, 249
Dishaw, M., 130
Dole, J., 257
Downing, J., 19
Doyle, C., 166

Dudley-Marling, C., 194
Duffy, G., 70, **108,** 116, 377
Dunn, L., 243
Durkin, D., 34, 39, 65, 255, 351, 386
Dykstra, R., 316
Dyson, A., 135, 206, 347

Early, M., 207, 208, 212
Ebbinghaus, H., 332
Edelsky, C., 110, 146, 163, 202, 211, 228, 229, 245, 365
Edge, J., 217
Edmonds, W., 269
Eisner, E., 277
Eldredge, J., 241, 383, 385, 387, 391
Elliott, D., 261
Ellis, D., 166
Ellis, R., 214
Emig, J., 249, 250
Enfield, M., 233
Englemann, S., 233
Englent, C., 261
Enright, D., 202

Fader, D., 241, 385, 388
Farest, C., 125
Farjeon, E., 123
Farr, M., 347
Farris, P., 180, 195, **223,** 366, **391**
Feeley, J., 285
Feelings, M., 122
Feelings, T., 122
Feitelson, D., 231
Felton, R., 236
Ferguson, P., 177, 179
Fernald, G., 233, 238
Ferreiro, E., 371, 378
Fielding, L., 130, 261, 262, 389, 392
Fields, M., 322, 327, **347**
Fillmore, L., 193
Finn, C., 231, 363
Fisher, A., 160
Fisher, C., 258, **278**
Fitzgerald, J., 164
Five, C., 181
Fleet, A., 74, 78
Fleisher, L., 98
Flesch, R., 56, 92, 230
Flickinger, G., 36, **39**
Flood, J., 67
Flood, S., 67
Flores, B., 163, 202
Flowers, B., 165
Forester, A., 386
Fountas, I., 220

Fox, M., 129
Fredericks, A., 321
Freedman, R., 124, 260, 263, 265
Freeman, D., 193, 207, 257
Freeman, Y., 160, 193, 207, 208, 257
Freisinger, R., 249, 250
Freppon, P., 69
Frew, A., 125
Frith, U., 93, 97
Fritz, J., 265
Froese, V., 55, 284
Fullan, M., 46
Fulps, J., 166, **180**
Fulwiler, T., 181, 226

Gage, N., 335
Galda, L., 123
Galindo, R., 313
Gamberg, R., 75, 76, 146
Ganopole, S., 197, **245**
Gardner, M., 160
Gaskins, I., 97
Gates, A., 104
Genishi, C., 185, 186, 187, 201
Gentile, J., 276, 277
George, J., 136
Gerhard, L., 260
Giamatti, A., 60
Gibbons, G., 263
Gibson, E., 241
Gill, K., 164
Gilles, C., 10
Gillingham, A., 233
Glass, G., 237
Glatthorn, A., 164, 165
Glickman, C., 342
Goffin, S., 51
Goldberg, D., 277
Goldberg, H., 238
Goldenberg, C., 6, **100**
Gollasch, F., 166
Gomez, M., 286
Goodman, J., 272
Goodman, K., 2, 7, 13, 18, 35, 43, 50, 68, 73, 74, 79, 80, 100, 108, 116, 146, 157, 177, 188, 194, 224, 228, 230, 245, 246, 247, 285, 292, 293, 294, 306, 309, 320, 325, 326, 329, 366, **369,** 370, 371, 373, 374, 377, 387
Goodman, Y., 3, 8, 10, 35, 228, 285, 307, 315, 320, 333, 347, 369, 371, 377, 379
Graue, M., 286

Graves, D., 78, 86, 88, 164, 166, 172, 173, 186, 250, 279, 304, 313, 326, 371, 396, 397
Gray, W., 375
Greaney, V., 389
Greenfield, E., 135
Greenlaw, M., 262
Grindler, M., 166, **177**
Groff, P., 230
Guba, E., 365
Gunderson, L., 397
Gunn, C., 166
Gunning, T., 284
Gutknecht, B., 285, **289,** 290, 294, 296

Hade, D., 125, **134**
Hajek, E., 396, 397
Hall, M., 332
Hall, N., 170
Hallahan, D., 196
Halliday, M., 207, 371, 375
Hamayan, E., 207
Hamman, V., 366, **407**
Hancock, J., 82
Hancock, M., 366, **391**
Handford, M., 135
Hansen, J., 55, 174, 286, **302,** 305
Hardy, B., 129
Hargreaves, A., 343
Harris, K., 303
Harris, T., 284
Harste, J., 2, 8, 18, 21, 39, 175, 181, 292, 329, 366
Hartwell, P., 250
Hazard, P., 157
Heald-Taylor, G., 291, 293
Heath, S., 139, 303
Hegge, T., 230
Heilman, A., 66, 67, 235, 236, 237, 256
Henderson, A., 351
Henderson, E., 204
Henke, L., 225
Henney, M., 125, **146**
Hennings, D., 272
Hepler, S., 122, 123, 134, 139, 143
Herber, H., 51, 61
Heward, W., 194, 196
Heymsfeld, C., 34, 43, 50, 228, 238
Hickman, J., 122, 123, 134, 139, 140, 143, 147
Hiebert, E., 67, 120, 163, 256, 258, **278,** 280, 284, 321
Hill, M., 303
Hillerich, R., 261, 262
Hindley, J., 304

Hipple, M., 180
Hoban, R., 81
Hoban, T., 122
Hoffman, J., 125
Hoffman, S., 204
Holdaway, D., 18, 78, 224, 383, 386, 387, 397
Hollingsworth, P., 2, **17**
Honig, B., 160
Hornsby, D., 78
Hoskisson, K., 164, 165, 387
Howe, K., 364
Howe-Tompkins, S., 315
Hubbard, R., 172
Huck, C., 70, 121, 122, 123, 170, 171, 262, 271, 272, 313, 395
Hudelson, S., 202, 208, 212
Hull, O., 315
Hulme, C., 233
Humes, A., 396
Hurd, P., 261
Hutchins, P., 171

Idol, L., 235
Irwin, J., 261

Jacobs, J., 366, **382**
Jacobsen, D., 312, 316
Jaggar, A., 178, 207
James, T., 364
Jensen, J., 82
Johns, J., 80, 286
Johnson, C., 193, **201**
Johnson, T., 82
Johnson, V., 257
Johnston, P., 290, 296, 343
Jongsma, K., 103, 366
Juel, C., 94, 95, 232
Judson, C., 272
Justen III, J., 196, **241**

Kalan, R., 135
Kamii, C., 204
Kantor, R., 261
Kantrowitz, B., 228, 231
Kaplan, S., 252
Kauffman, J., 196
Keats, E., 113
Keliher, A., 55
Kellaghan, T., 283
Kellogg, S., 78
Kelly, P., 181, 182, 183
Kemp, M., 80
Kennedy, M., 192
Kiefer, B., 134, 143

Kilpatrick, W., 372
King, D., 228
King, M., 397
Kirk, S., 230
Kline, L., 177
Kobrin, B., 262, 263
Koch, K., 79
Koeller, S., 226, 382, 389
Krashen, S., 202, 208, 236
Krathwohl, D., 364
Kreeft, J., 220
Krogness, M., 305
Krupp, J., 335
Kucer, S., 251
Kwak, W., 78

Labbo, L., 125
LaBrant, L., 389
Labuda, M., 197
Ladas, H., 236
Lamme, L., 147, 166, **170**
Lapkin, S., 208
LaPointe, A., 187
Lapp, D., 67
Larrick, N., 125, **157,** 384, 388
Lass, B., 39
Lauber, P., 264
Lawson, R., 265, 271, 272
Lee, D., 54
Lehman, B., 125
Leinhardt, G., 110, 392
Lester, J., 262
Leu, D., 185
Levin, T., 226
Levstik, L., 279
Liberman, I., 231, 233, 235
Lim, H., 193, **207**
Lincoln, Y., 365
Linek, W., 287, **309**
Linn, M., 277
Lobel, A., 79
Logan, N., 67
Lomox, R., 93
Long, E., 36, **39**
Lowe, K., 2
Luckasson, R., 195
Lundberg, I., 234
Lynch-Brown, C., 124

Mabbett, B., 69
Macauley, D., 124, 135, 260
MacGinitie, W., 37, **58,** 110, 237
MacGowan-Gilhooly, A., 193
MacLachlan, P., 124, 159
Maclean, M., 234

Author Index

Madaus, G., 283
Manning, G., 337
Manning, M., 192
Marek, A., 312
Markham, L., 164
Marshall, J., 123
Martin, B., 221
Martin, J., 178
Mason, G., 195
Mather, N., 195, **227**
Mathews, J., 80
Maxwell, J., 389
Mayer, M., 80
Mayher, J., 250, 251
McCaig, R., 396
McCallum, R., 34
McCarthy, B., 277
McCarty, B., 35
McCaslin, M., 344
McClure, A., 134, 136
McConkie, G., 235
McCord, D., 160
McCormick, C., 93
McCracken, R., 226, 388
McFarland, D., 365
McGee, L., 255
McGinley, W., 285
McGovern, A., 265
McKenna, M., 103, 228, 229, 312, 364, 365
McLoughlin, B., 201, 202
McLoughlin, J., 197
McLuhan, M., 84
Meek, M., 135, 136
Mehan, H., 185, 186
Melton, J., 327
Melton-Pagés, J., 321, **325**, 328, 330
Meltzer, M., 265
Merrian, E., 160, 272
Miller, J., 262
Miller, J. W., 364, 365
Mills, H., 68
Milz, V., 171, 373
Moffet, J., 226
Monjo, F., 265
Monroe, M., 233, 237
Monson, D., 242
Monson, R., 320, 321, **332**
Moore, D., 261
Morrow, C., 308
Morrow, L., 80, 178
Mosenthal, P., 401
Moss, B., 258, **260**
Murray, D., 164
Muskopf, A., 236
Myers, B., 114

Nagel, G., 67
Neilsen, L., 303
Nelson, K., 347
Ness, E., 158
Newman, P., 3, 8, 18, **24,** 30, 55, 73, 74, 78, 82, 92, 185, 228, 245, 327, 370, 407
Nhuong, H., 124
Norton, D., 122, 123, 124
Nurss, J., 219

O'Donnell, M., 2, 66, 67, 194
O'Keefe, T., 68
Olsen, W., 54
Orlansky, M., 194, 196
Orton, S., 232
Osborn, J., 42

Pace, G., 320
Padak, N., 312, 313
Pahl, M., 320, 321, **332**
Palincsar, A., 212
Pappas, C., 149, 262
Paradis, E., 67
Parry, J., 78
Parsons, L., 180, 181, 182
Paterson, K., 130
Patterson, L., 326, 365
Pearson, P., 3, 236, 237, 247, 285, 312, 313
Perfetti, C., 234, 236
Peyton, J., 202
Phenix, J., 185, 188
Pikulski, J., 286
Pinnell, G., 96, 103, 384
Platt, N., 134
Polacco, P., 133
Polloway, E., 196
Popham, W., 283
Pratt, C., 55
Prelutsky, J., 123
Pring, L., 235
Proett, J., 164
Pryor, E., 310, 312
Purves, A., 104, 262

Rasinski, T., 321, 322, **351,** 386
Rauch, S., 78
Rayner, K., 235
Read, C., 373
Readance, J., 255
Reed, S., 181
Renzulli, J., 196, 248
Resnick, L., 223
Reutzel, D., 2, **17,** 164, 223, 224, 248, 385, 386, 396, 397

Rhodes, L., 77, 78, 194, 365
Rice, J., 374, 375
Rich, S., 369, 397
Richard-Amato, P., 202
Richgels, D., 255
Ride, S., 262
Ridley, L., 293
Rief, L., 303
Rigg, P., 193, 207, 208
Robbins, P., 68
Robinson, R., 364, 365
Roe, B., 66, 67, 70, 121, 194
Rosberg, M., 407
Rosen, H., 130
Rosenblatt, L., 59, 125, **152,** 153, 155
Rosenshine, B., 116
Roser, N., 125
Ross, E., 66, 67, 70, 121, 194
Routman, R., 42, 82, 194, 326, 345, 407
Rowe, M., 204
Rubin, D., 194, 197
Ruddell, R., 119, 320, 397
Rupley, W., 66, 67, 256
Ruth, L., 180, 183
Rux, J., 67
Rynkofs, J., 313

Sachs, M., 124
Samuels, S., 98, 231
Sandburg, C., 160
Sarason, S., 345
Scarry, R., 221
Schwartz, A., 139
Schwartz, J., 40
Scott, J., 67, 120, 163, 256, 284, 321
Sebesta, S., 265
Seda, I., 193, **201,** 204
Sendak, M., 135
Shafer, R., 196
Shanahan, T., 252, 262
Shanklin, N., 177, 365
Shankweiler, D., 237
Shannon, P., 31, 319, 377
Share, D., 234
Sharmat, M., 81
Shavelson, R., 363
Shehan, M., 322, **351**
Shepherd, G., 241
Siera, M., 36, **43**
Silvern, S., 185
Silverstein, S., 79
Simpson, M., 181, 183
Slaughter, H., 68, 223, 396
Slavin, R., 59, 97, 103, 363, 364
Slingerland, B., 233

Author Index 415

Sloan, P., 74, 75
Smith, C., 181
Smith, E., 230, 232
Smith, F., 8, 18, 24, 36, 42, 135, 139, 144, 163, 174, 179, 292, 378
Smith, K., 366
Smith, P., 69, **83**
Smith, T., 196
Snow, C., 347
Snowling, M., 233
Sobol, D., 154
Spiegel, D., 68, 258, **267**
Spolsky, B., 106
Staab, C., 397
Stahl, S., 69, **92,** 94, 231, 234, 235, 238
Stanovich, K., 234, 235, 237, 364
Stansell, J., 365
Stein, L., 233
Steinle, J., 74
Stephens, D., 68
Stern, H., 217
Stevens, K., 272
Stewart-Dore, N., 82
Stewig, J., 120, 263
Stotsky, S., 252
Strackbein, D., 181, 182, 183
Stratton, B., 166, **177**
Strickland, D., 326
Sulzby, E., 203, 206, 347
Sutherland, Z., 124
Sweedler-Brown, C., 400
Sykes, G., 108

Taylor, B., 98, 232, 392
Taylor, D., 351
Taylor, P., 316
Teale, W., 93, 329, 330, 331
Thompson, R., 386
Thonis, E., 193
Thorndike, R., 387

Tiedt, I., 120, 193
Tiedt, P., 191, 193
Tierney, R., 251, 286, 343
Tomkins, G., 77
Tomlinson, 124, 257
Tompkins, G., 77, 164, 165, 182, 183
Tonjes, M., 247
Torrance, E., 247
Trachtenburg, P., 95, 96
Treiman, R., 96
Trelease, J., 225, 242, 389
Tschudi, S., 182
Tsutsui, Y., 77
Tunnell, M., 196, 224, **241,** 366, **382,** 385, 392
Tyson-Bernstein, H., 261

Urzua, C., 202

Vacca, J., 257
Vacca, R., 257
Valencia, S., 80, 285, 286, 289, 292, **298**
Van Allsburg, C., 122, 123, 135
Van Nostrand, A., 226
Varble, M., 366, **396**
Vassallo, P., 322, **358**
Veatch, J., 36, **51,** 264
Vellutino, F., 234
Viorst, J., 41, 78
von Glasersfeld, E., 278
Vygotsky, L., 185, 216, 370, 371, 378

Waber, B., 78, 137
Waldrop, P., 196, **241**
Wallace, G., 197
Walmsley, S., 321, **336,** 345
Wangberg, E., 397
Ward, L., 141
Watson, D., 2, **5,** 8, 9, 10, 73, 82, 193, **207,** 237, 246, 325, 344

Weaver, C., 7, 55, 292
Webb, N., 277
Weir, L., 177
Weiss, N., 78
Wells, G., 212
Wells, R., 76
Welty, E., 120
Wepner, S., 285
Westby, C., 232, 233, 236
Wetzel, N., 175
Williams, J., 135
White, E., 41, 123, 154
White, J., 384
Whitin, D., 171
Whitmore, K., 320
Wiesendanger, K., 67
Wilkerson, B., 223
Wilkinson, I., 67, 163, 223, 256, 284, 321
Willinsky, J., 175, 344
Winnicott, D., 138
Wiseman, D., 124, 284, 286
Witty, P., 197, 247
Wolf, D., 312
Wollman-Bonilla, J., 181, 182, 183
Wood, M., 2, 66, 67, 194
Woodley, J., 315, 316
Wortman, R., 315

Yager, R., 261
Yatvin, J., 68, 320
Young, E., 135
Young, T., 166, **180**

Zakaluk, B., 308
Zarrillo, J., 264, 284
Zemelman, S., 164
Zucker, C., 195

SUBJECT INDEX

The 4MAT System, 276
AAP Reading Initiative, 132
Ability grouping, 19–20, 379–380
Administrators
   as change agents, 28–29
   attitudes of, 44, 342
   roles of, 327–329
   support from, 320–321, 341–342
Adolescent literature, in social studies and science, 267–272
Aesthetic reading, 152–156
Alphabet books, 122
Alphabetic principle, 61–62
Alphabetic stage of learning, 93
Anecdotal records. *See* Assessment/evaluation
Art, children's, 210–211
Assessment/evaluation, 283–286, 309–317
   anecdotal records, 243, 285, 313, 314
   checklists, 91, 313
   conferences, 294, 313
   definition of, 284–285
   files, 312–313
   grading, 90–91, 309–317
   holistic grading, 315–316
   informal, 289–297
   kidwatching, 293
   literacy journals, 294–295
   portfolios, 91, 285–286, 296–297, 298–302, 302–305, 312–313
   purpose of, 13, 293
   record keeping, 311–316
   responsive, 293
   student conferences, 294
   surveys, 312
   traditional, formal, 291–292
      achievement tests, 283
      standardized tests, 283–284, 289–290
   teacher observation, 285

Authors
   children as, 170
   studying about, 147, 171
Author's chair, 88, 172–173, 179
Authorship, 170–176
Automaticity, 235–236

Basal reader(s), 33–34, 39, 382
   historical development of, 375
   literature-based, 40
   limitations of, 138, 224, 241, 246, 387
   oral reading with, 66
   silent reading with, 66
   teacher's manual for, 34
   textbooks, design of, 256–257
   using with gifted students, 246–247
   workbooks, limitations of, 41–42
Basalization of literature, 70, 157–161
Becoming a Nation of Readers, 67, 120, 163, 246, 256, 284, 376, 389, 392
Beginning to Read: Thinking and Learning about Print, 130–131
Behavioristic theory of learning, 35–36
Big books, 41, 387
Bilingual education, 192–193, 201–206, 207–218, 218–223
Biography, 124, 260, 265
Books for children
   core, in literature-based reading programs, 264
   information, *See* Nonfiction books
   natural (real), 157, 387
   reading aloud, 46, 143, 225, 387–388
   See also Children's literature

Caldecott award, 133
CALLA (Cognitive Academic Language Learning Approach), 207

Caretaker speech, 204
Child-centered learning, 88
Children's Book Council, 263
Children's Choices, 133
Children's literature
   activities related to books, 41, 76–78, 135–138, 268–272, 355–356
   classroom use, 76–81, 89–90, 119–128, 129–134, 135–138
   definition of, 120, 152
   genres, 122–124
   illustrations, 135
   literary elements, 121–122
   self-selection, 142–143, 388
Children's School, 358–360
Classroom environment, 13, 22
Collaborative learning, 88–89
Composition. *See* Writing
Computer(s)
   in the whole language classroom, 184–189
   in Writing to Read, 178
   word processing, 166, 175, 185–186, 220–221
   software, 185
Conferences, 294, 313
Constructivism versus behaviorism, 35–36
Contemporary realistic fiction, 123–124
Content area(s)
   expository material, 255, 278
   texts used
      compared to basal readers, 256–257
      limitations of, 261
   mathematics, 272–277
   science, 80, 260–267, 267–272
   social studies, 81, 260–267, 267–272
   using literature in, 260–272

416

Subject Index

Counting books, 122
Critical reading, 271
Cultural diversity, 192

DEAR (Drop Everything and Read), 148
Dialogue journals, 219–220, 252, 314
Direct instruction, 108–116
Directed Reading Activity (DRA), 34, 66–67

Early literacy, 351–357
Efferent reading, 152–156
Emergent literacy, 177–178
English-as-a-second-language (ESL), 192–193, 201, 207, 218–223
Evaluation. *See* Assessment/evaluation
Experience chart, 51, 53
Expository reading, 255, 278–279
Expository writing, 212
Expressive writing, 210–211, 249–250

Fernald Method, 233
Folders. *See* Assessment/evaluation, portfolios

Gifted students, 196–197
  reading and writing for, 245–253
Grading, 90–91, 309–317
Grouping children for learning
  in traditional classrooms, 19–20, 379–380
  in whole language classrooms, 19–20, 279–280

Historical fiction, 124
  social studies instruction, 269–270

Individualized reading, 51, 52, 265, 386
Information books, 124, 260–267
Instruction
  defined, 65–66
  direct, 108–116
  holistic, 108–116
  reflective, 208
  skill-based, 34–35
  traditional, 22–23
Interviews with whole language teachers, 336–346
Invented spelling, 97, 350, 353, 373

Journals, 204, 225–226. *See also* Writing, journals

Key Vocabulary, 51, 52, 53, 54, 56
Kidwatchers, 326
Kids Can Press, 132

Language acquisition and development, 19, 22, 347–351, 371
Language arts, 12–13, 20, 39
Language Experience Approach (LEA), 53, 56, 178, 208
Learning disabled (LD), 194–195, 223–227, 227–240
Libraries, 142, 242
Limited English proficient (LEP), 192–193, 201–206, 207–218, 218–223
Literacy journals, 294–295
Literacy Portfolios, 302–305
Literature. *See* Children's literature
Literature-based reading instruction, 134–145, 157–160, 224
  organizational patterns, 70, 264
  research on, 132–133, 382–390, 391–396
  theme units, 146–151, 264–265
Logographic stage of learning, 93

Mainstreamed students, 195–196, 241–244
Mathematics. *See* Content area(s)
Meaning-Centered reading, 84
Mental retardation, definition of, 195
Message Board, 80
Miscue analysis, 312,
Modern Fantasy, 123
Multicultural education, 191
Multicultural literature, 124
Multi-Layered Assessment Package (MAP), 306–309
Multiple-choice questions, 283–284

Narrative reading, 255, 278–279
Neurological impress method, 387
Newbery awards, 124, 133, 262
Nonfiction books, 124, 260–267

Organizing whole-language classrooms, 22–23, 379–380
  intermediate grades, 83–91
  primary grades, 72–83
Orthographic stage of learning, 93

Paperback book clubs, 394
Parents
  activities at home, 357
  communication with, 242–243, 327, 352–355
  involvement of, 321–322, 351–352, 358–360
  understanding language/writing development, 347–351
Parent-teacher conferences, 353–354, 358
Peer evaluation. *See* Writing, conferences
Phonics, 92–99
  debate over, 55–56, 61–62, 130–131, 228–231, 332–333
  direct instruction, 233
  and whole language, 68–69, 377
Phonological awareness, 69, 233–235
Picture books, 122–123
Play, in literary classrooms, 135–138
Poetry, 123, 135
Portfolios. *See* Assessment/evaluation
Potentially English proficient (PEP), 192, 207–218, *See also* Limited English proficient (LEP)

Questioning, 247–248

Reading
  achievement, 392–396
  aloud to children, 10, 225, 387–388
  collateral, 247
  conferences, 294, 313
  individualized, 51, 52, 265, 386
  literature for instruction, 134–145, 157–161, 224
  oral, 66, 101–102
  self-selection of books, 248, 388
  silent, 66, 130. *See also* Sustainted Silent Reading (SSR)
  stories, 10
Reading and writing, integrated, 177–180
Reading instruction, 58–63
  basal readers. *See* Basal reader(s)
  individualized, 51, 52, 265, 337, 386
  in New Zealand, 69, 100–107
  literature-based. *See* Literature-based reading instruction
  skill-based, 242, 290–291
  transition from basal readers to whole language, 43–50
Reading Recovery, 96, 103–104, 131, 237, 384

Subject Index

Reading research, 363–368. *See also* Literature-based reading instruction, research on; Whole language, research about
Reading response journals, 180–184
REAL (Readers and Writers of English as Another Language), 207
Record keeping, 311–316
Remedial reader, 194–195
Report cards. *See* Assessment/evaluation, portfolios
Research
 classroom, 372
 educational, 363–364
 interdisciplinary, 374
 qualitative versus quantitative, 364
 See also Whole language, research about; Reading research
Researchers, 365–366, 376

Scaffolding, 203–204
Scheduling. *See* Organizing whole language classrooms, primary grades
Science. *See* Content area(s), science
Shared book reading, 138–142
Silent reading, 66, 130
Social studies. *See* Content area(s)
Spelling, 97, 350, 353, 373
Stages of written language, 204, 347–351
Standardized tests, 283–284, 289–290
Student conferences, 294, 313
Sustained silent reading (SSR), 125, 226, 265, 268, 388

TAWL (Teachers Applying Whole Language), 7, 14
Teacher(s)
 empowerment, 115
 knowledge of reading terms, 407–410
 as researchers, 365–366, 376

 roles of, 20–21, 40, 88, 319–321, 326–327, 333–334, 336–346, 370–371, 380
Teachers's guides (manuals)
 for basal readers, 34
 with literature, 70, 157–160
Teaching reading in New Zealand, 69, 100–107
Thematic units, 91, 125, 146–151
 planning, 76, 149
 teaching ideas, 78–79
Trade books, 157
 selection and acquisition, 263–264.
 See also Children's literature
Traditional approaches to reading instruction, 21–23, 33–36, 51–58, 60–61
Traditional literature, 123
Transaction model of teaching/learning, 332–335
Transition from basals to books, 43–50
Transmission model of teaching/learning, 332–335

Uninterrupted Sustained Silent Reading (USSR), 125, 148

Videotapes about whole language, 32, 116

Wait-time strategy, 204–205
Whole language
 administrators' influence on, 319–321, 327–329
 cautions about, 2, 3, 51–58, 58–63, 336–346
 characteristics of, 245
 classroom, 9–11, 19–20, 325–326, 355–357
 contrasted to traditional beliefs, 19–23
 definitions of, 1–2, 5–9, 73, 325, 343–344
 implementing, 20–21, 43–50, 72–83, 83–91

 misconceptions about, 24–31
 parents involvement in, 321–322, 351–352, 358–360
 philosophy of, 2, 18, 22, 28, 52, 53
 principles supporting, 11–13
 research about, 129–130, 231, 364–366, 369–382, 396–407
 resources, 380
 teachers' views of, 336–346
Whole Language Umbrella (WLU), 43
Workbooks. *See* Basal reader(s)
Writer's Workshop, 85–87, 166
Writing
 audience for, 87–88, 171–172, 179
 conferences, 86–87, 170
 connection with reading, 163, 174, 177–180, 251–252
 drafting stage, 164–165
 expressive, 249–250
 folders, 296, 310. *See also* Assessment/evaluation, portfolios
 holistic grading, 315–316
 in intermediate grades, 83–91
 journals, 85, 180–184, 211–212, 252
 letters, 212
 poetic, 249
 prewriting stage, 164
 in primary grades, 355–357
 process, 163–166. *See also* Writer's Workshop
 publishing children's, 175
 research on, 396–407
 revising stage, 165, 172
 sharing stage, 165, 172
 spelling and, 97, 350, 353, 373
 transactional, 249–250
 whole language and traditional approaches, 396–407
 with computers, 186–187
Writing to Read, 178

Young author conferences, 175–176